T

MILESTONE DOCUMENTS IN WORLD HISTORY

Exploring the Primary Sources
That Shaped the World

MILESTONE DOCUMENTS
IN WORLD HISTORY

Exploring the Primary Sources
That Shaped the World

Volume 2
1082 – 1833

Brian Bonhomme
Editor in Chief

Cathleen Boivin
Consulting Editor

Schlager Group
Dallas, Texas

Milestone Documents in World History
Copyright © 2010 by Schlager Group Inc.

All rights reserved. No part of this book may be reproduced or utilized in any form or by any means, electronic or mechanical, including photocopying, recording, or by any information storage or retrieval systems, without permission in writing from the publisher. For information, contact:

Schlager Group Inc.
2501 Oak Lawn Avenue, Suite 440
Dallas, Tex. 75219
USA

You can find Schlager Group on the World Wide Web at
http://www.schlagergroup.com
Text and cover design by Patricia Moritz

Printed in the United States of America

10 9 8 7 6 5 4 3 2 1

ISBN: 978-0-9797758-6-4

This book is printed on acid-free paper.

Contents

Volume 1: 2350 BCE–1058 CE

Volume 2: 1082–1833

MILESTONE DOCUMENTS IN WORLD HISTORY

Exploring the Primary Sources
That Shaped the World

"Many a good slave may appear vile at first sight and many an extremely vile one appear to be good."

Overview

Kai Kaus ibn Iskandar, an eleventh-century ruler of provinces south of the Caspian Sea in what is today Iran, was the author of the *Qābūs nāmeh* (The Book of Qābūs), a history of his grandfather with extensive commentary, which includes a section on the purchase of slaves. It is a book that, along with Niẓām al-Mulk's *Siyāsat nāmeh* (The Book of Government), is considered one of the classics of early medieval Persian literature. The book itself contains many sections divided into forty-four chapters, providing advice on love, politics, sports, and everyday matters. Like the *Siyāsat nāmeh*, the *Qābūs nāmeh* is part of the Persian genre known as "Mirrors for Princes"—books intended to serve as guides for young princes on how to conduct affairs of state as well as their private lives. (In English translation, the *Qābūs nāmeh* has been given the title *A Mirror for Princes*.) Kai Kaus dedicated the text to his son Gilanshah.

Kai Kaus was in a good position to dispense advice to princes, as he ruled the territories of Gīlān and Māzandarān for twenty years before abdicating his throne. The section of the *Qābūs nāmeh* on purchasing slaves was one of the most important, as such advice was crucial to any nobleman in the medieval Middle East. One purchased slaves not only to serve in the household and for leisure but also as bodyguards and often as distinguished functionaries representing their masters. Beyond the slave's physical strength, it was necessary to consider others factors as well, depending on the slave's intended purposes. Kai Kaus's advice on the purchase of slaves contains practical information for a wide variety of circumstances likely experienced by princes in availing themselves of the slave market.

Context

The tenth and eleventh centuries were a time of tumult in the Islamic world, particularly in the region of modern-day Iran. Although the caliphs, or rulers, of the Abbasid Empire (750–1258) reigned over an expanse that stretched from Palestine to central Asia, their authority was dwindling; the empire was often wracked with rebellion, and more and more authority was devolving to the regional governors. Among those regional governors were the Ziyarids.

The Ziyarid Dynasty (967–1043), of which Kai Kaus would be a part, originally came from central Iran, but in the early tenth century they retreated to the mountainous region of Gīlān and Māzandarān, fleeing invasion. From there they ruled and attempted to reclaim their ancestral land around Rhagae, near modern-day Tehran, but with little success. Nonetheless, their efforts required significant resources and good governance to administer those resources. The greatest of the Ziyarid rulers was Qābūs ibn Wushmajir ibn Ziya (d. 1012), who proved himself a rare breed in that he possessed talent in both war and administration.

A fundamental component, albeit not a required one, of a government in the Middle East was the class of slaves. Slavery is typically viewed in light of what is commonly termed "Atlantic slavery," whereby in the early modern period, millions of Africans were shipped to the New World to perform labor on plantations. However, slavery in the Islamic world was quite different, being not nearly so cruel and inhumane. Agricultural slavery existed briefly, but the Zanj Rebellion (869–883), staged against the Abbasids in Iraq by slaves and immigrants of East African descent, abruptly ended that historical episode. Most slavery in the Islamic world tended to be one of three types: domestic, entertainment, or military. Slaves came from many areas, all of them outside the Dar al-Islam, or the Islamic world, as Islam prohibited making a slave of a Muslim (though less scrupulous individuals ignored this ban). Thus, slaves were made of Hindus from India, Africans, Russians, and various people from the steppes of Eurasia, particularly the Turks.

Slaves employed for domestic assistance and for entertainment were common throughout the Middle Eastern world even before the advent of Islam. Domestic slaves ranged from cooks and maids to majordomos, who ran the affairs of the household. Some slaves wielded considerable influence, often being of greater importance than many free people. Slaves held for entertainment purposes could be musicians or concubines who attended to the pleasures of their master. The most unusual form of slavery was military slavery.

The necessity for military slaves stemmed from many causes and began in the ninth century. Early in the 800s a

809
- Civil war begins in the Abbasid Empire.

CA. 813
- After al-Ma'mūn emerges victorious in the civil war, military slavery is introduced to the Islamic world.

977–981
- Qābūs ibn Wushmajir ibn Ziya, greatest of the rulers of the Ziyarid Dynasty, reigns for the first time.

998–1012
- Qābūs reigns for a second time.

1020
- Kai Kaus ibn Iskandar is born.

CA. 1040
- Kai Kaus travels to Afghanistan, to serve as a boon companion to Mawdud ibn Ma'ūd of Ghazna; at the Battle of Dandānqān, in present-day Turkmenistan near the town of Mary, the Seljuks defeat the Ghaznavid sultan Ma'ūd I.

1049
- After returning from Afghanistan, Kai Kaus begins twenty years of rule over Gīlān and Māzandarān.

1069
- Kai Kaus steps down from ruling.

civil war between sons of Caliph Hārūn ar-Rashīd (r. 786–809), arguably the greatest of the Abbasid caliphs, upset the balance of power within the empire. The victor, al-Ma'mūn (r. 813–833), had relied heavily on the armies of regional lords; in return for their support, he granted them increased power. Thus, much of his military power was drawn from other peoples rather than the central government. To offset this, al-Ma'mūn and his successor used *ghilman*, or slaves purchased for the express purposes of warfare, most of whom were Turks. At the time, the Turks were nomads who dwelt in the central Eurasian steppe, beyond the border of the Islamic world. They were the ideal military slaves, as life on the steppe made them tough, with extreme endurance and tolerance for hardship. In addition, they were not Muslims, and so Islam did not forbid their enslavement.

The idea was that an army of slaves would be loyal to their master. This may seem like a bizarre expectation, but there was legitimacy to it. The slaves, whether purchased or captured originally, in being sold to their final purchaser would be provided with food and clothing. As the *ghilman* were to guard their master, they would be well treated. Indeed, while they did not technically have legal rights, their status was considerably greater than that of a free peasant farmer. They received pay and often served in various positions of authority. From the master's perspective, since the *ghilman* were foreigners, they would have no local ties or affinities that might cloud their loyalty to him. Furthermore, since their status was directly tied to the master's, it would be in their best interest to serve him effectively.

Yet the system of military slavery was not perfect. Sometimes the *ghilman* would run afoul of the local populace as the result of their arrogance. Conflicts between *ghilman* and the population of Baghdad, the imperial capital, became so intense that Caliph al-Mu'tasim (r. 833–842) moved his palace and *ghilman* guard regiments to a new city— Sāmarrā'—seventy miles to the north. This plan also failed, however, as it isolated the *ghilman*, and they became involved with their own petty rivalries. Over time, al-Mu'tasim became more a prisoner of his slaves than their master. When he had the officers of the regiments killed in order to restore order, the rest of the men in the regiments revolted and terrorized the surrounding lands for a decade before order was restored. Military slaves continued to be used nonetheless—sometimes with similar results—but rarely in the vast numbers employed by the caliphs of the early ninth century. Indeed, afterward, military slaves tended to be used to form the caliphal bodyguard or the backbone of an army rather than the entire army. Thus, advice on how to select military slaves became important for every prince.

By the tenth century the central authority of the Abbasid Empire had collapsed, allowing local dynasties, who gave nominal allegiance to the Abbasid caliph in Baghdad, to flourish. Warfare between the local dynasts was frequent, which further necessitated the employment of military slaves. In addition, the Turks of central Asia began to enter the Middle East in increasing numbers, not always as slaves but rather as nomads seeking new pasturelands. The increasing Turkish presence led the Persian population to reconsider their status, especially upon the arrival of the Seljuk Turks, who conquered much of the Middle East in the eleventh century. Having previously been ruled by Arabs under the Abbasids, they were now ruled by the Turks.

In the eleventh century, then, the Persian-speaking population was beginning to reassert its cultural identity in the face of Turkic military superiority and the Arab identity characterized by the religion of Islam. In a sense, the Persians sought to establish their own identity before it was completely lost, and a major source of this identity was the pre-Islamic period, with its numerous empires and glorious culture. Thus, Kai Kaus wrote the *Qābūs nāmeh* in 1082–1083 in a simple, yet direct style rich in aphorisms and verses from poetry as well as the Qur'an. Aside from the section discussing slavery, the book also contains in its forty-four chapters sections with advice on love, politics, games, and other topics, making it part of the "Mirrors for Princes" genre. Although the book is primarily concerned with the history of Kai Kaus's grandfather, Qābūs, as part of the "mirror" genre the book is aptly named: *Qābūs* is also the Persian word for young men, more precisely young gentlemen or nobility in the British social sense. The ultimate goal of the book was to guide young princes in life—in making proper decisions not only in their private lives but also as rulers. Kai Kaus used his grandfather as the guiding example.

About the Author

Very little is known about Kai Kaus ibn Iskandar (1020–1083?), who lived in the region south of the Caspian Sea known as Gīlān and Māzandarān—a mountainous area in modern-day Iran with a strong independent streak. As a member of the Ziyarid Dynasty, which had ruled the region since the tenth century, he reigned from 1049 to 1069. It is not clear why he ceased to rule, but the fact that he continued a fairly active life until at least 1083 indicates that he left the throne peacefully. Prior to ruling the region, he served as a boon companion to the Ghaznavid prince Mawdud ibn Ma'ūd (r. 1041–1048). As a boon companion, Kai Kaus served to amuse, entertain, and even defend the prince. He was not part of the Ghaznavid government, in modern-day Afghanistan, though he may have learned many aspects of ruling from his time there. In 1049 Kai Kaus ascended the Ziyarid throne; however, his ascension coincided with the rise of the Seljuk Turks in the Middle East. As the Seljuks conquered Iran and eventually reached modern Turkey, smaller kingdoms found the Turks on their borders. The Seljuk presence and ultimate incorporation of Gīlān and Māzandarān into the Seljuk Empire may have been the cause of Kai Kaus's departure from the throne.

Once he no longer ruled a kingdom, Kai Kaus apparently spent his retirement contemplating the past and writing. In 1082–1083, at the age of sixty-three, Kai Kaus wrote the *Qābūs nāmeh* (The Book of Qābūs), centered on the life of his grandfather. Qābūs ibn Wushmajir ibn Ziya ruled the region from 977 to 981 and then again from 998 to 1012, marking the high point of Ziyarid power.

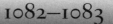
Explanation and Analysis of the Document

Dynastic histories were common enough, and it made sense that Kai Kaus would want to commemorate the golden age of the Ziyarids in the looming shadow of the Seljuks. Yet what makes the *Qābūs nāmeh* different is that Kai Kaus does much more than simply provide a narrative history of events and actors. In the text he attaches the glories of the Ziyarids not only to the region but also to the pre-Islamic past of Iran. The attachment to the pre-Islamic past solidifies the book's status as part of the pre-Islamic genre of "Mirrors for Princes," which served as guides to governance. In addition, unlike the authors of other such "mirrors," Kai Kaus emphasizes more than the running of a kingdom, providing advice on a wide range of topics and activities such as how to play polo. The passage on how to purchase slaves is but one example of the nature of the contents of the *Qābūs nāmeh*. Other chapters are similar, in that the advice is typically detailed yet to the point. Overall, Kai Kaus's "mirror" reflects not only the concerns of governing a territory but also the means to properly upholding the image of a gentleman and ruler outside the palace. This advice could have been utilized by princes as well as other young men and notables within and even outside the Islamic world.

◆ Paragraphs 1–5

The opening paragraphs discuss the fundamental process and problems associated with purchasing slaves. The author notes that one cannot simply compare buying men with buying other commodities as there are so many facets to human nature that one must rely on physiognomy. *Physiognomy* is the art or practice of determining a person's character by their physical features. Kai Kaus places particular emphasis on paying attention to a slave's face, especially the eyes and eyebrows. He mentions that God placed beauty in the eyes and eyebrows, calling to mind the adage "The eyes are the window to the soul." Most important, by judging the face, the buyer can evaluate the attitude and general health of the slave. While Kai Kaus's emphasis on beauty may seem a bit shallow, he is not necessarily speaking only about physical beauty. Nonetheless, for the sake of appearances, princes did choose the most comely slaves possible.

◆ Paragraphs 6–12

In the ensuing paragraphs, the author discusses the properties that one should look for in a slave and reminds the reader of the importance of considering that the desired physical characteristics will vary according to the intended occupation. In the first description, of a slave for "private service," Kai Kaus portrays a young and good-looking boy who can serve as a page and remain in the constant company of the prince. From the description, the specified slave would be Greek or perhaps Slavic. In fact, the word *slave* is in part rooted in the immense numbers of Slavs sold throughout the Middle East and the Mediterranean basin in medieval times.

The author then discusses clever slaves, who may be purchased to serve as treasurers or in other bureaucratic occupations. This physical description appears to indicate a man of Mediterranean origin, most likely Greek or perhaps Armenian—both were usually considered well educated and versed in commerce and thus ideal for such occupations. While the author is racially stereotyping slaves, there is some legitimate consideration behind each category, stemming from the realities of the medieval world. Slaves coming from the Byzantine Empire were much more likely to have been educated than, say, those from Russia or sub-Saharan Africa simply owing to the level of civilization and culture in those particular regions at the time.

With respect to slaves who would play musical instruments, the author again emphasizes physical appearance. To be a satisfactory entertainer, the slave must have a pleasing face and build. It is notable that in Kai Kaus's estimation, someone with a fleshy or rather fat face is incapable of learning. Most likely this stems from the notion that such persons would be lazy and not engaged in physical activities. The author also indicates that the fingers should be long, a common feature among successful musicians. Many slaves purchased for musical entertainment would not have had previous knowledge of the use of musical instruments and thus would need to learn. A facile mind and long dexterous fingers would offer them a better chance of success, particularly with the stringed instruments often played in the background at the court or in a prince's private chambers.

The next type of slave is a warrior, or *mamluk*. These slaves would typically serve as bodyguards for the prince, though often a prince would purchase sufficient quantities of warrior slaves to serve as an independent body in his army. Indeed, during the Crusades some princes possessed a regiment or more of *mamluks*. The physical description makes sense for any warrior—broad shoulders and a deep chest tell of a muscular upper body. Yet a closer examination reveals some indication for a racial preference. The broad shoulders and deep chest are very indicative of steppe archers, who would have drawn their powerful composite bows since childhood. Also the preference for black eyes and a round head gives a nod to the Turks, who, coming out of the Eurasian steppe, tended to have more of an Asian appearance than one might find in modern-day Turkey. Indeed, by the eleventh century, Turks—free and as *mamluks*—were the dominate military force owing to their status as horse-borne archers.

The description of the slave for employment clearly depicts a eunuch, or castrated male. Eunuchs were commonly employed in the harem, which was much more than a collection of women retained to pleasure the prince. The act of castration varied greatly; in some cases, the entire male genitalia was removed (to avoid the possibility of one

remaining "over-fond of women"). The creation of a eunuch was a costly endeavor, as one had to not only purchase the slave but also then hope he would survive the ordeal of becoming a eunuch. Thus, purchasing a slave who was already a eunuch was worth the cost. Should a slave survive his transformation into a eunuch, over time his body would change. The absence of testosterone would give his voice a higher pitch, and he would suffer from loss of muscle tone. Most eunuchs tended to be African. The comment on the eyes here is telling about an unspoken concern for all princes: access to the harem. Only the prince and young children whose mothers were in the harem could enter it; indeed, the Arabic *harīm* means "forbidden." Nonetheless, the women of the harem needed servants, and so intrigue abounded in the medieval courts. The primary purpose of the harem was to produce an heir to the throne, so the prince wanted to make sure that he was the only one copulating with the women there. Eunuchs could be coerced through a variety of means to allow a woman to slip out or even a man to slip in (often in disguise).

Kai Kaus next discusses herdsmen or grooms. It is clear that he has very little regard for this kind of slave, who will be dealing with livestock. The wide-eyed, open-browed, uncivilized description is indicative of Turks. They, being pastoral nomads with vast knowledge of livestock care. would be well suited to the task. Being a herdsman was a risky occupation, as one would face wild animals such as wolves and lions as well as livestock rustlers and bandits.

The final category of slave discussed by Kai Kaus is a common domestic slave. The eye color indicates that the slave should be either a northern European or a Slav and somewhat attractive. Again, as the slave would be employed in domestic duties within the palace, he would be seen by the public. Maintaining a certain public image was important in the demonstration of power.

◆ **Paragraphs 13–22**

The third section discusses racial attributes of the various peoples sometimes held as slaves: Turks, Slavs, Russians, Alans (from the steppes north of the Caucasus), Byzantines (Greeks), Armenians, Hindus (Indians), Abyssinians (Ethiopians), and Nubians (any other sub-Saharan Africans). For all of the races mentioned, Kai Kaus lists merits and faults, to aid princes in selecting the proper personality for the desired job. Interestingly, the author notes that the Turks were "not all of one race" but included groups understood by modern historians to be non-Turkic, such as Tibetans and Khutanese (from the city of Khotan near the Taklimakan Desert, north of Tibet). His inclusion of these peoples among those known as Turks may have been motivated by their physical appearance as well as their pastoral-nomadic lifestyle. Kai Kaus discusses the Turks more than any other race, which demonstrates the elevated importance of the Turks in the region, both as slaves generally and for their dominant military prowess.

The author then discusses the Slavs, Russians, and Alans, who lived between the Black and Caspian seas as seminomadic cultures and had Caucasian features, in contrast to

Qezal Owzan River flows through a valley of the Alborz Mountains north of Tehran in the province of Gilan.
(© Brian A. Vikander/CORBIS)

the Asian appearance of the Turks. As the Alans were a steppe culture, Kai Kaus was inclined to compare them to the Turks in terms of readiness for warfare. At the same time he also compares them in terms of artistic abilities to the Byzantines, another group with whom the Alans had considerable contact. He concludes that the Alans could be trained for more cerebral tasks, but one had to be careful with them in light of their less favorable qualities. Meanwhile, his assessments of the Byzantines and Armenians are very similar—much of their negative attributes should be understood to stem from two facets: First, both were enemies of the Persians, and, second, they were Christians. Nonetheless, Kai Kaus shows them grudging respect for their intellectual abilities, which, considering the complex bureaucracy of the Byzantine Empire, would have been impossible to ignore.

The final group that he discusses in detail are Hindus, or Indians. Although Muslims entered India in the seventh and eighth centuries, major penetration of India by Muslims did not occur until the eleventh century under the Ghaznavids, of modern-day Afghanistan. While the contact was ostensibly made under the guise of jihad, to defend the faithful or extend the domains of Islam, often the invasions of India were little more than plundering expeditions. Part of the loot included slaves—indeed, so many Indian slaves were carried back over the mountains into the Ghaznavid

kingdom that the range between the regions became known as the Hindu Kush, or "Killer of Hindus." Although India contains myriad ethnic groups, Kai Kaus chooses a religious identity for them—likely owing in part to the probable circumstance that he knew little about the racial or ethnic identities of India but also because some Indians had converted to Islam; thus it was simpler just to divide them on the basis of religion, which often served as the primary aspect of identity in much of the medieval world. He then subdivides Hindus much as he did with Turks. However, and perhaps unbeknownst to Kai Kaus, his divisions are based not on tribal affiliation but rather on caste. Indeed, he notes that Brahmans, one of the highest and accordingly most-educated castes in Hinduism, were clever. The attributes of the Rāwat, a warrior caste, and Kirār, a farmer caste, were also emphasized and preferred.

◆ Paragraphs 23–26

The following paragraphs deal with the actual buying and treatment of slaves, in particular with regard to checking the physical attributes of slaves for defects. While Kai Kaus earlier emphasizes the import of a pleasing physical appearance, here he tries to emphasize that a defect may be acceptable and that one should scrutinize even the finest-looking slave. The author notes defects that could be

> *"When you set out to buy slaves, be cautious."*
>
> (Paragraph 1)

> *"Whoever it may be that inspects the slave must first look at the face, which is always open to view, whereas the body can only be seen as occasion offers."*
>
> (Paragraph 4)

> *"Do not be content with a single look; many a good slave may appear vile at first sight and many an extremely vile one appear to be good. "*
>
> (Paragraph 23)

> *"And when a slave truly desires to be sold, do not dispute with him, but sell; when a slave demands to be sold or a wife to be divorced, then sell or divorce, because you will have no pleasure from either."*
>
> (Paragraph 28)

> *"Further, do not assemble a useless family about you; a small family is a second form of wealth."*
>
> (Paragraph 29)

> *"Set no store by the slave who always, when called to any work, demands to be sold and never has any fears with regard to being bought and sold; you will gain nothing good from him."*
>
> (Paragraph 31)

attributed to illness both physical and mental. In addition, he notes the dying of hair and other ruses employed by slave traders to mask defects in slaves.

Kai Kaus—who knew Persian and most likely Arabic as a second language—stresses that it is preferable to buy a slave who cannot speak Arabic, which was the language of Islam. Many non-Arabs knew enough Arabic to fulfill religious obligations but little beyond that. Kai Kaus's own feelings of inadequacy in this area seem to betray him here: There is indeed strategic merit to his suggestion that non-Arabic speakers are preferable, as in learning the language from scratch, their skill would always be inferior to the master's, thus demonstrating his mastery over them.

The author's last comments in this section have familiar yet different echoes in the modern world. Just as one should supposedly not go grocery shopping when hungry, Kai Kaus urges a prince not to purchase a slave girl when feeling amorous but to "abate your desires" first and then look. His advice demonstrates that in his view, a master ought to be mindful of the feelings of his slaves; in Islamic culture, slaves were not mere chattel.

◆ **Paragraphs 27–31**

In Islam, slaves did possess some basic rights and could serve in various positions of authority. Thus when Kai Kaus speaks of never purchasing slaves who have been treated with affection elsewhere, he is referring to a variety of levels of affection including love, friendship, and trust. He warns that if a slave was previously held in high esteem, that slave will have similar expectations from his or her new owner. This final portion of the excerpt also deals with what one should do after the slave has been purchased. The text indicates that one should be stern with a slave but not necessarily physical. Kai Kaus asserts that one should immediately sell a slave who will not work, for not only does the master solve a problem by ridding himself of a nuisance, but the act also serves as an example for other slaves should they neglect their duties.

Audience

Many people have read the *Qābūs nāmeh*, from the medieval era to the present. Indeed, it is considered, along with Niẓām al-Mulk's *Siyāsat nāmeh*, one of the essential works of the "Mirrors for Princes" genre. Being the primary audience, princes especially would read them, often as urged by their advisers, who were also likely to read them. The "mirrors" were very popular in medieval court circles and gained wide circulation throughout the Islamic world. Minor nobility and local notables, such as village elders, would sometimes possess a "mirror" so that they might learn how to better themselves. In the modern age, Kai Kaus's "mirror" is considered one of the greatest works of Persian prose.

Impact

The *Qābūs nāmeh* is an excellent model of the "mirror" genre but also captures the history of the Ziyarid Dynasty,

an often-overlooked yet important dynasty in Persian history. While the text became very popular in court circles throughout the Islamic world—particularly the eastern half, where Persian was largely used—it is difficult to assess how many people read or heeded Kai Kaus's advice. His descriptions of slaves and their characteristics are similar to those that appear in later sources, so at the very least it is safe to say that the work carried some influence.

Of greater importance, however, was the literary impact. As noted, the *Qābūs nāmeh* is considered a classic of early medieval Persian literature. This assessment is based not only on the wide-ranging content but also on the style and use of language. Kai Kaus wrote in a lucid and direct manner. Although he did incorporate some Arabic words, poetry, and verses from the Qur'an, as was common in all Persian literature at the time, he helped develop and maintain a Persian concept of literature, particular as part of the "Mirrors for Princes" genre.

Further Reading

■ Articles

Ayalon, David. "On the Term *Khādim* in the Sense of 'Eunuch' in the Early Muslim Sources." *Arabica* 32 (November 1985): 289–308.

Bosworth, C. E. "The Heritage of Rulership in Early Islamic Iran and the Search for Dynastic Connections with the Past." *Iran* 11 (1973): 51–62.

■ Books

Ayalon, David. "Preliminary Remarks on the Mamluk Military Instititution in Islam." In *War, Technology and Society in the Mid-*

Questions for Further Study

1. Compare this document with Machiavelli's work *The Prince* and with Niẓām al-Mulk's *Book of Government; or, Rules for Kings*. In what sense are these documents "Mirrors for Princes"? How do the documents reflect the differences in the cultures that produced them?

2. Compare and contrast slavery as the term was understood by Kai Kaus and slavery as it would have been understood by the authors of Act for the Abolition of Slavery throughout the British Colonies. Why are the similarities and differences important?

3. Many milestone documents are inspirational, making statements about the advance of human freedom, the development of law, and similar concerns. This document clinically discusses the purchasing of slaves—something that is abhorrent in the modern world—and compounds it with discussion of racial distinctions among slaves. In what sense is this a "milestone" document? Why should a modern reader be interested in it?

4. What historical factors surrounding the Ziyarid Dynasty made advice about the purchase of slaves timely?

dle East, eds. V. J. Parry and M. E. Yapp. London: Oxford University Press, 1975.

Crone, Patricia. *Slaves on Horses: The Evolution of the Islamic Polity*. Cambridge, U.K.: Cambridge University Press, 1980.

Irwin, Robert. *The Middle East in the Middle Ages: The Early Mamluk Sultanate, 1250–1382*. London: Croom Helm, 1986.

Lewis, Bernard. *Race and Slavery in the Middle East: An Historical Enquiry*. New York: Oxford University Press, 1990.

Lindsay, James E. *Daily Life in the Medieval Islamic World*. Westport, Conn.: Greenwood Press, 2005.

Segal, Ronald. *Islam's Black Slaves: The Other Black Diaspora*. New York: Farrar, Straus and Giroux, 2001.

■ **Web Sites**

"Islam and Slavery." Feminist Sexual Ethics Project, Brandeis University Web site.
   http://www.brandeis.edu/projects/fse/Pages/islamandslavery
   .html.

—Timothy May

KAI KAUS ON THE PURCHASE OF SLAVES

When you set out to buy slaves, be cautious. The buying of men is a difficult art; because many a slave may appear to be good, who, regarded with knowledge, turns out to be the opposite. Most people imagine that buying slaves is like any other form of trading, not understanding that the buying of slaves, or the art of doing so, is a branch of philosophy. Anyone who buys goods of which he has no competent understanding can be defrauded over them, and the most difficult form of knowledge is that which deals with human beings. There are so many blemishes and good points in the human kind, and a single blemish may conceal a myriad good points, while a single good point may conceal a myriad faults.

Human beings cannot be known except by the science of physiognomy and by experience, and the science of physiognomy in its entirety is a branch of prophecy that is not acquired to perfection except by the divinely directed apostle. The reason is that by physiognomy the inward goodness or wickedness of men can be ascertained.

Now let me describe to the best of my ability what is essential in the purchasing of slaves, both white and black, and what their good and bad points are, so that they may be known to you. Understand then that there are three essentials in the buying of slaves; first is the recognition of their good and bad qualities, whether external or internal, by means of physiognomy; second is the awareness of diseases, whether latent or apparent, by their symptoms; third is the knowledge of the various classes and the defects and merits of each.

With regard to the first requirement, that of physiognomy, it consists of close observation when buying slaves. (The buyers of slaves are of all categories: there are those who inspect the face, disregarding body and extremities; others look to the corpulence or otherwise of the slave.) Whoever it may be that inspects the slave must first look at the face, which is always open to view, whereas the body can only be seen as occasion offers. Then look at eyes and eyebrows, followed by nose, lips and teeth, and lastly at the hair. The reason for this is that God placed the beauty of human beings in eyes and eyebrows, delicacy in the nose, sweetness in the lips and teeth and freshness in the skin. To all these the hair of the head has been made to lend adornment, since [God] created the hair for adornment.

You must, consequently, inspect everything. When you see beauty in the eyes and eyebrows, delicacy in the nose, sweetness in the lips and teeth and freshness in the skin, then buy the slave possessing them without concerning yourself over the extremities of the body. If all of these qualities are not present, then the slave most possess delicacy; because, in my opinion, one that is delicate without having beauty is preferable to one that is beautiful but not possessed of delicacy.

The learned say that one must know the indications and signs by which to buy the slaves suited for particular duties. The slave that you buy for your private service and conviviality should be of middle proportions, neither tall nor short, fat nor lean, pale nor florid, thickset nor slender, curly-haired nor with hair overstraight. When you see a slave soft-fleshed, fine-skinned, with regular bones and wine-coloured hair, black eyelashes, dark eyes, black eyebrows, open-eyed, long-nosed, slender-waisted, round-chinned, red-lipped, with white regular teeth, and all his members such as I have described, such a slave will be decorative and companionable, loyal, of delicate character, and dignified.

The mark of the slave who is clever and may be expected to improve is this: he must be of erect stature, medium in hair and in flesh, broad of hand and with the middle of the fingers lengthy, in complexion dark though ruddy, dark-eyed, open-faced and unsmiling. A slave of this kind would be competent to acquire learning, to act as treasurer or for any other [such] employment.

The slave suited to play musical instruments is marked out by being soft-fleshed (though his flesh most not be over-abundant, especially on the back), with his fingers slender, neither lean nor fat. (A slave whose face is over fleshy, incidentally, is one incapable of learning.) His hands must be soft, with the middles of the fingers lengthy. He must be bright-visaged, having the skin tight; his hair must not be too long, too short or too black. It is better, also, for the soles of the feet to be regular. A slave of this kind will swiftly acquire a delicate art of whatever kind, particularly that of the instrumentalist.

The mark of the slave suited for arms-bearing is that his hair is thick, his body tall and erect, his build powerful, his flesh hard, his bones thick, his skin coarse and his limbs straight, the joints being firm. The tendons should be tight and the sinews and blood-vessels prominent and visible on the body. Shoulders must be broad, the chest deep, the neck thick and the head round; also for preference he should be bald. The belly should be concave, the buttocks drawn in and the legs in walking well extended. And the eyes should be black. Any slave who possesses these qualities will be a champion in single combat, brave and successful.

The mark of the slave suited for employment in the women's apartments is that he should be dark-skinned and sour-visaged and have withered limbs, scanty hair, a shrill voice, little [slender] feet, duck lips, a flat nose, stubby fingers, a bowed figure, and a thin neck. A slave with these qualities will be suitable for service in the women's quarters. He must not have a white skin nor a fair complexion; and beware of a ruddy-complexioned man, particularly if his hair is limp. His eyes, farther, should not be languorous or moist; a man having such qualities is either over-fond of women or prone to act as a go-between.

The mark of the slave who is callous [insensitive] and suited to be a herdsman or groom is that he should be open-browed and wide-eyed, and his eyelids should be flecked with red. He should, further, be long in lips and teeth and his mouth should be wide. A slave with these qualities is extremely callous, fearless and uncivilized.

The mark of the slave suited for domestic service and cookery is that he should be clean in face and body, round-faced, with hands and feet slender, his eyes dark inclining to blue, sound in body, silent, the hair of his head wine-colored and falling forward limply. A slave with these qualities is suitable for the occupations mentioned.

Each then, should have the essential characteristics which I have recounted. But I will also mention the defects and virtues which should be known in respect of each separate race. You must understand that Turks are not all of one race, and each has its own nature and essential character. Amongst them the most ill-tempered are the Ghuzz and the Qipchāqs; the best-tempered and most willing are the Khutanese, the Khallukhīs, and the Tibetans; the boldest and most courageous are the Turghay (?), the most inured to toil and hardship and the most active are the Tatars and the Yaghmā, whereas the laziest of all are the Chigil.

It is a fact well-known to all that beauty or ugliness in the Turks is the opposite of that in the Indians. If you observe the Turk feature by feature [he has] a large head, a broad face, narrow eyes, a flat nose, and unpleasing lips and teeth. Regarded individually the features are not handsome, yet the whole is handsome. The Indian's face is the opposite of this; each individual feature regarded by itself appears handsome, yet looked at as a whole the face does not create the same impression as that of the Turk. To begin with, the Turk has a personal freshness and clearness of complexion not possessed by the Indian; indeed the Turks win for freshness against all other races.

Without any doubt, what is fine in the Turks is present in a superlative degree, but so also is what is ugly in them. Their faults in general are that they are blunt-witted, ignorant, boastful, turbulent, discontented, and without a sense of justice. Without any excuse they will create trouble and utter foul language, and at night they are poor-hearted. Their merit is that they are brave, free from pretense, open in enmity, and zealous in any task allotted to them. For the [domestic] establishment there is no better race.

Slavs, Russians, and Alans are near in their temperament to the Turks, but are more patient. The Alans are more courageous than the Turks at night and more friendly disposed towards their masters. Although in their craftsmanship they are nearer to the Byzantines, being artistic, yet there are faults in them of various kinds; for example they are prone to theft, disobedience, betrayal of secrets, impatience, stupidity, indolence, hostility to their masters, and escaping. Their virtues are that they are soft-natured, agreeable, and quick of understanding. Further they are deliberate in action, direct in speech, brave, good road-guides, and possessed of good memory.

The defect of the Byzantines is that they are foul-tongued, evil-hearted, cowardly, indolent, quick-tempered, covetous, and greedy for worldly things. Their merits are that they are cautious, affectionate, happy, economically minded, successful in their undertakings, and careful to prevent loss.

The defect of the Armenians is that they are mischievous, foul-mouthed, thieving, impudent, prone to flight, disobedient, babblers, liars, friendly to misbelief, and hostile to their masters. From head to foot, indeed, they incline rather towards defects than to merits. Yet they are quick of understanding and learn their tasks well.

The defect of the Hindu is that he is evil-tongued and in the house no slave-girl is safe from him. But the various classes of the Hindus are unlike those that prevail amongst other peoples, because in other peoples the classes mingle with each other, whereas the Hindus, ever since the time of Adam (Upon whom be peace!), have practiced the following custom: namely, no trade will form an alliance with any outside it. Thus, grocers will give their daughters only to grocers, butchers to butchers, bakers to bakers, and soldiers to soldiers.

Each of these groups therefore has its own special character, which I cannot describe one by one because that would entail a book in itself.

However, the best of them, people benevolent, brave or skilled in commerce, are [respectively] the Brahman, the Rāwat and the Kirār. The Brahman is clever, the Rāwat brave, and the Kirār skilled in commerce, each class being superior to the one after. The Nubian and the Abyssinian are freer of faults, and the Abyssinian is better than the Nubian because many things were said by the Prophet in praise of the former.

These then are the facts concerning each race and the merits and defects of each.

Now the third essential is being completely alive to defects both external and internal through knowledge of symptoms, and this means that at the time of buying you may not be careless. Do not be content with a single look; many a good slave may appear vile at first sight and many an extremely vile one appear to be good. Further there is the fact that a human being's visage does not continually bear the same complexion. Sometimes it is more inclined to be handsome, at other times to be ugly. You must carefully inspect all the limbs and organs to ensure that nothing remains hidden from you. There are many latent diseases which are on the point of coming but have not yet appeared and will do so within a few days; such diseases have their symptoms.

Thus, if there is a yellowness in the complexion, the lips being changed [from the normal] in colour, and dry, that is the symptom of haemorrhoids. If the eyelids are continuously swollen, it is a symptom of dropsy. Redness in the eyes and a fullness of the veins in the forehead are the mark of epilepsy. Tearing out the hair, flickering of the eyelashes and chewing of the lips are the signs of melancholia. Crookedness in the bone of the nose or irregularity in it are the symptoms of fistula; hair that is extremely black, but more so in one place than another, shows that the hair has been dyed. If here and there upon the body you perceive the marks of branding where no branding should be, examine closely to ensure that there is no leprosy under it. Yellowness in the eyes and a change [from the ordinary] in the colour of the face are the symptoms of jaundice.

When you buy a slave, you must take and lay him down, press him on both sides and watch closely that he has no pain or swelling. If he has, it will be in the liver or spleen. Having looked for such hidden defects, seek further for the open ones, such as smells from the mouth and nose, hardness of hearing, hesitation in utterance, irregularity of speech, walking off the [straight] road, coarseness of the joints, and hardness at the base of the teeth, to prevent any trickery being practised on you.

When you have seen all that I have mentioned and have made certain, then if you should buy, do so from honest people, and so secure a person who will be of advantage to your household. As long as you can find a non-Arab do not buy an Arabic-speaking slave. You can mould a non-Arab to your ways, but never the one whose tongue is Arabic. Further, do not have a slave-girl brought before you when your appetites are strong upon you; when desire is strong, it makes what is ugly appear good in your eyes. First abate your desires and then engage in the business of purchasing.

Never buy a slave who has been treated with affection in another place. If you do not hold him dear, he will show ingratitude to you, or will flee, or will demand to be sold, or will nourish hatred in his heart for you. Even if you regard him with affection, he will show you no gratitude, in view of what he has experienced elsewhere. Buy your slave from a house in which he has been badly treated, so that he will be grateful for the least kindness on your part and will hold you in affection. From time to time make your slaves a gift of something; do not allow them to be constantly in need of money in such a way that they are compelled to go out seeking it.

Buy slaves of a good price, for each one's value is in accordance with his price. Do not buy a slave who has had numerous masters; a woman who has had many husbands and a slave who has had many masters are held in no esteem. Let those you buy be well-favoured. And when a slave truly desires to be sold, do not dispute with him, but sell; when a slave demands to be sold or a wife to be divorced, then sell or divorce, because you will have no pleasure from either.

If a slave is deliberately (and not through inadvertence or mistake) lazy or neglectful in his work, do not teach him under compulsion to improve; have no expectation of that, for he will in no wise become industrious or capable of improvement. Sell him quickly; you may rouse a sleeping man with a shout, but a dead body cannot be roused by the sound of a hundred trumpets and drums. Further, do not assemble a useless family about you; a small family is a second form of wealth.

Provide for your slaves in such fashion that they will not escape, and treat them that you have well, as befits your dignity; if you have one person in good condition it is better than having two in ill condition. Do not permit your male slave to take to himself in your household someone whom he calls "brother," nor permit slave-girls to claim sisterhood with each other; it leads to great trouble. On bond and free impose the burdens which they are able to bear, that they may not be disobedient through sheer weakness. Keep yourself ever adorned with justice, that you may be included amongst them that are honoured as such.

The slave must recognize your brother, sister, mother or father as his master. Never buy a dealer's exhausted slave; he is as fearful of the dealer as the ass is of the farrier. Set no store by the slave who always, when called to any work, demands to be sold and never has any fears with regard to being bought and sold; you will gain nothing good from him. Change him quickly for another, seeking out one such as I have described. Thus you will achieve your purpose and suffer no troubles.

Glossary

divinely directed apostle	Muhammad
prophecy	the disclosure, through divine inspiration, of the will of the deity

Domesday Book

"Anyone summoned on military service [who] did not go [should forfeit] all his land to the king."

Overview

The *Domesday Book*, commissioned by King William I (William the Conqueror) of England in 1085 and completed a year later, is the popular name given to a census and property register of England. Its formal name at the time was *Liber Wintoniensis* (*Book of Winchester*); Winchester was the location of the king's treasury, where the manuscript was stored. The *Domesday Book* recorded information about landholders and their tenants, the extent of their landholdings, and the number of people who lived on the land. It also detailed the extent of their resources: meadows, woodlands, and farm animals such as sheep and pigs. Further, it documented information such as the number of plows on the land and buildings, including mills, castles, churches, salt houses (where salt used for the preservation of meat was stored), and other structures. In the larger towns, the *Domesday Book* recorded the number of houses and information about the number of people engaged in trade. As a population census, though, it was incomplete because it counted only householders, not their families, and it omitted the population of England's major cities, including London. Additionally, the survey was never completed for four of England's northernmost counties and much of a fifth.

The book's peculiar name was not used until about 1176, when a chronicler of that era and treasurer for King Henry II, Richard Fitzneale (also called Richard Fitznigel, or Fitz Nigel, and Richard of Ely), stated in a treatise called *Dialogus de Scaccario* (*Dialogue concerning the Exchequer*) that the English called the book *Domesdai*. *Domesday* is an early form of the word *doomsday*, but the book is not a prophetic work about the end of the world. The book acquired the name because the English people began to compare it to the Last Judgment, or doomsday, of the Bible. It was believed that at the Last Judgment a person's deeds as recorded in the Book of Life would be used to determine whether that person merited entrance into heaven or would be condemned to hell. Because of its scope and finality, the *Domesday Book* was thought to be like the Book of Life—and as with the Book of Life, its findings could not be appealed. Indeed, one contemporary account from 1085 of the book's compilation suggested as much: "It is shame to tell what he thought it no shame for him to do. Ox, nor cow, nor swine was left that was not set down upon his writ" (qtd. at http://www.newadvent.org/cathen/05103a.htm). Nearly a century later, Fitzneale wrote: "This book is metaphorically called by the native English, Domesdai, the Day of Judgement. For as the sentence of that strict and terrible last account cannot be evaded by any subterfuge, so when this book is appealed to on those matters which it contains, its sentence cannot be quashed or set aside with impunity" (qtd. at http://www.history-magazine.com/domes day.html). Indeed, many English citizens resented the intrusion that the process of compiling the information represented.

To refer to the *Domesday Book* in the singular is slightly misleading, for there are in fact two such books. After the information was gathered, the intention was to compile and condense it into a more usable form. Much of that task was completed in two volumes, the larger of which is called *Great Domesday*, or sometimes the *Exchequer Domesday*. The process of compilation and condensation was not completed for five of England's counties, though, because William I died in 1087, so that material remained in raw form in the *Little Domesday*. Nevertheless, it has become customary to refer to the two volumes together in the singular. A third volume, called the *Inquisitio Eliensis*, or *Ely Inquest*, recorded similar information just for the abbey of Ely and thus could be considered part of the complete project.

Context

The chief event that provided the historical context for the creation of the *Domesday Book* was the turmoil surrounding the Norman Conquest of 1066, when various figures contended for the throne of England. Until this time, England was largely under the control of the Anglo-Saxons, the descendants of various Germanic tribes that had invaded and conquered much of England after the collapse of Roman control over Britannia in the fifth century. Anglo-Saxon nobles owned most of the land and were ruled by kings who came from their ranks, though Viking invaders also had a foothold in England and established what had come to be called the Danelaw, a swath of northern and

1016
- The Danish king Canute seizes the throne of England, driving Edward the Confessor into exile in Normandy.

CA. 1027—1028
- William I, known as William the Conqueror, is born in Falaise, Normandy.

1042
- Edward returns to England from exile in Normandy to claim the throne.

1066
- **January 5**
  Edward dies; Harold is crowned king of England.
- **October 14**
  William defeats English forces at the Battle of Hastings.
- **December 25**
  William is crowned king of England.

1085
- William commissions the process of gathering information that would be compiled into the *Domesday Book*.

1086
- The process of compiling the information for the *Domesday Book* is completed.

1087
- **September 9**
  William dies.

eastern England dominated by Vikings from Denmark. Contentions among the Anglo-Saxon nobles, however, enabled Canute the Great (also spelled Cnut, Knut, or Knud), the Viking king of Denmark, to invade England and declare himself king in 1016. In the process, he drove the Anglo-Saxon heir to the throne, Edward the Confessor (also spelled Eadward), into exile in Normandy in northwestern France. In Normandy, Edward was protected by his uncle, the duke of Normandy, until he returned to England and ascended the throne in 1042 after the death of Canute in 1035.

For the next twenty years, Edward tried to consolidate his power, though he ran into opposition in the person of Harold II, also known as Harold Godwin (sometimes spelled Godwine). Harold, the son of the powerful Earl of Wessex and Edward's brother-in-law, saw that Edward was likely to die without an heir and coveted the crown for himself. Meanwhile, Normandy was experiencing its own political upheavals, out of which the duke's illegitimate son, William, emerged as the most powerful figure. From the 1040s to the 1060s, William seized control of Normandy and neighboring French provinces and gained a reputation as a strong, ruthless ruler—and one who was loyal to Edward in England. Edward, for his part, knowing he would die childless (he hated his wife and had nothing to do with her, which perhaps explained his religious vow of celibacy), was equally loyal to William and promised the throne of England to him, although this point is a matter of some dispute. When Edward died in early 1066, the stage was set for William to invade England and defeat Harold, who had been crowned king of England shortly after Edward's death and to whom Edward may have promised the throne on his deathbed, although this point, too, is unclear.

In September 1066, William made his move to enforce his claim to the throne. The key battle took place on October 14, 1066, when William defeated the English forces at the Battle of Hastings. In the weeks that followed, William's armies consolidated his hold on England. On Christmas Day of 1066, William was crowned king of England. William, however, was not secure on his throne. In particular, he feared further invasions on the part of Scandinavians such as King Canute IV of Denmark, who in fact led raids on England, and King Olaf III of Norway. Additionally, William, as ruler of Normandy as well as England, continued to lead military campaigns in France, and the Scots were an ongoing source of rebellion.

Historians debate the purpose of the *Domesday Book*. The chief theory is that William commissioned it to compute the value of land and assets both before and after the Norman Conquest in 1066 for the purposes of taxation to fund military campaigns. Another theory is that he wanted to determine more precisely his own holdings as feudal overlord and thus whether the Crown or local landowners were responsible for such matters as road construction or bridge repair. A third theory is that he simply wanted to know what he had as a way to bring order out of the chaos following the Norman Conquest. Whatever the purpose, the book has survived to provide historians with a snapshot of the material life of people in medieval England. The *Domesday Book* contains a wealth of information and raw data that historians have used to understand medieval English economic and social life. It also sheds light on the position of the Catholic Church in medieval England by establishing the vast extent of church ownership of property and legal claim to services from other property. Most of the 13,418 places mentioned in the book still exist, although the spelling of names has evolved over the centuries, and people of British extraction have used the book to trace their family trees back to the eleventh century. The book also continued to be used into the twentieth century to settle legal disputes over land ownership.

About the Author

Specifying an "author" of the *Domesday Book* is impossible. After the information had been gathered, it was taken to Winchester, where a single anonymous scribe edited and recorded it with the assistance of a second scribe, who checked the first's work. The information was gathered by panels of officials and clerks who had been dispatched to the various parts of England. The officials were generally dukes or bishops; monks were often pressed into service as clerks. These people were given the information they needed by local sheriffs, reeves (officials who directed the affairs of a manor), and priests. Up to six villagers who lived on each manor also provided information.

All of this, of course, was done in the name of King William I, known to history as William the Conqueror. William was born in about 1027 or 1028, the illegitimate son of Robert I, the duke of Normandy. When William was eight years old, Robert died, but he had left instructions that William was to be his successor. A period of considerable anarchy followed, as William's enemies plotted to usurp the dukedom. William survived, with aid of King Henry I of France. After Henry knighted him in 1042, he began to assert control of Normandy as well as of neighboring provinces. His alliance with Edward the Confessor of England was based on blood; Edward's mother was the sister of William's grandmother. It is generally believed that Edward, who had taken a vow of celibacy and would therefore die without an heir, had promised the throne of England to William, though this is a matter of dispute. However, when Edward's brother-in-law, Harold II, assumed the throne in 1066 on Edward's death, William resolved to invade England and enforce his claim. He did just that and was crowned king of England on Christmas Day, 1066.

William, though illiterate and able to speak only French, took great interest in his new domains, which partially explains his motives for having the *Domesday Book* compiled. After the conquest, he had to put down a series of revolts, which he used as a pretext for seizing land from Anglo-Saxon nobles and conveying it to his Norman supporters. In time, Normans had largely replaced the Anglo-Saxon aristocracy, and this was a source of considerable resentment among England's historical nobility. The Nor-

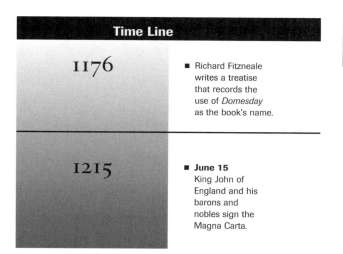

Time Line

1176
- Richard Fitzneale writes a treatise that records the use of *Domesday* as the book's name.

1215
- June 15 King John of England and his barons and nobles sign the Magna Carta.

man presence also altered the social and economic structure of England by imposing French feudalism. Despite Anglo-Saxon resentment, it is probably fair to say that William's imposition of order and administrative efficiency—of which the *Domesday Book* is an example—enabled England to become a major power. William died on September 9, 1087, while on a military campaign in France. Ultimately, every British monarch since then has been able to trace his or her ancestry (often in convoluted fashion) back to William the Conqueror.

Explanation and Analysis of the Document

The *Domesday Book* is not easy or inspirational reading. It contains a multitude of facts and figures about land ownership, usually couched in a vocabulary that is unfamiliar to modern readers. Additionally, the material was condensed, often with abbreviations. An understanding of what the *Domesday Book* contains requires an effort to understand the nature of land ownership in medieval England after the Norman Conquest.

◆ **"Surrey"**
The first excerpts from the document deal with the county of Surrey in southeastern England, south of London. Throughout these sections, the word *hundred* is often used. This word refers to a division of a county that comprised one hundred "hides," another unit of land measurement consisting of 120 acres. The entries thus specify how many hides of land various men held in a particular named hundred. Walter de Douai, for example, held two hides, or 240 acres, from the king. The entry also states that Walter's claim to the land was a matter of some dispute, for none of the residents of the hundred had ever seen a writ from the king. In some instances, the size of a person's landholdings was diminished, as in the case of Gilbert fitzRicher, whose holdings had shrunk from twenty to twelve hides. Numerous other land ownership terms are also used. The term *demesne* generally refers to land reserved for the use of the

Coronation of William I (© British Library Board. All Rights Reserved 064752)

owner and not occupied by tenants. The entry states that Gilbert's land was being worked by thirty-seven "villans," an alternative spelling of the word *villeins*, which generally refers to free peasants. The word *cottars* refers to slightly higher-ranking free peasants. "TRE" is a Latin abbreviation that means "in the time of King Edward" (Tempore Regis Edwardi); a corresponding abbreviation used elsewhere, "TRW," means "in the time of King William" (Tempore Regis Willelmi). Thus, the book records information both from before and after the Norman Conquest.

Geoffrey de Mandeville was one of King William's major tenants in chief and, incidentally, the constable of the Tower of London. As with the lands of Walter de Douai, the *Domesday Book* disputes Geoffrey de Mandeville's hold-

ings, for they were not regarded as part of the holdings of his predecessor, Esger, known as "Esger the Staller." Another entry states that Mandeville held the village of Wanborough, which also had not been part of Esger's land. Potentially, this was an important point, for it shed light on lands to which Geoffrey might have been entitled by inheritance and which ones he was not. The record further states that his ownership of the manor at the village of Carshalton was in dispute, for the "men of the shire"—an administrative district ruled by an alderman and sheriff—had never seen a writ granting his "seisin," or ownership.

At various points, reference is made to the value of holdings. Of course, the £ sign represents pounds in British currency, while "s" refers to shillings (there were twenty shillings in a pound) and "d" to pence (there were twelve pence in a shilling). While it is nearly impossible to establish modern equivalents for these units of currency, the purchasing power of a shilling at the time would have been equivalent to an amount perhaps more than $100 in U.S. currency today. Geoffrey, the record states, had sublet portions of his estate to free men, including a smith who held half a hide with his wife but was not required to perform service for it. This section introduces another term referring to a rank in the feudal system: *bordars*, meaning tenants who held a few acres of land and in exchange performed menial services.

Edward of Salisbury was a prominent citizen, for he was sheriff of the county. A sheriff at the time was less a law-enforcement officer and more an administrative official. What is noteworthy about the entry detailing his holdings is that they had been redistributed after the conquest such that by the time of the *Domesday Book* some two-fifths of the land was in the hands of the church and a further fifth was held by the king. Yet we need not feel sorry for Edward, who continued to hold various tracts of land in three hundreds and was deriving income from three mills as well as from various tenants residing on his land. Similarly, Robert Malet was a prominent baron and one of England's major landowners after the conquest. The excerpt from the *Domesday Book* records only a small portion of his holdings; in fact, he was the owner of an astonishing 257 manors throughout England and family property in Normandy. He would later lose most of his English property, likely because of a falling out with William's successor, William II. Another prominent Norman landowner was Miles Crispin, who held land in Wallingford Hundred, where he may have served as castellan, or warden, of Wallingford Castle, built by his father-in-law, who acquired the land through his wife. Again, the excerpt cites only a small portion of Crispin's holdings. Little is known about Hamo the sheriff, but the *Domesday* record of his landholdings would later become important in establishing the claims of a more prominent noble, Hamo de Crevequer, who held important royal offices in the thirteenth century. An interesting feature of the entry about the holdings of Humphrey the Chamberlain, brother of the sheriff of Dorset, is that the land was being held in the name of the queen.

The Tower of London, part of which—the White Tower—was built in 1078 for William I (© Museum of London)

◆ **"Berkshire"**

The entries for Berkshire introduce new vocabulary and are cast in a different style, perhaps reflecting differences in the way the king's various panels of officials had gone about their tasks. The records state that the deceased King Edward held eight "virgates of land" in the borough of Wallingford. The term *virgate* refers to either a quarter of an acre or a quarter of a hide; since the king had owned the land, it almost certainly refers to the latter. The term *close* refers either to the area around a cathedral or an enclosed pasture; again, the reference seems to be to the latter. The word *moneyer* means an authorized coiner of money, and *quit* probably refers to the transference of an ownership interest. *Messuage* means a dwelling house and its adjacent buildings, along with the land on which they are situated. Additionally, the record notes that Edward held fifteen acres on which dwelt "housecarls," that is, a small standing army.

Unlike the excerpts pertaining to Surrey, these excerpts show the extent of lands held by the church. Bishop Walkelin was a prominent Norman bishop who received grants from the king to build a new cathedral at Winchester, though he offended the king when the latter discovered that the bishop had essentially clear-cut a section of the king's forest to provide timbers for the cathedral. The "abbot of Abingdon" likely refers to Rainald, who earlier had served as King William's chaplain. "The archbishop" is no doubt the archbishop of Canterbury, a position held by Lanfranc at the time; Lanfranc is referred to later in the excerpt. An interesting feature of these excerpts is that they make reference to people whose names appear elsewhere, such as Miles Crispin and Robert d'Oilly, Crispin's father-in-law and the builder of Wallingford Castle. The significance is that there were prominent landowners who were tenants in chief of lands throughout England.

These excerpts also contain more detail about who was entitled to what income, including fines. The following excerpt might seem almost comical to modern ears:

Alweald and Godric have rent from their houses and [the fines due for] bloodshedding, if there is blood-

Milestone Documents

shed there, [and] if the man [accused] is received in them before claim is made by the king's reeve, except on Saturday, on account of the market, because then the king has the fine: and they have the fines for adultery and theft in their houses; other fines, however, are the king's.

Matters such as these were taken seriously at the time, and their mention in the *Domesday Book* is indicative of how the document provided a record of entitlements. Later in the document, detail is provided about the payment of fines for such crimes as murder or breaking into the city. Reference is made to a "tale," which was simply an enumeration or reckoning, related to the word *tally*. Reference is also made to "thegns," a form of the word *thane*. Prior to the conquest, the position of thegn had been relatively high. Thegns held grants of land from the king and were regarded as aristocratic royal retainers. After the conquest, however, there were so many thegns that the position had become devalued; besides the king, bishops began to acquire thegns. Nevertheless, the twelve senior thegns of a hundred sometimes functioned as a grand jury in criminal cases, and thegns were themselves subject only to the jurisdiction of the king. (The thegns "belonged" to the bishops, that is, served their will, but they were apparently under the king's jurisdiction.) The term *geld* is a reference to taxes levied by the king; earlier, King Canute had assessed geld as a form of tribute. The excerpts go into considerable detail about the obligations of thegns with regard to military service and the disposition of property in the event of a thegn's death.

◆ **"The Land of the King"**

The bare statement "King William holds Windsor in demesne" suggests the nature of the king's vast landholdings. From Anglo-Saxon times, Windsor had been the home of the English monarch, and it enjoyed the status of a so-called free borough. This meant that rather than its inhabitants having to pay taxes to the king, the borough itself was a recipient of taxes from other towns. Reference is made to "pannage," which is the right to pasture livestock on grazing land. One entry states that Albert the clerk held "the third part of a dene," which would have been valuable, for a dene was a wooded valley, typically with a stream running through it. The document also states that the king holds the town of Thatcham "in demesne"; Thatcham still has the distinction of being the oldest continuously inhabited place in England. In the entries for Gloucestershire, it is recorded that in the time of King Edward the city of Gloucester had owed the monarch some twelve sesters, or quarts, of honey and thirty-six "dickers of iron." The latter reference is somewhat puzzling, for the term *dicker* usually referred to ten animal hides; thus, a dicker of iron was probably equivalent in worth to ten animal hides. Interestingly, the document notes that the city of Gloucester also owed King William I a certain quantity of iron for use as nails in the king's ships, as well as "£60 at 20[d] to the ora," which refers to a unit of currency introduced by the Danes. The term *vill* means an administrative subdivision of a hun-

dred. Collectively, all of these entries are indicative of the extent of the king's holdings as well as changes in the king's holdings that had taken place from Edward's time and the obligations that the various tenants had to the king—or in some instances, no obligations at all. Notice that the entry for the king's jester, Berdic, records that he had rights to five vills and made no payment on them to the king; the position of jester was fairly lucrative. Several figures are said to have had rights to "carucates of land." A carucate was the same as a hide. Some entries also specify the king's alms. For example, it is recorded that the king gave to the church two pigs, one hundred loaves of bread, and beer on the feast of Saint Martin.

The entries about the property holdings of Saint-Denis of Paris are indicative of the extensive and growing influence of the French in England. Saint-Denis was a commune near Paris and the site of the Basilica of Saint Denis. Historically it had been closely associated with the French royal family, and after the Norman Conquest the basilica owned the rights to extensive property in England. So, too, did the Church of Lambeth, an important church whose property was held jointly by a French count. The church's holdings were extensive enough that in the twelfth century it became the seat of the archbishop of Canterbury. Yet another French church institution, the abbey at Saint-Evroul, held the rights to extensive tracts of land and was not required to pay geld to the king. Other religious institutions, such as the Church of the Nuns of Caen and the Church of Troarn, also had land holdings from the king. For example, the entry for Longtree Hundred notes that the Church of Troarn supported a "radknight," who was simply a feudal tenant who owed military service but was also required to do plowing.

The final excerpts pertain to "the land of Earl Hugh." Hugh was Hugh of Avranches (also spelled d'Avranches), the first earl of Chester. The entries indicate that Hugh was a man of considerable wealth, and in fact he was one of William's most influential barons. He held in Cheshire what were called "palatine powers," meaning that while he still owed allegiance to the king, he ruled with royal powers and was largely independent from the king. The purpose of granting palatine powers was to allow counties in western and northern England to deal, respectively, with the rebellious Welsh and Scots. Hugh and his cousin Robert of Rhuddlan used their position and wealth to deal brutally with the Welsh, which earned Hugh the sobriquet Hugh the Wolf. He was so fat that he could barely walk, so he was also called Hugh the Fat.

Audience

The *Domesday Book* presents the odd situation of its putative "author" and audience having been one and the same: King William I. The book was essentially a reference work; therefore, no one would actually have "read" it in the same way that a speech or a piece of diplomatic correspondence would have been read. William died before the book

Battle of Hastings (AP/Wide World Photos)

was fully compiled, but it provided his successors (most immediately his son, William II, followed by Henry I and then Stephen) with the information they needed to levy taxes, assert their control over royal lands, and determine whether the Crown or local landholders were responsible for outlays for improvements. Another audience, of course, consisted of the many nobles and landowners of England, who saw their claims and holdings recorded and thus legally fixed—or in some cases saw those claims to ownership denied. It is likely that each landholder had a copy of the segment of the book pertaining to his own holdings, as did local sheriffs and bailiffs, who used the book to adjudicate ownership disputes and other rights as well as obligations associated with property ownership. For centuries, the book was consulted to establish or dispute claims to land ownership. If a person believed that a piece of land belonged to him but a neighbor challenged this claim, the *Domesday Book* was consulted to see whether it could shed light on the matter. A chief audience has been modern historians, who have used the volumes to learn in detail about the nature of economic life in medieval England. Even the U.S. court system has consulted the *Domesday Book*. Since 1959 it has been cited as a precedent in at least six federal court cases, and in the twentieth century it was cited in at least fourteen state cases. The book has also proved useful to genealogists and people interested in their ancestry.

Impact

It is difficult to disentangle the impact of the *Domesday Book* from the impact of the Norman Conquest. The conquest put in place the Norman administrative structure that gave rise to the *Domesday Book*. In turn, the *Domesday Book* provided the factual and legal underpinnings for the social and economic structure that came to be called feudalism, particularly feudalism as it was practiced by the English under Norman French influence. A starting point for an understanding of this system is the word *feudalism* itself, a word that the medieval English did not use. It is derived from the word *fee*, a term that in feudal law referred to an estate in land from a lord in exchange for homage and service, particularly military service. After the conquest, King William I made numerous grants of land to his Norman supporters, who in exchange owed him homage and service. These "tenants in chief," in turn, granted lands to "mesne" tenants, who were obligated to perform some of the services the king required from the tenant in chief. These mesne tenants would then grant a portion of their holdings to subtenants, who could do the same to sub-subtenants. Thus, the system worked its way down from the king to people who were virtually peasants.

One of the problems with this arrangement was inheritance and the disposition of land for future generations.

> "Walter de Douai holds 2 hides of the king, as he says. But the men of the hundred say that they have never seen the writ or the king's commissioner who had given him seisin of II. But this they testify, that a certain free man holding this land, and able to go where he would, commended himself into Walter's hand for his own protection."
>
> ("Surrey, XXIII, The Land of Walter de Douai")

> "If anyone summoned on military service did not go be forfeited all his land to the king. But if anyone having to stay behind promised to sent another in his stead, and yet he who should have been sent stayed behind, his lord was quit for 50s."
>
> ("Surrey, XXXI, The Land of Humphrey the Chamberlain")

> "Berdic the king's jester has 3 vills, and there are 5 ploughs. He pays nothing."
>
> ("The Land of the King")

What happened if a tenant died without an heir or if his sole heir was a woman, who might marry a man who was an enemy of the lord? What obligations were transferred if land, or particularly a portion of land, changed hands by sale? Under what circumstances, if any, could a tenant hold property only for the term of his life? Under what circumstances, if any, could the lord reclaim title to land that had been granted to a tenant? What happened to land if the tenant was convicted of treason? If a lord allowed a deceased tenant's son to remain on the land, did this confer rights of hereditary ownership? To what extent could a tenant be relieved of military service by the payment of scutage—a tax levied for the king's military needs—and who would be required to pay scutage? The *Domesday Book* provided the factual information that formed the basis for answers to these and many other legal questions. Out of these legal questions and the answers that were provided emerged a body of common law that in time formed the basis of the English (and American) legal system. Common law refers to law that arises from precedent, that is, from the myriad decisions of judges over time; it stands in contrast to statutory law, which is law specified by decree.

A major impact of the *Domesday Book* was the signing in 1215 of the Magna Carta, an agreement between King John and his earls and barons. The Magna Carta was subsequently revised and reissued; the version of 1297 has been the one most commonly cited and is still part of English law. The Magna Carta, or Great Charter, was in effect an early constitution that specified the rights and obligations of the Crown and his nobles in relation to one another. It contained provisions such as the following:

> If any of our earls or barons, or anyone else holding from us in chief by military service should die, and should his heir be of full age and owe relief, the heir is to have his inheritance for the ancient relief, namely the heir or heirs of an earl for a whole county £100.... The keeper, for as long as he has the custody of the land of such (an heir), is to maintain the houses, parks, fishponds, ponds, mills and other things pertaining to that land from the issues of the same land, and he will restore to the heir, when the heir comes to full age, all his land stocked with ploughs and all other things in at least the same condition as when he received it. (http://www.archives.gov/exhibits/featured_documents /magna_carta/translation.html)

These principles, and the rights and obligations associated with them, could be enforced only if one had a comprehensive record of the "houses, parks, fishponds, ponds, mills and other things pertaining to that land." It was the *Domesday Book* that provided this information and thus laid the foundation for the legal system regarding property that still governs modern real estate transactions in common law countries.

Further Reading

■ Articles

King, Victoria. "The Domesday Book." *History Magazine* (October–November 2001). Also available online. http://www.history-magazine.com/domesday.html.

■ Books

Bartlett, Robert. *England under the Norman and Angevin Kings, 1075–1225.* New York: Oxford University Press, 2000.

Darby, H. C. *Domesday England.* New York: Cambridge University Press, 1977.

Forde, Helen. *Domesday Preserved.* London: HMSO, 1986.

Hallam, Elizabeth M. *Domesday Book through Nine Centuries.* New York: Thames and Hudson, 1986.

Reskine, R. W. H., and Ann Williams, eds. *The Story of Domesday Book.* Chichester, U.K.: Phillimore, 2003.

Rowley, Trevor. *Book of Norman England.* London: B. T. Batsford, 1997.

Wood, Michael. *Domesday: A Search for the Roots of England*, rev. ed. London: BBC, 1999.

■ Web Sites

"Domesday Book." New Advent Catholic Encyclopedia Web site. http://www.newadvent.org/cathen/05103a.htm.

"Magna Carta Translation." National Archives & Records Administration (United States) "Featured Documents" Web site. http://www.archives.gov/exhibits/featured_documents/magna_carta/translation.html.

"Research Guide for *Domesday Book.*" National Archives (United Kingdom) Web site. http://www.nationalarchives.gov.uk/catalogue/RdLeaflet.asp?sLeafletID=266&j=1.

—Michael J. O'Neal

Questions for Further Study

1. History textbooks generally provide readers with broad overviews of events, but the history they record is a mosaic of individual events and facts that historians have to assemble and interpret. How could a modern historian use the *Domesday Book* to write a history of medieval England? What can the *Domesday Book* teach modern readers about historiography, or the *process* of studying and writing about history?

2. What role did the Catholic Church play in medieval England? How can a historian ferret out an understanding of this role by reading the *Domesday Book*?

3. How did the *Domesday Book* help give rise to the system of English common law, the system used today not only in England but also in the United States and other countries that historically have had close associations with England?

4. An extraordinary emphasis was placed on land and land ownership in England during the eleventh century—and, indeed, throughout the entire medieval period, at least after the Norman Conquest. Why do you think land held such importance? Why and how was it a source of wealth?

5. The *Domesday Book* makes repeated references to commodities, rather than sums of money (although certainly sums of money are mentioned as well). Thus, reference is made to honey, nails, pigs, loaves of bread, iron, and the like. Why do you think these rather mundane items would be recorded in a book written for a king?

DOMESDAY BOOK

Surrey…

◆ XXIII. The land of Walter de Douai
In Wallington Hundred

Walter de Douai holds 2 hides of the king, as he says. But the men of the hundred say that they have never seen the writ or the king's commissioner who had given him seisin of II. But this they testify, that a certain free man holding this land, and able to go where he would, commended himself into Walter's hand for his own protection. This land is and was worth 20s.

◆ XXIIII. The land of Gilbert fitzRicher

Gilbert fitzRicher de l'Algle holds Witley. Earl Godwins held it. It was then assessed at 20 hides; now at 12 hides. There is land for 16 ploughs. In demesne are 2 ploughs; and 37 villans and 3 cottars with 13 ploughs. There is a church, and 3 acres of meadow, [and] woodland for 30 pigs. TRE, and afterwards, it was worth £15; now £16.

◆ XXV. The land of Geoffrey de Mandeville
In Brixton Hundred

Geoffrey de Mandeville holds Clapham. Thorbiorn held it of King Edward. It was then assessed at 10 hides; now at 3 hides. There is land for 7 ploughs. In demesne is 1 plough; and 8 villans and 3 bordars with 5 ploughs. There are 5 acres of meadow. TRE it was worth £10; afterwards the same; now £7.10s. The men say that Geoffrey has this manor wrongfully, because it does not belong to [his predecessor] Esger's land. What Geoffrey gave in alms from this manor is worth 20s.

In Wallington Hundred

Geoffrey himself holds Carshalton. 5 free men [held it] of King Edward, and they could go where they would. Of these, 1 held 2 hides, and 4 [held] 6 hides apiece. There were 5 manors. Now it is in 1 manor. It was then assessed at 27 hides; now at 3½ hides. There is land for 10 ploughs. In demesne is 1 [plough]; and 9 villans and 9 cottars with 5 ploughs. There is a church, and 7 slaves, and 12 acres of meadow. The men of the shire and of the hundred say that they have never seen the writ or the livery officer who on the king's behalf had given Geoffrey seisin of this manor. TRE it was worth £20; when he was seised of it, 100s; now £10. Of these hides, Wesman holds 6 hides of Geoffrey son of Count Eustace. Geoffrey de Mandeville gave him [i.e., Geoffrey] this land with his daughter. In demesne is 1 plough; and 3 villans and 1 cottar with 3 ploughs, and a mill rendering 35s, and 3 slaves, and 10 acres of meadow. [There is] woodland for 2 pigs. There is land for 2 ploughs. TRE it was worth £4; and afterwards 40s: now 110s. Of the same hides, a certain smith of the king's has half a hide, which TRE he received with his wife, but he has never done service for it.

In Woking Hundred

Geoffrey himself holds Wanborough. It is not (part) of Esger's land. Swein and Leofwine brothers, held it of King Edward. It was then assessed at 7 hides: now at 3 hides. There is land for 7 ploughs. There were 2 manors: now there is 1. In demesne is 1 plough: and 12 villans and 17 bordars with 8 ploughs. There is a church, and 8 slaves, and 6 acres of meadow, [and] woodland for 30 pigs. The whole TRE was worth £7; afterwards 100s; now £7.

Walter fitzOther holds West Horsley. Beorhtsige held it of King Edward. It was then assessed at 10 hides; now at 8 hides. There is land for 6 ploughs. In demesne are 2 ploughs: and 14 villans and 5 bordars with 5 ploughs. There is a church, and 8 slaves, [and] woodland for 20 pigs. TRE it was worth £8; afterwards 100s; now £6. Of this land, an Englishman holds 1 hide: and he has 1 plough there, with 1 bordar. It is worth 20s.

◆ XXVII. The land of Edward of Salisbury
In 'Elmbridge' Hundred

Edward of Salisbury holds Walton-on-Thames. Azur held it of King Edward. It was then assessed at 6 hides: now at 3 hides. There is land for 8 ploughs. In demesne are 2 ploughs: and 8 villans and 3 cottars with 7 ploughs. There are 8 slaves, and a mill rendering 1236d, and 40 acres of meadow, [and] woodland for 50 pigs. There is a forester, paying 10s. TRE it was worth £8; afterwards 100s; now £12, yet it renders £14.

In Godalming Hundred

Ranulph holds of Edward Hambledon. Azur held it of King Edward. It was then assessed at 5 hides: now at 3 hides. There is land for 4 ploughs. In demesne are 2 ploughs; and 8 villans and 1 cottar with 5 ploughs. There are 13 slaves, and a mill rendering 30d, and 3 acres of meadow, [and] woodland for 30 pigs. It is and always was worth 100s.

In Woking Hundred

Hugh holds of Edward West Clandon. Fulcwig held it TRE. It was then assessed, at 5 hides; now at 2½ hides. There is land for 3 ploughs. In demesne is 1 [plough]: and 4 villans and 5 bordars with 1½ ploughs. [There is] a mill rendering 3s. There is a church, and woodland for 5 pigs. It was worth 50s; now 60s.

◆ XXVIII. The land of Robert Malet
In Woking Hundred

Robert Malet holds Sutton [in Woking]. Wynsige held it of King Edward. It was then assessed at 5 hides; now at 3 hides. There is land for 3 ploughs. In demesne is 1 [plough]; and 5 villans and 5 bordars with 2 ploughs. There are 6 slaves, and a mill rendering 5s, and 20 acres of meadow, [and] woodland for 25 pigs. TRE, and afterwards, it was worth £8; now 100s. Durand was seised of this land, and the men say that he has it wrongfully, for none of them has seen the king's writ or livery officer.

◆ XXIX. The land of Miles Crispin
In Wallington Hundred

Miles Crispin holds Beddington, and William fitz-Turold [holds] of him. Ulf held it of King Edward. It was then assessed at 25 hides: now at 3 hides. There is land for 6 ploughs. In demesne is 1 plough; and 13 villans and 13 cottars with 6 ploughs. There is 1 slave, and 2 mills rendering 35s and 20 acres of meadow, [and] woodland for 5 pigs. TRE it was worth £10; afterwards £6; now £9.10s. From this manor … have been taken 21 messuages which Earl Roger holds, 13 in London, 8 in Southwark. They render 12s.

In Kingston Hundred

Miles himself holds Chessington. Magni Svert held it TRE. It was then assessed at 5 hides; now at 1 hide. When King William came into England, Vigot did not have it. There is land for 3 ploughs. This land belonged to Beddington. Villans held it. In demesne is now 1 plough: and 6 villans with 2 ploughs. TRE it was worth £4; afterwards 40s; now 70s.

◆ XXX. The land of Hamo the Sheriff
In Tandridge Hundred

Hamo the sheriff holds Titsey. Godtovi held it of King Edward. It was then assessed at 20 hides; now at 2 hides. There is land for 8 ploughs. In demesne are 4 ploughs; and 14 villans and 31 bordars with 5 ploughs. There is a church, and 9 slaves. For the pas-

ture, the seventh pig of the villans. TRE it was worth £10; afterwards £6; now £11.

In Brixton Hundred

Hamo himself holds Camber Well. Northmann held it of King Edward. It was then assessed at 12 hides; now at 6 hides and 1 virgate. There is land for 5 ploughs. In demesne are 2 [ploughs]: and 22 villans and 7 bordars with 6 ploughs. There is a church, and 63 acres of meadow, [and] woodland for 60 pigs. TRE it was worth £12; afterwards £6; now £14.

◆ XXXI. The land of Humphrey the Chamberlain
In Kingston Hundred

Humphrey the chamberlain holds of the queen's fief Coombe. Alfred held it of the king, and could go where he would. It was then assessed at 3 hides: now at nothing. There is land for 2 ploughs. In demesne is 1 [plough]; and 3 villans and 4 bordars with 1 plough. There are 8 acres of meadow. TRE it was worth £4; afterwards 20s; now 100s. TRW the woman who held this land put herself with it in the queen's hand.…

Berkshire…

In the Borough of Wallingford King Edward had 8 virgates of land, and in these were 276 closes rendering £11 from rent, and they who dwelt there did service for the king with horses or by water as far as Blewbury, Reading, Sutton Courtenay [and] Benson [Oxon.], and to those who did this the reeve gave cash or kind not from the rent of the king but from his own.

Now all the customs in this borough are as they were before; but of the closes there are 13 less: 8 were destroyed for the castle, and a moneyer has 1 quit so long as he does the coining: Sæwulf of Oxford has 1: the son of Alsige of Faringdon 1, which, he says, the king gave him; Humphrey Visdeloup has 1, for which he claims the king's warranty: Nigel [claims] 1 of Henry through inheritance from Swæting, but the burgesses give evidence that they never had it.

From these 13 the king does not have any customary due: and in addition William de Warenne has 1 close from which the king does not have any customary dues.

Over and above these are 22 messuages [held] by Frenchmen rendering 655d.

King Edward had 15 acres on which housecarls dwelt; Miles Crispin holds them, they do not know how. 1 of them belongs to Long Wittenham, a manor of Walter Giffard.

Bishop Walkelin has 27 closes rendering 25s, and they are appraised in his manor of Brightwell-cum-Sotwell.

The Abbot of Abingdon has 2 acres on which are 7 messuages rendering 4s, and belonging to Oxford.

Miles [has] 20 messuages rendering 12s10d, and they belong to Newnham Murren [Oxon.]; and also 1 acre on which are 6 closes rendering 18d. In [Great and Little] Haseley [Oxon.] 6 messuages rendering 44d. In North Stoke [Oxon.] 1 messuage rendering 12d. In Chalgrove [Oxon.] 1 messuage rendering 4d; and in Sutton Courtenay 1 acre on which are 6 messuages rendering 12d; and in Bray 1 acre, and there are 11 messuages rendering 35. The whole of this land belongs to Oxfordshire, and yet it is in Wallingford.

Reginald has 1 acre on which are 11 messuages rendering 26d, and they belong to Albury [Oxon.], which is in Oxford[shire].

The archbishop has 6 messuages rendering 26d; Walter Giffard has 1 acre and 10 messuages rendering 6s1½d; Robert d'Oilly 4 messuages rendering 20d; Gilbert de Ghent 1 messuage rendering 2½d; Hugh the Great 1 messuage rendering 4d; R. fitz-Seifrid 2 closes rendering 12d; Hugh de Bolbec 1 close rendering 4d; Ranulph Peverel 1 rendering 4d; Walter fitzOther 6 doses rendering 4d all but a halfpenny; William Lovet 1 plot of land rendering 4d; in [East and West] Ilsley 3 messuages rendering 3d. The Abbot of Battle [Abbey] has 5 messuages in Berkshire rendering 20d, [and there is] 1 close, which belonged to Bishop Peter, rendering 4d.

The king [has] 3 closes rendering 6d; Henry de Ferrers 6 closes which TRE and also TRW gave 62d customarily in the king's farm; now they give nothing.

Bishop Remigius [has] 1 close rendering 4d; Earl Hugh 1 close worth 16d;

Godric 1 close rendering 2d; Dodda 1 close rendering 2d; Algar 1 [close] rendering 2d; smiths [have] 5 closes rendering 10d.

The king [has] in Aldermaston 2 closes rendering 5d; the Count of Evreux 2 closes rendering 2½[d]; Hugh Bolbec 1 close rendering 2d; Roger de Lacy 1 close rendering 12d; Robert d'Oilly 1 close rendering 6d.

The king [has] 1 close rendering 6d; Bishop Osmund 7 closes rendering 28d; Robert d'Oilly 2 closes rendering 10d; Roger de Lacy 5 closes rendering 21d; Ralph Piercehedge 7 closes rendering 50d; Regenbald the priest 1 close rendering 4d; St Alban 1 close singa[sic], and it is in dispute; Beorhtric 1 close rendering 2d; Leofgifu 1 close rendering 2d; Godwine 1 close rendering 2d; Alwine 1 close rendering 2d; Almær the priest and another Almær the priest and Brunmann and Eadwig and Edmund and William son of Osmund and Leofflæd and Lambert the priest. Alweald and Godric have rent from their houses and [the fines due for] bloodshedding, if there is bloodshed there, [and] if the man [accused] is received in them before claim is made by the king's reeve, except on Saturday, on account of the market, because then the king has the fine: and they have the fines for adultery and theft in their houses; other fines, however, are the king's.

TRE it was worth £30; and afterwards £40; now £60, and yet it renders at farm £80 by tale. What belongs to Adbrei [is worth] 7s and the land of Miles Molay 24[s]; what the Abbot of Abingdon has, 8s: what Roger de Lacy [has], 7s; what Reginald [has], 4s.

The following thegns of Oxfordshire had land in Wallingford:

Archbishop Lanfranc 4 houses belonging to Newington [Oxon.] rendering 6s: Bishop Remigius 1 house belonging to Dorchester [Oxon.] rendering 12d: the Abbot of St Alban's 1 house rendering 4s: Abbot R […] 1 house [belonging] to Ewelme [Oxon.] rendering 3s.

Earl Hugh 1 house [belonging] to Pyrton [Oxon.] rendering 3s; Walter Giffard 3 houses [belonging] to Caversham rendering 2s; Robert d'Oilly 2 houses [belonging] to Watlington [Oxon.] rendering 2s and [belonging] to Waterperry [Oxon.] 1 house rendering 2s.

Ilbert de Lacy, Roger fitzSeifrid, and Ordgar. 3 houses rendering 4s; Hugh de Bolbec 3 houses [belonging] to [?] Crowmarsh Gifford [Oxon.] rendering 3s; Hugh the Great of Scoca 1 house rendering 12d: Drogo [has, belonging] to Shirburn [Oxon.], and [belonging] to South Weston [Oxon.], 3 houses rendering 4s; Robert d'Armentieres, [belonging] to Ewelme [Oxon.], 1 house rendering 12d; Wazo 1 house [belonging] to Ewelme [Oxon] rendering 3s.

When geld was commonly paid TRE, throughout the whole of Berkshire, a hide gave 3½d before [the Feast of] the Nativity of the Lord and as much at Pentecost. If the king sent out an army anywhere only 1 thegn went out from [each] 5 hides, and for his sustenance or pay 4s for 2 months was given him from each hide. This money, however, was not sent to the king but given to the thegns. If anyone summoned on military service did not go be forfeited all his land to the king. But if anyone having to stay behind promised to sent another in his stead, and yet he who should have been sent stayed behind, his lord was quit for 50s. When a thegn or a knight of the king's demesne was dying he left all his weapons to the king as heriot, and 1 horse with a saddle and 1 without a saddle. But if he possessed hounds or hawks these were presented to the king, to have if he wished. If any one slew a man having [the protection of] the king's peace, he forfeited both his person and all his possessions to the king. He who broke into the city at night paid a fine of 100s to the king, not to the sheriff. He who was summoned to [take part in] heading off [game] in the hunt [and] did not go, paid a fine of 50s to the king.

The Land of the King

King William holds Windsor in demesne. King Edward held it. There are 20 hides. There is land [...]. In demesne is 1 plough; and 22 villans and 2 bordars with 10 ploughs. There is 1 slave, and a fishery rendering 6s8d, and 40 acres of meadow. [There is] woodland for 50 pigs as pannage, and other woodland has been put in [the king's] preserve and there are, besides, 100 closes, less 5, in the vill. Of these, 26 are quit of rent and from the others come 30s.

Of the land of this manor Albert the clerk holds 1½ hides and the third part of a dene: Walter fitz-Other 1½ hides and 1 virgate, and as much woodland as provides 5 pigs as pannage. Gilbert Maminot [holds] 3 virgates. William Belet 1 hide, Ælfric 1 hide, and another Ælfric half a hide, and a priest of the vill 1½ hides, and 2 sergeants of the king's court half a hide. Eudo Dapifer 2 hides. TRE it was worth £15: and afterwards £7; now £15.

In Thatcham Hundred

The king holds Thatcham in demesne. King Edward held it. It was then assessed at 2 hides, and has never paid geld. There is land for 25 ploughs. There are 35 villans and 12 bordars with 25 ploughs, and there are 12 enclosures rendering at farm 55s, and 2 mills rendering 22s6d, and 147 acres of meadow. [There is] woodland for 60 pigs. The church of this manor 2 clerks hold with 3 hides which belong there; and these pay geld with the shire, and are worth £3. TRE it was worth £20: now £30: and yet it renders £34....

Gloucestershire

In the time of King Edward the city of Gloucester rendered £36 by tale, and 12 sesters of honey according to the measure of the same borough, and 36 dickers of iron, and 100 rods of iron, drawn out, for nails for the king's ships, and certain other small customary dues in the hall and in the king's chamber.

This city now renders the king £60 at 20[d] to the ora, and the king has £20 from the mint.

In the king's demesne land Roger of Berkeley holds 1 house and 1 fishery in this vill, and it is out of the king's hand. Baldwin held this TRE.

Bishop Osbern holds the land and messuages which Eadmær held; he pays 10s with other customary dues.

Geoffrey de Mandeville holds 6 messuages. TRE these rendered 6s8d with other customary dues. William [fitz] Baderon [holds] 2 messuages rendering 30d. William the scribe, 1 messuage rendering 1d. Roger de Lacy, 1 messuage rendering 26d. Bishop Osbern, 1 messuage rendering 41d. Bemer, 1 messuage rendering 14d. William the Bald, 1 messuage rendering 12d. Durand the sheriff, 2 messuages rendering 14d.

The same Durand holds 1 messuage rendering 26d, and in addition 1 messuage which renders no customary dues.

Hadewin holds 1 messuage which pays rent but withholds other customary dues.

Gosbert [holds] 1 messuage. Dunning 1 messuage. Widard 1 messuage. Arnulf the priest [holds] 1 messuage which pays rent and withholds other customary dues.

All these messuages rendered the royal customary dues TRE. Now King William has nothing from these, nor does Robert, his minister.

These messuages were in King Edward's farm on the day on which he was alive and dead. Now they have been removed from the king's farm and customary dues. TRE the whole of the king's demesne in the city was for lodging or clothing. When Earl William received it at farm, it was for clothing in the same way.

Where the castle stands were 16 houses which are not there now, and in the fortified area of the city 14 houses have been destroyed.

Earl William built the Castle of Chepstow [Mon.], and in his time it rendered only 40s from ships going into the woodland. In the time of his son, Earl Roger, however, the vill itself rendered £16, and Ralph de Limesy had half. Now the king has £12 from it.

All together from the renders of Caerleon [Mon.] and 1 plough *[sic]* which is there, and from 7 fisheries in the Wye and the Usk, come £7.10s.

In Wales are 3 hardwicks, Llanvair Discoed [Mon.], and Portskewett [Mon.] and Dinham [Mon.]. In these are 8 ploughs, and 11 half-villans and 15 bordars with 6 ploughs. For these 3 hardwicks Roger d'Ivry wished to have 100s.

Under Waswic the reeve are 13 vills; under Elmui 14 vills; under Bleio are 13 vills; under Iudichael are 14 vills.

These render 47 sesters of honey and 40 pigs and 41 cows and 28s, for hawks. The whole of this is worth £9 10s4d.

For a piece of waste land Walter the crossbowman renders 1 sester of honey and 1 pig.

Berdic the king's jester has 3 vills, and there are 5 ploughs. He pays nothing.

Morin [has] 1 vill; Cynesige 1; the son of Waswic 1; Sessisbert 1; Abraham the priest 2 vills; these men have 6 ploughs, and they pay nothing. Earl William placed these within the customary dues of King Gruffydd, with the leave of King William. Under the same reeves are 4 vills made waste by King Caradoc.

In the king's alms is 1 vill which renders to the church for his soul on the feast of St Martin 2 pigs and 100 loaves with beer.

I carucate of land belongs to St Michael, and 1 carucate to St David. These render no service except to the saints.

One Beluard of Caerwent has half a carucate of land and pays nothing.

From the pannage come 66 pigs, and they are valued at 44s. All these render £40.12s8d. Durand the sheriff gave these same things to William de EU for £55 at farm.

Walter the crossbowman holds 2 carucates of land of the king, and has there 3 ploughs, and 3 slaves and 3 female slaves. This is worth 20s.

Gerard has 2 carucates of land, and there are 2 ploughs. It is worth 20s.

Ows the king's reeve [has] 2 carucates of land, and there are 4 ploughs. It is worth 20s. There is in the king's demesne 1 carucate of land which Dagobert held.

Joscelin the Breton holds 5 carucates of land in Caerwent [Mon.], and there are 2 ploughs, with 2 Welshmen. It is worth 20s.

The Bishop of Coutances holds 5 carucates of land of the king, and one of his men [holds] of him. There are 2 ploughs in demesne; and 3 [ploughs] of the villans. It is worth 40s.

Roger of Berkeley holds 2 carucates of land at Rogerstone [Mon.], and has there 6 bordars with 1 plough. It is worth 20s.

Durand the sheriff holds of the king in Caerwent [Mon.] 1 estate called Caldicot [Mon.]. There he has in demesne 3 ploughs: and 15 half-villans and 4 slaves and 1 knight. All these have 12 ploughs. There is a mill rendering 10s. The whole of this is worth £6.

William de EU has, as he says, £9 as customary dues from Chepstow [Mon.]. But Gerard and other men say that he has no more by right from the £10 of customary dues of Chepstow, even if it should be valued at £100.

In Wales the same William has in fief 3 fisheries in the Wye [which] render 70s, and in the same fief Earl William gave Ralph de Limesy 50 carucates of land as it is done in Normandy, Hugh and other livery-officers attest that he granted it to Ralph thus. Now William de EU says that he has only 32 carucates of this land. There are in demesne 8 ploughs; and the men have 16 ploughs, There are 2 mills rendering 10s. The whole is worth £12.10s.

Roger de Lacy holds in the fief of Chepstow [Mon.] as much inhabited land with 1 mill as is worth 36s.

Turstin fitzRolf has 17 ploughs [sic] between the Usk and the Wye. 4½ of these are in demesne: the others are the men's. There are 11 bordars, and a mill rendering 7s. The whole is worth £9. The king's reeves claim 5½ carucates of this land, saying that Turstin took them without any grant.

The same Turstin has 6 carucates of land beyond the Usk, and there his men have 4 ploughs, and a mill rendering 15s, and [there is] half a fishery rendering 10s. The whole is worth 54s6d.

Alvred d'Epaignes has in fief 2 carucates of land, and there are 2 ploughs in demesne. The same Alvred has in Wales 7 vills which belonged to Earl William, and to Roger, his son, in demesne. These render 6 sesters of honey and 6 pigs and 10s.

The Borough of Winchcombe rendered £6 as farm TRE. Earl Harold had the third penny of this [6l], that is, 40s. Afterwards, it rendered £20 with the whole hundred of the same vill. Durand the sheriff added 100s. and Roger d'Ivry 60s. Now with the 3 hundreds associated with it, it renders £28 at 20[d] to the ora....

◆ XX. The land of Saint-Denis of Paris
In Deerhurst Hundred

The Church of Saint-Denis holds these vills in Deerhurst Hundred: Uckington 5 hides: Staverton 3 hides: Coln St Dennis and Calcot 5 hides; Little Compton [War.] 12 hides: Preston on Stour [War.] 10 hides; Welfordon-Avon [War.] 15 hides. In these lands 15 ploughs are in demesne: and 75 villans and 12 bordars with 39 ploughs. There are 38 slaves, and 4 mills rendering 40s, and 36 acres of meadow, [and] woodland 2½ leagues long and 1 league and 2 furlongs broad.

Of this above-mentioned land, 5 free men hold 4½ hides. To the same manor belong 2½ hides beyond the Severn. In Woolstone 5 hides; in The Leigh 1 hide; in Deerhurst Walton 1 hide: in Kemetton [Worcs.] half a hide. In these lands are 5 ploughs in demesne; and 5 villans and 18 bordars with 9 ploughs, 1 free man lives there. There are 38 acres of meadow, [and] woodland half a league long and 2 furlongs broad. To this manor belong 30 burgesses in Gloucester paying 15s8d, and 2 burgesses in Winchcombe paying 10d. TRE the whole manor was worth £10s; now £30.

◆ XXI. The land of the Church of Lambeth
In "Celfledetorn" Hundred

The Church of St Mary of Lamberth holds Aston Subedge. Countess Gode held it TRE. There are 4 hides. In demesne are 3 ploughs; and 6 villans and 1 knight with 3½ ploughs. There are 6 slaves and 3 female slaves. It was worth 100s: now £4.

◆ XXII. The land of Saint-Evroul
In 'Holford' Hundred

The Church of Saint-Evroul holds Roel of the king. Wulfweard held it TRE. There are 10 hides. In demesne are 4 ploughs: and 16 villans and 2 bordars with 6 ploughs. There are 3 slaves. It is and was worth £10. This manor has never paid geld.

◆ XXIII. The land of the Church of the Nuns of Caen
In Cirencester Hundred

The Church of the nuns of La Trinite of Caen holds Pinbury of the king. There are 3 hides. In demesne are 3 ploughs; and 8 villans and a smith with 3 ploughs. There are 9 slaves, and a mill rendering 40d. It is and was worth £4.

In Longtree Hundred

The church itself holds Minchinhampton. Countess Gode held it TRE. There are 8 hides. In demesne are 5 ploughs: and 32 villans and 10 bordars with 24 ploughs.

There is a priest and 10 slaves, and 8 mills rendering 45s, and 20 acres of meadow, [and] woodland 2 leagues long and half a league broad, It is worth £28.

◆ XXIIII. The land of the Church of Troarn
In Longtree Hundred

The Church of Saint-Martin of Troarn holds Horsley by gift of King William. Gode, the sister of King Edward, held it. There are 10 hides. In demesne are 4 ploughs: and 6 villans and 3 bordars with 6 ploughs, and 1 radknight, and in Gloucester 1 house rendering 6d. There is a mill rendering 50d. It was worth £12; now £14.

◆ XXVII. The land of Earl Roger
In "Gersdones" Hundred

Earl Roger holds Meysey Hampton, and Thorvald, the nephew of Vigot, [holds] of him.

◆ XXVIII. The land of Earl Hugh
In Bisley Hundred

Earl Hugh holds Bisley, and Robert [holds] of him. There are 8 hides. In demesne are 4 ploughs: and 20 villans and 28 bordars with 20 ploughs. There are 6 slaves and 4 female slaves. There are 2 priests and 8 radknights having 10 ploughs, and 23 other men paying 44s and 2 sesters of honey. There are 5 mills rendering 16s, and woodland rendering 20s, and in Gloucester 11 burgesses paying 66d. It was worth £24; now £20.

In the same place the earl himself holds 1 hide at Througham. Leofnoth held it of King Edward and could go where he would. This land pays geld. There are 4 bordars with 1 plough, and 4 acres of meadow. It is worth 20s.

In the same place the earl himself holds half a hide which Roger de Lacy claims In Edgeworth by witness of the shire. It is worth 10s, and it pays geld.

In 'Witley' Hundred

The earl himself holds Chipping Campden. Earl Harold held it. There are 15 hides paying geld. In

Glossary

close	the precinct of a cathedral
Earl William	son of William the Conqueror
hardwick	livestock farm
livery officer	a minor official in charge of a noble's livery, including pennons, flags, and heraldic colors

demesne [are] 6 ploughs; and 50 villans and 8 bordars with 21 ploughs. There are 12 slaves, and 2 mills rendering 6s2d. There are 3 female slaves. It was worth £30; now £20.

In Longtree Hundred

The earl himself holds 2 manors of 4 hides paying geld, and 2 of his men [hold] of him. Alnoth and Leofwine held them TRE. There has been no one to answer for these lands, but they are valued by the men of the shire at £8.

"It is the king's duty to enquire into the condition of his peasantry and army."

Overview

In 1091 Niẓām al-Mulk, *wazīr* (vizier) to the Seljuk sultans, wrote the *Siyāsat nāmeh* (*Book of Government; or, Rules for Kings*), a treatise on kingship and a model for governance, in response to a request by the Seljuk ruler Malik-Shāh that his ministers produce books on government and its administration in the face of various troubles facing the nation. He incorporated traditional Persian and Islamic modes of thought into his treatise, which became a classic of the genre known as the "Mirrors for Princes"—so called because the intent was that rulers should look into these books and see reflected in them the way in which to rule. The *Book of Government*, addressing politics and religion and the dangers facing the nation in some fifty chapters and giving practical and ethical advice for the conduct of the ruler, was given official sanction and established distinctly Persian forms of government and administration that endured for centuries. The excerpts chosen for inclusion here take up subjects varying from the role of spies and informants to the conduct of ambassadors to the payment of soldiers and the apportionment of government posts.

Context

In Islam, concepts of temporal kingship, or secular rule without any claim to rule by divine authority, developed in the tenth century—four hundred years after the rise of Islam. The first four caliphs did not rule merely as kings. (A king could claim that he ruled through divine right or that God had chosen the royal family, but he had no authority in religious matters.) Although the Umayyad caliphate essentially became a monarchy, as did the Abbasid caliphate after it, it still incorporated the spheres of both temporal and spiritual authority. The caliph was the deputy of God; he ruled by divine right and had authority in secular and religious affairs, even if most religious leaders challenged his religious authority. Only after the decline in the caliphs' power during the Abbasid period (750–1258) were governors able to assert their own temporal authority, independent of the caliph's.

Even then, temporal rulers felt a need or perhaps an obligation to be recognized by the caliph as a legitimate ruler.

The Abbasids ruled the Islamic empire from 750 to 1258 from the city of Baghdad. By the tenth century their empire had become decentralized, and local rulers at the periphery gradually increased their own power. Among them were the Shia Būyids. Most Muslims were Sunni, or those who followed the path of the prophet Muhammad. Shia Muslims differed from Sunnis less on religious grounds than on the interpretation of who should lead the Muslim world. The Shia believed that Muhammad had made his cousin Ali his successor, which had not happened. The Shia movement gradually evolved into a separate religious interpretation of Islam, in that the Shia believed that the Ali and his descendents were specially chosen because they could also interpret the will of God. The Shia, then, essentially challenged the basis of Abbasid authority.

In 1056 Baghdad and much of the land that is now Iran and Iraq were held by the Būyids, a Shia Muslim dynasty from Daylam, near the Caspian Sea. Although they were Shia Muslims, they controlled the actions of the Abbasid caliph, the titular head of the Sunni Muslim world. The position of the caliph existed primarily because the Būyids found it expedient to allow it to exist. This period of Shia dominance quickly came to an end, beginning in the early eleventh century, when Turkic nomads from central Asia crossed the Amu Dar'ya River and settled in northeastern Iran. Soon they became a force to reckon with under the leadership of the Seljuk clan.

By 1058 the Seljuks under Toghrïl Beg had forced the Būyids from Baghdad and conquered most of Iran and Iraq. Soon the empire stretched from modern-day Turkey into Afghanistan. Few, if any, could challenge Seljuk military supremacy, but administratively Seljuk rule was haphazard. Into this situation came a Persian, Niẓām al-Mulk. Like others among the conquered, he entered the service of the Seljuks and assisted in the administration of the empire. Having both witnessed and studied the history of less sophisticated groups who had established empires but proved largely unable (at least in his view) to rule them with any sophistication, Niẓām al-Mulk wrote a treatise on how to rule, encompassing both traditional Persian and Islamic modes of thought into his *Book of Government*.

1018
- Nizām al-Mulk is born near Tus in what is now Iran.

CA. 1044
- Nizām al-Mulk becomes adviser to a commander in Balkh (in modern-day Afghanistan).

CA. 1054
- Nizām al-Mulk becomes a minister to Alp Arslan.

1056
- Toghrïl Beg, sultan of the Seljuk Turks, conquers Baghdad and establishes the Seljuk Empire.

1063
- Toghrïl Beg dies, and his son Alp Arslan becomes the sultan, making Nizām al-Mulk *wazīr* of the empire.

1067
- Nizām al-Mulk founds Madrasa Nizāmiyyah, which would become the leading university among Sunni scholars, in Baghdad.

CA. 1073
- Alp Arslan is assassinated, and Malik-Shāh ascends the Seljuk throne.

1091
- Nizām al-Mulk writes the *Book of Government.*

1092
Nizām al-Mulk is assassinated, and Sultan Malik-Shāh dies. Civil war erupts among the Seljuk princes.

By the time of the Seljuks, the role of the caliph had diminished such that the caliph wielded only titular temporal and spiritual authority beyond Baghdad. The Seljuks did not seek to change the situation. Indeed, their capital was not Baghdad but Eşfahān, thus marginalizing the caliph. The Seljuk sultan (a title that means "power" in Arabic) was the true ruler. Most of the early sultans began as provincial governors and became increasingly independent but still sought the approval of the caliph. Symbolic gestures toward the caliph served to lend them legitimacy, but in reality the power of the Seljuk military was their true source of legitimacy. Armies of archers who aimed and fired from horseback gave the Seljuks all the authority they needed. They bolstered their armies with Turkic nomads migrating from the steppe in search of pasture land.

A proverb common to empires taken by nomads was that one could conquer but could not rule from horseback. There was a need for talented administrators to provide stability. Thus, individuals with administrative skills, like Nizām al-Mulk, filled a niche in the Seljuk Empire. In the medieval Middle East a rough caste system existed, although no laws or formal boundaries enforced it. Turks were the warriors, Persians the administrators, and Arabs the religious leaders. Gradually, an administration was erected, more or less along lines similar to those that had existed in the Abbasid Empire and the Ghaznavid Empire (977–1187) in eastern Iran and Afghanistan. Indeed, Nizām al-Mulk first took refuge in the Ghaznavid Empire during the early Seljuk period. It was only after the Seljuks conquered the Iranian regions and western portions of Afghanistan held by the Ghaznavid Empire that Nizām al-Mulk's family entered Seljuk service.

In its first fifty years, the Seljuk Empire grew at a breathtaking rate as the Seljuks directed other Turkic nomads westward to search for pastures. With the rapid advance and the ever-increasing numbers of Turks, many who were only recent converts to Islam, and—from the bureaucracy's standpoint—not civilized, it was a period of anxiety for urban and peasant populations. Indeed, one of the reasons the Seljuks sent the nomads westward was so that they would not be tempted to plunder Iran. By 1100 the Seljuk elite could not be considered nomadic, although their martial prowess provided them sufficient credibility among the nomadic population. In general, the warrior classes viewed the bureaucracy as effete. While the bureaucracy placed value on education, knowledge, and rational government, the warriors believed in rule through might and the sword. The sultan appreciated the need for bureaucracy but often preferred the company and advice of his generals. The bureaucracy felt a considerable amount of uncertainty in its position, because ultimately the military might of the sultan decided matters of legislation.

The ulema, or traditional religious elite consisting of scholars, jurists, and theologians, had previously had considerable influence in the running of the state, providing a moral compass. Its members had also developed certain ideas of how a temporal ruler should behave and rule. Above all, justice must be maintained. The people should

Dinar of the Seljuk rulers Toghrïl Beg and Malik-Shāh (© The Trustees of the British Museum)

obey the ruler, because the ruler had been chosen by God—even if he was not godly. Gradually, the ulema and the bureaucracy increasingly turned to an older Persian tradition termed the "Mirrors for Princes." These textual mirrors served as handbooks or guidebooks for rulers by providing examples of how to rule. Although many of the examples were idealistic and at times somewhat naive, they gave a model of what was considered to be a good ruler—in terms of both practical and ethical rule. It is fair to ask whether the majority of rulers governed according to the mirrors or whether the models offered were, in fact, wishful thinking on the part of their authors. It was in this milieu that Niẓām al-Mulk entered Seljuk service and wrote his own mirror, the *Book of Government*.

About the Author

Despite his importance, relatively little is known about Niẓām al-Mulk, who served as the *wazīr*, a position similar to prime minister, of the Seljuk Empire for thirty years. He was born in 1018 near Tus, in present-day Iran, and entered the service of the Seljuks in approximately 1044 as an adviser to a commander in Balkh, in modern-day Afghanistan. Around 1054 he became a minister to Alp Arslan, the heir to the Seljuk throne. It was the custom for the Seljuk princes to rule a portion of the empire in order to gain experience for running the entire empire. Niẓām al-Mulk quickly demonstrated his genius by advising the Turkic prince. Initially, he served as an underling to Alp Arslan's *wazīr*, but after the underling's death, Alp Arslan promoted him to chief *wazīr*. As such, he administered the

province of Khorāsān in what is now northeastern Iran and Afghanistan on Alp Arslan's behalf. Thus, when Alp Arslan became sultan in 1063, after his father, Toghrïl Beg, died, Niẓām al-Mulk became the *wazīr* of the empire.

Although Niẓām al-Mulk certainly carried out his own initiatives and advised the Seljuk sultan, it is questionable just how much he influenced the sultan's actions. His influence in the affairs of the empire grew considerably with the assassination of Alp Arslan in 1072 or 1073 by Ismailis—a group of Shia Muslims who resisted Seljuk domination. The sultan's son Malik-Shāh assumed the throne but not the power. Niẓām al-Mulk was able to dominate and control Malik-Shāh. Although Malik-Shāh enjoyed the freedom from having to govern, he eventually chafed under the watchful eye of his self-appointed guardian.

In his conversations and writings, Niẓām al-Mulk attempted to stress one primary concept to the Seljuk sultans: Justice was the most important attribute of a ruler. Indeed, Islamic philosophers and political thinkers down to the modern era have agreed on the preeminent importance of justice. Because he was a Persian and not a Turkic general or a member of the Seljuk ruling dynasty, Niẓām al-Mulk was not concerned with who ruled but rather how they governed. He believed that the maintenance of the social order was most important, because it produced stability. The key was a sultan who ruled with justice and not tyranny. In many ways Niẓām al-Mulk was an idealist. To reinforce the idea that justice was necessary for all, he assured the Seljuks that when kings die, they come before God and must answer for their rulership. The idea that rulers answer to God for their rule was one that Niẓām al-Mulk had derived not only from Islamic thought but also from older Persian concepts concerning the divine origins of kings. He believed that kings's power was absolute and thus that they were answerable to no one except God. Any power others, including the caliph, might have could not exceed that of the sultan, who was the "Shadow of God on Earth." The sultan ruled by the will of God and over a social system devised by God.

Although Niẓām al-Mulk served as the *wazīr* of the empire for thirty years and controlled the day-to-day affairs of the empire for most of that time, he also carried out his own private initiatives, accomplished with the aid of the immense power and wealth that came with his position. These initiatives were tied to his vision of the ideal state, his dedication to Sunni Islam, and the suppression of what he viewed as heresies. To this end, he established the Madrasah Niẓāmiyyah in Baghdad, which promoted the Shafii interpretation of Islamic law (one of four such schools of thought) in order to counter Shiism, of which he was an ardent opponent. Gradually, he funded or assisted in the establishment of additional religious schools throughout the Middle East. His ardor at combating the spread of Shiism in Iran, particularly the Ismaili variety, earned him the hatred of the Ismailis, who assassinated him in 1092.

Explanation and Analysis of the Document

Niẓām al-Mulk wrote the *Book of Government; or, Rules for Kings* in 1091 in order to guide the Seljuk sultans and set a model of government as well as to curb the excesses of the Turkic nomads, generals, and princes. In it, he wrote about the practice and art of governing, the qualities of kingship, and how to handle threats to the Seljuk Empire. In many ways, this work, which became a classic of Islamic political and governmental philosophy, is a memorial to what Niẓām al-Mulk failed to accomplish in his lifetime, despite his best efforts.

◆ Chapter X: "Concerning Intelligence Agents and Reporters and Their Importance in Administering the Affairs of the Country"

In this excerpt from the tenth chapter of the book, Niẓām al-Mulk stresses that it is important for a sultan to be involved in the matters of state, rather than simply enjoying the comforts and privileges that come with the crown. Here, he is perhaps showing regret for the way in which he treated Malik Shāh's early reign, encouraging his leisure pursuits rather than his governance of the empire. Although the actual running of most day-to-day affairs of the state was left to the *wazīr*, a good ruler paid attention to what happened in his kingdom. Niẓām al-Mulk also indicates the need for an intelligence network of informants who report back to the ruler. This network took shape in the form of the *barīd*, or the post. Unlike the modern postal service, the *barīd* consisted of riders who dispatched official documents to governors and generals. As they rode throughout the empire, they also were witnesses to how the

governors and other officials treated the subjects. Through them, the sultan could be reliably informed about the state of affairs throughout his kingdom—often in contradiction to what his officials told him. In addition, Niẓām al-Mulk stresses that the couriers should draw their salary from the treasury. In the modern era this may seem an odd thing to stress, but most officials received their pay from other sources—land grants, endowments, plunder, and rents, none of which were guaranteed. By insisting on payment derived from the treasury, Niẓām al-Mulk hoped to ensure adequate payment and ward off temptations to corruption.

◆ Chapter XIII: "On Sending Spies and Using Them for the Good of the Country and the People"

In addition to using the *barīd* as an intelligence network, in chapter XIII, Niẓām al-Mulk also recommends the use of spies to thwart government corruption and rebellion as well as the activities of foreign enemies. The recommendation that spies be disguised as merchants and Sufis is particularly noteworthy. Merchants, of course, traveled widely, and it was not uncommon for merchants from Seljuk territories to enter neighboring kingdoms. Sufis, or practitioners of Sufism, a mystical variant of Islam, also traveled widely through the Middle East. They gained access to the homes of local notables and officials because of their piety and the popularity of Sufism, particularly among the Turkic population. Indeed, the Turks converted to Islam primarily through the efforts of the Sufis, although mainstream Sunni religious leaders often did not trust them.

◆ Chapter XVII: "Concerning Boon-Companions and Intimates of the King and the Conduct of Their Affairs"

Niẓām al-Mulk places great emphasis on the topic of boon companions. A boon companion was a trusted friend but also a comrade in arms and confidant. In many instances, the friends of the sultan, or any ruler, gained high positions in the government. Because of their relationship with the ruler, they were often above criticism by anyone else. Unless boon companions had good morals and character, their positions might tempt them to abuse their power. This is what Niẓām al-Mulk wants to thwart.

It is clear that he sees a division between people with whom the sultan consorts during moments of leisure and those he consults in moments of work. "Where pleasure and entertainment are concerned … it is right that the king should consult with his boon-companions," he says. But "in everything to do with the country and its cultivation … it is better that he should take counsel with the ministers and nobles of the state and with experienced elders." In his mind, a clear separation is imperative so that government officials view the ruler as above them and not as an intimate friend. This demarcation stems from traditional Persian views of kingship in which the king is raised above all and is answerable only to God. The elevation of the ruler is contrary to the normal power structure among the Turks and steppe tribes, in which the khan ruled. The khan governed with the advice and cooperation of other tribal lead-

Eşfahān mosque, the south dome of which was commissioned by Niẓām al-Mulk (AP/Wide World Photos)

ers. Indeed, ruling the steppe tribes was very much a process of negotiation. Boon companions were crucial to this process, because they provided a support system for the khan—carrying out his orders, leading men into combat, and serving as intermediaries. In Niẓām al-Mulk's view, boon companions should not function in this way because it could lead them to be open to corruption.

In a sense, Niẓām al-Mulk is discussing not simply how to prevent the diminution of the sultan's authority or corruption. He is also changing the way in which the Seljuks thought of power. He establishes here that the king is the font of authority and does not share it with others. This is not to say that cronyism and nepotism did not occur within the Persian model of rulership, but Niẓām al-Mulk sees a clear need for a group of individuals entirely devoted to the king out of personal loyalty, who can defend him against the machinations of corrupt officials and who cannot corrupt the government through the king's favor—thus thwarting cronyism and nepotism.

◆ Chapter XXI: "On Ambassadors and Their Treatment"

In these two paragraphs, Niẓām al-Mulk attempts to formalize diplomatic activity. He is clearly disturbed by the lack of protocol that allows ambassadors from foreign powers (presumably the Byzantines) to arrive at the capital

unheralded, creating an awkward situation for the ruler. As he explains in the second paragraph, ambassadors also engaged in espionage and gauged troop strengths, wealth, and the condition of the people. As he puts it, "when kings send ambassadors to one another their purpose is not merely the message or the letter which they communicate openly, but secretly they have a hundred other points and objects in view." During any diplomatic visit, the host would want to create a favorable impression—that the sultan is all-powerful, that he possesses more wealth than his rivals, that his armies are countless, and that his palace and capital are the jewels of the world. Appearances could be everything. If the foreign ambassador were to see a good display, he would give a favorable report of the Seljuks. But if the ambassador were to find the sultan unprepared for his visit, the army in disarray, and no sumptuous gifts ready, then he would report back negatively concerning the affairs of the empire. This knowledge could invite invasion or persuade the ambassador to enlist malcontents seeking to overthrow the sultan.

If, however, the frontier commanders reported the impending arrival of an ambassador to the capital, the sultan could watch and control his movements. The orchestration of the state visit was crucial: It could disguise weakness—including the illness of the sultan—as well as highlight the strengths of the empire. At the end, Niẓām al-

Mulk alludes briefly to an incident involving himself and Alp Arslan. This is a reference to the fact that, because of intelligence gathered by ambassador spies, Alp Arslan overcame the Byzantines in 1071 at Malazgirt (in eastern Turkey) by exploiting their weaknesses.

◆ **Chapter XXIII: "On Settling the Dues of All the Army"**

The livelihood of a medieval soldier was always precarious. The troops risked their lives, and their pay was haphazard, in addition to which they often had to buy most of their own equipment. Niẓām al-Mulk was a strong proponent of paying troops regularly: two times a year. Twice-yearly payments had been more or less standard practice since the early days of the Abbasids. But the soldiers received large sums of money each time and often spent it all very quickly, then turning to mischief and even rioting in the capital. Should there be insufficient sums to pay the army, the risk was even greater, and sultans and caliphs had been slain in the rioting. Gradually, new methods were used in an attempt to lessen the dangers. The Seljuks adopted the Islamic practice of assigning an *iqṭāʿ*, or territorial domain of a sort, to troops, who were usually noble-born cavalry. This was not a true land grant. Essentially, taxes or a certain percentage of revenue from an area were assigned to a warrior. The warrior did not necessarily have to dwell there and certainly did not own the land, although sometimes an *iqṭāʿ* did become hereditary over time. Those who possessed an *iqṭāʿ* are referred to by Niẓām al-Mulik as "assignees." As an additional safeguard against rioting and rebellion Niẓām al-Mulk recommends that the soldiers not be paid by mere treasury officials but that they receive their money directly from the hands of the king. When the king paid his soldiers personally, it reminded them whose troops they were. Further, the simple act of having the king put money in their hands gave them access to him on a personal level, strengthening the bonds between warrior and commander. The king thus became much more than a distant figure, if only momentarily.

◆ **Chapter XLI: "On Not Giving Two Appointments to One Man; on Giving Posts to the Unemployed and Not Leaving Them Destitute; on Giving Appointments to Men of Orthodox Faith and Good Birth, and Not Employing Men of Perverse Sects and Evil Doctrine, Keeping the Latter at a Distance"**

Preventing governmental corruption is a constant theme in Niẓām al-Mulk's writing. His major advice is that no single person should hold more than one position and that no two people should share the same position. He is not simply speculating but indeed speaking from thirty years' experience—some of his acquired knowledge learned through his own mistakes. He had seen that some individuals attempted to accumulate positions and thus consolidate power in the court. Typically, in medieval Muslim governments, the bureaucracy was divided into several bureaus, including taxation, the chancellery, the army, and others. By holding several positions, individuals could

wield considerable influence and possible carry out their own policies—countering those of the chief *wazīr* or even the sultan. Furthermore, they would be able to acquire enormous wealth, not only from salaries but also from bribes given to them by others in order to gain favor.

Niẓām al-Mulk rails against what might be termed "hiring practices." He is clearly disturbed by the fact that qualified and educated people are unable to secure jobs in the government, whereas those who are unqualified can do so. His words also betray other concerns. By calling someone "unknown," he is most likely remarking on nepotism—that practice whereby an official's cousin, say, received a job despite lack of experience or qualifications. He also refers to people as "base-born" as opposed to those who have been born "noble." Niẓām al-Mulk came from a noble family and appears to have been displeased by the idea that commoners, whether Persians or Turks, could enter government in this way. Others from his social class had been passed over or given up even seeking government jobs. There are, he says, "well-known, noble, trusted, and experienced men who have no work at all, and are left deprived and excluded." Thus, the talented and qualified do not work for the government, and the mediocre have risen to the top. Finally, Niẓām al-Mulk's statements about Jews, Christians, Zoroastrians (an Iranian monotheistic religion worshipping Ahura Mazda), and Qarmatians (Shia Muslims) should not be surprising. All these groups could practice their religion but they did not serve in the military and were essentially second-class citizens. Niẓām al-Mulk was a devout Sunni Muslim who founded a system of religious schools that promulgated the Shafii interpretation of Islamic law. In his opinion, only Muslims (and in his view, only Sunnis were Muslims) should be employed in the government. He sees others as taking jobs away from Muslims.

Audience

The *Book of Government* was written for the Seljuk princes in an effort to educate them as true Islamic (and Persian) rulers who would govern wisely and justly. It is questionable, however, how many princes actually read these writings, though many scholars and bureaucrats did read them. The traditional training on governance (as well as military leadership) that princes received came not at their *wazīr's* feet but rather from an *atabeg*—a general and trusted companion of the sultan. Of course, some taught better than others, while others tacitly understood that their primary job was to keep an eye on a rebellious son. Thus, the quality of the rulers varied considerably with the quality of their mentors.

Impact

During his lifetime, Niẓām al-Mulk achieved considerable success in guiding the Seljuk Empire. It is notable that

> "It is the king's duty to enquire into the condition of his peasantry and army, both far and near, and to know more or less how things are."
>
> (Chapter X)

> "The troops must receive their pay regularly."
>
> (Chapter XXIII)

> "When two appointments are given to one man, one of the tasks is always inefficiently and faultily performed; and in fact you will usually find that the man who has two functions fails in both of them, and is constantly suffering censure and uneasiness on account of his shortcomings."
>
> (Chapter XLI)

after his assassination, the empire began to spiral into a series of civil wars. Nonetheless, many of the ideas and practices that he promoted in his tenure as *wazir*, and which can be found in the *Book of Government*, lasted long after his death and the end of the Seljuk Dynasty.

The Seljuks were not a native Middle Eastern dynasty but entered Iran bringing their own culture and traditions of kingship. Thus, they not only had to struggle to legitimize their rule according to Islamic tradition but also had to maintain their leadership over the Turkic tribes they ruled. Although the Seljuks had converted to Islam before becoming the preeminent power in the medieval Middle East, the traditions they inherited from the steppe still played a major role in the process of their empire building. Niẓām al-Mulk attempted to fully inculcate Islamic views into the minds of the Seljuk sultans, but Turkic concepts of kingship and sovereignty never went away. Essentially, the view of kingship and legitimacy that the Seljuks brought from the steppe was that the ruler had divine origins. Sovereign power and the ability to govern were granted by heaven and carried in the ruler's blood. All descendants of the ruler had an innate right and ability to rule.

From the time of Niẓām al-Mulk, however, whoever assumed control of the government did so by using the structures that he introduced to the Seljuks. How rigorously the sultans and their advisers applied his advice is open to question, but his ideas were widely known and had an impact on the way the public, from the commoners to the ulema, viewed the role of the ruler. These ideas spread to other parts of the Islamic world.

Niẓām al-Mulk's promotion of the Shafii interpretation of Islamic law and his fight against the Ismailis bore addi-

tional fruit under the rule of Saladin in Egypt and Syria. Before Saladin died in 1193—just over one hundred years after Niẓām al-Mulk's death—he built several Niẓāmiyyah madrassas in his realm. In addition, he attempted to stamp out the Ismailis' brand of Shia Islam, though he later tempered his actions after the Ismailis in Lebanon made it clear that they could harm Saladin no matter what precautions he took. It is clear that Saladin attempted to mold himself and his rule according to Niẓām al-Mulk's advice. Other rulers also used it, perhaps unwittingly through the advice of their own advisers who had read and debated this great work. Indeed, not everyone agreed with his philosophy of statecraft and governance, but the resulting discourse of later scholars and thinkers on Niẓām al-Mulk's ideals have made Islamic political thought much richer. One can find Nizam al-Mulk's influence in Iranian political thought even into the twenty-first century.

Further Reading

▪ Articles

Bosworth, C. E. "The Heritage of Rulership in Early Islamic Iran and the Search for Dynastic Connections with the Past." *Iran* 11 (1973): 51–62.

Lambton, Ann K. S. "Justice in the Medieval Persian Theory of Kingship." *Studia Islamica* 17 (1962): 91–119.

———. "*Quis custodiet custodes*: Some Reflections on the Persian Theory of Government." *Studia Islamica* 5 (1955): 125–148; 6 (1956): 125–146.

■ **Books**

Engineer, Asgharali. *Theory and Practise of the Islamic State*. Lahore, Pakistan: Vanguard Books, 1985.

Lambton, Ann K. S. *State and Government in Medieval Islam*. London: Oxford University Press, 1981.

——— *Continuity and Change in Medieval Persia: Aspects of Administrative, Economic, and Social History, 11th–14th Century*. Albany: State University of New York Press, 1988.

■ **Web Sites**

"Nizam al-Mulk." The Encyclopedia of Islam. Islamic Philosophy Web site.
   http://www.muslimphilosophy.com/ei2/nizam.htm.

—Timothy May

Questions for Further Study

1. Compare this document with Machiavelli's *Prince*. In what sense are both documents "Mirrors for Princes"? How do the two documents reflect the differences in the cultures that produced them?

2. What was the relationship between spiritual authority and temporal (earthly) authority in the Islamic nations of the Middle East in the eleventh century? Compare the views expressed in this document with modern views expressed by the Ayatollah Khomeini in "Islamic Government."

3. Why did Niẓām al-Mulk consider it necessary to write the *Book of Government; or, Rules for Kings*? What was it about the Seljuks and their relationship with the Middle East that required such a document?

4. In its early centuries, Islam split into various factions that differed on points of doctrine. What impact did this split have on governance and statecraft at the time of the *Book of Government*?

5. What is the meaning of the nomadic proverb that one could conquer but could not rule from horseback? What implications did the truth of this proverb have for governance in the Middle East at the time of *Book of Government*?

Nizām al-Mulk's Book of Government; or, Rules for Kings

[Chapter X: Concerning Intelligence Agents and Reporters and Their Importance in Administering the Affairs of the Country]

It is the king's duty to enquire into the condition of his peasantry and army, both far and near, and to know more or less how things are. If he does not do this he is at fault and people will charge him with negligence, laziness and tyranny, saying, "Either the king knows about the oppression and extortion going on in the country, or he does not know. If he knows and does nothing to prevent it and remedy it, that is because he is an oppressor like the rest and acquiesces in their oppression; and if he does not know then he is negligent and ignorant." Neither of these imputations is desirable. Inevitably therefore he must have postmasters; and in every age in the time of ignorance and of Islam, kings have had postmasters, through whom they have learnt everything that goes on, good and bad. For instance, if anybody wrongly took so much as a chicken or a bag of straw from another—and that five hundred farsangs away—the king would know about it and have the offender punished, so that others knew that the king was vigilant. In every place they appointed informers and so far checked the activities of oppressors that men enjoyed security and justice for the pursuit of trade and cultivation. But this is a delicate business involving some unpleasantness, it must be entrusted to the hands and tongues and pens of men who are completely above suspicion and without self-interest, for the weal or woe of the country depends on them. They must be directly responsible to the king and not to anyone else; and they must receive their monthly salaries regularly from the treasury so that they may do their work without any worries. In this way the king will know of every event that takes place and will be able to give his orders as appropriate, meting out unexpected reward, punishment or commendation to the persons concerned. When a king is like this, men are always eager to be obedient, fearing the king's displeasure, and nobody can possibly have the audacity to disobey the king or plot any mischief. Thus the employment of intelligence agents and reporters contributes to the justice, vigilance and prudence of the king, and to the prosperity of the country....

[Chapter XIII: On Sending Spies and Using Them for the Good of the Country and the People]

Spies must constantly go out to the limits of the kingdom in the guise of merchants, travellers, sufis, pedlars (of medicines), and mendicants, and bring back reports of everything they hear, so that no matters of any kind remain concealed, and if anything [untoward] happens it can in due course be remedied. In the past it has often happened that governors, assignees, officers, and army-commanders have planned rebellion and resistance, and plotted mischief against the king; but spies forestalled them and informed the king, who was thus enabled to set out immediately with all speed and, coming upon them unawares, to strike them down and frustrate their plans; and if any foreign king or army was preparing to attack the country, the spies informed the king, and he took action and repelled them. Likewise they brought news, whether good or bad, about the condition of the peasants, and the king gave the matter his attention, as did Adud ad Daula on one occasion....

[Chapter XVII: Concerning Boon-Companions and Intimates of the King and the Conduct of Their Affairs]

A king cannot do without suitable boon-companions with whom he can enjoy complete freedom and intimacy. The constant society of nobles [such as] margraves and generals tends to diminish the king's majesty and dignity because they become too arrogant. As a general rule people who are employed in any official capacity should not be admitted as boon-companions, nor should those who are accepted for companionship be appointed to any public office, because by virtue of the liberty they enjoy in the king's company they will indulge in high-handed practices and oppress the people. Officers should always be in a state of fear of the king, while boon-companions need to be familiar. If an officer is familiar he tends to oppress the peasantry; but if a boon-companion is not familiar the king will not find any pleasure or relaxation in his company. Boon-companions should have a fixed time for their appearance;

after the king has given audience and the nobles have retired, then comes the time for their turn.

There are several advantages in having boon-companions: firstly, they are company for the king; secondly, since they are with him day and night, they are in the position of bodyguards, and if any danger (we take refuge with Allah!) should appear, they will not hesitate to shield the king from it with their own bodies; and thirdly, the king can say thousands of different things, frivolous and serious, to his boon-companions which would not be suitable for the ears of his wazir or other nobles, for they are his officials and functionaries; and fourthly, all sorts of sundry tidings can be heard from boon-companions, for through their freedom they can report on matters, good and bad, whether drunk or sober; and in this there is advantage and benefit.

A boon-companion should be well-bred, accomplished, and of cheerful face. He should have pure faith, be able to keep secrets, and wear good clothes. He must possess an ample fund of stories and strange tales both amusing and serious, and be able to tell them well. He must always be a good talker and a pleasant partner; he should know how to play backgammon and chess, and if he can play a musical instrument and use a weapon, so much the better. He must always agree with the king, and whatever the king says or does, he must exclaim, "Bravo!" and "Well done!" He should not be didactic with "Do this" and "Don't do that," for it will displease the king and lead to dislike. Where pleasure and entertainment are concerned, as in feasting, drinking, hunting, polo and wrestling—in all matters like these it is right that the king should consult with his boon-companions, for they are there for this purpose. On the other hand, in everything to do with the country and its cultivation, the military and the peasantry, warfare, raids, punishment, gifts, stores and travels, it is better that he should take counsel with the ministers and nobles of the state and with experienced elders, for they are more skilled in these subjects. In this way matters will take their proper course....

[Chapter XXI: On Ambassadors and Their Treatment]

When ambassadors come from foreign countries, nobody is aware of their movements until they actually arrive at the city gates; nobody gives any information [that they are coming] and nobody makes any preparation for them; and they will surely attribute this to our negligence and indifference. So officers at the frontiers must be told that whenever anyone approaches their stations, they should at once despatch a rider and find out who it is who is coming, how many men there are with him, mounted and unmounted, how much baggage and equipment he has, and what is his business. A trustworthy person must be appointed to accompany them and conduct them to the nearest big city; there he will hand them over to another agent who will likewise go with them to the next city (and district), and so on until they reach the court. Whenever they arrive at a place where there is cultivation, it must be a standing order that officers, tax-collectors and assignees should give them hospitality and entertain them well so that they depart satisfied. When they return, the same procedure is to be followed. Whatever treatment is given to an ambassador, whether good or bad, it is as if it were done to the very king who sent him; and kings have always shewn the greatest respect to one another and treated envoys well, for by this their own dignity has been enhanced. And if at any time there has been disagreement or enmity between kings, and if ambassadors have still come and gone as occasion requires, and discharged their missions according to their instructions, never have they been molested or treated with less than usual courtesy. Such a thing would be disgraceful, as God (to Him be power and glory) says [in the Quran 24.53], "The messenger has only to convey the message plainly."

It should also be realized that when kings send ambassadors to one another their purpose is not merely the message or the letter which they communicate openly, but secretly they have a hundred other points and objects in view. In fact they want to know about the state of roads, mountain passes, rivers and grazing grounds, to see whether an army can pass or not; where fodder is available and where not; who are the officers in every place; what is the size of that king's army and how well it is armed and equipped; what is the standard of his table and his company; what is the organization and etiquette of his court and audience hall; does he play polo and hunt; what are his qualities and manners, his designs and intentions, his appearance and bearing; is he cruel or just, old or young; is his country flourishing or decaying; are his troops contented or not; are the peasants rich or poor; is he avaricious or generous; is he alert or negligent in affairs; is his wazir competent or the reverse, of good faith and high principles or of impure faith and bad principles; are his generals experienced and battle-tried or not; are his boon-companions polite and worthy; what are his likes and dislikes; in his cups is he jovial and good-natured or not; is he strict in religious matters and does he shew magnanimity and mercy, or is he careless; does he incline more to jesting or to gravity; and does he prefer boys or women. So that, if at any time they want to win over that king, or oppose his designs or criticize his faults, being informed of all his affairs they can think out their plan of campaign, and being aware of all the circumstances, they can take effective action, as happened to your humble servant in the time of The Martyr Sultan Alp Arslan (may Allah sanctify his soul)....

[Chapter XXIII: On Settling the Dues of All the Army]

The troops must receive their pay regularly. Those who are assignees of course have their salaries to hand independently as assigned; but in the case of pages who are not fit for holding fiefs, money for their pay must be made available. When the amount required has been worked out according to the number of troops, the money should be put into a special fund until the whole sum is in hand, and it must always be paid to them at the proper time. Alternatively the king may summon the men before him twice a year, and command that they be paid, not in such a way that the task be delegated to the treasury and they receive their money from there without seeing the king; rather the king should with his own hands put it into their hands (and skirts), for this increases their feelings of affection and attachment, so that they will strive more eagerly and steadfastly to perform their duties in war and peace....

[Chapter XLI: On Not Giving Two Appointments to One Man; on Giving Posts to the Unemployed and Not Leaving Them Destitute; on Giving Appointments to Men of Orthodox Faith and Good Birth, and Not Employing Men of Perverse Sects and Evil Doctrine, Keeping the Latter at a Distance]

Enlightened monarchs and clever ministers have never in any age given two appointments to one man or one appointment to two men, with the result that their affairs were always conducted with efficiency and lustre. When two appointments are given to one man, one of the tasks is always inefficiently and fault-

ily performed; and in fact you will usually find that the man who has two functions fails in both of them, and is constantly suffering censure and uneasiness on account of his shortcomings. And further, whenever two men are given a single post each transfers [his responsibility] to the other and the work remains forever undone. On this point there is a proverb which runs, "The house with two mistresses remains unswept; with two masters it falls to ruins." One of the two thinks to himself, "If I take pains to do the work expediently, and take care not to let anything go wrong, our master will think that this is due to the capability and skill of my partner, not to my own diligent and patient efforts." The other one has the same idea and thinks, "Why should I take trouble for nothing when it will go without praise or thanks? Whatever efforts and exertions I make, my master will suppose that my partner has done it." Actually there will be constant confusion in the work, and if the manager says, "What is the cause of this inefficiency?" each man will say that it is the other's fault. But when you go to the root of the matter and think intelligently, it is not the fault of either of them. It is the fault of the man who gave one appointment to two persons. And whenever a single officer is given two posts by the divan it is a sign of the incompetence of the wazir and the negligence of the king. Today there are men, utterly incapable, who hold ten posts, and if another appointment were to turn up, they would spend their efforts and money to get it; and nobody would consider whether such people are worthy of the post, whether they have any ability, whether they understand secretaryship, administration, and business dealings, and whether they can fulfill the numerous tasks which they have already accepted. And all the time there are capable, earnest, deserving, trustworthy, and experienced men left unemployed, sitting idle in their homes; and no one has the interest or judgment to enquire why one unknown, incapable, baseborn fellow should occupy so many appointments, while there are well-known, noble, trusted, and experienced men who have no work at all, and are left deprived and excluded, particularly men to whom this dynasty is greatly indebted for their satisfactory and meritorious services. This is all the more extraordinary because in all previous ages a public appointment was given to a man who was pure alike in religion and in origin; and if he was averse and refused to accept it, they used compulsion and force to make him take the responsibility. So naturally the revenue was not misappropriated, the peasants were unmolested, assignees enjoyed a good reputation and a safe existence, while the king lived a life of mental and bodily ease and tranquillity. But nowadays all distinction has vanished; and if a Jew administers the affairs of Turks or does any other work for Turks, it is permitted; and it is the same for Christians, Zoroastrians and Qarmatis. Everywhere indifference is predominant; there is no zeal for religion, no concern for the revenue, no pity for the peasants. The dynasty has reached its perfection; your humble servant is afraid of the evil eye and knows not where this state of affairs will lead.

Glossary

Adud ad Daula	known as the "Arm of the Empire," a Shia Muslim and the most important person of the Buyid Dynasty that controlled the Abbasid dynasty (r. 977–982)
farsang	a unit of measurement equaling approximately three miles; Baghdad to Samarqand is roughly 500 farsangs
lustre	in this context, evidence of great competence
Martyr Sultan Alp Arslan	Seljuk sultan who was killed by a prisoner taken while he and his troops were fighting north of the Amu Darya River; considered a martyr for his service to Islam

URBAN II'S CALL TO CRUSADE

"This royal city is now held captive by her enemies, and made pagan by those who know not God."

Overview

In 1095 Pope Urban II traveled northwest from Piacenza, in northern Italy, to preside over a church council at Clermont, in the Auvergne—the first time a pope had visited France in nearly fifty years. At the end of the council, on November 27, he preached a sermon to a large audience. He called on the faithful to aid the Christians of the East against the Turks and to liberate Jerusalem from Turkish rule. To those who took up the challenge, he offered a spiritual reward: forgiveness of all the sins they had committed to date. Although Urban's words would transform the course of world history, no official record of what he said is extant. Historians have to rely instead on later accounts, all of which were written after 1099, when the campaign he inspired resulted in the conquest of Jerusalem.

Context

Before traveling to France, Pope Urban II had held a church council at Piacenza in northern Italy in March 1095. There he received envoys from the Byzantine emperor Alexius I, who asked for military support against the Seljuk Turks on his eastern border. The Seljuk threat to Byzantium would provide the rationale for Urban's call to crusade.

The Seljuks were a powerful new force in the Near East. They had their roots north of the Oxus River (modern-day Amu Dar'ya), in what is now Uzbekistan. After converting to Sunni Islam in the tenth century, they embarked on a series of conquests that brought Iran, Iraq, and northern Syria under their control by the 1050s. Seljuk success came at the expense of the traditional ruling dynasty of the Islamic world—the Sunni Abbasid caliphs of Baghdad. When the Seljuks occupied Baghdad in 1055, they allowed the Abbasid caliph to carry on as a figurehead of Sunni orthodoxy but took real power into their own hands. Soon the Seljuks were making inroads westward, into Anatolia. Here they found the richest provinces of Byzantium, the eastern part of the Roman Empire that had survived the collapse of Roman political power in the West. In 1071 the Seljuks defeated the

Byzantines at Manzikert (now Malazgirt). In the aftermath, the Seljuks occupied much of Anatolia, establishing their capital at Nicaea (present-day Iznik), less than sixty miles from Constantinople (called Istanbul today).

The Christian response to the Seljuks was slow in coming for several reasons. First, the Seljuks had turned away from Constantinople. They headed east again and by 1079 occupied southern Syria and Palestine. In addition, the Byzantines chose to confront more urgent threats elsewhere. It was only after a powerful new emperor, Alexius I Comnenus, had stabilized the situation to the west and the north that Byzantine attention shifted to the eastern border. Mainly, though, authorities in Christian Europe were simply not prepared to respond. Alexius had actually requested papal help against "pagan" incursions before Piacenza; a few years earlier he had solicited support against the Pechenegs on the Balkan frontier. Urban denied that request but would respond differently in 1095, because his situation had changed since the early days of his pontificate.

Alexius's initial appeals for military aid had reached a pope in exile. Odo of Châtillon had been elected pope and had taken the name Urban II in 1088 at Terracina, south of Rome. No pope had lived in Rome since 1084, when Urban's predecessor and patron, Gregory VII, had been driven from the city by the German emperor Henry IV. The conflict between pope and emperor was over the Reform Movement—a radical effort to remake the church and Christian society—which the papacy had been leading since the mid-eleventh century. The slogans of the reformers were liberation and purification. Powerful secular rulers, such as Henry IV, were long accustomed to appointing bishops and abbots in their realms. By ending secular control over ecclesiastical appointments, the reformers hoped to free the church from the corrupting influence of worldly affairs. A purified clergy would then transform the fallen secular world into a genuinely Christian republic under papal leadership.

Urban II was a product of two centers of reform: the abbey of Cluny, where he rose to the office of prior, and the College of Cardinals around Gregory VII, where he served as cardinal-bishop of Ostia from around 1080. Urban spent the early years of his pontificate in southern Italy, pursuing reformist causes. By careful diplomacy he regained Rome in 1093, and two years later he presided over the first interna-

Time Line

1055
- The Seljuk Turks occupy Baghdad.

1071
- The Seljuk Turks defeat the Byzantines at the Battle of Manzikert.

1084
- Pope Gregory VII leaves Rome and goes into exile.

1088
- **March 12** Odo of Châtillon is elected pope at Terracina, taking the name Urban II.

1093
- Pope Urban II returns to Rome.

1095
- **March 1–7** The Council of Piacenza takes place.
- **November 18–28** The Council of Clermont is held.
- **November 27** Pope Urban II preaches the First Crusade.

1099
- **July 15** The crusaders take Jerusalem.

1104–1108
- Guibert of Nogent composes *Gesta Dei per Francos* (completing the final corrections in 1111).

tional church council of his pontificate at Piacenza. There, in response to Alexius's envoys, he urged many men to swear oaths to come to the emperor's aid against the Turks.

What Alexius expected from the pope was a small force of mercenaries. Urban's plan was much grander, however, and it was bound up with the aims of the Reform Movement. The campaign was to be a war of liberation, not of church offices from lay control but of Christian peoples and churches in the East. Urban's advocacy of violence to achieve this goal was consistent with reformist ideology. Gregory VII had recruited soldiers, whom he called "knights of Saint Peter," for the war with Henry IV. Urban II would recruit soldiers for a new campaign of liberation in the East. Such a project would demonstrate papal leadership over Christian Europe. It might even repair relations with the Byzantines, who had taken offense at the vigorous claims of the early reformist popes to spiritual primacy over their own Greek Orthodox Church.

The reformers wanted to purify as well as to liberate. The war in the East would be a vehicle of purification on two levels. For the individual volunteer, it would be a penitential exercise that would earn remission of sins. For Western Christian society as a whole, it would provide an outlet for the violence that had been an endemic feature of European life for two centuries. When Muslims, Magyars, and Vikings invaded Europe in the late ninth and early tenth centuries, central structures of authority broke down, and local warriors came to power. The violence of this warrior elite posed practical and moral problems for church leaders. Their first response had been to try to suppress it by imposing the Peace and Truce of God. At assemblies of churchmen and local people, a formal ban would be placed on waging war against vulnerable members of society and at certain times of year. The bans proved ineffective, however, and often led to more violence as local churches sought to impose their restrictions by force. When Urban came to Clermont, he began by enjoining the Peace and Truce of God upon the faithful. He then opened up a channel through which the pent-up violence of the knights could pour out of Europe: He preached the way of the cross to Jerusalem.

About the Author

The four main versions of Pope Urban's sermon are found in histories of the First Crusade written by churchmen within a decade of the expedition. Fulcher of Chartres was a cleric who may have been present at Clermont. He took the cross in response to Urban's preaching and joined the forces of Stephen of Blois when they departed for the East in October 1096. By October 1097 he had become chaplain to another powerful crusader, Baldwin of Boulogne; Fulcher retained that position after Baldwin became king of Jerusalem in 1100. In Jerusalem, Fulcher composed his history of the First Crusade, the *Historia Hierosolymitana*, completing the first version around 1106.

At the beginning of his *Historia Iherosolimitana*, Robert of Reims (called Robert the Monk in the document) indicates that he was present at the Council of Clermont. He is sometimes identified with an abbot of the Benedictine abbey of Saint Rémi of Reims who, though esteemed as a scholar, was expelled from his high office for administrative blunders in 1097 and eventually retired to the priory of Senuc, dying around 1122. Other scholars identify him instead with a simple monk of Saint Rémi. His history of the First Crusade is best dated to 1107.

Baldric of Dol was also present at Clermont. He was a learned monk who became abbot of the Benedictine abbey of Bourgueil in 1089. There he wrote verse in imitation of the poets of ancient Rome. In 1107 he was appointed archbishop of Dol in Brittany. He wrote his *Historia Jerosolimitana* in 1108.

Guibert of Nogent did not attend the Council of Clermont. He was from a noble family in northern France and entered the Benedictine abbey of Saint Germer-de-Fly as a youth. In 1104 he became abbot of Nogent-sous-Coucy. He was a prolific author, most famous today for his autobiography, *De vita sua*. He composed his history of the First Crusade, *Gesta Dei per Francos* (*The Deeds of God Performed through the Franks*), between 1104 and 1108, with final corrections completed in 1111.

Explanation and Analysis of the Document

It is natural to wonder how close the four authors come to what Urban said at Clermont. They are excellent sources in some respects. At least two and probably three of them (Robert, Baldric, and likely Fulcher) attended the Council of Clermont. The fourth, Guibert of Nogent, had access to eyewitness accounts. Despite being well positioned to record Urban's words, the authors present different versions of the sermon. While Guibert of Nogent, for example, has Urban describe the Crusade as a prelude to the Last Judgment, the others do not. We might expect eyewitness accounts to agree more closely, but even here there are variations. Urban speaks at length about Jerusalem in Robert's and Baldric's versions but says nothing about it in Fulcher's. Such differences among equally well-placed eyewitnesses make it impossible to declare one version more authentic than any other. Moreover, all of the versions are colored by the fall of Jerusalem to the crusaders in 1099, an event that took place between the delivery of the speech and its recordings. This unexpected triumph may have caused the authors to imbue the sermon with a momentousness that the original occasion lacked. Like many medieval historians, they felt free to recreate a famous speech according to what they believed should have been said at a moment of historical significance. These sources may not tell us what Urban said at Clermont, but they still have historical value because they reveal how contemporaries and participants understood the origins of the crusading movement.

◆ Fulcher of Chartres

Fulcher has Pope Urban address the mainly clerical participants in the Council of Clermont. These churchmen

Time Line

1106	■ Fulcher of Chartres finishes the first version of his *Historia Hierosolymitana*.
1107	■ Robert of Reims writes his *Historia Iherosolimitana*.
1108	■ Baldric of Dol completes his *Historia Jerosolimitana*.

were to serve as "Christ's heralds" in spreading the message of the Crusade to those who would actually do the fighting. The tone is terse and direct, with little figurative language. Fulcher offers the basic case for war against the Turks, presenting in outline form arguments that the other versions develop more fully.

In Fulcher's account Urban begins by appealing to the audience to help their Christian brothers living in the East. Medieval Europeans were comfortable with the idea of fighting for family members. In a world where governments were small and provided minimal law enforcement, family members looked to one another for protection. When a person was killed or injured, members of the injured party's family were obliged to exact vengeance from the offender or the offender's family. By having Urban speak of brotherhood, Fulcher brings this sense of obligation to the war against the Turks: It would be family feud writ large, a vendetta waged in the name of fraternal defense.

While couching Urban's appeal in the familiar language of feud and vengeance, Fulcher gives a new dimension to the idea of fighting for family. His concept of brotherhood transcends any particular fraternal bond—it is the tie that binds all Christian men to one another. In Fulcher's eyes, warfare within this Christian fraternity was illicit. It was wasteful, private war against supposed rivals who were actually, in Fulcher's expanded conception, Christian "brothers and relations." Christian men must turn away from internecine strife and fight the real enemy: the Turks whose conquests posed a threat to Christians everywhere. The cause of this new kind of war was so righteous that God himself commanded it and would grant remission of sins to those who died fighting it.

◆ Robert of Reims

In Robert's version Urban directly addresses those who would fight on the campaign. Speaking to knights, he makes sure to highlight the material rewards of participation. He

Pewter pilgrim badge of Saint George standing over a dragon and driving a spear into its mouth. The cult of Saint George was popular in England from 1098, when he is said to have appeared in the sky during the Battle of Antioch in the First Crusade. (© Museum of London)

compares Jerusalem, the land that "floweth with milk and honey," to a homeland that is too small for its population and that lacks food, natural resources, and wealth. Urban's main focus, though, as Robert presents it, is on another set of worldly concerns for the warriors of eleventh-century Europe: honor, reputation, and pride in family and ethnicity.

Urban begins by praising the Franks—the traditional name given to the tribes who settled in modern-day France during the later days of the Roman Empire, established successor states when the empire collapsed, converted to Catholic Christianity, and rose to new heights of power under the Merovingian and Carolingian dynasties. For Robert the Franks were a new chosen people, beloved of God for their devotion to the Roman church and blessed with all the martial virtues. They had a proud tradition of fighting for the faith, exemplified by the campaigns of Charlemagne and his son Louis the Pious in the eighth and ninth centuries. Urban's reference to these famous Frankish leaders does more than conjure up a heroic past. It invokes an alliance between the papacy and the Franks that dated back to the eighth century, when the papacy had recognized the legitimacy of the new rulers of the Frankish kingdom, the Carolingians, and they in return had conquered the central Italian lands that the popes would rule as independent sovereigns until the unification of Italy in 1870. The Crusade would offer a fresh opportunity for the Franks to come to the aid of the church. In Robert's version of the sermon, ethnic pride has replaced fraternal solidarity as the driving force behind the campaign.

To live up to their heroic past, the Franks must confront an enemy whose ravages would seem to mock their status as stalwart defenders of the faith. Briefly mentioned in Fulcher, here the Turks are denounced at length. Scholars now agree that these characterizations are far from accurate. The Seljuk campaigns of conquest disrupted typical patterns of life in the Middle East; however, the Seljuks did not systematically persecute Christians or radically disrupt European pilgrimage traffic to Jerusalem, which was, after all, a major revenue source for the city. Nevertheless, Urban describes a series of Turkish insults to the Christian faith. The Turks did not just destroy churches; they defiled them by circumcising Christian men and spreading their blood over the altars. They did not just kill Christian men; they tortured them by cutting open their stomachs, extracting their intestines, tying them to a stake, and walking the victim in a circle until the guts lay all over the ground. They did not just capture Christian women; they raped them. At the end of this litany, Urban challenges Frankish pride: Whose responsibility was it, if not theirs, to avenge these wrongs? The answer, when it comes at the end of the sermon, affirms the divine nature of the enterprise. In a famous moment, the audience shouted in unison, "It is the will of God!" (Thatcher and McNeal, p. 520).

◆ **Baldric of Dol**

In Baldric's version of the sermon, Urban offers a fuller justification for crusading violence, a more lavish description of Jerusalem, and a broader theological context for the campaign. In Baldric's day the most influential Christian

thinker on the use of force was Augustine of Hippo (354–430), an African bishop and a scholar in the last days of the Roman Empire. For Augustine a war was just if it met three conditions: just cause, such as fighting to defend oneself or to avenge an injury; legitimate authority, such as fighting at the command of a public authority (a Roman emperor, for example); and right intention, such as fighting for a loving, altruistic purpose. Augustine saw nothing good in violence. It was usually sinful and usually to be avoided, but it could be condoned under these limited conditions.

Baldric uses Augustine's categories to make a more radical claim for Christian violence: The war that Urban proclaims would not merely be blameless; it would be positively holy. The Crusade would be righteous because it would be fought for a just cause: the defense of Eastern Christians and the recovery of formerly Christian lands. The legitimate authority is Christ himself. He is the "Commander" and "our Leader"; the crusaders would be "His army." Those who joined him would fight with the right intention of helping their Christian brothers in the East. Baldric calls the Crusade "the only warfare that is righteous, for it is charity to risk your life for your brothers."

Jerusalem was at the heart of this new kind of holy war. Urban declares that Christians should be ashamed at allowing the Turks to possess the city and to pollute its holiest sites. Medieval maps located Jerusalem at the center of the world. The city was a growing source of concern to Europeans in the eleventh century. It was by far the most prestigious destination for pilgrims because of its remote location, its central role in the Last Judgment, and its links to Christ's life, Passion, and Resurrection. By the 1060s European pilgrims were traveling there in enormous bands, sometimes reaching into the thousands. In an age that venerated saints and their remains, the whole city could be described as a relic. Urban urges the Crusade in order to restore this holiest of cities to Christian control.

In the Old Testament, God promises the Holy Land to the Israelites. Urban holds up their experience as a model for the new Crusade. Just as the Israelites had conquered the Holy Land by force of arms, so must the crusaders conquer it again, but now with Jesus as their leader. Just as the Israelites had fought the peoples of Canaan—Baldric specifically mentions the Amalekites, a perennial Israelite foe, and the Jebusites, who controlled Jerusalem until King David conquered it—so must the crusaders fight the Turks. The force of Baldric's analogy is clear. Like the Israelites of old, the crusaders were part of God's plan for humankind; their providential role would be to restore the Holy Land to (Catholic) Christianity. In this way Baldric uses Christian providential history to make sense of the seemingly miraculous success of the First Crusade.

◆ **Guibert of Nogent**

Of all the versions of Urban's speech, Guibert's least resembles an actual sermon that a pope might have delivered at Clermont on November 27, 1095. It is less an emotional appeal to fight the Turks than a learned attempt to define the Crusade in a theologically satisfying way. The

Pool of Hezekiah, Church of the Holy Sepulchre, and Hospice of the Knights of Saint John, Jerusalem (Library of Congress)

title he gives his history of the First Crusade—*The Deeds of God Performed through the Franks*—sums up the message he has Urban deliver: The Crusade is God's work, and the crusaders are instruments of divine will. Like Baldric, Guibert dips into the Christian past to make his point. This time it is the Maccabees who show the way. Judah the Maccabee was the leader of a Jewish revolt against the Seleucid king Antiochus IV, who had outlawed Jewish religious rites in 167 BCE. After twenty-five years of war, the Maccabees liberated the Jews from Seleucid rule and rededicated their temple in Jerusalem. The crusaders, of course, lived under a new dispensation. Medieval theologians held that Christians had supplanted the Jews as God's chosen people. As a result, the Jewish homeland for which the Maccabees fought is now, as Urban declares to the "Christian soldiers" in his audience, "your country."

In trying to understand the Crusade as a manifestation of God's will, Guibert looks to the future as well as the past. Urban argues that the end of the world is near and that the

Antichrist will soon appear. As the name suggests, the Antichrist's appointed role is to fight against Christians: He is supposed to take up residence on the Mount of Olives and from there launch attacks that will destroy the Christians of Egypt, Africa, and Ethiopia. For the prophecy to come true, Christians had to be living in these countries. The crusaders, then, would conquer this vast region just in time for the Antichrist to come along and destroy them. Some commentators have wondered whether promoting the Crusade as a way of winning death at the hands of the Antichrist would have been an effective recruitment technique. By assigning the crusaders this glorious but ultimately doomed role, Guibert underscores his theological concerns.

Audience

The four authors envision slightly different audiences for Urban's call to the Crusade. For Fulcher the audience is

"O what a disgrace if such a despised and base race, which worships demons, should conquer a people which has the faith of omnipotent God and is made glorious with the name of Christ! With what reproaches will the Lord overwhelm us if you do not aid those who, with us, profess the Christian religion!"

(Fulcher of Chartres)

"This royal city is now held captive by her enemies, and made pagan by those who know not God. She asks and longs to be liberated and does not cease to beg you to come to her aid."

(Robert of Reims)

"You should shudder, brethren, you should shudder at raising a violent hand against Christians; it is less wicked to brandish your sword against Saracens. It is the only warfare that is righteous, for it is charity to risk your life for your brothers."

(Baldric of Dol)

"And you ought, furthermore, to consider with the utmost deliberation, if by your labors, God working through you, it should occur that the Mother of churches should flourish anew to the worship of Christianity, whether, perchance, He may not wish other regions of the East to be restored to the faith against the approaching time of the Antichrist."

(Guibert of Nogent)

mainly clerical, for Robert and Guibert it is military, and for Baldric it is a mixture of the two, with each group having a distinct role to play in the coming campaign. Other evidence suggests that Urban addressed a large, primarily clerical audience at Clermont. Attending the council were at least thirteen archbishops, eighty-two bishops, and numerous abbots and other clergy. After speaking at Clermont, Urban went on a long preaching tour, spreading the message of the Crusade through much of France while avoiding areas controlled directly by King Philip I, who had been excommunicated at Clermont for adultery. Urban preached the cross at Limoges in December 1095, at Le Mans in February 1096, and at Nîmes in July 1096. He did not return to Italy until August 1096. By then crusaders were marching to the East.

Impact

Urban's message at Clermont was revolutionary. By offering a spiritual reward to wage war, he was declaring that violence could be righteous and even a form of penance—a way of redressing sin akin to prayer or fasting. Urban's promotion of sacred violence marked a turning point in Christian thinking about the legitimate use of force. It certainly provoked a massive response. The first wave of crusaders set out in spring 1096. Sometimes called the People's Crusade, it consisted of some trained troops but many more poor and ill-prepared men and women under the leadership of popular preachers, such as Peter the Hermit. A second wave of crusaders departed for the East in late summer 1096. Dominating these forces were powerful nobles—among them Godfrey of Bouillon, Bohemond of Taranto, and Raymond of Saint Gilles—who commanded contingents of knights. We can only guess at the size of the First Crusade. Recent estimates suggest that around 120,000 people took the cross in response to Urban's appeal. Of these, roughly 85,000 departed for the East.

The crusaders who answered the pope's call remade the map of the Middle East and transformed relations among Christians, Muslims, and Jews in the process. On their way to the Holy Land in 1096, bands of crusaders attacked Jewish communities in the Rhineland, offering them the choice of conversion or death. The massacres and mass suicides that ensued set the stage for worsening Jewish-Christian relations in Europe through the later Middle Ages. Three years later, on July 15, 1099, the forces of the second wave of the Crusade captured Jerusalem. The conquest led to the establishment of crusader states that would survive for almost 200 years. The crusader presence in the Holy Land provoked a complex response in the Muslim world, combining indifference; misunderstanding; attempts at accommodation; and, in the late twelfth-century campaigns of Saladin, a "countercrusade" that aimed to restore Sunni Islam orthodoxy in the Middle East even as it sought to drive the European settlers into the sea. Over the twelfth and thirteenth centuries, crusading spread to frontier regions in Spain and the Baltic and even, in the form of campaigns against heretics, took root in the European heartland. It remained a characteristic feature of European life into the sixteenth century, bequeathing a controversial legacy to the modern world.

If the sermon itself was influential, so too were the ways in which it was recorded. The themes that Urban is made to address in the four main versions—renouncing unjust wars at home for righteous ones abroad, aiding Christian brethren in the East, and fighting out of love of God and neighbor—would appear repeatedly in later Crusade propaganda. The sermons also shaped contemporary understandings of the origins of the crusading movement. Especially influential was the idea—expressed briefly by Fulcher and developed more fully by the three French Benedictines—that the Crusade was a miraculous demonstration of God's will on earth. This notion was crucial to the emergence of a full-fledged ideology of Christian holy war.

Further Reading

■ Articles
Cowdrey, H. E. J. "Pope Urban II's Preaching of the First Crusade." *History* 55 (1970): 177–188.

Munro, Dana Carleton. "The Speech of Pope Urban II at Clermont, 1095." *American Historical Review* 11, no. 2 (January 1906): 231–242.

■ Books
Cole, Penny J. *The Preaching of the Crusades to the Holy Land, 1095–1270.* Cambridge, Mass.: Medieval Academy of America, 1991.

Questions for Further Study

1. The ostensible reason for Urban's call to the Crusade was to liberate the holy city of Jerusalem. Did Urban have other motives? If so, what were those motives?

2. In what particular ways did Urban appeal to knights and the nobility to join the Crusade? What promises did Urban hold out to the crusaders? What rhetorical devices did he use, at least according to some of the records of his sermon?

3. The records of Urban's sermon differ in several important ways. What are these differences? Explain the extent to which different listeners were, in effect, hearing different sermons. Further, explain how the various witnesses might have skewed their record of the pope's speech for particular motives.

4. Why do you think so many people responded to the pope's call for military action in a faraway land? What impulses did Urban seem to have tapped into?

5. It is said that Urban's call to the Crusade fundamentally transformed the relationships between Christians, Muslims, and even Jews and that the effects of this transformation are still being felt in the modern world. Do you believe that this is an accurate assessment? Do you believe that it is fair to essentially blame modern problems on thousand-year-old events? Explain.

Housley, Norman. *Fighting for the Cross: Crusading to the Holy Land*. New Haven, Conn.: Yale University Press, 2008.

Riley-Smith, Jonathan. *The First Crusade and the Idea of Crusading*. Philadelphia: University of Pennsylvania Press, 1986.

Thatcher, Oliver J., and Edgar H. McNeal. *A Source Book for Medieval History*. New York: Scribners, 1905.

Tyerman, Christopher. *God's War: A New History of the Crusades*. Cambridge, Mass: Harvard University Press, 2006.

■ **Web Sites**

"Crusades: A Guide to Online Resources." ORB: The Online Reference Book for Medieval Studies Web site.
    http://the-orb.net/encyclop/religion/crusades/crusade.html.

"A History of the Crusades." University of Wisconsin Digital Collections.
    http://digicoll.library.wisc.edu/History/subcollections/Hist CrusadesAbout.html.

—Michael Lower

Milestone Documents

URBAN II'S CALL TO CRUSADE

Urban II's Call to the Crusade according to Fulcher of Chartres

Most beloved brethren: Urged by necessity, I, Urban, by the permission of God chief bishop and prelate over the whole world, have come into these parts as an ambassador with a divine admonition to you, the servants of God. I hoped to find you as faithful and as zealous in the service of God as I had supposed you to be. But if there is in you any deformity or crookedness contrary to God's law, with divine help I will do my best to remove it. For God has put you as stewards over his family to minister to it. Happy indeed will you be if he finds you faithful in your stewardship. You are called shepherds; see that you do not act as hirelings. But be true shepherds, with your crooks always in your hands. Do not go to sleep, but guard on all sides the flock committed to you. For if through your carelessness or negligence a wolf carries away one of your sheep, you will surely lose the reward laid up for you with God. And after you have been bitterly scourged with remorse for your faults, you will be fiercely overwhelmed in hell, the abode of death. For according to the gospel you are the salt of the earth. But if you fall short in your duty, how, it may be asked, can it be salted? O how great the need of salting! It is indeed necessary for you to correct with the salt of wisdom this foolish people which is so devoted to the pleasures of this world, lest the Lord, when He may wish to speak to them, find them putrefied by their sins, unsalted and stinking. For if He shall find worms, that is, sins, in them, because you have been negligent in your duty, He will command them as worthless to be thrown into the abyss of unclean things. And because you cannot restore to Him His great loss, He will surely condemn you and drive you from His loving presence. But the man who applies this salt should be prudent, provident, modest, learned, peaceable, watchful, pious, just, equitable, and pure. For how can the ignorant teach others? How can the licentious make others modest? And how can the impure make others pure? If anyone hates peace, how can he make others peaceable? Or if anyone has soiled his hands with baseness, how can he cleanse the impurities of another? We read also that if the blind lead the blind, both will fall into the ditch. But first correct yourselves, in order that, free from blame, you may be able to correct those who are subject to you. If you wish to be the friends of God, gladly do the things which you know will please Him. You must especially let all matters that pertain to the church be controlled by the law of the church. And be careful that simony does not take root among you, lest both those who buy and those who sell [church offices] be beaten with the scourges of the Lord through narrow streets and driven into the place of destruction and confusion. Keep the church and the clergy in all its grades entirely free from the secular power. See that the tithes that belong to God are faithfully paid from all the produce of the land; let them not be sold or withheld. If anyone seizes a bishop let him be treated as an outlaw. If anyone seizes or robs monks, or clergymen, or nuns, or their servants, or pilgrims, or merchants, let him be anathema [that is, cursed]. Let robbers and incendiaries and all their accomplices be expelled from the church and anathematized. If a man who does not give a part of his goods as alms is punished with the damnation of hell, how should he be punished who robs another of his goods? For thus it happened to the rich man in the gospel; for he was not punished because he had stolen the goods of another, but because he had not used well the things which were his.

You have seen for a long time the great disorder in the world caused by these crimes. It is so bad in some of your provinces, I am told, and you are so weak in the administration of justice, that one can hardly go along the road by day or night without being attacked by robbers; and whether at home or abroad, one is in danger of being despoiled either by force or fraud. Therefore it is necessary to reenact the truce, as it is commonly called, which was proclaimed a long time ago by our holy fathers. I exhort and demand that you, each, try hard to have the truce kept in your diocese. And if anyone shall be led by his cupidity or arrogance to break this truce, by the authority of God and with the sanction of this council he shall be anathematized.

Although, O sons of God, you have promised more firmly than ever to keep the peace among yourselves and to preserve the rights of the church, there remains still an important work for you to do. Freshly quickened by the divine correction, you must apply the strength of your righteousness to another matter which concerns you as well as God. For your brethren who live in the east are in urgent need of your help, and you must hasten to give them the aid which has often been promised them. For, as the most of you have heard, the Turks and Arabs have attacked them and have conquered the territory of Romania [the Greek empire] as far west as the shore of the Mediterranean and the Hellespont, which is called the Arm of St George. They have occupied more and more of the lands of those Christians, and have overcome them in seven battles. They have killed and captured many, and have destroyed the churches and devastated the empire. If you permit them to continue thus for awhile with impunity, the faithful of God will be much more widely attacked by them. On this account I, or rather the Lord, beseech you as Christ's heralds to publish this everywhere and to persuade all people of whatever rank, foot-soldiers and knights, poor and rich, to carry aid promptly to those Christians and to destroy that vile race from the lands of our friends. I say this to those who are present, it is meant also for those who are absent. Moreover, Christ commands it.

All who die by the way, whether by land or by sea, or in battle against the pagans, shall have immediate remission of sins. This I grant them through the power of God with which I am invested. O what a disgrace if such a despised and base race, which worships demons, should conquer a people which has the faith of omnipotent God and is made glorious with the name of Christ! With what reproaches will the Lord overwhelm us if you do not aid those who, with us, profess the Christian religion! Let those who have been accustomed unjustly to wage private warfare against the faithful now go against the infidels and end with victory this war which should have been begun long ago. Let those who, for a long time, have been robbers, now become knights. Let those who have been fighting against their brothers and relatives now fight in a proper way against the barbarians. Let those who have been serving as mercenaries for small pay now obtain the eternal reward. Let those who have been wearing themselves out in both body and soul now work for a double honor. Behold! on this side will be the sorrowful and poor, on that, the rich; on this side, the enemies of the Lord, on that, his friends. Let those who go not put off the journey, but rent their lands and collect money for their expenses; and as soon as winter is over and spring comes, let them eagerly set out on the way with God as their guide.

Urban II's Call to the Crusade according to Robert of Reims

O race of the Franks. O people who live beyond the mountains [that is, reckoned from Rome], O people loved and chosen of God, as is clear from your many deeds, distinguished over all other nations by the situation of your land, your catholic faith, and your regard for the holy church, we have a special message and exhortation for you. For we wish you to know what a grave matter has brought us to your country. The sad news has come from Jerusalem and Constantinople that the people of Persia, an accursed and foreign race, enemies of God, "a generation that set not their heart aright, and whose spirit was not steadfast with God," have invaded the lands of those Christians and devastated them with the sword, rapine, and fire. Some of the Christians they have carried away as slaves, others they have put to death. The churches they have either destroyed or turned into mosques. They desecrate and overthrow the altars. They circumcise the Christians and pour the blood from the circumcision on the altars or in the baptismal fonts. Some they kill in a horrible way by cutting open the abdomen, taking out a part of the entrails and tying them to a stake; they then beat them and compel them to walk until all their entrails are drawn out and they fall to the ground. Some they use as targets for their arrows. They compel some to stretch out their necks and then they try to see whether they can cut off their heads with one stroke of the sword. It is better to say nothing of their horrible treatment of the women. They have taken from the Greek empire a tract of land so large that it takes more than two months to walk through it. Whose duty is it to avenge this and recover that land, if not yours? For to you more than to other nations the Lord has given the military spirit, courage, agile bodies, and the bravery to strike down those who resist you. Let your minds be stirred to bravery by the deeds of your forefathers, and by the efficiency and greatness of Karl the Great, and of Ludwig his son, and of the other kings who have destroyed Turkish kingdoms, and established Christianity in their lands. You should be moved especially by the holy grave of our Lord and Saviour which is now held by unclean peoples, and by the holy places which are treated with dishonor and irreverently befouled with their uncleanness.

O bravest of knights, descendants of unconquered ancestors, do not be weaker than they, but remember their courage. If you are kept back by your love for your children, relatives, and wives, remember what

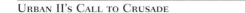

the Lord says in the Gospel: "He that loveth father or mother more than me is not worthy of me"; "and everyone that hath forsaken houses, or brothers, or sisters, or father, or mother, or wife, or children, or lands for my name's sake, shall receive a hundredfold and shall inherit everlasting life." Let no possessions keep you back, no solicitude for your property. Your land is shut in on all sides by the sea and mountains, and is too thickly populated. There is not much wealth here, and the soil scarcely yields enough to support you. On this account you kill and devour each other, and carry on war and mutually destroy each other. Let your hatred and quarrels cease, your civil wars come to an end, and all your dissensions stop. Set out on the road to the holy sepulchre, take the land from that wicked people, and make it your own. That land which, as the Scripture says, is flowing with milk and honey, God gave to the children of Israel. Jerusalem is the best of all lands, more fruitful than all others, as it were a second Paradise of delights. This land our Saviour made illustrious by his birth, beautiful with his life, and sacred with his suffering; he redeemed it with his death and glorified it with his tomb. This royal city is now held captive by her enemies, and made pagan by those who know not God. She asks and longs to be liberated and does not cease to beg you to come to her aid. She asks aid especially from you because, as I have said, God has given more of the military spirit to you than to other nations. Set out on this journey and you will obtain the remission of your sins and be sure of the incorruptible glory of the kingdom of heaven.

Urban II's Call to the Crusade according to Baldric of Dol

We have heard, most beloved brethren, and you have heard what we cannot recount without deep sorrow—how, with great hurt and dire sufferings our Christian brothers, members in Christ, are scourged, oppressed, and injured in Jerusalem, in Antioch, and the other cities of the East. Your own blood-brothers, your companions, your associates (for you are sons of the same Christ and the same Church) are either subjected in their inherited homes to other masters, or are driven from them, or they come as beggars among us; or, which is far worse, they are flogged and exiled as slaves for sale in their own land. Christian blood, redeemed by the blood of Christ, has been shed, and Christian flesh, akin to the flesh of Christ, has been subjected to unspeakable degrada-

tion and servitude. Everywhere in those cities there is sorrow, everywhere misery, everywhere groaning (I say it with a sigh). The churches in which divine mysteries were celebrated in olden times are now, to our sorrow, used as stables for the animals of these people! Holy men do not possess those cities; nay, base and bastard Turks hold sway over our brothers. The blessed Peter first presided as Bishop at Antioch; behold, in his own church the Gentiles have established their superstitions, and the Christian religion, which they ought rather to cherish, they have basely shut out from the hall dedicated to God! The estates given for the support of the saints and the patrimony of nobles set aside for the sustenance of the poor are subject to pagan tyranny, while cruel masters abuse for their own purposes the returns from these lands. The priesthood of God has been ground down into the dust. The sanctuary of God (unspeakable shame!) is everywhere profaned. Whatever Christians still remain in hiding there are sought out with unheard of tortures.

Of holy Jerusalem, brethren, we dare not speak, for we are exceedingly afraid and ashamed to speak of it. This very city, in which, as you all know, Christ Himself suffered for us, because our sins demanded it, has been reduced to the pollution of paganism and, I say it to our disgrace, withdrawn from the service of God. Such is the heap of reproach upon us who have so much deserved it! Who now serves the church of the Blessed Mary in the valley of Josaphat, in which church she herself was buried in body? But why do we pass over the Temple of Solomon, nay of the Lord, in which the barbarous nations placed their idols contrary to law, human and divine? Of the Lord's Sepulchre we have refrained from speaking, since some of you with your own eyes have seen to what abominations it has been given over. The Turks violently took from it the offerings which you brought there for alms in such vast amounts, and, in addition, they scoffed much and often at your religion. And yet in that place (I say only what you already know) rested the Lord; there He died for us; there He was buried. How precious would be the longed-for, incomparable place of the Lord's burial, even if God failed there to perform the yearly miracle! For in the days of His Passion all the lights in the Sepulchre and round about in the church, which have been extinguished, are related by divine command. Whose heart is so stony, brethren, that it is not touched by so great a miracle? Believe me, that man is bestial and senseless whose heart such divinely manifest grace does not move to faith! And yet the

Gentiles see this in common with the Christians and are not turned from their ways! They are, indeed, afraid, but they are not converted to the faith; nor is it to be wondered at, for a blindness of mind rules over them. With what afflictions they wronged you who have returned and are now present, you yourselves know too well, you who there sacrificed your substance and your blood for God.

This, beloved brethren, we shall say, that we may have you as witness of our words. More suffering of our brethren and devastation of churches remains than we can speak of one by one, for we are oppressed by tears and groans, sighs and sobs. We weep and wail, brethren, alas, like the Psalmist, in our inmost heart! We are wretched and unhappy, and in us is that prophecy fulfilled: "God, the nations are come into thine inheritance; thy holy temple have they defiled; they have laid Jerusalem in heaps; the dead bodies of thy servants have been given to be food for the birds of the heaven, the flesh of thy saints unto the beasts of the earth. Their blood have they shed like water round about Jerusalem, and there was none to bury them." Woe unto us, brethren! We who have already become a reproach to our neighbors, a scoffing, and derision to them round about us, let us at least with tears condole and have compassion upon our brothers! We who are become the scorn of all peoples, and worse than all, let us bewail the most monstrous devastation of the Holy Land! This land we have deservedly called holy in which there is not even a foot-step that the body or spirit of the Saviour did not render glorious and blessed; which embraced the holy presence of the mother of God, and the meetings of the apostles, and drank up the blood of the martyrs shed there. How blessed are the stones which crowned you, Stephen, the first martyr! How happy, O, John the Baptist, the waters of the Jordan which served you in baptizing the Saviour! The children of Israel, who were led out of Egypt, and who prefigured you in the crossing of the Red Sea, have taken that land by their arms, with Jesus as leader; they have driven out the Jebusites and other inhabitants and have themselves inhabited earthly Jerusalem, the image of celestial Jerusalem.

What are we saying? Listen and learn! You, girt about with the badge of knighthood, are arrogant with great pride; you rage against your brothers and cut each other in pieces. This is not the (true) soldiery of Christ which rends asunder the sheep-fold of the Redeemer. The Holy Church has reserved a soldiery for herself to help her people, but you debase her wickedly to her hurt. Let us confess the truth, whose heralds we ought to be; truly, you are not holding to the way which leads to life. You, the oppressors of children, plunderers of widows; you, guilty of homicide, of sacrilege, robbers of another's rights; you who await the pay of thieves for the shedding of Christian blood—as vultures smell fetid corpses, so do you sense battles from afar and rush to them eagerly. Verily, this is the worst way, for it is utterly removed from God! If, forsooth, you wish to be mindful of your souls, either lay down the girdle of such knighthood, or advance boldly, as knights of Christ, and rush as quickly as you can to the defence of the Eastern Church. For she it is from whom the joys of your whole salvation have come forth, who poured into your mouths the milk of divine wisdom, who set before you the holy teachings of the Gospels. We say this, brethren, that you may restrain your murderous hands from the destruction of your brothers, and in behalf of your relatives in the faith oppose yourselves to the Gentiles. Under Jesus Christ, our Leader, may you struggle for your Jerusalem, in Christian battle-line, most invincible line, even more successfully than did the sons of Jacob of old—struggle, that you may assail and drive out the Turks, more execrable than the Jebusites, who are in this land, and may you deem it a beautiful thing to die for Christ in that city in which He died for us. But if it befall you to die this side of it, be sure that to have died on the way is of equal value, if Christ shall find you in His army. God pays with the same shilling, whether at the first or eleventh hour. You should shudder, brethren, you should shudder at raising a violent hand against Christians; it is less wicked to brandish your sword against Saracens. It is the only warfare that is righteous, for it is charity to risk your life for your brothers. That you may not be troubled about the concerns of to-morrow, know that those who fear God want nothing, nor those who cherish Him in truth. The possessions of the enemy, too, will be yours, since you will make spoil of their treasures and return victorious to your own; or empurpled with your own blood, you will have gained everlasting glory. For such a Commander you ought to fight, for One who lacks neither might nor wealth with which to reward you. Short is the way, little the labor, which, nevertheless, will repay you with the crown that fadeth not away. Accordingly, we speak with the authority of the prophet: "Gird thy sword upon thy thigh, O mighty one." Gird yourselves, everyone of you, I say, and be valiant sons; for it is better for you to die in battle than to behold the sorrows of your race and of your holy places. Let neither property nor the alluring charms of your wives entice you from going; nor let the trials that are to be borne so deter you that you remain here.

You, brothers and fellow bishops; you, fellow priests and sharers with us in Christ, make this same announcement through the churches committed to you, and with your whole soul vigorously preach the journey to Jerusalem. When they have confessed the disgrace of their sins, do you, secure in Christ, grant them speedy pardon. Moreover, you who are to go shall have us praying for you; we shall have you fighting for God's people. It is our duty to pray, yours to fight against the Amalekites. With Moses, we shall extend unwearied hands in prayer to Heaven, while you go forth and brandish the sword, like dauntless warriors, against Amalek.

Urban II's Call to the Crusade according to Guibert of Nogent

If among the churches scattered about over the whole world some, because of persons or location, deserve reverence above others (for persons, I say, since greater privileges are accorded to apostolic sees; for places, indeed, since the same dignity which is accorded to persons is also shown to regal cities, such as Constantinople), we owe most to that church from which we received the grace of redemption and the source of all Christianity. If what the Lord says—namely, "Salvation is from the Jews"—accords with the truth, and it is true that the Lord has left us Sabaoth as seed, that we may not become like Sodom and Gomorrah, and our seed is Christ, in whom is the salvation and benediction of all peoples, then, indeed, the very land and city in which He dwelt and suffered is, by witness of the Scriptures, holy. If this land is spoken of in the sacred writings of the prophets as the inheritance and the holy temple of God before ever the Lord walked about in it, or was revealed, what sanctity, what reverence has it not acquired since God in His majesty was there clothed in the flesh, nourished, grew up, and in bodily form there walked about, or was carried about; and, to compress in fitting brevity all that might be told in a long series of words, since there the blood of the Son of God, more holy than heaven and earth, was poured forth, and His body, its quivering members dead, rested in the tomb. What veneration do we think it deserves? If, when the Lord had but just been crucified and the city was still held by the Jews, it was called holy by the evangelist when he says, "Many bodies of the saints that had fallen asleep were raised; and coming forth out of the tombs after His resurrection, they entered into the holy city and appeared unto many," and by the prophet Isaiah when he says, "It shall be His glorious sepulchre," then, surely, with this sanctity placed upon it by God the Sanctifier Himself, no evil that may befall it can destroy it, and in the same way glory is indivisibly fixed to His Sepulchre. Most beloved brethren, if you reverence the source of that holiness and glory, if you cherish these shrines which are the marks of His footprints on earth, if you seek (the way), God leading you, God fighting in your behalf, you should strive with your utmost efforts to cleanse the Holy City and the glory of the Sepulchre, now polluted by the concourse of the Gentiles, as much as is in their power.

If in olden times the Maccabees attained to the highest praise of piety because they fought for the ceremonies and the Temple, it is also justly granted you, Christian soldiers, to defend the liberty of your country by armed endeavor. If you, likewise, consider that the abode of the holy apostles and any other saints should be striven for with such effort, why do you refuse to rescue the Cross, the Blood, the Tomb? Why do you refuse to visit them, to spend the price of your lives in rescuing them? You have thus far waged unjust wars, at one time and another; you have brandished mad weapons to your mutual destruction, for no other reason than covetousness and pride, as a result of which you have deserved eternal death and sure damnation. We now hold out to you wars which contain the glorious reward of martyrdom, which will retain that title of praise now and forever.

Let us suppose, for the moment, that Christ was not dead and buried, and had never lived any length of time in Jerusalem. Surely, if all this were lacking, this fact alone ought still to arouse you to go to the aid of the land and city—the fact that "Out of Zion shall go forth the law and the word of Jehovah from Jerusalem!" If all that there is of Christian preaching has flowed from the fountain of Jerusalem, its streams, whithersoever spread out over the whole world, encircle the hearts of the Catholic multitude, that they may consider wisely what they owe such a well-watered fountain. If rivers return to the place whence they have issued only to flow forth again, according to the saying of Solomon, it ought to seem glorious to you to be able to apply a new cleansing to this place, whence it is certain that you received the cleansing of baptism and the witness of your faith.

And you ought, furthermore, to consider with the utmost deliberation, if by your labors, God working through you, it should occur that the Mother of churches should flourish anew to the worship of Christianity, whether, perchance, He may not wish other regions of the East to be restored to the faith against the approaching time of the Antichrist. For it is clear that Antichrist is to do battle not with the Jews, not with the Gentiles; but, according to the etymology of his name, He will attack Christians. And if Antichrist finds there no Christians (just as at present when scarcely any dwell there), no one will be there to oppose him, or whom he may rightly overcome. According to Daniel and Jerome, the interpreter of Daniel, he is to fix his tents on the Mount of Olives; and it is certain, for the apostle teaches it, that he will sit at Jerusalem in the Temple of the Lord, as though he were God. And according to the same prophet, he will first kill three kings of Egypt, Africa, and Ethiopia, without doubt for their Christian faith. This, indeed, could not at all be done unless Christianity was established where now is paganism. If, therefore, you are zealous in the practice of holy battles, in order that, just as you have received the seed of knowledge of God from Jerusalem, you may in the same way restore the borrowed grace, so that through you the Catholic name may be advanced to oppose the perfidy of the Antichrist and the Antichristians—then, who can not conjecture that God, who has exceeded the hope of all, will consume, in the abundance of your courage and through you as the spark, such a thicket of paganism as to include within His law Egypt, Africa, and Ethiopia, which have withdrawn from the communion of our belief? And the man of sin, the son of perdition, will find some to oppose him. Behold, the Gospel cries out, "Jerusalem shall be trodden down by the Gentiles until the times of the Gentiles be fulfilled." "Times of the Gentiles" can be understood in two ways: Either that they have ruled over the Christians at their pleasure, and have gladly frequented the sloughs of all baseness for the satisfaction of their lusts, and in all this have had no obstacle (for they who have everything according to their wish are said to have their time; there is that saying: "My time is not yet come, but your time is always ready," whence the lustful are wont to say "you are having your time"). Or, again, "the times of the Gentiles" are the fulness of time for those Gentiles who shall have entered secretly before Israel shall be saved. These times, most beloved brothers, will now, forsooth, be fulfilled, provided the might of the pagans be repulsed through you, with the co-operation of God. With the end of the world already near, even though the Gentiles fail to be converted to the Lord (since

according to the apostle there must be a withdrawal from the faith), it is first necessary, according to the prophecy, that the Christian sway be renewed in those regions, either through you, or others, whom it shall please God to send before the coming of Antichrist, so that the head of all evil, who is to occupy there the throne of the kingdom, shall find some support of the faith to fight against him.

Consider, therefore, that the Almighty has provided you, perhaps, for this purpose, that through you He may restore Jerusalem from such debasement. Ponder, I beg you, how full of joy and delight our hearts will be when we shall see the Holy City restored with your little help, and the prophet's, nay divine, words fulfilled in our times. Let your memory be moved by what the Lord Himself says to the Church: "I will bring thy seed from the East and gather thee from the West." God has already brought our seed from the East, since in a double way that region of the East has given the first beginnings of the Church to us. But from the West He will also gather it, provided He repairs the wrongs of Jerusalem through those who have begun the witness of the final faith, that is the people of the West. With God's assistance, we think this can be done through you.

If neither the words of the Scriptures arouse you, nor our admonitions penetrate your minds, at least let the great suffering of those who desired to go to the holy places stir you up. Think of those who made the pilgrimage across the sea! Even if they were more wealthy, consider what taxes, what violence they underwent, since they were forced to make payments and tributes almost every mile, to purchase release at every gate of the city, at the entrance of the churches and temples, at every side-journey from place to place: also, if any accusation whatsoever were made against them, they were compelled to purchase their release; but if they refused to pay money, the prefects of the Gentiles, according to their custom, urged them fiercely with blows. What shall we say of those who took up the journey without anything more than trust in their barren poverty, since they seemed to have nothing except their bodies to lose? They not only demanded money of them, which is not an unendurable punishment, but also examined the callouses of their heels, cutting them open and folding the skin back, lest, perchance, they had sewed something there. Their unspeakable cruelty was carried on even to the point of giving them scammony to drink until they vomited, or even burst their bowels, because they thought the wretches had swallowed gold or silver; or, horrible to say, they cut their bowels open with a sword and, spreading out the folds of the intestines, with frightful mutilation disclosed whatever nature held there in secret. Remember, I pray, the thousands who have perished vile deaths, and strive for the holy places from which the beginnings of your faith have come. Before you engage in His battles, believe without question that Christ will be your standard-bearer and inseparable fore-runner.

Glossary

Amalekites	a nomadic tribe who attacked the Hebrews in the desert during the flight from Egypt
blessed Peter	the apostle Peter
"a generation that set not their heart aright, …"	as in Psalms 78:9
Gentiles	in this context, persons neither Christian nor Jewish
God pays with the same shilling,…	an allusion to a parable of Jesus (Matthew 20:1–16)
"God, the nations are come…"	Psalm 79:1–3
Jebusites	Canaanite tribe conquered by King David, who renamed their city Jerusalem
Jerome	the prophet Jeremiah, an exponent of the prophet Daniel
Karl the Great	Charlemagne
Lord Himself says to the Church	through the prophet Isaiah, the source of the following quotation (Isaiah 43:5)
Ludwig	Louis I
Maccabees	the family of Jewish warriors who resisted the authority over their people of the kings of Syria in the second century BCE
"Out of Zion shall go forth…"	Prophecy in Isaiah 2:3
rich man in the gospel	as in a parable of Jesus (Luke 16:19–31)
Sabaoth	in this context, the Lord's armed hosts
…there must be a withdrawal from the faith	Guibert's interpretation of II Thessalonians 2:11–12

CONSTITUTIONS OF CLARENDON

"If the archbishop shall fail to render justice,
[appeals] must come finally to the lord king."

Overview

In January 1164, King Henry II of England held a council at his palace at Clarendon where he presented to his nobles and bishops a document now known as the Constitutions of Clarendon. The Constitutions were part of Henry II's effort to formalize and record unwritten laws that had previously been adhered to through custom and tradition alone. The Constitutions comprise sixteen clauses, or articles, that report and refine the standing laws of the kingdom with regard to judicial issues such as the jurisdiction of courts. Scholars generally agree that the Constitutions should not be seen as aggressive law reform. Henry hoped to clarify the jurisdictions of the church and the state by protecting the laws and customs he viewed to be his birthright as king. During the turmoil of the civil war that led up to Henry's reign, the church asserted its liberties. Henry wished to reclaim his rights and curtail some of the privileges given to the church. Throughout his reign, Henry was responsible for a vast body of legislation and has often been hailed as the founder of English common law.

Henry claimed that he was only formally recording the rights of the king that had previously been held through tradition and custom. However, these Constitutions met with great controversy. The archbishop of Canterbury, Thomas Becket, strongly objected to the Constitutions and refused to sign them, arguing that certain clauses limited the rights and freedoms of the church. Becket's refusal to sign and support the Constitutions resulted in his exile, and he did not return to England until 1170. Shortly after his arrival at Canterbury he was killed by four knights in the service of the king. Becket's martyrdom immortalized him as a true defender of ecclesiastical rights in England. After Becket's death, the finer points of these clauses were negotiated between Henry and Pope Alexander III.

Context

The twelfth century was a tumultuous time in England. Controversies surrounding the succession to the throne threw the country into a long civil war. Henry I died in 1135, leaving one legitimate daughter and heir, Matilda, and several illegitimate children. Matilda was quickly dismissed as Henry I's successor: She was married to Geoffrey of Anjou, a region in France, whose family was regarded as traditional enemies of the Normans, who had ruled England for a hundred years, so England's relationship with the rulers of France was strained. Also, ruling queens were rare at this time. Instead, Stephen, Henry I's nephew and a descendant of William the Conqueror, was chosen to rule. Matilda, though, had a large following of supporters and was able to contest Stephen's ascendance to the throne. The result was a civil war that would eventually see Stephen recognized as the legitimate ruler. Matilda relinquished her claim to the throne on the condition that Stephen would name her son, Henry, as successor. Stephen agreed, and following his death in 1154, Henry II was crowned king at the age of twenty-one.

After the long and turbulent civil war, the coronation of Henry II returned peace to England. Henry spent the first part of his reign establishing his rights as the new king. Henry's reign saw an increase in legal administration, the use of juries, and consistent record keeping. Two of the earliest legal treatises were also written during this period. The treatises are generally referred to by the names of their authors, Rannulf Glanvill and Henry de Bracton, though it remains uncertain which of these jurists wrote or revised what, so the treatises together are generally just called "Glanvill and Bracton." Thomas Becket served as chancellor to Henry II during the early part of his reign. The role of the chancellor was very important during this period, for the chancellor was in charge of numerous domestic and foreign affairs. When the archbishopric of Canterbury was left vacant by the death of Theobald in 1161, Henry supported and encouraged the election of Becket to replace him. Becket and Henry had been friends throughout the 1150s, and it was clear that Henry anticipated that the election of Becket would help to preserve royal interests. Contrary to Henry's expectations, Becket, once consecrated archbishop, defended the rights and liberties of the church.

On January 25, 1164, a council of bishops and nobles convened at Clarendon. The bishops were instructed to

- **August 5**
  Henry I is crowned king of England.

1133
- **March 5**
  Henry II is born.

1135
- **December 1**
  Henry I dies.
- **December 22**
  Stephen becomes king, marking the start of civil war.

1153
- **November 6**
  Stephen signs the Treaty of Winchester, ending the civil war.

1154
- **October 25**
  King Stephen dies.
- **December 19**
  Henry II is crowned king.

1162
- **June**
  Thomas Becket is consecrated archbishop of Canterbury.

1164
- **January**
  The Constitutions of Clarendon are drawn up at the Council of Clarendon.
- **October**
  Becket is placed on trial for refusing to acknowledge the Constitutions of Clarendon.

swear to uphold the customs of the realm. For two days Becket and the bishops refused, until Becket gave his promise to uphold the customs. The distinction between an oath and a promise was important: Although Becket was prepared to make a promise, he refused to put his name to the document in a more formal way. Henry's clerks were instructed to make a written record of the customs that included the names of the archbishops and bishops who had promised to uphold them. When the Constitutions were presented to Becket in written form, he refused to place his seal on the document. Although Becket had agreed to uphold the Constitutions, he refused the responsibilities that would have resulted from a more formal and documented recognition of the realm's customs.

Henry was forced to petition Pope Alexander III in the hope that the pope would entreat Becket to uphold the written version of the customs. Alexander III refused to do so and instead ordered the bishops to revoke their original agreement, though the pope did not challenge various clauses in the document. Becket was also notably silent on the clauses to which he did not object. The clauses that were disputed were those that limited the liberties of the church to a further extent than previous kings had limited them.

On October 8, 1164, Becket was placed on trial and found guilty of failing to obey a royal writ, the Constitutions. He was named a traitor to the Crown and forced into exile in France. Becket did not return to England until 1170, and shortly thereafter he was murdered in the cathedral at Canterbury. Soon after Becket's death, in January 1173, Becket was declared a martyr saint and was venerated throughout Europe, forcing Henry to enact a public penance at Becket's tomb and shrine. Henry II proved himself a strong ruler who was responsible for legislative improvements and successful military campaigns in France and Ireland, but now, as in the twelfth century, he is too often remembered solely for the Becket dispute

About the Author

There is no specific named author of the Constitutions of Clarendon. It is possible to assume, however, that the clauses were the result of the collaboration of Henry and his advisers, namely his baronial council and justiciars. The baronial council was made up of barons, important landowners who held their land directly from the king. Justiciars served as head executors of the judicial system and were often responsible for drawing up royal writs and other legal documents.

Henry II was born in 1133 in France. In 1150 he became the ruler of Normandy and Anjou. He married Eleanor of Aquitaine in 1153, shortly before his coronation as king of England in 1154. His son Richard (called the "Lion-Hearted" for his military prowess) would succeed him in 1189, and another son, John, best known for acceding to the demands of the English nobles in the Magna Carta in 1215, would be crowned after Richard's death in 1199. Henry launched several military campaigns to defend or gain territories in Wales, Scotland, Ireland, and France. Henry's sons caused great problems for him, waging several rebellions against him. He died on July 6, 1189, shortly after admitting defeat to his son, the soon-to-be Richard I.

Explanation and Analysis of the Document

The Constitutions consist of sixteen clauses that were rooted in the traditional customary laws of previous kings of England. Henry II wished to renew the laws and customs of his grandfather, Henry I, that would have been in place before the civil war. The Constitutions are a culmination of this tradition and also the contributions of the shrewd legal thinkers that surrounded Henry throughout his reign. The introduction of the Constitutions tells us that Henry has made the document from "the customs and liberties and dignities of his predecessors." The introduction continues further to explain that the Constitutions were drawn up in front of the barons, bishops, archbishops, and justices. The clergy present are named and then reported to have promised to "keep and observe" these customs. A list of names of those who have witnessed the clergy promise follows. The witness list serves to bind the promise of the clergy. Becket and his bishops revoked this promise shortly after the council at Clarendon.

◆ Clause 1
This clause allowed Henry to hold rights of advowson in order to prevent local disputes over the presentation of churches and also corruption within the system. Advowson was the right of a patron of a particular church or church office to appoint or nominate a candidate to hold a position within the church. A patron of a church would be a person who supported a church financially or by owning the land the church was built on. The right of a patron to appoint someone to be the priest in such a church often led to corruption. Sometimes people would try to buy their way in to a particular church or office. This clause allowed Henry and future kings of England to intervene and pass judgment on any such controversies in the court of the king.

◆ Clause 2
Clause 2 ensured that any church offices in the holding of the king could be given only with the king's approval. The king held the most land of anyone in the kingdom. (*Fee* refers to ownership of land or other real property.) On his many estates there would be churches that the king would sponsor directly. Although the king owned a great deal of land and many estates, he would not personally oversee their day-to-day management. The king would still be the patron of these churches and therefore responsible for appointing the churchmen who would run them.

◆ Clause 3
The third clause was perhaps the most controversial clause in the entire Constitutions. It states that clerics

Time Line	
1164	■ **November 2** Becket leaves for exile in France.
1170	■ **December 29** Becket is murdered in Canterbury Cathedral.
1172	■ **May** Henry reconciles with the church during meetings with Pope Alexander III at Avranches, Normandy.
1189	■ **July 6** Henry II dies.

("clerks") could be tried in the court of the king for what would be deemed secular crimes, though crimes against the church would still be tried in ecclesiastical courts. These distinctions had not always traditionally existed in English law, for in most cases clerics would be tried in ecclesiastical courts no matter what the crime was. The Crown viewed this as an unfair privilege of churchmen. If a priest were to be put on trial for murder in an ecclesiastical court, he could be thrown out of the church. A layman tried for murder in a secular court, however, could be put to death. In secular courts alleged criminals could be sentenced to "trial by ordeal," a physical test or battle to determine guilt. Clerics were previously exempt from this type of judgment, so churchmen would commonly get lighter sentences than people who were tried in secular courts. It is also important to note that the church viewed all crimes, even murder, as violations of its own canon law, that is, the law code that was applicable only to people in the church. Becket's strongest objections were voiced against the last part of the clause, which reads: "And if the clerk shall be convicted, or shall confess, the church ought not to protect him further." This sentence makes it clear that after a criminal is tried in the ecclesiastical courts, the church should not protect the criminal, and the king's court can intervene. This clause had various implications. It could have made a second trial in a secular court a possibility. If a priest was tried for murder, found guilty, and dismissed from the church, the Crown could then also try the priest as a layman because he would no longer be in the service of the

Pewter pilgrim badge of the head of Saint Thomas Becket (© Museum of London)

church. Henry was trying to limit ecclesiastical privileges, but Becket saw this "double punishment" as a step too far.

◆ Clause 4

This clause was meant to ensure that no one would leave Henry's kingdom without first obtaining the king's permission. The implication here is that churchmen would need the permission of the king even to answer the call of the pope. Henry would be able to limit the mobility of the clergy, giving him more control over their actions. The end of the clause demonstrates the Crown's concern over

treachery. The person applying to the king to leave the country had to take an oath to not do any harm to the king or country. There is some overlap between this clause and clause 8, which deals specifically with appeals and appeals to the papal court.

◆ Clause 5

Clause 5 states that oaths and promises made by an excommunicate (that is, a person denied the sacraments, such as Holy Communion, and thus essentially expelled from the church), while under excommunication, would be invalid. The "pledge of permanency" can be taken to mean a formal promise. The excommunicated person had to promise only that he would attend an ecclesiastical tribunal to be absolved of the excommunication. Any other actions that would need the support of an oath or pledge should not be undertaken. Only after persons were absolved of their sins would they be reinstated into the community. Throughout the 1160s excommunication was a major issue between Becket and Henry. Becket issued a series of excommunications from his exile in France, attempting to excommunicate several important clerics and supporters of Henry. Many of Becket's advisers, including Pope Alexander III, urged Becket to be more temperate and less ready to pronounce excommunication. Most of these excommunications would be overturned by the pope in efforts to procure peace between Henry and Becket.

◆ Clause 6

This clause relates to the process of accusation and trial in the case of criminal offences. The chief aim was to formalize legal procedures for trials and to create a judicial hierarchy. Accusations had to be made only by "reliable and legal accusers and witnesses." If no such people came forward to make the accusation, the sheriff would then be responsible for gathering twelve men to judge the matter. This clause makes formal mention of the use of juries for the purpose of indictment. The above-mentioned trial by ordeal was still in practice when juries became more formalized, but by the early thirteenth century juries would replace trial by ordeal.

◆ Clause 7

Clause 7, like clause 5, examines issues of excommunication. It states that people who hold lands from the king could not be placed under excommunication without first following a specific process. (*Demesne* refers to the portion of an estate set aside for the owner's personal use; *servitors* were those who performed official duties for the landowner.) The king must first be allowed to accuse and punish the person according to his courts. Only then might the individual be sent to the ecclesiastical courts to face the charges made by the church. For example, a dispute concerning the appointment of a candidate for a benefice occurred between Becket and the lord within whose lands the benefice lay. (A benefice is a particular post or church office given to a member of the clergy by a patron.) Becket presented a candidate whom the lord in turn expelled. Becket retaliated by excommunicating the lord. When Henry appealed to Becket to absolve the lord, Becket refused and stated that it was not within Henry's rights to intervene. According to the Constitutions, this should not have been allowed to take place. This clause clearly states that the king must be consulted about an interdict (an ecclesiastical censure) or excommunication when his land and the people who managed those lands were involved. An interdict could also be placed on lands. If an interdict were to be placed on lands, churches would be closed. All churches and church services would be suspended (except for the sacraments of baptism and extreme unction—the act of anointing and praying for a seriously ill person) until the interdict was lifted. Excommunication could be overturned only by a bishop or the pope, once the process of reconciliation with the church had ended.

◆ Clause 8

Becket also strongly objected to clause 8, which was intended to limit and also possibly censure the papal appeals process. Instead of bringing an appeal directly to the pope, the Constitutions stipulate that any appeal must first be reviewed by the king and only with his recommendation would it be referred to the judgment of the papacy. This clause, like clause 3, included more specific limitations than were customary in the reign of Henry's grandfather. Appeals to the pope were a common form of litigation, as the pope was the highest power anyone could appeal to in Europe. Money could be made in civil cases, and the Crown would have preferred to keep those revenues. The years after Becket's murder would see an increase in appeals made to the pope. This clause was viewed as a further assertion of royal rights over the English church, but it was unsuccessful in practice.

◆ Clause 9

Disputes between laymen and clerics about property would be resolved under clause 9. A jury would be responsible for determining whether property belonged to the church or to the laity. If the jury found that the property belonged to the church, the case would be heard in an ecclesiastical court. Conversely, if the property was found to belong to a member of the laity, the case would be heard in the king's court. *Fee* is a term often associated with the feudal system and designates land that is held by a lord in exchange for services, and *seisin* refers simply to feudal ownership of land. This clause helps determine jurisdiction, through the use of the chief justice of the king and the jury, for property disputes on church and lay property holdings.

◆ Clause 10

Clause 10 states that the church is allowed to place an interdict on an individual. If the church issued a summons to a person to answer for crimes punishable by excommunication and the person did not answer the summons, the arm of the secular law could intervene. The chief servitor, one in the service of the king, would first be given the chance to bring the individual before church officials before excommunication could be pronounced. If the king's servitor failed in this duty, he had to answer to the king, and the bishop would be allowed to impose ecclesiastical justice. This clause also allowed royal involvement in ecclesiastical justice.

◆ Clause 11

Bishops and greater churchmen of the time were sometimes barons of the king because of their lands and fealty to the Crown. This meant they would have held lands or estates directly from the king. They would owe the king loy-

Oak panel depicting King Stephen (© Museum of London)

alty, not only as their king but also as their feudal overlord. Barons would also be a part of the king's council. This clause was not disputed, because it appears to have been a standing custom of the realm. The clause concerns only land and possessions held by barons of the king and was therefore unchallenged by the church.

◆ **Clause 12**

Church property was included as part of the king's demense, the king's lands. Therefore, when a bishopric, abbey, or priory was vacant, the king was allowed to claim revenues from these properties until the seat was filled. Kings, though, could leave seats vacant for years and collect the revenues. The clergy objected to this abuse, which was a traditional right of the king. The clause also outlines the procedure for important church elections. The election was to take place in the king's chapel and only with the king's permission and agreement. The king had traditionally been involved in important elections. For example, Henry put forward Thomas Becket as his choice for archbishop, and his choice was confirmed by the pope. Throughout the Middle Ages kings and the

pope were in conflict about the king's appointments and those of the papacy.

◆ **Clause 13**

This clause helped ensure that both the king and the church would work to preserve the rights of each other. If the right of the king to administer justice was breached, the church would intervene on the king's behalf; the king would have the same obligation to the church. This clause was meant to protect the rights of both the king and the church.

◆ **Clause 14**

Clause 14 states that the church had no rights in the detention of chattels (personal property) that were under forfeiture, for the chattels were the property of the king. This clause did not attempt to limit or restrict the rights of the church. Because it was a traditional custom of the realm, it was another undisputed clause of the Constitutions.

◆ **Clause 15**

Debts, no matter their nature, were within the jurisdiction of the king, making them the responsibility of the king's

"*This memorandum or inquest was made of some part of the customs and liberties, and dignities of his predecessors, viz., of King Henry his grandfather and others, which ought to be observed and kept in the Kingdom.*"

(Introduction)

"*And these customs recognised by the archbishops and bishops and counts and barons and by the nobler ones and elders of the kingdom ... did grant; and upon the Word of Truth did orally firmly promise to keep and observe, under the lord King and under his heirs, in good faith and without evil wile.*"

(Introduction)

"*And if the clerk shall be convicted or shall confess, the church ought not to protect him further.*"

(Clause 3)

"*Concerning appeals, if they shall arise, from the archdean they shall proceed to the bishop, from the bishop to the archbishop. And if the archbishop shall fail to render justice, they must come finally to the lord king, in order that by his command the controversy may be terminated in the court of the archbishop, so that it shall not proceed further without the consent of the lord king.*"

(Clause 8)

men. According to clause 15, the king was the ultimate debt referee; all cases and litigation regarding debts would take place in the king's court. Becket objected to this clause. Controversy over this practice could have been the result, in part, of revenues to be gained from debt collection.

◆ **Clause 16**

The final clause states that the lord of the land could grant or deny permission to the son of a villein (a peasant who provides services in exchange for the use of land) who wished to be ordained as a priest. The permission had to be granted in order for the ordination into the priesthood to take place. This clause confirmed an aspect of control landowners would retain over persons tied to the land-tenure system. Peasants would have been tied to the land and therefore would need permission from the lord to leave

their duties. This clause records the long-standing custom-ary practice for a villein to seek his lord's permission to leave the land.

◆ **Closing Statement**

The ending sentences of the Constitutions allowed for further customs that are not recorded in the Constitutions: "There are, moreover, many other and great customs and dignities of the holy mother church, and of the lord king, and of the barons of the kingdom, which are not contained in this writ." This closing section makes it clear that the promise of the clergy was meant to cover the unrecorded customs as well. The clergy would be unable to object to these unmentioned customs. However, the disputes over the written customs demonstrate the power that written laws held over the laws that remained unwritten customs.

Audience

Barons, nobles, clerics, bishops, and archbishops were the initial intended audience of the Constitutions. These were the people whom Henry ordered to adhere to and swear to uphold the customs of his realm. Henry knew that by having these men of his kingdom attach their names to the document, the customs therein would be supported and upheld throughout his reign and future reigns. This is why the Constitutions needed approval from all of the bishops, barons, and witnesses at the Council of Clarendon.

Impact

The immediate impact of the Constitutions of Clarendon was that it led to a major conflict between Henry II and Thomas Becket. Becket's refusal to append his seal to the Constitutions and his later revocation of his promise to uphold them resulted in his trial in Northampton and his subsequent exile. The ongoing conflict between Becket and Henry led to Becket's murder, which increased papal power in England. Becket was proclaimed a saint who championed church rights and liberties. He became one of the most popular saints in Europe during the Middle Ages.

In 1172 Henry was ready to make peace with the church and met with Pope Alexander III in Avranches, Normandy. The pope ordered Henry to retract clause 8 of the Constitutions and allow open appeals with Rome once more. Further negotiations in 1176 led to the revocation of parts of clause 3. Henry agreed that clerks accused of crimes should be handed over to the bishop and not to the secular court.

Furthermore, clerks were not to be sentenced to a "trial by battle." By the thirteenth century, however, juries would proclaim a judgment before the member of the clergy was handed over to the bishop's jurisdiction. Henry would retain control over the appointment of bishops, as stipulated in clause 12. Although Becket's murder allowed a greater extent of papal involvement in English affairs, the power of the church should not be overestimated. Henry conceded relatively little compared with Becket's original demands.

The Assize of Clarendon, drafted in 1166, continued the process begun with the Constitutions. The Assize was a series of articles that focused on criminal behavior and the judicial system. Unlike the earlier Constitutions, the Assize met with very little controversy. Henry also outlined more thorough legislation dealing with criminal prosecutions. He introduced and refined existing laws pertaining to hereditary rights (the Assize of Northampton, 1176) and other property disputes (the Assize of Novel Disseisin, ca. 1188).

Despite the initial failure of the Constitutions, it is clear that they are part of the beginnings of law reform in England. Henry looked back to the customs of his grandfather's realm and tried to formalize them. Formerly, these customs were not necessarily the jurisdiction of the king. Instead, the laws were established according to local custom. The laws of Henry I contained distinctions between the areas of Wessex, Mercia, and the Danelaw (the area of northeastern England that was ruled primarily by Danish law as a result of earlier Viking invasions), whereas Henry II applied his legislation to the whole of England. Henry also attempted to apply common law to the clergy. Henry was keen to increase the bureaucracy to make the government stronger and more

Questions for Further Study

1. Based on the entry and the document, describe the relationship between church and state in England during the twelfth century. To what extent did politics play a role in this relationship?

2. To what extent did the Constitutions of Clarendon help shape the development of more modern legal concepts? Why is the document important in the history of law?

3. The Constitutions of Clarendon were Henry II's attempt to formalize legal customs and traditions. Why do you think Henry felt the need to "get it in writing" at this particular time? What factors might have influenced his desire to formalize these laws?

4. A thread that runs through the Constitutions of Clarendon has to do with land: who owns it, who holds rights in connection with it, what the nature of that ownership was. Why do you think land and land ownership were so important in England in the twelfth century? Why was land a source of power and influence?

5. To which clauses of the Constitutions did Thomas Becket object? Why did he object to these particular clauses? Why did his objections become a source of conflict with Henry II, ultimately leading to Becket's assassination?

centralized. It is undeniable that Henry's reign witnessed an avid interest in collecting, preserving, and reforming the laws of the kingdom. The desire to create more clearly defined boundaries between church and state jurisdictions was one of the lasting effects of the Constitutions. Some modern legal scholars have even seen Becket's objections to clause 3 as a precursor to the modern idea of "double jeopardy"—the right not to be tried twice for the same crime.

Further Reading

■ Articles

Maitland, F. W. "Henry II and the Criminous Clerks." *English Historical Review* 7, no. 26 (1892): 224–234.

■ Books

Bartlett, Robert. *England under the Norman and Angevin Kings, 1075–1225.* Oxford, U.K.: Clarendon Press, 2000.

Brand, Paul. "Henry II and the Creation of English Common Law." In *Henry II: New Interpretations*, ed. Christopher Harper-Bill and Nicholas Vincent. Woodbridge, U.K.: Boydell Press, 2007.

Clanchy, M. T. *England and Its Rulers, 1066–1307.* Malden, Mass.: Blackwell, 2006.

Duggan, Anne. *Thomas Becket.* London: Arnold Publishing, 2004.

Hudson, John. *The Formation of the English Common Law: Law and Society in England from the Norman Conquest to Magna Carta.* London: Longman, 1996.

Mortimer, Richard. *Angevin England, 1154–1258.* Oxford, U.K.: Blackwell, 1996.

Poole, A. L. *From Domesday Book to Magna Carta 1087–1216.* Oxford, U.K.: Clarendon Press, 1970.

Warren, W. L. *Henry II.* London: Eyre Methuen, 1973.

—Lauren Moreau

CONSTITUTIONS OF CLARENDON

In the year 1164 from the Incarnation of our Lord, in the fourth year of the papacy of Alexander, in the tenth year of the most illustrious king of the English, Henry II, in the presence of that same king, this memorandum or inquest was made of some part of the customs and liberties and dignities of his predecessors, viz., of king Henry his grandfather and others, which ought to be observed and kept in the kingdom. And on account of the dissensions and discords which had arisen between the clergy and the Justices of the lord king, and the barons of the kingdom concerning the customs and dignities, this inquest was made in the presence of the archbishops and bishops, and clergy and counts, and barons and chiefs of the kingdom. And these customs, recognized by the archbishops and bishops and counts and barons and by the nobler ones and elders of the kingdom, Thomas archbishop of Canterbury, and Roger archbishop of York, and Gilbert bishop of London, and Henry bishop of Winchester, and Nigel bishop of Ely, and William bishop of Norwich, and Robert bishop of Lincoln, and Hilary bishop of Chichester, and Jocelin bishop of Salisbury, and Richard bishop of Chester, and Bartholemew bishop of Exeter, and Robert bishop of Hereford, and David bishop of Mans, and Roger elect of Worcester, did grant; and, upon the Word of Truth did orally firmly promise to keep and observe, under the lord king and under his heirs, in good faith and without evil wile,—in the presence of the following: Robert count of Leicester, Reginald count of Cornwall, Conan count of Bretagne, John count of Eu, Roger count of Clare, count Geoffrey of Mandeville, Hugo count of Chester, William count of Arundel, count Patrick, William count of Ferrara, Richard de Luce, Reginald de St. Walelio, Roger Bigot, Reginald de Warren, Richer de Aquila, William de Braiose, Richard de Camville, Nigel de Mowbray, Simon de Bello Campo, Humphrey de Bohen Matthew de Hereford, Walter de Medway, Manassa Biseth—steward, William Malet, William de Curcy, Robert de Dunstanville, Jocelin de Balliol, William de Lanvale, William de Caisnet, Geoffrey de Vere, William de Hastings, Hugo de Moreville, Alan de Neville, Simon son of Peter William Malduit—chamberlain, John Malduit, John Marshall, Peter de Mare, and many other chiefs and nobles of the kingdom, clergy as well as laity.

A certain part, moreover, of the customs and dignities of the kingdom which were examined into, is contained in the present writing. Of which part these are the paragraphs;

1. If a controversy concerning advowson and presentation of churches arise between laymen, or between laymen and clerks, or between clerks, it shall be treated of and terminated in the court of the lord king.

2. Churches of the fee of the lord king cannot, unto all time, be given without his assent and concession.

3. Clerks charged and accused of anything, being summoned by the Justice of the king, shall come into his court, about to respond there for what it seems to the king's court that he should respond there; and in the ecclesiastical court for what it seems he should respond there; so that the Justice of the king shall send to the court of the holy church to see in what manner the affair will there be carried on. And if the clerk shall be convicted, or shall confess, the church ought not to protect him further.

4. It is not lawful for archbishops, bishops, and persons of the kingdom to go out of the kingdom without the permission of the lord king. And if it please the king and they go out, they shall give assurance that neither in going, nor in making a stay, nor in returning, will they seek the hurt or harm of king or kingdom.

5. The excommunicated shall not give a pledge as a permanency, nor take an oath, but only a pledge and surety of presenting themselves before the tribunal of the church, that they may be absolved.

6. Laymen ought not to be accused unless through reliable and legal accusers and witnesses in the presence of the bishop, in such wise that the archdean do not lose his right, nor any thing which he ought to have from it. And if those who are inculpated are such that no one wishes or dares to accuse them, the sheriff, being requested by the bishop, shall cause twelve lawful men of the neighbourhood or town to swear in the presence of the bishop that they will make manifest the truth in this matter, according to their conscience.

7. No one who holds of the king in chief, and no one of his demesne servitors, shall be excommunicat-

ed, nor shall the lands of any one of them be placed under an interdict, unless first the lord king, if he be in the land, or his Justice, if he be without the kingdom, be asked to do justice concerning him: and in such way that what shall pertain to the king's court shall there be terminated; and with regard to that which concerns the ecclesiastical court, he shall be sent thither in order that it may there be treated of.

8. Concerning appeals, if they shall arise, from the archdean they shall proceed to the bishop, from the bishop to the archbishop. And if the archbishop shall fail to render justice, they must come finally to the lord king, in order that by his command the controversy may be terminated in the court of the archbishop, so that it shall not proceed further without the consent of the lord king.

9. If a quarrel arise between a clerk and a layman or between a layman and a clerk concerning any tenement which the clerk wishes to attach to the church property but the layman to a lay fee: by the inquest of twelve lawful men, through the judgment of the chief Justice of the king, it shall be determined, in the presence of the Justice himself, whether the tenement belongs to the church property, or to the lay fee. And if it be recognized as belonging to the church property, the case shall be pleaded in the ecclesiastical court; but if to the lay fee, unless both are holders from the same bishop or baron, the case shall be pleaded in the king's court. But if both vouch to warranty for that fee before the same bishop or baron, the case shall be pleaded in his court; in such way that, on account of the inquest made, he who was first in possession shall not lose his seisin, until, through the pleading, the case shall have been proven.

10. Whoever shall belong to the city or castle or fortress or demesne manor of the lord king, if he be summoned by the archdean or bishop for any offense for which he ought to respond to them, and he be unwilling to answer their summonses, it is perfectly right to place him under the interdict; but he ought not to be excommunicated until the chief servitor of the lord king of that town shall be asked to compel him by law to answer the summonses. And if the servitor of the king be negligent in this matter, he himself shall be at the mercy of the lord king, and the bishop may thenceforth visit the man who was accused with ecclesiastical justice.

11. Archbishops, bishops, and all persons of the kingdom who hold of the king in chief have their possessions of the lord king as a barony, and answer for them to the Justices and servitors of the king, and follow and perform all the customs and duties as regards the king; and, like other barons, they ought to be present with the barons at the judgments of the court of the lord king, until it comes to a judgment to loss of life or limb.

12. When an archbishopric is vacant, or a bishopric, or an abbey, or a priory of the demesne of the

---

Glossary

advowson	the right of a patron of a particular church or church office to appoint or nominate a candidate to hold a position within the church
chattels	personal property
clerks	clerics
demesne	the portion of an estate set aside for the owner's personal use
fee	land that is held by a lord in exchange for services
inculpated	blamed
interdict	an ecclesiastical censure or prohibitory decree
pledge as a permanency	formal promise
seisin	feudal ownership of land
servitors	people who perform official duties for a landowner
wile	trick or stratagem

---

king, it ought to be in his hand; and he ought to receive all the revenues and incomes from it, as demesne ones. And, when it comes to providing for the church, the lord king should summon the more important persons of the church, and, in the lord king's own chapel, the election ought to take place with the assent of the lord king and with the counsel of the persons of the kingdom whom he had called for this purpose. And there, before he is consecrated, the person elected shall do homage and fealty to the lord king as to his liege lord, for his life and his members and his earthly honours, saving his order.

13. If any of the nobles of the kingdom shall have dispossessed an archbishop or bishop or archdean, the lord king should compel them personally or through their families to do justice. And if by chance any one shall have dispossessed the lord king of his right, the archbishops and bishops and archdeans ought to compel him to render satisfaction to the lord king.

14. A church or cemetery shall not, contrary to the king's justice, detain the chattels of those who are under penalty of forfeiture to the king, for they (the chattels) are the king's, whether they are found within the churches or without them.

15. Pleas concerning debts which are due through the giving of a bond, or without the giving of a bond, shall be in the jurisdiction of the king.

16. The sons of rustics may not be ordained without the consent of the lord on whose land they are known to have been born.

Moreover, a record of the aforesaid royal customs and dignities has been made by the foresaid archbishops and bishops, and counts and barons, and nobles and elders of the kingdom, at Clarendon on the fourth day before the Purification of the blessed Mary the perpetual Virgin; the lord Henry being there present with his father the lord king. There are, moreover, many other and great customs and dignities of the holy mother church, and of the lord king, and of the barons of the kingdom, which are not contained in this writ. And may they be preserved to the holy church, and to the lord king, and to his heirs, and to the barons of the kingdom, and may they be inviolably observed forever.

"I want you to send your son ... with me to my country, where he can observe the knights and acquire reason and chivalry."

Overview

Usama ibn Munqidh, a Muslim warrior during the early crusader era, was also a poet and a writer. At age ninety he dictated his memoirs in an entertaining and informative narrative called *Kitab al-itibar*, or *The Book of Contemplation*. Because his life spanned much of the early Crusades, Usama was an eyewitness to many of the events. Sections of the memoir include his observations of the European crusaders, and some of them are presented here as a selection titled "A Muslim View of the Crusaders," in which Usama relates both positive and negative views of the crusaders.

Were it not for a single manuscript found in El Escorial, Spain, all of this insight into daily Islamic life during the first two Crusades (1096–1099 and 1145–1149) would have been lost. While several other Islamic sources were written during the Crusades, they focus on Islamic leaders and are generally from the period following Usama's death. There are comparatively more European sources from the early Crusades, most notably the *Gesta Francorum* (The Deeds of the Franks) and Matthew of Edessa's *Chronicle*.

Context

The onset of Islam in the early seventh century decimated the Sassanian Empire in Iran and Iraq, and it greatly reduced the power of the Byzantine Empire. Within the region, the Byzantine Empire was known as "Rum" because it was a continuation of the Roman Empire. In the Middle East up until the time of the Crusades, populations of many religions and sects largely coexisted. By the late eleventh century the Byzantine Empire, based in the city of Constantinople, was faced with the encroaching threat of the Turks from the east. In 1071 the Byzantines were defeated at the Battle of Manzikert (Malazgirt), thereby allowing the Turks to establish a stronghold within Anatolia. In 1095 the Byzantine Empire sought military assistance from the papacy to battle the Turks, marking the start of Pope Urban II's plan to liberate Jerusalem from the Muslims. Jerusalem is a city of three religions, and each holds it in high regard. For Jews it

holds the site (Temple Mount) where God is said to have gathered the dust to create Adam, the first human being, and where two Jewish temples were consecutively built in ancient times—both long ago destroyed. For Christians, Jerusalem is where the Passion of Jesus took place and thus is the holiest site in Christianity. For Muslims, Jerusalem is the place from which Muhammad ascended to heaven (from Temple Mount) on a night journey with the angel Gabriel.

In a tour of France in 1095, Pope Urban II expanded upon the Byzantine call for assistance and preached the need for Christians to go to the Holy Land to liberate it from the Muslims. That same year the Council of Clermont proclaimed the Crusade. The members of the First Crusade were mostly nonwarriors who had answered Urban's call, and there was little coordination and cohesion among the crusaders. En route to the Holy Lands, they pillaged Constantinople and Byzantine lands, creating much tension between the Orthodox Christian and Catholic populations. However, a group of crusaders reached the city of Jerusalem and captured it in 1099. At this point some of the European nobility who had come on the Crusade settled and established crusader states throughout the Holy Land. Although the crusaders came from all around Europe, they were collectively called the Franks; they did not refer to themselves as crusaders, and in fact this term was not used until centuries after the Crusades occurred. Modern historians have numbered the Crusades, but the campaign spanned two hundred years, during which tensions rose, great battles were fought, and cities were conquered and reconquered. Simultaneously, trade relations between ethnic groups thrived, Europeans were reintroduced to Greco-Roman philosophy, and interreligious friendships and marriages took place. The period involved changes and growing influence on both sides. When Usama wrote his memoirs, the Islamic Middle East, under the leadership of Saladin, was in the early stages of retaking lands from the crusaders. As a witness to the events of the previous century, Usama must have recognized the significance of what was happening.

About the Author

Usama ibn Munqidh was born on July 4, 1095, in his family's Shayzar castle, which was located about fifteen

1095

- **July 4**
Usama ibn Munqidh is born in Shayzar, Syria.

- **November**
Pope Urban II begins preaching in France to gather support for a mission to liberate Jerusalem from the Muslims.

1099

- Jerusalem is captured by the crusaders.

1131

- Usama leaves Shayzar and joins Zangi's service.

1137

- Usama returns to Shayzar to defend the castle against a joint Byzantine-crusader siege. Afterward he is banished by his uncle and moves to Damascus.

1144

- After a political upheaval, Usama is forced out of Syria and relocates to Cairo.

1154

- Having been associated with a plot against the caliph, Usama flees to Damascus, where he is welcomed by Nureddin.

1164

- Usama enters retirement by joining the court of Qara Arslan in Hisn Kayfa. His attention shifts to literature and composition.

miles west of Hamah, Syria. This castle was an ancient city, known in Latin as Caesarea ad Orontem, and was home to about one hundred residents. Although he is sometimes referred to as the ruler of Shayzar, Usama had no actual claim to the title because his father had refused the position, which then passed to Usama's uncle Sultan. Because Sultan initially had no heir, he took Usama under his tutelage, educating his nephew in literature, religion, and warfare. Shayzar was located on the front line of Byzantium and the arriving crusaders, so Usama had many battles in which to develop his military abilities. Such remote outposts were the primary line of defense for the general Arab population, as neither the Abbasids (750–1258) nor the Seljuks (1037–1194) focused on fighting the crusaders, instead being occupied by internal politics and territorial expansion, respectively.

Tensions arose as Usama was displaced by Sultan's sons, and in 1131 Usama decided to leave Shayzar to join Zangi, the Turkic *atabeg* (regent) in Mosul. Usama enjoyed several years of service with Zangi's troops, but he abandoned his position in 1137, when his hometown came under attack by the Byzantine emperor John Comnenus and a group of crusaders. Along with his brothers, Usama helped his uncle Sultan defend the castle, but appreciation was not forthcoming. Possibly threatened by the military ability shown by Usama, Sultan banished his nephews from Shayzar. Unable to return to Zangi's service, Usama moved to Damascus and entered into service at the Burid court. Between 1140 and 1143 Usama and Muin al-Din, a Burid vizier, made several trips to Jerusalem and other crusader states to foster relations in the event that a combined Burid-crusader force would be needed to halt Zangi's expansion.

It was during this period that Usama made many of the observations and witnessed the anecdotes of the Franks that he relates in his memoir. By 1144 Usama had become loosely involved with internal politics, making his life in Damascus difficult, so he relocated to Cairo, Egypt. He enjoyed several years of service within the Fatimid court and, in 1150, was even an envoy to Nureddin, the son of Zangi and sultan of Syria and Egypt, but once again he became embroiled in political upheavals. Usama was associated with a conspiracy against the caliph al-Zafir and could no longer remain in Egypt. While Usama was in Egypt, Damascus had changed greatly. Nureddin had conquered the city, and he welcomed Usama to his court in 1154; for the next decade Usama served Nureddin. In 1164 he moved to Hisn Kayfa, where he served Qara Arslan, an associate of Nureddin. While residing in Hisn Kayfa, Usama turned his attention to literature. One of Usama's sons, Murhaf, became a close ally of Saladin, the rising power in the Middle East. In 1174 Saladin invited Usama to Damascus to join the court. There he spent the remainder of his life, enjoying a position of respect, and he had the time to continue his pursuits in literature.

Usama was much respected by fellow Muslims, both for his literary skills and for his noble nature as a warrior. Contemporary texts indicate that he was much better known for his writings than for his political career. His other compositions include literary anthologies, *Kitab al-asa* (Book of the Staff), *Kitab al-badia* (Book of Figures of Speech), *Kitab al-manazil wa al-diyar* (Book of Dwellings and Places), *and* Lubab al-adab (*Anthology of Literature*).

Explanation and Analysis of the Document

The Book of Contemplation is very loosely structured, based more on concepts than on chronology or location. The narrative writing is prose, giving it the feeling of an old man's ramblings, which it likely was. Throughout the memoir, Usama switches between curses and praises of the Franks, sometimes in the same stories. This might indicate that he felt obliged to demonstrate his enmity toward the Franks, when in actuality he may not have felt such strong animosity toward them. In some instances, Usama seems to attempt to relate a lesson or a moral, using the Franks as the negative subject of an exaggerated tale. The excerpts presented here provide some of Usama's views of the Franks who were in the Middle East. These selections include stories about some of the Franks with whom Usama had direct interaction. Most of the stories in which the Franks are presented in a positive manner were taken from events to which Usama was a direct witness. Conversely, most of the stories that belittle the Franks were secondhand.

◆ "Usama's Family Delivered. The Franks Seize His Property."

In this section Usama is in the service of Nureddin (called "Nur al-Din" in the excerpt), the son and heir of Zangi, who rules Mosul, Iraq, on behalf of the Abbasid leader. Having left his family in Egypt when he went to Syria to work for Nureddin, Usama seeks Nureddin's assistance in relocating his family. Although Usama mentions only his household and his sons, his household would have included the women of his family, his sons, male and female servants, and all of their personal belongings. Islamic decorum prevented direct discussion of female relatives. Ibn Ruzzik, the governor of southern Egypt with whom Usama corresponds, fears for the family's safety at the hands of the Franks and encourages Usama to return to Egypt, offering him the rulership of the frontier city of Aswan instead. Nurredin questions why Usama would consider returning to Egypt and "all her troubles." (Usama had tried to intervene on behalf of a fellow Syrian imprisoned in Egypt after a coup attempt and may have feared retribution.) Nureddin offers to send a message to the king of the Franks, Baldwin III of Jerusalem, requesting the safety of Usama's family. Baldwin sends back a document sealed with a cross, identifying the document as having come from him and granting safe passage for the family. It is unclear from the text whether the Frankish ship leaving Damietta, on the Egyptian coast, was provided solely for the transportation of Usama's family, but based on the account provided by Usama, it seems possible that it was and that there was a plan to sink it in order to acquire their possessions. According to Usama, Baldwin III justi-

Time Line

1174	■ Usama joins his son at Saladin's court.
CA. 1185	■ Usama composes his memoirs, which include "A Muslim View of the Crusaders."
1187	■ Saladin reconquers Jerusalem.
1188	■ **November 16** Usama dies in Damascus.

fied the event by arguing that such was the norm among the Muslims.

Indeed, this story may not be entirely true but perhaps was a means for Usama to vilify the Frankish king. It is clear throughout the story and especially by his cursing Baldwin that Usama did not hold the current Frankish king in high regard, despite the fact that there had been a close personal relationship between Usama's family and Baldwin's father, Fulk of Jerusalem. At the time of the shipwreck near Acre, a city on the Israeli coast, Usama was in eastern Anatolia with Nureddin, campaigning against the Seljuks. Usama concludes the story by reaffirming his faith in God and Fate, thankful for the safety of his family, but several decades later still lamenting the loss of his library. This first selection is notable because it is a clear portrayal of the negative traits of the Franks, in particular their lack of honesty and their untrustworthiness.

◆ "The 'Wonders' of the Frankish Race"

Earlier in the memoir, Usama tells the reader about specific events that occurred during the Crusades. At this point, however, he changes his focus to describing the crusaders, their traits, and, in his view, their lack of morality. The title, "The 'Wonders' of the Frankish Race," seems to imply a positive view of the Franks. Possibly a comparable and more accurate term for Usama's point of view would be *mysteries*; throughout the text Usama relates the negative aspects as well as the positive. He refers to the Franks as "mere beasts" because he feels that, like animals, they are good at fighting but lack morality. Throughout the text Usama occasionally dehumanizes the Franks by making such remarks because they are enemies, and dehumanizing enemies makes it easier to fight them. However, it is clear from other selections of the memoir that Usama held some

The angel Gabriel, who accompanied Muhammad on his night journey to heaven, as depicted in the medieval manuscript The Wonders of Creation and the Oddities of Existence (© The Trustees of the British Museum)

Franks in esteem, even if he did not always agree with them or understand their actions.

◆ "The Franks' Lack of Intelligence: An Invitation to Visit Europe"

This short story is about one of King Fulk's European knights who became a close friend of Usama, and it demonstrates the friendly relations that occasionally existed between Arabs and Franks. The story also reveals that even the soldiers who settled in the Holy Land and interacted with the Muslims failed to learn about their culture. When the knight prepares to return to Europe, he offers to take Usama's son along in order to provide the boy with "reason and chivalry." The knight assumes that Europe has a superior and broader education to offer Usama's son, while in fact at the time, Islamic philosophy and scientific knowledge surpassed that in Europe; it was Arab translations of Greco-Roman intellectual pursuits that reintroduced the knowledge to Europe. The request is an insult to Usama, albeit an unintentional one, because Usama has a gentle-

manly education, and many of his actions related throughout his memoir exemplify Islamic and Christian ideals. Just as Christian knights had a code of chivalry, so too did Muslim warriors. Usama responds to the suggestion in a polite manner by agreeing to the basis of the proposal but then explaining that it is not possible to accept because the boy's grandmother is waiting for their return. By offering the excuse of his mother, Usama avoids the situation, and the knight agrees that a mother should not be disobeyed.

◆ "The Marvels of Frankish Medicine"

In this story, the ruler of al-Munaytira, a town in Lebanon, requests of Usama's uncle the use of a physician. Usama's uncle employs a Christian physician named Thabit, further demonstrating that there were many levels of intersocietal relations. Thabit diagnoses a woman as having "dryness of humours," indicating that the Arab-Christian doctor practiced ancient Greek and Roman medicine based upon a balance of the four humors: blood, phlegm (mucus), black bile, and yellow bile. According to the medical practice, an imbalance in one of four humors resulted in illness. A dryness of humors would have referred to an imbalance of either yellow or black bile. The Arab doctor prescribes a special diet to balance the woman's humors, and it is successful until she resumes her normal diet. The Frankish doctor, failing to connect the resumption of previous eating habits to the illness, discredits Doctor Thabit and adopts a new treatment plan that results in the woman's death. The story also tells of a knight with a leg abscess, or open wound, who likely would have recovered following Thabit's remedy; however, the Frankish doctor intervenes and crudely amputates the leg, causing the knight's death. What particularly surprises Usama is the Frankish doctor's reliance on herbs and the lack of diagnostic measures as well as the absence of hygienic medical practices that were then common in the Middle East.

In opposition, Usama offers an example of sound Frankish medical practices. King Fulk's treasurer, Bernard, is injured by a horse. Presumably Bernard or someone who worked for him has applied ointments to the wound, but the Frankish doctor advises the patient to use vinegar as a disinfectant to clean the wound. This remedy heals the wound, despite Usama's hope that Bernard would die from the injury. A second example of effective Frankish medical practice also reveals positive personal traits among Franks. Abu al-Fath's son has festering sores on his neck. A Frankish man sees the boy and offers the father a remedy, on the condition that he not profit from the knowledge. This stipulation suggests that the Frank was a monk or a priest, as clerics were often called upon to treat ailments but would not accept money for helping someone in need. The remedy of glasswort (an herb), oil, and vinegar proves effective, and Usama himself treats people with this bit of Frankish medicine.

◆ "Newly Arrived Franks Are the Roughest"

As does the story about Frankish medicine, this tale presents both positive and negative views of the Franks.

Crusader castle fortification in Al Karak (in modern-day Jordan) (Library of Congress)

Usama refers to the Knights Templars as his friends; they obviously respect him and clear out Christians from the mosque so that he can pray. They also intervene on his behalf when a newly arrived Frank interrupts his prayers. The Frank, who tells Usama to face east during his prayers, is uninformed. The medieval European tradition held that during prayer, Christians should face east, toward the Holy Land. Although Muslims initially prayed facing toward Jerusalem, they soon began praying toward Mecca. Mecca is south of Jerusalem, so Usama would have been facing south. Jerusalem is the third-holiest site of the Islamic faith, and as such a mosque of great importance is located there—on Temple Mount. Al-Aqsa Mosque (the Farthest) is so named because during the prophet Muhammad's life it was the mosque located the farthest distance from Mecca, which is the holiest site in Islam. To commemorate Muhammad's night journey to heaven, a shrine, the Dome of the Rock, was also built in the same location.

◆ "When God Was Young"

This event, in which a Frank offers to show the Arab leader Muin al-Din and Usama a picture of "God when He was young," is insulting to Usama because according to Islamic theology, the Christian's implication that God and Jesus are the same being offends both God and Jesus. While Muslims revere Jesus and count him as one of the primary prophets, they do not believe that it is possible for Jesus, or anyone else, to be an embodiment of God.

◆ "Franks Have No Honour or Propriety"

Among Arabs the protection and preservation of personal and familial honor was of immense concern, and the examples of impropriety that Usama provides here would have been of great offense to an extended family as well as to the persons involved. Because there is a close connection between honor and courage, two highly valued traits among Arabs, Usama expresses amazement that the Franks can have one but not the other. In the first example, Frankish women and men freely socialize in public, which would not have taken place among the Muslims. The second story, which Usama claims to have witnessed, tells of a man in Nablus, Palestine, who returns home and finds his wife and another man in bed. The cuckolded husband tells the other man that should such an event occur again, they would "have an argument." It seems implausible that the first two stories are true; they are more like exaggerated rumors meant to shock the reader by illustrating the lack of morals among the Franks.

> "There was a respected Frankish knight who had come from their country just to go on pilgrimage and then return home.... He said to me: 'My brother, I am leaving for my country. I want you to send your son ... with me to my country, where he can observe the knights and acquire reason and chivalry. When he returns, he will be like a truly rational man.'"

("The Franks' Lack of Intelligence")

> "For the woman, I prescribed a special diet and increased the wetness of her humours. Then a Frankish physician came to them and said, 'This fellow don't know how to treat them.' ... So he took a razor and made a cut in her head in the shape of a cross. He then peeled back the skin so that the skull was exposed and rubbed it with salt. The woman died instantaneously."

("The Marvels of Frankish Medicine")

> "One day, I went into the little mosque, recited the opening formula 'God is great!' and stood up in prayer. At this, one of the Franks rushed at me and grabbed me and turned my face towards the east, saying, 'Pray like this!' ... So the Templars came in again, grabbed him and threw him out."

("Newly Arrived Franks Are the Roughest")

> "We came to the home of one of the old knights who came out in one of the first expeditions of the Franks.... He presented a very fine table, with food that was extremely clean and delicious. But seeing me holding back from eating, he said, 'Eat and be of good cheer!' For I don't eat Frankish food: I have Egyptian cooking-women and never eat anything except what they cook."

("Franks That Are Acclimatized Are Better")

The second story, in which a bathhouse keeper from Ma'arra, Syria, tells of what he witnessed of Franks in the bathhouse, expresses both Usama's surprise at and curiosity toward the crusaders. The story comes secondhand from one Salim, the bathhouse keeper, who tells Usama about a crusader who wanted to have his pubic hair shaved. Afterward, the crusader decided that he would like to have his wife similarly shaved, so he has an attendant fetch her, and Salim shaves her. In the Arab world it was unacceptable for a man to touch a woman who was not related to him, and it is shocking to hear of a man touching the most private body part of a woman, even if her husband was standing beside her.

In the final story, a woman accompanies her father to a bathhouse so that he can wash her hair. Despite the dishonor of allowing a daughter into a male bathhouse, Usama is touched by his affection for the motherless girl and the father's duty toward her. In the Middle Ages it would have been exceptionally rare for a widowed father to care for his daughter himself instead of relying on relatives or charitable institutions. Usama's companion lifts the woman's skirt to determine her gender, an unusual act, as the man supposedly lifts the skirt of a stranger. A skirt alone would not have indicated gender because men and women wore a similar one-piece, floor-length robe or gown. Usama presents the father's concern for his daughter as an example of the occasional high regard in which he held Franks.

◆ "Another Example of Their Medicine"

Told by the ruler of Tiberias, this story involves a sick knight, who is suffering. A priest is summoned to treat the man. Instead of treating the patient, the priest plugs his nose with wax, causing the man to suffocate; the priest justifies his action by stating, "'He was in great pain.'" It is unclear from the text whether Usama is taken aback by the death of the knight at the hands of a priest. However, because this story follows a tale of compassion, about the widower and his daughter in the bathhouse, it is more likely that Usama supported the action but may have been surprised by it.

◆ "Two Old Women Race"

In Tiberias, Usama witnesses the Franks abusing two old women by having them race each other to win the prize of a roasted pig. Despite its comical elements, this story has an important implied significance. Within Arab society there was great respect for elders, especially in terms of honor and preserving honor. Usama is quite shocked by the manner in which the two old women are treated because had such an incident occurred among the Arabs, the family members of the old women would have been viewed scornfully by others.

◆ "Examples of Frankish Jurisprudence"

Usama is obviously unimpressed with what he sees as the Frankish judicial system and how it resorts to barbaric duels and superstitious trials. What he does not account for is the fact that the crusader states were a less structured system than what existed at that time in Europe. The two examples that Usama relates may have been more the exception than the norm. When two men—a blacksmith and an old man—duel, Usama views the event as a misuse of power by the *vicomte* as well as disrespect of the elderly. In the story of a blind man who asks Muin al-Din for assistance, Usama explains that the man was blinded by the Franks as punishment for robbing and killing Christian pilgrims. While Usama expresses horror at the punishment given, a Muslim court would have imposed a similar sentence for robbery and murder. In the blinded man's story, it is not clear if his request to become a horseman instead of a religious scholar is meant in jest or as an example of overcoming adversity.

◆ "Franks That Are Acclimatized Are Better"

These stories are related to Usama by someone who serves him. The servant goes with Usama's friend Tadrus ibn al-Saffi to the home of an old Frankish knight. Seeing that Usama's servant is hesitant to eat for fear of violating Islamic dietary laws, the knight says that he uses only an Egyptian cook and does not allow pork, a restricted food for Muslims, in his home. Later, when the servant is walking in the street, in a case of mistaken identity, he is accused of having killed a knight, but the old knight comes to his rescue by telling the crowd that the servant is not a warrior and had not been part of the battle in question.

Audience

As implied by the title *The Book of Contemplation*, the reader is meant to absorb moral and religious wisdom and to apply it to life, much in the way that Usama learned by the examples of his father and his uncle. Readers can assume that Usama projected the image he desired, and therefore he was perhaps not overly concerned with proof and accuracy. Because of the multitude of favorable references to Saladin, it is possible that Usama dedicated the memoir to the ruler. However, because the first few dozen pages of the manuscript are missing, the intended recipient can only be guessed. Furthermore, the fact that there is but one remaining copy of the manuscript suggests that the memoir was not widely circulated.

Impact

Usama's memoir is unique in that it is the finest source available to describe the Islamic point of view during the early Crusades. While several sources from European crusaders, an Armenian monk, and other Christians are extant, Usama offers both positive and negative opinions of the Franks. It does not appear that his memoir had much of an impact on Arabic literature or on premodern historians. There is no evidence that his memoirs influenced any other texts or that the contents were even mentioned by another author until the twentieth century.

Further Reading

■ Articles

Cahen, Claude. "An Introduction to the First Crusade." *Past and Present* 6 (November 1954): 6–30.

Smail, R. C. "Latin Syria and the West, 1149–1187." *Transactions of the Royal Historical Society*, fifth series, 19 (1969): 1–20.

■ Books

Cobb, Paul. *Usama ibn Munqidh: Warrior-Poet of the Age of Crusades*. Oxford, U.K.: Oneworld, 2005.

Gabrieli, Francesco. *Arab Historians of the Crusades*. London: Routledge and Kegan Paul, 1969.

Goss, Vladimir P., and Christine V. Bornstein, eds. *The Meeting of Two Worlds: Cultural Exchange between East and West during the Period of the Crusades*. Kalamazoo: Western Michigan University, 1986.

Hillenbrand, Carole. *The Crusades: Islamic Perspectives*. Edinburgh: Edinburgh University Press, 1999.

Maalouf, Amin. *The Crusades through Arab Eyes*. New York: Schocken Books, 1985.

■ **Web Sites**

Laiou, Angeliki E., and Roy P. Mottahedeh, eds. "The Crusades from the Perspective of Byzantium and the Muslim World." Dumbarton Oaks Research Library Web site.

   http://www.doaks.org/publications/doaks_online_publications /CRcnts.html.

Winder, Viola H. "Memories of a Muslim Prince." Saudi Aramco World Web site.

   http://www.saudiaramcoworld.com/issue/197003/memories.of. a.muslim.prince.htm.

—Tia Wheeler

Questions for Further Study

1. What historical circumstances gave rise to the Crusades?

2. If you had to base an assessment of the relationship between the Franks and the Muslim Arabs entirely on Usama ibn Munqidh's "Muslim View of the Crusaders," how would you characterize that relationship?

3. Clearly, the period of the Crusades was a time of cultural clash between Christian Western Europe and Muslim Arab Palestine. In what ways does Usama's text illustrate that cultural clash? To what extent do you think the terms of that clash continue to exist in the twenty-first century?

3. Compare this document with Marco Polo's Description of Hangzhou. Both deal with the cross-cultural observations of their writers. In what ways are they similar? How do they differ?

4. According to Usama, in what different ways did the Franks and the Arabs regard women and their position in society?

5. Examine Usama's text in the context of Urban II's Call to Crusade. How do you think Usama would have reacted if he had been listening to Pope Urban's sermon urging European Christians to "liberate" Palestine?

USAMA IBN MUNQIDH'S "A MUSLIM VIEW OF THE CRUSADERS"

Usama's Family Delivered. The Franks Seize His Property

I then entered the service of Nur al-Din (may God have mercy upon him). He corresponded with Ibn Ruzzik about transporting my household and sons who had been left behind in Egypt, and who, I might add, had been treated very well. But Ibn Ruzzik sent the messenger back and begged off, claiming that he feared for their safety because of the Franks. He wrote to me, saying, "Come back to Egypt: you know what our relationship is like. If you are expecting any ill-will from the palace staff, then you can go to Mecca where I will send you a document granting you the city of Aswan, and I will send you all the reinforcements you need to combat the Abyssinians (for Aswan is one of the frontier-fortresses of the Muslims). Then I will let your household and sons come to join you."

So I consulted with Nur al-Din, seeking his advice on the matter. He said, "You are not seriously considering, having just left behind Egypt and all her troubles, going back there! Life is too short for that! I'll send a messenger to the king of the Franks to obtain safe-passage for your household, and I'll also send someone along to conduct them here." And so he (may God have mercy upon him) sent a messenger and obtained the safe-passage from the king, with his cross right on it, good for both land- and sea-travel.

So I sent along the safe-passage with a servant of mine, as well as a letter from Nur al-Din and my own letter for Ibn Ruzzik. Ibn Ruzzik then sent my family on to Damietta in one of his own personal launches, along with all the provisions and cash they would need, and his own letter of protection. From Damietta, they sailed in a Frankish ship. As they approached Acre, where the king was (may God *not* have mercy upon him), the king sent out a group of men in a small boat to sink the ship with axes, as my own companions looked on. The king rode out on his horse, stopped at the shore and took as pillage everything that was in the ship.

A servant of mine swam across to him, holding the safe-passage document, and said to him, "My lord king, is this not your document of safe-passage?"

"Indeed it is," he said. "But this is the procedure among the Muslims: if one of their ships is wrecked off one of their towns, then the inhabitants of that town get to pillage it."

My servant then asked, "So you are going to take us prisoner?" "No," the king replied, and he had my family (may God curse him) brought to a building, where he had the women searched and took everything they had with them. In the ship there had been jewellery that had been entrusted to the women, along with cloth and gems, swords and other weapons, and gold and silver amounting to something like thirty thousand dinars. The Franks took it all and then sent my household five hundred dinars, saying, "You can get to your country on this," even though the party totalled some fifty men and women.

As for me, I was at that very moment with Nur al-Din in the land of the king Mas'ud, in the region of Ra'ban and Kaysun. The news that my children and my brother's children and our women were safe made it easier to take the news about all the wealth that was lost. Except for my books: they totalled four thousand bound volumes of the most precious tomes. Their loss was for me a heartache that lasted all my life....

The "Wonders" of the Frankish Race

Glory be to the Creator, the Maker! Indeed, when a person relates matters concerning the Franks, he *should* give glory to God and sanctify him! For he will see them to be mere beasts possessing no other virtues but courage and fighting, just as beasts have only the virtues of strength and the ability to carry loads. I shall now relate something of their ways and the wonders of their intelligence.

The Franks' Lack of Intelligence: An Invitation to Visit Europe

In the army of King Fulk, son of Fulk, there was a respected Frankish knight who had come from their country just to go on pilgrimage and then return home. He grew to like my company and he became my constant companion, calling me "my brother." Between us there were ties of amity and sociability. When he resolved to take to the sea back to his country, he said to me:

"My brother, I am leaving for my country. I want you to send your son (my son, who was with me, was fourteen years old) with me to my country, where he can observe the knights and acquire reason and chivalry. When he returns, he will be like a truly rational man."

And so there fell upon my ears words that would never come from a truly rational head! For even if my son were taken captive, his captivity would not be as long as any voyage he might take to the land of the Franks.

So I said, "By your life, I was hoping for this very thing. But the only thing that has prevented me from doing so is the fact that his grandmother adores him and almost did not allow him to come here with me until she had exacted an oath from me that I would return him to her."

"Your mother," he asked, "she is still alive?"

"Yes," I replied.

"Then do not disobey her," he said.

The Marvels of Frankish Medicine

Here is an example of the marvellous nature of their medicine. The lord of al-Munaytira wrote to my uncle to request that he send him a physician to treat some of his companions who were ill. So my uncle sent him a native Christian physician called Thabit. He was barely gone ten days when he returned to Shayzar. So we said to him, "My, you healed your patients so quickly!" He explained:

They brought before me a knight in whose leg an abscess had formed and a woman who was stricken with a dryness of humours. So I made a small poultice for the knight and the abscess opened up and he was healed. For the woman, I prescribed a special diet and increased the wetness of her humours. Then a Frankish physician came to them and said, "This fellow don't know how to treat them." He then said to the knight, "Which would you like better: living with one leg or dying with both?" "Living with one leg," replied the knight. The physician then said, "Bring me a strong knight and a sharp axe." A knight appeared with an axe—indeed, I was just there—and the physician laid the leg of the patient on a block of wood and said to the knight with the axe, "Strike his leg with the axe and cut

it off with one blow." So he struck him—I'm telling you I watched him do it—with one blow, but it didn't chop the leg all the way off. So he struck him a second time, but the marrow flowed out of the leg and he died instantly.

He then examined the woman and said, "This woman, there is a demon inside her head that has possessed her. Shave off her hair." So they shaved her head. The woman then returned to eating their usual diet—garlic and mustard. As a result, her dryness of humours increased. So the physician said, "That demon has entered further into her head." So he took a razor and made a cut in her head in the shape of a cross. He then peeled back the skin so that the skull was exposed and rubbed it with salt. The woman died instantaneously. So I asked them, "Do you need anything else from me?" "No," they said. And so I left, having learned about their medicine things I had never known before.

Now, I have observed in their medicine a case exactly the opposite of this. Their king named as treasurer one of their knights, called Bernard (may God curse him), one of the most accursed and filthy Franks around. A horse kicked him in his leg and his lower leg started to fester and open up in fourteen different places. Every time these wounds would close in one place, another would open somewhere else. I prayed that he would just perish. But then a Frankish physician came and removed all the ointments that were on him and had him washed with strong vinegar. The wounds closed up and he was well and up again, like the very devil.

Here is another wondrous example of their medicine. We had at Shayzar an artisan called Abu al-Fath, who had a son on whose neck scrofula sores had formed. Every time one would close in one place, another would open up in another place. Once Abu al-Fath went to Antioch on an errand and his son accompanied him. A Frankish man noticed him and asked him about the boy. "He is my son," Abu al-Fath said.

The Frank said to him, "Do you swear to me by your religion that, if I prescribe for you some medicine that will cure your boy, you will not charge money from anyone else whom you yourself treat with it?"

Our man swore to that effect. The Frank then said, "Take him some uncrushed leaves of glasswort, burn them, then soak the ashes in olive oil and strong vinegar. Treat him, with this until it eats up the pustules in the affected area. Then take some fire-softened lead and soak it in butter. Then treat the boy with this and he will get well."

So our man treated the boy as he was told and the boy got well. The wounds closed up and he returned to his previous state of health. I have myself treated people afflicted by this ailment with this remedy, and it was beneficial and removed all of their complaints.

Newly Arrived Franks Are the Roughest

Anyone who is recently arrived from the Frankish lands is rougher in character than those who have become acclimated and have frequented the company of Muslims. Here is an instance of their rough character (may God abominate them!):

Whenever I went to visit the holy sites in Jerusalem, I would go in and make my way up to the al-Aqsa Mosque, beside which stood a small mosque that the Franks had converted into a church. When I went into the al-Aqsa Mosque—where the Templars, who are my friends, were—they would clear out that little mosque so that I could pray in it. One day, I went into the little mosque, recited the opening formula "God is great!" and stood up in prayer. At this, one of the Franks rushed at me and grabbed me and turned my face towards the east, saying, "Pray like *this*!"

A group of Templars hurried towards him, took hold of the Frank and took him away from me. I then returned to my prayers. The Frank, that very same one, took advantage of their inattention and returned, rushing upon me and turning my face to the east, saying, "Pray like *this*!"

So the Templars came in again, grabbed him and threw him out. They apologized to me, saying, "This man is a stranger, just arrived from the Frankish lands sometime in the past few days. He has never before seen anyone who did not pray towards the east."

"I think I've prayed quite enough," I said and left. I used to marvel at that devil, the change of his expression, the way he trembled and what he must have made of seeing someone praying towards Mecca.

When God Was Young

I saw one of the Franks come up to the amir Mu'in al-Din (may God have mercy upon him) while he was in the Dome of the Rock, and say, "Would you like to see God when He was young?"

"Why yes," Mu'in al-Din replied.

So this Frank walked in front of us until he brought us to an icon of Mary and the Messiah (Peace be upon him) when he was a child, sitting in her lap, "This is God when He was young," he said.

May God be exalted far beyond what the infidels say!

Franks Have No Honour or Propriety

The Franks possess nothing in the way of regard for honour or propriety. One of them might be walking along with his wife and run into another man. This other man might then take his wife to one side and chat with her, while the husband just stands there waiting for her to finish her conversation. And if she takes too long, he'll just leave her alone with her conversation partner and walk away! Here is an example that I myself witnessed. Whenever I went to Nablus, I used to stay at the home of a man called Mu'izz, whose home was the lodging-house for Muslims. The house had windows that opened onto the road and, across from it on the other side of the road, there was a house belonging to a Frankish man who sold wine for the merchants. He would take some wine in a bottle and go around advertising it, saying, "So-and-So the merchant has just opened a cask of this wine. Whoever wishes to buy some can find it at such-and-such a place." And the fee he charged for making that announcement was the wine in the bottle. So one day, he came back home and discovered a man in bed with his wife. The Frank said to the man, "What business brings you here to my wife?"

"I got tired," the man replied, "so I came in to rest."

"But how did you get into my bed?" asked the Frank.

"I found a bed that was all made up, so I went to sleep in it," he replied.

"While my wife was sleeping there with you?" the Frank pursued.

"Well, it's her bed," the man offered. "Who am I to keep her out of it?"

"By the truth of my religion," the Frank said, "if you do this again, we'll have an argument, you and I!"

And that was all the disapproval he would muster and the extent of his sense of propriety!

Here is another example. We had with us a bath-keeper called Salim, who was originally an inhabitant of Ma'arra, and who served in the bath-house of my father (may God have mercy upon him). He told me:

I once opened a bath-house in Ma'arra to earn my living. Once, one of their knights came in.

Now, they don't take to people wearing a towel about their waist in the bath, so this knight stretched out his hand, pulled off my towel from my waist and threw it down. He looked at me—I had recently shaved my pubic hair—and said, "Salim!" Then he moved in closer to me. He then stretched his hand over my groin, saying, "Salim! Good! By the truth of my religion, do that to me too!"

He then lay down on his back: he had it thick as a beard down in that place! So I shaved him and he passed his hand over it and, finding it smooth to the touch, said, "Salim, by the truth of your religion, do it to Madame!"—*madame* in their language means "the lady," meaning his wife. He then told one of his attendants, "Tell Madame to come here."

The attendant went and brought her and showed her in. She lay down on her back and the knight said, "Do her like you did me!" So I shaved her hair there as her husband stood watching me. He then thanked me and paid me my due for the service.

Now, consider this great contradiction! They have no sense of propriety or honour, yet they have immense courage. Yet what is courage but a product of honour and disdain for ill repute?

Here is an example close to that one. I once went to the baths in the city of Tyre and took a seat in a secluded room there. While I was there, one of my attendants in the bath said to me, "There are women here with us!" When I went outside, I sat down on the benches and, sure enough, the woman who was in the bath had come out and was standing with her father directly across from me, having put her garments on again. But I couldn't be sure if she was a woman. So I said to one of my companions, "By God, go have a look at this one—is she a woman?" What I meant was for him to go and ask about her. But instead he went—as I watched—and lifted her hem and pulled it up. At this, her father turned to me and explained, "This is my daughter. Her mother died, and so she has no one who will wash her hair. I brought her into the bath with me so that I might wash her hair."

"That's a kind thing you're doing," I assured him. "This will bring you heavenly reward."

Another Example of Their Medicine

Another example of their wondrous medicine was related to us by William de Bures, lord of Tiberias

and a man with some standing among the Franks. It happened that he travelled with the amir Mu'in al-Din (may God have mercy upon him) from Acre to Tiberias, and I accompanied him. On the way, he related to us the following story:

In our land there was a highly esteemed knight who took ill and was on the point of death. We went to one of our notable priests and asked him, "Will you come with us and have a look at Sir So-and-So?" "Yes," he replied and walked back with us. We were certain now that if only he would lay his hands upon him, he would recover. When the priest saw the knight he said, "Bring me some wax." So we brought him a bit of wax, which he softened and shaped like a knuckle-bone. Then he inserted one in each nostril and the knight died. "He's dead!" we remarked. "Yes," the priest replied. "He was in great pain, so I closed up his nose so that he could die and find relief."

Two Old Women Race

Let this go and bring the conversation back to Harim. And let us stop discussing their medical practices and move on to something else.

I was present in Tiberias during one of their feast-days. The knights had gone out to practise fighting with spears, and two decrepit old women went out with them. They positioned the two women at one end of the practice-field and at the other end they left a pig, which they had roasted and laid on a rock. They then made the two old women race one another, each one accompanied by a detachment of horsemen who cheered her on. At every step, the old women would fall down but then get up again as the audience laughed, until one of them overtook the other and took away the pig as her prize.

Examples of Frankish Jurisprudence

I was an eyewitness one day in Nablus when two men came forward to fight a duel. The reason behind it was that some Muslim bandits took one of the villages of Nablus by surprise, and one of the peasants there was accused of complicity. They said, "He guided the bandits to the village!" So he fled.

But the king sent men to arrest the peasant's sons, so the man came back before the king and said,

"Grant me justice. I challenge to a duel the man who said that I guided the bandits to the village."

The king said to the lord of the village, its fief-holder, "Bring before me the man whom he has challenged."

So the lord went off to his village, where a blacksmith lived, and took him, telling him, "You will fight in a duel." This was the fief-holder's way of making sure that none of his peasants would be killed and his farming ruined as a result.

I saw that blacksmith. He was a strong young man, but lacking resolve: he would walk a bit, then sit down and order something to drink. Whereas the other man, who had demanded the duel, was an old man but strong-willed: he would shout taunts as if he had no fears about the duel. Then the *vicomte* came—he is the governor of the town—and gave each one of the duellists a staff and a shield and arranged the people around them in a circle.

The two men met. The old man would press the blacksmith back until he pushed him away as far as the circle of people, then he would return to the centre. They continued exchanging blows until the two of them stood there looking like pillars spattered with blood. The whole affair was going on too long and the *vicomte* began to urge them to hurry, saying, "Be quick about it!"

The blacksmith benefited from the fact that he was used to swinging a hammer, but the old man was worn out. The blacksmith hit him and he collapsed, his staff falling underneath his back. The blacksmith then crouched on top of him and tried to stick his fingers in the old man's eyes, but couldn't do it because of all the blood. So he stood up and beat the man's head in with his staff until he had killed him. In a flash, they tied a rope round the old man's neck, dragged him off and strung him up. The blacksmith's lord now came and bestowed his own mantle upon him, let him mount behind him, on his horse and rode away with him.

And that was but a taste of their jurisprudence and their legal procedure, may God curse them!

On one occasion, I went with the amir Mu'in al-Din (may God have mercy upon him) to Jerusalem, and we stopped at Nablus. While there, a blind man—a young man wearing fine clothes, a Muslim—came out to the amir with some fruit and asked him for permission to be admitted into his service in Damascus. The amir did so. I asked about him and I was told that his mother had been married to a Frank, whom she had killed. Her son used to attempt various ruses on their pilgrims, and he and his moth-er used to work together to kill them. They finally brought charges against him for that and made him subject to the legal procedure of the Franks, to wit:

They set up a huge cask and filled it with water and stretched a plank of wood across it. Then they bound the arms of the accused, tied a rope around his shoulders and threw him into the cask. If he were innocent, then he would sink in the water and they would then pull him up by that rope so he wouldn't die in the water; if he were guilty, then he would not sink in the water. That man tried eagerly to sink into the water when they threw him in, but he couldn't do it. So he had to submit to their judgment—may God curse them—and they did some work on his eyes.

The man later arrived in Damascus, so the amir Mu'in al-Din (may God have mercy upon him) assigned him a stipend to meet all his needs and said to one of his attendants, "Take him to Burhan al-Din ibn al-Balkhi (may God have mercy upon him) and tell him to order someone to teach the Qur'an and some jurisprudence to this man."

At this the blind man said, "Victory and mastery be yours! This wasn't what I was thinking!"

"Then what were you thinking I would do?" asked the amir.

"That you would give me a horse, a mule and weapons, and make a horseman out of me!" the man answered.

The amir then said, "I never thought that a blind man would join the ranks of our cavalry."

Franks That Are Acclimatized Are Better

Among the Franks there are some who have become acclimatized and frequent the company of Muslims. They are much better than those recently arrived from their lands, but they are the exception and should not be considered representative.

Here is an example. I sent one of my men to Antioch on an errand. At the time, Chief Tadrus ibn al-Saffi was there, and his word had great influence in Antioch; there was a mutual bond of friendship between us. One day he said to my man, "A Frankish friend of mine has invited me to his home. You should come along so you can observe their ways." My man told me:

> I went along with him and we came to the home of one of the old knights who came out in one of the first expeditions of the Franks. He was since removed from the stipend-registry and dismissed

from service, but he had some property in Antioch off which he lived. He presented a very fine table, with food that was extremely clean and delicious. But seeing me holding back from eating, he said, "Eat and be of good cheer! For I don't eat Frankish food: I have Egyptian cooking-women and never eat anything except what they cook. And pork never enters my house." So I ate, though guardedly, and we left.

After passing through the market, a Frankish woman suddenly hung onto me while babbling at me in their language—I didn't understand what she was saying. Then a group of Franks began to gather around me and I was certain that I was going to perish. But suddenly, who should turn up but that knight, who saw me and approached. He came and said to that woman, "What's the matter with you and this Muslim?"

"This man killed my brother 'Urs." This 'Urs was a knight in Apamea whom someone from the army of Hama had killed.

The knight shouted at her and said, "This man is a *bourgeois* (i.e., a merchant), who neither fights nor attends battle." And he yelled at the assembled crowd and they dispersed. He then took me by the hand and went away. Thus, the effect of that meal was my deliverance from death.

amir	title of a ruler or chief in an Islamic country
dinars	small coins in gold or silver, introduced during the Caliphate period of Islam
Haram	forbidden to Muslims
King Fulk	the French count who became king of Jerusalem in 1129
Templars	the Knights Templars, members of a military religious order that arose during the Crusades and became very powerful in the Middle East

Portrait of Chinggis Khan (AP/Wide World Photos)

GREAT YASA OF CHINGGIS KHAN

"He ordered that all religions were to be respected and that no preference was to be shown to any of them."

Overview

The Great Yasa was the law code promulgated by Chinggis Khan (also known as "Genghis Khan" and spelled "Jenghiz Khan" in the document), who lived from 1162 to 1227 and was the founder of the Mongol Empire. At its height, the Mongol Empire was the largest contiguous kingdom in history, stretching from the Sea of Japan to the Carpathian Mountains in central and eastern Europe. Thus, the Mongols ruled an empire of extremely diverse cultures, religions, and ethnicities. To study the Mongols, one must use sources written in Mongolian, Chinese, Russian, Persian, Arabic, Japanese, Korean, Latin, Old French, Armenian, Turkic, Georgian, and Syriac. Fortunately, many of the primary sources have been translated, making it easier for English-speaking scholars and students of history to understand the Mongol Empire. Nonetheless, the Yasa remains one of the least understood aspects of the Mongol Empire.

Although the Mongols left many local rulers in place as they conquered various lands, they also paid great attention to the organization and running of the empire. Although government at the local level often remained unchanged, a Mongol-based and -managed government existed at the upper levels. For this they needed a law code. Chinggis Khan created a law system based on the customs of the steppe nomads of Mongolia, but he modified it and banned customs that threatened the stability of his unification of the Eurasian steppes. Many of the laws were suitable only for nomads. Unlike Hammurabi, the Babylonian ruler who is often credited with devising the first codified law (in the seventh century BCE), Chinggis Khan did not have his laws carved onto stelae (inscribed stones erected throughout the empire) but rather kept them on scrolls that were viewed only by the Mongol nobility. Local laws remained in place as long as they did not run contrary to the desires of the Mongols. In many aspects, the Mongols ruled, but their subjects did not know what the law of the land was.

In addition to the Yasa, another source of governance came from Chinggis Khan himself. These were his own maxims or sayings, known in Mongolian as *biligs* or *bileks*.

The maxims were not laws but were used to guide proper behavior and conduct. A person who did not follow or who strayed from them was often viewed in a negative light, while someone who adhered to them was considered a paragon of virtue. In many aspects the *biligs* are analogous to the hadiths in Islam. Islamic law is based primarily on two components. The first is the Qur'an, the holy book of Islam. The second are hadiths, which were the sayings and deeds of the Prophet Muhammad. Like Muhammad, Chinggis Khan served as a model of proper conduct, and people were encouraged to follow his example.

Context

The document reproduced is not the Yasa of Chinggis Khan, for there are no known surviving copies of it. Numerous primary sources call the Yasa a law code even if they do not make specific reference to a particular law. One of the major problems in studying the history of the Mongol Empire is that very few Mongolian sources survive. As the empire declined, the capitals of the four Mongol states into which the empires split after 1260 were often sacked and plundered. Also, climatic conditions often made it difficult for many documents to remain intact. In any case, the contents of the Mongolian imperial archives do not exist except in fragments.

Many historians who left chronicles of the Mongol Empire did not use sources from the imperial archives. Rather, they spoke with Mongolian princes and administrators to corroborate information. Although it is often said that history is written by the victors, for the Mongol Empire it was written by the conquered and by their enemies. The Mongolians did not have a writing system until around 1204, when Chinggis Khan ordered one to be adopted and adapted to the Mongolian language. He also directed that all of his sons and grandsons learn to read and write, even though he himself remained illiterate. Thus writing and the maintenance of documents was a relatively new concept from the onset of the empire. To ensure that it became an integral part of the court and the government, he appointed his adopted brother, Shigi-Qutuqtu, as the chief judge, with instructions to record the laws of the

CA. 1162

- Temüjin, who will become Chinggis Khan, is born.

1202

- First mention is made of the Yasa in Mongolian sources.

1206

- Temüjin is officially made the ruler of Mongolia and given the title of Chinggis Khan, meaning "fierce, or resolute, ruler."

- Shiqi-Qutuqtu is made chief judge and begins writing down the decrees of Chinggis Khan.

1210

- Xixia, modern-day Ningxia and Gansu provinces in China, becomes the first conquest of the Mongol Empire.

1227

- Chinggis Khan dies.

1228

- The Yasa of Chinggis Khan is codified.

1229

- The Yasa is promulgated at the coronation of Ögödei Khan, to confirm the validity of his rulership.

empire. Most documents were written in three languages, Mongolian, Persian, and Uighur (a Turkic language).

Nonetheless, most Mongols remained illiterate. In this light, it is not surprising that the Yasa was not promulgated across the empire. It was kept in the *Kok Debter*, or "Blue Book" (blue being a sacred and auspicious color for the Mongols) and locked away. Periodically, the *Kok Debter* was updated. The nomads, however, being a preliterate society, tended to memorize documents and thus had little need for written texts. Furthermore, many of the laws were based on timeless tradition, so the people adhered to them without any effort. The only changes that Chinggis Khan instituted were designed to promote unity among the nomadic tribes, which previously had been fractured and often engaged in seemingly endless cycles of war.

It appears that the Yasa was primarily applied to the nomadic population. Indeed, it remained a valid source of law for the Mongol world long after civil war split the empire into four powerful states in 1260. These four divisions included the empire of the Great Khan in East Asia, the Ilkhanate in the Middle East, the Jochid Khanate (popularly known as the Golden Horde but named after Chinggis Khan's eldest son) in the Eurasian steppes north of the Black and Caspian seas, and the Chaghatayid Khanate (named after Chinggis Khan's second son) in central Asia. In truth, the Mongols had very little concern for the vast majority of their subjects. The empire was viewed as the patrimony of the *altan uruk*, or Golden Family—that is, the family of Chinggis Khan—and a source of wealth for the ruling family. As long as rulers paid taxes, sent tribute and troops when requested, and did not rebel, the Mongols more or less left them to their own devices. If they did not do these things, the Mongols retaliated with the utmost violence. Typically, an area had only one attempt at rebelling, for the Mongols were not opposed to massacring entire populations.

The passages reproduced are not the Yasa as the Mongols knew it but rather the Yasa as viewed and interpreted by outsiders—both sedentary subjects in the empire and also populations beyond the borders of the Mongol Empire. Those authors who wrote from outside the empire needed to understand their enemy, while those who wrote from within the empire wrote to comprehend their masters. Those who wrote from a later period, after the empire had split, tried to understand the nature of empire at its height.

About the Author

The document as we have it is written by several authors: al-Makrizi (called simply "Makrizi" in the document), Mīrkhwānd ("Mirhond"), Ibn Battūtah ("ibn Batuta"), Vardan ("Vartang"), Mahakia, and, of course, Chinggis Khan ("Jenghiz Khan").

Taqi al-din Ahmad al-Makrizi (1364–1442) was a writer from the Mamluk Sultanate in Egypt and Syria. Although the Ilkhanate disappeared well before al-Makrizi was born, the Yasa remained an important topic. In addition to being the enemy of the Ilkhanate, the Mamluk Sultanate had long been an ally and (at least from the Golden Horde's perspective) vassal of the Golden Horde. Thus, an understanding of Mongol law was necessary. In addition, deserters from the Ilkhanate who could not flee to the Golden Horde took refuge in Mamluk territories, where they were received with honor. According to al-Makrizi, Chinggis Khan had the Yasa engraved onto steel tablets, although al-Makrizi drew most of his knowledge of the Yasa from Ata Malik Juvaini, a Persian who served in the Ilkhanate under Hülügü, including a period as governor of Baghdad. Although Juvaini worked for the Mongols, most of what he wrote concerning the Yasa consisted of some decrees and more maxims intended as guides rather than as absolute laws. Al-Makrizi interpreted Juvaini's writings differently.

Muḥammad ibn Kavand-Shāh ibn Mīrkhwānd (1433–1498) did not live under Mongol rule. Born in Bukhara in modern-day Uzbekistan, Mīrkhwānd lived and wrote in Balkh, in present-day Afghanistan. He enjoyed the patronage of various Timurid princes, the descendents of Emir Timur. The Yasa remained important in the Timurid Empire, although the Timurid prince Shah Rukh attempted to banish its use in 1411. Nonetheless, it remained the primary instrument of law among the nomadic soldiery of the Timurids. Mīrkhwānd eventually ended up in the employ of Sultan Ḥusayn Bayqarah (r. 1469–1506), the last ruler of Timurid Persia and eastern Afghanistan. Mīrkhwānd wrote a six-volume history known as the *Rowzat oṣ ṣafāl* (*Garden of Purity*), although there is some discussion about whether he wrote all of it or whether his grandson, Khwāndamīr, completed it.

Ibn Battūtah (1304–1368) traveled through much of the Mongol world, including all four of the khanates, in his many journeys. He spent considerable time in each of the khanates and had contact with high-ranking officials. He was thus in a good position to observe many details, though he wrote very little about Mongol legal proceedings.

Vartang is more properly known as Vardan (d. 1271), an Armenian monk and writer. Vardan wrote his thirteenth historical compilation around 1267, which is approximately when the chronicle ends. Most of the focus is on Armenia from the biblical era to the death of Hülegü in 1265. Vardan lived during the time of the Mongol conquest of Armenia in the 1230s and the subsequent rule of the Mongols. Vardan does not avoid describing the atrocities of the conquests, but he also recognized the security and practical rule of the Mongols.

Mahakia was another Armenian chronicler. We do not know much of his life other than that he wrote his chronicle in the thirteenth and fourteenth centuries.

Chinggis Khan was born in about 1162 in Mongolia, not far from today's capital of Ulaanbaatar. His family belonged to a nomad tribe, and he came to power by uniting various nomad tribes of northeastern Mongolia, beginning with an alliance formed with his father's blood brother Toghrul (also known as Wang Khan). By 1206 he had unified or subdued the Merkits, Naimans, Mongols, Keraits, Tatars, Uighurs, and several other tribes under his rule. When he set out to

Time Line

1267
- Vardan (also known as Vartang) writes his general history, including his comments on the Yasa.

1295
- Ghāzān Khan begins rule of the Ilkhanate in the Middle East and ends the use of the Yasa as a law code, instituting instead sharia, or rule by Islamic law.

1313
- Öz Beg Khan, ruler of the Golden Horde, begins a reign that will last until 1341; under his rule, which recognizes sharia, the nomads of the Russian steppes continue to use the Yasa.

1354
- Ibn Battūtah (sometimes called ibn Batuta) writes about his journeys, including his observations on the Yasa.

1363
- The Yasa is used occasionally in the Mamluk Sultanate of Egypt and Syria.

CA. 1400
- Mahakia comments about the Yasa in what exists only as fragments today.

1411

- During his reign, Shah Rukh abolishes the use of the Yasa in his empire and adopts sharia. His successors, however, still use the Yasa in central Asia.

CA. 1430s

- Al-Makrizi (also known as al-Maqrizi or simply Makrizi) records his comments on the Yasa.

1474

- Mīrkhwānd (also called Mirhond or Mirkhond) comments on the Yasa in his *Rowzat os safā\l* (*Garden of Purity*).

create the Mongol Empire, he realized the need for a rational legal system to maintain order. Beginning in 1202 the Mongolian sources refer to the Yasa, although it was not written down at that time, primarily because the Mongols were a preliterate society. Not until 1204 did Chinggis Khan order his scribes to adapt the Uighur writing system (a form of Syriac) to the Mongolian language. When he was crowned, he also decreed that his adopted brother, Shiqi-Qutuqtu, should be the chief judge of the empire and that he should record the decrees of the empire. In the ensuing years, Chinggis Khan consolidated his authority and pushed the empire westward to what is today Iran, Iraq, and part of Russia, among other lands. He died in 1227 during a military campaign against the Tangut people.

Explanation and Analysis of the Document

Although Chinggis Khan died in 1227, Shiqi-Qutuqtu continued to record his laws and completed his work in 1228. In 1229 the Yasa was officially promulgated at the coronation of Chinggis Khan's third son, Ögödei. While the laws had been recorded in the previous year, promulgating them at the coronation reaffirmed their validity and indicated that all rulers coming after Chinggis Khan had to abide by his Yasa. It is unclear whether Chinggis Khan

intended for the Yasa to be used for non-nomadic populations. In any case, his successors did use it, and the nomadic elite referred to it frequently. However, it was never published and disseminated broadly, and no single copy has been found. Thus, outsiders (non-Mongols) who lived in the empire or neighboring regions were left to deduce what the Yasa was and what it said. Indeed, the document reproduced here is not that of Chinggis Khan but represents instead the observations of non-Mongols, interpretations of the Yasa from the perspective of outsiders in terms not only of geography and culture but also of time.

That no copy of the Yasa exists makes an explanation of the laws difficult. Nonetheless, we can learn much from what others wrote of the Yasa, for these writings provide context for our understanding of how outsiders viewed the Mongols and their society. Indeed, many of the entries are not intended to provide a holistic view of the Mongols but rather what would be of interest to the authors' respective audiences. In all of the excerpts, "he" always refers to Chinggis Khan.

In addition to the royal decrees, Shiqi-Qutuqtu and others wrote down many of the sayings and advice of Chinggis Khan. These *biligs* (or "maxims") were not laws but rather pieces of what he considered commonsensical advice or rules for proper behavior. It remains unclear how many maxims Chinggis Khan actually uttered. Still, after he died, his shadow grew larger until he was venerated not only as an ancestor but also as a demigod who could intercede on behalf of his heirs, at least indirectly. Thus, like any hero, what he said and did and what others claimed he said and did began to blend. Whether or not Chinggis Khan actually spoke these words matters little, for they give insight into what the Mongols as a collective society, particularly the upper levels of society, viewed as important. Indeed, for many outside observers, the line between the Yasa and the maxims was blurred, particularly because much of their information about both came to them indirectly.

◆ "From Makrizi"

Al-Makrizi's fragments tend to focus on issues that would be of interest to his patrons, the Mamluk sultans and the educated Islamic public—primarily the ulema, or scholars, clergy, and jurists. It must be remembered that several Mongols dwelled in the Mamluk Sultanate and served in their military in high positions, so the Mamluks were not unfamiliar with Mongols. The first three entries correspond largely with Islamic law, while the next two are matters that speak to the Mongols' sense of pragmatism. As evidence in items 4 and 14, the purity of water was always crucial for the nomads because their livelihood depended on it; tainted water could cause massive loss among their herds and flocks.

Several sections take up social decorum. The sixth point refers specifically to hospitality. If an outsider was shown hospitality—given food, drink, or gifts no matter how innocuous—it meant they were protected. This was a trend that stretched across all of Eurasia among nomadic and seminomadic societies. The Mamluks, being of nomadic origin themselves, recognized it, as did Arabs. Other sections covering these issues include 7 and 12 through 16.

Many of the fragments also concern religion. Item 8 deals with the slaughtering of animals. Muslims, like Jews, slaughtered animals by cutting the jugular vein across the neck and allowing the blood to run out, whereas the Mongols stilled the heart with a hand or ripped the aorta by inserting a hand inside the animal's body. For Muslims, animals killed in the Mongol fashion were not considered safe to eat. The Mongols prepared meat on this way in order to save the blood for use in sausages and other foods. The threat of execution for slaughtering animals in the Muslim manner is found in other Muslim sources, intended to show that the Mongols were oppressive in their rule. It is possible that execution of Muslims for not slaughtering animals in the Mongol fashion did occur on occasion. For the Mongols, Muslims and Christians were generally viewed as nationalities based on their customs and were not considered in light of their individual religious practices. Thus, slaughtering animals signaled that one was abandoning the Mongol heritage. Still, sections 10, 11, and 17 reflect the Mongols' religious tolerance, for example, in saying that Chinggis Khan "ordered that all religions were to be respected and that no preference was to be shown to any of them." (Although section 10 emphasizes Muslim religious leaders in exempting them from taxation, it applied to clerics and devout members of all religions.) In this light, one would expect the death penalty to have applied only to nomads who slaughtered animals in the Muslim fashion.

The rest of al-Makrizi's Yasa fragments are concerned with military matters, which would be of the greatest interest to the Mamluks, although nothing described was a military secret. Indeed, the Mamluks had adopted many similar measures, most likely for pragmatic reasons rather than through Mongol influence. It is notable that al-Makrizi included sections about women and how they were expected to fight and perform the duties of men when the men were away. Sections 18 through 26 show the extent of Mongol discipline and the control that the Mongol khans had over their army, perhaps as a polite rebuttal of the situation in the Mamluk Sultanate, where the sultan was often chosen in a coup by disgruntled military officers.

◆ "From Mirhond"

The two entries of Mīrkhwānd, deal only with criminal justice. The first one concerns discipline for the army. Chinggis Khan imposed strict discipline on his army. The reference concerning the "community hunt" in section 27, in fact, applied to the military, as it was also a military exercise known as the *nerge*. Such punishments as are described here (beating with sticks and execution) are recorded elsewhere and are plausible; when compared with their mention in other sources, they appear here to be guidelines or advice given on how to maintain discipline rather than an actual law.

Item 28 deals with murder. The Mongols did allow the paying of a fine, most of which went to compensate the family of the victim. Although Mīrkhwānd indicates otherwise, payments were made either in cash or in kind, usually livestock. It is not surprising that Mīrkhwānd, a Muslim, placed a higher value on a Muslim than on a Chinese. The price for the life of a Chinese—a donkey—may have been less than one gold coin. That being said, the Mongols generally held the Chinese in low regard—in part, because there were so many of them and they feared being assimilated by the Chinese.

◆ "From ibn Batuta"

The compensation cited in section 29, written by Ibn Battūtah, also appears in a few other sources. It is probable that a person found in possession of a stolen horse had to repay the owner with additional horses, but the rest appears to be simply confirmation of the barbarity and draconian spirit of the Mongols. What is interesting about this passage is that it further demonstrates that the Yasa was intended for use among the nomads. Only nomads and rich sedentary people could possibly have nine horses. An average nomad would have at least five horses, while a noble could have hundreds if not thousands. Determining ownership of a horse was simple enough, for horses often were marked with the owner's brand or symbol. That nine horses would be given in addition to the stolen horse is significant, for Mongols considered the number nine auspicious.

◆ "From Vartang" and "From Mahakia"

The fragments included from Vardan and Mahakia are infused with Christian religious overtones. Vardan and Mahakia were both monks. Although the Mongols did kill many in their invasion of Armenia, their later rule was fairly tolerant. Many of the Armenian nobles found favor in the Mongol court, and Mongol religious toleration allowed the Armenians to practice their faith without oppression from Muslims, whose kingdoms surrounded them, or the Orthodox Byzantines, who viewed the Armenian Church as heretical. The reign of Hülegü was seen as a particularly beneficial period by Armenian Christians because Hülegü's wife was also a Christian. She helped finance the building of some churches, and Hülegü's rule was thus often considered a golden period. (Hülegü's wife also funded the building of mosques and Buddhist temples.) It is not surprising that parts of Vardan's and Mahakia's Yasa fragments resemble the Ten Commandments.

Most of the laws cited here are universal. Murder, theft, and adultery tend to be disruptive to society. The Mongols, like every other government, preferred a peaceful society, if only because it was more conducive to collection of taxes. From the perspective of Vardan and Mahakia, the fact that Mongol law seemed similar to the Ten Commandments help legitimate their rule and demonstrated that they were just and not infidels.

◆ "The Maxims of Jenghiz Khan"

The additional maxims of Chinggis Khan were used to advise subsequent rulers and princes descended from Chinggis Khan on proper behavior and conduct. The divi-

In 2006 Mongolian residents and foreign tourists visit the statue of Chinggis Khan unveiled as part of the eight hundredth anniversary of his forming the Great Mongolia State in Ulan Bator, Mongolia. (AP/Wide World Photos)

"If in battle, during an attack or a retreat, anyone let fall his pack, or bow, or any luggage, the man behind him must alight and return the thing fallen to its owner; if he does not so alight and return the thing fallen, he is to be put to death."

(Yasa 9)

"He ordered that all religions were to be respected and that no preference was to be shown to any of them. All this he commanded in order that it might be agreeable to God."

(Yasa 11)

"If unable to abstain from drinking, a man may get drunk three times a month; if he does it more than three times he is culpable; if he gets drunk twice a month it is better; if once a month, this is still more laudable; and if one does not drink at all what can be better?"

(Maxim 20)

"He also said: 'It is delightful and felicitous for a man to subdue rebels and conquer and extirpate his enemies, to take all they possess, to cause their servants to cry out, to make tears run down their faces and noses, to ride their pleasant-paced geldings, to make the bellies and navels of their wives his bed and bedding, to admire their rosy cheeks, to kiss them and to suck their red lips."

(Maxim 30)

sion in this document between what is considered the Yasa and what are maxims appears to be based on the nature of the entry. If it was linked to a punishment or phrased as a decree, the recorders deemed it to be part of the Yasa, whereas other pieces were considered simply advice or sayings from Chinggis Khan.

The maxims deal with a variety of topics. Several have to do with the leadership skills of a "Bek," or master, and his ability to command a tümen, or an army unit consisting of ten thousand men. The maxims prescribe behavior in times of war, enjoining proper deference to seniors and calling on soldiers to be "as a hungry falcon." The maxims also require the wives of soldiers to maintain a well-ordered household. Standards of heroism are also held up, with ref-

erence made to Yesun-Bey, a ruler of the Mongol Empire in the early fourteenth century. Nevertheless, Chinggis Khan was critical of Yesun-Bey, for he did not experience the hardships and fatigue of his men, so he was not fit to rule.

Many maxims are nostalgic in character, as Chinggis Khan reflects on past events as signposts pointing to proper and heroic behavior. Thus, in item 27, for example, he reflects on a previous battle and how he responded when he and his men were ambushed. He narrates a similar story in item 28. At times he seems to miss the sting of battle and the thrill of conquest. He sees his graying hair as a sign of seniority, but he can still look back to times when he and his multitudes could "conquer and extirpate his enemies, to take all they possess," and to "make the bellies and navels of their wives his bed and bedding." The Mongols were a harsh people, living in harsh conditions. Chinggis Khan was able to forge an empire and hold it together by adhering to the truth of the first maxim: "From the goodness of severity the stability of the government."

Audience

The audience for these writings varied considerably. As most, if not all, of al-Makrizi's work derives from Juvaini, an administrator in the Mongol Empire, there is some complexity to the question of the audience. Juvaini's work was written primarily for other Persians, although he received patronage from the Mongol court, and thus it is likely that the Mongol nobility also read it. Al-Makrizi wrote his work after the collapse of the Mongol Ilkhanate in Persia, and his audience was primarily intended to be the officials of the Mamluk Sultanate. Nonetheless, others also cribbed or plagiarized extensively from Juvaini, and Juvaini probably did the same, particularly with respect to the maxims. The maxims were intended exclusively for the nobility, to serve as foundational wisdom and standards of character.

Mīrkhwānd, also writing in a later period, had a different audience in the Timurid Dynasty. The Timurid, successors to the Mongols in central Asia and Iran, still held Chinggis Khan's legacy in high esteem. Mīrkhwānd's discussion of the Yasa was important to the Timurids' understanding of the past and the Mongol legacy that endured in the region. Indeed, Timur, the founder of the Timurid Dynasty, used the Yasa as he saw fit, for many Turko-Mongol nomads in the region, even as Muslims, still referred to it. Also, toward the end of Sultan Ḥusayn Bayqarah's reign, the realm was constantly threatened by invading Uzbeks, another successor to the Mongol Empire. Although many of the successors to the Mongols were Muslims and thus employed Islamic law, the Yasa still influenced their states. And in many areas of central Asia, where Muslims and non-Muslims intermixed, the Yasa was often the only legal code upon which both groups could agree.

Ibn Battūtah, Vardan, and Mahakia wrote for non-Mongol audiences. Ibn Battūtah wrote his work in North Africa, well away from the Mongol court, whereas Vardan and Mahakia wrote their works in Armenia. Other Armenians, primarily monks and priests, read them during the Middle Ages, so the audience was very narrow.

Impact

The impact of the Yasa and the maxims of Chinggis Khan is profound. Although no copy of the Yasa has been found, it was clearly the guiding beacon for the Mongol nobility in ruling their empire. Diverting from the Yasa sometimes led to conflict, and even the most ardent Muslim ruler often found ways to defer to the Yasa, in some cases to maintain the loyalty of the Turko-Mongol commanders. In addition, the maxims of Chinggis Khan remained an important litmus test for judging a person's character, particularly because over the centuries his legend outgrew the historic reality. Indeed, in some areas of the Eurasian steppes his image became that of an infallible leader, so that it would be reasonable to ask: "What would Chinggis do?"

The observations of outsiders concerning Mongol laws also demonstrate their impact outside the Mongol Empire. Neighboring states and travelers were curious about the Mongols and attempted to understand how they viewed the world. Furthermore, they also used what they could find to justify their various agendas—to determine whether the Mongols were infidels, to promote a belief that the Mongols supported Islam or Christianity, or even to assert that the Mongols were a punishment from God.

Many directives of the Yasa and the maxims continued to be obeyed in Mongolia and other parts of the steppe. Indeed, in later periods numerous cultural practices or laws were simply justified as having been introduced by Chinggis Khan. Even though it is questionable whether Chinggis Khan created the law code or maxims attributed to him, in many ways they are largely responsible for the way in which he and the Mongol Empire is envisioned in the popular imagination.

Further Reading

■ **Articles**

Ayalon, David. "The Great Yasa of Chingiz Khan: A Re-Examination." *Studia Islamica* 33 (1971): 97–140; 34 (1971): 151–180; 38 (1973): 107–156.

Morgan, David O. "The 'Great Yasa of Chingiz Khan' and Mongol Law in the Ilkhanate." *Bulletin of the School of Oriental and African Studies* 49, no. 1 (1986): 163–176.

Rachewiltz, Igor de. "Some Reflections on Cinggis Qan's Jasaq." *East Asian History* 6 (1993): 91–104.

Vernadsky, George. "The Scope and Contents of Chingis Khan's Yasa." *Harvard Journal of Asiatic Studies* 3 (1938): 337–360.

■ **Books**

Biran, Michal. *Chinggis Khan*. Oxford, U.K.: Oneworld, 2007.

Juvaini, Ata Malik. *Genghis Khan: The History of the World-Conqueror*, trans. John Andrew Boyle. Seattle: University of Washington Press, 1997.

Morgan, David O. "The 'Great Yasa of Chinggis Khan' Revisited." In *Mongols, Turks, and Others*, ed. Reuven Amitai and Michal Biran. Leiden, Netherlands: Brill, 2005.

Morgan, David O. *The Mongols*, 2nd ed. Malden, Mass.: Blackwell, 2007.

Rachewiltz, Igor de, trans. and ed. *The Secret History of the Mongols*. Leiden, Netherlands: Brill, 2004.

Ratchnevsky, Paul. *Genghis Khan: His Life and Legacy*, trans. Thomas Nivison Haining. Oxford, U.K.: Blackwell, 1991.

Riasonovsky, Valentine A. *Fundamental Principles of Mongol Law.* Bloomington: Indiana University Press, 1965.

Weatherford, Jack. *Genghis Khan and the Making of the Modern World.* New York: Crown Books, 2004.

■ **Web Sites**

"Explorations in Empire: Pre-Modern Imperialism Tutorial—The Mongols." San Antonio College History Department Web site.
    http://www.accd.edu/sac/history/keller/Mongols/index.html.

"The Legacy of Genghis Khan in Law and Politics." Mongolian Culture Web site.
    http://www.mongolianculture.com/ThelegacyofChinggis.htm.

—Timothy May

Questions for Further Study

1. Compare the Great Yasa of Chinggis Khan with another medieval law code, such as Wang Kŏn's Ten Injunctions or the Justice of the Rus. What cultural differences might account for differences in the law codes? What common concerns might account for any similarities?

2. To what extent might the nomadism that was prevalent in this part of the world at this time have contributed to the nature of the Great Yasa?

3. The name Chinggis Khan survives into the popular imagination of the twenty-first century as that of a cruel, violent conqueror, someone to be feared because he, in effect, plundered Asia. Based on what you have learned about the Great Yasa, do you think this view of Chinggis Khan is accurate?

4. There are no known surviving copies of the Great Yasa. The documents that survive are records that were kept by outsiders. How might this fact influence an interpretation of the Great Yasa? In what ways might it have been possible that the records that survive are biased?

5. Based on these excerpts from the Great Yasa, what was Chinggis Khan's attitude toward religion? Is his attitude surprising to you in any way? If so, how? If not, why not?

Great Yasa of Chinggis Khan

From Makrizi

1. An adulterer is to be put to death without any regard as to whether he is married or not.

2. Whoever is guilty of sodomy is also to be put to death.

3. Whoever intentionally lies, or practises sorcery, or spies upon the behaviour of others, or intervenes between the two parties in a quarrel to help the one against the other is also to be put to death.

4. Whoever urinates into water or ashes is also to be put to death.

5. Whoever takes goods (on credit) and becomes bankrupt, then again takes goods and again becomes bankrupt, then takes goods again and yet again becomes bankrupt is to be put to death after the third time.

6. Whoever gives food or clothing to a captive without the permission of his captor is to be put to death.

7. Whoever finds a runaway slave or captive and does not return him to the person to whom he belongs is to be put to death.

8. When an animal is to be eaten, its feet must be tied, its belly ripped open and its heart squeezed in the hand until the animal dies; then its meat may be eaten; but if anyone slaughter an animal after the Mohammedan fashion, he is to be himself slaughtered.

9. If in battle, during an attack or a retreat, anyone let fall his pack, or bow, or any luggage, the man behind him must alight and return the thing fallen to its owner; if he does not so alight and return the thing fallen, he is to be put to death.

10. He (Jenghiz Khan) decided that no taxes or duties should be imposed upon the descendants of Ali-Bek, Abu-Ta-leb, without exception, as well as upon fakirs, readers of the Al-Koran, lawyers, physicians, scholars, people who devote themselves to prayer and asceticism, muezzins and those who wash the bodies of the dead.

11. He ordered that all religions were to be respected and that no preference was to be shown to any of them. All this he commanded in order that it might be agreeable to God.

12. He forbade his people to eat food offered by another until the one offering the food tasted of it himself, even though one be a prince (Emir) and the other a captive; he forbade them to eat anything in the presence of another without having invited him to partake of the food; he forbade any man to eat more than his comrades, and to step over a fire on which food was being cooked or a dish from which people were eating.

13. When a wayfarer passes by people eating, he must alight and eat with them without asking for permission, and they must not forbid him this.

14. He forbade them to dip their hands into water and ordered them to use some vessel for the drawing of water.

15. He forbade them to wash their clothes until they were completely worn out.

16. He forbade them to say of anything that it was unclean, and insisted that all things were clean and made no distinction between the clean and unclean.

17. He forbade them to show preference for any sect, to pronounce words with emphasis, to use honorary titles; when speaking to the Sultan or anyone else simply his name was to be used.

18. He ordered his successors to personally examine the troops and their armament before going to battle, to supply the troops with everything they needed for the campaign and to survey everything even to needle and thread, and if any of the soldiers lacked a necessary thing that soldier was to be punished.

19. He ordered women accompanying the troops to do the work and perform the duties of the men, while the latter were absent fighting.

20. He ordered the warriors, on their return from the campaign (battle) to carry out certain duties in the service of the Sultan.

21. He ordered them to present all their daughters to the Sultan at the beginning of each year that he might choose some of them for himself and his children.

22. He put Emirs at the head of the troops and appointed Emirs of thousands, of hundreds, and of tens.

23. He ordered that the oldest of the Emirs, if he had committed some offence, was to give himself up to the messenger sent by the sovereign to punish him, even if he was the lowest of his servants; and prostrate himself before him until he had carried out

the punishment prescribed by the sovereign, even if it be to put him to death.

24. He forbade Emirs to address themselves to anyone except the sovereign. Whoever addressed himself to anyone but the sovereign was to be put to death, and anyone changing his post without permission was also to be put to death.

25. He ordered the Sultan to establish permanent postal communications in order that he might be informed in good time of all the events in the country.

26. He ordered his son, Jagatai-ben-Jenghiz Khan to see that the Yassa was observed.

From Mirhond

27. He ordered that soldiers be punished for negligence; and hunters who let an animal escape during a community hunt he ordered to be beaten with sticks and in some cases to be put to death.

28. In cases of murder (punishment for murder) one could ransom himself by paying fines which were: for a Mohammedan—40 golden coins (Balysh); and for a Chinese—one donkey.

From ibn Batuta

29. The man in whose possession a stolen horse is found must return it to its owner and add nine horses of the same kind: if he is unable to pay this fine, his children must be taken instead of the horses, and if he have no children, he himself shall be slaughtered like a sheep.

From Vartang

30. The Yassa of Jenghiz Khan forbids lies, theft and adultery and prescribes love of one's neighbour as one's self; it orders men not to hurt each other and to forget offences completely, to spare countries and cities which submit voluntarily, to free from taxes temples consecrated to God, and to respect the temples of God and their servants.

From Mahakia

31. (The Yassa prescribes these rules:) to love one another, not to commit adultery, not to steal, not to give false witness, not to be a traitor, and to respect old people and beggars. Whoever violates these commands is put to death.

The Maxims of Jenghiz Khan

1. From the goodness of severity the stability of the government.

2. If the Grandees, Knights and Beks of the children of the many sovereigns to come will not strictly observe the Yassa, the state will be shaken and collapse. People will again eagerly look for a Jenghiz Khan but will not find him.

3. He also said: "The Beks of a tümen (10,000 kibitkas), of a thousand and of a hundred who come to hear our thoughts at the beginning and at the end of the year and then return may command the troops; the state of those who sit in their yurts and do not hear these thoughts is like that of a stone that falls into deep water or an arrow shot into the reeds—they disappear. It is not fit for such men to command."

4. He also said: "Whoever can manage his own house well can also manage an estate, whoever can keep ten men in order in accordance with conditions may be given a thousand and a tümen and he will also keep them in order."

5. He also said: "Whoever can clean his own house can rid the country of thieves."

6. He also said: "Any Bek who cannot keep his ten men in order will, with his wife and children, be considered by us as guilty, and another man from his ten will be chosen and appointed Bek. In the same manner Beks of a hundred, a thousand and a tümen shall be dealt with."

7. He also said: "Any word on which three well-informed men are agreed may be spoken anywhere, otherwise it cannot be relied upon. Compare your words and the words of others with those of well-informed men, and if they agree you may speak them, otherwise you should by no means say them."

8. He also said: "Whoever goes to a senior must not say a word until the senior has addressed him; then let him answer according to the question. If he speaks first and is listened to it is well; otherwise he is like a man forging cold iron."

9. He also said: "Any horse that runs well when it is fat will also run well when it is fairly stout or fairly thin. Such a horse can be said to be a good one. But no horse can be said to be good that runs well in only one of these conditions."

10. He also said: "The senior Beks who will command, and also all warriors, must, in the same way as

they distinguish themselves when they occupy themselves with hunting, each distinguish his name and glory in war; and let each one always, praying fervently to Almighty God and keeping a meek heart, wish for the decoration of eight sides so that, by the power of the Lord ancient in days, it will be possible to take four limits in one place."

11. He also said: "Amongst people one must be like a calf, small and silent; but in the time of war one must be as a hungry falcon when it is hunting; he must go into battle shouting."

12. He also said: "As word that is said is considered to have been said seriously; if it is said jokingly it must not be carried out."

13. He also said: "As a man knows himself so should he know others."

14. He also said: "A man is not like the sun and therefore cannot appear everywhere before people; when the master is away hunting, or at war, the wife must keep the household in good condition and order so that if a messenger or a guest should happen to enter the house he may see that everything is in order; and she must prepare a good meal so that the guest may not want for anything. Thus she will win a good reputation for her husband and exalt his name in the assemblies like a mountain that rears its peak. Good husbands are known by their good wives. If a wife be stupid and dull, wanting in reason and orderliness, she makes obvious the badness of her husband. There is an adage-verse: 'In a house everything resembles its master.'"

15. In affairs caution is necessary.

16. He also said: "We go hunting and kill many mountain bulls. We go to war and kill many enemies. When Almighty God makes the ways smooth and work easy, men forget themselves and change."

17. He also said: "There is no hero equal to Yesun-Bey, and no man as skilful as he is. But not knowing fatigue and hardships in the campaign he thinks that everyone can have his endurance. Yet others cannot stand so much. Therefore Yesun-Bey is not fit to be chief over his troops. Only a man who feels hunger and thirst and by this estimates the feelings of others is fit to be a commander of troops, as he will see that the warriors do not suffer from hunger and thirst and that the four-legged beasts do not starve. The meaning of this is that the campaign and its hardships must be in proportion with the strength of the weakest of the warriors."

18. He also said: "As our merchants who import brocade garments and other good wares, expecting to make a profit, become very experienced in these goods

and garments, so the Beks must teach boys to shoot arrows well and to ride well and must train the boys in warlike deeds in order to make them as fearless and daring as the merchants are cunning in their trade."

19. He also said: "After us the descendants of our clan will wear gold embroidered garments, eat rich and sweet food, ride fine horses, and embrace beautiful women but they will not say that they owe all this to their fathers and elder brothers, and they will forget us and those great times."

20. He also said: "If unable to abstain from drinking, a man may get drunk three times a month; if he does it more than three times he is culpable; if he gets drunk twice a month it is better; if once a month, this is still more laudable; and if one does not drink at all what can be better? But where can such a man be found? If such a man were found he would be worthy of the highest esteem."

21. He also said: "...Lord ancient in days! You know and are aware that formerly Altan Khan raised a rebellion and that he began the enmity. He slew the innocent Ukin-Barchach and Ambagai-Kaan whom the tribe of Tatars seized and sent to him and who were the elder brothers of my sire and grandsire. I am athirst for their blood in retribution and vengeance. If you know that my intention is just, send me power and victory from above and order that your angels, men, peris and spirits above give me their aid...."

22. He also said: "My bowmen and warriors loom like thick forests: their wives, sweethearts and maidens shine like red flames. My task and intention is to sweeten their mouths with gifts of sweet sugar, to decorate their breasts, backs and shoulders with garments of brocade, to seat them on good geldings, give them to drink from pure and sweet rivers, provide their beasts with good and abundant pastures, and to order that the great roads and highways that serve as ways for the people be cleared of garbage, tree-stumps and all bad things; and not to allow dirt and thorns in the tents."

23. He also said: "If anyone of our clan act in violation of the approved Yassa let him be admonished verbally; if he does it again, let him be persuaded by eloquence; if he does it a third time, let him be sent to the remote place Baljuin-Khuljur. When he returns thence, he will be attentive. But if he be not brought to his senses, let him be put in irons and imprisoned. If he comes out of imprisonment good-tempered and reasonable, well and good. If not, let his relations assemble and deliberate as to what is to be done with him."

24. He also said: "The commanders of a tümen, of a thousand and of a hundred must each keep their troops in readiness and in order; so that whenever a decree or order reaches them, they may mount their horses without delay, even at night."

25. He also said: "Every boy born in Bargudjin Tukum, on the Onon and Kerulen, will be wise, manly and heroic without guidance, instruction or experience: he will be knowing and comely; and every maiden born there will, without combing or adornment, be handsome and beautiful."

26. He also said: "After the return of the messenger (he had sent) Muhuli-Govan asked: 'When you came to pay your respects to Jenghiz Khan and reported my speech to him what did he do?' The other replied: 'He bent his thumb.' He asked: 'Did he also put out a finger for me.'—He answered: 'He did.' Then Muhuli said: 'For this reason it is not in vain that I serve to the very death and demonstrate the greatest energy and eagerness.' He asked also: 'For whom else did he put out a finger?' The putting out of a finger is on the road to exaltation. He said: 'He put out a finger for Burji, Burgul, Kublai, Jilogen, Harajar, Jadai, Badai and Kyshlyk, to them all, and said: 'They all served, before and behind me, skilfully with aid and reinforcement, they shot arrows well and kept pedigreed horses on the lead, hunting birds on their hands, and hunting dogs on the leash.'"

27. He also said: "Once Bala-Halaja, who was one of the honoured Beks, asked him: 'You are called the master of power and a hero: what signs of conquest and victory are there to be seen on your hand?' Jenghiz Khan condescended to answer: 'Before I assumed the throne of the kingdom I was once riding along one of the roads. Six men who had laid an ambush at the bridge-passage made an attempt upon me. When I heard them I drew my sabre and rushed to the attack. They rained arrows upon me, but none of the arrows reached their target and not a single one touched me. I put them to death with my sabre and rode on unharmed. On my return it was necessary for me to pass by these slain. Their six geldings wandered masterless. I led away all six geldings.'"

28. He also said: "Once I was riding with Burji. Twelve men sat in ambush on a peak of the mountain range. Burji rode behind. I did not await him and, relying on my own power and strength, rushed to attack them. Suddenly all twelve of them shot off arrows and their arrows flew by me on all sides, but I proceeded to the attack when suddenly one arrow struck me in the mouth. I fell and was rendered senseless by this severe wound. At this moment Burji sped up and saw me and the fact that the wound had rendered me like a man in agony, jerking my legs and rolling over like a ball. He immediately warmed some water and brought it. I washed my throat and spat out the clotted blood. My soul, which had left my body, once more returned to it and I recovered feeling and motion. I rose and rushed to the attack. They were frightened by my hardiness, threw themselves down from that mountain, and gave up the ghost. The reason for the status of Tarkhan awarded to Burji-Noyon is that at such a time he made a laudable effort."

29. He also said: "During his youth Jenghiz Khan rose one morning extremely early. Several of the dark hairs in his locks became white. Those near him asked: 'O King! Your age is youthfully happy and you have not yet reached the beginning of old age. How is it that a trace of greyness has appeared in your locks?' He said in reply: 'Since the Almighty God has willed to make me the elder and chief of tümens and thousands and to raise through me the banner of well-doing, he has also put on me the sign of old age (greyness) which is also the sign of seniority.'"

30. He also said: "It is delightful and felicitous for a man to subdue rebels and conquer and extirpate

Glossary

Mohammedan	Muslim
wish for the decoration of eight sides so that . . . it will be possible to take four limits in one place	a reference to invoking the might of Tengri (the Heavens or the Sky God), which extends everywhere, and in this way being able to close or cut off all four avenues of escape (north, south, east, west)
Yesun-Bey	a famous warrior in his day

his enemies, to take all they possess, to cause their servants to cry out, to make tears run down their faces and noses, to ride their pleasant-paced geldings, to make the bellies and navels of their wives his bed and bedding, to admire their rosy cheeks, to kiss them and to suck their red lips."

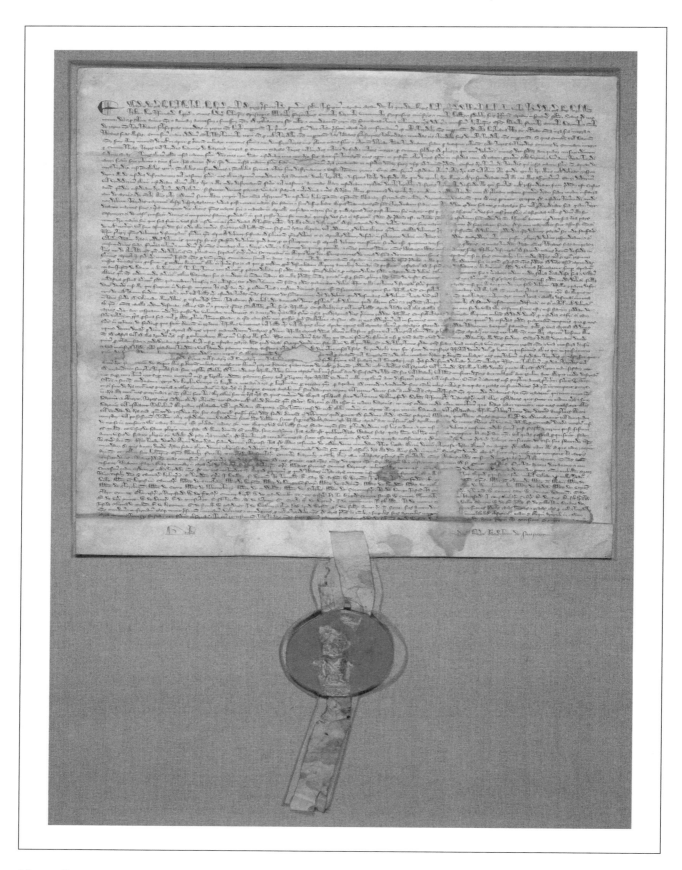

Magna Carta (AP/Wide World Photos)

MAGNA CARTA

"No Freeman shall be taken, or imprisoned, ...
but by lawful Judgment of his Peers, or by the Law of the Land."

Overview

In June 1215 a group of English barons forced King John of England to accept the sixty-three provisions of the Magna Carta ("Great Charter") at Runnymede, England. The Magna Carta was not originally intended to secure rights for all English citizens. Rather, it was meant to assert the feudal rights of England's barons, who had become disenchanted with King John's rule. Soon after it was signed, John ignored the tenets of the charter and began warring with his barons again. Despite the motivations of the authors and signers, the document contains political principles that remain important today. After its original issuance in 1215, the charter was revised and reissued. The 1297 version of the charter, which is the version used here, was renewed under King Edward I and remains on the statute books to this day, although numerous provisions have been repealed by specific legislation.

The Magna Carta has gained significance as the centuries have passed and has come to symbolize the very foundation of civil liberties. It limited royal power and asserted that monarchs also were subject to the rule of law. During the Tudor period (1485–1603), the Magna Carta faded into the background. In the later seventeenth century, it was revived by lawyers and parliamentarians. By that point, it had taken on a different level of meaning and had been transformed into a symbol. This new significance was not lost on British colonists in North America, who drew upon the Magna Carta as they came into conflict with King George III over rights and taxation.

Context

On October 14, 1066, William, Duke of Normandy, also known as William the Conqueror, defeated the recently crowned King Harold II of England at the Battle of Hastings. On Christmas Day, 1066, he was crowned King William I of England. The Norman Conquest ushered in many changes in England, particularly with respect to government. The Normans brought a more centralized style of

rule than had previously existed in England. William set up the Great Council, which would eventually become Parliament. The Anglo-Saxon nobles were dispossessed of their lands, which were then given to a much smaller group of Norman barons. This concentrated a degree of power and wealth among these barons, and they were thus often emboldened to resist royal authority.

In the century that followed the Norman Conquest, power had become more centralized in the hands of the monarch, oftentimes at the expense of baronial authority. Taxes continually increased to finance numerous endeavors. The issues that led to the signing of the Magna Carta at Runnymede in 1215 grew in importance during the rule of King John's predecessor, King Richard I, who was his brother. Richard ruled England from 1189 to 1199, but he spent much of his reign in Aquitaine, a region in western France where he had grown up with his mother, Eleanor of Aquitaine. He also spent time outside his realm as a crusader. For fourteen months beginning in December 1192, he was the prisoner of Duke Leopold V of Austria, who held him for ransom after his capture by pirates while returning home from the Third Crusade. Since Richard was mostly an absentee monarch, he put ministers in charge of the day-to-day administration of his kingdom. These ministers had to raise taxes continually to support Richard's endeavors overseas, including money for the ransom, which nearly bankrupted England. After his return from captivity, Richard spent most of the remainder of his life in combat in France. The barons and ministers who ran the country in his stead became very comfortable with this arrangement, but it would cause considerable trouble for the next king, John, who ascended the throne after Richard died on April 6, 1199. John's rule was often heavy-handed and despotic, and the barons were naturally resentful. In many regards, John was set up to fail, since he was always compared with his iconic brother, who was nicknamed "Richard the Lion-Hearted."

Trouble had begun in 1190, when Richard I had named as his successor Duke Arthur of Brittany, a nephew. Upon Richard's death, John acted quickly and declared himself king. After years of fighting to resolve the succession issue, he captured his teenage nephew and imprisoned him. The story goes that in 1203 John murdered his captive nephew

1066

- **December 25**
  The Norman Conquest is completed when William, duke of Normandy, is crowned King William I of England.

1199

- **May 27**
  John is crowned king of England.

1204

- **June**
  Normandy is captured by French forces.

1206

- **December**
  Pope Innocent III chooses Cardinal Stephen Langton as archbishop of Canterbury; John refuses to comply with the pope's decision.

1208

- **March 24**
  Pope Innocent III places England under a papal interdict.

1212

- Pope Innocent III formally deposes King John.

1213

- John surrenders his kingdom to the pope and then receives it back as the pope's vassal in exchange for payment of annual tribute.

in cold blood. This act of cowardice was not lost on his barons and cost John a great deal of political capital. John also was not as effective a military tactician as his brother and father, King Henry II, had been. King Philip II of France, also known as Philip Augustus, managed to take most of England's territorial possessions in France, including Normandy itself, the land of John's ancestors.

The next major controversy of John's rule was his conflict with Pope Innocent III over the election of the archbishop of Canterbury, Cardinal Stephen Langton. Innocent III refused to accept John's candidate, the bishop of Norwich John de Grey, and a confrontation ensued. John saw this as a direct assault on his power, and after he refused to back down, the pope put England under a papal interdict, which meant that no sacraments could be performed in England except baptism and the last rites. John essentially ignored the interdict, prompting the pope to depose him—in effect, to strip him of his crown. After a protracted struggle that saw John excommunicated and church lands seized by the Crown, John capitulated in 1212 and allowed Langton to assume his duties as archbishop of Canterbury. The damage to John's reputation, however, was already done.

During this same period, John had come into increasing conflict with his nobles and had begun to resort to ever more cruel and unusual tactics to control his barons, such as holding hostage the wives and children of those with whom he was quarrelling. John thus cultivated considerable antagonism among the barons on whom he greatly depended for financial and military support. John also continued the burdensome tax-collection policies of Richard I.

In 1214 John suffered a major military defeat at the hands of the French and returned to England in disgrace. Once again, his standing in the eyes of his people had suffered, and the stage was set for his acceptance of the Magna Carta the following year. As part of the uprising against him, the barons seized control of the Tower of London in May 1215. One month later at Runnymede, a meadow along the Thames west of London, the barons persuaded John to affix his seal to a charter of liberties intended to rein in the king's power.

About the Author

The authorship of the Magna Carta is not entirely known. Some historians believe that a document called the "Articles of Barons" formed the basis of the Magna Carta. The consensus is that these articles were worked into a final document by a group of learned men, most likely headed by Stephen Langton, William Marshal, and Robert Fitzwalter.

Langton was born around 1150. After the death of the archbishop of Canterbury, Hubert Walter, in 1205, Langton became embroiled in a power struggle between King John and Pope Innocent III. Langton was the pope's choice to succeed Walter, but John had another candidate in mind. Eventually, John capitulated, and Langton became the archbishop of Canterbury. During the baronial conflict with John, Langton supported and advised the barons. However, he extricated himself from the conflict when the opposition turned to violence, and he was one of the king's emissaries at Runnymede. He died in 1228.

William Marshal, the First Earl of Pembroke, was born in about 1146 and died in 1219. He was considered one of the greatest warriors of his day, and his bravery in battle became the stuff of legend. Marshal aided in the succession of John after the death of Richard I. By 1213 he had become one of John's most important counselors, and he remained loyal to the king during the baronial conflict. He represented the king at Runnymede and was probably among the authors of the final document. After John's death, Marshal acted as the regent for the underage Henry III and thus became the de facto ruler of England.

The birth date of Robert Fitzwalter is unknown. It is known, however, that he died on November 9, 1235. He came to prominence as the leader of the opposition to John. In 1212 he was accused of actions against the king and fled to France. His lands were seized and his castles destroyed. The following year, his lands were restored by John, but he remained a staunch opponent of the king. He was one of the chief negotiators of the Magna Carta, though it is not known exactly how much input he had.

Explanation and Analysis of the Document

The Magna Carta originally contained sixty-three "chapters," or clauses, that asserted what the barons considered to be their ancient rights in an effort to protect themselves and their property. By the time Edward I agreed to reissue the Magna Carta in 1297, there were thirty-seven clauses. The clauses that pertained solely to the conflict leading up to the signing of the document in 1215 had been eliminated, and all clauses concerned with the administration of forests had been transferred to a separate Forest Charter in 1217.

The document commences with a preamble, which states that it is a declaration of liberties granted to "Archbishops, Bishops, Abbots, Priors, Earls, Barons, and ... all freemen of this our realm." The clauses that follow enumerate various types of liberties, including freedom of the church, feudal law regarding the holding of land, the rights of widows, the reformation of the justice system, property rights, the rights of people accused of crimes, and the rights of merchants. They appear in no particular order, and the language of the clauses often reflects the influence of Norman French legal and feudal practices.

◆ Clause 1

Clause 1 contains at least two important provisions. The first is its assertion that "the Church of England shall be free." Stephen Langton was in all likelihood the architect of this clause. After the bitter confrontation between Pope Innocent III and King John over Langton's appointment as archbishop of Canterbury, Langton wanted to prevent any such confrontations in the future. This provision would become an antecedent to later concepts of the division of

Time Line

1214

- **October**
  John returns to England from France in defeat.

1215

- **A group of barons** gathers at Stamford and renounces allegiance to John.

- **June 10**
  The barons meet John at Runnymede to negotiate a settlement.

- **June 15**
  King John agrees to the Magna Carta.

1216

- **October 18**
  John dies; his nine-year-old son, Henry III, becomes king.

- **November 12**
  The first revision of the Magna Carta is issued to garner support for the regime of Henry III.

1225

- **February 11**
  Henry III, now old enough to rule, issues a revision of the Magna Carta.

1297

- **October 12**
  King Edward I confirms Henry III's 1225 version of the Magna Carta.

1628

- **June**
  Sir Edward Coke promulgates the Petition of Right, a proclamation of liberties issued by Parliament and agreed to by King Charles I.

1679

■ **May 27**
Parliament passes the Habeas Corpus Act, based on the principles of the Magna Carta and cementing the right to not be imprisoned without cause.

1689

■ **December 16**
The English Bill of Rights is passed by Parliament and given royal assent; the bill provides for civil and political rights in England.

church and state. The phrase "Church of England" assigned an idiosyncratic nature to the Church of England, distinguishing it from the Roman Catholic Church. This concept of a distinct Church of England would be played out in the sixteenth century during the reign of Henry VIII.

A second important aspect of Clause 1 is the use of the word *freemen*. Although it is not entirely clear what the authors meant by this term at the time, what is important is what it later came to mean. Over time, the category of freemen came to apply to an increasingly broad range of people, and this usage is one of the features that has allowed the Magna Carta to be interpreted flexibly over the centuries.

◆ **Clauses 2–7**

These clauses address feudal relationships and rights. In the early thirteenth century English society was defined by feudal relationships and agreements. The nobility held their lands as direct grants from the king in exchange for military service and payment of taxes. These taxes came in many forms, many of which involved the transference of estates from one generation to the next. Many of the barons' complaints against John pertained to the king's having overstepped his authority. These clauses define the boundaries of feudal relationships with the king and protect the rights of the nobles from abuses by royal authority.

Clauses 2 and 3, for example, deal with issues of inheritance and who may profit from the transference of property. Both address the amount of "relief" that could be assessed to someone receiving an inheritance. Relief was a fee paid in order to collect one's inheritance, but there was no limit on the amount of relief to be paid, which Clause 2 tried to correct. Clause 3 prevented the king from receiving

relief when he had already profited from having been the guardian of an inheritance. Clauses 4 and 5 protected the rights of heirs who were too young to collect their inheritance from king's representatives, who might otherwise have tried to profit dishonestly from the property of their charges.

In Clause 6 the marriage of heirs is addressed. The king had made a practice of selling female heirs to men wishing to gain the women's title and fortune. In many cases these marriages were seen as inequitable because the man was from a lower social station than the woman. The barons wanted to curtail this practice. Clause 7 stipulates the rights of widows and states that a widow could not have her inheritance denied to her. The implication of the second portion of the clause is perhaps more significant. The clause states, "No widow shall be distrained to marry herself." In other words, no widow had to marry if she chose not to do so. Allowing widows autonomy in deciding whether to remarry represented a small step toward granting rights not just to men but also to women.

◆ **Clauses 8–14**

This sequence of clauses deals with a variety of issues. Clause 8 spells out the relationship between debtors and sureties. A surety was someone who was responsible for a debt if the debtor could not pay. This clause says that a debt collector could not go to the surety without first endeavoring to collect the debt from the debtor. It further states that if a surety satisfied the debt, he was entitled to compensation from the debtor equal to the amount settled.

The city of London played a major role in the conflict between King John and the barons. By siding with the barons in the conflict, the people of London earned a special position with the barons, and that position earned them Clause 9 of the Magna Carta. Clause 9 stipulates that London was granted all of the traditional rights and privileges that the city had previously enjoyed. These rights and privileges were protected now by law.

Clause 10 reflected an effort to define the terms of military service under the feudal code. The exact amount of service was not well defined, and the Magna Carta did not do much to rectify this murkiness. However, this clause put in writing the principle that the amount of service required was to be based on the amount of land a noble had been granted.

Clauses 11 through 14 deal with issues of justice. Clause 11, for example, was intended to limit the expenses individuals incurred while seeking justice. Prior to 1215, individuals who had to go to court literally had to go to court—that is, to the location of the king. If the king was moving from place to place, those seeking justice had to follow him at their own expense. This clause fixed where court would be held and limited expenses. Clause 12 was aimed at making justice more convenient by stating that certain trials would be held in the county. It names two types of legal proceedings, using language that had been imported from Norman French. "Assises of novel disseisin" were court proceedings for the recovery of land of which a person had recently lost ownership; an "assise," spelled "assize" now, was simply a sitting of the court. Assises of

The castle where King John resided prior to signing the Magna Carta (© James Emmerson/Robert Harding World Imagery/Corbis)

"Mortdancestor," usually spelled *mort d'ancestor*, were actions to recover land of which a person had been deprived by the death of an ancestor. Clause 13 introduces another legal term: "Assises of Darrein Presentment." "Darrein Presentment" translates to "last presentation" and had to do with legal complications that could ensue over conflicting claims to a benefice, or an ecclesiastical office.

Clause 14 expresses the view that there should not be excessive punishment for those convicted of a crime. The clause addresses the assessment of fines, and its thrust is that the fine should be commensurate with the severity of the crime. The principle that the punishment should fit the crime has become important in the judicial systems of democratic nations and was later set forth in the Eighth Amendment to the U.S. Constitution.

◆ **Clauses 15–24**

These clauses define the feudal rights of the king and the barons, particularly as they pertained to property and matters of civil justice. It was the practice of the day in England for the king's subjects to build and maintain bridges. Villages and individuals had no option to refuse when the king ordered them to build a bridge. Clause 15 sought to end this practice. Clause 16 deals with riverbanks and fishing rights, stating that fishing rights were not to be curtailed, save on those rivers that were designated in

the time of King Henry II. Later, Clause 23 deals with fish weirs, or traps that were used to catch fish by placing wooden posts in the riverbed. Since these wooden posts often were impediments to commerce, the barons wanted them removed.

Clause 17 returns to the administration of justice by stating that trials must be conducted by the proper authorities. This instruction was to ensure that proper justice would be dispensed and people would be protected from the brand of justice doled out by local officials, whose sentences were often much harsher than those passed by the king's officials. Clause 18 deals with estates of Crown tenants who owed debts to the Crown. It specifies how a Crown tenant would be protected from abuses by royal authorities who tried to collect debts. The clause states that documentation was required from royal officials in order to settle debts. An escheator was a royal official responsible for holding an inquest on the death of a tenant in chief and determining who should inherit the property.

Clauses 19 through 21 share the common theme of property rights. In general, they established the principle that property could not be taken from a person arbitrarily without proper remuneration. This concept later became the linchpin in English philosopher John Locke's understanding of property and enumeration of "natural rights" in the seventeenth century.

Clause 22 represented another attempt to define the scope of the king's power and make that power less arbitrary. The clauses pertaining to feudal relationships do not say that the king did not have certain powers; rather, they defined and limited those powers. Clause 22 limited the king's power to take away the land of a noble convicted of a felony. By attaching a specific timetable to when a baron's land could be taken from him after conviction of a felony, another safeguard was put in place against the abuse of royal power. Clause 24 deals with Writs Praecipe, also called writs of covenant. These writs, issued by the king, gave local sheriffs the authority to take away a noble's land and remit it to another party who claimed the land. Practices such as these had been at the heart of the conflict between the barons and King John.

◆ **Clauses 25–29**

Clauses 25 through 29 deal with fundamental issues of fairness. The purpose of Clause 25, one of the more straightforward of the Magna Carta's clauses, was to establish standard measurements for the sale of certain items in order to protect buyers. A "haberject" was a type of dyed cloth. Clause 26 pertains to the subject of trial by combat. A "Writ of Inquisition" was the right to trial by combat for an accuser, an important function of justice at that time. Governments had not yet fully developed their judicial function, and trial by combat was one of the main forms of redress for someone wronged by another. This clause simply provided that this right could not be taken away and would be granted without charging a fee. The Magna Carta takes up this issue again later, in Clause 34. Clause 27 reined in the king's ability to collect a tax from guardianship when it was not within the scope of the law to do so. The term *fee-ferm* means "fee-farm," or a farm on which a farmer paid rent. Under the practice of socage, a farmer held land in exchange for service; the term *burgage* referred to property in towns on which the holder paid rent.

Clauses 28 and 29 would later become quite influential in the practice of criminal law. The most accepted interpretation of Clause 28 is that a bailiff (meaning any number of different officials) may not charge a person with a crime without first producing a credible witness. Clause 29 is perhaps the most well-known clause and the one that was seized on by later legal scholars, for from it the concept of trial by jury evolved:

No Freeman shall be taken, or imprisoned, or be disseised of his Freehold [have his property taken away], or Liberties, or free Customs, or be outlawed, or exiled, or any otherwise destroyed; nor will we pass upon him, nor condemn him, but by lawful Judgment of his Peers, or by the Law of the Land.

In other words, a person could not be convicted by the arbitrary whim of another person but must be found guilty of a legitimate crime by a group of his peers. Trial by jury has since become the foundation of democratic judicial systems. The clause concludes with a strong statement that justice may not be bought.

◆ **Clauses 30–37**

Clause 30 provided for free trade with merchants of all nations not at war with the king. It states that trade was to be unencumbered by excessive royal taxation. Another clause designed to rein in the power of the king, Clause 31, enabled barons to regain rights that they had held under previous kings but that had not been recognized by King John. Before John's reign, the rights to property ownership and inheritance of subtenants, another layer of the feudal order, had been recognized. John ignored these rights when land was escheated (left without an heir). Instead of allowing the land to pass to the proper tenant, John claimed the land for himself. An addition to the original 1215 version, Clause 32, deals with the practice of subdividing fiefs (feudal estates) in order to break down the feudal order. Extreme fragmentation of estates could have broken down the feudal order and made tenants independent of their feudal lords. Clause 32 sought to end this practice.

Clause 33 specifies who would have guardianship over churches and thus have had the right to an appointment at a church. Churches were founded by either the king or a lesser feudal lord. The founder of a particular church had the right to appoint its head. In certain cases, John ignored this and appointed heads of the churches. This clause was meant to define legally another feudal relationship and protect the feudal rights of the barons. Taking up again the issue of trial by combat, Clause 34 eliminated the advantage women were seen to have, for female accusers had been able to hire a champion to fight in their stead, but an accused man had to fight for himself. Clause 34 sought to end this practice.

Clause 35 returns to the issue of judicial procedure. It makes reference to two institutions: "Frankpledge" and "Tything." The latter was a group of ten men; the former referred to the obligation of the ten to stand as sureties for the members of the group and to produce any one of the members if he was summoned to a legal proceeding. The purpose of this clause was to specify when and under what circumstances these institutions could be invoked while preventing their misuse to harass people. Clause 36 attempted to prevent another abuse: in this case, abuse over the ownership of church lands, particularly the practices of granting land to a church and taking it back and of the church's taking land and leasing it back to the donor. Finally, Clause 37 regulated the practice of escuage, also called scutage. This term referred to the obligation of a tenant to follow his lord in military service at his own expense.

Audience

The original audience for the Magna Carta consisted of the barons—possibly around 165 men, including some thirty-nine in rebellion—and the king. Additionally, the audience included advisers to the king and, to a lesser extent, ecclesiastical authorities. As the years passed, the audience for the Magna Carta grew. By using the word *freemen* in its introduction and first clause and "all Men of this our

> "A Widow, after the death of her husband, incontinent, and without any Difficulty, shall have her marriage and her inheritance, and shall give nothing for her dower, her marriage, or her inheritance, which her husband and she held the day of the death of her husband."
>
> (Clause 7)

> "The city of London shall have all the old liberties and customs, which it hath been used to have. Moreover we will and grant, that all other Cities, Boroughs, Towns, and the Barons of the Five Ports, and all other Ports, shall have all their liberties and free customs."
>
> (Clause 9)

> "No Bailiff from henceforth shall put any man to his open Law, nor to an Oath, upon his own bare saying, without faithful Witnesses brought in for the same."
>
> (Clause 28)

> "No Freeman shall be taken, or imprisoned, or be disseised of his Freehold, or Liberties, or free Customs, or be outlawed, or exiled, or any otherwise destroyed; nor will we pass upon him, nor condemn him, but by lawful Judgment of his Peers, or by the Law of the Land. We will sell to no man, we will not deny or defer to any man either Justice or Right."
>
> (Clause 29)

Realm" in Clause 37, the charter potentially had an audience that was much larger than the assemblage of men at Runnymede. There has been much dispute about what this language implied and to whom the rights granted by the Magna Carta applied. The jurist and legal scholar Sir Edward Coke used the term to include almost all men and, in 1628, promulgated the Magna Carta as a constitution by which the rights of Englishmen were guaranteed. Regardless of what the writers of Magna Carta may have originally intended, its scope came to include all men and eventually all people. The Magna Carta would have its heyday not in the thirteenth century but rather hundreds of years later during the Enlightenment, when political thinkers drew on the Magna Carta to resist absolute monarchy and advocate more representative constitutional government.

Impact

Upon its inception, the Magna Carta did not make much of an impact, as King John largely ignored it. It faded in importance during the Tudor period of English history, but the document was revived in the seventeenth century during the Stuart period, when Parliament was at odds with the king. Sir Edward Coke was the seventeenth-century champion of the Magna Carta. He asserted that it was proof of an ancient set of liberties that English people possessed. Coke invoked an ideal of the Magna Carta, rather than the probable intention of its authors. Although Coke died in 1634, his view of the Magna Carta was used as a spark to ignite the English Civil War of the 1640s and later the Glorious Revolution of 1688, which brought King

William III and Queen Mary II from the Netherlands to the English throne and produced the English Bill of Rights. It was also the inspiration behind the Habeas Corpus Act of 1679. As time went on, power shifted increasingly from the king to Parliament, and many historians argue that the Magna Carta was at the center of this evolution. Coke's idealized interpretation of the Magna Carta would eventually become reality.

In the American colonies, the Magna Carta became a symbol. Many colonies were being founded and settled concurrently with the strife between Parliament and the Stuart kings James I and Charles I in the seventeenth century. As a result, colonists were often mindful of the Magna Carta when colonial charters were being drawn up. Colonists saw themselves as entitled to the ancient rights granted to them by the Magna Carta, and they invoked the Magna Carta in their arguments against British taxation and infringements upon their rights. The ideal of the Magna Carta remained powerful in the writing of the U.S. Constitution, and many interpretations of the Magna Carta live on in the American Constitution and Bill of Rights.

Further Reading

■ Books

Daniell, Christopher. *From Norman Conquest to Magna Carta: England, 1066–1215.* New York: Routledge, 2003.

Danziger, Danny, and John Gillingham. *1215: The Year of Magna Carta.* New York: Simon & Schuster, 2004.

Erickson, Carolly. *Royal Panoply: Brief Lives of the English Monarchs.* New York: St. Martin's Press, 2006.

Howard, A. E. Dick. *Magna Carta: Text and Commentary.* Rev. ed. Charlottesville: University Press of Virginia, 1998.

Turner, Ralph V. *Magna Carta: Through the Ages.* New York: Pearson/Longman, 2003.

■ Web Sites

"Magna Carta: A Commentary on the Great Charter of King John, with an Historical Introduction [1215]." Online Library of Liberty Web site.
    http://oll.libertyfund.org/index.php?option=com_staticxt&staticfile=show.php%3Ftitle=338&Itemid=27.

Sommerville, J. P. "The Crisis of John's Reign." University of Wisconsin Web site.
    http://history.wisc.edu/sommerville/123/123%20114%20John%20in%20crisis.htm.

"Treasures in Full: Magna Carta." British Library Web site.
    http://www.bl.uk/treasures/magnacarta/index.html.

—Matthew Fiorello and Michael J. O'Neal

Questions for Further Study

1. Why do some historians date the beginning of Western democracy, specifically Anglo-American democracy, to the Magna Carta? What "modern" rights are asserted in the Magna Carta?

2. Read the Magna Carta in conjunction with another medieval English document, the Domesday Book. How do the two documents, taken together, give modern readers a portrait of life in feudal medieval England? What would the life of a noble or landowner have been like? Of a peasant? Of a priest or nun?

3. What impact did the Norman Conquest of 1066 have on the Anglo-Saxon nobles already living in England? How did that impact give rise to the Magna Carta?

4. In what respects did the Magna Carta improve the condition of women?

5. The legend of Robin Hood—the medieval English outlaw and his band of "merry men" who stole from the rich and gave to the poor—continues to be widely known, the subject of movies and television series. How do you think someone like Robin Hood would have reacted to the Magna Carta? Would he have applauded any of its clauses? Would he have condemned others? Why?

MAGNA CARTA

[Preamble] Edward by the grace of God, King of England, Lord of Ireland, and Duke of Guyan, to all Archbishops, Bishops, etc. We have seen the Great Charter of the Lord Henry, sometimes King of England, our father, of the Liberties of England, in these words: Henry by the grace of God, King of England, Lord of Ireland, Duke of Normandy and Guyan, and Earl of Anjou, to all Archbishops, Bishops, Abbots, Priors, Earls, Barons, Sheriffs, Provosts, Officers, and to all Bailiffs and other our faithful Subjects , which shall see this present Charter, Greeting. Know ye that we, unto the honour of Almighty God, and for the salvation of the souls of our progenitors and successors, Kings of England, to the advancement of holy Church, and amendment of our Realm, of our meer and free will, have given and granted to all Archbishops, Bishops, Abbots, Priors, Earls, Barons, and to all freemen of this our realm, these liberties following, to be kept in our kingdom of England for ever.

[1] First, We have granted to God, and by this our present Charter have confirmed, for us and our Heirs for ever, That the Church of England shall be free, and shall have her whole rights and liberties inviolable. We have granted also, and given to all the freemen of our realm, for us and our Heirs for ever, these liberties underwritten, to have and to hold to them and their Heirs, of us and our Heirs for ever.

[2] If any of our Earls or Barons, or any other, which holdeth of Us in chief by Knights service, shall die and at the time of his death his heir be of full age, and oweth us Relief, he shall have his inheritance by the old Relief; that is to say, the heir or heirs of an Earl, for a whole Earldom, by one hundred pound; the heir or heirs of a Baron, for a whole Barony, by one hundred marks; the heir or heirs of a Knight, for one whole Knights fee, one hundred shillings at the most; and he that hath less, shall give less, according to the custom of the fees.

[3] But if the Heir of any such be within age, his Lord shall not have the ward of him, nor of his land, before that he hath taken him homage. And after that such an heir hath been in ward (when he is come of full age) that is to say, to the age of one and twenty years, he shall have his inheritance without Relief, and without Fine; so that if such an heir, being within age, be made Knight, yet nevertheless his land shall remain in the keeping of his Lord unto the term aforesaid.

[4] The keeper of the land of such an heir, being within age, shall not take of the lands of the heir, but reasonable issues, reasonable customs, and reasonable services, and that without destruction and waste of his men and goods. And if we commit the custody of any such land to the Sheriff, or to any other, which is answerable unto us for the issues of the same land, and he make destruction or waste of those things that he hath in custody, we will take of him amends and recompence therefore, and the land shall be committed to two lawful and discreet men of that fee, which shall answer unto us for the issues of the same land, or unto him whom we will assign. And if we give or sell to any man the custody of any such land, and he therein do make destruction or waste, he shall lose the same custody; and it shall be assigned to two lawful and discreet men of that fee, which also in like manner shall be answerable to us, as afore is said.

[5] The keeper, so long as he hath the custody of the land of such an heir, shall keep up the houses, parks, warrens, ponds, mills, and other things pertaining to the same land, with the issues of the said land; and he shall deliver to the Heir, when he cometh to his full age, all his land stored with ploughs, and all other things, at the least as he received it. All these things shall be observed in the custodies of the Archbishopricks, Bishopricks, Abbeys, Priories, Churchs, and Dignities vacant, which appertain to us; except this, that such custody shall not be sold.

[6] Heirs shall be married without Disparagement.

[7] A Widow, after the death of her husband, incontinent, and without any Difficulty, shall have her marriage and her inheritance, and shall give nothing for her dower, her marriage, or her inheritance, which her husband and she held the day of the death of her husband, and she shall tarry in the chief house of her husband by forty days after the death of her husband, within which days her dower shall be assigned her (if it were not assigned her before) or that the house be a castle; and if she depart from the castle, then a competent house shall be forthwith provided for her, in the which she may

honestly dwell, until her dower be to her assigned, as it is aforesaid; and she shall have in the meantime her reasonable estovers of the common; and for her dower shall be assigned unto her the third part of all the lands of her husband, which were his during coverture, except she were endowed of less at the Church-door. No widow shall be distrained to marry herself: nevertheless she shall find surety, that she shall not marry without our licence and assent (if she hold of us) nor without the assent of the Lord, if she hold of another.

[8] We or our Bailiffs shall not seize any land or rent for any debt, as long as the present Goods and Chattels of the debtor do suffice to pay the debt, and the debtor himself be ready to satisfy therefore. Neither shall the pledges of the debtor be distrained, as long as the principal debtor is sufficient for the payment of the debt. And if the principal debtor fail in the payment of the debt, having nothing wherewith to pay, or will not pay where he is able, the pledges shall answer for the debt. And if they will, they shall have the lands and rents of the debtor, until they be satisfied of that which they before paid for him, except that the debtor can show himself to be acquitted against the said sureties.

[9] The city of London shall have all the old liberties and customs, which it hath been used to have. Moreover we will and grant, that all other Cities, Boroughs, Towns, and the Barons of the Five Ports, and all other Ports, shall have all their liberties and free customs.

[10] No man shall be distrained to do more service for a Knights fee, nor any freehold, than therefore is due.

[11] Common Pleas shall not follow our Court, but shall be holden in some place certain.

[12] Assises of novel disseisin, and of Mortdancestor, shall not be taken but in the shires, and after this manner: If we be out of this Realm, our chief Justicer shall send our Justicers through every County once in the Year, which, with the Knights of the shires, shall take the said Assises in those counties; and those things that at the coming of our foresaid Justicers, being sent to take those Assises in the counties, cannot be determined, shall be ended by them in some other place in their circuit; and those things, which for difficulty of some articles cannot be determined by them, shall be referred to our Justicers of the Bench, and there shall be ended.

[13] Assises of Darrein Presentment shall be alway taken before our Justices of the Bench, and there shall be determined.

[14] A Freeman shall not be amerced for a small fault, but after the manner of the fault; and for a great fault after the greatness thereof, saving to him his contenement; and a Merchant likewise, saving to him his Merchandise; and any other's villain than ours shall be likewise amerced, saving his wainage, if he falls into our mercy. And none of the said amerciaments shall be assessed, but by the oath of honest and lawful men of the vicinage. Earls and Barons shall not be amerced but by their Peers, and after the manner of their offence. No man of the Church shall be amerced after the quantity of his spiritual Benefice, but after his Lay-tenement, and after the quantity of his offence.

[15] No Town or Freeman shall be distrained to make Bridges nor Banks, but such as of old time and of right have been accustomed to make them in the time of King Henry our Grandfather.

[16] No Banks shall be defended from henceforth, but such as were in defence in the time of King Henry our Grandfather, by the same places, and the same bounds, as they were wont to be in his time.

[17] No Sheriff, Constable, Escheator, Coroner, nor any other our Bailiffs, shall hold Pleas of our Crown.

[18] If any that holdeth of us Lay-fee do die, and our Sheriff or Bailiff do show our Letters Patents of our summon for Debt, which the dead man did owe to us; it shall be lawful to our Sheriff or Bailiff to attach or inroll all the goods and chattels of the dead, being found in the said fee, to the Value of the same Debt, by the sight and testimony of lawful men, so that nothing thereof shall be taken away, until we be clearly paid off the debt; and the residue shall remain to the Executors to perform the testament of the dead; and if nothing be owing unto us, all the chattels shall go to the use of the dead (saving to his wife and children their reasonable parts).

[19] No Constable, nor his Bailiff, shall take corn or other chattels of any man, if the man be not of the Town where the Castle is, but he shall forthwith pay for the same, unless that the will of the seller was to respite the payment; and if he be of the same Town, the price shall be paid unto him within forty days.

[20] No Constable shall distrain any Knight to give money for keeping of his Castle, if he himself will do it in his proper person, or cause it to be done by another sufficient man, if he may not do it himself for a reasonable cause. And if we lead or send him to an army, he shall be free from Castle-ward for the time that he shall be with us in fee in our host, for the which he hath done service in our wars.

[21] No Sheriff nor Bailiff of ours, or any other, shall take the Horses or Carts of any man to make carriage, except he pay the old price limited, that is to say, for carriage with two horse, x.d. a day; for three horse, xiv.d. a day. No demesne Cart of any Spiritual person or Knight, or any Lord, shall be taken by our Bailiffs; nor we, nor our Bailiffs, nor any other, shall take any man's wood for our Castles, or other our necessaries to be done, but by the licence of him whose wood it shall be.

[22] We will not hold the Lands of them that be convict of Felony but one year and one day, and then those Lands shall be delivered to the Lords of the fee.

[23] All Wears from henceforth shall be utterly put down by Thames and Medway, and through all England, but only by the Sea-coasts.

[24] The Writ that is called Praecipe in capite shall be from henceforth granted to no person of any freehold, whereby any freeman may lose his Court.

[25] One measure of Wine shall be through our Realm, and one measure of Ale, and one measure of Corn, that is to say, the Quarter of London; and one breadth of dyed Cloth, Russets, and Haberjects, that is to say, two Yards within the lists. And it shall be of Weights as it is of Measures.

[26] Nothing from henceforth shall be given for a Writ of Inquisition, nor taken of him that prayeth Inquisition of Life, or of Member, but it shall be granted freely, and not denied.

[27] If any do hold of us by Fee-ferm, or by Socage, or Burgage, and he holdeth Lands of another by Knights Service, we will not have the Custody of his Heir, nor of his Land, which is holden of the Fee of another, by reason of that Fee-ferm, Socage, or Burgage. Neither will we have the custody of such Fee-ferm, or Socage, or Burgage, except Knights Service be due unto us out of the same Fee-ferm. We will not have the custody of the Heir, or of any Land, by occasion of any Petit Serjeanty, that any man holdeth of us by Service to pay a Knife, an Arrow, or the like.

[28] No Bailiff from henceforth shall put any man to his open Law, nor to an Oath, upon his own bare saying, without faithful Witnesses brought in for the same.

[29] No Freeman shall be taken, or imprisoned, or be disseised of his Freehold, or Liberties, or free Customs, or be outlawed, or exiled, or any otherwise destroyed; nor will we pass upon him, nor condemn him, but by lawful Judgment of his Peers, or by the Law of the Land. We will sell to no man, we will not deny or defer to any man either Justice or Right.

[30] All Merchants (if they were not openly prohibited before) shall have their safe and sure Conduct to depart out of England, to come into England, to tarry in, and go through England, as well by Land as by Water, to buy and sell without any manner of evil Tolts, by the old and rightful Customs, except in Time of War. And if they be of a land making War against us, and such be found in our Realm at the beginning of the Wars, they shall be attached without harm of body or goods, until it be known unto us, or our Chief Justice, how our Merchants be intreated there in the land making War against us; and if our Merchants be well intreated there, theirs shall be likewise with us.

[31] If any man hold of any Eschete, as of the honour of Wallingford, Nottingham, Boloin, or of any other Eschetes which be in our hands, and are Baronies, and die, his Heir shall give none other Relief, nor do none other Service to us, than he should to the Baron, if it were in the Baron's hand. And we in the same wise shall hold it as the Baron held it; neither shall we have, by occasion of any such Barony or Eschete, any Eschete or keeping of any of our men, unless he that held the Barony or Eschete hold of us in chief.

[32] No Freeman from henceforth shall give or sell any more of his Land, but so that of the residue of the Lands the Lord of the Fee may have the Service due to him, which belongeth to the Fee.

[33] All Patrons of Abbies, which have the King's Charters of England of Advowson, or have old Tenure or Possession in the same, shall have the Custody of them when they fall void, as it hath been accustomed, and as it is afore declared.

[34] No Man shall be taken or imprisoned upon the Appeal of a Woman for the Death of any other, than of her husband.

[35] No County Court from henceforth shall be holden, but from Month to Month; and where greater time hath been used, there shall be greater: Nor any Sheriff, or his Bailiff, shall keep his Turn in the Hundred but twice in the Year; and nowhere but in due place, and accustomed; that is to say, once after Easter, and again after the Feast of St. Michael. And the View of Frankpledge shall be likewise at the Feast of St. Michael without occasion; so that every man may have his Liberties which he had, or used to have, in the time of King Henry our Grandfather, or which he hath purchased since: but the View of Frankpledge shall be so done, that our Peace may be kept; and that the Tything be wholly kept as it hath been accustomed; and that the Sheriff seek no Occasions, and that he be content with so much as the

Sheriff was wont to have for his Viewmaking in the time of King Henry our Grandfather.

[36] It shall not be lawful from henceforth to any to give his Lands to any Religious House, and to take the same Land again to hold of the same House. Nor shall it be lawful to any House of Religion to take the Lands of any, and to lease the same to him of whom he received it. If any from henceforth give his Lands to any Religious House, and thereupon be convict, the Gift shall be utterly void, and the Land shall accrue to the Lord of the Fee.

[37] Escuage from henceforth shall be taken like as it was wont to be in the time of King Henry our Grandfather; reserving to all Archbishops, Bishops, Abbots, Priors, Templers, Hospitallers, Earls, Barons, and all persons, as well Spiritual as Temporal, all their free liberties and free Customs, which they have had in time passed. And all these Customs and Liberties aforesaid, which we have granted to be holden within this our Realm, as much as appertaineth to us and our Heirs, we shall observe; and all Men of this our Realm, as well Spiritual as Temporal (as much as in them is) shall observe the same against all persons in like wise. And for this our Gift and Grant of these Liberties, and of other contained in our Charter of Liberties of our Forest, the Arch-

Glossary

Advowson	the right, in English ecclesiastical law, to nominate a person to fill a vacant benefice
contenement	property other than real estate necessary to maintaining one's present way of life
evil Tolts	excessive royal taxes
Five Ports	the confederation, established in 1155, of five towns in southeastern England located where the channel was narrowest, hence crossing to the Continent quickest
Guyan	old spelling of Guyenne, or Aquitaine
Haberjects	the materials from which chain mail was made
incontinent	person not under control; in this context, describing a woman not under the authority of a male relative or guardian
Justicer	person appointed to administer justice
King Henry our Grandfather	King Henry II of England
Lay-fee	debt owed to the Crown by a Crown tenant
Lord Henry ... King Henry our father	King Henry III of England
meer	pure
keep his Turn in the Hundred	hold court in the county
Viewmaking	the process of gathering and inspecting the men in the Frankpledge
villain	villein; a free common villager of the peasant class
wainage	vehicles a freeman needed to make a living
wears ... utterly put down	weirs taken down or removed
without Disparagement	without being assigned to a lower class

bishops, Bishops, Abbots, Priors, Earls, Barons, Knights, Freeholders, and other our Subjects, have given unto us the Fifteenth Part of all their Moveables. And we have granted unto them for us and our Heirs, that neither we, nor our Heirs shall procure or do anything whereby the Liberties in this Charter contained shall be infringed or broken; and if anything be procured by any person contrary to the premisses, it shall be had of no force nor effect. These being Witnesses; Lord B. Archbishop of Canterbury, E. Bishop of London, J. Bishop of Bathe, P. of Winchester, H. of Lincoln, R. of Salisbury, W. of Rochester, W. of Worester, J. of Ely, H. of Hereford, R. of Chichester, W. of Exeter, Bishops; the Abbot of St. Edmunds, the Abbot of St. Albans, the Abbot of Bello, the Abbot of St. Augustines in Canterbury, the Abbot of Evesham, the Abbot of Westminster, the Abbot of Bourgh St. Peter, the Abbot of Reading, the Abbot of Abindon, the Abbot of Malmsbury, the Abbot of Winchcomb, the Abbot of Hyde, the Abbot of Certefey, the Abbot of Sherburn, the Abbot of Cerne, the Abbot of Abbotebir, the Abbot of Middleton, the Abbot of Seleby, the Abbot of Cirencester; H. de Burgh Justice, H. Earl of Chester and Lincoln, W. Earl of Salisbury, W. Earl of Warren, G. de Clare Earl of Gloucester and Hereford, W. de Ferrars Earl of Derby, W. de Mandeville Earl of Essex, H. de Bygod Earl of Norfolk, W. Earl of Albermarle, H. Earl of Hereford, J. Constable of Chester, R. de Ros, R. Fitzwalter, R. de Vyponte, W. de Bruer, R. de Muntefichet, P. Fitzherbert, W. de Aubenie, F. Grefly, F. de Breus, J. de Monemue, J. Fitzallen, H. de Mortimer, W. de Beauchamp, W. de St. John, P. de Mauly, Brian de Lisle, Thomas de Multon, R. de Argenteyn, G. de Nevil, W. de Mauduit, J. de Balun, and others.

We, ratifying and approving these Gifts and Grants aforesaid, confirm and make strong all the same for us and our Heirs perpetually, and, by the Tenour of these Presents, do renew the same; willing and granting for us and our Heirs, that this Charter, and all and singular his Articles, for ever shall be stedfastly, firmly, and inviolably observed; although some Articles in the same Charter contained, yet hitherto peradventure have not been kept, we will, and by Authority Royal command, from henceforth firmly they be observed. In witness whereof we have caused these our Letters Patents to be made. T. Edward our Son at Westminster, the Twenty-eighth Day of March, in the Twenty-eighth Year of our Reign.

Boniface VIII's Clericis Laicos and Unam Sanctam

"It is altogether necessary to salvation for every human creature to be subject to the Roman pontiff."

Overview

Clericis laicos and Unam sanctam are examples of official letters, known as bulls, issued by a pope. Such a letter is called a "bull" because it is sealed with what is known in Latin as *bulla*—made of clay, wax, lead, or gold—which attests to the document's authenticity. The two papal bulls discussed here illustrate conflicting claims of power between the pope and kings of emerging European nation-states at the end of the thirteenth century, especially France and England. Pope Boniface VIII, King Philip IV (also known as Philip the Fair) of France, and King Edward I of England were among the figures involved.

The bull Clericis laicos was intended to prohibit kings from taxing the clergy in order to finance their wars. This prohibition so angered Philip IV that Boniface VIII subsequently issued another bull that allowed the French king to tax the clergy. However, Boniface was still displeased with the continued monarchal efforts to assert power over the clergy. Therefore, in 1302 he issued Unam sanctam, proclaiming that the pope possessed spiritual as well as temporal power over secular rulers and that submission to the office of the pope was necessary for salvation. Claims such as these would become lasting points of contention between future popes and secular rulers.

Context

Boniface VIII played an important role in effecting change in the balance of power between the papacy and the rulers of emerging European nation-states. When Boniface was born around 1235, nation-states were still in their infancy, and Catholic bishops held power in small feudal domains and fiefdoms across much of Europe. The spiritual authority of the papacy over secular rulers had been established when Pope Gregory VII had Holy Roman Emperor Henry IV submit to him at Canossa in 1077 after protracted power struggles. By the time Boniface was elected pope in 1294, though, papal power had already been much reduced. Papal supremacy had been established in

practice, through the accumulation of benefices (estates from which rents and other fees were paid to the clergy) and other property, as well as in theory, through the legal and theological writings of clergymen and friars such as Duns Scotus and Saint Thomas Aquinas. But with the rise of the Capetian kings in France, the royal house of Plantagenet in England, and the city-states and merchant class in Italy, secular power had increased, while the power of the clergy had begun to diminish. Expanding globalization in trade and international banking meant that resistance to papal authority would grow throughout the late 1290s and continue into the fourteenth century.

When Boniface VIII was elected pope in 1294, Philip IV had ruled France since 1285, Edward I had been king of England since 1272, and Adolf of Nassau had proclaimed himself Holy Roman Emperor–elect in 1292. James II (or Jaime II) had ruled the kingdom of Aragon in northeastern Spain since 1291, and Sancho IV would remain as sovereign of the Spanish kingdom of Castile until 1295, when Ferdinand IV ascended the throne under the regency of his mother. In all of these kingdoms were duchies, in which nobles vied for power, land, and wealth. Bishops and monasteries within these lands also held power, but the rapid growth of mendicant monastic orders—Franciscans and Dominicans, who lived in cities and survived by begging—was changing the face of the clergy. These kingdoms also had cardinals and other clergy who lived and worked at the Vatican. These clerics were not disinterested members of a politically neutral religious body; they all harbored strong ties to their homelands. There was thus a network of rivalries across Europe that was often manifested in political and religious power plays. All of the rulers mentioned were Christian, and although they proclaimed allegiance to the church, they were also keenly focused on protecting their own interests.

In 1294 Philip IV provoked a war with Edward I in order to reclaim Gascony (a region on the west coast of France near the Spanish border) from English control. Boniface VIII tried to arbitrate between the two monarchs, most likely because both of them had levied taxes on the clergy to raise funds for their war. The taxation had been met with resistance and appeals for help from the clergy to the pope, who responded by issuing Clericis laicos in 1296. In

CA. 1235

- Pope Boniface VIII is born Benedetto Caetani in Anagni, Italy.

1276

- Caetani is nominated papal notary by Pope Innocent V.

1281

- Caetani is made a cardinal deacon by Pope Martin IV.

1286

- **January 6** Philip IV is crowned king of France, after having ascended the throne following the death of his father, Philip III, in 1285.

1291

- Caetani is elevated to cardinal priest.

1294

- **December 24** Caetani is elected pope in Naples.

1295

- **January 23** Caetani is consecrated as Pope Boniface VIII in Rome.

1296

- **February 25** Clericis laicos is promulgated.

response to the bull, Philip prohibited the exportation of gold, silver, arms, and merchandise from France and prevented foreigners from working in his realm. This not only damaged England and Flanders—with whom France was at war—but also rallied Tuscan bankers and other Italian merchants against the papacy. Boniface realized the severity of potential financial damage and rescinded Clericis laicos by issuing a new bull (Ineffabilis amoris) that allowed Philip to tax the clergy as long as he requested the permission of the pope. This was not an entirely conciliatory move, as in the newly issued bull Boniface threatened to excommunicate Philip.

Threats went back and forth between Philip and Boniface throughout 1297. Boniface made further capitulations to Philip in two other bulls. (Etsi de statu and Ab olim ante) One allowed rulers to tax the clergy without papal consent as long as the clergy agreed to be taxed, and the other allowed rulers to determine the necessity of taxing the clergy without discussing the matter with the pope. In the latter bull, Boniface explained that at no time had he tried to lessen the rights of the kings or the secular powers within kingdoms. One scholar has suggested that the reason for Boniface's capitulation lay in the problems he had been facing within Italy from the noble Colonna family of Rome, a powerful rival of his own family, the Caetani. However, it seems that a combination of factors, not the least of which had been the economic hardship Philip had brought on with the embargo on exports, caused the pope to reconsider.

Tensions abated for a few years, and in 1300 Boniface declared the first Jubilee Year, which allowed for general pardon of sins upon pilgrimage to Rome. Pilgrims descended upon the city, and the event was seen as having been very successful. However, Philip had not given up in his determination to demonstrate his power. In 1301 he had the French bishop Bernard Saisset arrested, tried, and condemned on charges of heresy, blasphemy, and treason. Philip was deliberately provoking Boniface again, since in accordance with canon law only popes were allowed to put bishops on trial. When Philip requested papal approval of his actions, Boniface was incensed and demanded the release of Saisset. He further ordered the French bishops to attend a special council regarding religion in France that was to be held in Rome the following year. Boniface, who had been trained in law, was well aware that if he allowed Philip to set a precedent in trying Saisset, the future of papal power in France was grim. In order to demonstrate his spiritual authority over the king, he sent Philip a bull titled Ausculta fili, which translates as "Listen, My Son." When Philip received the bull, he was infuriated at Boniface's assertion that the king was subject to the pope. He responded by burning the bull and having his agents create missives, purportedly written by Boniface, in which the pope asserted his power over the king, as well as other letters attributed to Philip in which he denied papal authority. These forged letters enabled Philip to sway public opinion in his favor.

Philip called for a meeting of the Estates-General (an assembly that included the clergy, nobles, and the people) that took place in Paris in April 1302. This was the first meeting of the three tiers of society with representation from all levels, although various groups of nobles and clergy had convened before. At the meeting, it was declared that Boniface had attempted to assert power over France and should be declared a heretic. After the French cardinals in Rome received news from France that they should turn against Boniface, they informed the pope that they would prefer not to attend the upcoming council. Boniface then addressed the cardinals and denied that he had ever made the statements in the letters forged by Philip's advisers and attributed to him—but he added that he would not be averse to Philip's being removed from power.

When the council met in November 1302, over half of the French bishops did not attend, and no useful resolutions emerged from the meeting. Boniface then issued Unam sanctam. Although he made no specific reference in this bull to the problems he had with Philip, Boniface wanted to demonstrate that the unity of the church took precedence over temporal affairs. However, it seems likely that his unhappiness with the French bishops—who had obeyed the king instead of the pope—led him to issue Unam sanctam. Boniface must have been aware that the unity of the church would be endangered if bishops placed national sovereignty above ecclesiastical supremacy.

Philip and his minister, Guillaume de Nogaret, then accused the pope of having been a heretic, usurper, and criminal. In retaliation, Boniface decided to excommunicate Philip and then moved from Rome to his hometown, Anagni. With the help of Sciarra Colonna, of the powerful Colonna family, and his mercenaries, Nogaret besieged Boniface's palace, where he had been spending the summer of 1303. Nogaret and his soldiers entered the pope's home, where they found him, fully dressed in his papal robes, waiting for them. Various letters and histories claimed that they physically attacked Boniface and that he did not resist. However, Nogaret and Colonna delayed too long in deciding whether to try Boniface immediately, kill him, or bring him back to France. The pope's supporters in the area seized the opportunity to fight back and rescued him. Boniface returned to Rome, where he died shortly afterward.

About the Author

In about 1235 Pope Boniface VIII was born Benedetto Caetani in the town of Anagni, near Rome, a younger son of noble parents. His mother's ancestors included three previous popes. Since the laws of primogeniture meant that only his older brothers would inherit his parents' wealth and titles, Benedetto went into the church. He must have had private tutoring in history, Latin, and religion before he began to study law at the University of Bologna, the top school for legal studies at the time. At the age of twenty-five, he was appointed canon of the Cathedral of Todi, having already held a similar position in Anagni.

Caetani rose rapidly through the ranks of the church. In Paris in 1264 he served as the secretary to Cardinal Simon de Brie, who later became Pope Martin IV, and in 1265 he

Time Line

1297

- **July**
  Clericis laicos is rescinded by Etsi de statu.

1300

- Boniface VIII declares a Jubilee Year.

1302

- **November 18**
  Unam sanctum is promulgated.

1303

- Boniface VIII excommunicates Philip IV.

- **September 7**
  Troops led by Guillaume de Nogaret and Sciarra Colonna force their way into the palace of Boniface VIII in Anagni and take him prisoner.

- **September 9**
  The townspeople of Anagni rise up against Nogaret and his force, putting them to flight and freeing the pope.

- **October 11 or 12**
  Boniface VIII dies.

1310

- **March 16**
  Boniface VIII is tried posthumously for heresy by Pope Clement V at the instigation of Philip IV; the charge is abandoned, but Clement consents to repudiate the acts of Boniface that had injured Philip.

Time Line

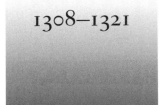

1308–1321

- Dante Alighieri includes Boniface VIII in the eighth circle of hell in *The Inferno*, the first part of his epic poem the *Divine Comedy*.

traveled to England in the capacity of secretary to Cardinal Ottobono Fieschi, the future Pope Adrian V. In England he was able to participate in negotiations between Henry III and the barons who were rebelling against his rule. In 1281 Pope Martin IV made Caetani a cardinal deacon. This meant that he could earn money from the benefices attached to the position, many of which were in France. When he was made cardinal priest on September 22, 1291, he gained yet more benefices in addition to those he already had. In a spirit of nepotism typical of the time, Caetani used his riches to promote his family, and this would later create problems for him. He also invested heavily in land to ensure the continued wealth and stability of his family, the longtime rival of the rich Colonna family.

Caetani's election as pope was marred by scandal. When Pope Nicolas IV died in 1292, the cardinals could not decide who should become pope, and the position remained vacant for two years. Finally, in 1294, Pietro da Morrone, a Benedictine hermit monk, was elected pope and chose the name Celestine V. Papal appointments were—and still are—for life, though at the time conclaves were held outside Rome. Celestine V was uncomfortable with the power and attention that the papacy brought him. After having been pope for only five months, he made the unprecedented decision to abdicate. Caetani was known for his legal skills and knowledge, and he helped the pope determine the validity of his decision. Subsequently, he would be accused of having facilitated the abdication of Celestine in order to serve his own interests. However, it has also been suggested that Celestine had requested the assistance of Caetani, a well-known expert in canon law.

In any event, Caetani did benefit from Celestine V's abdication. On December 24, 1294, he was elected pope in Naples. He left for Rome in early January, and on January 23 was led in procession to the Church of Saint John Lateran in Rome by King Charles II of Naples, and the king's son, Charles Martel (named after the famous eighth-century king). This action (which put the king and his son in a servile position) might be seen as foreshadowing Caetani's later assertions as Pope Boniface VIII of the spiritual power of the pope over the secular power of kings.

Before he left Naples, Boniface had ordered that Celestine be placed under the custody of the abbot of Monte Cassino and taken to Rome. He claimed that he was doing this for the protection of Celestine, whose abdication had created an uproar among the clergy and nobles. Celestine

escaped and went into hiding in his cave outside Sulmona. He was soon caught but managed to escape again, only to be apprehended a second time and taken to Boniface at his home in Anagni. The former pope was then confined to the Castle of Fumone near Anagni, where he died in 1296.

Authoritarian and stubborn, Boniface worked to consolidate the power of the papacy, in part to remove questions about the validity of his election after the unprecedented abdication of Celestine and in part to assert the rights of the pope over secular rulers. Personal motives also drove him, and his granting of land and offices to his nephews exacerbated the rivalry between his family and the powerful Roman noble family, the Colonnas. Boniface was also a noted patron of art and education. In 1303 he founded Studium Urbis, which later became Sapienza, the University of Rome.

Explanation and Analysis of the Document

Boniface VIII issued Clericis laicos on February 25, 1296, and Unam sanctam on November 18, 1302. The titles of the bulls come from their opening sentences; naming bulls thus was typical. "Clericis laicos" comes from the phrase "laymen are in a high degree hostile to the clergy" ("clericis laicos infestos oppido tradit antiquitas"), while "Unam sanctam" comes from "one holy catholic and apostolic church" ("unam sanctam ecclesiam catholicam"). Both bulls assert the supreme authority of the pope over secular rulers.

◆ Clericis laicos

The bull's opening statement about lay people's hostility toward the clergy is taken from the Decretum Gratiani (Decretals of Gratian, "decretals" being decrees in the form of papal letters), a document compiled by a monk named Gratian in about 1140. Prior to that time, canon law—the laws followed by the church—had not been uniform across Europe. In the Decretals, Gratian had attempted to codify and organize canon law along the lines of the Code of Justinian, which dated to 534. Justinian was a Byzantine Roman emperor who had codified Roman laws into the Corpus juris civilis as part of his attempt to revive the Roman Empire. The Code of Justinian became the basis for all secular Roman law and would later influence canon law. Boniface's allusion to the Decretals of Gratian about hostility toward the clergy has been seen as indicative of his "new inflexibility" and desire to have powers legalized that previously had been granted to the pope through "tacit consent" (Langlois, p. 35). In the introduction, Boniface refers to himself as bishop because one of his roles as pope was to act as the bishop of Rome. In the Catholic tradition, a bishop is in charge of a diocese, or a group of churches. Because Saint Peter, considered the first pope, was believed to have been the bishop of Rome, all subsequent popes have held this title.

Boniface issued the bull in part because Philip IV was taxing the clergy, who had agreed to pay at risk of offending him. In Clericis laicos, Boniface states that secular rulers should not levy taxes on the clergy without first asking his permission. However, it is important to note that although Boniface observes that some clergy had paid these taxes out of fear, many French clerics supported Philip out of loyalty to their king and were not in agreement with the pope.

In the next sentence, in which Boniface proclaims that "such iniquitous acts" as Philip's taxation of the clergy had to stop, he is careful to point out that this decree came not from him alone but was based on the "the counsel of our brothers, of the apostolic authority." This declaration was most likely included to forestall accusations of imperial behavior on Boniface's part, but it did not work, as the king and many of the clergy rebelled. His legal training is revealed in his careful listing of all the titles and types of members of religious orders no matter what their rank: "whatever prelates, or ecclesiastical persons, monastic or secular, of whatever grade, condition, or standing." This group included canons, cardinals, monks, and friars belonging to the recently formed mendicant orders of the Dominicans and Franciscans. The bull also lists all ranks of secular rulers: "emperors, kings or princes, dukes, counts or barons, podestas, captains, or officials or rectors—by whatever name they are called, whether of cities, castles, or any places whatever, wherever situated." This exhaustive catalog covered all of the political situations found in Christian Western Europe at that time. For example, France retained the feudal system in which dukes, counts, and barons held sway, while in Italy the landscape was divided between feudal and royal holdings in the south and newly formed city-states ruled by podestas, or magistrates, in the north.

Clericis laicos decrees that anyone involved in taxing the clergy at any level—whether by imposing the payments or collecting them and whether in the form of cash or goods—was to be held responsible and excommunicated. Boniface adds that anyone who dared to take church goods or money kept in the church treasury was also to be excommunicated. Likewise, clergy who paid these taxes were to be excommunicated. These were serious charges, indeed, as excommunication meant that one could no longer receive any of the sacraments of the church, which included remission of one's sins after making confession, partaking in Holy Communion, exchanging marriage vows, receiving last rites (administered to a person thought to be close to death), and burial in a Christian cemetery. Excommunication was a serious punishment for Christians, many of whom believed that salvation lay in participating in religious life.

The bull stipulates that "corporations, moreover, which shall be guilty in these matters" are to be placed "under the ecclesiastical interdict." Here Boniface was trying to alleviate the damage caused by Philip's decree in 1296 that currency and metals could not be exported from France. This embargo had seriously damaged the Vatican's ability to conduct business and engage in diplomacy.

The bull concludes with the threat of the wrath of God on anyone who would dare to counteract it: "Let no man at all, then, infringe this page of our constitution, prohibition or decree, or, with rash daring, act counter to it; but if any

Pope Boniface (© Bettmann/CORBIS)

one shall presume to attempt this, he shall know that he is about to incur the indignation of Almighty God and of His blessed apostles Peter and Paul." This passage has the flavor of a curse, which was not unusual for the times. By invoking the special relationship with God that he held as pope, Boniface was able to threaten both the clergy and the secular powers with a supernatural power whom none of them could command.

◆ Unam sanctam

The statements in Unam sanctam include quotations from the writings of Saint Bernard, Hugh of Saint Victor, and Saint Thomas Aquinas as well as scriptural quotations. In the first sentence, the phrase "we do firmly believe and simply confess—that there is one holy catholic and apostolic church" comes from the Apostle's Creed, which is recited during Mass. The phrase where the spouse proclaims, "My dove, my undefiled is but one, she is the choice one of her that bare her," is taken from the Song of Solomon 6:9; this verse has been interpreted as a paean to the church—which often is referred to as the spouse of Christ. Boniface's statement that "she [the church] is that seamless garment of the Lord which was not cut but which fell by lot" is a reference to the soldiers who gambled for Christ's clothes before the Crucifixion. All of these phrases would have been familiar to readers of the bull and those who heard it read aloud.

Boniface aroused antipapal sentiment with his commentary on the "two swords" and his proclamation that the pope holds both the secular and the spiritual swords. The quotation "put up the sword in its scabbard" comes from John 18:11 and Matthew 26:52. In these passages, Jesus is being arrested by the high priests. In an attempt to stop them, Peter cuts off the ear of a slave belonging to one of the priests. Jesus then tells Peter to put his sword away, as the Lord would have defended him if necessary. These passages assert the power of God—in Boniface's view, embodied in the office of the pope—over the actions of men. The implication is that God and the church have supremacy over secular rulers, who are meant to support the church by defending its territories and submitting to its greater authority. Likewise, the bull states that kings and military leaders should act only under the direction of priests, who in turn are subject to the will and rule of the pope.

Boniface's quotation of Saint Dionysius comes from *The Celestial Hierarchy*. This writing is now attributed to Dionysius the Pseudo-Areopagite, who lived during the fifth century CE, but in Boniface's time it was ascribed to Saint Dionysius (also known as Saint Denis), a Christian martyr who lived during the third century CE and was the first bishop of Paris. The epithet Pseudo-Areopagite comes from the biblical reference to Dionysius, a judge of Areopagus who questioned Saint Paul and was converted by him (Acts of the Apostles 17:34). *The Celestial Hierarchy* was influenced by Neoplatonism, a school of thought derived from Plato's writings. Dionysus the Pseudo-Areopagite believed that the celestial hierarchy was determined by God. In alluding to Dionysius's claim that "the law of divinity is to lead the lowest through the intermediate to the highest things," Boniface provides more evidence for his view of the supremacy of a spiritual leader.

Boniface's statement that "a spiritual man judges all things, but he himself is judged by no one" drew the most ire. According to Boniface, no one could judge the actions of the pope, whose power is divinely given. While this claim of spiritual authority had been tacitly understood and many

previous scholars had written on the topic, Boniface was the first to officially declare it in a bull. Although Boniface was accused of having been polemical in this bull, it has been noted that in many ways he was less adversarial than other theorists who were his contemporaries. Both Giles of Rome and James of Viterbo issued tracts dedicated to Boniface on the power of the church, and it has been suggested that they influenced him. Giles, an Augustinian monk, may have even had a hand in helping draft Unam sanctam, although he was close to Philip as well and also wrote tracts on the French king's behalf.

Audience

Addressed to all of Christendom, the bulls of Boniface VIII were also intended to speak specifically to Philip IV of France and his advisers, including Guillaume de Nogaret, who was opposed to the pope; Edward I; and all other rulers who thought to resist the pope. A papal bull was sent in numerous manuscript copies to secular rulers and all members of the clergy. During church services it was read aloud to the general public, most of whom were illiterate. Boniface also intended Clericis laicos to be read by canonists (those who studied and wrote on canon law), since he included it in the Liber sextus decretalium of 1298, a collection of decretals that was sent out to universities with the requirement that it be used in the study of canon law. This inclusion ensured that it would be taught to students and, more important, that future clerics would submit to the pope rather than to secular rulers.

Impact

Boniface VIII's reputation in history was damaged by the two bulls Clericis laicos and Unam sanctam, both of which asserted the supremacy of the pope and church over secular rulers. Dante Alighieri alluded to Boniface's infamy in the *Inferno*, the first part of his epic poem the *Divine Comedy*, when Pope Nicolas III, after having been confined to the eighth circle of hell (a realm reserved for simoniacs, or those who had paid for ecclesiastical positions) remarked that a space would also be reserved there for Boniface. Notwithstanding his reputation, it is important to note that Boniface canceled Clericis laicos in July 1297 by issuing another bull (Etsi de statu) so that Philip IV could collect taxes from the clergy. Boniface's successor, Pope Clement V, canceled Unam sanctam in order to placate Philip.

The promulgation of Clericis laicos and Unam sanctam had serious repercussions for the relationship between secular rulers and the papacy. Power struggles between popes and Christian kings continued for generations afterward. The resistance of Philip IV to the policies advanced in Clericis laicos might be seen as presaging King Henry VIII's rejection of Pope Clement VII's refusal to validate his divorce and recognize his second marriage. Martin Luther, though he was a clergyman, rejected the claims of Pope Leo X for lay people to fund the church. Boniface VIII's declaration of papal superiority over the entire Christian world—especially in economic terms—was unpopular and thus sowed the seeds of dissent for future arguments with secular rulers. His claim of Christian superiority allowed rulers to justify the invasion and conquest of non-Christian lands. The fiscal separation of church and state is still observed in many countries, with religious groups remaining exempt from governmental taxation.

Boniface's issuance of these bulls signaled a point of change from the medieval to the early modern era; his term as pope marked the end of claims of papal supremacy based on spiritual authority. Philip did not yield to the authority of God as embodied in the office of the pope, as Henry IV had done earlier at Canossa, but instead asserted his political power and attempted to stem papal power within his territories. Boniface's bull forbidding the taxation of clergy was nothing new, but the resistance of secular powers and Philip's success in compelling the pope to capitulate was novel and would have lasting repercussions on political and religious life.

Further Reading

■ Books

Izbicki, Thomas M. "Clericis laicos and the Canonists." In *Popes, Teachers, and Canon Law in the Middle Ages*, eds. James Ross Sweeney and Stanley Chodorow. Ithaca, N.Y.: Cornell University Press, 1989.

Luscombe, David. "The Lex divinitatis in the Bull Unam sanctam of Pope Boniface VIII." In *Church and Government in the Middle Ages: Essays Presented to C. R. Cheney on His 70th Birthday*, ed. Christopher Brooke, et al. New York: Cambridge University Press, 1976.

Questions for Further Study

1. To modern readers, the disputes between the papacy and secular rulers in the thirteenth and fourteenth centuries—marked by scandal, taxation of the clergy, warfare, the besieging of a pope's home, accusations of heresy, and the like—seem unthinkable. What religious, cultural, and historical factors allowed these kinds of events to happen?

2. What role did Pope Boniface VIII play in the ultimate transition from medievalism to modernism, specifically in the emergence of more modern, secular nation-states?

3. Compare this document with the Rock and Pillar Edicts of Aśoka, written in the third century BCE in India. How do the two documents differ in terms of the attitude they express to religion and the spiritual welfare of the people the documents affected? Why do you think these differences existed?

4. Read this document in conjunction with the Capitulary of Charlemagne, the Domesday Book, the Constitutions of Clarendon, the Magna Carta, and Martin Luther's *Ninety-five Theses*. Trace the development of the position and role of the Catholic Church and the relationship between ecclesiastical and secular power in western Europe.

5. Major historical figures often become mere names in history books, but modern readers should remind themselves that they were actual people. In what sense was Boniface VIII a real-life human figure? Put differently, how did his background and temperament influence his attitude to the papacy? How might history have evolved differently had Boniface been a different type of person?

Mastnak, Tomaž. *Crusading Peace: Christendom, the Muslim World, and Western Political Order*. Berkeley: University of California Press, 2002.

Muldoon, James. "Boniface VIII as Defender of Royal Power: Unam Sanctam as a Basis for the Spanish Conquest of the Americas." In *Popes, Teachers, and Canon Law in the Middle Ages*, eds. James Ross Sweeney and Stanley Chodorow. Ithaca, N.Y.: Cornell University Press, 1989.

Tierney, Brian. *The Crisis of Church and State, 1050–1300*. Toronto: University of Toronto Press, 1988.

Tierney, Brian, and Sidney Painter. *Western Europe in the Middle Ages, 300–1475*. 6th ed. New York: McGraw-Hill, 1999.

■ **Web Sites**

"Pope Boniface VIII." New Advent "Catholic Encyclopedia" Web site. http://www.newadvent.org/cathen/02662a.htm.

"Unam Sanctam." New Advent "Catholic Encyclopedia" Web site. http://www.newadvent.org/cathen/15126a.htm.

"Clericis Laicos." New Advent "Catholic Encyclopedia" Web site. http://www.newadvent.org/cathen/04050b.htm.

—M. Callahan

BONIFACE VIII's CLERICIS LAICOS AND UNAM SANCTAM

Clericis Laicos

Bishop Boniface, servant of the servants of God, in perpetual memory of this matter.

Antiquity teaches us that laymen are in a high degree hostile to the clergy, a fact which also the experiences of the present times declare and make manifest; inasmuch as, not content within their own bounds, they strive after what is forbidden, and loose the reins in pursuit of what is unlawful. Nor have they the prudence to consider that all jurisdiction is denied them over the clergy—over both the persons and the goods of ecclesiastics. On the prelates of the churches and on ecclesiastical persons, monastic and secular, they impose heavy burdens, tax them and declare levies upon them. They exact and extort from them the half, the tenth or twentieth or some other portion or quota of their revenues or of their goods; and they attempt in many ways to subject them to slavery and reduce them to their sway. And, with grief do we mention it, some prelates of the churches and ecclesiastical persons, fearing where they ought not to fear, seeking a transitory peace, dreading more to offend the temporal than the eternal majesty, without obtaining the authority or permission of the apostolic chair, do acquiesce, not so much rashly, as improvidently, in the abuses of such persons. We, therefore, wishing to put a stop to such iniquitous acts, by the counsel of our brothers, of the apostolic authority, have decreed: that whatever prelates, or ecclesiastical persons, monastic or secular, of whatever grade, condition, or standing, shall pay, or promise, or agree to pay as levies or talliages to laymen the tenth, twentieth, or hundredth part of their own and their churches' revenues of goods—or any other quantity, portion or quota of those same revenues or goods, of their estimated or of their real value—under the name of an aid, loan, subvention, subsidy or gift, or under any other name, manner or clever pretence, without the authority of that same chair: likewise emperors, kings or princes, dukes, counts or barons, podestas, captains, or officials or rectors – by whatever name they are called, whether of cities, castles, or any places whatever, wherever situated; and any other persons, of whatever pre-eminence, condition or standing who shall impose, exact or receive such payments, or shall anywhere arrest, seize or presume to take posses-

sion of the belongings of churches or ecclesiastical persons which are deposited in the sacred buildings, or shall order them to be arrested, seized or taken possession of, or shall receive them when taken possession of, seized or arrested—also all who shall knowingly give aid, counsel or favour in the aforesaid things, whether publicly or secretly:—shall incur, by the act itself, the sentence of excommunication. Corporations, moreover, which shall be guilty in these matters, we place under the ecclesiastical interdict. The prelates and above-mentioned ecclesiastical persons we strictly command, by virtue of their obedience and under penalty of deposition, that they by no means acquiesce in such demands, without express permission of the aforesaid chair; and that they pay nothing under pretext of any obligation, promise and confession made hitherto, or to be made hereafter before such constitution, notice or decree shall come to their notice; nor shall the aforesaid secular persons in their way receive anything. And if they shall pay, or if the aforesaid persons shall receive, they shall fall by the act itself under sentence of excommunication. From the aforesaid sentences of excommunication and interdict, moreover, no one shall be able to be absolved, except in the throes of death, without the authority and special permission of the apostolic chair; since it is our intention by no means to pass over with dissimulation so horrid an abuse of the secular powers. Notwithstanding any privileges whatever—under whatever tenor, form, or manner or conception of words—that have been granted to emperors, kings, and other persons mentioned above; as to which privileges we will that, against what we have here laid down, they in no wise avail any person or persons. Let no man at all, then, infringe this page of our constitution, prohibition or decree, or, with rash daring, act counter to it; but if any one shall presume to attempt this, he shall know that he is about to incur the indignation of Almighty God and of His blessed apostles Peter and Paul.

Given at Rome at St. Peter's on the sixth day before the Calends of March [February 25] in the second year of our pontificate.

◆ Unam Sanctam

We are compelled, our faith urging us, to believe and to hold—and we do firmly believe and simply confess—

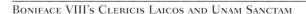

that there is one holy catholic and apostolic church, outside of which there is neither salvation nor remission of sins; her Spouse proclaiming it in the canticles: "My dove, my undefiled is but one, she is the choice one of her that bare her"; which represents one mystic body, of which body the head is Christ; but of Christ, God. In this church there is one Lord, one faith and one baptism. There was one ark of Noah, indeed at the time of the flood, symbolizing one church; and this being finished in one cubit had, namely, one Noah as helmsman and commander. And, with the exception of this ark, all things existing upon the earth were, as we read, destroyed. This church, moreover, we venerate as the only one, the Lord saying through his prophet: "Deliver my soul from the sword, my darling from the power of the dog." He prayed at the same time for His soul, that is, for Himself the Head—and for His body,—which body, namely, he called the one and only church on account of the unity of the faith promised, of the sacraments, and of the love of the church. She is that seamless garment of the Lord which was not cut but which fell by lot. Therefore of this one and only church there is one body and one head—not two heads as if it were a monster:—Christ, namely, and the vicar of Christ, St. Peter, and the successor of Peter. For the Lord Himself said to Peter, Feed my sheep. My sheep, he said, using a general term, and not designating these or those particular sheep; form which it is plain that He committed

to Him all His sheep. If, then, the Greeks or others say that they were not committed to the care of Peter and his successors, they necessarily confess that they are not of the sheep of Christ; for the Lord says, in John, that there is one fold, one shepherd, and one only. We are told by the word of the gospel that in this His fold there are two swords,—a spiritual, namely, and a temporal. For when the apostles said "Behold here are two swords"—when, namely, the apostles were speaking in the church—the Lord did not reply that this was too much, but enough. Surely he who denies that the temporal sword is in the power of Peter wrongly interprets the word of the Lord when He says: "Put up the sword in its scabbard." Both swords, the spiritual and the material, therefore, are in the power of the church; the one, indeed, to be wielded for the church, the other by the church; the one by the hand of the priest, the other by the hand of the kings and knights but at the will and sufferance of the priest. One sword, moreover, ought to be under the other, and the temporal authority to be subjected to the spiritual. For when the apostle says "there is no power but of God, and the powers that are of God are ordained," they would not be ordained unless sword were under sword and the lesser one, as it were, were led by the other to great deeds. For according to St. Dionysius the law of divinity is to lead the lowest through the intermediate to the highest things. Not therefore, according to the law

apostolic chair	the sitting pope
being finished in one cubit	an allusion to the eighteen inches (one cubit), cited as the height of Noah's ark above the waterline in Genesis 6:16
canticles	chapters in the biblical book entitled Canticle of Canticles (more often known as Song of Solomon); in the time of Boniface, Christians interpreted the passage quoted as an allegory of the love of Christ for the church
her Spouse	Christ
his prophet	King David, to whom the verse that follows (Psalm 22:20) is credited
prophecy of Jeremiah	quotation truncated from Jeremiah 1:10, "seamless garment of the Lord … " (see John 19:23–24)
successor of Peter	the sitting pope
talliages	tallages, the levies just referred to
the apostle says "there is no power but of God,…"	the apostle Paul, in Romans 13:1

of the universe, are all things reduced to order equally and immediately; but the lowest through the intermediate, the intermediate through the higher. But that the spiritual exceeds any earthly power in dignity and nobility we ought the more openly to confess the more spiritual things excel temporal ones. This also is made plain to our eyes from the giving of tithes, and the benediction and the sanctification; from the acceptation of this same power, from the control over those same things. For, the truth bearing witness, the spiritual power has to establish the earthly power, and to judge it if it be not good. Thus concerning the church and the ecclesiastical power is verified the prophecy of Jeremiah: "See, I have this day set thee over the nations and over the kingdoms," and the other things which follow. Therefore if the earthly power err it shall be judged by the spiritual power; but if the lesser spiritual power err, by the greater. But if the greatest, it can be judged by God alone, not by

man, the apostle bearing witness. A spiritual man judges all things, but he himself is judged by no one. This authority, moreover, even though it is given to man and exercised through man, is not human but rather divine, being given by divine lips to Peter and founded on a rock for him and his successors through Christ himself whom he has confessed; the Lord himself saying to Peter: "Whatsoever thou shall bind," etc. Whoever, therefore, resists this power thus ordained by God, resists the ordination of God, unless he makes believe, like the Manichean, that there are two beginnings. This we consider false and heretical, since by the testimony of Moses, not "in the beginnings," but "in the beginning" God created the heavens and the earth. Indeed we declare, announce and define, that it is altogether necessary to salvation for every human creature to be subject to the Roman pontiff.

The Lateran, Nov. 14, in our 8th year. As a perpetual memorial of this matter.

Bust of Marco Polo (AP/Wide World Photos)

MARCO POLO'S DESCRIPTION OF HANGZHOU

"The city of Kinsay has some 3000 baths, the water of which is supplied by springs."

Overview

The Travels of Marco Polo was dictated by Marco Polo to his cellmate Rustichello da Pisa, an Arthurian romance writer, while they were in a prison in Genoa, Italy, in about 1298. It details the approximately twenty-four years (including travel time) that Polo and his father and uncle spent in China working for Kublai Khan, the Mongol emperor during China's Yuan Dynasty (1279–1368). Historians contest whether Polo actually visited all the locales that he wrote about, and the reader cannot be sure which parts of the book are in his voice and which represent Rustichello's embellishments or various copyists' additions or revisions. There are approximately 150 slightly differing versions, none of which is the certified original version. The consensus, however, is that Polo did work as a tax collector and administrator for Kublai Khan, while his numerous visits to and enthusiastic description of Kinsay (modern-day Hangzhou, China) are not parts of the book that engender historical criticism. Polo's description of Kinsay is the longest and most famous chapter in the book, representing about 4 percent of the total.

The fact that there is no certified original manuscript of the book Polo dictated to Rustichello presents various problems of verification. The book was subsequently copied, recopied, translated, and retranslated numerous times, with additions and changes depending on the whims of the copyists and the beliefs of the times. Of the remaining 150 manuscripts, reportedly no two are identical. Scholars have divided the manuscripts into Group A, which are believed to be closest to the original version dictated in prison, and Group B, which feature many additions and occasional omissions and were probably recorded sometime after Polo returned from Genoa to Venice. In other chapters of the book, Polo describes various wonders of China, including the Yangtze River (now called the Chang River), which he calls the largest in the world. It is, in fact, the third largest in the world, but it is highly unlikely that he had heard of the Amazon or Nile rivers. Regardless of these discrepancies, Polo's extensive narrative of Hangzhou is a positive and admiring description of a large, well-organized, and prosperous Chinese city.

Context

Marco Polo was not the first Christian European traveler to write a book about Kublai Khan and China during the Yuan Dynasty. Friar Giovanni da Pian del Carpini, a contemporary of Polo's, was sent by Pope Innocent IV to meet with the Mongols (referred to as the Tartars) to analyze their military power as well as to convert them to Christianity. He wrote *The Story of the Mongols Whom We Call the Tartars* in about 1248, although very few medieval Europeans ever read his book. Later, in May 1330, the Franciscan missionary Odorico da Pordenone wrote that during his stay in China he visited Quinsai (another variant spelling for Hangzhou), which he described as the largest city in all the world. In certain respects these and other accounts are in contrast with the extremely popular *Travels of Marco Polo*, which was copied and recopied by hand in the time before the invention of the European printing press.

The predominant Christian sect in China and western Asia during Polo's time was the Nestorian Christians. In the fifth century, Nestorius, the Greek patriarch of Constantinople, was condemned as a heretic by the Greek and Latin Catholic churches. This condemnation was the result of his belief that the Virgin Mary should be considered the "mother of Christ" instead of the "mother of God." He and his followers established churches in the Middle East, central Asia, and Africa, and by the eighth century there were Nestorian churches in Turkestan and China. Some historians speculate that it may have been along the caravan routes of Asia that in 1141 the victories of a ruler of the partially Christianized Khitans (from the north of China) over a Muslim king and a Seljuk sultan started the tales of Prester John. Prester John was rumored to be a rich and successful Christian king, who in some stories was able to defeat Muslims and in some stories was able to live peacefully with Muslims. From the twelfth to the seventeenth centuries in Europe the legends of Prester John inspired papal missions as well as individual and group treks in search of this mythical Christian king who was imagined in many different places, including India, central Asia, China, and Africa.

China's Yuan Dynasty was founded by Kublai Khan, grandson of the Mongol leader Genghis Khan. Genghis

1122

- A man claiming to be Patriarch John of India arrives in Rome asking for papal confirmation of his office.

BEFORE 1180

- *Letter of Prester John*, a romance tale supposedly written to the Byzantine emperor Manuel I Comnenus, reaches Rome.

1206

- Genghis Khan, called Temüjin at the time, unites the nomadic tribes that come to be referred to as the Mongols.

1237

- The Mongols first invade Europe, where they are called the Tartars.

1245

- **April 16** Friar Giovanni da Pian del Carpini leaves Lyon, France, at Pope Innocent IV's command to meet with the Tartars (Mongols).

CA. 1248

- On his return from China, Friar Giovanni writes *The Story of the Mongols Whom We Call the Tartars.*

Khan was able to conquer the northern part of China, but it was not until 1279 that Kublai Khan conquered the southern part of China as well and fully established the Yuan Dynasty. During this dynasty, the Mongol administration of the Han Chinese was something less than beneficent. Han Chinese constitute 91 percent of the population of China today, and during the time of Kublai Khan they likewise vastly outnumbered the Mongols. The Mongols did not trust the Han Chinese and turned to fellow Mongols and non-Chinese, including Muslims and outsiders from central Asia, the Middle East, and even Europe— among them Polo and his father and uncle—to fill important governmental posts. This was one reason, apart from the trade opportunities offered by the vast and rich country, that Polo and his family spent almost a quarter century in China. China was more advanced than Europe in many ways during Polo's time. Most Europeans had not heard of paper money or of burning coal for heat, and they dressed in rough homespun clothing in contrast to the silks and finery of many of the Chinese. Among other achievements, Kublai Khan's Yuan Dynasty accomplished one of the hallmarks of a successful Chinese dynasty, upkeep of and improvements to the Grand Canal (or Da Yunhe) between Beijing and Hangzhou, the city described using the name of Kinsay in *The Travels of Marco Polo.*

Debate continues even to the present day about whether Polo truly was a traveler to the court of Kublai Khan or was merely a teller of tall tales and merchant stories who never made it to China. The few historians who disbelieve that Polo visited China cite several of his omissions, including his lack of reference to the Great Wall, to using chopsticks, to drinking tea, or to Chinese women's bound feet. He also fails to mention fishing with cormorants, Chinese characters, acupuncture, or Confucianism. In turn, there are no Chinese sources referring to Marco Polo. Still, the vast majority of historians believe that Polo did spend time in China and that the Mongol Yuan Dynasty's propensity to mistrust Han Chinese made him valuable as a trusted administrator who yet may not have had a great deal of contact with the Han Chinese who bound their daughters' feet, ate with chopsticks, and drank tea.

About the Author

Marco Polo is the author of his travel accounts, while Rustichello da Pisa is the Arthurian romance writer and scribe who wrote down and probably embellished what Polo dictated. The two jointly produced *The Travels of Marco Polo*, sometimes referred to by the title *Description of the World*. Rustichello is given credit for making the text more acceptable and readable for medieval audiences. Rustichello was born in Pisa, Tuscany, in western Italy sometime in the late thirteenth century and spent time in France as an adult. He was famous as a romance writer before he met Marco Polo, having written a romance about King Arthur in a mixture of French and Italian. It is believed that he was captured by the Genoese at the Battle of Meloria in 1284, during a conflict between the Republic of Genoa and his native Pisa.

Marco Polo was born in Venice in about 1254, the son of a Venetian merchant, Niccolò Polo, who had traveled to central Asia and then to China with his brother Maffeo Polo. After they returned to Venice and picked up the seventeen-year-old Marco, they spent about three years traveling to China, where Marco Polo served in Kublai Khan's court for the next two decades while traveling extensively in different parts of China and beyond. When the three returned to Venice in 1295, Marco Polo was forty-one, having spent the majority of his adult life in China. Historians believe it was in about 1298 that Polo was taken prisoner by the Genoese, who were then at war with the Venetians, stemming from the historic trade rivalry between the two cities. Scholars believe that as a Venetian, Polo was captured by the Genoese during the naval Battle of Curzola. Polo was released from prison in 1299 and returned to Venice. He married and had three daughters and continued as a successful merchant, but he did not leave Venice again before he died in 1324.

Explanation and Analysis of the Document

The Travels of Marco Polo ranges as widely as the terrain Polo covered in his journeys—from the modern-day Middle East to India to China (for which he uses the name "Cathay"). He discusses the history of the Mongols, with particular emphasis on Kublai Khan (whom he calls the "Great Kaan") and his court (as well as his own place in it) and describes the many regions and provinces he visited. In Chapters 76 and 77 of the fourth part of the *Travels*, he focuses on the city of Hangzhou, referred to as "Kinsay" at the time.

◆ **Chapter 76: Description of the Great City of Kinsay, Which Is the Capital of the Whole Country of Manzi**

From the beginning, Polo is very complimentary of Kinsay, which he refers to as the "City of Heaven," and of the Chinese living there. His respect for Kublai Khan is shown in his reference to the "Great Kaan" and in his entreating Kublai not to destroy the beauty of the city. Historians believe that Polo made notes for this chapter shortly after the Mongols conquered Kinsay. He encourages Kublai Khan to avoid undue destruction, since the residents are sophisticated, rich, and peaceful; do not bear arms; and represent more of a financial boon to the Mongols than any type of threat.

According to a document that was written by the "Queen of this Realm" (a captive princess of the Song Dynasty, taken from Hangzhou to the Kublai Khan's court) and which Polo relies on, the city of Kinsay is said to be one hundred miles in circumference with twelve thousand bridges of stone. This description, in the third paragraph, is no doubt an exaggeration. However, Kinsay was indeed a very large city, perhaps the largest in the world at that time, and many historians believe his description is standard

Time Line	
1253	■ Genghis Khan's grandson Kublai Khan begins to take over China.
CA. **1254**	■ Marco Polo is born in Venice.
1271	■ **April** At age seventeen, Polo begins his journey to China along with his father, Niccolò, and uncle Maffeo.
CA. **1275**	■ The Polos arrive in China.
1279	■ Kublai Khan takes over the southern part of China, fully establishing the first alien dynasty of China, the Yuan Dynasty.
1295	■ Having been gone for twenty-four years, the Polos reach Venice on their return journey from China.
1298	■ Marco Polo is imprisoned in Genoa and there dictates an account of his travels in China to Rustichello da Pisa.

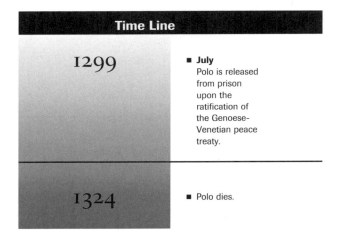

medieval verbiage for a very large city with many bridges. Others see the figure of one hundred miles as an inaccurate inequivalent to one hundred Chinese *li*, a measure actually equal to about a third of a mile. Kinsay certainly had many bridges, which were often very high so that large Chinese barges could pass underneath. Hangzhou is situated at the end of the Grand Canal, and historians speculate that part of Polo's attraction to the city is based on his childhood in Venice with its many canals and bridges.

Polo writes in paragraphs 4 and 5 of successful tradesmen and craftsmen organized in guilds and of merchants who have become very wealthy. Such persons would have been important to the Polos, since they themselves were merchants and did business in China; also, in working for Kublai Khan, traveling where assigned and bringing back detailed reports of the various sights, Polo would have been accustomed to recording such societal particulars. The Chinese women of Kinsay receive special attention from Polo, who describes them as dainty, angelic, and beautiful, wearing an abundance of silk.

In modern times, West Lake in Hangzhou is considered one of the most beautiful parts of China, and Polo writes expansively of it, with its beautiful palaces and mansions. Polo gives the non-Christian, Buddhist Chinese—whom he calls "Idolaters"—credit for their beautiful temples around West Lake. In the medieval Western mind, any religion other than Christianity, especially one featuring the worship of idols such as a statue of the Buddha, would have been considered a practice of idolaters.

The only openly critical aspect of this chapter is the reference to the dining habits of the Chinese, who Polo says persist in eating "dogs and other unclean beasts" that a Christian would never consume. Medieval Europeans wrote frequently about their pet dogs and the loyalty and love that these pets offer. Eating dog has never been a part of European cuisine, so it is not surprising that Polo would denounce the habit. Polo also reports in paragraph 8 that the Chinese in Kinsay use paper money—which was not in use in medieval Europe at the time—since Kublai Khan has control of the city and paper money is mandated by the Mongols. From Polo's description, Hangzhou is evidently a

city that has a curfew, is under careful military control, and offers protection from fire.

Polo mentions richly endowed state hospitals, where the authorities take "poor cripples" to stay; alternatively, they find work for them if they are able to work. By contrast, medieval European hospitals were often religious institutions that were part of monasteries, staffed by monks and nuns. Some medieval European hospitals were independent, with their own land endowments; others were leper sanatoriums or hospitals for the poor. Still others operated as hostels for travelers or religious pilgrims or homes for the elderly, the mentally ill, the lame and the blind.

Historians speculate that Polo's role for Kublai Khan was to inspect provinces and collect taxes. He describes in paragraph 12 that Kublai pays special attention to Hangzhou because of the size of the city and the volume of its trade, which makes it a very profitable part of the empire. He writes later that Kinsay is a city with many hot baths, leading to another positive assessment of the Han Chinese, whom he calls "very cleanly in their persons." In medieval Europe, while there were a few communal baths, plumbing was neither advanced nor sophisticated, and Europeans were not easily able to bathe regularly.

Speaking as a merchant (beginning in paragraph 15), Polo notes the proximity of Kinsay to the ocean and the large volume of shipping to and from India and the rest of the world. Medieval trade routes were dominated by Venice and Genoa at the time, and silk and spices topped the list of desired trading goods from the Far East and Southeast Asia. While Polo was working for Kublai Khan, his uncle and father continued to trade within China, and they became very wealthy during their time there. The nine kingdoms of Manzi to which Polo refers included all Chinese territory south of the Yellow River and in the West today's Shaanxi Province. Polo describes this territory as vast, with more than twelve hundred cities, each with its own garrison.

Polo makes special notice in paragraph 18 of the Chinese attachment to astrology, a practice that was important in Europe at this time as well. In Chinese astrology, the twelve animal signs are based on the moon's phases as recorded through a lunisolar calendar, as opposed to the solar calendar of the West. Polo refers in paragraph 19 to the Buddhist practice of cremation and the associated funeral ceremonies. In Europe, bodies were not cremated. From the seventh century, burial was a Christian church function. Most bodies of the poor were buried in mass graves, and after decomposition, the bones were dug up and stored along the walls of the graveyard or within the church under the floors or behind the walls. The rich could afford their own crypts. Polo speaks of the Chinese custom of burning paper money for the dead, a practice that many Chinese still follow today.

In paragraph 21, Polo describes the "palace of the king who fled"— the thirteenth-century Song Dynasty Emperor Duzong, who fled when Kublai Khan and the Mongols invaded. There is no evidence today that the "greatest palace in the world," which had a "compass of ten miles" and "20 great and handsome halls," still stands. Polo also

Portuguese translation of 1502 version of Marco Polo's travels in China (AP/Wide World Photos)

briefly mentions the only Christian church in the city, that of the Nestorian Christians.

Polo the tax collector certainly appreciated that the population of the city was carefully counted, with the names of entire families and their slaves listed above the front doors of homes and with guests being registered for stays at inns. This was another element of control by the Khan; hostelers were required to keep detailed records of their guests, such that the movements of people could be monitored.

◆ Chapter 77: Further Particulars concerning the Great City of Kinsay

Polo opens this chapter by again extolling the beauty of the lake, speaking of the system of canals that serves as a sewer system to "carry away all impurities." The canals are large enough that one is able to travel the city via canal as well as on the streets. He devotes two paragraphs to the "vast number" of markets, supplied by "merchants from India and other foreign parts." On market days, held three times a week, an "ample supply" of game is available to the city—ranging from roebuck to rabbit to quail. In para-

graphs 4 and 5 he writes enthusiastically of the fresh fruits and vegetables and the fish from the sea. "Owing to the impurities of the city which pass through the lake," he says, the fish is "remarkably fat and savory."

Polo is especially fascinated with the women of Hangzhou, beautifully attired and "abundantly perfumed." He writes that they are also practiced in the "arts of allurement"; male visitors are so bewitched by them that they when they return home, they say that they have been to the "City of Heaven." By contrast, women in medieval Europe were often defined religiously, in their devotion to the Virgin Mary, or in chivalrous terms, by being placed on a pedestal.

Other sections of the city are occupied, Polo tells us, by doctors and astrologers, among other professionals. Chinese astrologers were greatly admired for the depth of their knowledge and were the "teachers of reading and writing." They devised detailed charts for prediction of the future, calculating auspicious days to marry, start a new business, build a new home, and so on. In his description of the neighborhoods and squares of the city, Polo impresses the reader with the size of the city. He uses the sale of huge quantities of

"Within the city there is an eminence on which stands a Tower, and at the top of the tower is hung a slab of wood. Whenever fire or any other alarm breaks out in the city a man who stands there with a mallet in his hand beats upon the slab, making a noise that is heard to a great distance. So when the blows upon this slab are heard, everybody is aware that fire has broken out, or that there is some other cause of alarm."

(Chapter 76, Paragraph 11)

"You must know also that the city of Kinsay has some 3000 baths, the water of which is supplied by springs. They are hot baths, and the people take great delight in them, frequenting them several times a month, for they are very cleanly in their persons. They are the finest and largest baths in the world; large enough for 100 persons to bathe together."

(Chapter 76, Paragraph 14)

"They burn the bodies of the dead.... And when they come to the burning place, they take representations of things cut out of parchment, such as caparisoned horses, male and female slaves, camels, armour suits of cloth of gold (and money), in great quantities, and these things they put on the fire along with the corpse, so that they are all burnt with it."

(Chapter 76, Paragraph 19)

"The position of the city is such that it has on one side a lake of fresh and exquisitely clear water (already spoken of), and on the other a very large river. The waters of the latter fill a number of canals of all sizes which run through the different quarters of the city, carry away all impurities, and then enter the Lake; whence they issue again and flow to the Ocean, thus producing a most excellent atmosphere."

(Chapter 77, Paragraph 1)

"These women are extremely accomplished in all the arts of allurement, and readily adapt their conversation to all sorts of persons, insomuch that strangers who have once tasted their attractions seem to get bewitched, and are so taken with their blandishments and their fascinating ways that they never can get these out of their heads."

(Chapter 77, Paragraph 7)

pepper to illustrate the immense extent of Hangzhou, saying that the daily consumption of pepper amounted to forty-three loads, each load made up of 223 pounds. Historians speculate that Hangzhou had between one million and two million people in the thirteenth century.

Polo comments that the inhabitants of the city are peaceful and that they are honest in their commercial dealings. If, as he reports, residents of Hangzhou treat foreigners very well, one can understand his fondness for returning to the city. Indeed, he ends his description of the city by returning to the lake and reporting on the recreational "parties of pleasure" that take place on barges of all sizes. From the lake, he points out, one can take in the whole city, "in its full beauty and grandeur, with its numberless palaces, temples, monasteries, and gardens."

Audience

The Travels of Marco Polo was written for the Christian European medieval audience to learn of the glories of the great Kublai Khan and the wonders of Asia and China. The medieval Christian mind is fascinating to historians, who describe it as being wrapped around biblical influences, recurring stories of Alexander the Great and his exploits, stories of Saint Thomas the Apostle traveling to India, and the legend of Prester John. Even though there were various travel writers prior to Marco Polo, many of them were Islamic and writing with an emphasis on Muslim trade with Asia, and practically none of their books or tales were read by Europeans before Polo's book found widespread popularity. Travel for the average medieval citizen was practically nonexistent, even though most had heard of "the Seres" (the Chinese) and silk garments.

Historians believe that Polo's book, as dictated to Rustichello, was originally written in French intermingled with Italian and was then translated into various languages, including Tuscan, Venetian, German, Latin, Irish, and back into Venetian. Historians point out that the Latin versions are usually more scholarly, wherein copyists varied the manuscript to appeal to a more educated audience, while versions in other languages are more lively and copied with additions and deletions to appeal to less-educated audiences. Until the eleventh century, education in Europe was limited to monasteries and cathedral schools. The establishment of universities in major European cities during the eleventh century made education available to wider classes of Europeans, allowing for a wider reading audience for a book with a popular orientation such as Polo's. Historians speculate that Rustichello's literary expertise and flourishes made the book more approachable and appreciated by all audiences of the day.

Impact

Some historians believe that Marco Polo influenced Christopher Columbus in his desire to sail west over the Atlantic to China, since Columbus is known to have owned a copy of Polo's book. Columbus may have also received a

Questions for Further Study

1. Medieval Asia was the object of intense curiosity in Europe, which sent explorers and missionaries into China, Mongolia, India, and other nations. Why do you think Asia held such fascination for westerners?

2. What problems do contemporary historians face when confronted with a text that was written hundreds of years ago, before the development of the printing press? Speculate as to how the historian might separate fact from fiction in reading and interpreting such a text.

3. During the medieval period the Christian church was bent on extending its reach in the world by converting people in far-flung nations to Christianity. In your opinion, were church authorities interested entirely in saving souls, or did they have other motives?

4. What differences between European culture and Chinese culture did Marco Polo observe? Which Chinese practices did he approve of? Which did he condemn and why? Overall, what was Polo's attitude to China and its culture?

5. The Travels of Marco Polo was as much an adventure tale as it was a sober, factual account of the author's observations of China. In this respect, it bore similarities to the adventurous, chivalric romances that were common in the medieval period. What characteristics of an adventure tale do you see in the document? Why would the accounts of travelers at that time have taken on characteristics of adventure tales?

second copy after returning from his first voyage to the Americas. It is contested whether Polo's book had an impact on pre-Columbian mapmakers; his name did appear in the *Catalan Atlas* composed in 1375 and given to Charles V of France. Although Marco Polo was writing of the Chinese as "the other," this is not the negative "other" that developed later in European history, out of a belief in the superiority of Western civilization. Polo's is a magnificent and glorious "other" that by all accounts fired the imaginations of its readers. The name of Marco Polo continues to reverberate in the twenty-first century. A "Marco Polo traveler" today is a reference to one traveling first class, on the best flights and in the best hotels and cruise staterooms.

Further Reading

■ Articles

Di Cosmo, Nicola. "State Formation and Periodization in Inner Asian History." *Journal of World History* 10, no. 1 (Spring 1999): 1–40.

Zhou, Gang. "Small Talk: A New Reading of Marco Polo's *Il milione*." *Modern Language Notes* 124, no. 1 (January 2009): 1–22.

■ Books

Bergreen, Laurence. *Marco Polo: From Venice to Xanadu.* New York: Alfred A. Knopf, 2007.

Carpini, Giovanni da Pian del. *The Story of the Mongols Whom We Call the Tartars*, trans. Erik Hildinger. Boston: Branden Publishing Company, 1996.

Gordon, Stewart. *When Asia Was the World: Traveling Merchants, Scholars, Warriors, and Monks Who Created the "Riches of the East."* Philadelphia: Da Capo Press, 2008.

Hart, Henry H. *Marco Polo, Venetian Adventurer.* Norman: University of Oklahoma Press, 1967.

Larner, John. *Marco Polo and the Discovery of the World.* New Haven, Conn.: Yale University Press, 1999.

Rachewiltz, Igor de. *Papal Envoys to the Great Khans.* Stanford, Calif.: Stanford University Press, 1971.

Riddle, John. *Marco Polo.* Broomall, Pa.: Mason Crest Publishers, 2003.

Wood, Frances. *Did Marco Polo Go to China?* Boulder, Colo.: Westview Press, 1996.

■ Web Sites

"Marco Polo and His Travels." Silkroad Foundation Web site. http://www.silk-road.com/artl/marcopolo.shtml.

—Carole Schroeder

MARCO POLO'S DESCRIPTION OF HANGZHOU

Milestone Documents

Chapter 76: Description of the Great City of Kinsay, Which Is the Capital of the Whole Country of Manzi

When you have left the city of Changan and have travelled for three days through a splendid country, passing a number of towns and villages, you arrive at the most noble city of Kinsay, a name which is as much as to say in our tongue "The City of Heaven," as I told you before.

And since we have got thither I will enter into particulars about its magnificence; and these are well worth the telling, for the city is beyond dispute the finest and the noblest in the world. In this we shall speak according to the written statement which the Queen of this Realm sent to Bayan the conqueror of the country for transmission to the Great Kaan, in order that he might be aware of the surpassing grandeur of the city and might be moved to save it from destruction or injury. I will tell you all the truth as it was set down in that document. For truth it was, as the said Messer Marco Polo at a later date was able to witness with his own eyes. And now we shall rehearse those particulars.

First and foremost, then, the document stated the city of Kinsay to be so great that it hath an hundred miles of compass. And there are in it twelve thousand bridges of stone, for the most part so lofty that a great fleet could pass beneath them. And let no man marvel that there are so many bridges, for you see the whole city stands as it were in the water and surrounded by water, so that a great many bridges are required to give free passage about it. And though the bridges be so high the approaches are so well contrived that carts and horses do cross them.

The document aforesaid also went on to state that there were in this city twelve guilds of the different crafts, and that each guild had 12,000 houses in the occupation of its workmen. Each of these houses contains at least 12 men, whilst some contain 20 and some 40—not that these are all masters, but inclusive of the journey-men who work under the masters. And yet all these craftsmen had full occupation, for many other cities of the kingdom are supplied from this city with what they require.

The document aforesaid also stated that the number and wealth of the merchants, and the amount of goods that passed through their hands, was so enormous that no man could form a just estimate thereof. And I should have told you with regard to those masters of the different crafts who are at the head of such houses as I have mentioned, that neither they nor their wives ever touch a piece of work with their own hands, but live as nicely and delicately as if they were kings and queens. The wives indeed are most dainty and angelical creatures! Moreover it was an ordinance laid down by the King that every man should follow his father's business and no other, no matter if he possessed 100,000 bezants.

Inside the city there is a Lake which has a compass of some 30 miles, and all round it are erected beautiful palaces and mansions, of the richest and most exquisite structure that you can imagine, belonging to the nobles of the city. There are also on its shores many abbeys and churches of the Idolaters. In the middle of the Lake are two Islands, on each of which stands a rich, beautiful and spacious edifice, furnished in such style as to seem fit for the palace of an Emperor. And when anyone of the citizens desired to hold a marriage feast, or to give any other entertainment, it used to be done at one of these palaces. And everything would be found there ready to order, such as silver plate, trenchers, and dishes, and whatever else was needful. The King made this provision for the gratification of his people, and the place was open to everyone who desired to give an entertainment. Sometimes there would be at these palaces an hundred different parties; some holding a banquet, others celebrating a wedding; and yet all would find good accommodation in the different apartments and pavilions, and that in so well ordered a manner that one party was never in the way of another.

The houses of the city are provided with lofty towers of stone in which articles of value are stored for fear of fire; for most of the houses themselves are of timber, and fires are very frequent in the city.

The people are Idolaters; and since they were conquered by the Great Kaan they use paper-money. Both men and women are fair and comely, and for the most part clothe themselves in silk, so vast is the supply of that material, both from the whole district of Kinsay, and from the imports by traders from other provinces. And you must know they eat every kind of flesh, even that of dogs and other unclean beasts, which nothing would induce a Christian to eat.

Since the Great Kaan occupied the city he has ordained that each of the 12,000 bridges should be provided with a guard of ten men, in case of any disturbance, or of any being so rash as to plot treason or insurrection against him. Each guard is provided with a hollow instrument of wood and with a metal basin, and with a time-keeper to enable them to know the hour of the day or night. And so when one hour of the night is past the sentry strikes one on the wooden instrument and on the basin, so that the whole quarter of the city is made aware that one hour of the night is gone. At the second hour he gives two strokes, and so on, keeping always wide awake and on the lookout. In the morning again, from the sunrise, they begin to count anew, and strike one hour as they did in the night, and so on hour after hour.

Part of the watch patrols the quarter, to see if any light or fire is burning after the lawful hours; if they find any they mark the door, and in the morning the owner is summoned before the magistrates, and unless he can plead a good excuse he is punished. Also if they find anyone going about the streets at unlawful hours they arrest him, and in the morning they bring him before the magistrates. Likewise if in the daytime they find any poor cripple unable to work for his livelihood, they take him to one of the hospitals, of which there are many, founded by the ancient kings, and endowed with great revenues. Or if he be capable of work they oblige him to take up some trade. If they see that any house has caught fire they immediately beat upon that wooden instrument to give the alarm, and this brings together the watchmen from the other bridges to help to extinguish it, and to save the goods of the merchants or others, either by removing them to the towers above mentioned, or by putting them in boats and transporting them to the islands in the lake. For no citizen dares leave his house at night, or to come near the fire; only those who own the property, and those watchmen who flock to help, of whom there shall come one or two thousand at the least.

Moreover, within the city there is an eminence on which stands a Tower, and at the top of the tower is hung a slab of wood. Whenever fire or any other alarm breaks out in the city a man who stands there with a mallet in his hand beats upon the slab, making a noise that is heard to a great distance. So when the blows upon this slab are heard, everybody is aware that fire has broken out, or that there is some other cause of alarm.

The Kaan watches this city with especial diligence because it forms the head of all Manzi; and because he has an immense revenue from the duties levied on the transactions of trade therein, the amount of which is such that no one would credit it on mere hearsay.

All the streets of the city are paved with stone or brick, as indeed are all the highways throughout Manzi, so that you ride and travel in every direction without inconvenience. Were it not for this pavement you could not do so, for the country is very low and flat, and after rain 'tis deep in mire and water. But as the Great Kaan's couriers could not gallop their horses over the pavement, the side of the road is left unpaved for their convenience. The pavement of the main street of the city also is laid out in two parallel ways of ten paces in width on either side, leaving a space in the middle laid with fine gravel, under which are vaulted drains which convey the rain water into the canals; and thus the road is kept ever dry.

You must know also that the city of Kinsay has some 3000 baths, the water of which is supplied by springs. They are hot baths, and the people take great delight in them, frequenting them several times a month, for they are very cleanly in their persons. They are the finest and largest baths in the world; large enough for 100 persons to bathe together.

And the Ocean Sea comes within 25 miles of the city at a place called Ganfu, where there is a town and an excellent haven, with a vast amount of shipping which is engaged in the traffic to and from India and other foreign parts, exporting and importing many kinds of wares, by which the city benefits. And a great river flows from the city of Kinsay to that sea-haven, by which vessels can come up to the city itself. This river extends also to other places further inland.

Know also that the Great Kaan hath distributed the territory of Manzi into nine parts, which he hath constituted into nine kingdoms. To each of these kingdoms a king is appointed who is subordinate to the Great Kaan, and every year renders the accounts of his kingdom to the fiscal office at the capital. This city of Kinsay is the seat of one of these kings, who rules over 140 great and wealthy cities. For in the whole of this vast country of Manzi there are more than 1200 great and wealthy cities, without counting the towns and villages, which are in great numbers. And you may receive it for certain that in each of those 1200 cities the Great Kaan has a garrison, and that the smallest of such garrisons musters 1000 men; whilst there are some of 10,000, 20,000 and 30,000; so that the total number of troops is something scarcely calculable. The troops forming these garrisons are not all Tartars.

Many are from the province of Cathay, and good soldiers too. But you must not suppose they are by any means all of them cavalry; a very large proportion of them are foot-soldiers, according to the special requirements of each city. And all of them belong to the army of the Great Kaan.

I repeat that everything appertaining to this city is on so vast a scale, and the Great Kaan's yearly revenues therefrom are so immense, that it is not easy even to put it in writing, and it seems past belief to one who merely hears it told. But I *will* write it down for you.

First, however, I must mention another thing. The people of this country have a custom, that as soon as a child is born they write down the day and hour and the planet and sign under which its birth has taken place; so that everyone among them knows the day of his birth. And when anyone intends a journey he goes to the astrologers, and gives the particulars of his nativity in order to learn whether he shall have good luck or no. Sometimes they will say *no*, and in that case the journey is put off till such day as the astrologer may recommend. These astrologers are very skilful at their business, and often their words come to pass, so the people have great faith in them.

They burn the bodies of the dead. And when anyone dies the friends and relations make a great mourning for the deceased, and clothe themselves in hempen garments, and follow the corpse playing on a variety of instruments and singing hymns to their idols. And when they come to the burning place, they take representations of things cut out of parchment, such as caparisoned horses, male and female slaves, camels, armour suits of cloth of gold (and money), in great quantities, and these things they put on the fire along with the corpse, so that they are all burnt with it. And they tell you that the dead man shall have all these slaves and animals of which the effigies are burnt, alive in flesh and blood, and the money in gold, at his disposal in the next world; and that the instruments which they have caused to be played at his funeral, and the idol hymns that have been chaunted, shall also be produced again to welcome him in the next world; and that the idols themselves will come to do him honour.

Furthermore there exists in this city the palace of the king who fled, him who was Emperor of Manzi, and that is the greatest palace in the world, as I shall tell you more particularly. For you must know its demesne hath a compass of ten miles, all enclosed with lofty battlemented walls; and inside the walls are the finest and most delectable gardens upon earth, and filled too with the finest fruits. There are numerous fountains in it also, and lakes full of fish. In the middle is the palace itself, a great and splendid building. It contains 20 great and handsome halls, one of which is more spacious than the rest, and affords room for a vast multitude to dine. It is all painted in gold, with many histories and representations of beasts and birds, of knights and dames, and many marvellous things. It forms a really magnificent spectacle, for over all the walls and all the ceiling you see nothing but paintings in gold. And besides these halls the palace contains 1000 large and handsome chambers, all painted in gold and divers colours.

Moreover, I must tell you that in this city there are 160 *tomans* of fires, or in other words 160 *tomans* of houses. Now I should tell you that the *toman* is 10,000, so that you can reckon the total as altogether 1,600,000 houses, among which are a great number of rich palaces. There is one church only, belonging to the Nestorian Christians.

There is another thing I must tell you. It is the custom for every burgess of this city, and in fact for every description of person in it, to write over his door his own name, the name of his wife, and those of his children, his slaves, and all the inmates of his house, and also the number of animals that he keeps. And if anyone dies in the house then the name of that person is erased, and if any child is born its name is added. So in this way the sovereign is able to know exactly the population of the city. And this is the practice also throughout all Manzi and Cathay.

And I must tell you that every hosteler who keeps an hostel for travellers is bound to register their names and surnames, as well as the day and month of their arrival and departure. And thus the sovereign hath the means of knowing, whenever it pleases him, who come and go throughout his dominions. And certes this is a wise order and a provident.

Chapter 77: Further Particulars Concerning the Great City of Kinsay

The position of the city is such that it has on one side a lake of fresh and exquisitely clear water (already spoken of), and on the other a very large river. The waters of the latter fill a number of canals of all sizes which run through the different quarters of the city, carry away all impurities, and then enter the Lake; whence they issue again and flow to the Ocean, thus producing a most excellent atmosphere.

By means of these channels, as well as by the streets, you can go all about the city. Both streets and canals are so wide and spacious that carts on the one and boats on the other can readily pass to and fro, conveying necessary supplies to the inhabitants.

At the opposite side the city is shut in by a channel, perhaps 40 miles in length, very wide, and full of water derived from the river aforesaid, which was made by the ancient kings of the country in order to relieve the river when flooding its banks. This serves also as a defence to the city, and the earth dug from it has been thrown inwards, forming a kind of mound enclosing the city.

In this part are the ten principal markets, though besides these there are a vast number of others in the different parts of the town. The former are all squares of half a mile to the side, and along their front passes the main street, which is 40 paces in width, and runs straight from end to end of the city, crossing many bridges of easy and commodious approach. At every four miles of its length comes one of those great squares of 2 miles (as we have mentioned) in compass. So also parallel to this great street, but at the back of the market places, there runs a very large canal, on the bank of which towards the squares are built great houses of stone, in which the merchants from India and other foreign parts store their wares, to be handy for the markets. In each of the squares is held a market three days in the week, frequented by 40,000 or 50,000 persons, who bring thither for sale every possible necessary of life, so that there is always an ample supply of every kind of meat and game, as of roebuck, red-deer, fallow-deer, hares, rabbits, partridges, pheasants, francolins, quails, fowls, capons, and of ducks and geese an infinite quantity; for so many are bred on the Lake that for a Venice groat of silver you can have a couple of geese and two couple of ducks. Then there are the shambles where the larger animals are slaughtered, such as calves, beeves, kids, and lambs, the flesh of which is eaten by the rich and the great dignitaries.

Those markets make a daily display of every kind of vegetables and fruits; and among the latter there are in particular certain pears of enormous size, weighing as much as ten pounds apiece, and the pulp of which is white and fragrant like a confection; besides peaches in their season both yellow and white, of every delicate flavour.

Neither grapes nor wine are produced there, but very good raisins are brought from abroad, and wine likewise. The natives, however, do not much care about wine, being used to that kind of their own made from rice and spices. From the Ocean Sea also come daily supplies of fish in great quantity, brought 25 miles up the river, and there is also great store of fish from the lake, which is the constant resort of fishermen, who have no other business. Their fish is of sundry kinds, changing with the season; and, owing to the impurities of the city which pass into the lake, it is remarkably fat and savoury. Anyone who should see the supply of fish in the market would suppose it impossible that such a quantity could ever be sold; and yet in a few hours the whole shall be cleared away; so great is the number of inhabitants who are accustomed to delicate living. Indeed they eat fish and flesh at the same meal.

All the ten market places are encompassed by lofty houses, and below these are shops where all sorts of crafts are carried on, and all sorts of wares are on sale, including spices and jewels and pearls. Some of these shops are entirely devoted to the sale of wine made from rice and spices which is constantly made fresh, and is sold very cheap.

Certain of the streets are occupied by the women of the town, who are in such a number that I dare not say what it is. They are found not only in the vicinity of the market places, where usually a quarter is assigned to them, but all over the city. They exhibit themselves splendidly attired and abundantly perfumed, in finely garnished houses, with trains of waiting women. These women are extremely accomplished in all the arts of allurement, and readily adapt their conversation to all sorts of persons, insomuch that strangers who have once tasted their attractions seem to get bewitched, and are so taken with their blandishments and their fascinating ways that they never can get these out of their heads. Hence it comes to pass that when they return home they say they have been to Kinsay or the City of Heaven, and their only desire is to get back thither as soon as possible.

Other streets are occupied by the Physicians, and by the Astrologers, who are also teachers of reading and writing; and an infinity of other professions have their places round about those squares. In each of the squares there are two great palaces facing one another, in which are established the officers appointed by the King to decide differences arising between merchants, or other inhabitants of the quarter. It is the daily duty of these officers to see that the guards are at their posts on the neighbouring bridges, and to punish them at their discretion if they are absent.

All along the main street that we have spoken of, as running from end to end of the city, both sides are lined with houses and great palaces and the gardens pertaining to them, whilst in the intervals are the houses of tradesmen engaged in their different crafts. The crowd of people that you meet here at all hours, passing this way and that on their different errands, is so vast that no one would believe it possible that victuals enough could be provided for their consumption, unless they should see how, on every market-day, all those squares are thronged and crammed with purchasers, and with the traders who have brought in stores of provision by land or water; and everything they bring in is disposed of.

To give you an example of the vast consumption in this city let us take the article of *pepper*, and that will enable you in some measure to estimate what must be the quantity of victual, such as meat, wine, groceries, which have to be provided for the general consumption. Now Messer Marco heard it stated by one of the Great Kaan's officers of customs that the quantity of pepper introduced daily for consumption into the city of Kinsay amounted to 43 loads, each load being equal to 223 lbs.

The houses of the citizens are well built and elaborately finished; and the delight they take in decoration, in painting and in architecture, leads them to spend in this way sums of money that would astonish you.

The natives of the city are men of peaceful character, both from education and from the example of their kings, whose disposition was the same. They know nothing of handling arms, and keep none in their houses. You hear of no feuds or noisy quarrels or dissensions of any kind among them. Both in their commercial dealings and in their manufactures they are thoroughly honest and truthful, and there is such a degree of good will and neighbourly attachment among both men and women that you would take the people who live in the same street to be all one family.

And this familiar intimacy is free from all jealousy or suspicion of the conduct of their women. These they treat with the greatest respect, and a man who should presume to make loose proposals to a married woman would be regarded as an infamous rascal. They also treat the foreigners who visit them for the sake of trade with great cordiality, and entertain them in the most winning manner, affording them every help and advice on their business. But on the other hand they hate to see soldiers, and not least those of the Great Kaan's garrisons, regarding them as the cause of their having lost their native kings and lords.

On the Lake of which we have spoken there are numbers of boats and barges of all sizes for parties of pleasure. These will hold 10, 15, 20, or more persons, and are from 15 to 20 paces in length with flat bottoms and ample breadth of beam, so that they always keep their trim. Anyone who desires to go a-pleasuring with the women, or with a party of his own sex, hires one of these barges, which are always to be

Glossary

bezants	gold coins
Cathay	in Marco Polo's time, northern China
Chagan	ancient imperial capital of China; eastern terminus of the Silk Road
chaunted	chanted
demesne	the palace grounds
eminence	a natural elevation
francolins	birds in the pheasant family
Ganfu	ancient name for Canton but here meant to designate a port of Kinsay
Great Kaan	Kublai Khan
Manzi	in Marco Polo's time, southern China
Ocean Sea	the South China Sea
Venice groat of silver	a thick silver coin issued by Venice in the thirteenth century
women of the town	prostitutes

found completely furnished with tables and chairs and all the other apparatus for a feast. The roof forms a level deck, on which the crew stand, and pole the boat along whithersoever may be desired, for the lake is not more than 2 paces in depth. The inside of this roof and the rest of the interior is covered with ornamental painting in gay colours, with windows all round that can be shut or opened, so that the party at table can enjoy all the beauty and variety of the prospects on both sides as they pass along. And truly a trip on this Lake is a much more charming recreation than can be enjoyed on land. For on the one side lies the city in its entire length, so that the spectators in the barges from the distance at which they stand, take in use whole prospect in its full beauty and grandeur, with its numberless palaces, temples, monasteries, and gardens, full of lofty trees, sloping to the shore. And the Lake is never without a number of other such boats, laden with pleasure parties; for it

is the great delight of the citizens here, after they have disposed of the day's business, to pass the afternoon in enjoyment with the ladies of their families, or perhaps with others less reputable, either in these barges or in driving about the city in carriages.

Of these latter we must also say something, for they afford one mode of recreation to the citizens in going about the town, as the boats afford another in going about the Lake. In the main street of the city you meet an infinite succession of these carriages passing to and fro. They are long covered vehicles, fitted with curtains and cushions, and affording room for six persons; and they are in constant request for ladies and gentlemen going on parties of pleasure. In these they drive to certain gardens, where they are entertained by the owners in pavilions erected on purpose, and there they divert themselves the livelong day, with their ladies, returning home in the evening in those same carriages.

IBN KHALDŪN'S "SOCIAL SOLIDARITY"

"Social solidarity is found only in groups related by blood ties or by other ties which fulfil the same functions."

Overview

In the fourteenth century, Abū Zaid 'Abd ar-Rahmān ibn Khaldūn wrote a landmark universal history, his *Kitāb al-'ibar* (Book of Examples). Ibn Khaldūn was a a member of the inner circle of several royal courts and an eminent scholar of Islamic history, and he excelled as a philosopher. The theories he presented in the *Muqaddimah*—the first book of the *Kitāb al-'ibar*, also known as the *Prolegomena* (Introduction)—has earned him the title "father of sociology" among some scholars. The purpose of his seven-volume text was to understand the rise and fall of civilizations. Within the *Muqaddimah*, Ibn Khaldūn introduced his sociological theories, identifying the characteristics of civilization and outlining how an empire may rise and fall. A central feature is the cohesion of a social group: *'asabiyyah*, or "social solidarity." The extracts presented here highlight aspects of this notion of social solidarity.

Context

Although some of Ibn Khaldūn's analysis of society and the state may seem self-evident to modern readers, it is important to consider the time and culture in which he lived and wrote. At the time in the Islamic world, it was widely held that God was responsible for all actions and that the actions of a society could not alter predetermined fate. While not unseating God from his prescribed position, Ibn Khaldūn offered rational explanations for the mechanisms of society, including dynastic rise and fall.

During the mid- and late fourteenth century, portions of the Islamic world were stable, while others were in turmoil. Syria and Palestine, which had experienced the devastation of the Crusades, were controlled by the Mamluks in Cairo. The Ottoman Empire was emerging in Anatolia (modern-day Turkey), and Iraq and Persia were rapidly falling to the Turkic conqueror Timur. In Andalusia (Islamic Spain), Alfonso XI fought the Islamic kingdom of Granada from 1312 to 1350. The fall of the Almohads in the previous century had led to the emergence of a number of smaller states in North Africa, the most dominant being the Hafsids and

Marinids; eventually the Marinids came to dominate. Within the span of a century, many dynasties ended and new empires began. It was into this rapidly changing world that Ibn Khaldūn was born, and doubtless these conditions fueled his interest in the rise and fall of civilizations.

About the Author

In 1332 Ibn Khaldūn was born into a prominent family that had left Yemen in the Arabian Peninsula during the eighth century, immigrating to Andalusia and later resettling in North Africa. The family served many generations of Andalusian and North African royals as political advisers, until Ibn Khaldūn's father gave up life at court for the secluded life of a scholar, focusing on providing a thorough education to his sons, Ibn Khaldūn and Yahyā. As a young child, Ibn Khaldūn received a traditional education, studying the Qur'an, Islamic jurisprudence (law), and the Arabic language. Later he attended Zaytuna University in Tunis, where he was introduced to the rational sciences, philosophy, and mathematics. It was at the university that Ibn Khaldūn experienced a devastating life event: the loss of his parents and his teachers to the plague, which swept through North Africa at that time, claiming the lives of a third of the population. This may have been the precipitating event that led him to analyze society and civilization outside the confines of traditional Islamic thought. It is clear from his later writings that Ibn Khaldūn was a rationalist, that is, that he required explanations for events and situations to be supported by evidence. This was diametrically opposed to the predominant philosophical outlook in Islamic philosophy, which was that all events were the will or doing of God. Unlike the rationalists in medieval Europe, who faced tremendous opposition from the Catholic Church and sometimes even death for their subversive viewpoints, Ibn Khaldūn and other rationalists in North Africa were tolerated.

At the age of twenty, Ibn Khaldūn entered into the service of Ibn Tāfrākīn, the ruler of Tunis, and shortly thereafter he moved to Fez, Morocco, where he served the Maranid sultan Abū Inan Farés. These auspicious events marked the beginning of a tumultuous twenty-year career of political service. Ibn Khaldūn transferred from court to

1332

■ **May 12**
Abū Zaid 'Abd ar-Raḥmān ibn Khaldūn is born in Tunis.

1352

■ Ibn Khaldūn is appointed to the Marinid court, beginning a life of continuous political turmoil, including a two-year imprisonment.

1364

■ Ibn Khaldūn is sent by Muḥammad al-Ḥmar, the Nasrid ruler of Granada in Andalusia, on a diplomatic mission to the Castilian King Pedro the Cruel.

1375

■ Following the assassination of a friend, Ibn Khaldūn retreats to Frenda, Algeria. While there, he begins work on his history book.

1379

■ Ibn Khaldūn returns to his native city of Tunis, with the intention of leading a quiet academic life as a professor of Islamic jurisprudence.

1382

■ Having once again become entangled in political intrigues, Ibn Khaldūn leaves Tunis and settles in Cairo, where he is appointed chief *qadi*, or judge, of the Maliki Islamic school of thought.

court in North Africa and Andalusia, riding the waves of political fortune and even spending two years in prison after finding himself on the wrong side of a palace coup. Ibn Khaldūn's personal participation in politics and frequent moves between courts enabled him to develop his political theories; the moves also had the useful effect of keeping him from developing long-term loyalty to any one dynasty, which in turn left him free to write without the need to please a royal patron.

Ibn Khaldūn's political difficulties reached a climax in 1375 when a close friend and political ally, Ibn al-Khaṭīb, was assassinated. He regarded this event as a warning and began his first retirement, retreating to Frenda, Algeria, where he wrote the *Muqaddimah* in less than six months. However, he was forced to end his self-imposed isolation in order to gain access to the sources and libraries he needed to complete the remaining sections of his great work. In 1379 Ibn Khaldūn returned to his native Tunis to continue his scholarship and, in 1382, presented the first draft of his historical work to Sultan Abū al-'Abbās of Tunis. In 1382 he departed Tunis for the hajj, the annual Islamic pilgrimage to Mecca. En route, he stopped in Alexandria, Egypt, and then traveled to Cairo, at that time a leading city of the Islamic world and the capital of the Mamluk Empire. He was awed by the city and its religious and academic institutions, and there he eventually settled and spent his last years.

Ibn Khaldūn lectured on his theories from the *Muqaddimah* at Cairo's Al Azhar University, joined the faculty of several other educational institutions, and was appointed Ibn chief *qadi*, or justice, of the Maliki branch of Islamic jurisprudence. (The Maliki school, one for the four main schools of Islamic jurisprudence, predominated in North and West Africa.) Ibn Khaldūn's career as a jurist, like his career at court, was stormy, and he was removed from and then reinstated to the position of *qadi* six times. Some religious leaders criticized what they regarded as nonreligious elements in his writings, while scholars criticized him because of his position as a *qadi*. In 1400 Ibn Khaldūn was in Damascus, Syria, on an official mission when Timur and his army surrounded the city. He offered to serve as a negotiator and spent more than a month in the Turkic camp, during which time he engaged in a series of interviews with the conqueror. According to Ibn Khaldūn's autobiography, the two men enjoyed their conversations, Timur because he knew of Ibn Khaldūn's history and wanted to learn from the scholar and Ibn Khaldūn because he was anxious to meet the leader from central Asia whom he believed might have the power to reunite the Islamic world.

Explanation and Analysis of the Document

When Ibn Khaldūn began his retirement in 1375, his intention was to write a history of North Africa and the Arabs. He realized that in order to properly analyze and explain history, he first needed to develop a framework that would make it possible to understand past and current events methodically. This framework is the *Muqaddimah*.

An important idea presented in the *Muqaddimah* is that just as there is a human life cycle, dynasties have a life cycle. Ibn Khaldūn suggests that dynasties last for three generations, or approximately 120 years, during which time they experience a childhood, reach an apex during maturity, and decline during old age. Citing specific examples, Ibn Khaldūn demonstrates that there is often a dynamic leader who solidifies the political structure. The next generation focuses on social development, and the second-generation leadership enjoys the benefits of the previous generation's military and political ability. The second generation's attention to arts and culture leads to a weakened political structure by the time the third and final generation takes power. Society weakens under the lax state structure brought on by luxury, and a new group arises to take power. Thus begins a new cycle of dynasty or empire. Even within a long-lasting empire, smaller dynastic divisions are common.

In considering the cycle of dynasties, Ibn Khaldūn proposes that stable government will lead to urban development, which in turn brings about cultural evolution once security and basic needs are being met. He also proposes various ways in which urban development, or the lack of it, have an impact on the development of civilization. As a survivor of the plague that killed so many people in the mid-fourteenth century, Ibn Khaldūn focuses on public health, suggesting that cities might be made healthier by allowing for proper airflow and ventilation.

◆ **Chapter 1**

Human society is necessary because people must cooperate in order to accomplish daily activities such as making food, building homes, and creating tools for the previous two activities. When referring to philosophers in the second sentence, Ibn Khaldūn indicates that Islamic scholars largely accept the notion that humans automatically form societal alliances to meet social need. However, he chooses to offer an explanation for why humans need social interaction. In others words, he is proposing that humans are not social by nature but by necessity. Cooperation is the means by which humans can more efficiently meet their needs.

Following on the need for security, Ibn Khaldūn next introduces the notion of organized defense in the form of a "restraining force to keep men off each other." He notes that most humans have access to comparable weapons, so in cases of conflict between people, there is a need for a restraining force. From this need arises a person or group of people who exert authority over others, and this, he says, is the basis of sovereignty among humans. He differentiates his theory of human society from that of contemporary philosophers by showing that humans are the only ones to recognize the need for cooperation and to form a society to address the need deliberately, as opposed to bees and locusts, who do so instinctively.

◆ **Chapter 2**

This chapter introduces the concept of *'aṣabiyyah*, a term for which there is no single equivalent English word. The most common definitions are "group feeling," "group

Time Line

1400	■ Ibn Khaldūn acts as a negotiator on behalf of the people of Damascus, Syria, when they are besieged by Timur.
1406	■ **March 16** Ibn Khaldūn dies in Cairo.
1806	■ Silvestre de Sacy translates selections of Ibn Khaldūn's *Muqaddimah* and *Kitāb al-'ibar* (Book of Examples). This is the first general circulation in Europe of Ibn Khaldūn's writings.
1858	■ The first Arabic printing of the *Muqaddimah* is published, followed soon after by the first full French translation.

solidarity," "social solidarity," and "a need for belonging." This document translates the term as "social solidarity."

Aggression, according to Ibn Khaldūn, is "a common characteristic of men." He says that humans will always desire what others have and that therefore there must be some means to prevent them from taking what belongs to others. Among settled populations, the authority that prevents aggression within the community is the political structure and its representatives, while external aggression is prevented by state-supported defensive measures, such as walls and troops. Nomadic societies have chiefs and elders who serve as authorities, but not having walls with which to protect themselves, nomadic communities must rely on their social solidarity to unite themselves in defense.

According to his theory, there are various levels of association, and the solidarity of these levels changes according to need. The three main levels are blood ties, or immediate

Cairo tomb of the Mamluks, slave soldiers who fought to win political control of several Muslim states, including Egypt and Syria (© Bettmann/CORBIS)

family; kinship, or the extended family, such as the clan or tribe; and, commonality, or nonfamilial alliances, such as companionship, proximity of habitation, or patronage. A person will first and foremost be loyal to those with whom they share blood ties, next to those with whom they share kinship, and finally to those with whom they share some commonality; a threat to any of these levels will be seen as a threat to the individual, except in cases where a threat is to several levels of associations. For example, when there is a threat to a brother by a cousin, the individual will ally with the brother instead of the kin, as this is the more personal threat. Ibn Khaldūn explains the significance of the words of the Prophet Mohammad "Learn your genealogies to know who are near of kin" by saying that kinship serves a function only if it leads to actual cooperation. He notes that "if the kinship is evident it acts as a natural urge leading to solidarity," but if it is based merely on "knowledge of descent from a common ancestor it is weakened and has little influence on the sentiments and hence little practical effect."

Because the Bedouins, or nomadic peoples, require a greater sense of social solidarity in order to unify themselves in matters of survival and defense, ties of kinship are particularly important for them. Ibn Khaldūn points out that the nomadic life is a hard one and remarks that humans prefer a settled lifestyle; he observes that the easier life of settled peoples lessens the importance of blood ties and thereby changes the basis of social solidarity. He quotes the caliph 'Umar I (called "Omar" in the document), the second leader of the Islamic community after the death of Muhammad, who urged people not become "like the Nabateans," who forgot their familial relations and embraced a geographic identity. But Ibn Khaldūn acknowledges that as populations in towns and cities grow, intermarriage increases, and identification with a particular family weakens.

Eventually this concept of social solidarity is replaced by the concept of sovereignty when one person asserts his authority over the others in the group. Ibn Khaldūn says that given the opportunity, most people will seek to assert sovereignty, as humans desire power. In other works, he distinguishes between a chief and a sovereign: A sovereign has the ability to coerce other people, whereas a chief does not. For example, a sovereign may unilaterally impose taxes on the population, but a chief cannot. A society under the authority of a chief may decide as a whole to levy taxes, or, more likely, a select group within that society may decide to, but it would not be a unilateral decision.

◆ Chapter 3

A group needs cohesive social solidarity in order to defeat or overtake another group, for, as Ibn Khaldūn observes, "Victory ... goes to the side which has most solidarity." Similarly, the person with the most support is the one who is able to rise above the rest and become a sovereign. The authority of a successful dynasty comes over time to be accepted by the population as the norm, so that military might is no longer the foundation of the sovereign's authority. At this point, as Ibn Khaldūn notes, "rule is accepted as the will of God." He mentions that theological books often will discuss the importance of the Islamic state only after a discussion of religious beliefs as a means of bolstering the state's authority.

Ibn Khaldūn provides two examples of the fall of dynastic fortunes: the Abbasid (the document uses the variant spelling "Abbaside") dynasty (750–1258) and the experience of the Ummayad (or Omayyad) dynasty (661–750). In the case of the Abbasids, he notes, the dynasty began relying on the talents of people from the fringes of the empire, leading to decentralization and growing authority among these clients of the caliph. Ibn Khaldūn points out that while the Abbasids retained nominal authority, real power fell into a succession of other hands. The Mongols (whom he refers to as Tatars) brought the dynasty down in name as well as in fact in 1258.

◆ Chapter 4

A society and the state that governs it are interdependent. Ibn Khaldūn holds that the state is the authority that preserves the essence of the society: "The state is therefore to society as form is to matter, for the form by its nature preserves the matter and ... the two are inseparable." The weakening of one will cause the waning of the other. He proposes that the decline of society leads to the crumbling of empires, and in this respect he mentions the Roman, Persian, and Arab empires. He asserts that the primary factors that binds a society are "solidarity and power," as wielded by a ruler. When the ruling class loses that power, a new solidarity must arise, and Ibn Khaldūn notes that the disturbance to society is very great.

Audience

There is no indication that Ibn Khaldūn's *Kitāb al-'ibar* was commissioned by a particular ruler; rather, his composition was for personal satisfaction and for posterity. He did present an incomplete draft to the Hafsid ruler of Tunis, Abū al-'Abbās, but more as a peace offering, to mend fractured relations, than an obligation to a patron. To Ibn

Khaldūn, knowledge was of great importance, possibly even more important than his own life. After all, this was the man who, when nearly seventy years old, asked to be lowered in a basket down the outside wall of the Damascus citadel to request an audience with the ruthless Turkic conqueror Timur. His political position did not obligate him to attempt negotiations, nor was he the most senior ranking official within the city. He volunteered as a way to gather information about Timur and the Turkic camp, which he later incorporated into his voluminous history.

During his lifetime, the primary audience for Ibn Khaldūn's works consisted of students and other scholars. In the autobiographical section, he refers to using the *Muqaddimah* in teaching, first in Tunis and later in Cairo. Furthermore, contemporary Muslim scholars mention attending lectures given by Ibn Khaldūn or reading his theories, and several Mamluk historians proudly name Ibn Khaldūn among their teachers in Cairo.

Impact

Between the founding of Islam in the seventh century and the time that Ibn Khaldūn wrote in the fourteenth century, Muslims tended to believe that since God was responsible for all actions and knew the future, individuals and society could not alter predetermined fate. By offering an explanation for the mechanisms of society, Ibn Khaldūn contributed to a more modern understanding of the relationship between free will and a God who is all-knowing—what Muslims call *al-'Alim*—and all-powerful, or *al-Qadir*. Muslims begin with the notion that everything that takes place in the universe happens because it is part of God's plan. This view is expressed by the phrase *al-qada' wa al-qadar*, translated as "the decision and determination of Allah." But does this mean that humans have no free will? Orthodox Islam would respond no. While there have been Islamic thinkers who have taken this position, their view has been largely rejected. Orthodox Islam teaches that while God has power over and knowledge about all things, he has given humans freedom of choice. This freedom is not in any way inconsistent with God's foreknowledge and power. While humans are still under God's power, humans are free to act, and God will judge humans based on the amount of responsibility and freedom he has granted us. These distinctions become important to a proper understanding of Ibn Khaldūn's theories, for they have a bearing on the distinctively Islamic view of history. Ibn Khaldūn may have established what amount to "laws" of historical development and change, but those laws do not in any way diminish the role of God in human affairs.

The genius of Ibn Khaldūn's theories was not known in Europe before the nineteenth century, largely because his life was concurrent with general decline in the Islamic world. Had he written his seminal work a few hundred years earlier or later, his theories might have found their way into Europe. Even within the Islamic world, Ibn Khaldūn was more well known for the rest of the *Kitāb al-*

> "Social solidarity is found only in groups related by blood ties or by other ties which fulfil the same functions."
>
> (Chapter 2)

> "The end of social solidarity is sovereignty. This is because ... it is solidarity which makes men unite their efforts for common objects, defend themselves, and repulse or overcome their enemies."
>
> (Chapter 2)

> "Once consolidated the state can dispense with social solidarity. The reason is that newly founded states can secure the obedience of their subjects only by much coercion and force ... Once kingship has been established, however, and inherited by successive generations or dynasties, the people forget their original condition [and] the rulers are invested with the aura of leadership."
>
> (Chapter 3)

> "The two [state and society] being inseparable, any disturbance in either of them will cause a disturbance in the other; just as the disappearance of one leads to the disappearance of the other. The greatest source of disturbance is in the breakdown of such empires as the Roman, Persian, or Arab; or in dynasty, such as the Omayyad or Abbaside."
>
> (Chapter 4)

> "It is evident that men are by nature in contact with and tied to each other, even where kinship is absent; though, as we have said before, in such cases such ties are weaker than where they are reinforced by kinship. Such contact may produce a solidarity nearly as powerful as that produced by kinship."
>
> (Chapter 4)

'ibar than for the *Muqaddimah*. It was only during the latter half of the Ottoman Empire that Islamic scholars sought to apply Ibn Khaldūn's theories, and those theories did not become known in Europe until 1806, when Baron Silvestre de Sacy, a French linguist and student of the Middle East, published a biography of Ibn Khaldūn and translated portions of the *Muqaddimah*, in particular the *Prolegomena*. He published a fuller translation in 1816.

Some of Ibn Khaldūn's theories, including those on urban development and economics, were never given much examination, though today scholars of both the East and the West have come to regard him as a pioneer in these subjects, demonstrating deep insight and vision. European economic and political theory might have developed earlier had Europeans utilized his writings, which have similarities to the works of the political theorist Niccolò Machiavelli and the economist Adam Smith. Some historians see the seeds of the work of Edward Gibbon, whose monumental work, *The History of the Decline and Fall of the Roman Empire* (1776–1788), traces a similar arc in history and continues to reverberate in discussions of cultural decay. Other historians find in Khaldūn a progenitor of Karl Marx, coauthor of the *Das Kapital*, and his view that historical progression is the result of clashes between social classes that give rise to the decline of an old social order and the rise of a new one.

Even in the twentieth century, the economist Arthur Laffer acknowledged that Ibn Khaldūn was the source of his famous Laffer curve, which continues to be invoked in discussions of taxation. The curve illustrates an economic theory that attempts to find an optimal tax rate somewhere between 0 percent and 100 percent that will generate the most revenue for a government. Laffer reputedly sketched it on a napkin during a meeting with key U.S. policy makers in 1974. He later stated that his source for the curve was a statement from Ibn Khaldūn, which he quoted as "It should be known that at the beginning of the dynasty, taxation yields a large revenue from small assessments. At the end of the dynasty, taxation yields a small revenue from large assessments" (http://www.heritage.org/research/taxes/bg1765.cfm).

Overall, Ibn Khaldūn's influence has been profound. The famed historian Arnold Toynbee wrote, "He has conceived and formulated a philosophy of history which is undoubtedly the greatest work of its kind that has ever yet been created by any mind in any time or place" (qtd. in Izzeddin, p. 61). The British philosopher Robert Flint seconded this view when he wrote: "As a theorist on history he had no equal in any age or country.... Plato, Aristotle and Augustine were not his peers" (qtd. at http://www.islamawareness.net/Science/muslims_contributions.html).

Further Reading

■ Articles

Boulakia, Jean David. "Ibn Khaldun: A Fourteenth-Century Economist." *Journal of Political Economy* 79, no. 5 (September–October 1971): 1105–1118.

Gibb, H. A. R. "The Islamic Background of Ibn Khaldun's Political Theory." *Bulletin of the School of Oriental Studies* 7, no. 1 (1933): 23–31.

Rosen, Lawrence. "Theorizing from Within: Ibn Khaldun and His Political Culture." *Contemporary Sociology* 34, no. 6 (November 2005): 596–599.

■ Books

Al-Azmeh, Aziz. *Ibn Khaldūn, An Essay in Reinterpretation.* London: Frank Cass, 1982.

Brett, Michael. *Ibn Khaldun and the Medieval Maghreb.* Aldershot, U.K.: Ashgate, 1999.

Enan, Mohammad Abdullah. *Ibn Khaldūn: His Life and Works.* Kuala Lumpur, Malaysia: Other Press, 2007.

Fischel, Walter J. *Ibn Khaldūn in Egypt: His Public Functions and His Historical Research, 1382–1406—A Study in Islamic Historiography.* Berkeley: University of California Press, 1967.

Questions for Further Study

1. On what basis do some scholars regard Ibn Khaldūn as the "father of sociology"?

2. What were the historical circumstances that would have made the rise and fall of empires a topic of interest to scholars such as Ibn Khaldūn?

3. How relevant do you believe Ibn Khaldūn's theories are in the modern world? Do you believe that those theories have applicability to the United States in the twenty-first century? Why or why not?

4. Ibn Khaldūn wrote: "Social solidarity is found only in groups related by blood ties or by other ties which fulfil the same functions." In contemporary life, what "other ties" serve the same function that "blood ties" might have served in former eras?

5. Although Ibn Khaldūn has been highly praised for the originality of his thinking, his name and theories are not widely known in the West. Why do you think that is so?

Izzeddin, Nejla, and William Ernest Hocking. *The Arab World: Past, Present and Future*. Whitefish, Mont.: Kessinger Publishing, 2006.

Talbi, M. "Ibn Khaldun." In *Encyclopedia of Islam*, 2nd ed., ed. P. J. Bearman, et al., 825–831. Leiden, Netherlands: E. J. Brill, 1999.

■ **Web Sites**

Anthony, John. "The Scholar from Algeria." Saudi Aramco World Web site.
http://www.saudiaramcoworld.com/issue/196605/the.scholar.from.algeria.htm.

Laffer, Arthur B. "The Laffer Curve: Past, Present, and Future," Heritage Foundation Web site.
http://www.heritage.org/research/taxes/bg1765.cfm.

"Muslim Contributions to Science." Islam Awareness Web site.
http://www.islamawareness.net/Science/muslims_contributions.html.

Stone, Caroline. "Ibn Khaldun and the Rise and Fall of Empires," Saudi Aramco World Web site.
http://www.saudiaramcoworld.com/issue/200605/ibn.khaldun.and.the.rise.and.fall.of.empires.htm.

—Tia Wheeler and Michael J. O'Neal

Ibn Khaldūn's "Social Solidarity"

Chapter 1

Human society is necessary. Philosophers express this truth by saying that man is social by nature, i.e., he needs a society, or "city" as they call it....

The reason for this is that ... each individual's capacity for acquiring food falls short of what is necessary to sustain life. Even taking a minimum, such as one day's supply of wheat, it is clear that this requires operations (grinding and kneading and baking) each of which necessitates utensils and tools, which presuppose the presence of carpenters, smiths, potmakers, and other craftsmen. Even granting that he eat the wheat unground, he can only obtain it in that state after many more operations, such as sowing and reaping and threshing, to separate the grain from the chaff, all of which processes require even more tools and crafts.

Now it is impossible for an individual to carry out all the above-mentioned work, or even part of it. Hence it becomes necessary for him to unite his efforts with those of his fellow men who by cooperating can produce enough for many times their number....

And unless he so cooperate with others he cannot obtain the food without which he cannot live, nor defend himself, for want of weapons, but will fall a prey to the beasts and his species will be extinct. Cooperation, however, secures both food and weapons, thus fulfilling God's will of preserving the species. Society is therefore necessary to man ... and it is society which forms the subject of this science....

Human society having, as we have shown, been achieved and spread over the face of the earth, there arises the need of a restraining force to keep men off each other in view of their animal propensities for aggressiveness and oppression of others. Now the weapons with which they defend themselves against wild beasts cannot serve as a restraint, seeing that each man can make equal use of them. Nor can the restraint come from other than men, seeing that animals fall far short of men in their mental capacity. The restraint must therefore be constituted by one man, who wields power and authority with a firm hand and thus prevents anyone from attacking anyone else, i.e. by a sovereign. Sovereignty is therefore peculiar to man, suited to his nature and indispensable to his existence.

According to certain philosophers, sovereignty may also be found in certain animal species, such as bees and locusts, which have been observed to follow the leadership of one of their species, distinguished from the rest by its size and form. But in animals sovereignty exists in virtue of instinct and divine providence, not of reflection aiming at establishing a political organization....

Chapter 2

... Aggressiveness and the lust for power are common characteristics of men, and whenever a man's eye dwells on the goods of his neighbour his hand is apt to follow it, unless he be checked by some restraint.

As regards towns and villages, their mutual aggressiveness is checked by the governors and the state, which restrain their subjects from attacking or oppressing each other; in other words, the power of the rulers preserves the people from oppression, unless it be the oppression of those same rulers. External aggression, for its part, is warded off by means of walls and fortifications, which protect a city by night, prevent surprises, and moreover supplement an otherwise inadequate defence; while the garrisons of the State carry out a prepared and prolonged resistance.

In nomadic societies, intra-group aggressiveness is checked by the chiefs and elders, owing to the prestige and respect with which they are regarded by the tribesmen. Aggression from outside, aimed at their possessions, is warded off by those of their young men who are noted for their bravery. And such defence can succeed only when they are united by a strong social solidarity arising out of kinship, for this greatly increases their strength....

Social solidarity is found only in groups related by blood ties or by other ties which fulfil the same functions. This is because blood ties have a force binding on most men, which makes them concerned with any injury inflicted on their next of kin. Men resent the oppression of their relatives, and the impulse to ward off any harm that may befall those relatives is natural and deep rooted in men.

If the degree of kinship between two persons helping each other is very close, it is obviously the blood tie, which by its very evidence, leads to the required solidarity. If the degree of kinship is distant, the blood tie is somewhat weakened but in its place there exists a family feeling based on the widespread knowledge of kinship. Hence each will help the other for fear of the dishonour which would arise if he failed in his duties towards one who is known by all to be related to him.

The clients and allies of a great nobleman often stand in the same relationship towards him as his kinsmen. Patron and client are ready to help each other because of the feeling of indignation which arises when the rights of a neighbour, a kinsman, or a friend are violated. In fact, the ties of clientship are almost as powerful as those of blood.

This explains the saying of the Prophet Mohammad, 'Learn your genealogies to know who are your near of kin,' meaning that kinship only serves a function when blood ties lead to actual cooperation and mutual aid in danger—other degrees of kinship being insignificant. The fact is that such relationship is more of an emotional than an objective fact in that it acts only by bringing together the hearts and affections of men. If the kinship is evident it acts as a natural urge leading to solidarity; if it is based on the mere knowledge of descent from a common ancestor it is weakened and has little influence on the sentiments and hence little practical effect....

Ties of kinship come out most clearly among savage peoples living in wildernesses, such as the Bedouins and other like peoples. This is because of the peculiarly hard life, poor conditions and forbidding environment which necessity has imposed upon such peoples. For their livelihood is based upon the produce of camels, and camel breeding draws them out into the wilderness where the camels graze on the bushes and plants of the desert sands....

Now the wilderness is a hard and hungry home, to which such men adapted their nature and character in successive generations. Other peoples, however, do not try to go out into the desert or to live with the nomads and share their fate; nay, should a nomad see the possibility of exchanging his condition for another he would not fail to do so.

As a result of all this, the genealogies of nomads are in no danger of being mixed or confused but remain clear and known to all....

The above [i.e. purity of race and tribal solidarity] holds true only for nomadic Arabs. The caliph Omar said: "Learn your genealogies and be not like the Nabateans of Mesopotamia who, if asked about their origin, reply: 'I come from such and such a village.'" Those Arabs who took up a more sedentary life, however, found themselves, in their quest for more fertile lands and rich pastures, crowding in on other peoples—all of which led to a mixture [of blood] and a confusion of genealogies.

This is what happened at the beginning of the Muslim era, when men began to be designated by the localities [in which they dwelt]. Thus people would refer to the military province of Qinnasrin or the military province of Damascus or that of al-'Awasim. The usage then spread to Spain.

This does not mean, however, that the Arabs were no longer designated by their genealogies; they merely added to their tribal name a place-name which allowed their riders to distinguish between them more easily. Later on, however, further mixture took place, in the cities, between Arabs and non-Arabs. This led to a complete confusion of genealogies, and a consequent weakening of that solidarity which is the fruit of tribal kinship; hence tribal names tended to be cast aside. Finally, the tribes themselves were absorbed and disappeared and with them all traces of tribal solidarity.

The nomads, however, continued as they had always been. "And God shall inherit the earth and all that are upon it...."

The end of social solidarity is sovereignty. This is because, as we have said before, it is solidarity which makes men unite their efforts for common objects, defend themselves, and repulse or overcome their enemies. We have also seen that every human society requires a restraint, and a chief who can keep men from injuring each other. Such a chief must command a powerful support, else he will not be able to carry out his restraining function. The domination he exercises is sovereignty, which exceeds the power of a tribal leader; for a tribal leader enjoys leadership and is followed by his men whom he cannot however compel. Sovereignty, on the other hand, is rule by compulsion, by means of the power at the disposal of the ruler.

[Now rulers always strive to increase their power], hence a chief who secures a following will not miss the chance of transforming, if he can, his rule into sovereignty; for power is the desire of men's souls. And sovereignty can be secured only with the help of the followers on whom the ruler relies to secure the acquiescence of his people, so that kingly sovereignty is the final end to which social solidarity leads....

Chapter 3

Kingship and dynasties can be founded only on popular support and solidarity. The reason for this is, as we have seen before, that victory, or even the mere avoidance of defeat, goes to the side which has most solidarity and whose members are readiest to fight and to die for each other. Now kingship is an honoured and coveted post, giving its holder all worldly goods as well as bodily and mental gratifications. Hence it is the object of much competition and is rarely given up willingly, but only under compulsion. Competition leads to struggle and wars and the overthrow of thrones, none of which can occur without social solidarity.

Such matters are usually unknown to, or forgotten by, the masses, who do not remember the time when the dynasty was first established, but have grown up, generation after generation, in a fixed spot, under its rule. They know nothing of the means by which God set up the dynasty; all they see is their monarchs, whose power has been consolidated and is no longer the object of dispute and who do not need to base their rule any more on social solidarity. They do not know how matters stood at first and what difficulties were encountered by the founders of the dynasty....

Once consolidated the state can dispense with social solidarity. The reason is that newly founded states can secure the obedience of their subjects only by much coercion and force. This is because the people have not had the time to get accustomed to the new and foreign rule.

Once kingship has been established, however, and inherited by successive generations or dynasties, the people forget their original condition, the rulers are invested with the aura of leadership, and the subjects obey them almost as they obey the precepts of their religion, and fight for them as they would fight for their faith. At this stage the rulers do not need to rely on a great armed force, since their rule is accepted as the will of God, which does not admit of change or contradiction. It is surely significant that the discussion of the Imamate is inserted [in theological books] at the end of the discussion of doctrinal beliefs, as though it formed an integral part of them.

From this time onward the authority of the king is based on the clients and freedmen of the royal household, men who have grown up under its protection; or else the king relies on foreign bands of warriors whom he attaches to himself.

An example of this is provided by the Abbaside dynasty. By the time of the Caliph Al-Mu'taṣim and his son Al-Wāthiq, the spirit and strength of the Arabs had been weakened, so that the kings relied mainly on clients recruited from Persians, Turks, Deylamites, Seljuks, and others. These foreigners soon came to control the provinces, the Abbasides' rule being confined to the neighbourhood of Baghdad. Then the Deylamites marched on Baghdad and occupied it, holding the Caliphs under their rule. They were succeeded by the Seljuks, who were followed by the Tatars, who killed the Caliph and wiped out that dynasty.

The same is true of the Omayyad dynasty in Spain. When the spirit and solidarity of the Arabs weakened, the feudal lords pounced on the kingdom and divided it up among themselves. Each of them set himself up as supreme lord in his region and, following the example of the foreigners in the Abbaside empire, usurped the emblems and titles of sovereignty.... They upheld their authority by means of clients and freedmen and with the help of tribesmen recruited from the Berbers, Zenata, and other North Africans....

Clientship and the mixing with slaves and allies can replace kinship [as the basis of solidarity]. For although kinship is natural and objective, it is also emotional. For group ties are formed by such things as living together, companionship, prolonged acquaintance or friendship, growing up together, having the same foster parents, and other such matters of life and death. Such ties once formed lead to mutual help and the warding off of injuries inflicted on others; as can be commonly seen to occur. An example of this is provided by the relation of dependence. For there arises a special tie between a patron and those in his service which draws them close together so that although kinship is absent the fruits of kinship are present....

Chapter 4

... The state is therefore to society as form is to matter, for the form by its nature preserves the matter and, as philosophers have shown, the two are inseparable.

For a state is inconceivable without a society; while a society without a state is well-nigh impossible, owing to the aggressive propensities of men, which require a restraint. A polity therefore arises, either theocratic or kingly, and this is what we mean by state.

The two being inseparable, any disturbance in either of them will cause a disturbance in the other;

just as the disappearance of one leads to the disappearance of the other. The greatest source of disturbance is in the breakdown of such empires as the Roman, Persian, or Arab; or in [the breakdown of a whole] dynasty, such as the Omayyad or Abbaside....

The real force which operates on society is solidarity and power, which persists through [successive] rulers. Should such a solidarity disappear, and be replaced by another solidarity which acts on society, the whole Ruling Class would disappear and the disturbance thus caused be very great....

It is evident that men are by nature in contact with and tied to each other, even where kinship is absent; though, as we have said before, in such cases such ties are weaker than where they are reinforced by kinship. Such contact may produce a solidarity nearly as powerful as that produced by kinship.

Now many city dwellers are interrelated by marriage, thus forming groups of kinsmen, divided into parties and factions, between which there exist the same relations of friendship and enmity as exist between tribes.

Christopher Columbus (AP/Wide World Photos)

CHRISTOPHER COLUMBUS'S LETTER TO RAPHAEL SANXIS ON THE DISCOVERY OF AMERICA

"If I am supported by our most invincible sovereigns, ... as much gold can be supplied as they will need."

Overview

Christopher Columbus, a mariner from Genoa, Italy, set sail from Spain in 1492 in command of three ships—the *Niña*, the *Pinta*, and the *Santa María*—and a crew of about eighty-seven men. His goal was to find a trade route to India, in the East, by sailing in a westerly direction. He arrived in the West Indies, the numerous islands that border the Caribbean Sea between southeastern North America and northeastern South America. Columbus, though, believed that he had circled the world and arrived in Asia, which is why he called the islands the Indies and referred to their inhabitants as Indians. In Columbus's day, Europeans referred to all lands east of the Indus River as the Indies. In March 1493, after having returned to Europe, he wrote a letter reporting what he had found. His letter provided the first European glimpse of the New World.

Ironically, the letter's common title, "Letter to Raphael Sanxis," perpetuates another mistake. The letter's addressee was Gabriel Sanxis, the treasurer of Aragon under the rulers of Spain, King Ferdinand II and Queen Isabella I, who had funded Columbus's voyage. The letter was translated into Latin for wider dissemination. Latin could be read by educated people throughout Europe regardless of their native tongue. The translator, Leander de Cosco, made a mistake, one of several in the translation; although "Raphael" survives in the title, the addressee's first name should have been Gabriel. The letter has been reproduced under other names, most commonly the "First Letter of Columbus," "The Latin Letter of Columbus," and "The Spanish Letter of Columbus." This letter is not to be confused with a nearly identical earlier letter Columbus had sent in February 1493 to Luis de Santángel, Ferdinand II's finance minister, who had persuaded the king and queen to agree to Columbus's proposal and finance his voyage.

Context

Columbus wrote his letter in the context of an age of European world exploration. In the fifteenth century the region around the Mediterranean Sea was dominated by great maritime powers, including Spain, Portugal, and Italian cities such as Venice, Naples, and Genoa. Rulers and merchants were interested in establishing trade routes, in large part because goods could be moved more quickly and efficiently along sea routes than by land, where roads were uncertain and rivers and mountains posed obstacles. Particularly nettlesome to Europeans was the fall of Constantinople (modern-day Istanbul, Turkey) to the Ottoman Empire in the fifteenth century. Constantinople had been the center of the Orthodox Christian Byzantine Empire and an important trade link between Europe and Asia for centuries, but the Islamic Ottomans had closed it. Merchants in Europe could still buy products from Asia in such places as Egypt, but many wanted to cut out the middleman and find a way to access Asian markets directly. An additional factor that encouraged finding new trade routes was that public treasuries throughout Europe had been depleted by war (for example, the Hundred Years' War of 1337–1453), disease (the bubonic plague, or the Black Death), and famine. Thus, the race was on for a sea route to Asia and the wealth it promised.

As the Middle Ages ended, many Europeans became intensely curious about the wider world. This curiosity had been sparked in large part by the Crusades, the two-hundred-year series of wars in the eleventh and twelfth centuries between Christian Europeans and Muslim Arabs over control of Palestine. During the Crusades, legions of Europeans had traveled to the Middle East, either on pilgrimage to the holy sites in and around Jerusalem or simply to make their fortunes. Their travels had introduced them to new terrain, new languages, new religions, and new cultures. As books about Palestine and cultural contact with Asian cultures became more widely disseminated in Europe, including works by Marco Polo and Sir John Mandeville in the fourteenth century, explorers and adventurers became determined to see these lands for themselves. In the view of some historians, the voyage of Christopher Columbus, which established the first link between two worlds, marked the separation between the ignorance and isolation of the Middle Ages and the European Renaissance (or "rebirth"), a period of intense scientific, literary, intellectual, and geographical awakening.

1451

- Christopher Columbus is born in Genoa, Italy, sometime between August 25 and October 31.

1486

- Columbus petitions the Spanish court to fund his voyage but is refused.

1487

- Columbus submits his plans to King Charles VIII of France and King Henry VII of England, but both decline his proposals.

1492

- **April 17**
Columbus signs an agreement with King Ferdinand II and Queen Isabella I of Spain to finance his expedition to the West.

- **August 3**
Columbus sets sail from Palos de la Frontera, Spain.

- **October 12**
Columbus arrives in the New World, making landfall in the Bahamas.

1493

- **January 6**
Columbus completes his initial explorations and sets sail for home.

- **February 15**
Columbus writes a letter about his voyage to Luis de Santángel, King Ferdinand's finance minister.

During the fifteenth century and well into the sixteenth, the Portuguese were the leaders in world exploration. They achieved this status in large part because of the influence of Prince Henry the Navigator, the son of Portugal's King John I. In 1415 the Portuguese gained a toehold in Africa by subduing the Muslim trading center of Ceuta, located on the Moroccan side of the Strait of Gibraltar. From about 1418 to 1421, João Gonçalves Zarco and Tristão Vaz Teixeira explored the Madeira Islands; in 1427 Diogo de Sevilha discovered the Azores Islands; in 1434 the Portuguese began to explore the western African coast, and they were the first Europeans to sail south of the equator. Around 1444 Dinís Dias sighted Cape Verde, the westernmost point of Africa, and in 1482 Diogo Cão discovered the mouth of the Congo River. From 1487 to 1488 Bartolomeu Dias led an expedition around Africa's southern tip, the Cape of Good Hope. The Portuguese continued their explorations after Columbus's voyage; Fernão de Magalhães, known to English speakers as Ferdinand Magellan, led a voyage around the world from 1519 to 1522. Portuguese explorers became the first Europeans to land in Japan in 1542, and they established the first European trading outposts in India in the early seventeenth century.

Meanwhile, the Italians were not to be outdone. Marco Polo was a Venetian who introduced Europeans to central Asia and the Far East in *The Travels of Marco Polo*. One of the most prominent Italian explorers was Amerigo Vespucci. During his voyage in 1497, the details of which are unclear, he may have sailed as far north as Canada and may have explored the Gulf of Mexico; it is known that he landed in Brazil and explored the Amazon River. Perhaps his chief legacy was that his name, Amerigo, inspired the name of the New World, America. At about the same time, Giovanni Caboto, known in English as John Cabot, became the first to explore the eastern coast of North America. Later, in 1524, the Florentine navigator Giovanni da Verrazzano explored the Atlantic seaboard of North America from Cape Fear as far north as Nova Scotia. The Verrazzano Narrows Bridge connecting the boroughs of Brooklyn and Staten Island in New York City was named after him. Christopher Columbus, thus, was one of several prominent Italian explorers.

Two qualifications should be made. First, the word *discover* is often used in connection with European exploration. Clearly, indigenous peoples had already "discovered" the land on which they lived; the native peoples of Brazil had found the Amazon River long before Amerigo Vespucci did. The word *discover* in this context is merely a shorthand way of saying that Europeans made contact with a land and its people for the first time. The second is the role of Leif Eriksson in European discovery of the Americas. Eriksson, born in Iceland, was a Norse explorer in the late tenth and early eleventh centuries. It is generally believed that he was the first European to set foot in North America; he arrived in Newfoundland very early in the eleventh century. He tends to get less credit than Columbus and others for "discovering" North America in large part because the records and details of his travels are sketchy and because his countrymen did not act on his discoveries.

Columbus began to plan his expedition in the 1480s when he started accumulating maps, charts revealing ocean currents, and papers documenting interviews with sailors who had ventured away from Europe into the Atlantic. His own travels to Africa had provided him with firsthand information about Atlantic currents, and he had learned about Viking legends surrounding Leif Eriksson. He was knowledgeable about ancient Greek and Roman theories that the world was connected by a single body of water. The reason he believed that he had landed in Asia, however, was that early scientists such as the second-century Greco-Roman astronomer and mathematician Ptolemy had seriously underestimated distances and the circumference of the world. No one suspected that two continents stood in the way of a western route to Asia.

As early as 1484, Columbus began to seek a patron for his voyage. His first choice was the Portuguese, particularly because he was living in Portugal and was married to a woman whose family had connections with the Portuguese nobility. The Portuguese king, John II, heard his proposal but ultimately turned Columbus down. He then sought patronage in Spain from Ferdinand II, the king of Aragon, and Isabella I, the queen of Castile and Léon, but initially they, too, turned him down, preoccupied as they were with efforts to reclaim by war the region of Granada from the Moors, or Spanish Muslims. He also tried to persuade King Henry VII of England and King Charles VIII of France to fund his plan, but they refused as well. Finally, in April 1492 Ferdinand and Isabella agreed to Columbus's proposal. They may have been motivated partly by their expulsion of as many as two hundred thousand Jews from Spain earlier that year; Jews had constituted a large portion of the nation's business, financial, and entrepreneurial classes.

The expedition set sail from Palos de la Frontera, Spain, on August 3, 1492. The three small ships sailed west, and on October 12, 1492, history changed when land was spotted and, later that day, the sailors stepped ashore on an island the inhabitants called Guanahani. It remains unclear exactly at which island in the Bahamas Columbus and his crew made landfall; Watling Island, or modern-day San Salvador, is the leading contender. In the weeks and months that followed, he explored other islands in the region, principally modern-day Cuba (which Columbus initially thought was the coast of China) and Hispaniola (comprising modern-day Haiti and the Dominican Republic). On January 6, 1493, the *Niña* and *Pinta* began the return voyage; the *Santa María* had been badly damaged when it had run aground on Christmas Day. After a storm-tossed voyage home, the ships made it to Lisbon, Portugal, where Columbus was arrested by Portuguese authorities for having violated Portuguese sovereignty in the Atlantic. He was eventually released and on March 15 arrived back at Palos de la Frontera, the day after he had written his letter to Sanxis. He appeared before Ferdinand and Isabella and was accorded a hero's welcome. The letter was first published in Barcelona in April 1493. Later that month, it

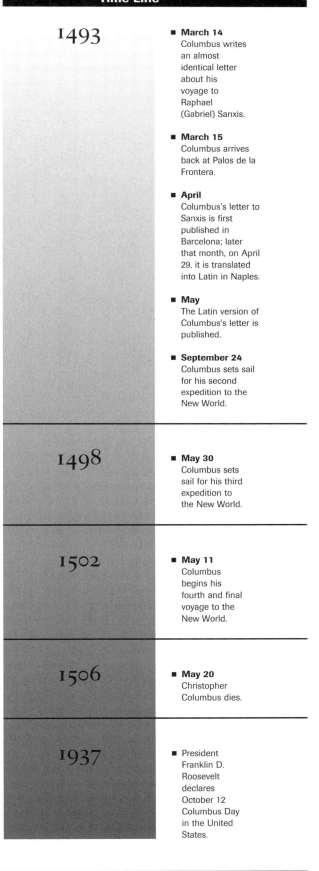

Time Line

1493

- **March 14**
  Columbus writes an almost identical letter about his voyage to Raphael (Gabriel) Sanxis.

- **March 15**
  Columbus arrives back at Palos de la Frontera.

- **April**
  Columbus's letter to Sanxis is first published in Barcelona; later that month, on April 29, it is translated into Latin in Naples.

- **May**
  The Latin version of Columbus's letter is published.

- **September 24**
  Columbus sets sail for his second expedition to the New World.

1498

- **May 30**
  Columbus sets sail for his third expedition to the New World.

1502

- **May 11**
  Columbus begins his fourth and final voyage to the New World.

1506

- **May 20**
  Christopher Columbus dies.

1937

- **President Franklin D. Roosevelt declares October 12 Columbus Day in the United States.

arrived in Naples, Italy, where Leander de Cosco translated it into Latin. The Latin version was then published in May of that year.

About the Author

Christopher Columbus (Cristoforo Colombo being the Italian form of his name and Cristóbal Colón the Spanish) was born in 1451 in Genoa, Italy, the son of a wool weaver. He apparently acquired a good education, for he spoke several languages and had read the works of such early scientists as Ptolemy. At the age of fourteen he took his first sea voyage, and in his twenties he worked on trading ships that took him to northern Europe, the Aegean Sea, and perhaps as far west as Iceland.

After having married and become a father, Columbus settled in Lisbon, Portugal, where he and his brother, Bartholomeo (Spanish form, Bartolomé), ran a shop that sold maps and charts. In 1485 he moved to Spain and began the process of seeking a patron to fund his search for a western trade route. It was not until 1492, after King Ferdinand II and Queen Isabella I had expelled the Moors from Spain, that they were prepared to listen seriously to his proposals, which included the promises to spread Christianity and to bring back gold, spices, and silk from Asia. The king and queen finally agreed, the contract reading in part:

> that of all and every kind of merchandise, whether pearls, precious stones, gold, silver, spices, and other objects and merchandise whatsoever, of whatever kind, name and sort, which may be bought, bartered, discovered, acquired and obtained within the limits of the said Admiralty, Your Highnesses grant from now henceforth to the said Don Cristóbal [Christopher Columbus] ... the tenth part of the whole, after deducting all the expenses which may be incurred therein. (qtd. in Bourne, p. 79)

Columbus set sail in August of that year. He arrived in the Bahamas on October 12 and returned to Spain in March the following year.

Columbus's explorations of the New World did not end with this voyage. In 1493 he launched a second voyage in which he commanded seventeen ships and twelve hundred men; this voyage introduced horses to the New World. During this expedition, he created the colony of Santo Domingo and in 1495 subdued the entire island of Hispaniola and thus became governor of its Spanish colony. Two more voyages followed. In 1498, following a more southerly route, he came across Trinidad and Tobago, Margarita, and Grenada, and he touched the South American mainland. Oddly, in 1500 he was arrested in Santo Domingo on charges that he and his men had abused native people and that he himself had abused Spaniards. Back in Spain, he successfully defended himself against these charges, although he was removed as governor of the colony. In 1502 he took his fourth voyage, during which he arrived in Panama. This voyage was fraught with problems. He was forced to wait a year in Jamaica while his ships were being repaired. Finally, he departed for Europe in 1504. He fell ill in 1505 and died on May 20, 1506, in Valladolid, Spain.

Explanation and Analysis of the Document

Christopher Columbus realized that he would need backing for future expeditions to the New World and thus was eager to report that his journey had been an unqualified success. Accordingly, in his letter he submitted a glowing account of the lands he had discovered and the people he had encountered, all with a view to impressing on his readers the many reasons why Spain should continue efforts to colonize the lands he had found.

◆ Introduction

The text begins with an introduction, which notes the details of the voyage. As has been noted, however, the translator, Leander de Cosco, mistakenly used the name Raphael rather than Gabriel Sanxis. It is also noted that the translation was made on "the third of the kalends of May 4, 1493." The term *kalends* is a variant of *calends* and refers to the first day of the ancient Roman month, from which days were counted backward. In this case, the date in this complicated calendar system would be April 29. This version of the letter pays tribute to King Ferdinand II, but other published versions of the letter made certain to acknowledge Queen Isabella I as well.

◆ Paragraphs 1 and 2

The text of Columbus's letter begins with another translation mistake. Columbus appears to say that he had departed from Cadiz, but in fact he had departed from Palos de la Frontera, with a stop at the Canary Islands before having sailed westward. In a straightforward way, Columbus notes that he arrived at the islands, which he then claimed for the king. He also states that he renamed them in honor of Christ (San Salvador); Christ's mother, Mary; and the king and queen. The island on which he first landed was called Guanahany (or Guanahani), which in the language of the indigenous people, the Taínos ("the friendly people"), meant "cradle of life." He gave the name Juana to what turned out to be Cuba, naming the island probably for Juana of Castile, the daughter of Ferdinand and Isabella and mother of Holy Roman Emperor Charles V. Which of the islands corresponded to each of the other names is uncertain. In the second paragraph he provides some details about his exploration of Cuba, which he believed was "the continental country of Cathay," or China.

◆ Paragraph 3

After having found the coast of Cuba to be isolated, Columbus sailed on to what he called Hispana, or Hispaniola (a corruption of La Isla Española), which he details in the third paragraph. He believed that he had come across Japan. He describes the island's landscape, extolling its

Replica of the Nina (AP/Wide World Photos)

beauty, its "salubrious rivers" and high mountains, the bays that provided harbors, the flora and fauna (nightingales, palm trees, fruit trees), resources such as spices and metals, and the "vast fields, groves, fertile plains, very suitable for planting and cultivating, and for the building of houses." Columbus was already looking forward to the prospect of Spain's colonizing the land with farmers and planters, and he wanted to impress on his readers the suitability of the islands for this purpose.

◆ **Paragraphs 4 and 5**

With the fourth paragraph, Columbus turns to a description of the inhabitants he encountered. Modern readers can only imagine the reactions of the crew from Catholic Spain once they saw the nakedness of the islanders. Columbus notes that the islands had no iron and therefore the inhabitants did not use iron weapons, but he adds that they did arm themselves with spears. He makes much of the timidity and fear of the islanders. While modern readers may be challenged to imagine the reactions of

Spanish sailors, it takes little imagination to picture the reactions of the islanders to what must have struck them as the explorers' massive ships, strange clothing, and fearful weapons. Perhaps with a view to reassuring his countrymen that the islanders would be pliant, Columbus stresses their simple manners, trustworthiness, "excellent and acute understanding," and liberality with their goods. He details some of the exchanges he made, emphasizing that the islanders were willing to give gold for trifling items. Again, perhaps Columbus was trying to whet the appetite of his countrymen for future expeditions.

In the fourth paragraph, too, Columbus touches on the religious aspect of his mission. He reports that he gave the islanders goods to make them "friendly to me, that they might be made worshippers of Christ." He notes that the islanders did not practice "idolatry" and suggests that they would be "favorably inclined" to conversion to Christianity, especially since they had greeted the explorers as "celestial people" and offered food and drink with "great love and extraordinary goodwill." In the fifth paragraph, he details the characteristics of the boats and canoes the islanders used for trading and commerce. Columbus was thus emphasizing that trade already existed in the islands and that networks of transportation and trade could later be exploited by the Spanish. He happily reports that the natives of different islands spoke languages that were mutually intelligible, which would facilitate the process of Christian conversion.

◆ **Paragraph 6**

The sixth paragraph provides details about further exploration of the islands, along with specifications of distances. Columbus extols the immensity of Hispaniola, comparing the length of its coastline to that of Spain: the distance between "Colonia," or Cátalonia, and "Fontarabia," or Fuenterrabía on Spain's northeastern coast near the French border. He reports that he came across a city that he renamed for the "Lord of the Nativity," or La Navidad. He ordered that a fort be built and thus established the very first colony in the New World. Hispaniola would become the most significant Spanish colony in the region—and the most lucrative. Despite Columbus's protestations that the soldiers remaining at the fort faced no danger as long as they did not "transgress the regulations and command which we gave," in fact, Columbus and later his brother, Bartholomeo, turned out to be poor administrators of the colony. Eventually, Spanish colonists would rise up in arms against them, and both Christopher and his brother would be arrested. The chief sufferers in these disputes, though, were the Taíno, who were subjected to what was called *encomienda*, a system that required them to mine designated quotas of gold that were shipped to Spain as tribute to the Spanish Crown. In effect, the Taíno became slaves.

◆ **Paragraph 7**

The seventh paragraph returns to the islanders and a discussion of their customs. Columbus notes, for example, that with the exception of chiefs the people are monogamous and that he was uncertain of the extent to which they owned personal property—a characteristic the Spanish could exploit to their advantage. Again with a view to reassuring the Spanish, he stresses that he found no "monstrosities." He is compelled to note the existence of one warlike tribe on the island of Dominica, though he dismisses them as a threat. He describes the physical appearance of the islanders and touches on the roles of women relative to men. Further tempting the Spanish, he alludes to the legend about a nearby island that supposedly abounded in gold.

◆ **Paragraph 8**

In the final paragraph of the letter, Columbus shifts into what might be characterized as the role of salesman. He notes that he has brought along men who can attest to the truth of his observations. He speculates that the men he left behind at the fort have already discovered products that will be valuable to the Spanish. He observes that he would have been able to bring back more bounty if he had

been outfitted with "as many ships as the occasion required." In his following request to his "most invincible sovereigns" for "a little of their help," he holds out the promise of future bounty: "as much gold can be supplied as they will need, indeed as much of spices, of cotton, of chewing gum (which is only found in Chios) ... and as many slaves for the navy, as their majesties will wish to demand." He goes on to cast the expedition in religious terms as a manifestation of divine will. He virtually compels the king and queen to fund future expeditions when he declares, "Let Christ rejoice on earth, as he rejoices in heaven, when he foresees coming to salvation so many souls of people hitherto lost." Soon, Christendom would not only expand its boundaries but also partake in an increase in temporal, or worldly, advantages.

Audience

The nominal audience of Columbus's letter was Gabriel Sanxis, King Ferdinand II's treasurer. The true audience, however, comprised the king and his consort, Queen Isabella I, who had funded the expedition and could be counted on to fund further expeditions if Columbus reported a successful first journey. It is unknown whether Columbus anticipated that his letter would be published, but he likely knew that its contents, if not the letter itself, would be disseminated to others who might finance future expeditions. Surely, he realized that his broader audience was the Spanish people, who would take pride in Columbus's accomplishment and be gratified to know that the people he had encountered in the New World could potentially be the source of wealth and become Christian converts. Yet another member of the letter's audience was the pope, Alexander VI, who must have read the letter either in Spanish or the Latin translation, or perhaps its contents were reported to him. His response on May 4, 1493, was to issue a papal bull (thus called because the document was authenticated with a round leaden seal called a *bulla*) granting Ferdinand and Isabella perpetual ownership of the New World.

Impact

The impact of Columbus's letter cannot be disentangled from the impact of the voyage itself. Europeans learned for the first time of the existence of an entirely new world, one that held the potential for the acquisition of great wealth and the spread of Christianity. Columbus described this new world as a land of immense beauty and richness, and within a hundred years of his death the route he had charted had been followed by many adventurers, traders, colonists, planters, fortune seekers, missionaries, and others willing to abandon their life in the Old World for the possibilities opened by the New World.

Historians and others continue to debate a fundamental question: Was Columbus a hero or a villain? That he was an accomplished mariner is clear, though he went to his

"I proceeded along [Juana's] coast towards the west for some distance; I found it so large and without perceptible end, that I believed it to be not an island, but the continental country of Cathay."

(Paragraph 2)

"In the one which was called Hispana ... there are great and beautiful mountains, vast fields, groves, fertile plains, very suitable for planting and cultivating, and for the building of houses."

(Paragraph 3)

"Yet when they perceive that they are safe, putting aside all fear, they are of simple manners and trustworthy, and very liberal with everything they have, refusing no one who asks for anything they may possess, and even themselves inviting us to ask for things."

(Paragraph 4)

"I gave to them many beautiful and pleasing things that I had brought with me, no value being taken in exchange, in order that I might the more easily make them friendly to me, that they might be made worshippers of Christ, and that they might be full of love towards our king, queen, and prince, and the whole Spanish nation."

(Paragraph 4)

"I promise this, that if I am supported by our most invincible sovereigns with a little of their help, as much gold can be supplied as they will need, indeed as much of spices, of cotton, of chewing gum (which is only found in Chios),... and as many slaves for the navy, as their majesties will wish to demand."

(Paragraph 8)

"Let Christ rejoice on earth, as he rejoices in heaven, when he foresees coming to salvation so many souls of people hitherto lost."

(Paragraph 8)

death continuing to believe that he had found Asia. That Columbus had the vision to believe that the world was round and that the earth could be circumnavigated makes him an important figure of the early Renaissance, although if he had never lived, in time someone else would have made the same discoveries. He was a poor administrator, and he shared the racist views of Europeans of his day. His discoveries changed the course of world history and led to what historians call the Columbian exchange, in which foodstuffs, plants, herbal remedies, livestock, fruit trees, tobacco, chewing gum (made from chicle, a natural tree gum), technologies, and cultures passed back and forth over the Atlantic. But the legacy of Columbus was also one of slavery and disease—populations were decimated by smallpox carried by Europeans, a disease to which American indigenous peoples had no immunity. According to some historians, the population of Hispaniola dropped from approximately one million to thirty thousand within twenty years after Columbus's arrival, and as early as 1502 African slaves were being imported to replace the shrinking labor population. Some historians believe that in return European syphilis may have originated in Central America.

Nevertheless, Columbus's legacy came to be celebrated in the United States. In 1792 the Society of Saint Tammany in New York City organized a celebration to commemorate the three hundredth anniversary of Columbus's voyage. In 1869 Italians in San Francisco organized an October 12 celebration. Since 1920 Americans have annually celebrated October 12 in honor of Columbus, and in 1937 President Franklin D. Roosevelt designated October 12 "Columbus Day." Columbus's name survives in the U.S. capital (the District of Columbia), a Canadian province (British Columbia), and in the names of numerous cities, counties, natural landmarks, and such institutions as Columbia University. Many activists who speak for indigenous peoples, though, decry the celebration of Columbus Day, believing that it is a symbol of colonization and exploitation.

The process of colonizing the Americas did not take long. Spaniards first settled Hispaniola and then moved on to Puerto Rico, Cuba, and Jamaica. By 1519, Hernando Cortés, from his base in Cuba, was leading the conquest of the Aztec empire. He and his conquistadors razed Tenochtitlán, the Aztec capital city, and forged Mexico as the capital of the viceroyalty of New Spain. In the 1520s Spain's Francisco Pizarro explored the western coast of South America and in the 1530s conquered the Inca capital at Cuzco. Because the city was too high and remote, the Spaniards established a new capital, Lima, near the coast of Peru. Meanwhile, Portugal laid claim to Brazil, while Spaniards established Santa María del Buen Aire (which later became Buenos Aires, the capital of Argentina) in 1536 and Asunción (the capital of Paraguay) in 1537. Also in the sixteenth century, the French, Spanish, Portuguese, Dutch, Swedish, and English arrived in North America, establishing the first European colonies there. Ponce de León of Spain explored Florida during expeditions in 1513 and 1521, and French Huguenots (Calvinist Protestants) arrived in the 1560s. By the early 1600s the British and Dutch were colonizing what would become the eastern seaboard of the United States. In time, this would bring to North America a flood of African

Questions for Further Study

1. It is widely noted that Columbus believed that he had arrived in Asia when in fact he was in the Caribbean. Do you believe that this misapprehension on Columbus's part in any way diminishes his accomplishment?

2. Columbus Day is celebrated as a minor holiday in the United States. Many Native American activists and others oppose this celebration, arguing that Columbus's voyage led to the decimation of Amerindian populations and that Columbus himself was guilty of atrocities against Amerindians. What is your position on this issue?

3. In what ways might politics and economics have influenced, and perhaps biased, Columbus's account of his discovery?

4. Some historians make the suggestion that if one had to choose a single event that marked the beginning of the European Renaissance, it would be Columbus's voyage to the New World. On what basis could this assertion be considered true, if slightly exaggerated?

5. History's grand events can sometimes be the outcome of a mosaic of details—unimportant in themselves—that comes together at just the right time and in just the right place to produce a momentous outcome. What historical and personal details led to Columbus's voyage of discovery? How might this history of exploration of the New World have been different had these occurrences not coalesced?

slaves and of Irish, Scandinavian, German, Italian, and Eastern European immigrants.

At about 2:00 am on October 12, 1492, a sailor named Rodrigo de Triana was at his post as a lookout onboard the *Pinta*. He strained to see what appeared to him to be a sandbank and then shouted "Tierra! Tierra!" ("Land! Land!"). The echo of those words continues to reverberate throughout the world.

Further Reading

▪ Books

Bourne, Edward G., and Julius E. Olson, eds. *The Northmen, Columbus, and Cabot, 985–1503: The Voyages of the Northmen, the Voyages of Columbus and of John Cabot*. 1906. Reprint. Boston: Adamant Media Corporation, 2001.

Cohen, J. M., ed. and trans. *The Four Voyages of Christopher Columbus: Being His Own Log-Book, Letters and Dispatches with Connecting Narrative Drawn from the Life of the Admiral by His Son Hernando Colon and Others*. London: Penguin Classics, 1969.

Crosby, A. W. *The Columbian Voyages: The Columbian Exchange, and Their Historians*. Washington, D.C.: American Historical Association, 1987.

Davidson, Miles H. *Columbus Then and Now: A Life Reexamined*. Norman: University of Oklahoma Press, 1997.

Fuson, Robert H., ed. and trans. *The Log of Christopher Columbus*. Camden, Maine: International Marine Publishing, 1987.

Keen, Benjamin, ed. and trans. *The Life of the Admiral Christopher Columbus by his Son Ferdinand*. 1959. Reprint. Westport, Conn.: Greenwood Press, 1978.

Markham, Clements R., ed. and trans. *The Journal of Christopher Columbus (During His First Voyage, 1492–93) and Documents Relating the Voyages of John Cabot and Gaspar Corte Real*. 1893. Reprint. Boston: Adamant Media Corporation, 2001

Morison, Samuel Eliot. *Christopher Columbus, Mariner*. Boston: Little, Brown, 1955.

Phillips, William D., Jr., and Carla Rahn Phillips. *The Worlds of Christopher Columbus*. New York: Cambridge University Press, 1992.

Wilford, John Noble. *The Mysterious History of Columbus: An Exploration of the Man, the Myth, the Legacy*. New York: Knopf, 1991.

▪ Web Sites

"1492: An Ongoing Voyage." Library of Congress Web site. http://www.loc.gov/exhibits/1492/intro.html.

—Michael J. O'Neal

CHRISTOPHER COLUMBUS'S LETTER TO RAPHAEL SANXIS ON THE DISCOVERY OF AMERICA

Letter of Christopher Columbus, to whom our age owes much, concerning the islands recently discovered in the Indian sea. For the search of which, eight months before, he was sent under the auspices and at the cost of the most invincible Ferdinand, king of Spain. Addressed to the magnificent lord Raphael Sanxis, treasurer of the same most illustrious king, and which the noble and learned man Leander de Cosco has translated from the Spanish language into Latin, on the third of the kalends of May 4, 1493, the first year of the pontificate of Alexander the Sixth.

Because my undertakings have attained success, I know that it will be pleasing to you: these I have determined to relate, so that you may be made acquainted with everything done and discovered in this our voyage. On the thirty-third day after I departed from Cadiz, I came to the Indian sea, where I found many islands inhabited by men without number, of all which I took possession for our most fortunate king, with proclaiming heralds and flying standards, no one objecting. To the first of these I gave the name of the blessed Saviour, on whose aid relying I had reached this as well as the other islands. But the Indians call it Guanahany. I also called each one of the others by a new name. For I ordered one island to be called Santa Maria of the Conception, another Fernandina, another Isabella, another Juana, and so on with the rest.

As soon as we had arrived at that island which I have just now said was called Juana, I proceeded along its coast towards the west for some distance; I found it so large and without perceptible end, that I believed it to be not an island, but the continental country of Cathay; seeing, however, no towns or cities situated on the sea-coast, but only some villages and rude farms, with whose inhabitants I was unable to converse, because as soon as they saw us they took flight. I proceeded farther, thinking that I would discover some city or large residences. At length, perceiving that we had gone far enough, that nothing new appeared, and that this way was leading us to the north, which I wished to avoid, because it was winter on the land, and it was my intention to go to the south, moreover the winds were becoming violent, I therefore determined that no other plans were practicable, and so, going back, I returned to a certain bay that I had noticed, from which I sent two of our men to the land, that they might find out whether there was a king in this country, or any cities. These men traveled for three days, and they found people and houses without number, but they were small and without any government, therefore they returned.

Now in the meantime I had learned from certain Indians, whom I had seized there, that this country was indeed an island, and therefore I proceeded towards the east, keeping all the time near the coast, for 322 miles, to the extreme ends of this island. From this place I saw another island to the east, distant from this Juana, 54 miles, which I called forthwith Hispana; and I sailed to it; and I steered along the northern coast, as at Juana, towards the east, 564 miles. And the said Juana and the other islands there appear very fertile. This island is surrounded by many very safe and wide harbors, not excelled by any others that I have ever seen. Many great and salubrious rivers flow through it. There are also many very high mountains there. All these islands are very beautiful, and distinguished by various qualities; they are accessible, and full of a great variety of trees stretching up to the stars; the leaves of which I believe are never shed, for I saw them as green and flourishing as they are usually in Spain in the month of May; some of them were blossoming, some were bearing fruit, some were in other conditions; each one was thriving in its own way. The nightingale and. various other birds without number were singing, in the month of November, when I was exploring them. There are besides in the said island Juana seven or eight kinds of palm trees, which far excel ours in height and beauty, just as all the other trees, herbs, and fruits do. There are also excellent pine trees, vast plains and meadows, a variety of birds, a variety of honey, and a variety of metals, excepting iron. In the one which was called Hispana, as we said above, there are great and beautiful mountains, vast fields, groves, fertile plains, very suitable for planting and cultivating, and for the building of houses. The convenience of the harbors in this island, and the remarkable number of rivers contributing to the healthfulness of man, exceed belief, unless one has seen them. The trees, pasturage, and fruits of this island differ greatly from those of Juana. This Hispana, moreover, abounds in different kinds of spices, in gold, and in metals.

On this island, indeed, and on all the others which I have seen, and of which I have knowledge, the inhabitants of both sexes go always naked, just as they came into the world, except some of the women, who use a covering of a leaf or some foliage, or a cotton cloth, which they make themselves for that purpose. All these people lack, as I said above, every kind of iron; they are also without weapons, which indeed are unknown; nor are they competent to use them, not on account of deformity of body, for they are well formed, but because they are timid and full of fear. They carry for weapons, however, reeds baked in the sun, on the lower ends of which they fasten some shafts of dried wood rubbed down to a point; and indeed they do not venture to use these always; for it frequently happened when I sent two or three of my men to some of the villages, that they might speak with the natives, a compact troop of the Indians would march out, and as soon as they saw our men approaching, they would quickly take flight, children being pushed aside by their fathers, and fathers by their children. And this was not because any hurt or injury had been inflicted on any one of them, for to every one whom I visited and with whom I was able to converse, I distributed whatever I had, cloth and many other things, no return being made to me; but they are by nature fearful and timid. Yet when they perceive that they are safe, putting aside all fear, they are of simple manners and trustworthy, and very liberal with everything they have, refusing no one who asks for anything they may possess, and even themselves inviting us to ask for things. They show greater love for all others than for themselves; they give valuable things for trifles, being satisfied even with a very small return, or with nothing; however, I forbade that things so small and of no value should be given to them, such as pieces of plates, dishes and glass, likewise keys and shoe-straps; although if they were able to obtain these, it seemed to them like getting the most beautiful jewels in the world. It happened, indeed, that a certain sailor obtained in exchange for a shoestrap as much worth of gold as would equal three golden coins; and likewise other things for articles of very little value, especially for new silver coins, and for some gold coins, to obtain which they gave whatever the seller desired, as for instance an ounce and a half and two ounces of gold, or thirty and forty pounds of cotton, with which they were

already acquainted. They also traded cotton and gold for pieces of bows, bottles, jugs and jars, like persons without reason, which I forbade because it was very wrong; and I gave to them many beautiful and pleasing things that I had brought with me, no value being taken in exchange, in order that I might the more easily make them friendly to me, that they might be made worshippers of Christ, and that they might be full of love towards our king, queen, and prince, and the whole Spanish nation; also that they might be zealous to search out and collect, and deliver to us those things of which they had plenty, and which we greatly needed. These people practice no kind of idolatry; on the contrary they firmly believe that all strength and power, and in fact all good things are in heaven, and that I had come down from thence with these ships and sailors; and in this belief I was received there after they had put aside fear. Nor are they slow or unskilled, but of excellent and acute understanding; and the men who have navigated that sea give an account of everything in an admirable manner; but they never saw people clothed, nor these kind of ships. As soon as I reached that sea, I seized by force several Indians on the first island, in order that they might learn from us, and in like manner tell us about those things in these lands of which they themselves had knowledge; and the plan succeeded, for in a short time we understood them and they us, sometimes by gestures and signs, sometimes by words; and it was a great advantage to us. They are coming with me now, yet always believing that I descended from heaven, although they have been living with us for a long time, and are living with us today. And these men were the first who announced it wherever we landed, continually proclaiming to the others in a loud voice, "Come, come, and you will see the celestial people." Whereupon both women and men, both children and adults, both young men and old men, laying aside the fear caused a little before, visited us eagerly, filling the road with a great crowd, some bringing food, and some drink, with great love and extraordinary goodwill.

On every island there are many canoes of a single piece of wood; and though narrow, yet in length and shape similar to our row-boats, but swifter in movement. They steer only by oars. Some of these boats are large, some small, some of medium size. Yet they row many of the larger row-boats with eighteen cross-benches, with which they cross to all those islands, which are innumerable, and with these boats they perform their trading, and carry on commerce among them. I saw some of these row-boats or canoes which were carrying seventy and eighty rowers. In all these islands there is no difference in the appearance of the people, nor in the manners and language, but all understand each other mutually; a fact that is very important for the end which I suppose to be earnestly desired by our most illustrious king, that is, their conversion to the holy religion of Christ, to which in truth, as far as I can perceive, they are very ready and favorably inclined.

I said before how I proceeded along the island Juana in a straight line from west to east 322 miles, according to which course and the length of the way, I am able to say that this Juana is larger than England and Scotland together; for besides the said 322 thousand paces, there are two more provinces in that part which lies towards the west, which I did not visit; one of these the Indians call Anan, whose inhabitants are born with tails. They extend to 180 miles in length, as I have learned from those Indians I have with me, who are all acquainted with these islands. But the circumference of Hispana is greater than all Spain from Colonia to Fontarabia. This is easily proved, because its fourth side, which I myself passed along in a straight line from west to east, extends 540 miles. This island is to be desired and is very desirable, and not to be despised; in which, although as I have said, I solemnly took possession of all the others for our most invincible king, and their government is entirely committed to the said king, yet I especially took possession of a certain large town, in a very convenient location, and adapted to all kinds of gain and commerce, to which we give the name of our Lord of the Nativity. And I commanded a fort to be built there forthwith, which must be completed by this time; in which I left as many men as seemed necessary, with all kinds of arms, and plenty of food for more than a year. Likewise one caravel, and for the construction of others men skilled in this trade and in other professions; and also the extraordinary good will and friendship of the king of this island toward us. For those people are very amiable and kind, to such a degree that the said king gloried in calling me his brother. And if they should change their minds, and should wish to hurt those who remained in the fort, they would not be able, because they lack weapons, they go naked, and are too cowardly. For that reason those who hold the said fort are at least able to resist easily this whole island, without any imminent danger to themselves, so long as they do not transgress the regulations and command which we gave.

In all these islands, as I have understood, each man is content with only one wife, except the princes or kings, who are permitted to have twenty. The women appear to work more than the men. I was not able to find out surely whether they have individual property, for I saw that one man had the duty of distributing to the others, especially refreshments, food, and things of that kind. I found no monstrosities among them, as very many supposed, but men of great reverence, and friendly. Nor are they black like the Ethiopians. They have straight hair, hanging down. They do not remain where the solar rays send out the heat, for the strength of the sun is very great here, because it is distant from the equinoctial line as it seems, only twenty-six degrees. On the tops of the mountains too the cold is severe, but the Indians, however, moderate it, partly by being accustomed to the place, and partly by the help of very hot victuals, of which they eat frequently and immoderately. And so I did not see any monstrosity, nor did I have knowledge of them any where, excepting a certain island named Charis, which is the second in passing from Hispana to India. This island is inhabited by a certain people who are considered very warlike by their neighbors. These eat human flesh. The said people have many kinds of row-boats, in which they cross over to all the other Indian islands, and seize and carry away every thing that they can. They differ in no way from the others, only that they wear long hair like the women. They use bows and darts made of reeds, with sharpened shafts fastened to the larger end, as we have described. On this account they are considered warlike, wherefore the other Indians are afflicted with continual fear, but I regard them as of no more account than the others. These are the people who visit certain women, who alone inhabit the island Mateunin, which is the first in passing from Hispana to India. These women, moreover, perform no kind of work of their sex, for they use bows and darts, like those I have described of their husbands; they protect themselves with sheets of copper, of which there is great abundance among them. They tell me of another island greater than the aforesaid Hispana, whose inhabitants are without hair, and which abounds in gold above all the others.

I am bringing with me men of this island and of the others that I have seen, who give proof of the things that I have described. Finally, that I may compress in few words the brief account of our departure and quick return, and the gain, I promise this, that if I am supported by our most invincible sovereigns with a little of their help, as much gold can be supplied as they will need, indeed as much of spices, of cotton, of chewing gum (which is only found in Chios), also as much of aloes wood, and as many slaves for the navy, as their majesties will wish to demand. Likewise rhubarb and other kinds of spices, which I suppose these men whom I left in the said fort have already found, and will continue to find; since I remained in no place longer than the winds forced me, except in the town of the Nativity, while I provided for the building of the fort, and for the safety of all. Which things, although they are very great and remarkable, yet they would have been much greater, if I had been aided by as many ships as the occasion required. Truly great and wonderful is this, and not corresponding to our merits, but to the holy Christian religion, and to the piety and religion of our sovereigns, because what the human understanding could not attain, that the divine will has granted to human efforts. For God is wont to listen to his servants who love his precepts, even in impossibilities, as has happened to us on the present occasion, who have attained that which hitherto mortal men have never reached. For if any one has written or said any thing about these islands, it was all with obscurities and conjectures; no one claims that he had seen them; from which they seemed like fables. Therefore let the king and queen, the princes and their most fortunate kingdoms, and all other countries of Christendom give thanks to our Lord and Saviour Jesus Christ, who has bestowed upon us so great a victory and gift. Let religious processions be solemnized; let sacred festivals be given; let the churches be covered with festive garlands. Let Christ rejoice on earth, as he rejoices in heaven, when he foresees coming to salvation so many souls of people hitherto lost. Let us be glad also, as well on account of the exaltation of our faith, as on account of the increase of our temporal affairs, of which not only Spain, but universal Christendom will be partaker. These things that have been done are thus briefly related. Farewell. Lisbon, the day before the ides of March.

Christopher Columbus, admiral of the Ocean fleet.

Niccolò Machiavelli's *The Prince*

"A prince wishing to keep his state is very often forced to do evil."

Overview

Niccolò Machiavelli was a Renaissance Italian politician, diplomat, and writer—that is, a "Renaissance man," a phrase still used to describe an educated person versed in a variety of practical and creative endeavors. He remains best known for his treatise on the acquisition, maintenance, and use of political power, *The Prince*, or *Il Principe* in Italian. He is considered one of the most famous thinkers of the Renaissance and is thought by some to be the founder of modern political science, since his goal in writing *The Prince* was to divorce politics from morality. For some readers, Machiavelli was the consummate political realist. For others, he was a cynic, and his name has survived in the adjective *Machiavellian*, which denotes the use of sly cunning and manipulation in order to achieve one's ends.

The Prince is a prominent document in a literary genre called "Mirrors for Princes." In this context, the word *princes* has been used to refer to rulers in general, not just princes. Writers in this genre in antiquity examined politics by asking series of questions: What defines the good state? What characteristics define the good citizen? Among early church fathers such as Saint Augustine, the key issue was what defined a good prince. Augustine's answer was the beginning of a Christian "Mirrors for Princes" literary tradition that would continue up to the Renaissance. These treatises were written to advise a Christian prince about how to rule so that in conducting the affairs of state the prince did not lose his soul. A Renaissance example of such a treatise was *The Education of a Christian Prince* by the Dutch humanist scholar Desiderius Erasmus, who had written it as a textbook for the young Spanish Habsburg prince who would become Charles I of Spain as well as the Holy Roman Emperor Charles V. The critical difference between Machiavelli and Erasmus had to do with ethical concerns. For Erasmus, success was goodness. By following Christian ethical principles, a prince should leave the kingdom or principality in better condition than when he had come to power. Machiavelli, in contrast, sought political success. What mattered was getting, using, and keeping power. Power was an end in itself rather than a means to an end.

Machiavelli drew upon two sources to develop his political thought: his political experiences as a government official during a tumultuous time in the history of Florence—which was mirrored in the turmoil in other Italian city-states and much of Europe—and from his study of classical history, especially that of the Romans. As he watched the political machinations of his contemporaries and studied the rise and fall of ancient Roman figures, he concluded that the Augustinian tradition continued by Erasmus and others was based far too much on an idealistic religious framework. What was needed, in his view, was a more realistic approach to politics based on human nature as it could be understood in a historical framework. The result was *The Prince* as well as many other historical works, the most prominent being *Discourses on Livy* (a Roman writer) and *The Art of War*. Machiavelli himself stated the unifying theme of his works in a document titled *Words to Be Spoken on the Law for Appropriating Money*:

> All the cities that ever at any time have been ruled by an absolute prince, by aristocrats or by the people, as is this one, have had for their protection force combined with prudence, but the latter is not enough alone, and the first either does not produce things or, when they are produced, does not maintain them. (qtd. in Gilbert, vol. 3, p. 1439)

Context

Machiavelli's life coincided with political turmoil in his home city of Florence (Italian: Firenze), one of the most important city-states in the region of central Italy called Tuscany. On the surface, Florence was a democracy, but in reality it was more of an oligarchy or plutocracy, with power lodged in the hands of a few prominent and wealthy citizens. Chief among these wealthy citizens were the Medicis, a family of bankers and merchants led by Cosimo de' Medici, sometimes called Cosimo the Elder, who came to power in 1434. The Medicis manipulated elections through fear and favor and created a patronage network that relied on a combination of cunning, deception, persuasion, leniency, force, and social astuteness—all oiled by

1434

- Cosimo de' Medici (1389–1464) takes control of the Republic of Florence.

1469

- Lorenzo ("the Magnificent") de' Medici (1449–1492), Cosimo's grandson, becomes ruler of Florence.

- **May 3** Niccolò Machiavelli is born in Florence.

1494

- King Charles VIII of France invades northern Italy; the Medicis are expelled, and Girolamo Savonarola takes power.

1497

- **February 7** Many works of art and luxury items are destroyed in the Bonfire of the Vanities sponsored by Savonarola.

1498

- Savonarola is burned at the stake; soon afterward, Machiavelli is appointed head of the second chancery and later secretary to the Signoria (governing council of Florence).

1500

- Machiavelli makes his first diplomatic mission to France.

money—to manage Florence for generations without establishing an overt dictatorship.

Machiavelli came of age during a time of rapid change. Piero di Cosimo de' Medici, Cosimo's son, succeeded his father in 1464, but he was soon followed in 1469 by Cosimo's grandson, Lorenzo the Magnificent, an important patron of the arts. When Lorenzo died in 1492, his son, Piero di Lorenzo, succeeded him but ruled only until 1494, when King Charles VIII of France invaded Italy to enforce his claim to the kingdom of Naples. In the meantime, the papacy fell into the hands of the infamous and cunning Borgias, a family of Spanish origin who maintained their power in Rome and in their home state of Venice through virtually every crime imaginable. Rodrigo Borgia became Pope Alexander VI in 1492. With his backing, his son, Cesare, brutally tried to assert rule over Romagna and the Marches in central Italy. It is thought that the conduct of Borgias—in particular Cesare—was Machiavelli's major inspiration for *The Prince*.

With the Medici family overthrown, power was seized by Girolamo Savonarola, an ascetic Dominican friar who ruled Florence as both a secular leader and a priest and who sought to remake Florence into a Christian theocracy. Savonarola is perhaps best known for an incident that took place on February 7, 1497, when a large number of items associated with moral laxity—books, cosmetics, statues and paintings, gaming pieces, mirrors, musical instruments, women's finery—were destroyed in the "Bonfire of the Vanities." Under his regime, which regarded trade and the making of money as "vanities," Florence became a grim and poverty-stricken place. Alexander VI and the Florentine aristocracy had soon had enough. Savonarola was arrested on charges that included heresy; he was tortured and then burned at the stake on May 23, 1498.

Meanwhile, the Medici family, led by Piero di Lorenzo de' Medici (nicknamed by some sources "Piero the Unfortunate"), continued to live in exile in Venice. Florence remained free of Medici rule until 1512, but the intervening years were chaotic. Discord existed among the groups who opposed Savonarola's vision of a democratic government; similar discord arose among the various factions that supported the Medicis. War with France over control of Pisa dragged on—and drained the resources of the aristocracy. Florence lacked a strong executive authority, leading to the restoration of the Medicis under Lorenzo de' Medici. The following year, Giovanni de' Medici, the second son of Lorenzo the Magnificent, was installed as Pope Leo X. This was during a time when the pope was the de facto ruler of Italy's Papal States and exerted influence over much of the Italian peninsula. The Medicis retained the papacy after Leo X's death in 1521; his cousin, Giulio de' Medici, was elected Pope Clement VII in 1523.

As if this internal turmoil, warfare, and intrigue were not enough, Machiavelli was witness to considerable turmoil beyond the borders of Florence. The chief Italian city-states—Milan, Venice, Florence, Naples, and the Papal States (the regions of central Italy under the direct rule of the papacy), along with lesser city-states and duchies such as Pisa, Mantua, Genoa, Siena, Verona, and others—engaged in intense competition that frequently erupted into warfare, both on land and at sea. These rivalries were the source of political maneuvering, plots to overthrow rulers, attempted assassinations, and other examples of skullduggery. The papacy often acted as a power broker in these disputes. Constant wars between the Italian states as well as invasions by armies from France and the Holy Roman Empire greatly hindered unity and peaceful development for centuries.

About the Author

Niccolò Machiavelli was born in Florence on May 3, 1469. Little is known of his early life. Since his father's financial problems prevented him from receiving an education that would have matched his abilities, he was largely self-taught. During his twenties he witnessed the rise and fall of Girolamo Savonarola. In the new republican government that was created after Savonarola's execution, he was appointed head of the second chancery (*cancelleria*) in Florence. The post was less important than other posts, but its responsibilities grew when it was merged with the Secretariat of the Ten (*i Dieci*), which was the executive council. He was also secretary to the magistracy, and as such he was ultimately responsible to the Signoria, the governing council, which assigned him duties concerning foreign relations and defense.

In the course of performing his duties, Machiavelli went on several diplomatic missions. The first was to France in 1500. Upon his return, he served as the Florentine representative to the court of Cesare Borgia in 1502 and 1503. In Machiavelli's writings, Borgia would later emerge as a model for the kind of authoritarian prince who could bring unity to Italy by sheer force. However, not long afterward Cesare was imprisoned and stripped of his lands; he soon escaped from captivity but died in exile in Spain.

From 1507 to 1512, Machiavelli remained busy with efforts to dislodge the French from Italy and to dissuade the Holy Roman Emperor, Maximilian I, from invading Italy. He also led the Florentine militia he had organized, and in June 1509 it subdued the rival city of Pisa. When the Medici family was restored to power in Florence in 1512, Machiavelli was dismissed and then arrested soon afterward and imprisoned after a conspiracy against the Medici had come to light. He was tortured as a suspect in the plot to overthrow the Medici but later released for lack of evidence. He was then confined to his home in Florence. Impoverished, he returned to his father's small piece of land outside Florence, where he wrote a number of works to win the favor of the Medici, including *The Prince* and a broader study of politics, *Discourses on Livy*.

While Machiavelli was a republican in sympathies, he was also a practical politician who sought power and an office in which to exert it. He dedicated *The Prince* to Lorenzo di Piero de' Medici but to no avail. He had more success courting favor with Giulio de' Medici, who became

Time Line

1502	■ Machiavelli visits Cesare Borgia and draws lessons from his conduct that later will be developed in *The Prince*.
1506	■ Machiavelli helps muster a citizen's militia in Florence.
1509	■ Machiavelli leads Florentine military operations against Pisa.
1512	■ The Medicis are restored to power in Florence, and Machiavelli is dismissed from office.
1513	■ Giovanni de' Medici becomes Pope Leo X. Machiavelli is arrested, tortured, and briefly imprisoned; after his release, he writes *The Prince*.
1520	■ Machiavelli's book *The Art of War* is published.
1527	■ **June 21** Machiavelli dies.
1532	■ *The Prince* is published.

Cesare Borgia with Machiavelli (Library of Congress)

Pope Clement VII in 1523, in part by writing an official history of Florence for him. Machiavelli also wrote many literary works, especially comedies. After Rome was sacked in 1527 by troops from the Holy Roman Empire, the Medicis were expelled from Florence again, leaving Machiavelli without a position. Disappointed and ill, he died on June 21, 1527.

Explanation and Analysis of the Document

The Prince is not a long book. It has twenty-six chapters that are compact and clearly written; however, it is not thoroughly systematic. It was based upon study of modern events and ancient history from which the author drew political lessons. The selection is from Chapters XIV to XIX.

◆ Chapter XIV: That Which Concerns a Prince on the Subject of the Art of War

In this chapter, Machiavelli discusses war as the central subject of study for a prince, stating, "A prince ought to have no other aim or thought, nor select anything else for his study, than war and its rules and discipline." Machiavelli reasons that wars have usually been waged by princes;

war enabled them to win and keep kingdoms—or to lose them. He points out that princes who submersed themselves in pleasure rather than war often lost power and adds that history contains many stories of kingdoms and empires that were conquered by battle-hardened invaders. Ineptitude in manipulating violence usually meant not just defeat but also destruction.

Machiavelli cites historical examples such as Francesco Sforza, whose success at arms enabled him to become the duke of Milan. A prince wins respect, Machiavelli contends, by being armed, but an unarmed prince engenders the suspicion of those who are armed. Likewise, for a prince to be unarmed and unskilled in the use of weapons would not lead to respect, and such a prince could not rely on his armed men. Accordingly, arms and warfare were the proper study of a prince, even more so in peace than in wartime, and a prince should practice with his men the drills and activities that harden the body. Machiavelli also observes that a prince should know how to read the terrain and make use of this knowledge in developing military strategy.

In Machiavelli's view, conducting war games during peacetime would familiarize a prince and his troops with the geography of their territory. This familiarity, he observes, not only could aid in defensive operations against invaders but also could be applicable to fighting in foreign lands. Machiavelli cites the example from ancient Greece of Philopoemen, the prince of the Achaeans in the third century BCE, who continually treated the countryside as a maneuvers map, especially in peacetime. Philopoemen's objective was to learn war and eliminate the possibility of surprise attack. Citing further examples such as Xenophon, Alexander the Great, and Julius Caesar, Machiavelli recommends that princes read histories "and study there the actions of illustrious men, to see how they have borne themselves in war, to examine the causes of their victories and defeat, so as to avoid the latter and imitate the former."

◆ Chapter XV: Concerning Things for Which Men, and Especially Princes, Are Praised or Blamed

Chapter XV discusses "the rules of conduct for a prince towards subject and friends." Machiavelli offers a new method for discussing the subject. He rejects imaginary republics and principalities—perhaps like the one imagined in Thomas More's influential book *Utopia*, published in 1516—in favor of those that are real. It is a mistake, he says, to neglect what people actually do by focusing on what they *ought* to do. The reason is that ignoring reality increases the likelihood of destruction; therefore, it is vital for a prince to "know how to do wrong, and to make use of it or not according to necessity." Remarks such as this have historically earned Machiavelli a reputation for cynicism.

In the course of conducting public affairs, the actions of princes—what they do— may bring them either praise or blame, Machiavelli states, and he cites numerous terms that are used to describe the character of princes who are considered either praiseworthy or blameworthy. However, in his view, those characteristics often counted as virtues might cause a prince's defeat, while those seen as vices could lead to security and prosperity. As Machiavelli puts it: "It will be found that something which looks like virtue, if followed, would be his ruin; whilst something else, which looks like vice, yet followed brings him security and prosperity."

◆ Chapter XVI: Concerning Liberality and Meanness

Chapter XVI discusses liberality versus meanness or, in modern terms, generosity versus parsimony. Machiavelli begins by saying that it is good to have a reputation for liberality and adds that a prince should exercise his liberality in ways that enhance his subjects' perception of him, for ignorance of a prince's good deeds otherwise may create a negative impression. However, Machiavelli notes that it is easy for a prince to exhaust his means by giving money to good causes and then to try to recoup his expenditures by collecting higher taxes. The result would be to engender hatred and poverty among his subjects, which would spark complaints of miserliness. Thus, Machiavelli concludes, if a prince cannot be liberal effectively, then it is better to be mean. Further, by not squandering money to no political benefit, a prince would have money for emergencies. He thus "exercises liberality towards all from whom he does not take, who are numberless, and meanness towards those to whom he does not give, who are few."

Machiavelli cites two examples of "mean" princes who accomplished great things. One is Pope Julius II, who won the papacy with a reputation for liberality but then forsook that liberality. The other is King Charles I of Spain, who as Holy Roman Emperor Charles V was able to conduct extensive military campaigns because he had not spent his fortune by doling it out among his petitioners. For Machiavelli, liberality is essentially a perishable commodity in the reputations market. If the wealth needed to be liberal was lost, a prince might become despised or even hated. Therefore, to have a reputation for meanness would bring reproach but not hatred, which is better than a failed policy of liberality. A prince "ought to hold of little account a reputation for being mean, for it is one of those vices which will enable him to govern." Machiavelli then refutes the example of Julius Caesar, who had achieved power in Rome by sustaining a reputation for liberality, by asserting that Caesar "moderated his expenses" once he had gained power. Machiavelli encapsulates the paradox of liberality thus: "For even whilst you exercise it you lose the power to do so, and so become either poor or despised, or else, in avoiding poverty, rapacious and hated." In other words, liberality is ultimately self-defeating.

◆ Chapter XVII: Concerning Cruelty and Clemency, and Whether It Is Better to Be Loved Than Feared

In Chapter XVII, Machiavelli offers a lesson on the adage that sometimes it is necessary to be cruel to be kind. Machiavelli counsels clemency rather than cruelty, but he notes that there are limits because cruelty might achieve political gains such as peace and loyalty. He cites the pacifying effects of Cesare Borgia's successful use of cruelty in imposing unity and loyalty during his military campaigns in Romagna. If unity and loyalty are maintained, Machiavelli argues, then a reputation for cruelty is nothing, and excessive leniency can lead to violence such as robberies and murders that "are wont to injure the whole people." In contrast, misguided clemency benefits only the few. To buttress his point, Machiavelli cites the Roman writer Virgil's characterization in *The Aeneid* of Dido's defense of her conduct as the queen of Carthage. The quotation may be loosely translated thus: "The difficulty of my position and the novelty to me of being a ruler, of being invested with the powers of a governor, compel me to do these things to adopt this course."

In order to be wise, Machiavelli advises, a prince should believe and act slowly but not show fear. A prince should act temperately, without overconfidence and distrustful suspicion, which could render him intolerable. Several key questions for Machiavelli—and later political theorists as well—center on whether it is better to be feared or loved. Is it safer to be feared than loved? Can a prince be feared but not hated? Machiavelli again takes the realist rather than idealist view. Men, he writes, "are ungrateful, fickle, false, cowardly, covetous, and as long as you succeed they are yours entirely; they will offer you their blood, property, life and children." In other words, a prince's subjects will remain loyal only as long as he is successful.

Pope Leo X (© Bettmann/CORBIS)

Thus, says Machiavelli, a prince needs to inspire fear without creating hatred. He must "keep his hands off the property of others," for an individual is more likely to resent appropriation of his "patrimony" than the execution of his father. He cites the example of Hannibal, the brilliant Carthaginian commander and tactician from the third century BCE, best known for his successes in the Second Punic War and his use of elephants to cross the Pyrenees and Alps. Machiavelli also cites the example of Scipio Africanus the Elder, the Roman general who gained fame in the Second Punic War and brought Hannibal's string of stunning victories to an end at the Battle of Zama in 202 BCE. Both generals were later criticized for the very qualities that had made them so successful.

◆ **Chapter XVIII: Concerning the Way in Which Princes Should Keep Faith**

Machiavelli begins by observing "how praiseworthy it is in a prince to keep faith, and to live with integrity and not with craft." He points out, though, that the most successful princes have not been men who kept their word if it was expedient to break it. As Machiavelli sees it, there are two ways to act: One is to follow the law; the other is to use force. Since following the law is often not sufficient for achieving justice, taking action after the manner of beasts is the way to be successful. He draws an extended analogy

of the fox and the lion. The fox can avoid traps and snares that the lion cannot; however, the fox cannot defend himself against wolves, while the lion can. Machiavelli insists that a prince needs to cultivate the qualities of both the fox (cunning) and the lion (force) because human beings are untrustworthy. To demonstrate this precept, Machiavelli discusses treaties. Because treaties are frequently broken, a prince should practice deception when agreeing to them. It is not necessary to actually be "merciful, faithful, humane, religious, [and] upright." Rather, it is necessary only to appear to have those qualities. Most people, including princes, are usually known by appearances, Machiavelli observes; consequently, a prince should preach peace and good faith but act according to his own best interest.

◆ **Chapter XIX: That One Should Avoid Being Despised and Hated**

In this chapter Machiavelli discusses those characteristics in a prince that cause people to despise and hate him. He begins by stating several rather obvious examples of how a prince might instill hatred among his subjects. Rapaciousness and stealing people's property would engender hatred quickly. Violating the women of his subjects would also cause him to be hated. To be fickle, frivolous, effeminate, and indecisive are all examples of conduct that could engender dislike. However, Machiavelli stresses, a prince who appears courageous and resolute in judgment will be esteemed, and an esteemed prince is more secure from conspiracies than one who is despised. Conspiracies, Machiavelli notes, require agreement among a growing number of people committed to rebellion. Therefore, a prince ought to be supportive of his nobles, but not to the point that it outraged the people. Machiavelli details numerous contemporary and ancient examples of rulers who were able to avoid the appearance of characteristics that engendered hatred as well as those who were "lovers of justice, enemies to cruelty, humane, and benignant" but nevertheless "came to a sad end."

It is probably impossible, Machiavelli concedes, for a prince to avoid being hated by at least someone. The key rule is to avoid being hated by everyone—and hatred, in Machiavelli's view, could be caused as easily by doing good works as by doing bad ones. Therefore, a prince should do evil if that is the best practical policy.

Audience

Machiavelli's immediate audience for *The Prince* was Giuliano de' Medici, to whom the book was originally dedicated, but after Giuliano died in 1516, Machiavelli quickly changed the dedication to Lorenzo di Piero de' Medici. At first glance it appears that he dedicated the book to members of the Medici family in order to curry favor as an office seeker. It is possible, though, that Machiavelli did not have a specific audience in mind. What he sought was a hearing from those who would use his lessons to unite Italy. However, his broader intentions in writing the book have puzzled numerous scholars.

"*A prince ought to have no other aim or thought, nor select anything else for his study, than war and its rules and discipline; for this is the sole art that belongs to him who rules, and it is of such force that it not only upholds those who are born princes, but it often enables men to rise from a private station to that rank.*"

(Chapter XIV)

"*Hence it is necessary for a prince wishing to hold his own to know how to do wrong, and to make use of it or not according to necessity.*"

(Chapter XV)

"*Therefore it is wiser to have a reputation for meanness which brings reproach without hatred, than to be compelled through seeking a reputation for liberality to incur a name for rapacity which begets reproach with hatred.*"

(Chapter XVI)

"*Our experience has been that those princes who have done great things have held good faith of little account, and have known how to circumvent the intellect of men by craft, and in the end have overcome those who have relied on their word.*"

(Chapter XVIII)

"*Hatred is acquired as much by good works as by bad ones, therefore, as I said before, a prince wishing to keep his state is very often forced to do evil.*"

(Chapter XIX)

Impact

Machiavelli has been vilified since before his death. Some historians have seen *The Prince* as a kind of sword that smote the body politic of Renaissance Europe, revealing the secrets of dirty politics. In many quarters he has been regarded as "Old Nick" (the devil) and the ideal theorist for evil dictators. Stories have historically circulated that tyrants such as Catherine de Médicis (great-granddaughter of Lorenzo the Magnificent who became queen of France and was known particularly for her ruthless perse-

cution of the French Huguenots) and the Italian Fascist dictator Benito Mussolini carried *The Prince* with them at all times and that Joseph Stalin, dictator of the Soviet Union, kept a copy on his nightstand.

Some historians have believed that Machiavelli was just a foolish and inconsistent man. Others have argued that *The Prince* was nothing but a long-winded job-wanted advertisement, or possibly even a work of satire. Still others credit him with having envisioned a unified Italy liberated from foreign influences. And still others have seen his approach as a portrait of the brokenness of political reality. Perhaps the enduring impact of Machiavelli's *The Prince* is that it has prompted many generations of political and even business leaders throughout the world to ponder the age-old question of whether the ends justify the means. Was Machiavelli—or any leader who has since been attracted to his views—merely a cold-blooded liar willing to deceive in order to achieve and hold power? Or did he propose a model for a coolly practical ruler, one ready to do what was necessary to achieve noble ends in a world filled with deception and duplicity?

It is possible to discern a direct correspondence between Machiavelli's views and the realpolitik of nineteenth-century and early twentieth-century Europe. This was an approach to politics, developed chiefly by German theorists and politicians, based on pragmatism rather than ideology. The term has often been associated with coercive and amoral uses of power—with pure power politics—but this definition is slightly misleading. The political situation in Europe in the mid-nineteenth century was in many respects similar to that of Italy in the sixteenth century. European leaders had been faced with a series of revolts, particularly in 1848. The principles of realpolitik demanded that leaders not only make concessions but also use power to restore social order, and it was these principles that enabled Otto von Bismarck to unify Germany's numerous principalities into a single strong state in 1871.

Machiavelli has often been credited with having devised the concept of "reason of state," or "raison d'état," as a justification for rulers to pursue their goals—and do so under a cloak of secrecy. Philosophers today continue to debate the fundamental issue of whether a state—or a political party—should remain "pure" in its pursuit of ethical ends or be willing to exercise power, sometimes covertly, to achieve a worthwhile end. Political candidates wrestle with the question of whether to "tell the voters what they want to hear" in order to get elected. The alternative of candidness could spell defeat and thus failure to carry out an agenda that the candidate believes will benefit the nation. It was Niccolò Machiavelli who first defined the terms of these types of questions.

Further Reading

■ Articles

Mattingly, Garrett. "Machiavelli's Prince: Political Science or Political Satire?" *American Scholar* 27 (1958): 482–491.

■ Books

Chabod, Federico. *Machiavelli and the Renaissance*, trans. David Moore. New York: Harper & Row, 1965.

De Grazia, Sebastian. *Machiavelli in Hell*. Princeton, N.J.: Princeton University Press, 1989.

Fleisher, Martin, ed. *Machiavelli and the Nature of Political Thought*. New York: Atheneum, 1972.

Questions for Further Study

1. In the modern world, Machiavelli's name is connected with cunning, deceit, and manipulation. Based on what you have read, do you believe this legacy is fair?

2. Read this document in conjunction with Niẓām al-Mulk's *Book of Government; or, Rules for Kings*. How are the two documents similar as "Mirrors for Princes"? How are they different? Speculate as to what you think each author would have thought about the other's work.

3. Machiavelli wrote *The Prince* at a time of immense political turmoil in Italy. Trace the events that would have played an important role in Machiavelli's thinking about politics and governance.

4. Just four years after Machiavelli wrote *The Prince*, Martin Luther's *Ninety-five Theses* were issued in Germany, launching the Protestant Reformation. What characteristics of the Catholic Church, particularly as it played a role in the political climate surrounding Machiavelli in Italy, do you think Luther would have objected to?

5. In the same year that Machiavelli wrote *The Prince* (1513), the Spanish Crown issued the *Requerimiento* to enforce its dominion over Spanish colonies in the Caribbean. Based on what you have read, how do you think Machiavelli would have gone about enforcing rule in similar colonies?

6. Do you believe that Machiavelli has anything to say to rulers in the modern world? Under what circumstances, if any, do you think such rulers should ever act in a "Machiavellian" way?

Gilbert, Allan H, ed. and trans. *Machiavelli: The Chief Works and Others*. 1965. Reprint. Durham, N.C.: Duke University Press, 1989.

Hale, J. R. *Machiavelli and Renaissance Italy*. New York: Macmillan, 1960.

Hexter, J. H. *The Vision of Politics on the Eve of the Reformation: More, Machiavelli, Seyssel*. New York: Basic Books, 1973.

Lucas-Dubreton, Jean. *Daily Life in Florence in the Time of the Medici*. New York: Macmillan, 1961.

■ **Web Sites**

Erb, Scott. "Machiavelli and Power Politics." University of Maine at Farmington "Reading Revolutions: Intellectual History" Web site. http://hua.umf.maine.edu/Reading_Revolutions/Machiavelli.html.

—Andrew J. Waskey and Michael J. O'Neal

Milestone Documents

Niccolò Machiavelli's *The Prince*

Chapter XIV. That Which Concerns a Prince on the Subject of the Art of War

A Prince ought to have no other aim or thought, nor select anything else for his study, than war and its rules and discipline; for this is the sole art that belongs to him who rules, and it is of such force that it not only upholds those who are born princes, but it often enables men to rise from a private station to that rank. And, on the contrary, it is seen that when princes have thought more of ease than of arms they have lost their states. And the first cause of your losing it is to neglect this art; and what enables you to acquire a state is to be master of the art. Francesco Sforza, through being martial, from a private person became Duke of Milan; and the sons, through avoiding the hardships and troubles of arms, from dukes became private persons. For among other evils which being unarmed brings you, it causes you to be despised, and this is one of those ignominies against which a prince ought to guard himself, as is shown later on. Because there is nothing proportionate between the armed and the unarmed; and it is not reasonable that he who is armed should yield obedience willingly to him who is unarmed, or that the unarmed man should be secure among armed servants. Because, there being in the one disdain and in the other suspicion, it is not possible for them to work well together. And therefore a prince who does not understand the art of war, over and above the other misfortunes already mentioned, cannot be respected by his soldiers, nor can he rely on them. He ought never, therefore, to have out of his thoughts this subject of war, and in peace he should addict himself more to its exercise than in war; this he can do in two ways, the one by action, the other by study.

As regards action, he ought above all things to keep his men well organized and drilled, to follow incessantly the chase, by which he accustoms his body to hardships, and learns something of the nature of localities, and gets to find out how the mountains rise, how the valleys open out, how the plains lie, and to understand the nature of rivers and marshes, and in all this to take the greatest care. Which knowledge is useful in two ways. Firstly, he learns to know his country, and is better able to undertake its defence; afterwards, by means of the knowledge and observation of that locality, he understands with ease any other which it may be necessary for him to study hereafter; because the hills, valleys, and plains, and rivers and marshes that are, for instance, in Tuscany, have a certain resemblance to those of other countries, so that with a knowledge of the aspect of one country one can easily arrive at a knowledge of others. And the prince that lacks this skill lacks the essential which it is desirable that a captain should possess, for it teaches him to surprise his enemy, to select quarters, to lead armies, to array the battle, to besiege towns to advantage.

Philopoemen, Prince of the Achaeans, among other praises which writers have bestowed on him, is commended because in time of peace he never had anything in his mind but the rules of war; and when he was in the country with friends, he often stopped and reasoned with them: "If the enemy should be upon that hill, and we should find ourselves here with our army, with whom would be the advantage? How should one best advance to meet him, keeping the ranks? If we should wish to retreat, how ought we to set about it? If they should retreat, how ought we to pursue?" And he would set forth to them, as he went, all the chances that could befall an army; he would listen to their opinion and state his, confirming it with reasons, so that by these continual discussions there could never arise, in time of war, any unexpected circumstances that he could deal with.

But to exercise the intellect the prince should read histories, and study there the actions of illustrious men, to see how they have borne themselves in war, to examine the causes of their victories and defeat, so as to avoid the latter and imitate the former; and above all do as an illustrious man did, who took as an exemplar one who had been praised and famous before him, and whose achievements and deeds he always kept in his mind, as it is said Alexander the Great imitated Achilles, Caesar Alexander, Scipio Cyrus. And whoever reads the life of Cyrus, written by Xenophon, will recognize afterwards in the life of Scipio how that imitation was his glory, and how in chastity, affability, humanity, and liberality Scipio conformed to those things which have been written of Cyrus by Xenophon. A wise prince ought to observe some such rules, and never in peaceful times stand idle, but increase his resources with industry in such a way that they may be available to him in adversity, so that if fortune changes it may find him prepared to resist her blows.

Chapter XV. Concerning Things for Which Men, and Especially Princes, Are Praised or Blamed

It remains now to see what ought to be the rules of conduct for a prince towards subject and friends. And as I know that many have written on this point, I expect I shall be considered presumptuous in mentioning it again, especially as in discussing it I shall depart from the methods of other people. But, it being my intention to write a thing which shall be useful to him who apprehends it, it appears to me more appropriate to follow up the real truth of a matter than the imagination of it; for many have pictured republics and principalities which in fact have never been known or seen, because how one lives is so far distant from how one ought to live, that he who neglects what is done for what ought to be done, sooner effects his ruin than his preservation; for a man who wishes to act entirely up to his professions of virtue soon meets with what destroys him among so much that is evil.

Hence it is necessary for a prince wishing to hold his own to know how to do wrong, and to make use of it or not according to necessity. Therefore, putting on one side imaginary things concerning a prince, and discussing those which are real, I say that all men when they are spoken of, and chiefly princes for being more highly placed, are remarkable for some of those qualities which bring them either blame or praise; and thus it is that one is reputed liberal, another miserly, using a Tuscan term (because an avaricious person in our language is still he who desires to possess by robbery, whilst we call one miserly who deprives himself too much of the use of his own); one is reputed generous, one rapacious; one cruel, one compassionate; one faithless, another faithful; one effeminate and cowardly, another bold and brave; one affable, another haughty; one lascivious, another chaste; one sincere, another cunning; one hard, another easy; one grave, another frivolous; one religious, another unbelieving, and the like. And I know that every one will confess that it would be most praiseworthy in a prince to exhibit all the above qualities that are considered good; but because they can neither be entirely possessed nor observed, for human conditions do not permit it, it is necessary for him to be sufficiently prudent

that he may know how to avoid the reproach of those vices which would lose him his state; and also to keep himself, if it be possible, from those which would not lose him it; but this not being possible, he may with less hesitation abandon himself to them. And again, he need not make himself uneasy at incurring a reproach for those vices without which the state can only be saved with difficulty, for if everything is considered carefully, it will be found that something which looks like virtue, if followed, would be his ruin; whilst something else, which looks like vice, yet followed brings him security and prosperity.

Chapter XVI. Concerning Liberality and Meanness

Commencing then with the first of the above-named characteristics, I say that it would be well to be reputed liberal. Nevertheless, liberality exercised in a way that does not bring you the reputation for it, injures you; for if one exercises it honestly and as it should be exercised, it may not become known, and you will not avoid the reproach of its opposite. Therefore, any one wishing to maintain among men the name of liberal is obliged to avoid no attribute of magnificence; so that a prince thus inclined will consume in such acts all his property, and will be compelled in the end, if he wish to maintain the name of liberal, to unduly weigh down his people, and tax them, and do everything he can to get money. This will soon make him odious to his subjects, and becoming poor he will be little valued by any one; thus, with his liberality, having offended many and rewarded few, he is affected by the very first trouble and imperiled by whatever may be the first danger; recognizing this himself, and wishing to draw back from it, he runs at once into the reproach of being miserly.

Therefore, a prince, not being able to exercise this virtue of liberality in such a way that it is recognized, except to his cost, if he is wise he ought not to fear the reputation of being mean, for in time he will come to be more considered than if liberal, seeing that with his economy his revenues are enough, that he can defend himself against all attacks, and is able to engage in enterprises without burdening his people; thus it comes to pass that he exercises liberality towards all from whom he does not take, who are numberless, and meanness towards those to whom he does not give, who are few.

We have not seen great things done in our time except by those who have been considered mean; the rest have failed. Pope Julius the Second was assisted in reaching the papacy by a reputation for liberality, yet he did not strive afterwards to keep it up, when he made war on the King of France; and he made many wars without imposing any extraordinary tax on his subjects, for he supplied his additional expenses out of his long thriftiness. The present King of Spain would not have undertaken or conquered in so many enterprises if he had been reputed liberal. A prince, therefore, provided that he has not to rob his subjects, that he can defend himself, that he does not become poor and abject, that he is not forced to become rapacious, ought to hold of little account a reputation for being mean, for it is one of those vices which will enable him to govern.

And if any one should say: Caesar obtained empire by liberality, and many others have reached the highest positions by having been liberal, and by being considered so, I answer: Either you are a prince in fact, or in a way to become one. In the first case this liberality is dangerous, in the second it is very necessary to be considered liberal; and Caesar was one of those who wished to become pre-eminent in Rome; but if he had survived after becoming so, and had not moderated his expenses, he would have destroyed his government. And if any one should reply: Many have been princes, and have done great things with armies, who have been considered very liberal, I reply: Either a prince spends that which is his own or his subjects' or else that of others. In the first case he ought to be sparing, in the second he ought not to neglect any opportunity for liberality. And to the prince who goes forth with his army, supporting it by pillage, sack, and extortion, handling that which belongs to others, this liberality is necessary, otherwise he would not be followed by soldiers. And of that which is neither yours nor your subjects' you can be a ready giver, as were Cyrus, Caesar, and Alexander; because it does not take away your reputation if you squander that of others, but adds to it; it is only squandering your own that injures you.

And there is nothing wastes so rapidly as liberality, for even whilst you exercise it you lose the power to do so, and so become either poor or despised, or else, in avoiding poverty, rapacious and hated. And a prince should guard himself, above all things, against being despised and hated; and liberality leads you to both. Therefore it is wiser to have a reputation for meanness which brings reproach without hatred, than to be compelled through seeking a reputation for liberality to incur a name for rapacity which begets reproach with hatred.

Chapter XVII. Concerning Cruelty and Clemency, and Whether It Is Better to Be Loved than Feared

Coming now to the other qualities mentioned above, I say that every prince ought to desire to be considered clement and not cruel. Nevertheless he ought to take care not to misuse this clemency. Cesare Borgia was considered cruel; notwithstanding, his cruelty reconciled the Romagna, unified it, and restored it to peace and loyalty. And if this be rightly considered, he will be seen to have been much more merciful than the Florentine people, who, to avoid a reputation for cruelty, permitted Pistoia to be destroyed. Therefore a prince, so long as he keeps his subjects united and loyal, ought not to mind the reproach of cruelty; because with a few examples he will be more merciful than those who, through too much mercy, allow disorders to arise, from which follow murders or robberies; for these are wont to injure the whole people, whilst those executions which originate with a prince offend the individual only.

And of all princes, it is impossible for the new prince to avoid the imputation of cruelty, owing to new states being full of dangers. Hence Virgil, through the mouth of Dido, excuses the inhumanity of her reign owing to its being new, saying:

Res dura, et regni novitas me talia cogunt
Moliri, et late fines custode tueri.
[Against my will, my fate, / A throne unsettled, and an infant state, / Bid me defend my realms with all my pow'rs, / And guard with these severities my shores.]

Nevertheless he ought to be slow to believe and to act, nor should he himself show fear, but proceed in a temperate manner with prudence and humanity, so that too much confidence may not make him incautious and too much distrust render him intolerable.

Upon this a question arises: whether it be better to be loved than feared or feared than loved? It may be answered that one should wish to be both, but, because it is difficult to unite them in one person, is much safer to be feared than loved, when, of the two, either must be dispensed with. Because this is to be asserted in general of men, that they are ungrateful, fickle, false, cowardly, covetous, and as long as you succeed they are yours entirely; they will offer you their blood, property, life and children, as is said above, when the need is far distant; but when it approaches they turn against you. And that prince who, relying entirely on their promises, has neglected other precautions, is ruined; because friendships that are obtained by payments, and not by greatness or nobility of mind, may indeed be earned, but they are not secured, and in time of need cannot be relied upon; and men have less scruple in offending one who is beloved than one who is feared, for love is preserved by the link of obligation which, owing to the baseness of men, is broken at every opportunity for their advantage; but fear preserves you by a dread of punishment which never fails.

Nevertheless a prince ought to inspire fear in such a way that, if he does not win love, he avoids hatred; because he can endure very well being feared whilst he is not hated, which will always be as long as he abstains from the property of his citizens and subjects and from their women. But when it is necessary for him to proceed against the life of someone, he must do it on proper justification and for manifest cause, but above all things he must keep his hands off the property of others, because men more quickly forget the death of their father than the loss of their patrimony. Besides, pretexts for taking away the property are never wanting; for he who has once begun to live by robbery will always find pretexts for seizing what belongs to others; but reasons for taking life, on the contrary, are more difficult to find and sooner lapse. But when a prince is with his army, and has under control a multitude of soldiers, then it is quite necessary for him to disregard the reputation of cruelty, for without it he would never hold his army united or disposed to its duties.

Among the wonderful deeds of Hannibal this one is enumerated: that having led an enormous army, composed of many various races of men, to fight in foreign lands, no dissensions arose either among them or against the prince, whether in his bad or in his good fortune. This arose from nothing else than his inhuman cruelty, which, with his boundless valour, made him revered and terrible in the sight of his soldiers, but without that cruelty, his other virtues were not sufficient to produce this effect. And short-sighted writers admire his deeds from one point of view and from another condemn the principal cause of them. That it is true his other virtues would not have been sufficient for him may be proved by the case of Scipio, that most excellent man, not of his own times but within the memory of man, against whom, nevertheless, his army rebelled in Spain; this arose from nothing but his too great forbearance, which gave his soldiers more licence than is consistent with military discipline. For this he was upbraid-ed in the Senate by Fabius Maximus, and called the corrupter of the Roman soldiery. The Locrians were laid waste by a legate of Scipio, yet they were not avenged by him, nor was the insolence of the legate punished, owing entirely to his easy nature. Insomuch that someone in the Senate, wishing to excuse him, said there were many men who knew much better how not to err than to correct the errors of others. This disposition, if he had been continued in the command, would have destroyed in time the fame and glory of Scipio; but, he being under the control of the Senate, this injurious characteristic not only concealed itself, but contributed to his glory.

Returning to the question of being feared or loved, I come to the conclusion that, men loving according to their own will and fearing according to that of the prince, a wise prince should establish himself on that which is in his own control and not in that of others; he must endeavour only to avoid hatred, as is noted.

Chapter XVIII. Concerning the Way in Which Princes Should Keep Faith

Every one admits how praiseworthy it is in a prince to keep faith, and to live with integrity and not with craft. Nevertheless our experience has been that those princes who have done great things have held good faith of little account, and have known how to circumvent the intellect of men by craft, and in the end have overcome those who have relied on their word. You must know there are two ways of contesting, the one by the law, the other by force; the first method is proper to men, the second to beasts; but because the first is frequently not sufficient, it is necessary to have recourse to the second. Therefore it is necessary for a prince to understand how to avail himself of the beast and the man. This has been figuratively taught to princes by ancient writers, who describe how Achilles and many other princes of old were given to the Centaur Chiron to nurse, who brought them up in his discipline; which means solely that, as they had for a teacher one who was half beast and half man, so it is necessary for a prince to know how to make use of both natures, and that one without the other is not durable. A prince, therefore, being compelled knowingly to adopt the beast, ought to choose the fox and the lion; because the lion cannot defend himself against snares and the fox cannot defend himself against wolves. Therefore, it is necessary to be a fox to discover the snares and a lion to terrify the wolves. Those who rely simply on the lion do not understand what they are about. Therefore a wise lord cannot, nor ought he to, keep faith when such observance may be turned against him, and when the reasons that caused him to pledge it exist no longer. If men were entirely good this precept would not hold, but because they are bad, and will not keep faith with you, you too are not bound to observe it with them. Nor will there ever be wanting to a prince legitimate reasons to excuse this nonobservance. Of this endless modern examples could be given, showing how many treaties and engagements have been made void and of no effect through the faithlessness of princes; and he who has known best how to employ the fox has succeeded best.

But it is necessary to know well how to disguise this characteristic, and to be a great pretender and dissembler; and men are so simple, and so subject to present necessities, that he who seeks to deceive will always find someone who will allow himself to be deceived. One recent example I cannot pass over in silence. Alexander VI did nothing else but deceive men, nor ever thought of doing otherwise, and he always found victims; for there never was a man who had greater power in asserting, or who with greater oaths would affirm a thing, yet would observe it less; nevertheless his deceits always succeeded according to his wishes, because he well understood this side of mankind.

Therefore it is unnecessary for a prince to have all the good qualities I have enumerated, but it is very necessary to appear to have them. And I shall dare to say this also, that to have them and always to observe them is injurious, and that to appear to have them is useful; to appear merciful, faithful, humane, religious, upright, and to be so, but with a mind so framed that should you require not to be so, you may be able and know how to change to the opposite.

And you have to understand this, that a prince, especially a new one, cannot observe all those things for which men are esteemed, being often forced, in order to maintain the state, to act contrary to faith, friendship, humanity, and religion. Therefore it is necessary for him to have a mind ready to turn itself accordingly as the winds and variations of fortune force it, yet, as I have said above, not to diverge from the good if he can avoid doing so, but, if compelled, then to know how to set about it.

For this reason a prince ought to take care that he never lets anything slip from his lips that is not replete with the above-named five qualities, that he may appear to him who sees and hears him altogeth-

er merciful, faithful, humane, upright, and religious. There is nothing more necessary to appear to have than this last quality, inasmuch as men judge generally more by the eye than by the hand, because it belongs to everybody to see you, to few to come in touch with you. Every one sees what you appear to be, few really know what you are, and those few dare not oppose themselves to the opinion of the many, who have the majesty of the state to defend them; and in the actions of all men, and especially of princes, which it is not prudent to challenge, one judges by the result.

For that reason, let a prince have the credit of conquering and holding his state, the means will always be considered honest, and he will be praised by everybody because the vulgar are always taken by what a thing seems to be and by what comes of it; and in the world there are only the vulgar, for the few find a place there only when the many have no ground to rest on.

One prince of the present time, whom it is not well to name, never preaches anything else but peace and good faith, and to both he is most hostile, and either, if he had kept it, would have deprived him of reputation and kingdom many a time.

Chapter XIX. That One Should Avoid Being Despised and Hated

Now, concerning the characteristics of which mention is made above, I have spoken of the more important ones, the others I wish to discuss briefly under this generality, that the prince must consider, as has been in part said before, how to avoid those things which will make him hated or contemptible; and as often as he shall have succeeded he will have fulfilled his part, and he need not fear any danger in other reproaches.

It makes him hated above all things, as I have said, to be rapacious, and to be a violator of the property and women of his subjects, from both of which he must abstain. And when neither their property nor honour is touched, the majority of men live content, and he has only to contend with the ambition of a few, whom he can curb with ease in many ways.

It makes him contemptible to be considered fickle, frivolous, effeminate, mean-spirited, irresolute, from all of which a prince should guard himself as from a rock; and he should endeavour to show in his actions greatness, courage, gravity, and fortitude; and in his private dealings with his subjects let him show that his judgments are irrevocable, and maintain himself in such reputation that no one can hope either to deceive him or to get round him.

That prince is highly esteemed who conveys this impression of himself, and he who is highly esteemed is not easily conspired against; for, provided it is well known that he is an excellent man and revered by his people, he can only be attacked with difficulty. For this reason a prince ought to have two fears, one from within, on account of his subjects, the other from without, on account of external powers. From the latter he is defended by being well armed and having good allies, and if he is well armed he will have good friends, and affairs will always remain quiet within when they are quiet without, unless they should have been already disturbed by conspiracy; and even should affairs outside be disturbed, if he has carried out his preparations and has lived as I have said, as long as he does not despair, he will resist every attack....

But concerning his subjects, when affairs outside are disturbed he has only to fear that they will conspire secretly, from which a prince can easily secure himself by avoiding being hated and despised, and by keeping the people satisfied with him, which it is most necessary for him to accomplish, as I said above at length. And one of the most efficacious remedies that a prince can have against conspiracies is not to be hated and despised by the people, for he who conspires against a prince always expects to please them by his removal; but when the conspirator can only look forward to offending them, he will not have the courage to take such a course, for the difficulties that confront a conspirator are infinite. And as experience shows, many have been the conspiracies, but few have been successful; because he who conspires cannot act alone, nor can he take a companion except from those whom he believes to be malcontents, and as soon as you have opened your mind to a malcontent you have given him the material with which to content himself, for by denouncing you he can look for every advantage; so that, seeing the gain from this course to be assured, and seeing the other to be doubtful and full of dangers, he must be a very rare friend, or a thoroughly obstinate enemy of the prince, to keep faith with you.

And, to reduce the matter into a small compass, I say that, on the side of the conspirator, there is nothing but fear, jealousy, prospect of punishment to terrify him; but on the side of the prince there is the majesty of the principality, the laws, the protection of friends and the state to defend him; so that, adding to all these things the popular goodwill, it is impossible that any one should be so rash as to conspire. For whereas in general the conspirator has to fear before the execution of his plot, in this case he has also to fear the sequel to the crime; because on account of it he has the people for an enemy, and thus cannot hope for any escape.

Endless examples could be given on this subject, but I will be content with one, brought to pass within the memory of our fathers. Messer Annibale Bentivoglio, who was prince in Bologna (grandfather of the present Annibale), having been murdered by the Canneschi, who had conspired against him, not one of his family survived but Messer Giovanni, who was in childhood: immediately after his assassination the people rose and murdered all the Canneschi. This sprung from the popular goodwill which the house of Bentivoglio enjoyed in those days in Bologna; which was so great that, although none remained there after the death of Annibale who were able to rule the state, the Bolognese, having information that there was one of the Bentivoglio family in Florence, who up to that time had been considered the son of a blacksmith, sent to Florence for him and gave him the government of their city, and it was ruled by him until Messer Giovanni came in due course to the government.

For this reason I consider that a prince ought to reckon conspiracies of little account when his people hold him in esteem; but when it is hostile to him, and bears hatred towards him, he ought to fear everything and everybody. And well-ordered states and wise princes have taken every care not to drive the nobles to desperation, and to keep the people satisfied and contented, for this is one of the most important objects a prince can have.

Among the best ordered and governed kingdoms of our times is France, and in it are found many good institutions on which depend the liberty and security of the king; of these the first is the parliament and its authority, because he who founded the kingdom, knowing the ambition of the nobility and their boldness, considered that a bit in their mouths would be necessary to hold them in; and, on the other side, knowing the hatred of the people, founded in fear, against the nobles, he wished to protect them, yet he was not anxious for this to be the particular care of the king; therefore, to take away the reproach which he would be liable to from the nobles for favouring the people, and from the people for favouring the nobles, he set up an arbiter, who should be one who could beat down the great and favour the lesser without reproach to the king. Neither could you have a better or a more prudent arrangement, or a greater source of security to the king and kingdom. From this one can draw another important conclusion, that princes ought to leave affairs of reproach to the management of others, and keep those of grace in their own hands. And further, I consider that a prince ought to cherish the nobles, but not so as to make himself hated by the people.

It may appear, perhaps, to some who have examined the lives and deaths of the Roman emperors that many of them would be an example contrary to my opinion, seeing that some of them lived nobly and showed great qualities of soul, nevertheless they have lost their empire or have been killed by subjects who have conspired against them. Wishing, therefore, to answer these objections, I will recall the characters of some of the emperors, and will show that the causes of their ruin were not different to those alleged by me; at the same time I will only submit for consideration those things that are noteworthy to him who studies the affairs of those times.

It seems to me sufficient to take all those emperors who succeeded to the empire from Marcus the philosopher down to Maximinus; they were Marcus and his son Commodus, Pertinax, Julian, Severus and his son Antoninus Caracalla, Macrinus, Heliogabalus, Alexander, and Maximinus.

There is first to note that, whereas in other principalities the ambition of the nobles and the insolence of the people only have to be contended with, the Roman emperors had a third difficulty in having to put up with the cruelty and avarice of their soldiers, a matter so beset with difficulties that it was the ruin of many; for it was a hard thing to give satisfaction both to soldiers and people; because the people loved peace, and for this reason they loved the unaspiring prince, whilst the soldiers loved the warlike prince who was bold, cruel, and rapacious, which qualities they were quite willing he should exercise upon the people, so that they could get double pay and give vent to their greed and cruelty. Hence it arose that those emperors were always overthrown who, either by birth or training, had no great authority, and most of them, especially those who came new to the principality, recognizing the difficulty of these two opposing humours, were inclined to give satisfaction to the soldiers, caring little about injuring the people. Which course was necessary, because, as princes cannot help being hated by someone, they ought, in the first place, to avoid being hated by every one, and when they cannot compass this, they ought to endeavour with the utmost diligence to avoid the hatred of the most powerful. Therefore, those emperors who through inexperience had need of special favour adhered more readily to the soldiers than to the people; a course which turned out advantageous to them or not, accordingly as the prince knew how to maintain authority over them.

From these causes it arose that Marcus [Aurelius], Pertinax, and Alexander, being all men of modest life, lovers of justice, enemies to cruelty, humane, and benignant, came to a sad end except Marcus; he alone lived and died honoured, because he had succeeded to the throne by hereditary title, and owed nothing either to the soldiers or the people; and afterwards, being possessed of many virtues which made him respected, he always kept both orders in their places whilst he lived, and was neither hated nor despised.

But Pertinax was created emperor against the wishes of the soldiers, who, being accustomed to live licentiously under Commodus, could not endure the honest life to which Pertinax wished to reduce them; thus, having given cause for hatred, to which hatred there was added contempt for his old age, he was

Glossary

King of France [who fought Pope Julius II]	Louis XII
Marcus the philosopher	Roman emperor Marcus Aurelius
Pertinax	a Roman emperor who was assassinated after reigning less than a year
present King of Spain	Ferdinand V

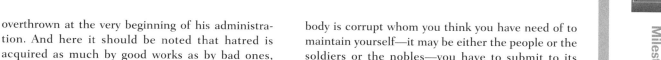

overthrown at the very beginning of his administration. And here it should be noted that hatred is acquired as much by good works as by bad ones, therefore, as I said before, a prince wishing to keep his state is very often forced to do evil; for when that body is corrupt whom you think you have need of to maintain yourself—it may be either the people or the soldiers or the nobles—you have to submit to its humours and to gratify them, and then good works will do you harm.

REQUERIMIENTO

"We shall powerfully enter into your country, and ...
subject you to the yoke and obedience of the Church and of their Highnesses."

Overview

The Requerimiento—a Spanish word meaning "requirement" or "demand"—was a document that was read aloud by the Spanish conquistadores of the early sixteenth century to native peoples in the Americas, demanding that they submit themselves to Spanish rule and to Christianity. In 1493 Pope Alexander VI, in the wake of Christopher Columbus's first voyage across the Atlantic Ocean, had claimed the authority to grant the Spanish monarchy dominion over the New World. The Spanish jurist Juan López de Palacios Rubios then composed the Requerimiento in 1513 to justify the subjugation of the American peoples in the name of God, forcing them to convert to the Catholic Church or face the Spaniards in war.

In Spain people were beginning to debate the morality of colonization of the Americas. Some supported colonization, in large part because of the wealth it would bring to Spain but also because colonists and missionaries would win new souls for Christ. Since the 700s Spain had been embroiled in war with the Moors—Spanish Muslims—in trying to expel them from Granada, in southern Spain. Proponents of that war, principally clerics, justified it by saying that the Moors knew of Christ but consciously rejected him; accordingly, they had no rights. The war against the Moors was then used as precedent and justification for subjugating the peoples of the New World. Other Spaniards, however, pointed out that the Amerindians (a modern term for the indigenous peoples of the Americas) had never heard of Christ, so religious warfare against them was unjustifiable. These Spaniards opposed colonization because of its violence, slavery, exploitation, and crime. Nevertheless, the prospect of enrichment won out, with disastrous consequences for the indigenous peoples of South, Central, and North America.

Context

In the fifteenth century, maritime powers such as Spain, Portugal, and the Italian cities of Venice, Naples, and Genoa dominated the region around the Mediterranean Sea. Merchants and traders were interested in establishing trade routes, particularly a sea route to Asia in view of the wealth it promised. Rulers wanted to replenish their public treasuries, which had been depleted by war (such as the Hundred Years' War of 1337–1453), disease (especially the bubonic plague—the Black Death), and famine. Additionally, Europeans were growing intensely curious about the wider world, a curiosity sparked in large part by the Crusades, the two-hundred-year series of wars in the eleventh through thirteenth centuries between Christian Europeans and Muslim Arabs over control of Palestine. Thousands of crusaders traveled to the Middle East, either on pilgrimage to the holy sites in and around Jerusalem or simply to make their fortunes through war, and their travels introduced them to entirely new cultures. The result of these factors was that the fifteenth century was an age of widespread exploration.

During the fifteenth century—and well into the sixteenth—the Portuguese led Europe in world exploration. They were the first Europeans to sail south of the equator, discovering the islands of Madeira, the Azores, the Cape Verde Islands, and the Congo River in Africa; and in 1487–1488 Bartolomeu Dias led an expedition around the Cape of Good Hope at Africa's southern tip. Meanwhile, others, including the Italians, were conducting similar explorations.

It was in this context that Christopher Columbus, a Genoan, made his voyage of discovery to the New World in 1492. Columbus initially had difficulty finding a patron for the voyage, the actual purpose of which was to find a sea route to Asia by sailing west. He approached the king of Portugal, John II, as well as King Henry VII of England and King Charles VIII of France, but all turned him down. He then sought support in Spain from Ferdinand II, the king of Aragon, and Isabella I, the queen of Castile and León. They declined his proposal at first because they were preoccupied with efforts to reclaim Granada from the Moors. Finally, in April 1492, the Spanish king and queen agreed to Columbus's plan. Part of their motivation may have been to recoup the income lost from that year's expulsion from Spain of some 160,000 to 200,000 Jews, who had formed a major portion of the nation's business, financial, and entrepreneurial class. The expedition set sail to the west

1479

- **September 4**
The Treaty of Alcáçovas ends the War of the Castilian Succession and establishes the territorial claims of Portugal and Spain.

1492

- **August 11**
Rodrigo Borgia becomes Pope Alexander VI.

- **October 12**
Christopher Columbus makes landfall in the Bahamas.

1493

- **May 4**
Pope Alexander VI issues the papal bull *Inter caetera*, granting Spain sovereignty over the New World.

- **September 24**
Columbus sets sail on his second expedition to the New World.

- **September 26**
The papal bull *Dudum siquidem* grants Spain virtually unlimited rights over the New World.

1494

- **June 7**
The Treaty of Tordesillas establishes the boundary line between Spanish and Portuguese territories in the Atlantic.

1498

- **May 30**
Columbus sets sail on his third expedition to the New World.

from Palos de la Frontera, in southwestern Spain, on August 3, 1492, and the history of the Americas changed forever when sailors stepped ashore on an island in the Bahamas on October 12. In the weeks that followed, Columbus explored other islands, principally modern-day Cuba (which he thought was Japan) and Hispaniola, before departing in January 1493 and arriving back in Spain, via Portugal, to a hero's welcome. In the years that followed, Columbus made three more voyages to the New World.

One of the major players in European politics at the time was the pope, particularly because the early Renaissance was a time of "secular popes"—that is, popes who were politicians and kings rather than religious leaders (and whom history has derided for their greed, extravagance, illegitimate children, and outright criminal behavior, including murder). Since the mid-fifteenth century, popes had inserted themselves into the unstable relationship between Spain and Portugal as they competed for control of the Atlantic. In 1452, 1455, 1456, 1481, and 1484, popes issued papal bulls whose purpose was to divide spheres of influence between these two nations, particularly along the western coast of Africa. (A bull is a papal pronouncement, so named because it was secured with a round leaden seal called a *bulla*.) The conflict between Spain and Portugal gained added intensity after Columbus's voyage, and in the months after his return, Spanish and Portuguese negotiators attempted to hammer out an agreement over the rights to possess and rule the new lands. Portuguese authorities had actually arrested Columbus after he returned from his first voyage, on the charge that he had violated Portuguese territorial sovereignty under the terms of the 1479 Treaty of Alcáçovas, which had been sanctioned by a bull issued by Pope Sixtus IV on June 21, 1481.

The pope at the time of Columbus's voyage was Alexander VI, a member of the infamous Borgia family who spent his papal career mired in political intrigue, shifting alliances and brokering agreements that would preserve his power and that of the papacy. Alexander was born in Valencia, Spain, as Roderic Llançol, but he later adopted the Italian name Rodrigo Borgia. He assumed the papacy on August 11, 1492—just eight days after Columbus set sail on his first voyage. As a Spaniard by birth, he had a close personal relationship with the Spanish king, who urged him to issue a new papal bull favorable to Spain's interests. Alexander agreed and issued *Inter caetera* (Among Other Works) on May 4, 1493, giving Spain sovereignty in the New World, specifically the right to acquire any lands that lay to the west of a meridian one hundred miles west of the Azores and Cape Verde. In essence, Portugal would keep its islands, but Spain was granted dominion over two continents. This bull was supplemented by a later one, dated September 26, 1493, and titled *Dudum siquidem* (Some Time Ago), which granted Spain virtually unlimited rights in the Americas and beyond; for this reason the bull is often referred to by the title "Extension of the Apostolic Grant and Donation of the Indies," or simply "Extension of the Donation." Meanwhile, Spain proved willing to compromise and signed the Treaty of Tordesillas on June 7, 1494, which moved the dividing meridian line to the west, enabling Portugal eventually to colonize Brazil. In January 1506, Alexander's successor, Pope Julius II, issued the bull *Ea quae* (This Which), confirming the terms of the Treaty of Tordesillas. But *Inter caetera* and *Dudum siquidem* were what provided the legal underpinnings of the Requerimiento.

The colonization of the New World began apace. The earliest colonies were built on Hispaniola, inhabited by the Taínos, an Arawak people. On his first voyage, Columbus established the settlement of La Navidad on what is today Haiti's northern coast. On his second voyage, in 1493, he brought some thirteen hundred to fifteen hundred men and established La Isabela in today's Dominican Republic. Another settlement, Nueva Isabela, was built in 1496; after being destroyed by a hurricane, it was rebuilt as Santo Domingo, which survives as the oldest permanent European settlement in the Americas. At first the Taínos were cooperative, helping the colonists build their settlements. Rapidly, however, treatment of the Taínos turned harsh, with the Taínos forced to work in gold mines and subjected to beatings, starvation, and mass killings. Additionally, disease, especially smallpox, began to ravage the population; some historians assert that the population of Hispaniola dropped from a million to just thirty thousand within twenty years after Columbus's arrival and to as few as six thousand by 1535. As early as 1502, African slaves were imported to replace the shrinking labor population. Additionally, turmoil surrounded the governorship of the island, so Spanish settlers began dispersing throughout the islands of the Caribbean, establishing new settlements wherever they landed, primarily in modern Cuba, Puerto Rico, Trinidad, and Jamaica.

As of 1513, Spain's colonies in the New World were relatively new. Columbus's initial voyage had occurred just twenty years earlier, and during the early years of the 1500s Spain had little in the way of legal and administrative infrastructure in place in Central and South America. Reports began to reach Spain that Spanish settlers were abusing the Amerindians. The cardinal archbishop of Seville and president of the royal council, Domingo de Mendoza, tried to stop this abuse by dispatching a group of Dominican priests to Hispaniola. The priests, led by Antonio de Montesinos, were unable to end the abuses, but they were able to disturb the comfort of the colonists by preaching that their treatment of the Amerindians was sinful. In response, the colonists selected a Franciscan friar named Alonso de Espina to return to Spain and defend their interests to the king. Ferdinand responded with outrage, and to address the problem he appointed a group of theologians and professors to make recommendations for solving it.

On December 27, 1512, the group promulgated the Laws of Burgos, named after the city where they met. The Laws of Burgos, the first legal code designed to regulate the activities of the Spanish colonists, was a set of thirty-five laws enacted to ensure that the Amerindians were converted to Christianity and to forbid their mistreatment, initially on Hispaniola but later in Puerto Rico and Jamaica as well. The chief effect of the laws was to create a system called

Time Line

1502
- **May 11**
  Columbus begins his fourth and final voyage to the New World.

1506
- **January 6**
  Pope Julius II issues the bull *Ea quae*, confirming the terms of the Treaty of Tordesillas.

1512
- **December 27**
  The Laws of Burgos are promulgated to regulate the behavior of Spanish colonists in the New World.

1513
- Palacios Rubios composes the Requerimiento, demanding that the native peoples of the Americas submit to Spain and Christianity.
- Vasco Núñez de Balboa crosses the Isthmus of Panama, leading the first European expedition to the Pacific Ocean and the western coast of the New World.

1521
- **August 13**
  Hernán Cortés declares victory over the Aztec Empire in Mexico after the fall of Tenochtitlán.

1532

■ **November 16**
Spanish forces
commanded by
Francisco
Pizarro defeat
the Incas of
Peru at the
Battle of
Cajamarca.

1542

■ **November 20**
The Leyes
Nuevas, or the
New Laws of
the Indies for
the Good
Treatment and
Preservation of
the Indians, are
passed in Spain.

encomiendas. Under this system, Amerindians were placed under the supervision of a master in groups ranging in size from forty to 150. The laws regulated how the Amerindians would be paid, fed, and housed, and they required that any punishments be carried out not by the settlers themselves but by public officials. The requirement that Amerindians be converted to Christianity and practice the faith was one of the chief aspects of the Laws of Burgos. The laws thus necessitated the construction of churches, each containing a picture of the Virgin Mary and a bell used to call the Amerindians to prayer. Amerindians were obliged to sing hymns, cross themselves, and pray. Further, each native was to be tested periodically to ensure that he or she knew the Ten Commandments, the seven deadly sins, and the Catholic articles of faith. Any *encomendero,* or master, who failed to enforce these rules could be fined.

Although from a modern perspective the imposition of Spanish laws on the indigenous peoples of the Americas was indefensible, at the time the laws were relatively humane—or at least were intended to be. For example, children under the age of fourteen and women who were more than four months pregnant were not required to work, and Amerindians were allowed to continue to perform their sacred dances. Further, in the laws the Amerindians were given the promise of independence upon conversion to Christianity:

> We declare and command and say that it is our will that those Indians who thus become competent to live by themselves, under the direction and control of our said judges of the said Island, present or future, shall be allowed to live by themselves and shall be obliged to serve [only] in those things in which our vassals in Spain are accustomed to serve, so that they may serve and pay the tribute which they [our vas-

sals] are accustomed to pay to their princes. (http://faculty.smu.edu/bakewell/bakewell/texts/burgoslaws.html)

Overall, the Laws of Burgos had little effect. In the minds of many settlers, they simply sanctioned the system of *encomiendas,* and abuses continued. The matter would not be addressed again until 1542 and the Leyes Nuevas, or the New Laws of the Indies for the Good Treatment and Preservation of the Indians. These laws strictly limited the power of Spanish landowners. Meanwhile, though, it was decided that something more was needed than the Laws of Burgos. Spanish missionaries argued that the settlers could not simply descend on the Amerindians and conquer them. Rather, they needed some sort of legal and spiritual justification. Thus, the Requerimiento was composed to be read to the native populations and on Christian grounds legitimize their destruction.

About the Author

The Requerimiento was written by Juan López de Palacios Rubios, a Spanish jurist who was born Juan López de Vivero in 1450. He was a professor at the University of Salamanca and later at the University of Valladolid. He served as president of the Mesta, more formally called the Honored Council of the Mesta, an influential association of sheep owners in the Kingdom of Castile. He served as a judge in the city of Valladolid, as a minister of the Royal and Supreme Council of the Indies, as an ambassador to Rome, and as a member of the Royal Council of Castile. He was a committed supporter of the monarchy, writing such documents as *Libellus de insulis oceanis* (Book of the Ocean Isles), a legal treatise that defended the legitimacy of Castilian sovereignty in the Americas. He died in 1524.

Explanation and Analysis of the Document

The Requerimiento is written in the second person, as addressed to the indigenous peoples of the Americas. It lays out what the Spanish believed to be the legal and spiritual foundations of Spanish claims to the Americas. It urges the Amerindians to submit themselves to Spanish rule and to convert to Catholicism. It threatens the people with war and conquest if they do not submit.

◆ **Paragraphs 1–3**
The first paragraph announces that the source of the declaration is King Ferdinand, or Don Fernando, and his daughter, Doña Juana. The latter became queen of Castile (spelled "Castille" in the document) and León in 1504 after the death of Isabella, and later she would become queen of Aragon (as well as the mother of Holy Roman Emperor Charles V). She is often referred to by the Latin form of her name, Joanna, and she acquired the sobriquet Joanna the Mad (Juana la Loca) because of her obsession with her

A finger ring with the portrait of Pope Alexander VI, pictured through a magnifying glass (AP/Wide World Photos)

husband. The paragraph refers to the monarchs as "subduers of the barbarous nations" and begins to make the argument justifying this view, noting that God created heaven and earth as well as Adam and Eve, the progenitors of the whole human race. Over time, a "multitude" sprang from Adam and Eve, requiring the establishment of kingdoms and provinces because all the world's people could not be "sustained" in a single entity.

Paragraph 2 makes reference to the Catholic doctrine of apostolic succession. In the New Testament, Christ says to his apostle Peter that he is the "rock" on which Christ's church will be built (in fact, the name Peter means "rock"). Peter, then, is generally regarded as the first pope of the Catholic Church, and his successors hold their authority over the church as part of a line of succession from Christ through Saint Peter. Peter and his successors were given dominion over the human race, regardless of "law, sect, or belief."

The third paragraph develops the argument of apostolic succession. As would be the case with his successors, Peter had his seat in Rome, but God "permitted him to have his seat in any other part of the world, and to judge and govern all Christians, Moors, Jews, Gentiles, and all other sects." The document then informs listeners that this person is called "Pope," a word analogous to "Great Father." This line of popes who govern the universe "will continue till the end of the world."

◆ **Paragraphs 4 and 5**

Paragraph 4 makes the claim that one of Saint Peter's successors—Pope Alexander VI—donated "these isles and Tierra-firme" to the king and queen of Spain. "Tierra-firme," meaning "solid ground," is derived from the Latin *terra firma* and at the time referred to land around the Isthmus of Panama, which was under a grant dating to 1509. Already by this time, a number of provinces had been created in the region, and "Tierra-firme" referred specifically to the province on the westernmost portion of Honduras. Later, the term would be used to encompass a number of other islands and provinces, including Panama, Jamaica, the Cayman Islands, and various islands now under the control of Columbia. The paragraph goes on to make the rather absurd suggestion that if they wish, the Amerindians can examine the documents—written in Latin—granting these territories to Spain. The word "donation" is used, alluding to the papal bulls that gave Spain dominion over the New World, which collectively have been called the "Bulls of Donation."

In paragraph 5 the claim is made that numerous peoples in the New World have voluntarily submitted themselves to Spanish rule and have converted to Catholicism. They have done so "in the way that subjects ought to do, with good will, without any resistance, immediately, without delay." The monarchs have "joyfully and benignantly received them" as subjects and vassals, and the people have willingly listened to

A Dominican Navy soldier provides security to the tomb of Christopher Columbus in Santo Domingo (AP/Wide World Photos)

"Of all these nations God our Lord gave charge to one man, called St. Peter, that he should be Lord and Superior of all the men in the world, that all should obey him, and that he should be the head of the whole human race."

(Paragraph 2)

"One of these Pontiffs, who succeeded that St. Peter as Lord of the world, in the dignity and seat which I have before mentioned, made donation of these isles and Tierra-firme to the aforesaid King and Queen and to their successors, our lords."

(Paragraph 4)

"So their Highnesses are kings and lords of these islands and land of Tierra-firme by virtue of this donation."

(Paragraph 5)

"If you do not do this, and maliciously make delay in it, I certify to you that, with the help of God, we shall powerfully enter into your country, and shall make war against you in all ways and manners that we can, and shall subject you to the yoke and obedience of the Church and of their Highnesses."

(Paragraph 7)

the monarchs' priests, who have come to preach the "Holy Faith." The document then requires the listeners to do the same: to acknowledge the supremacy of the Catholic Church, to recognize the Spanish monarchs as lords and superiors, and to submit to the monarchs' emissaries.

◆ **Paragraphs 6 and 7**

The remainder of the Requerimiento presents the listeners with two alternatives. One is to submit. If they do, the Spanish will receive them with "love and charity." The promise is made that the people will not be reduced to a condition of servitude. The document also makes the somewhat dubious claim that if people submit themselves to the Spanish, they will not be required to convert to Catholicism: "They shall not compel you to turn Christians, unless you yourselves, when informed of the truth, should wish to be converted to our Holy Catholic Faith." The document points

out, though, that nearly everyone else in the isles has already chosen to do so. The paragraph concludes with another dubious claim, that the monarchs will grant the people "privileges," "exemptions," and "benefits" if they submit.

The document concludes with threats. If the people do not submit, the Spanish will make war and "subject you to the yoke and obedience of the Church and of their Highnesses." People will be forced into slavery, and their goods will be seized. At this point the document makes a perplexing legal claim: "We protest that the deaths and losses which shall accrue from this are your fault, and not that of their Highnesses, or ours." In other words, the accountability for any killings or losses will lie with the Amerindians, not the Spanish—as if to say that the Requerimiento has provided the colonizers with legal justification to perpetrate atrocities on the Amerindians in the name of God and country. The document concludes with the rather absurd request that the listeners bring forward a "notary" to assent in writing to the terms of the Requerimiento.

Audience

Ostensibly, the audience for the Requerimiento consisted of the native peoples of the Americas. The notion was that colonizers would arrive at an island or village and read the document publicly, particularly to anyone who seemed resistant to Spanish rule. Usually, the document was read in Spanish, which the Amerindians were unable to understand, although occasionally the document was translated. In reality, the true underlying audience for the document was the Spanish colonizers themselves. The earliest colonizers believed that they had a right to conquest. By tradition, they felt justified in simply arriving, seizing desired property, and subjugating the indigenous peoples. Spanish clerics and missionaries fought this belief, as in their view naked conquest was unjustifiable. King Ferdinand wanted to rein in the excesses of the early colonizers, so Palacios Rubios, a member of his royal council, composed the Requerimiento to provide the colonizers with the spiritual justification they needed, basing conquest not on raw subjugation but on the authority of the pope to grant the lands of the Americas to the Spanish.

Impact

Somewhat paradoxically, the impact of the Requerimiento was both negligible and profound. It was negligible in the sense that the intended audience was unable to understand the document, for it was read in Spanish to people who did not know Spanish. Observers noted that the document was often read to trees, empty beaches, and abandoned villages as well as from the decks of ships far out of earshot of land. One of these observers was Bartolomé de Las Casas, a Dominican friar who was appalled by Spanish treatment of the Amerindians. He wrote that when he first read the document, he did not know "whether to laugh or cry" (qtd. in Kamen, p. 97). Even the document's author, Palacios Rubios, believed that it was faintly ridiculous. One of his contemporaries wrote that Rubios "could not stop laughing when I told him what some commanders had done with it" (qtd. in Kamen, p. 97). From this point of view, the Requerimiento itself had virtually no impact at all.

From another perspective, the impact of the document was profound and far reaching. In its wake, the conquest of the New World continued. In 1513 Vasco Núñez de Balboa crossed the Isthmus of Panama, leading the first European expedition to the western coast of the New World and the Pacific Ocean. In Mexico the Spanish subdued the Aztec Empire, launching an invasion under Hernán Cortés in

Questions for Further Study

1. Read the Requerimiento in conjunction with Columbus's Letter to Raphael Sanxis on the Discovery of America. What do the two documents, taken together, tell modern readers about Spanish attitudes to the people of the Caribbean?

2. What role did the rivalry between Spain and Portugal play in events as they unfolded in the New World? How might the politics of the time differed in a way that would have enabled Portugal to become the ascendant power in the New World?

3. The intended audience for the Requerimiento was unable to understand it, for it was written in Spanish, which the native peoples of the New World did not speak. Thus, the document itself had little direct impact. In what sense, then, can the impact of the document be regarded as profound and far reaching? Resolve this apparent paradox.

4. Compare the Requerimiento with the Diplomatic Correspondence between Muhammad al-Kānāmi and Muhammad Bello (1810–1812). To what extent are the two documents similar in terms of religion, specifically the issue of one culture's imposing its religious beliefs on another? How are they fundamentally different?

5. A widely noted truism in the twenty-first century is that colonization of the New World by the Spanish and by Europeans in general had a devastating impact on Amerindians. How fair do you think this charge is? Do you think that colonization, or at least invasion, of the New World was inevitable? To what extent was the clash between the Old World and the New World part of a pattern of cultural clashes that took place throughout history before the concept of the nation-state was formed?

1519 and declaring victory in 1521 after the fall of Tenochtitlán (rebuilt as Mexico City). In 1532 Spaniards under the command of Francisco Pizarro defeated the Incas at the Battle of Cajamarca, completing the conquest of Peru. Estimates hold that during the 1500s, about a quarter million Spaniards settled in the New World, with devastating effects on indigenous populations. In Mexico, for example, according to some estimates the indigenous population declined by about 90 percent during the 1500s. Over the same period, the native population of Peru declined from about 6.5 million to about 1 million. Spanish hegemony lasted until the 1800s, when independence movements in South America broke Spain's hold on the New World. In 1898 the United States defeated Spain in the Spanish-American War, driving it out of its last colonies in Cuba and Puerto Rico and thus ending Spanish rule in the Americas.

Further Reading

■ Books

Benjamin, Thomas, et al., eds. *The Atlantic World in the Age of Empire*. Boston: Houghton Mifflin, 2001.

Francis, John Michael, ed. *Iberia and the Americas: Culture, Politics, and History; A Multidisciplinary Encyclopedia*. Santa Barbara, Calif.: ABC-CLIO, 2006.

Kamen, Henry. *Empire: How Spain Became a World Power, 1492–1763*. New York: HarperCollins, 2004.

Las Casas, Bartolomé de. *A Short Account of the Destruction of the Indies*, trans. Nigel Griffin. New York: Penguin, 1999.

Milanich, Jerald T., and Susan Milbrath, eds. *First Encounters: Spanish Explorations in the Caribbean and the United States, 1492–1570*. Gainesville: University of Florida Press, 1989.

Newcomb, Steven T. *Pagans in the Promised Land: Decoding the Doctrine of Christian Discovery*. Golden, Colo.: Fulcrum, 2008.

Paiewonsky, Michael. *Conquest of Eden, 1493–1515: Other Voyages of Columbus; Guadeloupe, Puerto Rico, Hispaniola, Virgin Islands*. Rome: Mapes Monde, Editore, 1993.

Rouse, Irving. *The Tainos: Rise and Decline of the People Who Greeted Columbus*. New Haven, Conn.: Yale University Press, 1993.

Sale, Kirkpatrick. *The Conquest of Paradise: Christopher Columbus and the Columbian Legacy*. New York: Knopf, 1990.

Schmidt-Nowara, Christopher, and John M. Nieto-Phillips. *Interpreting Spanish Colonialism: Empires, Nations, and Legends*. Albuquerque: University of New Mexico Press, 2005.

Williams, Eric. *From Columbus to Castro: The History of the Caribbean, 1492–1969*. New York: Vintage, 1984.

■ Web Sites

"1512–1513. The Laws of Burgos." Colonial Latin America, Southern Methodist University Web site.
http://faculty.smu.edu/bakewell/bakewell/texts/burgoslaws.html.

—Michael J. O'Neal

REQUERIMIENTO

On the part of the King, Don Fernando, and of Doña Juana, his daughter, Queen of Castille and León, subduers of the barbarous nations, we their servants notify and make known to you, as best we can, that the Lord our God, Living and Eternal, created the Heaven and the Earth, and one man and one woman, of whom you and we, all the men of the world, were and are descendants, and all those who came after us. But, on account of the multitude which has sprung from this man and woman in the five thousand years since the world was created, it was necessary that some men should go one way and some another, and that they should be divided into many kingdoms and provinces, for in one alone they could not be sustained.

Of all these nations God our Lord gave charge to one man, called St. Peter, that he should be Lord and Superior of all the men in the world, that all should obey him, and that he should be the head of the whole human race, wherever men should live, and under whatever law, sect, or belief they should be; and he gave him the world for his kingdom and jurisdiction.

And he commanded him to place his seat in Rome, as the spot most fitting to rule the world from; but also he permitted him to have his seat in any other part of the world, and to judge and govern all Christians, Moors, Jews, Gentiles, and all other sects. This man was called Pope, as if to say, Admirable Great Father and Governor of men. The men who lived in that time obeyed that St. Peter, and took him for Lord, King, and Superior of the universe; so also they have regarded the others who after him have been elected to the pontificate, and so has it been continued even till now, and will continue till the end of the world.

One of these Pontiffs, who succeeded that St. Peter as Lord of the world, in the dignity and seat which I have before mentioned, made donation of these isles and Tierra-firme to the aforesaid King and Queen and to their successors, our lords, with all that there are in these territories, as is contained in certain writings which passed upon the subject as aforesaid, which you can see if you wish.

So their Highnesses are kings and lords of these islands and land of Tierra-firme by virtue of this donation: and some islands, and indeed almost all those to whom this has been notified, have received and served their Highnesses, as lords and kings, in the way that subjects ought to do, with good will, without any resistance, immediately, without delay, when they were informed of the aforesaid facts. And also they received and obeyed the priests whom their Highnesses sent to preach to them and to teach them our Holy Faith; and all these, of their own free will, without any reward or condition, have become Christians, and are so, and their Highnesses have joyfully and benignantly received them, and also have commanded them to be treated as their subjects and vassals; and you too are held and obliged to do the same. Wherefore, as best we can, we ask and require you that you consider what we have said to you, and that you take the time that shall be necessary to understand and deliberate upon it, and that you acknowledge the Church as the Ruler and Superior of the whole world, and the high priest called Pope, and in his name the King and Queen Doña Juana our lords, in his place, as superiors and lords and kings of these islands and this Tierra-firme by virtue of the said donation, and that you consent and give place that these religious fathers should declare and preach to you the aforesaid.

If you do so, you will do well, and that which you are obliged to do to their Highnesses, and we in their name shall receive you in all love and charity, and shall leave you, your wives, and your children, and your lands, free without servitude, that you may do with them and with yourselves freely that which you like and think best, and they shall not compel you to turn Christians, unless you yourselves, when informed of the truth, should wish to be converted to our Holy Catholic Faith, as almost all the inhabitants of the rest of the islands have done. And, besides this, their Highnesses award you many privileges and exemptions and will grant you many benefits.

But, if you do not do this, and maliciously make delay in it, I certify to you that, with the help of God, we shall powerfully enter into your country, and shall make war against you in all ways and manners that we can, and shall subject you to the yoke and obedience of the Church and of their Highnesses; we shall take you and your wives and your children, and shall make slaves of them, and as such shall sell and dispose of them as their Highnesses may command; and we shall take away your goods, and shall do you all the mischief and damage that we can, as to vassals who do not obey, and refuse to receive their lord, and resist and contradict him; and we protest that the deaths and losses which shall accrue from this are your fault, and not that of their Highnesses, or ours, nor of these cavaliers who come with us. And that we have said this to you and made this Requisition, we request the notary here present to give us his testimony in writing, and we ask the rest who are present that they should be witnesses of this Requisition.

Glossary

One of these Pontiffs   Pope Alexander VI

Martin Luther (Library of Congress)

"Those preachers of indulgences are in error who say that by the pope's indulgences a man is freed from every penalty, and saved."

Overview

According to legend, on October 31, 1517, Martin Luther, a Catholic monk of the Augustinian order serving in Wittenberg, Germany, nailed a document containing ninety-five theses (points for discussion and debate) to the door of a chapel in Wittenberg. Luther's motive for this act was to provoke debate about what he regarded as errors in church teachings and practices and to correct abuses in the church, particularly the practice of selling indulgences. The issues that Luther raised generated a much wider debate, which in time split Western Christianity. The immediate outcome of that split was to be Lutheranism, a form of Protestant Christianity that enlisted millions of people with its appeal to freedom of conscience and freedom of speech.

Luther's *Ninety-five Theses* unintentionally sparked a powder keg that led to the Protestant Reformation, the sixteenth-century movement that rejected many of the teachings of Catholicism and led to the formation of numerous Protestant denominations, including the Lutheran Church. The theses called for religious reform (note that the word *Protestant* is derived from "protest"), but in an age when religion and politics were often one and the same, their implications were also political. Religious wars erupted that were not to cease until the Peace of Westphalia in 1648. When the fighting stopped, Germany and Scandinavia were Lutheran. England continued to hold to Anglicanism, while Scotland joined fellow Calvinists in France, Switzerland, Holland, and elsewhere in Presbyterianism. Spain, Portugal, Italy, and most of France and Switzerland remained Roman Catholic.

Context

Martin Luther, an ordained Catholic priest with a doctorate in theology, joined the theology faculty at Wittenberg University, at the same time serving as a parish priest at Schlosskirche, or Castle Church, in Wittenberg. In the years that followed, Luther came to dispute many of the theological principles of Catholicism and concluded that

the church had gone astray by becoming worldly and corrupt. At the core of his reexamination of Catholicism was the issue of how a person achieved salvation in heaven. According to church teaching, salvation could be achieved in part through good works, that is, by leading an exemplary life. This teaching was based on a theological principle called supererogation, which states that Jesus; his mother, Mary; and the church's saints had performed a great many good works—far in excess of what was needed to achieve their own salvation—and these good works were stored as treasure in heaven. An ordinary person typically died with more sin than merits on his or her soul, so in effect the merits of Jesus, Mary, and the saints were used to cleanse the soul, allowing a person's soul to enter heaven. This is why a deceased person's living relatives and loved ones prayed and offered masses for the dead; prayers and masses were their supplication to God to transfer these stored-up merits to the deceased. This doctrine, then, was the foundation of the belief in good works as one path to salvation.

Based on his reading of the Bible, particularly the book of Romans, Luther came to conclude that this view was erroneous. He insisted instead on the doctrine of justification by grace through faith, which is now usually phrased more simply as "justification through faith." According to this view, salvation in heaven is an unconditional gift of God's love and grace. A person receives it through faith alone and acceptance of Jesus Christ as the source of salvation; it cannot be "earned" through the performance of good works, for that would imply that a well-behaved, charitable atheist could be admitted to heaven. The doctrine of justification by faith became a central doctrine of the Protestant Reformation.

Luther's teachings about indulgences began to attract the attention of church authorities. Catholic theology teaches that when a penitent confesses a sin to a priest and is given absolution (or forgiveness from God through the priest), the sin is forgiven, the person is now in a state of grace, and the person's soul can enter heaven. (The church distinguishes between mortal sins, or severe sins that merit punishment in hell, and venial sins, or minor transgressions that by themselves do not preclude entrance to heaven.) According to the church, however, the stain of sin is not fully taken away by the sacrament of penance, or con-

1483

■ **November 10**
Martin Luther is born in Eisleben, Germany.

1505

■ **July 2**
Luther is struck by lightning but lives and vows to become a monk.

■ **July 17**
Luther enters the Augustinian cloister at Erfurt.

1517

■ **October 31**
Luther, according to tradition, nails his *Ninety-five Theses* to the chapel door of Castle Church in Wittenberg.

1520

■ **July 15**
Pope Leo X issues a papal bull proclaiming forty-one of Luther's theses heretical.

1521

■ **January 3**
Luther is excommunicated from the church.

■ **April 18**
At the Diet of Worms, Luther declares he cannot renounce his teachings on salvation.

■ **May 25**
Holy Roman Emperor Charles V issues the Edict of Worms, declaring Luther a wanted heretic.

fession. After death, a person's soul has to spend time in purgatory, an intermediate state between this world and heaven. In purgatory, a word related to the word *purge* through the Latin word *purgare*, a person is shut out from God's presence, a form of punishment that enables the person to give satisfaction for past sins and become fit to enter heaven. An indulgence, which is typically in the form of a prayer or some other type of religious observance, earns the soul a reduction in the time spent in purgatory. Church teaching distinguishes between partial and plenary indulgences. A partial indulgence reduces the time spent in purgatory; a plenary indulgence remits all of the time the person's soul would otherwise have spent in purgatory.

In the sixteenth century the practice of granting indulgences was much abused. The church often sold them by granting letters of indulgence (or what Luther called letters of pardon) to people who donated money to the church. Among the worst offenders was Johann Tetzel, a Dominican friar who traveled about selling indulgences to raise funds for the renovation of Saint Peter's Basilica in Rome. Tetzel was reported to have often said, "As soon as the coin in the coffer rings, the soul from purgatory springs" (qtd. in Estep, p. 119). Luther was deeply troubled by this practice, along with other indications that the church had grown greedy and worldly, and he preached sermons against it. He objected to what he saw as Pope Leo X's greed and wealth, for the pope had struck a bargain with an ambitious German nobleman, Alfred of Mainz, who was trying to buy a bishopric and who took part in the Tetzel scheme in Germany as part of his payment to the pope for the position. Luther, meanwhile, feared that Catholics would neglect confession, absolution, and penance because they believed that buying indulgences would serve the same purpose—that, in effect, they would believe they could buy their way into heaven.

Put simply, conflict was brewing between Luther and the church hierarchy. The growing dispute was not just with a faraway pope, for the Wittenberg church at which Luther served contained one of the largest collections of sacred relics in Europe, some seventeen thousand items at the time, including a purported twig from the burning bush of Moses and a fragment of bread from the Last Supper. The church had a special dispensation from the pope allowing it to sell indulgences to people who came to view the relics—and who paid a stipulated fee. The church hierarchy actually computed that a person who visited the relics on All Saints' Day (November 1) and paid the fee would have the time spent in purgatory reduced by 1,902,202 years and 270 days. Luther had had enough of this practice and was determined to provoke debate and public discussion about it. It was for this reason that he published his *Ninety-five Theses*.

About the Author

Luther was born on November 10, 1483, as Martin Luder (later Latinizing his name) in the town of Eisleben in what is now Germany. (At the time, Germany was a loose collection of independent states, each ruled by a noble, that were part of the Holy Roman Empire.) Early in life, he was content to follow his family's wishes and enter the family copper business. But on July 2, 1505, his life was altered when, according to legend, he was knocked off his horse by a lightning bolt. Grateful that his life had been spared, he vowed to become a monk and entered the monastery of the Augustinian monks at Erfurt, where he devoted himself to an ascetic life of fasting, prayers, and pilgrimages.

In 1507 Luther was ordained as a Catholic priest. After earning bachelor's degrees in theology in 1508 and 1509 and a doctorate in theology in 1512, he joined the theology faculty at Wittenberg University. He also served as a parish priest at Castle Church in Wittenberg. On October 31, 1517, he purportedly nailed the *Ninety-five Theses* to the door of Castle Church, though many historians dispute that he actually nailed the document to the church door (a story started by a fellow theologian but never confirmed by others), believing instead that he sent it to a small number of bishops. Soon the theses were translated from Latin and, with the help of the recently invented printing press, distributed throughout Germany and then all of Europe. Luther's life was tumultuous after the publication of the *Ninety-five Theses*: He was excommunicated from the Catholic Church and branded a heretic and an outlaw. Eventually, he settled in Wittenberg, Germany. On June 13, 1525, he married Katharina von Bora, who in time gave birth to their three sons and three daughters.

In the final years of his life, Luther, who was often known to be rude, who had an irascible temper, and whose anti-Semitism modern Lutherans are quick to repudiate, continued to preach and write, publishing a German translation of the complete Bible in 1534 and numerous books and tracts. He engaged in disputes with various religious factions that, he believed, were advocating extreme views, among them the Baptists. In his final years, he suffered from health problems, and the death of one of his daughters in 1542 was a blow from which he never fully recovered. In early 1546 he was traveling to his birthplace, Eisleben, when he began complaining of chest pains. He died early on February 18, 1546, and on February 22 was laid to rest at Castle Church in Wittenberg.

Explanation and Analysis of the Document

Nailing a document such as the *Ninety-five Theses* to the door of Wittenberg Castle Church was not a particularly unusual act in Martin Luther's day. The door served as a kind of billboard, and it was a common way to announce a meeting to discuss matters concerning Christendom and Christianity. It is uncertain whether Luther actually nailed the document to the church door or simply sent it to select bishops, including Albert of Mainz, the German nobleman who took part in the Tetzel scheme for selling indulgences. The document opens with an announcement that for the love of the truth and with a desire to bring truth to light, Doctor Martin Luther, professor of theology, planned to hold a meeting

Time Line	
1524	■ The Peasants' War erupts; the war ends the following year.
1534	■ Luther's translation of the Bible into German is published.
1546	■ **February 18** Luther dies at Eisleben.
1555	■ **September 25** The Lutheran Church is officially recognized by the Holy Roman Empire in the Peace of Augsburg.
1618	■ **May 23** The Thirty Years' War begins.
1648	■ **October 24** The Thirty Years' War ends with the signing of the Peace of Westphalia.

where the points he raised would be discussed. He invited all interested parties to attend or to send their arguments to him via letter to be included in the discussion.

◆ Theses 1–9

Luther first takes up the issue of repentance. He uses the Latin phrase *Poenitentiam agite*, which is generally translated as simply "repent," though sometimes it is translated as "do penance." The distinction was important to Luther, for it pointed to the difference between being truly penitent and simply performing outward acts of penance, such as sacramental penance—that is, receiving the sacrament of penance after confessing to a priest. He argues that true inward repentance consists of self-hatred caused by sin. A crucial thesis is number 5, which states: "The pope does not intend to remit, and cannot remit any penalties other than those which he has imposed either by his own authority or by that of the Canons." In other words, the pope (and by extension priests) can impose penalties on the faithful only for violation of the "Canons," that is, canon law or church law. Nor, as Thesis 6 states, can the pope remit guilt except insofar as guilt has been remitted by God. Further, the portions of canon law that pertain to repentance can be imposed only on the living, not on the dead. In sum, Luther is making a clear distinction between the pope and God in matters of repentance and in the applicability of church law to penitents. Ultimately, this view would lead to the Protestant rejection of the Catholic Church's sacrament of penance, that is, confession of sins to a priest.

◆ Theses 10–26

In this group of theses, Luther turns to the theological concept of purgatory. He calls those priests who impose canonical penances on the dying "ignorant and wicked" and characterizes this practice as "tares," or weeds that are sown in a field of wheat or other grain—that is, an undesirable element. His use of this word is an allusion to Jesus' parable of the wheat and the tares in the Gospel of Matthew 13:24–30. Luther says that canonical penalties used to be imposed before penitents were given absolution (forgiveness) in the sacrament of penance, not after, as a test of their sincerity. Luther maintains that when people die, they are released from all earthly penalties as embodied in canon law. The penalty of purgatory is imposed not by earthly law but by the person's own fear, even despair, brought about by his or her own sinfulness. Purgatory is a process by which souls increase in love and decrease their own fear as they become more assured of their own blessedness. Accordingly, when the pope remits all penalties in purgatory, he can remit only those that he himself has imposed—again, according to earthly or canon law. This line of argument leads to another crucial thesis, number 21: "Therefore those preachers of indulgences are in error who say that by the pope's indulgences a man is freed from every penalty, and saved." The pope can free souls only from earthly penalties. Luther goes on to argue that if the pope could remit all penalties, only the most perfect could gain entrance to heaven, meaning that most people are deceived by "that indiscriminate and high-sounding promise of release from penalty." The pope does not hold the keys to heaven, but he can intercede, that is, pray for the souls of the deceased.

◆ Theses 27–38

Luther at this point turns specifically to the practice of selling indulgences and, what amounts to the same thing, letters of pardon. He refers to Johann Tetzel's rhyme quoted earlier about the penny jingling or ringing in the coffer, noting that the practice of paying for indulgences is a mark of "avarice" and citing a central doctrine of Protestantism—that "the intercession of the Church is in the power of God alone." As a result of what Luther is laying out here, it can be said that, in general, Protestantism believes in a more personal relationship with God, in contrast to Catholicism, which traditionally saw the church as a necessary mediator between people and God at a time when people in general could not read and, even if they could, had no copy of the Bible to read for themselves. Luther states that no one can know whether people wish to be bought out of purgatory. Pointing to the rarity of true contrition, Luther makes a bold statement in Thesis 32: He says that people who depend on letters of pardon will be "condemned eternally" and that people should be cautious in believing that such letters from the pope will have any effect on a person's salvation. Letters of pardon are ineffective without true contrition; the soul cannot be bought out of purgatory by indulgences and "confessionalia," another term for letters of pardon. Luther contends that every Christian has a right to remission of guilt and to the blessings of Christ without letters of pardon.

◆ Theses 39–55

A common theme in this group of theses is the deleterious effect of the practice of selling indulgences and letters of pardon. Luther sees an inconsistency in the effort to preach true contrition while selling letters of pardon. True contrition actually loves penalties, but letters of pardon "relax" people and make them hate penalties. In several theses, Luther argues that the performance of good works and acts of charity are preferable to purchasing "apostolic" pardons, or pardons from the pope and the church hierarchy. Money that is spent on indulgences and letters of pardon would be better spent by helping the poor and would be even better spent to meet the needs of one's own family. Indulgences and letters of pardon fail to make people better; instead, they only make them free from penalty, and spending money on them merits only God's "indignation." Luther is particularly concerned about the possibility that in purchasing indulgences, people will lose their "fear of God." It leads to a failure to emphasize the word of God in churches, which is far more significant than the effort to sell from the pulpit pardons and remissions from punishment. Luther alludes to his particular quarrel with the pope—that money gained from the selling of indulgences is being used for the church of Saint Peter in Rome at the expense of the German people. He even suggests boldly that it would be better for the pope to sell the church of Saint Peter and give the money to those from whom "hawkers" of indulgences take it.

◆ Theses 56–80

In this group of theses, Luther walks a fine line between condemnation of the pope—and, by extension, the entire church hierarchy—and his recognition of the pope's authority. Indeed, the power of the pope became a key issue in the Protestant Reformation, one of the results of which was the growing belief among the laity that the hierarchy of bishops, archbishops, cardinals, and popes interfered with a person's individual relationship with God. As a result, many Protestant denominations explicitly disavow

Luther nails his theses to the door of the All Saints' Church in Wittenburg. (Library of Congress)

hierarchies and the mandated forms of worship they prescribe (such as the Catholic mass) in favor of scriptural reading and more personal forms of worship.

Thus, on the one hand, Luther acknowledges the power of the pope in the remission of penalties in certain cases. A person is "accursed" if he speaks against the validity of apostolic pardons. The pope has "graces" at his disposal, including the Gospel and gifts of healing. But while acknowledging the authority of the pope, Luther condemns practices that the pope condones and that lead to corruption, greed, and false doctrine. He discusses the "treasures" of the church, arguing that the treasures consist of the keys of the church and the holy Gospel, not of material goods. Luther turns ironic when he says that not enough clerics recognize this supremacy of the Gospel, for the Gospel makes the last first and the first last, an allusion to Matthew 20:16: "So the last shall be first, and the first last." In other words, the emphasis on material things rather than the Gospel of Jesus inverts priorities and turns the Gospel into a tool used as a net to catch riches from men—again a biblical allusion, this time to Matthew 4:19 and Mark 1:17, where Jesus invites his apostles to follow him and be fishers of men. The core of Luther's view is contained in Thesis 72: "But he who guards against the lust and license of the pardon-preachers, let him be blessed!"

◆ **Theses 81–95**

Much of the remainder of the document is taken up with questions that Luther believes the laity would put to church authorities. If the pope has the power to remit time in purgatory through the sale of indulgences, why does he not simply empty purgatory? Why does the practice of saying masses for the dead at the time of their death and on anniversaries of their death have to continue if indulgences can be purchased? Why do God and the pope allow sinners to buy others' way out of purgatory? Why does not the pope use his own riches to build his church in Rome? Why does the pope suspend pardons and indulgences that have not been paid for? Luther then goes on to call for discussion of these matters, believing that the church should answer these questions. He concludes by urging the faithful to "be diligent in following Christ," confident that they can overcome tribulations and enter heaven.

Audience

The immediate audience for Luther's *Ninety-five Theses* included members of the local academic and ecclesiastical community. The document was also directed at preachers and others who supported the sale of indulgences. The burden of Luther's concern was for the Christian laity, but he was also concerned for the purity of the theology and practice of the church. As word of the theses spread, knowledge of them extended to all orders of society, especially in northern Europe. For many reformers, including the French theologian John Calvin (who gave his name to Calvinism and is regarded as a spiritual force behind Presbyterianism), the German reformer Martin Bucer, and the French reformer Guillaume Farel, Luther's teachings, expressed in part in the *Ninety-five Theses*, gave them reasons for pressing ahead with ecclesiastical reform.

Impact

Luther himself expressed surprise at the firestorm the *Ninety-five Theses* set off. He once said, "I would never have thought that such a storm would rise from Rome over one simple scrap of paper" (PBS, http://www.pbs.org/empires/martinluther/about_driv.html). Luther could not have known the far-reaching impact his scrap of paper would have, for it launched the Protestant Reformation, breaking the hold of the Catholic Church on Europe.

The impact on his life and on the Catholic Church was almost immediate. In response to the publication of the theses, Pope Leo X ordered a prominent Italian theologian, Sylvester Mazzolini of Prierio (also known as Prierias), to investigate the dispute. Mazzolini concluded that Luther's teachings were opposed to the church's doctrine on indulgences and branded Luther a heretic (that is, a dissenter from official teachings). The pope demanded that Luther submit to the pope's authority by recanting his heretical views. To that end he dispatched his representative to confront Luther at Augsburg, Germany, in October 1518. Over the next two years, the dispute grew more heated until the pope threatened to excommunicate Luther. In response, Luther burned the papal bull that contained the pope's warning. (A "bull" is an official papal letter, so called because it is sealed with a lead seal called a bulla.) On January 3, 1521, the pope issued a bull excommunicating Luther.

That same month, Charles V, the emperor of the Holy Roman Empire, convened the Diet of Worms, an assembly similar to a parliament and held in a small town on the Rhine River. Luther appeared before the diet. When he was asked whether he still believed his "errors," he replied the next day (April 18, 1521):

Unless I am convinced by the testimony of Scripture or by plain reason (for I believe in neither the pope nor in councils alone, for it is well-known, not only that they have erred, but also have contradicted themselves) … my conscience is captive to the Word of God. I cannot and will not recant, for it is neither safe nor honest to violate one's conscience.

According to legend, he then said, "I can do no other. Here I take my stand" (qtd. in Estep, pp. 132–133).

On May 25, 1521, the Diet of Worms issued the Edict of Worms, declaring Luther a heretic and an outlaw. He took refuge in Eisenach, where he lived for the next year under the protection of a German prince, occupying his time by translating the New Testament of the Bible into simple German that ordinary people could understand—another step in his efforts to free the faithful from the grip of church authority. Groups from all over Europe sent him letters soliciting his comments on assorted matters of church doctrine or seeking his support for their own reform movements.

But the impact of the "scrap of paper" extended far beyond Luther's own life. By the early 1520s, like-minded people in Europe were already calling themselves "Lutherans," although Luther did not regard himself as the creator of a new religion and even urged his followers to call themselves Christians, not Lutherans. They rejected his advice, and today there are some sixty-six million Lutherans in the world. His conflicts with the church helped spark the so-called Peasants' War of 1524–1525. At the time, Europe was in a state of upheaval. Since at least the fourteenth century, European peasants had been in rebellion against their landowning masters. They regarded Luther's challenge to the church as an attack as well on the social and economic system that oppressed them. Accordingly, they believed that if they rose up in revolt, they would gain the support of Protestant Reformers like Luther. Aiding the peasants were poor nobles who had no way to repay the debts they owed to the Catholic Church.

Initially, Luther supported the peasants, but he withdrew this support when the revolts turned bloody. Critics blamed Luther for the revolts, so he succumbed to increasing pressure to condemn the peasants, which he did, with characteristic vehemence, in 1525 in *Against the Murderous, Thieving Hordes of Peasants*—though part of his motivation was to lend his support to the German nobility who, like him, questioned the authority of the pope and who offered him protection. The revolt was put down in 1525, though henchmen continued to ransack churches, abduct church officials, and commit other atrocities.

The Peasants' War was only a harbinger of things to come. In the years and decades that followed, Catholicism and Protestantism formed the two sides in an ongoing battle that frequently erupted into warfare. Throughout the 1500s, tensions between Catholics and Protestants increased, erupting into violence in 1606 when Catholics and Protestants clashed in the German city of Donauwörth. Nations on the European continent, many of them—such as Spain and Italy—still Catholic, looked on the swelling influence of Protestant Germans with fear and distrust. In 1618 these tensions erupted into the Thirty Years' War, a series of conflicts that embroiled most of Europe and that led to the death of nearly a third of the

> "Our Lord and Master Jesus Christ, when He said Poenitentiam agite, willed that the whole life of believers should be repentance."
>
> (Thesis 1)

> "The pope does not intend to remit, and cannot remit any penalties other than those which he has imposed either by his own authority or by that of the Canons."
>
> (Thesis 5)

> "Therefore those preachers of indulgences are in error who say that by the pope's indulgences a man is freed from every penalty, and saved."
>
> (Thesis 21)

> "Every true Christian, whether living or dead, has part in all the blessings of Christ and the Church; and this is granted him by God, even without letters of pardon."
>
> (Thesis 37)

> "Injury is done the Word of God when, in the same sermon, an equal or a longer time is spent on pardons than on this Word."
>
> (Thesis 54)

> "But he who guards against the lust and license of the pardon-preachers, let him be blessed!"
>
> (Thesis 72)

German population before it ended with the signing of the Peace of Westphalia in 1648.

These kinds of religious conflicts continued. Protestant England was wracked with religious dissension that erupted into armed insurrection, which ended when the Catholic king, Charles I, was beheaded by Protestant revolutionaries in 1649. The monarchy was restored in 1660, but Catholic-Protestant animosity continued, and in 1688 the Catholic James II fled England into exile, to be replaced by King William and Queen Mary, both Protestants. For decades English Protestants feared that James's Catholic heirs would return to reclaim the throne. Until the nineteenth century, Catholics (and Jews) in England were not allowed to attend universities or hold public office. In the largely Protestant United States, similar anti-Catholic prejudice was commonplace throughout the nineteenth century and well into the twentieth. Throughout the twentieth century, Catholics and Protestants in Northern Ireland died in bloody bombings and assassinations.

The Protestant Reformation in Europe had as its by-products bloodshed, conflict, and discrimination. Nevertheless, historians agree that the Reformation Luther and others launched made an important contribution to the development of Europe. The Reformation freed the nations of Europe from the grip the Catholic Church had on most aspects of life: government, education, scientific research, publication of books, among others. The emphasis on personal belief rather than church authority sparked a renewed interest in learning. This interest, in turn, fueled the rapid artistic, intellectual, and social advancement of Europe.

Further Reading

■ Books

Atkinson, James. *The Great Light: Luther and the Reformation*. Grand Rapids, Mich.: Eerdmans, 1968.

Bainton, Roland. *Here I Stand: A Life of Martin Luther*. London: Penguin, 2002.

Brecht, Martin. *Martin Luther*. 3 vols., trans. James L. Schaaf. Minneapolis, Minn.: Fortress Press, 1985–1993.

Ebeling, Gerhard. *Luther: An Introduction to His Thought*. Philadelphia: Fortress Press, 1970.

Edwards, Mark U., Jr. *Luther's Last Battles: Politics and Polemics, 1531–46*. Ithaca, N.Y.: Cornell University Press, 1983.

Estep, William Roscoe. *Renaissance and Reformation*. Grand Rapids, Mich.: Eerdmans, 1986.

Kolb, Robert. *Martin Luther: Confessor of the Faith*. New York: Oxford University Press, 2009.

Krey, Philip D. W., and Peter D. S. Krey, eds. *Luther's Spirituality*. New York: Paulist Press, 2007.

Lohse, Bernhard. *Martin Luther: An Introduction to His Life and Work*. Philadelphia: Fortress Press, 1986.

Wilson, Derek. *Out of the Storm: The Life and Legacy of Martin Luther*. New York: St. Martin's Press, 2008.

■ Web Sites

Kreis, Steven. "Lectures on Early Modern European History—Lecture 3: The Protestant Reformation." History Guide Web site. http://www.historyguide.org/earlymod/lecture3c.html.

"Martin Luther: The Reluctant Revolutionary." PBS Web site. http://www.pbs.org/empires/martinluther.

—Andrew J. Waskey and Michael J. O'Neal

Questions for Further Study

1. What were the intersections between politics and religion in the context surrounding Luther's theses? What were the intersections between money and religion in the same context?

2. What were some of the church abuses to which Luther objected? On what specific grounds did he object to them?

3. Luther's beliefs, and the actions he took on those beliefs, might seem almost tame today. He did not deny the existence of God, the divinity of Christ, or most other fundamental church doctrines. Yet his actions attracted a great deal of attention from Rome, led to the Diet of Worms, and caused his excommunication from the church. Why was the church so troubled by the teachings of one priest in Germany?

4. Why do you think Catholics in Europe and North America were held in such suspicion in the centuries following the Protestant Reformation?

5. In the modern world, there are numerous Protestant denominations, among them Methodists, Baptists, Seventh-day Adventists, various Reformed churches, and Anabaptists (including the Amish, Mennonites, and Quakers). Additionally, there are numerous small sects, such as the Churches of Christ, the Zion Christian Church, and the Free Apostolic Church of Pentecost, among many others. What do you believe Luther would have thought about this proliferation of Protestant denominations and sects? What do you believe he would have thought about the prominence of nondenominational televangelists in the modern world?

MARTIN LUTHER'S NINETY-FIVE THESES

Disputation of Doctor Martin Luther on the Power and Efficacy of Indulgences

October 31, 1517

Out of love for the truth and the desire to bring it to light, the following propositions will be discussed at Wittenberg, under the presidency of the Reverend Father Martin Luther, Master of Arts and of Sacred Theology, and Lecturer in Ordinary on the same at that place. Wherefore he requests that those who are unable to be present and debate orally with us, may do so by letter.

In the Name our Lord Jesus Christ. Amen.

1. Our Lord and Master Jesus Christ, when He said Poenitentiam agite, willed that the whole life of believers should be repentance.

2. This word cannot be understood to mean sacramental penance, i.e., confession and satisfaction, which is administered by the priests.

3. Yet it means not inward repentance only; nay, there is no inward repentance which does not outwardly work divers mortifications of the flesh.

4. The penalty [of sin], therefore, continues so long as hatred of self continues; for this is the true inward repentance, and continues until our entrance into the kingdom of heaven.

5. The pope does not intend to remit, and cannot remit any penalties other than those which he has imposed either by his own authority or by that of the Canons.

6. The pope cannot remit any guilt, except by declaring that it has been remitted by God and by assenting to God's remission; though, to be sure, he may grant remission in cases reserved to his judgment. If his right to grant remission in such cases were despised, the guilt would remain entirely unforgiven.

7. God remits guilt to no one whom He does not, at the same time, humble in all things and bring into subjection to His vicar, the priest.

8. The penitential canons are imposed only on the living, and, according to them, nothing should be imposed on the dying.

9. Therefore the Holy Spirit in the pope is kind to us, because in his decrees he always makes exception of the article of death and of necessity.

10. Ignorant and wicked are the doings of those priests who, in the case of the dying, reserve canonical penances for purgatory.

11. This changing of the canonical penalty to the penalty of purgatory is quite evidently one of the tares that were sown while the bishops slept.

12. In former times the canonical penalties were imposed not after, but before absolution, as tests of true contrition.

13. The dying are freed by death from all penalties; they are already dead to canonical rules, and have a right to be released from them.

14. The imperfect health [of soul], that is to say, the imperfect love, of the dying brings with it, of necessity, great fear; and the smaller the love, the greater is the fear.

15. This fear and horror is sufficient of itself alone (to say nothing of other things) to constitute the penalty of purgatory, since it is very near to the horror of despair.

16. Hell, purgatory, and heaven seem to differ as do despair, almost-despair, and the assurance of safety.

17. With souls in purgatory it seems necessary that horror should grow less and love increase.

18. It seems unproved, either by reason or Scripture, that they are outside the state of merit, that is to say, of increasing love.

19. Again, it seems unproved that they, or at least that all of them, are certain or assured of their own blessedness, though we may be quite certain of it.

20. Therefore by "full remission of all penalties" the pope means not actually "of all," but only of those imposed by himself.

21. Therefore those preachers of indulgences are in error who say that by the pope's indulgences a man is freed from every penalty, and saved;

22. Whereas he remits to souls in purgatory no penalty which, according to the canons, they would have had to pay in this life.

23. If it is at all possible to grant to any one the remission of all penalties whatsoever, it is certain that this remission can be granted only to the most perfect, that is, to the very fewest.

24. It must needs be, therefore, that the greater part of the people are deceived by that indiscriminate and high-sounding promise of release from penalty.

25. The power which the pope has, in a general way, over purgatory, is just like the power which any bishop or curate has, in a special way, within his own diocese or parish.

26. The pope does well when he grants remission to souls [in purgatory], not by the power of the keys (which he does not possess), but by way of intercession.

27. They preach only human doctrines who say that so soon as the penny jingles into the money-box, the soul flies out [of purgatory].

28. It is certain that when the penny jingles into the money-box, gain and avarice can be increased, but the result of the intercession of the Church is in the power of God alone.

29. Who knows whether all the souls in purgatory wish to be bought out of it, as in the legend of Sts. Severinus and Paschal.

30. No one is sure that his own contrition is sincere; much less that he has attained full remission.

31. Rare as is the man that is truly penitent, so rare is also the man who truly buys indulgences, i.e., such men are most rare.

32. They will be condemned eternally, together with their teachers, who believe themselves sure of their salvation because they have letters of pardon.

33. Men must be on their guard against those who say that the pope's pardons are that inestimable gift of God by which man is reconciled to Him;

34. For these "graces of pardon" concern only the penalties of sacramental satisfaction, and these are appointed by man.

35. They preach no Christian doctrine who teach that contrition is not necessary in those who intend to buy souls out of purgatory or to buy confessionalia.

36. Every truly repentant Christian has a right to full remission of penalty and guilt, even without letters of pardon.

37. Every true Christian, whether living or dead, has part in all the blessings of Christ and the Church; and this is granted him by God, even without letters of pardon.

38. Nevertheless, the remission and participation [in the blessings of the Church] which are granted by the pope are in no way to be despised, for they are, as I have said, the declaration of divine remission.

39. It is most difficult, even for the very keenest theologians, at one and the same time to commend to the people the abundance of pardons and [the need of] true contrition.

40. True contrition seeks and loves penalties, but liberal pardons only relax penalties and cause them to be hated, or at least, furnish an occasion [for hating them].

41. Apostolic pardons are to be preached with caution, lest the people may falsely think them preferable to other good works of love.

42. Christians are to be taught that the pope does not intend the buying of pardons to be compared in any way to works of mercy.

43. Christians are to be taught that he who gives to the poor or lends to the needy does a better work than buying pardons;

44. Because love grows by works of love, and man becomes better; but by pardons man does not grow better, only more free from penalty.

45. Christians are to be taught that he who sees a man in need, and passes him by, and gives [his money] for pardons, purchases not the indulgences of the pope, but the indignation of God.

46. Christians are to be taught that unless they have more than they need, they are bound to keep back what is necessary for their own families, and by no means to squander it on pardons.

47. Christians are to be taught that the buying of pardons is a matter of free will, and not of commandment.

48. Christians are to be taught that the pope, in granting pardons, needs, and therefore desires, their devout prayer for him more than the money they bring.

49. Christians are to be taught that the pope's pardons are useful, if they do not put their trust in them; but altogether harmful, if through them they lose their fear of God.

50. Christians are to be taught that if the pope knew the exactions of the pardon-preachers, he would rather that St. Peter's church should go to ashes, than that it should be built up with the skin, flesh and bones of his sheep.

51. Christians are to be taught that it would be the pope's wish, as it is his duty, to give of his own money to very many of those from whom certain hawkers of pardons cajole money, even though the church of St. Peter might have to be sold.

52. The assurance of salvation by letters of pardon is vain, even though the commissary, nay, even though the pope himself, were to stake his soul upon it.

53. They are enemies of Christ and of the pope, who bid the Word of God be altogether silent in some Churches, in order that pardons may be preached in others.

54. Injury is done the Word of God when, in the same sermon, an equal or a longer time is spent on pardons than on this Word.

55. It must be the intention of the pope that if pardons, which are a very small thing, are celebrated with one bell, with single processions and ceremonies, then the Gospel, which is the very greatest thing, should be preached with a hundred bells, a hundred processions, a hundred ceremonies.

56. The "treasures of the Church," out of which the pope grants indulgences, are not sufficiently named or known among the people of Christ.

57. That they are not temporal treasures is certainly evident, for many of the vendors do not pour out such treasures so easily, but only gather them.

58. Nor are they the merits of Christ and the Saints, for even without the pope, these always work grace for the inner man and the cross, death, and hell for the outward man.

59. St. Lawrence said that the treasures of the Church were the Church's poor, but he spoke according to the usage of the word in his own time.

60. Without rashness we say that the keys of the Church, given by Christ's merit, are that treasure;

61. For it is clear that for the remission of penalties and of reserved cases, the power of the pope is of itself sufficient.

62. The true treasure of the Church is the Most Holy Gospel of the glory and the grace of God.

63. But this treasure is naturally most odious, for it makes the first to be last.

64. On the other hand, the treasure of indulgences is naturally most acceptable, for it makes the last to be first.

65. Therefore the treasures of the Gospel are nets with which they formerly were wont to fish for men of riches.

66. The treasures of the indulgences are nets with which they now fish for the riches of men.

67. The indulgences which the preachers cry as the "greatest graces" are known to be truly such, in so far as they promote gain.

68. Yet they are in truth the very smallest graces compared with the grace of God and the piety of the Cross.

69. Bishops and curates are bound to admit the commissaries of apostolic pardons, with all reverence.

70. But still more are they bound to strain all their eyes and attend with all their ears, lest these men preach their own dreams instead of the commission of the pope.

71. He who speaks against the truth of apostolic pardons, let him be anathema and accursed!

72. But he who guards against the lust and license of the pardon-preachers, let him be blessed!

73. The pope justly thunders against those who, by any art, contrive the injury of the traffic in pardons.

74. But much more does he intend to thunder against those who use the pretext of pardons to contrive the injury of holy love and truth.

75. To think the papal pardons so great that they could absolve a man even if he had committed an impossible sin and violated the Mother of God—this is madness.

76. We say, on the contrary, that the papal pardons are not able to remove the very least of venial sins, so far as its guilt is concerned.

77. It is said that even St. Peter, if he were now Pope, could not bestow greater graces; this is blasphemy against St. Peter and against the pope.

78. We say, on the contrary, that even the present pope, and any pope at all, has greater graces at his disposal; to wit, the Gospel, powers, gifts of healing, etc., as it is written in I. Corinthians xii.

79. To say that the cross, emblazoned with the papal arms, which is set up [by the preachers of indulgences], is of equal worth with the Cross of Christ, is blasphemy.

80. The bishops, curates and theologians who allow such talk to be spread among the people, will have an account to render.

81. This unbridled preaching of pardons makes it no easy matter, even for learned men, to rescue the reverence due to the pope from slander, or even from the shrewd questionings of the laity.

82. To wit:—"Why does not the pope empty purgatory, for the sake of holy love and of the dire need of the souls that are there, if he redeems an infinite number of souls for the sake of miserable money with which to build a Church? The former reasons would be most just; the latter is most trivial."

83. Again:—"Why are mortuary and anniversary masses for the dead continued, and why does he not return or permit the withdrawal of the endowments founded on their behalf, since it is wrong to pray for the redeemed?"

84. Again:—"What is this new piety of God and the pope, that for money they allow a man who is impious and their enemy to buy out of purgatory the pious soul of a friend of God, and do not rather, because of that pious and beloved soul's own need, free it for pure love's sake?"

85. Again:—"Why are the penitential canons long since in actual fact and through disuse abrogated and dead, now satisfied by the granting of indulgences, as though they were still alive and in force?"

86. Again:—"Why does not the pope, whose wealth is to-day greater than the riches of the richest, build just this one church of St. Peter with his own money, rather than with the money of poor believers?"

87. Again:—"What is it that the pope remits, and what participation does he grant to those who, by perfect contrition, have a right to full remission and participation?"

88. Again:—"What greater blessing could come to the Church than if the pope were to do a hundred times a day what he now does once, and bestow on every believer these remissions and participations?"

89. "Since the pope, by his pardons, seeks the salvation of souls rather than money, why does he suspend the indulgences and pardons granted heretofore, since these have equal efficacy?"

90. To repress these arguments and scruples of the laity by force alone, and not to resolve them by giving reasons, is to expose the Church and the pope to the ridicule of their enemies, and to make Christians unhappy.

91. If, therefore, pardons were preached according to the spirit and mind of the pope, all these doubts would be readily resolved; nay, they would not exist.

92. Away, then, with all those prophets who say to the people of Christ, "Peace, peace," and there is no peace!

93. Blessed be all those prophets who say to the people of Christ, "Cross, cross," and there is no cross!

94. Christians are to be exhorted that they be diligent in following Christ, their Head, through penalties, deaths, and hell;

95. And thus be confident of entering into heaven rather through many tribulations, than through the assurance of peace.

Glossary

Apostolic pardon	an indulgence, given by a priest, for the remission (releasing from guilt) of sins
commissary	in this context, person responsible for executing a function of a superior
greater graces	as enumerated in 1 Corinthians 12:4–11
mortuary and anniversary masses	respectively, masses for the dead individually and for all those who have died in a given year
St. Lawrence	a bishop who was tortured and martyred in the third century, during the reign of the Roman emperor Valerian
St. Peter's church	the Catholic (that is, universal) Church
Sts. Severinus and Paschal	respectively, a French abbot of the sixth century, famed for his exercise of penance, and an Italian pope (Paschal I) of the eighth century who oversaw restoration of basilicas in Rome
tares that were sown	an allusion to the parable of Jesus given in Matthew 13:24–30
true contrition	repentance that includes the firm will never to sin again

DUTCH DECLARATION OF INDEPENDENCE

"When he does not behave thus, ... then he is no longer a prince, but a tyrant, and the subjects are to consider him in no other view."

Overview

The Dutch Declaration of Independence, signed on July 26, 1581, was formally called the Act of Abjuration or, in Dutch, the Plakkaat van Verlatinghe. A coalition of Dutch provinces in the northern portion of the federation called the United Provinces issued the declaration to pronounce their independence from Spanish rule under King Philip II. A literal English translation of Plakkaat van Verlatinghe would be "Placard of Desertion"; this title was given to the document because Dutch rebels believed that Philip had essentially deserted the Low Countries, like a shepherd who had deserted his flock, and the document outlines his abuses against the provinces.

The declaration, regarded as the first modern declaration of independence, was forged during the Eighty Years' War, often called the Dutch War of Independence. The first phase of this war was the Dutch Revolt of 1568–1609, during which the Netherlands' northern provinces achieved independence from Spain. After Spain and the northern provinces signed the Twelve Years' Truce in 1609 at Antwerp, ending hostilities, the southern provinces continued to live under Spanish domination until the Treaty of Münster was signed in 1648. This treaty, part of the realignment brought about that year by the Treaty of Westphalia—which ended the Eighty Years' War as well as the Thirty Years' War, fought in central Europe—confirmed the existence of the Dutch provinces as an independent nation variously called the Dutch Republic, the Republic of the Seven United Netherlands, or the Republic of the Seven United Provinces.

In the twenty-first century, the names of Holland and the Netherlands tend to be used interchangeably. The terminology, though, is complex and oftentimes confusing. *Netherlands* literally means "Low Countries" or "Lowlands" and historically dates to the period when the Dutch Republic consisted of a loose confederation of seven provinces; the declaration refers to this confederation in the opening line as the United Provinces of the Low Countries. In 1830 two of those provinces broke off from the recently established United Kingdom of the Netherlands to form Belgium. Today, the phrase "Low Countries" is often used to refer col-

lectively to the countries of the Netherlands, Belgium, and Luxembourg. The phrase actually has little to do with the countries' "lowness" relative to sea level; rather, it refers to the provinces' originally being the more southerly portions of earlier empires. Holland is a name commonly used to refer to the country of the Netherlands, but more accurately it reflects the names of two provinces, North Holland and South Holland, that historically were the most prominent members of the Dutch Republic. Finally, "Dutch" refers to the language spoken in the Netherlands, though the word is also used to refer to the people and the nation's institutions; it is etymologically related to "Deutsche," or German.

Context

The Dutch Declaration of Independence was signed in the midst of a complex set of events that would radically alter the balance of power in Western Europe. In the fifteenth century, the successive dukes of Burgundy held control of what were called the Seventeen Provinces, a collection of counties and fiefdoms roughly corresponding to the Dutch Republic and also including small portions of modern-day France and Germany. Accordingly, the region was often called the Burgundian Netherlands. The Burgundian Netherlands were inherited by Charles, the duke of Burgundy, in 1506. Charles was a descendant of the House of Habsburg, a branch of the Austrian royal succession that ruled a large portion of central Europe, and as such he became King Charles I of Spain in 1516; he was also the grandson of King Ferdinand II of Aragon and Isabella I of Castile, famous for backing Christopher Columbus's voyage to the New World in 1492. Charles was Spanish, but he was born in Ghent (in Flanders, now part of Belgium), so he spoke Dutch and was sympathetic to Dutch concerns. In 1519, upon the death of his grandfather, he became the head of the House of Habsburg and was elected the monarch of the Holy Roman Empire as Charles V (though the pope did not officially crown him until 1530). He thus presided over a large swath of western, central, and southern Europe, including the Netherlands. He asserted his control over the Netherlands in 1549 when he issued the Pragmatic Sanction, which recognized the Sev-

1519

- **June 28**
  Charles V of
  Spain is elected
  Holy Roman
  Emperor.

1544

- **William I inherits
  the title "prince
  of Orange."**

1549

- Charles V issues
  the Pragmatic
  Sanction,
  recognizing the
  Seventeen
  Provinces as a
  unified political
  entity to which
  the Habsburgs
  were heirs.

1556

- **January 16**
  Philip II is
  crowned king
  of Spain upon
  the abdication
  of his father,
  Charles V.

1566

- **April 5**
  Dutch nobles
  present a
  petition to
  Margaret of
  Parma, Philip's
  governor of the
  Netherlands, to
  end persecution
  of Protestants.

1567

- **August 22**
  Troops under
  the command of
  Fernando
  álvarez de
  Toledo, third
  duke of Alba,
  enter Brussels
  and begin to
  take harsh
  measures
  against rebels.

enteen Provinces as a unified political entity to which the Habsburgs were heirs.

During the sixteenth century, three major issues caused friction in Charles V's Dutch domains. One issue was taxation. Flanders had become a particularly wealthy province, but the other Dutch provinces were affluent as well, largely through trade and industry as spurred by an entrepreneurial ethic. Charles became embroiled in a series of wars, particularly against France as part of the Italian Wars and against the Turks in the Mediterranean. He needed funds to finance these wars, and the affluent Dutch bore more than their fair share of the tax burden, although they opposed the wars because France and the Turkish Ottoman Empire were important trading partners. The second issue that caused friction was the rise of Protestantism, which Catholic Spain regarded as heresy. Protestantism had been tolerated locally throughout the Dutch provinces, but Charles believed that it had to be suppressed and sent troops into the provinces to that end. He enacted harsh measures against Dutch Protestants, creating numerous grievances. His attempts to suppress Dutch Protestantism took place against the backdrop of the notorious Spanish Inquisition, the oftentimes cruel effort to root out heresy, blasphemy, witchcraft, sodomy, and other departures from Catholic orthodoxy.

The third source of friction was efforts to centralize the government. The Netherlands had historically consisted of numerous principalities operating more or less autonomously under the control of local nobles. Charles wanted to increase efficiency in his empire, so he attempted to impose more centralized rule over these principalities. Charles replaced local Dutch stadtholders (heads of state) and members of the States-General, the governing body of the Seventeen Provinces, with his own appointments. He also replaced bishops and other religious authorities. Both the nobles and the increasingly influential merchants of the Netherlands resented these encroachments on their traditional prerogatives.

Thus did matters stand when Charles relinquished the throne of Spain to his son, Philip II, in 1556. While the Dutch had grown annoyed with Charles, they grudgingly tolerated his rule, for he spoke Dutch and appeared to be at least somewhat interested in Dutch welfare. Philip II, though, was more Spanish than Dutch and showed little interest in the Netherlands. The issues that had arisen during the first half of the sixteenth century became more pronounced under Philip, who governed the Dutch provinces harshly; he was at loggerheads with the Dutch nobles throughout his first decade of rule. They resisted his efforts to increase taxes. They demanded the withdrawal of Spanish troops. They resented Antoine Perrenot de Granvelle, Philip's appointed head of the States-General, and several prominent nobles resigned from the States-General in protest. Religious protests increased, as Dutch Protestants—and even Dutch Catholics—called for an end to persecution of Protestantism. In 1566 a petition to that end was submitted by some four hundred nobles to Philip's governor of the Netherlands, Margaret of Parma, who passed it along to Philip—who promptly ignored it.

As if matters were not troubled enough, they turned worse in 1566 when rioting broke out in Flanders and other provinces. These riots were led by Dutch Calvinists and were part of a so-called iconoclastic ("image breaking") movement. Calvinists in numerous cities looted churches and destroyed religious images of Catholic saints, which Calvinists thought of as idols. In response to the vandalism, in 1567 Philip sent troops to Brussels under the command of Fernando Álvarez de Toledo, the third duke of Alba. Given broad license by Philip, the duke of Alba created the Council of Troubles (in Dutch, Raad van Beroerten) to enforce harsh measures against anyone he thought to be disloyal to the king. Numerous nobles were executed, including most prominently Lamoraal, the count of Egmond, and Filips van Montmorency, the count of Hoorn, who were decapitated in Brussels in 1568. Over the next year, a thousand people were executed, prompting Netherlanders to refer to the Council of Troubles as the "Council of Blood."

Amid this turmoil, William I, the prince of Orange and an influential stadtholder, assumed leadership of the opposition to Philip, though William was politically savvy and did not renounce his allegiance to the king. Initially, he fled to his domains in Germany to avoid the wrath of the duke of Alba. In 1568 he returned in an effort to drive Alba out, invading the Netherlands in concert with armies led by his two brothers and a fourth army led by French Huguenots. On May 23, 1568, his forces defeated a Spanish force at the Battle of Heiligerlee, marking the first Dutch victory of the Dutch Revolt and the Eighty Years' War. Although William was victorious, the other invading armies were not. William ran out of money, his army fell apart, and the rebellion was effectively quelled until 1572.

The duke of Alba meanwhile retained his position of authority. He provoked the ire of Netherlanders anew when he instituted a tax to fund the Spanish king's war against the Ottoman Empire. The Ottoman Turks, for their part, offered direct aid to the Dutch rebels, hoping thereby to counter Habsburg hegemony over Europe. Discontent continued to grow until Dutch rebels seized the town of Brielle on April 1, 1572. This victory, entirely unexpected, emboldened the rebels, who reappointed William of Orange as their leader. William faced a difficult challenge, for he needed to find a way to unite three different factions: Calvinists who wanted to impose Dutch Protestantism, Catholics who yet remained loyal to Philip, and a large group of Catholics and Protestants who were primarily interested in ending Spanish rule over their country and restoring their privileges.

Throughout the 1570s, Philip had problems of his own. His wars were bankrupting Spain; his unpaid soldiers mutinied, and in 1576 they sacked and looted Antwerp in an event called the Spanish Fury. Again the rebels were emboldened. That same year the Seventeen Provinces signed an internal treaty called the Pacification of Ghent, an agreement to join forces against the Spanish and to enforce religious tolerance. The union, however, was still in disarray. In early 1579 the southern provinces, through the Union of Arras, withdrew from the greater union and confirmed their loyalty to the Spanish king, largely because they were uncomfortable

Time Line

1568

- **May 23**
The Dutch achieve their first victory in their revolt and the Eighty Years' War when William's forces defeat the Spanish at the Battle of Heiligerlee.

1576

- **November 4**
Mutinous Spanish troops launch the three-day sack of Antwerp.

- **November 8**
Dutch rebels sign the Pacification of Ghent, an agreement to join forces against the Spanish and to enforce religious toleration.

1579

- **January 6**
The southern provinces reject the Pacification of Ghent and withdraw from the union of the Seventeen Provinces in the Union of Arras.

- **January 23**
The Union of Utrecht formally unites the rebellious northern provinces as the United Provinces.

- **May 7**
The Congress of Cologne is convened to mediate a settlement between the rebellious Dutch provinces and Philip II of Spain; the congress disbands at the end of the year.

1581

■ **July 26**
The Act of Abjuration, or Dutch Declaration of Independence, is signed.

1584

■ **July 10**
William I of Orange is assassinated.

1609

■ **April 9**
The Dutch Revolt ends with the signing of the Twelve Years' Truce at Antwerp.

1648

■ **October 24**
The Treaty of Münster is signed, ending Spanish control over the Netherlands.

with the fundamentalist religious fervor of the Calvinists. In response, the northern provinces of Holland, Zeeland, Utrecht, and Groningen formed the Union of Utrecht on January 23, 1579, leaving the Seventeen Provinces divided between north and south. Over the next year and a half, Gelder, Overijssel, and Friesland also joined with the northern provinces, which then declared their independence from Spain as the Republic of the Seven United Provinces in the Act of Abjuration on July 26, 1581. (*Abjuration* denotes a formal renunciation or repudiation, in this case, of Philip II of Spain.) One of the alliance's first tasks was to find a monarch to rule. The position was offered to Queen Elizabeth I of England, but she turned the Dutch down, unwilling to alienate the Spanish king. Accordingly, the rebel provinces turned to Hercule François, the duke of Anjou, the French king's younger brother, who agreed on the condition that the provinces renounce all allegiance to Spain.

About the Author

The Dutch Declaration of Independence was drafted by a committee of four men; details of their lives are sketchy. Andries Hessels held the position of *greffier*, or secretary, of

Brabant. Jacques Tayaert was a pensionary, or chief functionary and legal adviser, in the city of Ghent. Jacob Valcke held the same position in the city of Ter Goes, now called Goes. Finally, Pieter van Dieven was pensionary of the city of Mechelen. A fifth name is often mentioned, that of Jan de Asseliers, the *audiencer* of the States-General (the official charged with drafting its declarations), who may have physically written out the declaration and may have composed the preamble. His name appears at the very end of the document as a signer.

Although he was not strictly speaking an author of the declaration, William I of Orange, often called William the Silent, reputedly for his circumspection in negotiations with the king of France, was the leader of the Dutch Revolt and thus can be considered the inspiration behind the document. (This William of Orange is not to be confused with the William of Orange who assumed the throne of England in 1689 through the Glorious Revolution; the latter was William III of Orange.) William I of Orange was born on April 24, 1533, in Germany. Upon the death of his cousin in 1544, as the family's only recognized heir, he assumed the title of prince of Orange. Later, through marriage, he gained additional royal titles. In 1555 Charles V appointed him to the Council of State; later, Philip appointed him stadtholder of Holland, Zeeland, Utrecht, and Burgundy. During the religious disturbances that followed the accession of Philip, he refused to appear before the Council of Troubles and was declared an outlaw. He then became leader of the armed resistance to Spain and won several important battles. His leadership of the Dutch was validated by the signing of the Act of Abjuration in 1581. Philip, though, had placed a bounty on his head, which proved too hard to resist on the part of one Balthasar Gérard, a Catholic Frenchman who believed that William had betrayed his king, Philip. On July 10, 1584, Gérard presented himself at William's home and shot him with a handgun—one of the earliest political assassinations by handgun in history.

Explanation and Analysis of the Document

The Dutch Declaration of Independence begins with a lengthy exposition detailing the abuses of the Spanish king, Philip II, and the historical circumstances that led to the signing of the document. This is followed by the "declaration of independence" per se, indicating that the duke of Anjou agreed to function as the Netherlands' monarch, listing specific ways in which Spanish influence was to be eliminated, and outlining provisions for the governance of the provinces.

◆ Paragraphs 1–7
The first seven paragraphs of the declaration effectively constitute a preamble, although the section is not specifically identified as such. In the preamble, the Dutch rebels outline in detail the historical circumstances that led to their renunciation of Spanish rule. After a very brief introduction, the document opens with harsh criticism of Spain's King

Philip. Using traditional Christian imagery, the document compares the king to a shepherd and the Netherlands to his flock. Paragraph 2 argues that a king is supposed to look to the welfare of his flock. In contrast, Philip has subjected the Dutch to oppression, slavery, and tyranny and has infringed upon "their ancient customs and privileges." Accordingly, the Dutch have decided to "disallow his authority" and choose another prince to rule over them. They have been forced to take this step because their "humble petitions and remonstrances" to the king have been ignored. The paragraph asserts that the provinces accept a ruler only "upon certain conditions, which he swears to maintain"; if the prince violates these conditions, "he is no longer sovereign."

In a small gesture of political goodwill, the third paragraph casts the blame for the current circumstances less on the king and more on his "evil counselors," who, according to the document, wanted to exploit the Netherlands for their own gain, as they had in other realms. Nevertheless, the king is culpable because he listened to those counselors and took steps to subdue the Netherlands. The paragraph makes reference to the Spanish Inquisition, which locally was part of a broad effort to subjugate the Dutch by imposing church authorities on them. The fourth paragraph continues this theme, referring to the Inquisition as being "as dreadful and detested in these provinces as the worst of slavery." The document then makes reference to various petitions for religious toleration submitted by the nobles to Margaret of Parma, Philip's appointed governor of the Netherlands. Margaret, born in 1522, was Charles V's illegitimate daughter and became the duchess of Parma, in Italy, when she married Ottavio Farnese, the duke of Parma, who happened to be Pope Paul III's grandson. (The duke was just thirteen at the time, while Margaret was just sixteen—and this was her second marriage.) Philip responded to the nobles' petitions with more oppression through the Inquisition, which was charged with enforcing the doctrines enunciated at the Council of Trent—a Catholic ecumenical council that ran from 1545 to 1563 and whose primary purpose was to answer and resist Protestant heresy.

The fifth paragraph makes reference to the events that took place in 1566 and the immediate aftermath. Yet another petition for religious toleration was submitted to Margaret and, through her, to the Spanish king. Envoys were dispatched to seek relief from the king, but the king, rather than receiving them to discuss the matter and find common ground, declared that anyone who had taken part in the effort to remonstrate with him was a rebel and an outlaw, subject to punishment by death and the confiscation of his estates. It was at this point that the king empowered the duke of Alba (spelled Alva in the document), who cruelly enforced the Inquisition and later boasted that he had put to death over eighteen thousand men. Alba's rule became prominent in the so-called Black Legend, a term coined in 1914 by the Spanish writer Julián Juderías to refer to the reputation of the Spanish during the sixteenth century as cruel, oppressive, tyrannical, and intolerant. Paragraph 6 continues to outline Alba's abuses. Because so many people had been executed, there would have been little reason to

William the Silent (© Bettmann/CORBIS)

send an invading army into the Netherlands, yet such an army did invade under Alba's generalship with the purpose of ruling the country as tyrannically as Spain ruled the "Indies," or its colonies in the New World. The document states that throughout all this turmoil, the people of the Netherlands yet tried to find ways to submit themselves to the king and treat his representative with courtesy. In response, they were subjected to conquest, violence, and executions.

The seventh and final paragraph of the preamble lists numerous other abuses. Dutch nobles, including William of Orange and "diverse gentlemen," were forced to flee into exile, and their lands were then confiscated by the Spanish. Spanish soldiers were quartered in people's houses. Dutch citizens were forced to pay taxes for the construction of military posts; the "tenth penny" was a 10 percent tax levied on merchandise. German mercenaries were brought into the Netherlands, again with the purpose of waging war and denying the Dutch their traditional liberties.

◆ **Paragraphs 8 and 9**

Having catalogued the abuses of the Spanish king, the document states in paragraph 8 that the provinces have

"When he does not behave thus, but, on the contrary, oppresses them, seeking opportunities to infringe their ancient customs and privileges, exacting from them slavish compliance, then he is no longer a prince, but a tyrant, and the subjects are to consider him in no other view. And particularly when this is done deliberately, unauthorized by the states, they may not only disallow his authority, but legally proceed to the choice of another prince for their defense."

(Paragraph 2)

"This being come to the knowledge of the people gave just occasion to great uneasiness and clamor among them, and lessened that good affection they had always borne toward the king and his predecessors. And, especially, seeing that he did not only seek to tyrannize over their persons and estates, but also over their consciences, for which they believed themselves accountable to God only."

(Paragraph 5)

"All these considerations give us more than sufficient reason to renounce the King of Spain, and seek some other powerful and more gracious prince to take us under his protection; and, more especially, as these countries have been for these twenty years abandoned to disturbance and oppression by their king, during which time the inhabitants were not treated as subjects, but enemies, enslaved forcibly by their own governors."

(Paragraph 8)

"So, having no hope of reconciliation, and finding no other remedy, we have, agreeable to the law of nature in our own defense, and for maintaining the rights, privileges, and liberties of our countrymen, wives, and children, and latest posterity from being enslaved by the Spaniards, been constrained to renounce allegiance to the King of Spain, and pursue such methods as appear to us most likely to secure our ancient liberties and privileges."

(Paragraph 10)

"more than sufficient reason to renounce the King of Spain, and seek some other powerful and more gracious prince to take us under his protection." In paragraph 9, still more abuses are listed. Reference is made to Don Juan of Austria, yet another illegitimate child of Charles V. Don Juan was a military commander who was sent to the Netherlands to fulfill the role of governor-general. Like Alba, he directed a number of campaigns that led to the sacking of various Dutch cities and the execution of large numbers of rebels, until his death in 1578. His mandate in the Netherlands was to disrupt and destroy the alliance created by the Pacification of Ghent of 1576. Again, the document emphasizes that efforts were made to secure peace, particularly through the Congress of Cologne, convened in 1579. Although it was mediated by Pope Gregory XIII, the congress was unsuccessful; again, Spain refused to back down, to the extent that a price was put on William of Orange's head.

◆ **Paragraphs 10–13**

Paragraph 10 constitutes the actual declaration of independence from Spanish rule. The authors, representing "the greater part of the United Provinces," proclaim that the Dutch are renouncing their allegiance to the Spanish king, who "has forfeited, ipso jure, all hereditary right to the sovereignty of those countries." None of the members of the States-General aligned with the document would thenceforth recognize the authority of the Spanish king. All inhabitants of the Low Countries, including civil servants, the nobility, and the common people, were relieved from their oaths of allegiance to Spain. The document then indicates that the duke of Anjou—François, the youngest son of King Henry II of France—agreed to accept sovereignty over the Netherlands, replacing the authority of Archduke Matthias, a member of the House of Habsburg who had succeeded the duke of Alba but had since resigned his position as governor of the Netherlands (to later become Holy Roman Emperor). The duke of Anjou never proved popular in the Netherlands, holding but limited power; he died in 1584.

The remaining paragraphs outline the specific political steps that the rebellious provinces were taking. Paragraph 11 establishes a council that was to govern the affairs of the Netherlands until the duke of Anjou could assume his responsibilities. Paragraph 12 turns to specific issues of governance, such as the coining of money, justice, financial affairs, and the like. Paragraph 13 gives specifics relating to the establishment, membership, and powers of the president and governing council.

Audience

The audience for the Dutch Declaration of Independence was threefold. First was the Spanish king, Philip II. The declaration represented the northern provinces' formal renunciation of the authority of the king to rule in the Netherlands. A second audience, of course, consisted of the citizens of the northern provinces, including everyone from minor nobility through the merchant class to peasants. A final audience was

international. The Dutch rebels needed aid, in the forms of manpower, finances, and supplies for the ongoing Dutch Revolt as well as political or royal leadership; the need for the latter would become even more pressing upon the assassination of William of Orange three years later. Although they eventually became a republic, their initial instinct was to have the country ruled by a monarch. For these reasons, France's duke of Anjou, England's Queen Elizabeth I, the Turkish Ottoman Empire, and other international figures and states were a significant part of the audience.

Impact

The Dutch Declaration of Independence by no means brought peace to the United Provinces. Through the 1580s, Spain continued to send troops to the Netherlands. Yet Spanish forces were being stretched thin; they continued to fight Islam in the Mediterranean, and the Spanish Armada was defeated by the British navy in 1588—just as the northern provinces of the Netherlands were building up their own navy. Spain was virtually bankrupt, and the Spanish people, burdened with high taxes and war casualties, grew increasingly unwilling to back the war in the Netherlands. Finally, Spain capitulated and agreed to a suspension of hostilities at Antwerp in 1609, a treaty known as the Twelve Years' Truce. War erupted again, however, in 1621 over issues of religious toleration—of Protestants in the Catholic south and Catholics in the Protestant north—and sea trade routes. In 1639 the Dutch dealt the Spanish a decisive defeat in the last major campaign of the Eighty Years' War. The war officially ceased with the 1648 Treaty of Münster, which ended Spanish control over the Netherlands. This treaty was part of the larger realignment in Europe brought about by the Peace of Westphalia, which also ended the Thirty Years' War—a complex war between Catholics and Protestants in the Holy Roman Empire that engulfed most of Europe.

Ultimately, the Dutch Revolt and the Dutch Declaration of Independence would have a far-reaching impact on Europe. The Dutch Revolt essentially challenged the divine right of kings to rule. As of 1648 the Netherlands was no longer a monarchy, a circumstance that sowed seeds of discontent with monarchial rule throughout the continent. The ultimate results of these antiroyalist sentiments were the decline of the Spanish Empire, the English Civil Wars of the mid-seventeenth century, and the French Revolution of the late eighteenth century. It has also been argued that the Dutch Declaration of Independence, read by Thomas Jefferson, had a significant effect on the crafting of the American Declaration of Independence of 1776.

Further Reading

■ **Articles**

Brandon, Pepijn. "The Dutch Revolt: A Social Analysis." *International Socialism* 116 (Autumn 2007): 139–164.

■ Books

Arnade, Peter. *Beggars, Iconoclasts, and Civic Patriots: The Political Culture of the Dutch Revolt.* Ithaca, N.Y.: Cornell University Press, 2008.

Darby, Graham, ed. *The Origins and Development of the Dutch Revolt.* London: Routledge, 2001.

Geyl, Pieter. *History of the Dutch-Speaking Peoples, 1555–1648.* London: Phoenix Press, 2001.

———. *The Revolt of the Netherlands, 1555–1609.* Lanham, Md.: Rowman & Littlefield, 1980.

Israel, Jonathan I. *The Dutch Republic: Its Rise, Greatness and Fall, 1477–1806.* Oxford, U.K.: Clarendon Press, 1998.

Koenigsberger, H. G. *Monarchies, States Generals and Parliaments: The Netherlands in the Fifteenth and Sixteenth Centuries.* Cambridge, U.K.: Cambridge University Press, 2001.

Limm, Peter. *The Dutch Revolt, 1559–1648.* London: Longman, 1999.

Parker, Geoffrey. *The Dutch Revolt.* New York: Penguin, 1977.

———. *Spain and the Netherlands, 1559–1659: Ten Studies.* London: Collins, 1979.

Tracy, James D. *The Founding of the Dutch Republic: War, Finance, and Politics in Holland, 1572–1588.* Oxford, U.K.: Oxford University Press, 2008.

Van Gelderen, Martin. *The Political Thought of the Dutch Revolt, 1555–1590.* Cambridge, U.K.: Cambridge University Press, 2002.

■ Web Sites

Wolff, Barbara. "Was Declaration of Independence Inspired by Dutch?" University of Wisconsin–Madison News Web site. http://www.news.wisc.edu/3049.

—Michael J. O'Neal

Questions for Further Study

1. What role did religion play in the Dutch independence movement?

2. Trace the history of the Spanish Empire using the Dutch Declaration of Independence along with Columbus's Letter to Raphael Sanxis on the Discovery of America, the Requerimiento, and the Cartagena Manifesto.

3. The Dutch Revolt was one of the earliest efforts in Europe to unite smaller principalities into a nation. Compare the process in the Netherlands with the process of unification in Germany as reflected in events surrounding the Carlsbad Decrees.

4. The Dutch Revolt and the Dutch Declaration of Independence challenged the divine right of kings to rule. How was the Dutch challenge different from, or similar to, the challenge issued in such documents as John Locke's *Second Treatise on Civil Government* or the French Declaration of the Rights of Man and of the Citizen?

5. During the sixteenth and seventeenth centuries, the Dutch were among the world's leaders in artistic accomplishment, trade, science, and industry. Why do you think such a small country was capable of such achievements?

DUTCH DECLARATION OF INDEPENDENCE

The States General of the United Provinces of the Low Countries, to all whom it may concern, do by these Presents send greeting:

As it is apparent to all that a prince is constituted by God to be ruler of a people, to defend them from oppression and violence as the shepherd his sheep; and whereas God did not create the people slaves to their prince, to obey his commands, whether right or wrong, but rather the prince for the sake of the subjects (without which he could be no prince), to govern them according to equity, to love and support them as a father his children or a shepherd his flock, and even at the hazard of life to defend and preserve them. And when he does not behave thus, but, on the contrary, oppresses them, seeking opportunities to infringe their ancient customs and privileges, exacting from them slavish compliance, then he is no longer a prince, but a tyrant, and the subjects are to consider him in no other view. And particularly when this is done deliberately, unauthorized by the states, they may not only disallow his authority, but legally proceed to the choice of another prince for their defense. This is the only method left for subjects whose humble petitions and remonstrances could never soften their prince or dissuade him from his tyrannical proceedings; and this is what the law of nature dictates for the defense of liberty, which we ought to transmit to posterity, even at the hazard of our lives. And this we have seen done frequently in several countries upon the like occasion, whereof there are notorious instances, and more justifiable in our land, which has been always governed according to their ancient privileges, which are expressed in the oath taken by the prince at his admission to the government; for most of the Provinces receive their prince upon certain conditions, which he swears to maintain, which, if the prince violates, he is no longer sovereign.

Now thus it was that the king of Spain after the demise of the emperor, his father, Charles the Fifth, of the glorious memory (of whom he received all these provinces), forgetting the services done by the subjects of these countries, both to his father and himself, by whose valor he got so glorious and memorable victories over his enemies that his name and power became famous and dreaded over all the world, forgetting also the advice of his said imperial majesty, made to him before to the contrary, did rather hearken to the counsel of those Spaniards about him, who had conceived a secret hatred to this land and to its liberty, because they could not enjoy posts of honor and high employments here under the states as in Naples, Sicily, Milan and the Indies, and other countries under the king's dominion. Thus allured by the riches of the said provinces, wherewith many of them were well acquainted, the said counselors, we say, or the principal of them, frequently remonstrated to the king that it was more for his Majesty's reputation and grandeur to subdue the Low Countries a second time, and to make himself absolute (by which they mean to tyrannize at pleasure), than to govern according to the restrictions he had accepted, and at his admission sworn to observe. From that time forward the king of Spain, following these evil counselors, sought by all means possible to reduce this country (stripping them of their ancient privileges) to slavery, under the government of Spaniards having first, under the mask of religion, endeavored to settle new bishops in the largest and principal cities, endowing and incorporating them with the richest abbeys, assigning to each bishop nine canons to assist him as counselors, three whereof should superintend the inquisition.

By this incorporation the said bishops (who might be strangers as well as natives) would have had the first place and vote in the assembly of the states, and always the prince's creatures at devotion; and by the addition of the said canons he would have introduced the Spanish inquisition, which has been always as dreadful and detested in these provinces as the worst of slavery, as is well known, in so much that his imperial majesty, having once before proposed it to these states, and upon whose remonstrances did desist, and entirely gave it up, hereby giving proof of the great affection he had for his subjects. But, notwithstanding the many remonstrances made to the king both by the provinces and particular towns, in writing as well as by some principal lords by word of mouth; and, namely, by the Baron of Montigny and Earl of Egmont, who with the approbation of the Duchess of Parma, then governess of the Low Countries, by the advice of the council of state were sent several times to Spain upon this affair. And, although the king had by fair words given them grounds to hope that their request should be complied with, yet by his letters he ordered the contrary, soon after expressly commanding, upon pain of his displeasure, to admit the new bishops immediately, and put them in possession of their bishoprics and incorporated abbeys, to hold the court of the inquisition in the places where it had been before, to obey and follow the decrees and ordinances of the Council of Trent, which in many articles are destructive of the privileges of the country.

This being come to the knowledge of the people gave just occasion to great uneasiness and clamor among them, and lessened that good affection they had always borne toward the king and his predecessors. And, especially, seeing that he did not only seek to tyrannize over their persons and estates, but also over their consciences, for which they believed themselves accountable to God only. Upon this occasion the chief of the nobility in compassion to the poor people, in the year 1566, exhibited a certain remonstrance in form of a petition, humbly praying, in order to appease them and prevent public disturbances, that it would please his majesty (by showing that clemency due from a good prince to his people) to soften the said points, and especially with regard to the rigorous inquisition, and capital punishments for matters of religion. And to inform the king of this affair in a more solemn manner, and to represent to him how necessary it was for the peace and prosperity of the public to remove the aforesaid innovations, and moderate the severity of his declarations published concerning divine worship, the Marquis de Berghen, and the aforesaid Baron of Montigny had been sent, at the request of the said lady regent, council of state, and of the states-general as ambassadors to Spain, where the king, instead of giving them audience, and redress the grievances they had complained of (which for want of a timely remedy did always appear in their evil consequences among the common people), did, by the advice of Spanish council, declare all those who were concerned in preparing the said remonstrance to be rebels, and guilty of high treason, and to be punished with death, and confiscation of their estates; and, what is more (thinking himself well assured of reducing these countries under absolute tyranny by the army of the Duke of Alva), did soon after imprison and put to death the said lords the ambassadors, and confiscated their estates, contrary to the law of nations, which has been always religiously observed even among the most tyrannic and barbarous princes.

And, although the said disturbances, which in the year 1566 happened on the aforementioned occasion, were now appeased by the governess and her ministers, and many friends to liberty were either banished or subdued, in so much that the king had not any show of reason to use arms and violence, and further oppress this country, yet for these causes and reasons, long time before sought by the council of Spain (as appears by intercepted letters from the Spanish ambassador, Alana, then in France, writ to the Duchess of Parma), to annul all the privileges of this country, and govern it tyrannically at pleasure as in the Indies; and in their new conquests he has, at the instigation of the council of Spain, showing the little regard he had for his people, so contrary to the duty which a good prince owes to his subjects), sent the Duke of Alva with a powerful army to oppress this land, who for his inhuman cruelties is looked upon as one of its greatest enemies, accompanied with counselors too like himself. And, although he came in without the least opposition, and was received by the poor subjects with all marks of honor and clemency, which the king had often hypocritically promised in his letters, and that himself intended to come in person to give orders to their general satisfaction, having since the departure of the Duke of Alva equipped a fleet to carry him from Spain, and another in Zealand to come to meet him at the great expense of the country, the better to deceive his subjects, and allure them into the toils, nevertheless the said duke, immediately after his arrival (though a stranger, and no way related to the royal family), declared that he had a captain-general's commission, and soon after that of governor of these provinces, contrary to all its ancient customs and privileges; and, the more to manifest his designs, he immediately garrisoned the principal towns and castles, and caused fortresses and citadels to be built in the great cities to awe them into subjection, and very courteously sent for the chief nobility in the king's name, under pretense of taking their advice, and to employ them in the service of their country. And those who believed his letters were seized and carried out of Brabant, contrary to law, where they were imprisoned and prosecuted as criminals before him who had no right, nor could be a competent judge; and at last he, without hearing their defense at large, sentenced them to death, which was publicly and ignominiously executed.

The others, better acquainted with Spanish hypocrisy, residing in foreign countries, were declared outlawed, and had their estates confiscated, so that the poor subjects could make no use of their fortresses nor be assisted by their princes in defense of their liberty against the violence of the pope; besides a great number of other gentlemen and substantial citizens, some of whom were executed, and others banished that their estates might be confiscated, plaguing the other honest inhabitants, not only by the injuries done to their wives, children and estates by the Spanish soldiers lodged in their houses, as likewise by diverse contributions, which they were forced to pay toward building citadels and new fortifications of towns even to their own ruin, besides the taxes of the hundredth, twentieth, and tenth penny, to pay both the foreign and those raised in the country, to be employed against their fellow-citizens and against those who at the hazard of their lives defended their liberties. In order to impoverish the subjects, and to incapacitate them to hinder his design, and that he might with more ease execute the instructions received in Spain, to treat these countries as new conquests, he began to alter the course of justice after the Spanish mode, directly contrary to our privileges; and, imagining at last he had nothing more to fear, he endeavored by main force to settle a tax called the tenth penny on merchandise and manufacture, to the total ruin of these countries, the prosperity of which depends upon a flourishing trade, notwithstanding frequent remonstrances, not by a single province only, but by all of them united, which he had effected, had it not been for the Prince of Orange with diverse gentlemen and other inhabitants, who had followed this prince in his exile, most of whom were in his pay, and banished by the Duke of Alva with others who between him and the states of all the provinces, on the contrary sought, by all possible promises made to the colonels already at his devotion, to gain the German troops, who were then garrisoned in the principal fortresses and the cities, that by their assistance he might master them, as he had gained many of them already, and held them attached to his interest in order, by their assistance, to force those who would not join with him in making war against the Prince of Orange, and the provinces of Holland and Zealand, more cruel and bloody than any war before. But, as no disguises can long conceal our intentions, this project was discovered before it could be executed; and he, unable to perform his promises, and instead of that peace so much boasted of at his arrival a new war kindled, not yet extinguished.

All these considerations give us more than sufficient reason to renounce the King of Spain, and seek some other powerful and more gracious prince to take us under his protection; and, more especially, as

these countries have been for these twenty years abandoned to disturbance and oppression by their king, during which time the inhabitants were not treated as subjects, but enemies, enslaved forcibly by their own governors.

Having also, after the decease of Don Juan, sufficiently declared by the Baron de Selles that he would not allow the pacification of Ghent, the which Don Juan had in his majesty's name sworn to maintain, but daily proposing new terms of agreement less advantageous. Notwithstanding these discouragements we used all possible means, by petitions in writing, and the good offices of the greatest princes in Christendom, to be reconciled to our king, having lastly maintained for a long time our deputies at the Congress of Cologne, hoping that the intercession of his imperial majesty and of the electors would procure an honorable and lasting peace, and some degree of liberty, particularly relating to religion (which chiefly concerns God and our own consciences), at last we found by experience that nothing would be obtained of the king by prayers and treaties, which latter he made use of to divide and weaken the provinces, that he might the easier execute his plan rigorously, by subduing them one by one, which afterwards plainly appeared by certain proclamations and proscriptions published by the king's orders, by virtue of which we and all officers of the United Provinces with all our friends are declared rebels and as such to have forfeited our lives and estates. Thus, by rendering us odious to all, he might interrupt our commerce, likewise reducing us to despair, offering a great sum to any that would assassinate the Prince of Orange.

So, having no hope of reconciliation, and finding no other remedy, we have, agreeable to the law of nature in our own defense, and for maintaining the rights, privileges, and liberties of our countrymen, wives, and children, and latest posterity from being enslaved by the Spaniards, been constrained to renounce allegiance to the King of Spain, and pursue such methods as appear to us most likely to secure our ancient liberties and privileges. Know all men by these presents that being reduced to the last extremity, as above mentioned, we have unanimously and deliberately declared, and do by these presents declare, that the King of Spain has forfeited, ipso jure, all hereditary right to the sovereignty of those countries, and are determined from henceforward not to acknowledge his sovereignty or jurisdiction, nor any act of his relating to the domains of the Low Countries, nor make use of his name as prince, nor suffer others to do it. In consequence whereof we also declare all officers, judges, lords, gentlemen, vassals, and all other the inhabitants of this country of what condition or quality soever, to be henceforth discharged from all oaths and obligations whatsoever made to the King of Spain as sovereign of those countries. And whereas, upon the motives already mentioned, the greater part of the United Provinces have, by common consent of their members, submitted to the government and sovereignty of the illustrious Prince and Duke of Anjou, upon certain conditions stipulated with his highness, and whereas the most serene Archduke Matthias has resigned the government of these countries with our approbation, we command and order all justiciaries, officers, and all whom it may concern, not to make use of the name, titles, great or privy seal of the King of Spain from henceforward; but in lieu of them, as long as his highness the Duke of Anjou is absent upon urgent affairs relating to the welfare of these countries, having so agreed with his highness or otherwise, they shall provisionally use the name and title of the President and Council of the Province.

And, until such a president and counselors shall be nominated, assembled, and act in that capacity, they shall act in our name, except that in Holland and Zealand where they shall use the name of the Prince of Orange, and of the states of the said provinces until the aforesaid council shall legally sit, and then shall conform to the directions of that council agreeable to the contract made with his highness. And, instead of the king's seal aforesaid, they shall make use of our great seal, center-seal, and signet, in affairs relating to the public, according as the said council shall from time to time be authorized. And in affairs concerning the administration of justice, and transactions peculiar to each province, the provincial council and other councils of that country shall use respectively the name, title, and seal of the said province, where the case is to be tried, and no other, on pain of having all letters, documents, and despatches annulled. And, for the better and effectual performance hereof, we have ordered and commanded, and do hereby order and command, that all the seals of the King of Spain which are in these United Provinces shall immediately, upon the publication of these presents, be delivered to the estate of each province respectively, or to such persons as by the said estates shall be authorized and appointed, upon peril of discretionary punishment.

Moreover, we order and command that from henceforth no money coined shall be stamped with the name, title, or arms of the King of Spain in any of these United Provinces, but that all new gold and silver pieces, with their halfs and quarters, shall only bear such impressions as the states shall direct. We order likewise and command the president and other lords of the privy council, and all other chancellors, presidents, accountants-general, and to others in all the chambers of accounts respectively in these said countries, and likewise to all other judges and officers, as we hold them discharged from henceforth of their oath made to the King of Spain, pursuant to the tenor of their commission, that they shall take a new oath to the states of that country on whose jurisdiction they depend, or to commissaries appointed by them, to be true to us against the King of Spain and all his adherents, according to the formula of words prepared by the states-general for that purpose. And we shall give to the said counselors, justiciaries, and officers employed in these provinces, who have contracted in our name with his highness the Duke of Anjou, an act to continue them in their respective offices, instead of new commissions, a clause annulling the former provisionally until the arrival of his highness. Moreover, to all such counselors, accomptants, justiciaries, and officers in these Provinces, who have not contracted with his highness, aforesaid, we shall grant new commissions under our hands and seals, unless any of the said officers are accused and convicted of having acted under their former commissions against the liberties and privileges of this country or of other the like maladministration.

We farther command of the president and members of the privy council, chancellor of the Duchy of Brabant, also the chancellor of the Duchy of Guelders, and county of Zutphen, to the president and members of the council of Holland, to the receivers of great officers of Beoostersheldt and Bewestersheldt in Zealand, to the president and council of Friese, and to the Escoulet of Mechelen, to the president and members of the council of Utrecht, and to all other justiciaries and officers whom it may concern, to the lieutenants all and every of them, to cause this our ordinance to be published and proclaimed throughout their respective jurisdictions, in the usual places appointed for that purpose, that none may plead ignorance. And to cause our said ordinance to be observed inviolably, punishing the offenders impartially and without delay; for so it is found expedient for the public good. And, for better maintaining all and every article hereof, we give to all and every one of you, by express command, full power and authority. In witness

Document Text

whereof we have hereunto set our hands and seals, dated in our assembly at the Hague, the six and twentieth day of July, 1581, indorsed by the orders of the states-general, and signed J. De Asseliers.

Glossary

Escoulet of Mechelen	governing body of this small region of southern Holland
ipso jure	automatically (literally: by the law itself)
king of Spain	Philip II
Zealand	misspelling of Zeeland, the Dutch province comprising a strip of coastline that borders on Belgium

LAWS GOVERNING MILITARY HOUSEHOLDS

"Law is the foundation of social order."

Overview

In 1615 Tokugawa Hidetada, the second shogun of Japan's Tokugawa *bakufu*, or military government, promulgated the Laws Governing Military Households, or Buke Shohatto, a set of instructions or rules for members of Japan's large military class. The laws were meant to maintain peace and regulate all aspects of the behavior of warriors, extending from the lords of domains to the lesser samurai who served them. Although they are correctly interpreted as a set of laws, only a few of the stipulations laid out in the thirteen articles of this document were meant to be enforced in the sense that a law governing the crime of murder or burglary would be. Instead, most of the laws were broadly prohibitive or hortatory in nature; they were meant to give general guidelines for behavior rather than proscribe specific acts.

The significance of the laws lay in the new standards set forth for military rule in Japan's early-modern era, also known as the Tokugawa Period (1600–1868). The laws essentially had four aims. First, they signified the determination of the Tokugawa government to enforce the peace, to ensure that Japan not return again to the warfare and decentralized rule that had characterized it in the preceding century. Second, they set forth the importance of Confucian social and political ideals at the same time that they stressed the need to maintain distinctions of rank and status; in this manner, the document was conservative in nature. Third, in an indirect but powerful way, they contributed to the rapid urbanization of Japan that took place in the seventeenth century. And, finally, they played a role in the eventual demise of the samurai, or warrior, class as a whole. Few of these effects were immediately realized, and few of them would have occurred without other policies or practices enacted either by the *bakufu* or the great lords (daimyo), but the Laws Governing Military Households was at the same time the basis for all of them.

Context

Between 1467 and 1477 war between two factions of the largely defunct Ashikaga *bakufu* took place within the boundaries of Kyoto, the capital (and only major city) in Japan at the time. Besides decimating much of the capital, the war ushered in the so-called Warring States Period, a century-long period of upheaval in which Japan was ruled piecemeal by feudal lords, approximately two hundred in number. Given Japan's relatively small size (an area equivalent to the state of Montana, though the northernmost island of Japan, Hokkaido, was largely uninhabited at the time and outside of Japanese control), these two hundred domains were small in area. The lords of these domains were spoken of as *daimyo*, meaning "great name," and they established their authority by means of military prowess.

The Warring States Period was a transitional time in Japanese history, dividing the medieval and early-modern worlds, and it was unique in several distinguishing ways. Accordingly, the establishment of Tokugawa rule in the seventeenth century, and the accompanying practices, policies, and laws—such as Laws Governing Military Households—can be understood only in the context of developments during this critical era. Four developments were particularly significant

First, prior to the Warring States Period, Japan was ruled by an aristocratic elite that included Kyoto courtiers (among them, the hereditary emperor), powerful temples and clerics of the Buddhist and Shinto faiths, and the upper echelon of the warrior class. Although the balance of power between these three blocs changed over the centuries, its members had long been the dominant players in the world of politics and economics. That changed after 1467. With full-scale warfare throughout the land, traditional distinctions of hereditary status and rank lost much of their importance. Instead, military might came to define both political power and social influence as never before, and, of course, it was the warriors alone who wielded the sword. Never before had an individual's genealogy or hereditary status meant so little in Japan. People of the time recognized this shift and coined a new word, *gekokujo*, meaning "the low overthrowing the high," reflecting the radical changes they were seeing. Whereas in the past, warriors of influence were men with distinguished pedigrees, linked back to elite families, now many of the greatest warriors were upstarts, individuals whose immediate ancestors may have been farmers or minor warriors serving greater lords.

Time Line

1568
- **November 11**
  Oda Nobunaga marches into Kyoto.

1582
- **June 6**
  Nobunaga is killed at Honnoji Temple in Kyoto.

1590
- **July 7**
  Toyotomi Hideyoshi succeeds in bringing all of Japan under his control.

1598
- **August 8**
  Hideyoshi dies at age sixty-three, leaving a five-year-old heir, Toyotomi Hideyori.

1600
- **September 9**
  At the Battle of Sekigahara, Tokugawa Ieyasu establishes himself as the new military head.

1603
- **February 2**
  Ieyasu receives from the emperor the title of shogun.

1605
- **April 4**
  Ieyasu retires at the age of sixty-three, and his twenty-six-year-old son Tokugawa Hidetada succeeds him as shogun.

1615
- **July 7**
  Laws Governing Military Households is issued.

Second, prior to the Warring States Period, much of the land in the country was held in the form of private estates by courtier families and temples. Many warriors held extensive fiefs, too, but the proportion of land under their control increased dramatically in the century after the civil war began in 1467, as they confiscated estates and incorporated them within their domains. In short, by 1568 most of the land and its economic capacity was in warrior hands.

Third, despite the growth of warrior power, the position of the great lords (daimyo) was by no means secure. They were, of course, often at war with neighboring daimyo; were at pains to maintain the loyalty of their vassals, who were not against seeking a new lord if it was to their advantage; and were challenged, and in some cases threatened, by the rise of leagues of commoners, who likewise sought expanded influence in this period of upheaval. More than a few daimyo lost their heads at the hands of one of their own men (or sons), others were overthrown or defeated, and some daimyo families survived much of the century of warfare only to be destroyed near its end. Instability and insecurity were watchwords of the period.

Fourth, despite the upheaval of the century, it was also a time of economic and population growth and technological progress. This was possible because war was not going on everywhere all the time. Many regions went decades with little or no fighting, and much of the fighting that did occur, at least until late in the period, was small in scale and limited in destruction. This allowed some daimyo to extend and build their economic and political bases. In the process, local economies grew, and new technologies led to increased prosperity. In this manner the Warring States Period provided a solid foundation for the remarkable growth in these areas that would take place in the seventeenth century.

In 1568 Oda Nobunaga, having established a sizable domain in central Japan, marched his army into Kyoto, making it known that he intended to once again bring Japan under single rule. He is known as the first of the "three unifiers." By the time of his death in 1582, Nobunaga controlled more than two-thirds of the country, but he was stopped short by one of his own vassals, who attacked him while he was staying the night at a Kyoto temple. His successor, the second unifier, was Toyotomi Hideyoshi, another of Nobunaga's vassals. Hideyoshi was able to grasp power and eventually unify all Japan under a system that has been defined as "federal," in that he held a major portion of power but allowed daimyo to maintain their domains as long as they pledged loyalty to him. Tokugawa Ieyasu, the third unifier, continued this approach after grasping power in 1600. The result was that the early-modern system of government consisted of a shogun at its head (though nominally under the authority of the hereditary emperor in Kyoto), with approximately two hundred daimyo beneath him, each of whom controlled his own domain, which varied in size depending on his status and the goodwill of the shogun. It was a rather odd system, structured largely upon military ideals and organization, with the shogun serving as "the greatest among equals."

Man dressed in replica samurai armor (AP/Wide World Photos)

The more immediate context of the promulgation of Laws Governing Military Households was Tokugawa Ieyasu's assertion of unchallenged control after defeating the armies of Toyotomi Hideyori in the summer of 1615. Hideyori, the heir of the second unifier, Hideyoshi, was just five years of age when his father died in 1598. In the battles for supremacy that ended in Tokugawa Ieyasu's victory in 1600, the great warriors sidestepped Hideyori and the question of his legitimacy as Hideyoshi's political heir. He was allowed to continue to reside in his castle in Osaka, and it was there that he eventually reached adulthood. But by 1614 he had become a potential threat, and Ieyasu decided that he must be destroyed. With that accomplished by mid-year of 1615, the Tokugawa *bakufu* was finally in a position to promulgate laws governing the behavior of the military houses.

About the Author

Although they were issued by the Tokugawa government when Hidetada was shogun, the Laws Governing Military Households was a product of Ieyasu's efforts. This is not surprising, since Ieyasu, even though he was formally retired, continued to rule the country and shape and define the new political system. Ieyasu did not actually draft the laws. Instead, drafting was the work of Ishin Suden (1569–1633), a Zen monk and close adviser to Ieyasu. Suden spent several decades of his early life in the Kyoto temple Nanzenji but from 1608 formed ties with Ieyasu and was used in various capacities by the shogun in the years that followed. Like many others within the Buddhist priesthood, Suden was highly educated and thus was in a position to assist Ieyasu in preparing laws. It would be wrong, however, to speak of Suden as the author, because ultimately these were Ieyasu's laws, put into written form by Suden after much discussion with and instruction from Ieyasu.

Explanation and Analysis of the Document

The Laws Governing Military Households was promulgated by being formally read to a gathering of Japan's daimyo at Fushimi Castle, outside Kyoto, on July 7, 1615. The document consists of thirteen articles. Each begins with a statement of exhortation or prohibition. There then follows a brief explanatory section, often drawing upon classical sources (both Chinese and Japanese) or traditional principles to support the argument. This was to be expected. In the year previous to the laws' issuance, Suden and numerous associates among the Buddhist priesthood and Kyoto nobility had been busily engaged in copying and studying such classical sources from the country's libraries, all at Ieyasu's behest. Close analysis also reveals that precedents for most of the articles can be found in previous law codes; many, in fact, originated with the daimyo "house codes" (laws governing the behavior of a daimyo's retainers or vassals) of the Warring States Period, evidence that the

Tokugawa were confronted with many of the same issues as their daimyo predecessors, particularly when it came to the control and management of vassals.

In brief, the laws' thirteen articles stipulated the following: (1) Warriors were to study both literary and military arts; (2) excessive drinking and partying were forbidden; (3) criminals were not to be sheltered in any domain; (4) warrior lords had to expel from their domains any warriors charged with treason or murder; (5) outsiders to the domains were not to be allowed to fraternize or reside therein; (6) castles could be repaired, if reported, but new construction was forbidden; (7) warrior factions of any type were forbidden; (8) marriages could not be arranged without *bakufu* approval; (9) daimyo had to follow regulations when calling on the shogun; (10) one's dress had to accord with one's status; (11) only those of appropriate rank were allowed to ride in palanquins; (12) samurai of the various domains had to be frugal; and (13) lords of domains should select men of talent as their officials.

Articles 1 and 13 address the question of wise rule and how to accomplish it. Article 1 is justifiably considered the most important article of the laws. The approach to rulership that it lays out can be interpreted both as a standard that the Tokugawa expected the daimyo to uphold and as a declaration of the intentions of the central holders of power, the Tokugawa shoguns themselves. The declaration of the need not just for literary arts but for military arts as well provides a clear signal that the Tokugawa expected that the existing governmental system of 1615, structured largely upon a military organization with which all daimyo were familiar, would continue. In other words, the Tokugawa foresaw neither themselves nor the daimyo abandoning their weapons or martial attitude and training. The system was to remain military at heart. In this sense, the Tokugawa affirmed the position of the warrior class. And although this affirmation might not have seemed significant at the time, it became so during the next two centuries, as Japan enjoyed a period of remarkable peace, free of war, from the late 1630s until the 1850s. During these years the samurai and their institutions became rusty and antiquated and in many ways irrelevant to the early modern society that developed. Nonetheless, their position was confirmed and bolstered by the sort of ideals expressed in article 1 of the laws.

At the same time that it confirms the military arts, article 1 also stresses the literary arts as crucial to good rulership. Another way to put this, commonly used at the time, was that one came to power by the sword but then ruled (if he was wise) with the brush (that is to say, the pen). As defined by Confucian philosophy, wise rulers were cultivated and educated, characteristics that allowed them to draw on past examples to meet the challenges of the present, understand the needs of the people, and show compassion to their subjects. In article 1, the Tokugawa assert that they intend to be rulers of this type. It was an assertion they needed to make because, in contrast to the Kyoto courtiers, Japan's warriors were often seen as boorish and uncultivated. It was a stigma that was not easily overcome, particularly as the court, with emperor and courtiers, continued to

A view of Fushimi Castle in Kyoto, where the laws were formally read in 1615 (© Charles and Josette Lenars/CORBIS)

exist (supported, in fact, by the *bakufu*), a symbol of the height of cultivation.

Articles 2 and 12 are concerned with the proper behavior of individuals. Although exhortations to avoid drinking and gambling or to live frugally might seem petty or overly intrusive into the private affairs of individuals, they were not viewed as such at the time. According to Confucian teachings, moral behavior is at the heart of good government, and Ieyasu was determined that his rule, and that of the daimyo beneath him, follow that model.

Articles 3 through 8 hark back to the Warring States Period and the dangers of that time. In light of the stable, peaceful, and prosperous society that was well in place by the middle of the seventeenth century, the stipulations in these articles can appear quaint or archaic to historians. But it is important to keep in mind that warriors in 1615 had lived lives in which warfare was the norm, intrigue and treason against one's lord were common occurrences, and peace was as fleeting as the clouds of autumn. Accordingly, the Tokugawa issued these grave warnings and severe decrees to counteract such tendencies. By all measures, the results were positive and impressive.

Article 3 provides a powerful philosophical background to the specific stipulations that follow in later articles. The assertions that "law is the foundation of social order" and "reason may be violated in the name of law, but law may not

be violated in the name of reason" reveal the overriding concern for peace and stability. In essence, the author of the statement acknowledges that law is not perfect, that at times reason might suggest that the law could be ignored or sidestepped. Yet that is unacceptable. Imperfect though it may be, law, if followed, would ensure stability in society.

Articles 6 and 8 are the two laws in this section that had the most practical significance. Article 6, with its restrictions on new castle construction by daimyo, is best understood in conjunction with another law, known as the One Domain, One Castle Decree, issued under the name of the shogun's three top advisers less than a month before the issuance of Laws Governing Military Households. That edict explicitly decreed that within each domain all castles except that in which the daimyo resided were to be destroyed. The purpose was clear: to limit the military capabilities of daimyo, ensuring that they did not establish fortified states capable of challenging the Tokugawa *bakufu*. The need for this limitation was a reflection of developments in the Warring States Period, during which time castles became fortlike structures, used as much for fortifications for troops on the offensive as for defensive bulwarks.

The intent of article 8, with its regulation of marriages among daimyo, is clear, given the common practice in earlier centuries and in many places around the world of forging political and military alliances through the means of matrimony. No alliances could be made without the consent of the *bakufu*.

Articles 9–11 deal with questions of status. Simply put, they require all warriors, from daimyo to foot soldiers, to act in accordance with their position in society. The specific examples given—concerning the number of attendants a daimyo might employ when calling on the shogun, the quality and luxuriousness of one's dress, and the privilege of riding in a palanquin (in short, being carried by menials rather than riding a horse or moving under one's own power)—were surely not meant to be exclusive. The quality of food one ate and the entertainment one engaged in were also governed by one's status, as was the privilege of taking additional wives. Moreover, similar, but more restrictive laws of this nature regulated the manners of merchants and others of means, extending to the size and style of their residences. It was believed in Japan at the time, and backed by Confucian ideology, that in a well-ordered society people knew their place and acted accordingly. To fail to do so would invite commotion and disharmony. Moreover, as these three articles suggest, distinctions in status existed *within* classes as much as *between* classes. In other words, although class could be an important marker in distinguishing groups and individuals, in many cases the divisions between individuals of different statuses within a class were sharper than those between individuals of different classes. Low-level samurai, for instance, were much closer in status to commoners, such as merchants, than they were to their own daimyo or to the shogun, neither of whom they could have ever had the opportunity of meeting.

Audience

As named in the title of the Laws Governing Military Households, the main audience for this set of regulations was the military households. Just what the term *military households* (*buke* in Japanese) meant, however, particularly when considered in light of the laws themselves, is open to question. They were initially read to the great lords, the daimyo, in Fushimi Castle. A *daimyo* was defined as a lord whose domain produced rice in the amount of 10,000 koku or more (a koku equaling approximately five bushels), and, as noted earlier, the daimyo numbered about two hundred during the Tokugawa era, with rice yields of the greatest lords reaching over 1 million koku. Evidence of how many of those two hundred daimyo attended the gathering at Fushimi Castle in 1615 when the laws were read is unavailable, but it is highly unlikely that all were there. For one thing, that many daimyo, with their attendants, would have overwhelmed the castle. In light of the Tokugawa rulers' emphasis upon status distinctions, it seems fair to assume that few of the minor daimyo (perhaps those with domains producing under 75,000–100,000 koku) were invited. So the immediate audience of the laws were important daimyo, the sorts of people who could have constituted a serious threat to the *bakufu*. In addition to having heard them read, they also received written copies of the laws

either at that time or shortly thereafter, as did daimyo who were not in attendance.

Examination of the document itself reveals a much more diverse view of the audience. Although some of the articles were directed specifically at the great lords, others were clearly applicable to warriors of all levels. Viewed accordingly, the *buke*, or "military households," truly meant all warriors, regardless of status. Those articles specific to the daimyo are article 5, the ban on outsiders to the domain (in that daimyo were responsible for enforcing this ban); article 6, the stipulations concerning the repair and construction of castles; article 8, the prohibition on marriage without *bakufu* approval (the *bakufu* was uninterested and unconcerned about marriages formed by those beneath daimyo status); article 9, the regulations governing visits to the shogun (here the subject is specifically given as "the daimyo," leaving no question as to the audience); and article 13, the exhortation to select men of talent to serve in government (in this case, the term "lords of domains" is used, which was analogous to "daimyo"). All the remaining articles are as appropriate to minor samurai scraping by on stipends of 50 koku annually as to the grandest daimyo. Of course, some of these articles, like articles 10 or 11, with their restrictions on dress or riding in palanquins, would serve to remind minor samurai of their low status and keep them firmly low. But many of the others would serve to tie warriors together as a class, counteracting the articles that stress differentiations in status. Thus, any warrior could read article 1 and work to cultivate the literary and military arts, thereby making him a better and more useful servant of the state.

Impact

Many of the articles in Laws Governing Military Households are moralistic and hortatory in nature. Did warriors take it to heart to follow both literary and military arts, as stipulated in article 1? Did they avoid heavy drinking and wild parties, as laid out in article 2? And were they frugal in their daily lives, as decreed in article 12? In short, did members of the warrior class follow Confucian political and social ideals, as interpreted by Tokugawa Ieyasu and his associates, as seen in these articles? There are no simple answers to these questions, but there is good evidence that Confucian ideology, thus defined, played a prominent role in shaping the lives and ideals of the warrior class in Tokugawa Japan. As early as 1651, for example, a warrior named Yui Shosetsu planned and undertook a rebellion against the *bakufu* because its contemporary leaders failed, he claimed, to follow the high ideals laid out by Ieyasu. Of course, the Laws Governing Military Households was just one among many forums in which Confucian ideals were expressed at the time; nonetheless, the document was part of a larger and influential discourse.

In a more practical sense, the 1615 Laws Governing Military Households (along with those for emperor and courtiers and for religious institutions) laid the foundation for Tokugawa rule. With their regulation of inter-daimyo

"*The study of literature and the practice of the military arts, including archery and horsemanship, must be cultivated diligently. 'On the left hand literature, on the right hand use of arms' was the rule of the ancients. Both must be pursued concurrently.*"

(Law 1)

"*Anyone who violates the law must not be harbored in any domain. Law is the foundation of social order. Reason may be violated in the name of law, but law may not be violated in the name of reason.*"

(Law 3)

"*The castles in various domains may be repaired, providing the matter is reported without fail. New construction of any kind is strictly forbidden.*"

(Law 6)

"*Marriage must not be contracted in private [without approval from the* bakufu*].*"

(Law 8)

relations, castle building, and marriage, the laws severely limited the potential of any lords to challenge the *bakufu*. And none did, for more than 250 years. Viewed in this manner, the laws summarized in the document were stunningly successful.

The Laws Governing Military Households also provided an important model for later laws. In fact, each of the succeeding fourteen Tokugawa shoguns (excepting two whose rule was very brief) reissued the Laws Governing Military Households, with fewer or more changes depending upon the needs of the time. During the first half of the period, this was done in Edo Castle with daimyo in attendance; later that was seen as unnecessary. Nonetheless, the Laws Governing Military Households remained a standard for the age, a set of rules and instructions by which warriors of all ranks were to gauge their actions.

Some of the effects of the Laws Governing Military Households were surely unexpected, at least to Tokugawa Ieyasu and his associates who drafted them. Article 6 is striking in this regard. By restricting new castle construction—and limiting castles to one per domain, as decreed in the earlier law of 1615—the *bakufu* set in motion developments that would dramatically change the makeup of Japan-

ese society. Each limited to one castle within his domain, daimyo began to build large and sumptuous edifices, hardly the sort of fortified structures from which they could carry out military offensives. At the same time, daimyo worked to ensure that their own vassals did not become a threat, by removing them from lands in the countryside to the castle towns, in exchange for stipends. The result was rapid urbanization as castle towns became cities virtually overnight, replete with new commercial goods, new forms of culture, and large warrior and merchant classes. This was an unintended, yet unmistakable result of a seemingly straightforward law. The largest castle town, by the way, was the shogun's headquarters at Edo (present-day Tokyo), which by 1700 was home to over one million inhabitants.

Another unexpected effect, which by no means can be attributed solely to the laws, was the eventual demise of the warrior class. Despite the warrior ideals of "military arts" seen in article 1, the overall thrust of the Laws Governing Military Households (coupled with the more general policies and practices of the Tokugawa *bakufu*) was to make the warrior class anachronistic. Law and order and absolute loyalty to one's lord were the ideals of the new age, and there was no room for those who thought or acted otherwise.

Everything that had made the Warring States Period one of continual upheaval was now outlawed: treasonous plans, murder, lawlessness, questionable associations, excessive numbers of castles, "innovations," factions, and marriage alliances. Most of all, hierarchy and status differentiations were to be maintained. By no means could *gekokujo* ("the low overthrowing the high") be tolerated. The result was a warrior class that became increasingly unnecessary and obsolete. The very success of the Tokugawa *bakufu*, and in a sense the Laws Governing Military Households, meant the inevitable end of Japan's warring class.

Further Reading

■ Articles

Butler, Lee. "Tokugawa Ieyasu's Regulations for the Court: A Reappraisal." *Harvard Journal of Asiatic Studies* 54, no. 2 (1994): 509–551.

Hall, J. Carey. "Japanese Feudal Laws, III: The Tokugawa Legislation." *Transactions of the Asiatic Society of Japan* 38, no. 4 (1911): 269–331.

■ Books

Hall, John Whitney. *Cambridge History of Japan*. Volume 4: *Early Modern Japan*. New York: Cambridge University Press, 1991.

Sansom, George. *A History of Japan, 1615–1867*. Stanford, Calif.: Stanford University Press, 1963.

Totman, Conrad. *Tokugawa Ieyasu: Shogun*. San Francisco: Heian International, 1983.

Steenstrup, Carl. *A History of Law in Japan until 1868*. Leiden, Netherlands: Brill, 1991.

—Lee Butler

Questions for Further Study

1. What were the motives behind the Laws Governing Military Households? What social and historical forces led to their enactment?

2. What were the ultimate effects of the Laws Governing Military Households? Specifically, how did they contribute to urbanization in Japan, and why was this development important?

3. Historians note that in many early cultures, rank and social class played crucial roles in government, the economy, religion, and other social institutions. What role did social class play in seventeenth-century Japan? How did this class system affect the lives of ordinary citizens?

4. Historians also note that the history of early societies was the history of efforts to consolidate smaller domains into a functioning central state, with domains living in peace. To what extent did the Laws Governing Military Households contribute to the consolidation of Japan as a nation?

5. What role did the ideals of Confucianism play in the Laws Governing Military Households? Why did Confucianism, a Chinese religious philosophy, take root in Japan?

LAWS GOVERNING MILITARY HOUSEHOLDS

1. The study of literature and the practice of the military arts, including archery and horsemanship, must be cultivated diligently.

"On the left hand literature, on the right hand use of arms" was the rule of the ancients. Both must be pursued concurrently. Archery and horsemanship are essential skills for military men. It is said that war is a curse. However, it is resorted to only when it is inevitable. In time of peace, do not forget the possibility of disturbances. Train yourselves and be prepared.

2. Avoid group drinking and wild parties.

The existing codes strictly forbid these matters. Especially, when one indulges in licentious sex, or becomes addicted to gambling, it creates a cause for the destruction of one's own domain.

3. Anyone who violates the law must not be harbored in any domain.

Law is the foundation of social order. Reason may be violated in the name of law, but law may not be violated in the name of reason. Anyone who violates the law must be severely punished.

4. The *daimyō*, the lesser lords (*shōmyō*), and those who hold land under them (*kyūnin*) must at once expel from their domains any of their own retainers or soldiers who are charged with treason or murder.

Anyone who entertains a treasonous design can become an instrument for destroying the nation and a deadly sword to annihilate the people. How can this be tolerated?

5. Hereafter, do not allow people from other domains to mingle or reside in your own domain. This ban does not apply to people from your own domain.

Each domain has its own customs different from others. If someone wishes to divulge his own domain's secrets to people of another domain, or to report the secrets of another domain to people of his own domain, he is showing a sign of his intent to curry favors.

6. The castles in various domains may be repaired, provided the matter is reported without fail. New construction of any kind is strictly forbidden.

A castle with a parapet exceeding ten feet in height and 3,000 feet in length is injurious to the domain. Steep breastworks and deep moats are causes of a great rebellion.

7. If innovations are being made or factions are being formed in a neighboring domain, it must be reported immediately.

Men have a proclivity toward forming factions, but seldom do they attain their goals. There are some who [on account of their factions] disobey their masters and fathers, and feud with their neighboring villages. Why must one engage in [meaningless] innovations, instead of obeying old examples?

8. Marriage must not be contracted in private [without approval from the *bakufu*].

Marriage is the union symbolizing the harmony of *yin* and *yang*, and it cannot be entered into lightly. The thirty-eighth hexagram *kuei* [in the *Book of Changes*], says, "Marriage is not to be contracted to create disturbance. Let the longing of male and female for each other be satisfied. If disturbance is to take hold, then the proper time will slip by." The "Peach Young" poem of the *Book of Odes* says, "When men and women observe what is correct, and marry at the proper time, there will be no unattached women in the land." To form a factional alliance through marriage is the root of treason.

9. The *daimyō*'s visits (*sankin*) to Edo must follow the following regulations:

The *Shoku Nihongi* [Chronicles of Japan] contains a regulation saying that "Unless entrusted with some official duty, no one is permitted to assemble his clansmen at his own pleasure. Furthermore no one is to have more than twenty horsemen as his escort within the limits of the capital...." Hence it is not permissible to be accompanied by a large force of soldiers. For the *daimyō* whose revenues range from 1,000,000 *koku* down to 200,000 *koku* of rice, not more than twenty horsemen may accompany them. For those whose revenues are 100,000 *koku* or less, the number is to be proportionate to their incomes. On official business, however, the number of persons accompanying him can be proportionate to the rank of each *daimyō*.

10. The regulations with regard to dress materials must not be breached.

Lords and vassals, superiors and inferiors, must observe what is proper within their positions in life. Without authorization, no retainer may indiscriminately wear fine white damask, white wadded silk garments, purple silk kimono, purple silk linings, and kimono sleeves which bear no family crest. Lately retainers and soldiers have taken to wearing rich damask and silk brocade. This was not sanctioned by the old laws, and must now be kept within bounds.

11. Persons without rank are not to ride in palanquins.

Traditionally there have been certain families entitled to ride palanquins without permission, and there have been others receiving such permission. Lately ordinary retainers and soldiers have taken to riding in palanquins, which is a wanton act. Hereafter, the *daimyō* of various domains, their close relatives, and their distinguished officials may ride palanquins without special permission. In addition, briefly, doctors and astrologers, persons over sixty years of age, and those who are sick or invalid may ride palanquins after securing necessary permission. If retainers and soldiers wantonly ride palanquins, their masters shall be held responsible. The above restrictions do not apply to court nobles, Buddhist prelates, and those who have taken the tonsure.

12. The samurai of all domains must practice frugality. When the rich proudly display their wealth, the poor are ashamed of not being on a par with them. There is nothing which will corrupt public morality more than this, and therefore it must be severely restricted.

13. The lords of all domains must select as their officials men of administrative ability.

The way of governing a country is to get the right men. If the lord clearly discerns between the merits and faults of his retainers, he can administer due rewards and punishments. If the domain has good men, it flourishes more than ever. If it has no good men, it is doomed to perish. This is an admonition which the wise men of old bequeathed to us.

Take heed and observe the purport of the foregoing rules.

First year of Genna [1615], seventh month.

Glossary

Book of Changes	Yi jin or I Ching, one of the Confucian Five Classics, also called the Classic of Changes
Book of Odes	Shi jing, one of the Confucian Five Classics, also called the Classic of Poetry
First year of Genna, seventh month	The Japanese dating system does not correspond to Western dating methods. "Genna" refers to the era, and the month can be construed as August.

"No Japanese is permitted to go abroad."

Overview

In 1635 the Tokugawa government (commonly referred to as the Tokugawa *bakufu*, meaning Japan's military government at that time) issued a regulatory code known as the Closed Country Edict, or Sakokurei. This was one of several sets of laws issued during the 1630s that caused Japan to become largely closed off from the rest of the world for over two centuries. During the sixteenth and seventeenth centuries, European exploration had begun to radically alter both the shape of the world and relations between peoples from different parts of the globe. Accordingly, the fact that Japan's rulers took steps to halt those developments as they affected Japan was significant.

The Closed Country Edict of 1635 was one of several codes that led to Japan's status as a "closed country." Because Japanese rulers tended to reissue laws, often with only slight modifications, whenever they deemed it necessary, certain subjects were addressed on a number of occasions. Such was the case with regulations concerning Japan's foreign relations. Between 1633 and 1639, the Tokugawa government issued five edicts related to the matter; the first four were similar, with slight additions and modifications, and the last was a brief supplement meant to be observed in conjunction with the previous codes.

Although historians have long debated the impetus behind the Closed Country Edict and its effectiveness and results, they are nonetheless in agreement that its impact was immense. Without it, Japan's early modern history might have developed in a dramatically different manner. Among the edict's effects were the following: (1) It limited Japan's relations with other nations and peoples from 1635 until the 1850s; (2) it forced the country as a whole to focus on internal developments during these centuries; (3) it added to the country's stability, since it was one of a number of measures that gave the Tokugawa *bakufu* increased control over the Japanese people; (4) it gave the government power to regulate all aspects of foreign relations, which it did to its advantage (and to the detriment of the great lords).

Context

In the autumn of 1543 a Portuguese ship arrived in southern Japan; it was the first Western vessel to reach that land. At the time, Japan was in the midst of the Warring States Period, a century (1467–1568) of decentralized power. The land was divided among two hundred feudal lords, or daimyo, each of whom ruled a domain of limited size and periodically vied with neighboring lords for control of a larger area. Lacking a central government at the time, Japan conducted no formal foreign relations. However, there was much international activity in the area, and the Japanese were part of it. A number of the daimyo, particularly those in southwestern Japan, were active in overseas trade. Many Japanese pirates (and pirates of other nationalities) plied the waters of Southeast Asia and East Asia, and there were a number of small Japanese colonies established by traders at ports throughout the region. The arrival of the westerners saw the emergence of a robust intra-Asian trade network, in which goods and precious metals moved between China, Japan, South Asia, and Southeast Asia on boats of many nationalities. This trade would thrive for another century, with the Portuguese and later the Dutch acquiring most of their wealth in Asia by becoming major trade participants in the region, rather than by sending spices and other luxury items back to Europe.

For Japan, the Warring States Period was in many ways a time of remarkable openness. Not only was foreign trade open to those with the means to conduct it, but society and politics were open too. Members of the lower classes, who had always been put in their place in previous centuries, were now free to contest the upper classes as long as they had the will and the weapons to do so. Freedom was the order of the day, but it came with the price of political instability. It was into this world that the Portuguese entered. Christian missionaries—members of the Society of Jesus, or Jesuits—first came to Japan in 1549, only six years after the first Portuguese ship arrived. The Jesuits were part of the Counter-Reformation, the Catholic Church's effort to regain Europe from the Protestants and spread the Gospel to the far reaches of the earth. They were learned and devout, dedicated to the cause they had joined. And they were supported in their efforts by the Por-

Time Line

1543
- The Portuguese arrive in Japan.

1549
- Francis Xavier, a Jesuit missionary, arrives in Japan and begins preaching Christianity.

1568
- Oda Nobunaga marches into Kyoto.

1587
- **Summer** Toyotomi Hideyoshi issues an edict that calls for the expulsion of Christian missionaries.

1600
- The period of Tokugawa rule begins.

1604
- The *ito wappu*, or "raw silk apportionment" system, is established.

1609
- The daimyo of southwestern Japan are forbidden to keep large ships.

1614
- **Winter** Tokugawa Ieyasu issues the edict to ban Christianity and expel missionaries.

tuguese traders, who gave them passage and donated funds to their work. Thus, as the Portuguese traders worked to enlarge their portion of trade with Japan, their Jesuit associates worked to convert the Japanese to Christianity.

Because the Portuguese brought wealth to the regions in which they stopped, the daimyo of southwestern Japan were anxious that the traders make use of their harbors. Some, like Omura Sumitada, who controlled Nagasaki, even donated lands and harbors, which, in effect, allowed the Portuguese to establish foreign enclaves within the country. Some daimyo also converted to Christianity and encouraged (occasionally with a heavy hand) their subjects to do likewise. The result was that by 1580 there may have been as many as one hundred thousand Japanese Christians and by 1600 as many as three hundred thousand, though what percentage of those were committed to the faith is difficult to say. Nonetheless, Christianity and the foreigners who brought it had begun to have an impact upon Japan.

Politically, Japan began to change during this time as well. In 1568 the daimyo Oda Nobunaga led his army into the capital of Kyoto and undertook the process of unifying the country. By the time of his death in 1582, Oda Nobunaga was master of two-thirds of the land. His successor, Toyotomi Hideyoshi, completed the unifying process under a system in which he allowed the lords to retain their lands and local authority as long as they were supportive of and subordinate to him. Tokugawa Ieyasu succeeded Toyotomi Hideyoshi in 1600 and used his model of rulership. Ieyasu's heirs followed in his footsteps for the next 250 years as the shoguns (fifteen in number) of the Tokugawa *bakufu*.

With reunification in the late sixteenth century, the "big three"—Oda Nobunaga, Toyotomi Hideyoshi, and Tokugawa Ieyasu—were forced to consider ways of bringing lasting stability to Japan. The government needed steady sources of revenue, the daimyo needed to be controlled, lawlessness needed to be brought to an end, and foreign affairs and foreign trade needed to be regulated. A major concern was the foreign trade activity of the southwestern daimyo, men with large domains and large armies; their ability to dominate foreign trade added to the threat they posed to the central regime.

In this regard, the foreigners and the new foreign religion, Christianity, warranted careful consideration for reasons not only of security and stability but also of economics. One possibility was to do nothing about these matters, which is how Oda Nobunaga reacted. But he had not established complete political authority by his death; without that authority, issues such as foreign relations were unlikely to be addressed. Toyotomi Hideyoshi's position was different, and he came to view foreign influence with concern. In 1587 he issued an order that called for the expulsion of Christian missionaries from Japan, but he took no steps to enforce the order. Perhaps it was because of his strong interest in foreign trade as well as his concern that it might end or be dramatically curtailed if the missionaries were forced to leave. Given the close ties between the Portuguese traders and Jesuits, his concern was justified.

However, around the turn of the century the situation became more complex, eventually leading both Toyotomi Hideyoshi and Tokugawa Ieyasu to turn against the foreigners. The main factors were the arrival of other westerners: Spanish (both traders and Franciscan missionaries), Dutch, and English. The Franciscans and Jesuits were soon at odds, and there was evidence to suggest that many of the foreigners presented a threat to the peace—a threat that needed to be addressed. As a result of a dispute in 1596–1597, Hideyoshi put to death twenty-six Christians, six of whom were Spanish Franciscans and the rest Japanese. With Ieyasu's assertion of power in 1600, the same pattern ensued: reconciliation with the foreigners and then conflict and rejection. In 1614 Ieyasu finally issued an edict banning Christianity and expelling all missionaries. With the death of Ieyasu in 1616, persecution of Christians began in earnest, carried out under the direction of Hidetada and Iemitsu, the second and third Tokugawa shoguns. Particularly noteworthy was the "Great Martyrdom" of 1622, in which 132 Christians, both Jesuits and Japanese converts, were executed in Nagasaki.

One reason the Tokugawa shoguns were willing to undertake such harsh measures is that foreign trade was unlikely to be hurt, since the Dutch had begun to supplant the Iberian powers on the seas. And whereas the Portuguese and Spanish were zealous in their religion, the Dutch were not. Moreover, in order to solidify their position, the Dutch took steps to undermine their European rivals, playing off Tokugawa fears of Christianity.

From an economic standpoint, a key aspect of Tokugawa policy in these early decades was the regulation of the silk trade under *ito wappu*, or the "raw silk apportionment" system. Because the Portuguese had been able to gain restricted access to trade with China in the late sixteenth century, they were the sole purveyors of raw silk to Japan, the most highly prized and profitable of goods in this market. Stiff competition for silk among Japanese merchants led to steep prices and enormous profits for the Portuguese. In order to change this situation and regulate the import silk market, in 1604 the Tokugawa *bakufu* established the *ito wappu* system, which took control away from the Portuguese and gave it to powerful Japanese merchants from several of the large cities (at first Kyoto, Nagasaki, and Sakai, to which were shortly added Osaka and Edo: thus the "five trading cities" referred to in article 12 of the edict). These merchants negotiated terms, set prices, and allocated goods both to their benefit and the benefit of the government. The Portuguese continued to make a profit from the silk trade, but it was much reduced.

This was the general context in which the Closed Country Edict was issued in 1635. Its issuance (as well as those edicts that preceded and followed it in the same decade) was not immediately precipitated by a particular incident or crisis, involving, for example, foreign affairs, Christianity, or international commerce—suggesting that these laws reflected a set of policies that had been many years in the making, here at last put into final form.

Time Line

1622
- **Autumn**
  The "Great Martyrdom" of 132 Christians in Nagasaki occurs.

1623
- The British decide that its Japan trade is unprofitable and close their warehouses and administrative offices there.

1624
- The Spanish are expelled from Japan.

1633–1639
- The five documents making up the edicts that closed Japan to the world are issued.

1639
- The Portuguese are expelled from Japan.

1854
- The "closed country" policy is formally ended following the forceful intervention of the American commodore Matthew Perry in 1853 and the signing of the Kanagawa Treaty the following year.

About the Author

Just who the author or authors of this document were is hard to know. The edict was issued under the rule of the third shogun, Tokugawa Iemitsu (1604–1651). Although it is highly unlikely that he wrote it (common practice was to

The foundation of the tower of what was formerly Edo Castle in the Imperial Palace compound in Tokyo, built by Shogun Tokugawa Ieyasu (AP/Wide World Photos)

have learned advisers or high officials draft edicts), he no doubt had a large say in what was in it. Like the other early Tokugawa shoguns, Iemitsu was a personal ruler who took an active role in establishing policy and laying down laws. Iemitsu differed from his two predecessors, however, in that he was the first shogun to have no experience in battle. Probably for this reason he did much to establish the bureaucratic structure of the Tokugawa *bakufu*, shifting it away from the military organization that had characterized it under his father and grandfather. In this sense, the Closed Country Edict was appropriate to him. Accordingly, it is fair to say that the content reflected Iemitsu's concerns and ideas and that it had been worked out in conjunction with his advisers.

As for the five individuals who signed the edict of 1635—Hotta Masamori, Abe Tadaaki, Matsudaira Nobutsuna, Sakai Tadakatsu (1587–1662), and Doi Toshikatsu (1573–1644)—we must be careful not to ascribe authorship to them without appropriate caveats. In the first place, since most of the 1635 edict had already appeared in a decree of 1633, the authorship of the earlier document must also be considered. At that time, only two of these men (Sakai and Doi) were serving as senior councillors (the council being the governmental body that issued these edicts). Sakai and Doi may, in fact, have been the principal authors, as they were influential daimyo with close ties to

the Tokugawa. Moreover, both were longtime appointees, having served as senior councillors for more than a decade. Sakai Tadakatsu had established his worth to the Tokugawa in 1600 when he fought with Tokugawa Ieyasu in the battle that brought Ieyasu to power. Doi Toshikatsu had even longer and closer connections to the Tokugawa, having become a powerful retainer to Tokugawa Hidetada in 1579. Both men were rewarded with large fiefs and eventually important positions in the early *bakufu* government.

Explanation and Analysis of the Document

The Closed Country Edict of 1635 consists of seventeen articles and can be roughly divided into three sections. Understanding these divisions provides a key to understanding the concerns and intent of the Tokugawa leadership that produced the document. Three articles address the question of Japanese travel and trade abroad, both of which are prohibited, five articles deal with Christian missionaries and their teachings, and the remaining nine articles are directed at foreign trade and the protocols and requirements associated with it.

It is important to note that the title given the document, Closed Country Edict, was a later addition ascribed by histo-

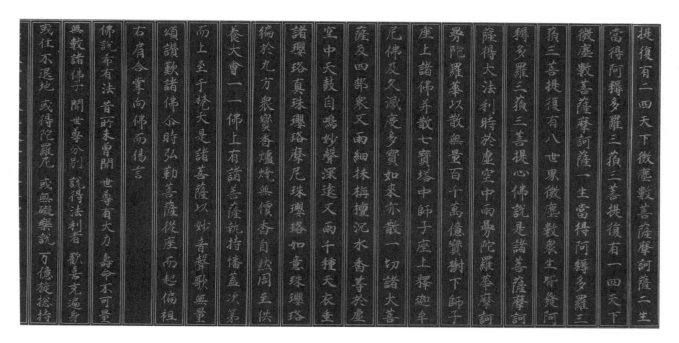

***Scroll of a portion of the Lotus Sutra, commissioned to commemorate the anniversary of the death of the third
Tokugawa shogun, Iemitsu*** (Freer Gallery of Art, Smithsonian Institution, Washington, D.C.: Purchase, F1962.27)

rians as they attempted to classify it. To call this document the Closed Country Edict suggests an interpretation that the authors may not have expected or desired, and this is something that must be kept in mind. The edict, in fact, had no title beyond the simple "Items: for Nagasaki," meaning a list of articles or instructions. Considered in that light, we might also ask which of the seventeen articles actually established policy that led to Japan's becoming a closed country.

◆ Articles 1–3

The first three articles, those that address Japanese travel and trade abroad, clearly do establish policy leading to a closed country. By restricting both Japanese ships and individuals of Japanese birth from traveling to foreign countries, or returning from foreign countries after having resided there, the Tokugawa government made it clear that if foreign relations and trade were maintained, they would be conducted by foreigners *in their ships*, not by Japanese in Japanese vessels. In this sense, the edict did indeed define one type of closed country, a country in which resident nationals must remain. Leaving for any purpose, long-term or short-term, was unacceptable. It also put an end to (or at least cut off irrevocably) the several small Japanese colonies in the Southeast Asian coastal region, which meant that Japan would remain limited in size and space to more traditional borders.

Beyond the first three articles, there is very little in this edict that specifies or decrees, implicitly or explicitly, that Japan is to be a closed country. Only article 14 hints at this; it stipulates that foreign vessels must depart for home by the autumn, unless they reached Japan late, in which case they must leave within fifty days of arrival. From this alone, it is

difficult to know just when in a given year foreign vessels arrived in Japan, but it must have been during the first week or so of the seventh month (as the Japanese dated it), since article 16 states that Japanese merchants are to arrive in Nagasaki by the summer. Taken together, these two articles suggest that foreign trading vessels were probably allowed in Japan for approximately two months each summer, but the edict says nothing further about foreign relations or foreign residents except where Christianity is at issue.

◆ Articles 4–8

The five articles that deal with Christianity are not the harsh, strongly prohibitive declarations about the religion or threats against missionaries and believers that one might expect. Article 4, for example, requires the two Nagasaki commissioners (to whom the Closed Country Edict is addressed) to carry out investigations into suspected gatherings of believers, while article 5 notes that those who inform on Christians should be given rewards, and article 6 suggests that precedence be followed in having the Omura domain guard any foreign ship that has an objection to *bakufu* policy (usually related to Christianity, the reason the article is placed here). Finally, article 7 concerns the protocol surrounding the incarceration of Christians and instructs the commissioners to have suspects placed in the prison of the Omura domain. In short, these articles deal with secondary or administrative matters. Prohibitions against Christianity, missionaries, and Japanese Christian believers had all been explicitly stated in earlier edicts, beginning with that of Ieyasu in 1613. The authors of the 1635 edict saw no need to reiterate those prohibitions.

Painting of the Dutch and Chinese Settlements at Nagasaki (© The Trustees of the British Museum)

◆ **Articles 9–17**

The remaining nine articles deal with foreign trade. The detailed stipulations suggest that much here is new or at least had not already been made explicit in edict form, and that was in fact the case. Officials could turn back to earlier laws and edicts to chart policies that regulated and prohibited Christianity, but that was not true of the *ito wappu* system, which had been laid out in rudimentary form in 1604 but lacked specific prohibitions and regulations until the five edicts of the 1630s.

Closer examination of these nine articles reveals that three are directed at Japanese merchants, three at foreign merchants (those who brought the goods in their ships), and three at both groups. Articles 9 and 16 define acceptable behavior for Japanese merchants, ensuring that no merchants from one city monopolize trade, and require Japanese merchants to arrive in Nagasaki by a certain day (in the summer) in order to be able to purchase goods. As the Tokugawa *bakufu* stipulate here and elsewhere, things are to be done with order. Those who failed to do so would inevitably lose their privileges. Article 10 is likewise directed at Japanese merchants, though it is more difficult to understand. It prohibits samurai from purchasing goods from Chinese vessels, suggesting that at least some warriors in the new and peaceful world of Tokugawa Japan were engaged in commerce, an activity the *bakufu* did not look highly upon. The reason was that trade and commercial activities were regarded as unbefitting the warrior (that is, gentlemanly) class, whose work was to be noble and uplifting.

The three articles directed at foreign merchants are article 14, which sets the date of departure for foreign ships; article 15, which prohibits the deposit of unsold goods in Nagasaki; and article 17, which requires traders on foreign ships arriving in Hirado (another port in southwestern Japan) to sell their silk at the price established in Nagasaki. At this point in time, given the extent of *bakufu* control over the sale of raw silk, none of these articles was particularly onerous; they merely ensured that no irregularities would occur in the system as already established. Also, as suggested in article 17, foreign trade in Japan was becoming limited in location; no longer could traders on a foreign vessel arrive at any harbor that they wished and there carry out trade with local inhabitants.

The articles that are relevant to both foreign and Japanese merchants are articles 11–13; they all deal with the protocols of foreign trade regarding silk and other commodities. Article 11 confirms an earlier practice regarding permission to engage in buying and selling, while article 12 reiterates the privileged position of the "five trading cities" in the silk market. Article 13 states that non-silk merchandise may be traded after the price on raw silk is set. It also provides two caveats: It gives the local commissioners discretion to regulate the quantity of goods brought for sale in Chinese ships, since the vessels are small and can carry only limited loads, and it requires purchasers to pay for their goods within twenty days of the date when the price for the item is set.

Audience

The Closed Country Edict of 1635 was addressed to the Nagasaki commissioners Sakakibara Motonao (who held the title of Lord of Hida) and Sengoku Hisataka (Lord of Yamato). These two individuals were the highest-ranking officials in Nagasaki. The Tokugawa leadership had appointed them and placed them under the direction of the senior councillors in Edo, which was evidence of the importance of their role as commissioners. At the beginning of the Tokugawa Era, there had been just one commissioner, and he had carried out duties in Nagasaki only while foreign ships were in port. But in 1633 (the year that the first Closed Country Edict was issued), the shift was made to two commissioners, one of whom spent the year in Nagasaki and the other in Edo; the next year they would switch places, a practice that would be followed throughout the Tokugawa Era. Appointments to these posts were for just two years, though they were occasionally renewed.

For the commissioners Sakakibara and Sengoku, the edict's articles were their "standing orders," as it were. They were direct instructions from government leaders on the policies to be followed and enforced in Nagasaki. In that sense, they were narrowly formulated, yet there was noth-

> "*Japanese ships are strictly forbidden to leave for foreign countries.*"
>
> (Article 1)

> "*No Japanese is permitted to go abroad. If there is anyone who attempts to do so secretly, he must be executed. The ship so involved must be impounded and its owner arrested, and the matter must be reported to the higher authority.*"
>
> (Article 2)

> "*If there is any place where the teachings of the padres (Christianity) is practiced, the two of you must order a thorough investigation.*"
>
> (Article 4)

> "*After settling the price, all white yarns (raw silk) brought by foreign ships shall be allocated to the five trading cities and other quarters as stipulated.*"
>
> (Article 12)

> "*Ships arriving in Hirado must sell their raw silk at the price set in Nagasaki, and are not permitted to engage in business transactions until after the price is established in Nagasaki.*"
>
> (Article 17)

ing secret about these instructions. In fact, it was imperative that the information within the edict be disseminated. A common practice in Tokugawa Japan was to post edicts or instructions on signboards at the edge of town, and it was likely that this was done in Nagasaki (and perhaps throughout the southwestern region) with the Closed Country Edict of 1635. With those public postings in place, individuals would have had no excuse for ignoring or breaking these laws.

Similarly, the articles dealing with foreign trade, buying and selling of raw silk, the merchants of the "five trading cities," and related issues would have been presented to the affected parties. Copies of the edict would have been sent to Japanese merchants before their arrival in Nagasaki and delivered to captains of foreign trading vessels upon arrival. Ignorance of the law was no excuse in Tokugawa Japan.

Impact

Without the Closed Country Edict (and accompanying policies such as the ban on Christianity), early modern Japan might have developed in radically different ways than it did. For example, Christianity might have become an influential religious and social force, altering Japan's culture in fundamental ways. Likewise, relations with foreign peoples might have increased in extent and depth, with Japanese travelers journeying frequently to other parts of Asia, the Near East, and even Europe. Another possibility is that an open Japan would have been less internally stable than it was. Perhaps the Tokugawa *bakufu* would have had difficulty ruling such a state, and rather than lasting centuries the *bakufu* might have lasted only decades. Those were all possibilities, but they did not occur. Instead, Japan was closed (if imperfectly), and it followed a distinct path largely unshaped by foreign intercourse for well over two hundred years.

Although the Tokugawa leadership may have considered its policy of prohibiting foreign travel by Japanese vessels and individuals (as seen in articles 1–3) merely a matter of security, there is no question that the impact of these articles was considerable. The measures forced the Japanese to turn inward, to consider first themselves and their world rather than the broader world beyond their borders. As a result, the rich and unique early-modern culture of Tokugawa Japan—with its kabuki theater, ukiyo-e woodblock prints, and distinctive crafts—developed within a closed country, a land in which foreign ideas and habits had limited influence.

Although the Closed Country Edict was effective at "keeping Japanese in," it was less effective at "keeping foreigners out," primarily because that was not its intent. Nonetheless, there was constriction over time, some of it brought about by *bakufu* decree and some the result of external factors. Important factors included the *bakufu*'s decision to ban entry to all Europeans of the Catholic faith; the English decision early in the seventeenth century to abandon Japan as unprofitable, which left only the Dutch on the European side and the Chinese among the Asians; and a Tokugawa decree of 1639, which restricted the Dutch and Chinese to the harbor of Nagasaki, where small numbers of them resided in foreign enclaves and carried out trade annually when their ships arrived from abroad. The only other foreign intercourse the *bakufu* allowed was trade between the daimyo of Tsushima and Korea (which faced each other across the straits of Japan) and trade between the daimyo of Satsuma and the Kingdom of the Ryukyus (islands to the south of Japan, the most prominent being Okinawa). Despite these annual contacts, Japan was indeed a land that saw and housed very few foreigners during the Tokugawa era. Native Japanese could not help but feel that the rest of the world was far away and its peoples very different.

Because Japan became largely closed off to outsiders, by the late eighteenth century the idea of *sakoku*, or "Japan as a closed country," had become accepted policy, despite the fact that no formal declaration of closure had ever been made. This was a case in which a practice had become doctrine over time, a tradition shaped by years of acceptance.

For the Tokugawa *bakufu*, the Closed Country Edict was one of a handful of critical policies that gave it firm control over the country. One might contend that by restricting travel and trade abroad, the *bakufu* weakened Japan and cut off its people from opportunity or that by limiting and confining trade perhaps the *bakufu* gave up many of the benefits of a more open society and marketplace. Those arguments are not without merit, but it is difficult to find fault with the *bakufu*'s political successes. The *bakufu* created a society in which peace reigned for 250 years, during which time Japan experienced unprecedented population growth and commercial activity. The Tokugawa Period was not without problems, some of them severe, but it was also a remarkable period, a time when Japan moved from having been a medieval society to being an early-modern one, and at least some of the credit for that must go to the influence of the Closed Country Edict.

Questions for Further Study

1. Why did Japan's rulers decide to close their country to foreign influences through the Closed Country Edict? What characteristics of Japanese society at the time gave rise to the edict?

2. The sixteenth century was a time of great European exploration of the world, including Japan. Why were European explorers and traders interesting in the Far East in general and Japan in particular?

3. What role did Christianity play in relations between Japan and Europe in the sixteenth and seventeenth centuries? Compare this dynamic in Japan with events that occurred in connection with European exploration and colonization in the Americas by consulting two entries: Columbus's Letter to Raphael Sanxis on the Discovery of America and *Requerimiento*.

4. How might the history of Japan in the nineteenth and twentieth centuries have been different had the Closed Country Edict not been issued?

5. The title "Closed Country Edict" was a later attempt to classify the document; the drafters of the document called it simply "Items: for Nagasaki." In your opinion, did the document have the effect of closing Japan to outsiders? Or did the drafters of the document have a different end in view?

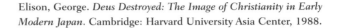

Finally, it is important to note that Japan's closed country policy led to confrontations with the West in the early and middle nineteenth century. These confrontations nearly resulted in Japan's subjugation, as it stubbornly held to a practice that was shortsighted and impractical, at least by the 1850s. Nonetheless, Japan emerged independent and largely unscathed, though the Tokugawa government and the old military order collapsed in the process.

Further Reading

▪ Articles

Tashiro, Kazui. "Foreign Relations during the Edo Period: Sakoku Reexamined." *Journal of Japanese Studies* 8, no. 2 (1982): 283–306.

Toby, Ronald. "Reopening the Question of Sakoku: Diplomacy in the Legitimation of the Tokugawa Bakufu." *Journal of Japanese Studies* 3, no. 2 (1977): 323–364.

▪ Books

Boxer, Charles. *The Christian Century in Japan, 1549–1650*. Berkeley: University of California Press, 1951.

Elison, George. *Deus Destroyed: The Image of Christianity in Early Modern Japan*. Cambridge: Harvard University Asia Center, 1988.

Hall, John Whitney. *The Cambridge History of Japan*. Volume 4: *Early Modern Japan*. New York: Cambridge University Press, 1991.

Sansom, George. *A History of Japan, 1615–1867*. Stanford, Calif.: Stanford University Press, 1963.

Toby, Ronald. *State and Diplomacy in Early Modern Japan: Asia in the Development of the Tokugawa Bakufu*. Princeton, N.J.: Princeton University Press, 1984.

—Lee Butler

Milestone Documents

JAPAN'S CLOSED COUNTRY EDICT

Items: for Nagasaki

1. Japanese ships are strictly forbidden to leave for foreign countries.

2. No Japanese is permitted to go abroad. If there is anyone who attempts to do so secretly, he must be executed. The ship so involved must be impounded and its owner arrested, and the matter must be reported to the higher authority.

3. If any Japanese returns from overseas after residing there, he must be put to death.

4. If there is any place where the teachings of padres (Christianity) is practiced, the two of you must order a thorough investigation.

5. Any informer revealing the whereabouts of the followers of padres (Christians) must be rewarded accordingly. If anyone reveals the whereabouts of a high ranking padre, he must be given one hundred pieces of silver. For those of lower ranks, depending on the deed, the reward must be set accordingly.

6. If a foreign ship has an objection [to the measures adopted] and it becomes necessary to report the matter to Edo, you may ask the Omura domain to provide ships to guard the foreign ship, as was done previously.

7. If there are any Southern Barbarians (Westerners) who propagate the teachings of padres, or otherwise commit crimes, they may be incarcerated in the prison maintained by the Omura domain, as was done previously.

8. All incoming ships must be carefully searched for the followers of padres.

9. No single trading city shall be permitted to purchase all the merchandise brought by foreign ships.

10. Samurai are not permitted to purchase any goods originating from foreign ships directly from Chinese merchants in Nagasaki.

11. After a list of merchandise brought by foreign ships is sent to Edo, as before you may order that commercial dealings may take place without waiting for a reply from Edo.

12. After settling the price, all white yarns (raw silk) brought by foreign ships shall be allocated to the five trading cities and other quarters as stipulated.

13. After settling the price of white yarns (raw silk), other merchandise [brought by foreign ships] may be traded freely between the [licensed] dealers. However, in view of the fact that Chinese ships are small and cannot bring large consignments, you may issue orders of sale at your discretion. Additionally, payment for goods purchased must be made within twenty days after the price is set.

14. The date of departure homeward of foreign ships shall not be later than the twentieth day of the ninth month. Any ships arriving in Japan later than usual shall depart within fifty days of their arrival. As to the departure of Chinese ships, you may use your discretion to order their departure after the departure of the Portuguese *galeota*.

15. The goods brought by foreign ships which remained unsold may not be deposited or accepted for deposit.

16. The arrival in Nagasaki of representatives of the five trading cities shall not be later than the fifth day of the seventh month. Anyone arriving later than that date shall lose the quota assigned to his city.

17. Ships arriving in Hirado must sell their raw silk at the price set in Nagasaki, and are not permit-

Glossary

fifth day of the seventh month	The Japanese dating system is not equivalent to Western dating. This date can be construed as sometime in the summer.
galeota	galleon
twentieth day of the ninth month	The Japanese dating system is not equivalent to Western dating. This date can be pinpointed to the autumn.

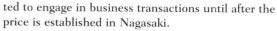

ted to engage in business transactions until after the price is established in Nagasaki.

You are hereby required to act in accordance with the provisions set above. It is so ordered.

From:
Lord of Kaga, seal [Hotta Masamori]
Lord of Bungo, seal [Abe Tadaaki]
Lord of Izu, seal [Matsudaira Nobutsuna]
Lord of Sanuki, seal [Sakai Tadakatsu]
Lord of Oi, seal [Doi Toshikatsu]

To:
Sakakibara, Lord of Hida [Motonao]
Sengoku, Lord of Yamato [Hisataka]

"No King of France can ... usurp any Right or Power over the said Countrys situated on this and the other side the Rhine."

Overview

The Treaty of Westphalia set the year 1648 as the ultimate diplomatic and religious break between the medieval and early modern periods. The rupture, however, was neither simple nor accomplished by mutual consent, as demonstrated by the attitudes of two leaders of the time. The Habsburg Archduke Ferdinand, who in 1619 became Holy Roman Emperor, had declared in 1596 that he would sooner die than make any concessions to the sectarians on the topic of religion. His contemporary, Cardinal Richelieu of France, wrote: "The state has no immortality; its salvation is now or never" (Wedgwood, 1949, p. 191). In twenty-first century terms, the former would be derided as a fanatic, while the latter would be considered a political realist.

The Treaty of Westphalia was actually a pair of treaties negotiated in the Westphalian towns of Münster and Osnabrück and concluded on October 24, 1648. These agreements ended the Thirty Years' War (1618–1648), a period of violence and destruction unmatched in Europe until the twentieth century. The war had brought about a perspectival change in the way states dealt with one another. The medieval notion of universality, whereby rulers acted in the best interests of the church, had given way to the brutal emergence of raison d'état, or the view that state interests trump all other concerns. The treaty was the European community's first attempt to reign in national aggression through fostering a balance of power and collective peace.

Context

In the broadest sense, the Treaty of Westphalia may be considered the culmination of the European medieval experience. The significance of this ambitious document is often neglected, since it cannot be read simply as the treaty that ended the Thirty Years' War. It addressed social, political, economic, and religious trends, as well as other issues arising from domestic and international perspectives, in order to create a collective and enduring peace.

In the sixteenth century the Protestant Reformation had split much of Europe into opposing camps defined by religion. The rulers of Spain, France, and the Holy Roman Empire had initially pledged their support to the papacy against the then-heretical position of Martin Luther and his followers. Within a short time, however, many rulers—particularly German electors and princes from the northern states and principalities of the Holy Roman Empire as well as the kings of Sweden and Denmark—had decided to embrace Lutheranism, whether they were motivated by religious conviction, humanist inclinations, antipapal sentiment, or territorial greed.

The situation was most problematic for the Holy Roman Empire, since its Habsburg emperor, Charles V, was also King Charles I of staunchly Catholic Spain. In the early seventeenth century, the Holy Roman Empire encompassed modern-day Germany, Austria, the Czech Republic, Slovenia, Luxembourg and parts of Poland, Slovakia, eastern France, and northern Italy. It also included the United Provinces, or the modern-day Netherlands; the Spanish Netherlands, or present-day Belgium; and the Swiss Confederation, or what was to become Switzerland. Charles V undertook a series of wars to root out Protestantism. Since the empire never enjoyed the political unity of other European states, the outcome of these conflicts was compromise. The most significant treaty resulting from Charles V's wars was the Peace of Augsburg (1555), in which the empire was effectively divided between Lutheran and Catholic principalities. The Peace of Augsburg established the principle of *cuius regio, eius religio*, which meant that the prince or elector of a certain territory would determine the religion for all of its inhabitants. This peace agreement, however, was more of a truce and demonstrated the weakness of the empire. Additionally, by 1555, the range of Protestant confessions had come to include not only Lutherans but also groups not permitted under the Peace of Augsburg: Calvinists, Anabaptists, and Unitarians.

The climate was thus far from tolerant. After 1577, Calvinists were expelled from Lutheran states. The elector Frederick III, a Calvinist, then made the University of Heidelberg into a Calvinist seminary in the Palatinate, an important principality consisting of the Lower Palatinate along the Rhine and Neckar rivers and the Upper Palatinate

1555

■ September 25
The Peace of Augsburg, between the Holy Roman Emperor and an alliance of Lutheran princes, provides a legal basis for the existence of Lutheranism within the Holy Roman Empire.

1589

■ April 13
The Edict of Nantes restores civil rights to French Calvinists (Huguenots) in the predominantly Catholic France of Henry IV.

1619

■ Ferdinand II, staunch supporter of the Catholic cause, becomes Holy Roman Emperor.

1625–1629

■ The Lutheran king of Denmark, Christian IV, assists the Lutheran princes of Saxony against imperial forces.

1629

■ March 6
The Edict of Restitution is meant to revert to the religious distribution at the time of the Peace of Augsburg and prevent the further spread of Protestantism following the imperial victories under Albrecht von Wallenstein.

to the east on the Bohemian border. Catholics were allowed to live in the Palatinate only if they worshiped in homes, while Unitarians were suppressed altogether. The struggle between Lutherans and Calvinists was as hard fought in the second half of the sixteenth century as the conflict between Luther and the papacy in the first half. As princes and electors endorsed one creed over another, a rivalry that the religious reformer and scholar Philipp Melanchthon called *rabies theologica*, or theological rabies, was infecting the empire and laying the groundwork for religious war.

In lands neighboring the Holy Roman Empire, the Reformation continued to spread and incite conflict. Throughout the Swiss Confederation, Protestantism was becoming entrenched in city governments and public education. The situation in France was more problematic. While the French monarchy tolerated Protestantism at first, by 1534 it had begun a crackdown on French Protestants, who were known as Huguenots. The second half of the sixteenth century witnessed the French Wars of Religion (1552–1598) and culminated in the Edict of Nantes (1598), whereby King Henry IV, seeing the economic value of granting liberties to Protestants, gave rights and privileges to the Huguenots. The United Provinces and Flanders (now the Netherlands, northwestern Belgium, and the French department of Nord) saw considerable growth of Protestantism among the literate merchant classes. Dutch economic concerns would later be major diplomatic considerations at the Congress of Westphalia.

Charles V's abdication shortly after the Peace of Augsburg temporarily settled religious controversy in the Holy Roman Empire. Other Habsburgs, though, saw themselves as defenders of Catholicism against the growing threats of both the Protestants and the Ottoman Turks. The tension between Protestants and Catholics in Europe, therefore, ought to be seen from the perspective of a wider threat to the Catholic faith, which was under attack on many fronts. In 1564 the imperial crown fell to Charles V's nephew, Maximilian II, who only added to the cauldron by preferring Lutheran to Catholic preachers and protecting Protestants from persecution. His son and successor, Rudolf II, believed that moderation and toleration served to undermine the unity of the empire. In contrast, Protestant and Catholic leaders in the Swiss Confederation, having endured the strict rule of Calvinism in Geneva, followed a more conciliatory path.

By the early seventeenth century, the empire was far from unified. As of 1600, the Jesuits had restored the authority of Catholicism in many Austrian parishes that had adopted Luther's reforms. A good example of religious division can be seen in the kingdom of Bohemia, which then included Lusatia and Silesia (encompassing the present-day Czech Republic as well as parts of eastern Germany, Slovakia, and southern Poland). By the mid-sixteenth century, most of Bohemia was Protestant. Holy Roman Emperors Ferdinand I and Rudolf II had attempted to outlaw Protestantism in Bohemia. However, they were unable to enforce such edicts, since most members of the nobility and burgeoning middle class were Protestants and only the peasants remained firmly Catholic.

The seeming religious freedom that existed in Bohemia and other areas not only strengthened the princes but also guaranteed instability, which threatened the Holy Roman Empire and eventually invited outside influence. In addition, by the early seventeenth century, the economic prosperity once enjoyed by many German states had been undermined. The bulk of economic trade no longer flowed from the Mediterranean across the Alps and up through the German principalities but instead was being routed directly to northern Europe by sea. This was largely because England and the Netherlands, rather than Spain and Portugal, had come to dominate the Atlantic and many trade routes. Major German banking families were in steady decline. By 1600, the various currencies used within the empire were becoming unstable. As the economic situation worsened, the population continued to increase, which amplified the potential for unrest among the peasantry.

As is often typical during periods of economic instability, many tenaciously clung to religious beliefs. This served to rekindle strife over religious divisions. What formerly had been more of an academic debate between Catholics and Protestants was quickly becoming more heated. In the Rhineland, for example, Jesuits in Cologne argued that Luther should have been burned at the stake, while in Heidelberg a Calvinist theologian suggested a crusade against the papacy. Protestant princes formed the Protestant Union in 1608. In response, Catholic leaders formed the Catholic League the following year. Both had outside support; the French king, Henry IV, offered support to the Protestant Union, while the Spanish Habsburgs stood ready to help fellow Catholics. In 1617 the Habsburg Archduke Ferdinand, a fervent Catholic, was made king of Bohemia and two years later became Holy Roman Emperor Ferdinand II.

By the second decade of the century, Europe was a tinderbox brimming with economic turmoil, social unrest, and religious division. It merely needed some rapid series of events to set it alight. In Prague on May 23, 1618, a group of Protestant nobles, angry at the growing influence of Catholicism—and particularly the appointment of Archduke Ferdinand to the Bohemian throne—tossed two representatives of Holy Roman Emperor Matthias and their secretary out of a window. The three survived, but the action was an affront not only to the empire but also Ferdinand and the Catholic League. Ferdinand immediately sent two armies into Bohemia. In response, the Calvinist elector of the Palatinate, Frederick V, organized a counterforce. By the end of November 1618, Protestant forces had captured Pilsen, the Catholic stronghold in Bohemia. The following spring, Matthias was dead and Ferdinand had become his presumptive heir as Holy Roman Emperor. The Bohemian Diet declared that Ferdinand was deposed as king and offered the Bohemian crown to Frederick V, who accepted.

The deposal of Ferdinand as Bohemian king should have solidified Catholic and Protestant factions, but instead it demonstrated that religion was one of several factors in the conflict. Frederick V's father-in-law, James I of England, a Protestant, advised him not to accept the Bohemian crown. Dutch Protestants offered no real assis-

Time Line	
1630	■ When the forces of the Lutheran Swedish King Gustavus II Adolph successfully invade the Holy Roman Empire, the Swedes intervene in order to support Lutheran princes, protect Swedish trade, and check the power of the empire, an intervention that lasts five years.
1631	■ **September 17** The Battle of Breitenfeld, the first major Protestant victory of the war, leads many German states to ally with Gustavus II.
1634	■ **September 6** The Battle of Nördlingen is a crushing defeat for the Protestant forces after the death of Gustavus II; the outcome persuades France to become more directly involved in the war.
1635	■ **May 30** The Peace of Prague between Ferdinand II and many of the defeated Protestant princes in the Holy Roman Empire is meant to restore peace by granting widespread amnesty, preventing private armies, and restoring the conditions of the Peace of Augsburg.

1636

- The French Cardinal Richelieu begins a costly twelve-year attempt to reduce Hapsburg influence in the Holy Roman Empire by supporting the Protestants there after the defeat of the Swedes.

1643

- **May 19**
The Battle of Rocroi represents a major defeat for the Spanish Habsburgs by the French.

1648

- **October 24**
The Treaty of Westphalia, a pair of treaties negotiated in the Westphalian towns of Münster and Osnabrück is concluded, ending the Thirty Years' War.

tance, and the Lutheran Duke of Saxony Elector George I (a populous eastern German duchy on Bohemia's northern border) sided with Ferdinand rather than Frederick. This was most likely because the duke not only hated the Calvinists but also saw the potential for territorial gain. With little backing and his forces defeated by the Catholic League at the Battle of White Mountain in November 1620, Frederick V was forced into exile. The Bohemian Protestants were defeated, and their land was confiscated. Ferdinand, who had become Holy Roman Emperor Ferdinand II by this time, was restored as Bohemian king, and he proceeded to sell former Protestant estates to Catholics, thereby creating a new Catholic nobility in Bohemia. The initial salvos of the Thirty Years' War in Bohemia were over, but many yearned for vengeance.

In the second phase of the conflict, the mantle of Protestant resistance was taken up by King Christian IV of Denmark. He intervened not so much to assist his fellow Protes-

tants but primarily to acquire territory in northern Germany. Christian received nominal support from England, France, and the Netherlands, then known as the United Provinces, although none of these lands provided significant financial or military support. Unfortunately for Christian, the Holy Roman Empire found a brilliant general in Albrecht von Wallenstein, a Bohemian nobleman who sought to increase his own power by supporting Ferdinand II. In 1625 Wallenstein was commissioned to supply twenty thousand troops for the emperor's cause. By mid-1629, imperial forces had gained the upper hand, forcing Christian to renounce any claims to northern Germany. Ferdinand then confiscated the lands of those who had supported the Danish king and gave land to Wallenstein, including the North German duchy of Mecklenburg. Ferdinand also issued the Edict of Restitution in 1629, which prohibited Calvinist worship but, more important, restored all Catholic property that had been secularized since 1552, much of which had been bought and paid for. This edict convinced even Catholic princes that Ferdinand had overstretched his authority. Many had benefited economically from the decentralized structure of the empire, but Ferdinand's centralization of power, enforced by Wallenstein, was perceived as a threat.

Like Christian IV of Denmark, the Swedish king, Gustavus II Adolph, was primarily concerned about his state's political independence and economic development. For these reasons, in 1630 he positioned Sweden as the rescuer of Protestantism in the northern German states and a check against the power of the Habsburgs under Ferdinand II. While Gustavus, a Lutheran, prohibited forced conversions and tolerated Catholicism, the forces of the empire were brutal. For example, in 1631 an imperial army under Johann Tserclaes (also known as Count Tilly) massacred twenty thousand in the Protestant archbishop city of Magdeburg and even destroyed its cathedral. After the first major Protestant victory in this phase of the war at Breitenfeld in Saxony in September 1631, many of Ferdinand's allies began entering the Swedish alliance. Gustavus moved into central and southern Germany, devastating the countryside as he marched, but he was mortally wounded in battle in 1632. Wallenstein was assassinated two years later, but thanks to the imperial army's reinforcement with Spanish troops, Sweden's military advance was halted at the South German town of Nördlingen in September 1634. In May 1635, Ferdinand II signed the Peace of Prague with the Saxons; this treaty also suspended the Edict of Restitution and prohibited German princes from forming military alliances with foreign powers.

The final phase of the Thirty Years' War came as a result of France's fear of being surrounded by powerful Habsburgs in both the Holy Roman Empire and Spain. The first minister of France, Cardinal Richelieu, supported Sweden and garnered the support of Pope Urban VIII, who feared that Habsburg power might threaten his holdings in Italy. Thus, leadership of the Protestant forces passed from Sweden to France, and the war became a wider European conflict. Since the entry of France meant the infusion of forces superior to those of the emperor, many Protestant leaders began to defect from their alliance with Ferdinand III, Ferdinand II's son who had become Holy Roman Emperor upon his father's death in 1637. At the Battle of Breitenfeld outside Vienna in 1642, the imperial army suffered a loss of ten thousand troops at the hands of the Swedes. In 1643 the French won a decisive victory at the Battle of Rocroi over the Spanish on the border of the Spanish Netherlands (modern-day Belgium). By 1646, Ferdinand III had sent representatives to Westphalia to seek peace negotiations.

The war had devastated most of central Europe. The six armies—of the Holy Roman Empire, Denmark, Sweden, Bohemia, Spain, and France—were made up primarily of mercenaries who had no attachment to the places where the fighting occurred; they would fight for any faith for a fee. These armies did not respect the right of surrender; they treated civilians as legitimate targets and made rape and torture general instruments of war. As armies traveled, so did disease. Typhus, dysentery, bubonic plague, and syphilis added to the demographic catastrophe. The war, the flight of refugees, and the ravages of disease brought about a drastic population decline. By the war's end in Germany and Austria, the population had fallen by nearly one-third, from an estimated 21 million to 13.5 million. Starvation was also a consequence of the long war. Farmers saw no reason to plant crops, since there was no assurance they would still be alive to harvest them. As at Versailles at the end of World War I, diplomats gathered in Westphalia at the end of 1644 in the hope of creating a lasting peace.

About the Author

There is no solitary author of the treaty. However, since the treaty's original language was French and considering France's advantageous position at the war's end, the French delegation perhaps had the most influence. It was headed by Henri II d'Orléans, the duke of Longueville, who, as a French prince, had previously served in the French military in both Italy and the Holy Roman Empire. Usually cast as a rebel of sorts, he used his role at Westphalia not only for the benefit of France but also to secure the independence of the Swiss Confederation. He was joined by the French diplomat Abel Servien, marquis de Sablé, and Claude de Mesmes, the count d'Avaux, a diplomat and public administrator.

While Sweden was in a rather advantageous position at war's end, the Swedish attempt to secure one of the electoral college votes within the empire was thwarted by the stronger influence of France at the conference. The Swedish representatives were Johann Adler Salvius and Count Bengt Gabrielsson Oxenstierna. The Holy Roman Empire's chief delegate was Count Maximilian von Trauttmansdorff. Trauttmansdorff had a long tenure in the service of the Habsburgs, securing both the Bohemian and the Hungarian crowns for the future Ferdinand II and, later, serving as the most influential minister to Ferdinand III.

The Spanish delegation was headed by Gaspar de Bracamonte y Guzmán. Many delegations were sent from the German principalities of the Holy Roman Empire. The rep-

Ferdinand II (© Bettmann/CORBIS)

resentative of the Catholic Church, Fabio Chigi (later Pope Alexander VII), and the Venetian envoy, Alvise Contarini (who became the doge, or duke, of Venice), served as mediators. Many of the imperial states of the Holy Roman Empire also sent delegations. The most important was Brandenburg, which was represented by Count Johann von Sayn-Wittgenstein, the most prominent of the empire's Protestant representatives. He was able to increase the holdings of Brandenburg by obtaining eastern Pomerania as well as other smaller territories.

Explanation and Analysis of the Document

The Treaty of Westphalia is named for the northern German region where the negotiations were conducted. Representatives did not gather at one location, however. At the town of Münster, the delegates from France and the Holy Roman Empire met under the mediation of the papacy and the republic of Venice. A mere fifty kilometers away in Osnabrück, the delegates of France, the Holy Roman Empire, and Sweden gathered with Christian IV of Denmark as mediator. This segregation of powers was necessary, since Sweden refused to be mediated by a representative of the papacy and the papal representative refused to sit in the same room with a "heretic."

The Congress of Westphalia opened in December 1644 and was concluded with much fanfare on October 24, 1648. The comprehensive treaty's introduction declares a "universal Peace," which, according to article I, is to be founded not on a common religion or dictated by religious authority but is to occur "between all and each of the Allies … that each Party shall endeavour to procure the Benefit, Honour and Advantage of the other." In other words, abiding by the principles of the treaty was intended to benefit all parties. In order to halt the cycle of violence, articles II and VI provided for amnesty and pardon for all offenses committed since the beginning of the war while avoiding the rhetoric typical of an imposed peace.

The language of the treaty was new to diplomatic discourse in that it is conciliatory toward different religious sects. This was clearly an effort to remove religious difference as a cause of conflict. To this end, article XLV proclaims "the Liberty of the Exercise of Religion" throughout the Holy Roman Empire, thus strengthening the position of the Protestants. Article XXVIII specifically granted religious freedom to Lutherans (called "those of the Confession of Augsburg" in the document) and restored ecclesiastical property to them based on their holdings as of 1624. Articles XXII, XXV, and XXVI offered an olive branch to Charles I Louis of the Lower Palatinate, who was the son of Frederick V, the Calvinist elector whom the Protestants had selected as Bohemian king in 1619 in their attempted rebellion against Ferdinand II.

The monetary cost of the war had been significant, and the treaty attempted to anticipate and address economic concerns. Article XXXIX gave all parties a period of two years to show claim, after which debts were to be considered settled. Since economic conditions had worsened throughout the Holy Roman Empire during the war, the signatories wanted to ensure that indemnities either would be paid quickly or would be forgiven to avoid future strife and acts of vengeance. For similar reasons, article XLI upheld secular judicial pronouncements issued during the war.

The latter half of the treaty dealt, in particular, with the Holy Roman Emperor and his subjects. Article XLIV repeated the earlier proclamation of general amnesty, and article XLV provided for the return of some royal land but without compensation for damages. Herein the overriding influence of France and Sweden in drafting the document is evident; while the emperor and Austria, whom the delegates wanted to conciliate, could regain lost property, these provisions implied that others within the empire who lost property might not have it returned. Article XLIX restated the principle regarding religious liberty and the return of church land. It refers to an agreement among those powers that were meeting at Münster and extended it to apply to the Swedish delegation at Osnabrück.

Specific regions and allies are mentioned in the treaty. For example, article LVI stipulated the repayment of a sum to "Madam the Landgravine," whose family had been a long-term supporter of the Protestant cause in the state of Hesse. Article XCIX absolved the House of Savoy, which assisted in the French cause, of any retribution on the part

of the empire. Article LVIII stipulated that fortresses of war throughout the empire were to be dismantled as long as they did not leave an area lacking in security. Article LXXXII called upon each prince of the empire to respect the traditions and rights of other states, participate in the empire's assemblies, and regard the authority of the Holy Roman Emperor.

Territorial realignments were recognized in the treaty. For example, the United Provinces of the Netherlands were pronounced independent of Spain. Article LXXVI recognized France's right to the towns of Metz, Toul, and Verdun on the western border of the empire, as well as most of Alsace, although article LXXXIX required France to renounce further claims to territory in the vicinity of the Rhine. Article LXXVII stipulates that the French king is obligated to "preserve" Catholicism in areas where it is dominant. Contrary to the Edict of Restitution, only territory that the empire had conquered by 1624 was to be returned to the Catholic Church. French territorial gains were small, but the treaty assured that France, while being obliged to respect religious traditions, could achieve its security goals by maintaining a buffer between itself and the Holy Roman Empire.

Articles CIV through CXIX provided for the implementation of peace. Specifically, articles CIV and CV spelled out the time and method for cessation of hostilities, CVI the publication of the peace, CVII through CXIV the restoration or transfer of property, CXV the responsibilities of local inhabitants toward departing soldiers, and CXVIII the demobilization of troops and the maintenance of those necessary for security.

With respect to the treaties and covenants established during the course of the war, such as the Edict of Restitution and Peace of Prague, article CXXI made clear that the Treaty of Westphalia superseded all other provisions, treaties, and agreements. Article CXXXII warned anyone who might infringe on what the treaty termed "Publick Peace." While no specific punishment was given, Article CXXIII enjoined all signatories to "defend and protect all and every Article of this Peace." This provision gave France and Sweden the ability to frustrate the Habsburgs. France and Sweden thus became the guarantors of the new imperial constitution with the obligation to protect the rights of princes against the Holy Roman Emperor. They became the counterbalance to ensure that future conflict over or within the empire would be quelled.

Audience

The audience of this treaty were the signatories themselves. The Westphalian delegates comprised a veritable who's who of European statesmen, future heads of state, and a future pope. This, in fact, may be the reason the treaty endured and also represented a fundamental shift in modern diplomatic statecraft. For the signatories, a major consideration was the sheer expense of the conflict itself. None of the major combatant states—the Holy Roman

Heads of state and royals of twenty European countries walk through a street of Münster, Germany, on October 24, 1998, in celebration of the 350th anniversary of the Treaty of Westphalia. (AP/Wide World Photos)

"*And to prevent for the future any Differences arising in the Politick State, all and every one of the Electors, Princes and States of the Roman Empire, are so establish'd and confirm'd in their antient Rights, Prerogatives, Libertys, Privileges, free exercise of Territorial Right, as well Ecclesiastick, as Politick Lordships, Regales, by virtue of this present Transaction: that they never can or ought to be molested therein by any whomsoever upon any manner of pretence.*"

(Article LXIV)

"*No King of France can or ought ever to; pretend to or usurp any Right or Power over the said Countrys situated on this and the other side the Rhine.*"

(Article LXXXIX)

"*And for the Remainder of their Rights and Privileges, Ecclesiastical and Secular, which they enjoy'd before these Troubles, they shall be maintain'd therein; save, nevertheless the Rights of Sovereignty, and what depends thereon, for the Lords to whom they belong.*"

(Article CXVII)

Empire, Spain, France, or Sweden—had profited economically from the war. Thus, the peace would open important opportunities for commerce between at least some of the former enemies and enable the United Provinces and France to concentrate on overseas trade. The best example was the explosive growth in the second half of the century of the United Provinces into the Dutch Empire. Within a generation, however, the treaty's designs would become a source of contention. By 1672, for example, the French-Dutch War had broken out, even drawing England into the conflict. The dividend of peace was profit, and profit, like religion, was a strong motive for conflict.

Impact

The significance of the Treaty of Westphalia is often underestimated. It would serve as a model for resolving future European conflicts. Six armies had participated in the conflict. Those six states as well as many princes of the empire participated in a gathering that brought together more than one hundred delegations. For the first time, a congress with representatives from all parties involved in a multinational conflict not only addressed international disputes but also agreed to abide by the resulting settlement.

France and Sweden gained the most from the treaty. Ultimately, France would replace Spain as the dominant power on the continent (and the two countries would not officially cease hostilities until 1659). Sweden emerged as the major power in the Baltic, a position it would enjoy for a half-century until military defeat by Czar Peter I of Russia. The Habsburgs lost the most. The Austrian branch, the traditional rulers of the Holy Roman Empire, agreed to the independence of the Swiss Confederation. In addition, German princes were not only recognized as independent but also were given the right to establish Lutheranism, Catholicism, or Calvinism within their territories. The treaty also required the Spanish Habsburgs to recognize the independence of a Dutch Republic, which included two provinces taken from the Spanish Netherlands (present-day Belgium).

These territorial and political realignments were significant, and many would last well into the nineteenth century. The treaty also determined religious distribution within the empire by confirming the Peace of Augsburg, which had first established the principle that the prince's religion would determine the religion of his people and expanded it to include Calvinism. As a result, the northern parts of the empire remained largely Lutheran and the area along the Rhine Calvinist, and Catholicism prevailed in the south.

With the catastrophic decline in agriculture, many farmers lacked the capital to remain independent and were forced to become day laborers. In parts of central Europe, especially areas east of the Elbe River, the loss of peasant holdings resulted in the consolidation of large estates and the expansion of serfdom.

The treaty also brought about a formal break between German principalities and territories controlled by the Austrian Habsburgs. Princely power demonstrated during the war and guaranteed by the treaty revealed how little most German states and principalities had to offer the Habsburgs. After 1648, the Austrian Habsburgs increasingly focused attention on their own territories, both inside and outside the empire, and expanded farther into southeastern Europe. This absence of Habsburg influence coupled with the religious and territorial provisions of the treaty enabled a former weak principality, such as Brandenburg-Prussia, to begin the process of state building, especially under the Calvinist Frederick William who was both the elector of Brandenburg and the duke of Prussia.

Finally, the Treaty of Westphalia signaled the loss of power of the papacy. Since late antiquity, the church had battled for supremacy over European princes and kings, in particular, the Holy Roman Emperor. Even though the Holy Roman Empire had fought on behalf of the Catholic religion in the Thirty Years' War, its loss and the emergence of Richelieu's version of statecraft left little room for the Catholic Church as a power player after 1648.

Further Reading

■ Articles

Croxton, Derek. "The Peace of Westphalia of 1648 and the Origins of Sovereignty." *International History Review* 21, no. 3 (September 1999): 569–591.

Falk, Richard. "Revisiting Westphalia, Discovering Post-Westphalia." *Journal of Ethics* 6, no. 4 (2002): 311–352.

■ Books

Forster, Marc R. *The Counter-Reformation in the Villages: Religion and Reform in the Bishopric of Speyer, 1560–1720.* Ithaca, N.Y.: Cornell University Press, 1992.

Grimmelshausen, Hans Jakob Christoffel von. *The Adventures of Simplicius Simplicissimus,* trans. George Schulz-Behrend. Columbia, S.C.: Camden House, 1993.

Ingrao, Charles W. *The Habsburg Monarchy, 1618–1815.* New York: Cambridge University Press, 1994.

Schiller, Friedrich. *The Robbers* and *Wallenstein,* trans. F. J. Lamport. New York: Penguin, 1979.

Wedgwood, C. V. *Richelieu and the French Monarchy.* London: Hodder and Staughton, 1949.

———. *The Thirty Years' War.* New York: Methuen, 1981.

—Christopher Ohan

Questions for Further Study

1. In what ways did the Treaty of Westphalia transform Europe? Put differently, how did the treaty mark a transition from medieval to more modern modes of thought in the political sphere?

2. Read the Treaty of Westphalia in conjunction with the Dutch Declaration of Independence, which began an independence movement in the Netherlands that culminated in the Treaty of Münster, which was part of the Treaty of Westphalia. What contribution did the Dutch make to the political events that led to the Treaty of Westphalia?

3. Would the Treaty of Westphalia and the events leading to it have taken place if Martin Luther had not posted his *Ninety-Five Theses* in Germany? Explain.

4. Like the Treaty of Westphalia, the Treaty of Versailles in 1919 tried to impose a lasting peace in Europe. How were the events that led to the treaties similar, and how were they different? Did the two treaties succeed? What were their fundamental weaknesses?

5. Discussions of the Treaty of Westphalia and the events surrounding it often focus on kings, popes, and empires. But how did the treaty—and the events surrounding it—affect the ordinary person?

TREATY OF WESTPHALIA

In the name of the most holy and individual Trinity: Be it known to all, and every one whom it may concern, or to whom in any manner it may belong, That for many Years past, Discords and Civil Divisions being stir'd up in the Roman Empire, which increas'd to such a degree, that not only all Germany, but also the neighbouring Kingdoms, and France particularly, have been involv'd in the Disorders of a long and cruel War:... It has at last happen'd, by the effect of Divine Goodness, seconded by the Endeavours of the most Serene Republick of Venice, who in this sad time, when all Christendom is imbroil'd, has not ceas'd to contribute its Counsels for the publick Welfare and Tranquillity; so that on the side, and the other, they have form'd Thoughts of an universal Peace....

I. That there shall be a Christian and Universal Peace, and a perpetual, true, and sincere Amity, between his Sacred Imperial Majesty, and his most Christian Majesty; as also, between all and each of the Allies.... That this Peace and Amity be observ'd and cultivated with such a Sincerity and Zeal, that each Party shall endeavour to procure the Benefit, Honour and Advantage of the other; that thus on all sides they may see this Peace and Friendship in the Roman Empire, and the Kingdom of France flourish, by entertaining a good and faithful Neighbourhood.

II. That there shall be on the one side and the other a perpetual Oblivion, Amnesty, or Pardon of all that has been committed since the beginning of these Troubles ...

III. And that a reciprocal Amity between the Emperor, and the Most Christian King, the Electors, Princes and States of the Empire, may be maintain'd ... the one shall never assist the present or future Enemys of the other under any Title or Pretence whatsoever, either with Arms, Money, Soldiers, or any sort of Ammunition; nor no one, who is a Member of this Pacification, shall suffer any Enemys Troops to retire thro' or sojourn in his Country.

IV. ... That if for the future any Dispute arises between these two Kingdoms, the abovesaid reciprocal Obligation of not aiding each others Enemys, shall always continue firm ... but yet so as that it shall be free for the States to succour; without the bounds of the Empire, such or such Kingdoms, but still according to the Constitutions of the Empire.

V. That the Controversy touching Lorain shall be refer'd to Arbitrators nominated by both sides or it shall be terminated by a Treaty between France and Spain, or by some other friendly means; and it shall be free as well for the Emperor, as Electors, Princes and States of the Empire, to aid and advance this Agreement by an amicable Interposition, and other Offices of Pacification, without using the force of Arms.

VI. According to this foundation of reciprocal Amity, and a general Amnesty, all and every one of the Electors of the sacred Roman Empire, the Princes and States (therein comprehending the Nobility, which depend immediately on the Empire) their Vassals, Subjects, Citizens, Inhabitants (to whom on the account of the Bohemian or German Troubles or Alliances, contracted here and there, might have been done by the one Party or the other, any Prejudice or Damage in any manner, or under what pretence soever, as well in their Lordships, their fiefs, Underfiefs, Allodations, as in their Dignitys, Immunitys, Rights and Privileges) shall be fully re-establish'd on the one side and the other, in the Ecclesiastick or Laick State, which they enjoy'd, or could lawfully enjoy, notwithstanding any Alterations, which have been made in the mean time to the contrary....

VII. It shall also be free for the Elector of Treves, as well in the Quality of Bishop of Spires as Bishop of Worms, to sue before competent Judges for the Rights he pretends to certain Ecclesiastical Lands, situated in the Territorys of the Lower Palatinate, if so be those Princes make not a friendly Agreement among themselves....

XXII. Further, that all the Palatinate House, with all and each of them, who are, or have in any manner adher'd to it; and above all, the Ministers who have serv'd in this Assembly, or have formerly serv'd this House; as also all those who are banish'd out of the Palatinate, shall enjoy the general Amnesty here above promis'd, with the same Rights as those who are comprehended therein, or of whom a more particular and ampler mention has been made in the Article of Grievance....

XXV. That the said Lord Charles Lewis shall give no trouble to the Counts of Leiningen and of Daxburg, nor to their Successors in the Lower Palatinate; but he shall let them peaceably enjoy the

Rights obtain'd many Ages ago, and confirm'd by the Emperors.

XXVI. That he shall inviolably leave the Free Nobility of the Empire, which are in Franconia, Swabia, and all along the Rhine, and the Districts thereof, in the state they are at present....

XXVIII. That those of the Confession of Augsburg, and particularly the Inhabitants of Oppenheim, shall be put in possession again of their Churches, and Ecclesiastical Estates, as they were in the Year 1624. as also that all others of the said Confession of Augsburg, who shall demand it, shall have the free Exercise of their Religion, as well in publick Churches at the appointed Hours, as in private in their own Houses, or in others chosen for this purpose by their Ministers, or by those of their Neighbours, preaching the Word of God....

XXXIX. That the Debts either by Purchase, Sale, Revenues, or by what other name they may be call'd, if they have been violently extorted by one of the Partys in War, and if the Debtors alledge and offer to prove there has been a real Payment, they shall be no more prosecuted, before these Exceptions be first adjusted. That the Debtors shall be oblig'd to produce their Exceptions within the term of two years after the Publication of the Peace, upon pain of being afterwards condemn'd to perpetual Silence.

XL. That Processes which have been hitherto enter'd on this Account, together with the Transactions and Promises made for the Restitution of Debts, shall be look'd upon as void; and yet the Sums of Money, which during the War have been exacted bona fide, and with a good intent, by way of Contributions, to prevent greater Evils by the Contributors, are not comprehended herein.

XLI. That Sentences pronounc'd during the War about Matters purely Secular, if the Defect in the Proceedings be not fully manifest, or cannot be immediately demonstrated, shall not be esteem'd wholly void; but that the Effect shall be suspended until the Acts of Justice (if one of the Partys demand the space of six months after the Publication of the Peace, for the reviewing of his Process) be review'd and weigh'd in a proper Court, and according to the ordinary or extraordinary Forms us'd in the Empire: to the end that the former Judgments may be confirm'd, amended, or quite eras'd, in case of Nullity.

XLII. In the like manner, if any Royal, or particular Fiefs, have not been renew'd since the Year 1618. nor Homage paid to whom it belongs; the same shall bring no prejudice, and the Investiture shall be renew'd the day the Peace shall be concluded.

XLIII. Finally, That all and each of the Officers, as well Military Men as Counsellors and Gownmen, and Ecclesiasticks of what degree they may be, who have serv'd the one or other Party among the Allies, or among their Adherents, let it be in the Gown, or with the Sword, from the highest to the lowest, without any distinction or exception ... shall be restor'd by all Partys in the State of Life, Honour, Renown, Liberty of Conscience, Rights and Privileges, which they enjoy'd before the abovesaid Disorders; that no prejudice shall be done to their Effects and Persons, that no Action or accusation shall be enter'd against them; and that further, no Punishment be inflicted on them, or they to bear any damage under what pretence soever: And all this shall have its full effect in respect to those who are not Subjects or Vassals of his Imperial Majesty, or of the House of Austria.

XLIV. But for those who are Subjects and Hereditary Vassals of the Emperor, and of the House of Austria, they shall really have the benefit of the Amnesty, as for their Persons, Life, Reputation, Honours: and they may return with Safety to their former Country; but they shall be oblig'd to conform, and submit themselves to the Laws of the Realms, or particular Provinces they shall belong to.

XLV. As to their Estates that have been lost by Confiscation or otherways, before they took the part of the Crown of France, or of Swedeland, notwithstanding the Plenipotentiarys of Swedeland have made long instances they may be also restor'd. Nevertheless his Imperial Majesty being to receive Law from none, and the Imperialists sticking close thereto, it has not been thought convenient by the States of the Empire, that for such a Subject the War should be continu'd: And that thus those who have lost their Effects as aforesaid, cannot recover them to the prejudice of their last Masters and Possessors. But the Estates, which have been taken away by reason of Arms taken for France or Swedeland, against the Emperor and the House of Austria, they shall be restor'd in the State they are found, and that without any Compensation for Profit or Damage.

XLIX. And since for the greater Tranquillity of the Empire, in its general Assemblys of Peace, a certain Agreement has been made between the Emperor, Princes and States of the Empire, which has been inserted in the Instrument and Treaty of Peace, ... touching the Differences about Ecclesiastical Lands, and the Liberty of the Exercise of Religion; it has been found expedient to confirm, and ratify it by this present Treaty, in the same manner as the abovesaid Agreement has been made with the said Crown of

Swedeland; also with those call'd the Reformed, in the same manner, as if the words of the abovesaid Instrument were reported here verbatim....

LVI. ... That if within the term of nine Months, the whole Sum be not paid to Madam the Landgravine, not only Cuesfeldt and Newhaus shall remain in her Hands till the full Payment, but also for the remainder, she shall be paid Interest at Five per Cent. and the Treasurers and Collectors of the Bayliwicks appertaining to the abovesaid Arch-bishopricks, Bishopricks and Abby, bordering on the Principality of Hesse, ... they shall yearly pay the Interest of the remaining Sum notwithstanding the Prohibitions of their Masters. If the Treasurers and Collectors delay the Payment, or alienate the Revenues, Madam the Landgravine shall have liberty to constrain them to pay, by all sorts of means, always saving the Right of the Lord Proprietor of the Territory....

LVIII. ... The Fortifications and Ramparts, rais'd during the Possession of the Places, shall be destroy'd and demolish'd as much as possible, without exposing the Towns, Borroughs, Castles and Fortresses, to Invasions and Robberys....

LXIII. And as His Imperial Majesty, upon Complaints made in the name of the City of Basle, and of all Switzerland, in the presence of their Plenipotentiarys deputed to the present Assembly, touching some Procedures and Executions proceeding from the Imperial Chamber against the said City, and the other united Cantons of the Swiss Country, and their Citizens and Subjects having demanded the Advice of the States of the Empire and their Council; these have, by a Decree of the 14th of May of the last Year, declared the said City of Basle, and the other Swiss-Cantons, to be as it were in possession of their full Liberty and Exemption of the Empire; so that they are no ways subject to the Judicatures, or Judgments of the Empire, and it was thought convenient to insert the same in this Treaty of Peace, and confirm it, and thereby to make void and annul all such Procedures and Arrests given on this Account in what form soever.

LXIV. And to prevent for the future any Differences arising in the Politick State, all and every one of the Electors, Princes and States of the Roman Empire, are so establish'd and confirm'd in their antient Rights, Prerogatives, Libertys, Privileges, free exercise of Territorial Right, as well Ecclesiastick, as Politick Lordships, Regales, by virtue of this present Transaction: that they never can or ought to be molested therein by any whomsoever upon any manner of pretence.

LXV. They shall enjoy without contradiction, the Right of Suffrage in all Deliberations touching the Affairs of the Empire; but above all, when the Business in hand shall be the making or interpreting of Laws, the declaring of Wars, imposing of Taxes, levying or quartering of Soldiers, erecting new Fortifications in the Territorys of the States, or reinforcing the old Garisons; as also when a Peace of Alliance is to be concluded, and treated about, or the like, none of these, or the like things shall be acted for the future, without the Suffrage and Consent of the Free Assembly of all the States of the Empire: Above all, it shall be free perpetually to each of the States of the Empire, to make Alliances with Strangers for their Preservation and Safety; provided, nevertheless, such Alliances be not against the Emperor, and the Empire, nor against the Publick Peace, and this Treaty, and without prejudice to the Oath by which every one is bound to the Emperor and the Empire.

LXVI. That the Diets of the Empire shall be held within six Months after the Ratification of the Peace; and after that time as often as the Publick Utility, or Necessity requires. That in the first Diet the Defects of precedent Assemblys be chiefly remedy'd; and that then also be treated and settled by common Consent of the States, the Form and Election of the Kings of the Romans, by a Form, and certain Imperial Resolution; the Manner and Order which is to be observ'd for declaring one or more States, to be within the Territorys of the Empire, besides the Manner otherways describ'd in the Constitutions of the Empire; that they consider also of re-establishing the Circles, the renewing the Matricular-Book, the re-establishing suppress'd States, the moderating and lessening the Collects of the Empire, Reformation of Justice and Policy, the taxing of Fees in the Chamber of Justice, the Due and requisite instructing of ordinary Deputys for the Advantage of the Publick, the true Office of Directors in the Colleges of the Empire, and such other Business as could not be here expedited.

LXVII. That as well as general as particular Diets, the free Towns, and other States of the Empire, shall have decisive Votes; they shall, without molestation, keep their Regales, Customs, annual Revenues, Libertys, Privileges to confiscate, to raise Taxes, and other Rights, lawfully obtain'd from the Emperor and Empire, or enjoy'd long before these Commotions, with a full Jurisdiction within the inclosure of their Walls, and their Territorys: making void at the same time, annulling and for the future prohibiting all Things, which by Reprisals, Arrests, stopping of Passages, and other prejudicial Acts, either during the War, under what pretext soever they have been done and attempted hitherto by private Authority, or may hereafter without any preceding formality of Right be enterpris'd. As for the rest, all laudable Customs of the sacred Roman Empire, the fundamental Constitutions and Laws, shall for the future be strictly observ'd, all the Confusions which time of War have, or could introduce, being remov'd and laid aside....

LXX. The Rights and Privileges of Territorys, water'd by Rivers or otherways, as Customs granted by the Emperor, with the Consent of the Electors, and among others, to the Count of Oldenburg on the Viserg, and introduc'd by a long Usage, shall remain in their Vigour and Execution. There shall be a full Liberty of Commerce, a secure Passage by Sea and Land: and after this manner all and every one of the Vassals, Subjects, Inhabitants and Servants of the Allys, on the one side and the other, shall have full power to go and come, to trade and return back, by Virtue of this present Article, after the same manner as was allowed before the Troubles of Germany; the Magistrates, on the one side and on the other, shall be oblig'd to protect and defend them against all sorts of Oppressions, equally with their own Subjects, without prejudice to the other Articles of this Convention, and the particular laws and Rights of each place. And that the said Peace and Amity between the Emperor and the Most Christian King, may be the more corroborated, and the publick Safety provided for, it has been agreed with the Consent, Advice and Will of the Electors, Princes and States of the Empire, for the Benefit of Peace....

LXXII. That Monsieur Francis, Duke of Lorain, shall be restor'd to the possession of the Bishoprick of Verdun, as being the lawful Bishop thereof; and shall be left in the peaceable Administration of this Bishoprick and its Abbys (saving the Right of the King and of particular Persons) and shall enjoy his Patrimonial Estates, and his other Rights, wherever they may be situated (and as far as they do not contradict the present Resignation) his Privileges, Revenues and Incomes; having previously taken the Oath of Fidelity to the King, and provided he undertakes nothing against the Good of the State and the Service of his Majesty.

LXXIII. In the second place, the Emperor and Empire resign and transfer to the most Christian King, and his Successors, the Right of direct Lordship and Sovereignty, and all that has belong'd, or might hitherto belong to him, or the sacred Roman Empire, upon Pignerol....

LXXVI. Item, All the Vassals, Subjects, People, Towns, Boroughs, Castles, Houses, Fortresses, Woods, Coppices, Gold or Silver Mines, Minerals, Rivers, Brooks, Pastures; and in a word, all the Rights, Regales and Appurtenances, without any reserve, shall belong to the most Christian King, and shall be for ever incorporated with the Kingdom France, with all manner of Jurisdiction and Sovereignty, without any contradiction from the Emperor, the Empire, House of Austria, or any other: so that no Emperor, or any Prince of the House of Austria, shall, or ever ought to usurp, nor so much as pretend any Right and Power over the said Countrys, as well on this, as the other side the Rhine.

LXXVII. The most Christian King shall, nevertheless, be oblig'd to preserve in all and every one of these Countrys the Catholick Religion, as maintain'd under the Princes of Austria, and to abolish all Innovations crept in during the War....

LXXXI. For the greater Validity of the said Cessions and Alienations, the Emperor and Empire, by virtue of this present Treaty, abolish all and every one of the Decrees, Constitutions, Statutes and Customs of their Predecessors, Emperors of the sacred Roman Empire, tho they have been confirm'd by Oath, or shall be confirm'd for the future; particularly this Article of the Imperial Capitulation, by which all or any Alienation of the Appurtenances and Rights of the Empire is prohibited: and by the same means they exclude for ever all Exceptions hereunto, on what Right and Titles soever they may be grounded.

LXXXII. Further it has been agreed, That besides the Ratification promis'd hereafter in the next Diet by the Emperor and the States of the Empire, they shall ratify anew the Alienations of the said Lordships and Rights: insomuch, that if it shou'd be agreed in the Imperial Capitulation, or if there shou'd be a Proposal made for the future, in the Diet, to recover the Lands and Rights of the Empire, the abovenam'd things shall not be comprehended therein, as having been legally transfer'd to another's Dominion, with the common Consent of the States, for the benefit of the publick Tranquillity; for which reason it has been found expedient the said Seigniorys shou'd be ras'd out of the Matricular-Book of the Empire....

LXXXIX. ... No King of France can or ought ever to; pretend to or usurp any Right or Power over the said Countrys situated on this and the other side the Rhine:...

XCII. That the most Christian King shall be bound to leave not only the Bishops of Strasburg and

Basle, with the City of Strasburg, but also the other States or Orders, ... so that he cannot pretend any Royal Superiority over them, but shall rest contented with the Rights which appertain'd to the House of Austria, and which by this present Treaty of Pacification, are yielded to the Crown of France. In such a manner, nevertheless, that by the present Declaration, nothing is intended that shall derogate from the Sovereign Dominion already hereabove agreed to....

XCIX. Who hereafter, with the Authority and Consent of their Imperial and most Christian Majestys, by virtue of this solemn Treaty of Peace, shall have no Action for this account against the Duke of Savoy, or his Heirs and Successors....

CIV. As soon as the Treaty of Peace shall be sign'd and seal'd by the Plenipotentiarys and Ambassadors, all Hostilitys shall cease, and all Partys shall study immediately to put in execution what has been agreed to;... That when it shall be known that the signing has been made in these two Places, divers Couriers shall presently be sent to the Generals of the Armys, to acquaint them that the Peace is concluded, and take care that the Generals chuse a Day, on which shall be made on all sides a Cessation of Arms and Hostilitys for the publishing of the Peace in the Army; and that command be given to all and each of the chief Officers Military and Civil, and to the Governors of Fortresses, to abstain for the future from all Acts of Hostility: and if it happen that any thing be attempted, or actually innovated after the said Publication, the same shall be forthwith repair'd and restor'd to its former State.

CV. The Plenipotentiarys on all sides shall agree among themselves, between the Conclusion and the Ratification of the Peace, upon the Ways, Time, and Securitys which are to be taken for the Restitution of Places, and for the Disbanding of Troops; of that both Partys may be assur'd, that all things agreed to shall be sincerely accomplish'd.

CVI. The Emperor above all things shall publish an Edict thro'out the Empire, and strictly enjoin all, who by these Articles of Pacification are oblig'd to restore or do any thing else, to obey it promptly and without tergi-versation, between the signing and the ratifying of this present Treaty; commanding as well the Directors as Governors of the Militia of the Circles, to hasten and finish the Restitution to be made to every one, in conformity to those Conventions, when the same are demanded....

CVII. If any of those who are to have something restor'd to them, suppose that the Emperor's Commissarys are necessary to be present at the Execution of some Restitution (which is left to their Choice) they shall have them. In which case, that the effect of the things agreed on may be the less hinder'd, it shall be permitted as well to those who restore, as to those to whom Restitution is to be made, to nominate two or three Commissarys immediately after the signing of the Peace, of whom his Imperial Majesty shall chuse two, one of each Religion, and one of each Party, whom he shall injoin to accomplish without delay all that which ought to be done by virtue of this present Treaty....

CVIII. Finally, That all and every one either States, Commonaltys, or private Men, either Ecclesiastical or Secular, who by virtue of this Transaction and its general Articles, or by the express and special Disposition of any of them, are oblig'd to restore, transfer, give, do, or execute any thing, shall be bound forthwith after the Publication of the Emperor's Edicts, and after Notification given, to restore, transfer, give, do, or execute the same, without any Delay or Exception, or evading Clause either general or particular, contain'd in the precedent Amnesty, and without any Exception and Fraud as to what they are oblig'd unto....

CXII. That the very Places, Citys, Towns, Boroughs, Villages, Castles, Fortresses and Forts ... shall be restor'd without delay to their former and lawful Possessors and Lords, whether they be mediately or immediately States of the Empire, Ecclesiastical or Secular, comprehending therein also the free Nobility of the Empire: and they shall be left at their own free disposal, either according to Right and Custom, or according to the Force this present Treaty....

CXIII. And that this Restitution of possess'd Places, as well by his Imperial Majesty as the most Christian King, and the Allys and Adherents of the one and the other Party, shall be reciprocally and bona fide executed.

CXIV. That the Records, Writings and Documents, and other Moveables, be also restor'd....

CXV. That the Inhabitants of each Place shall be oblig'd, when the Soldiers and Garisons draw out, to furnish them without Money the necessary Waggons, Horses, Boats and Provisions, to carry off all things to the appointed Places in the Empire....

CXVII. That it shall not for the future, or at present, prove to the damage and prejudice of any Town, that has been taken and kept by the one or other Party; but that all and every one of them, with their Citizens and Inhabitants, shall enjoy as well the general Benefit of the Amnesty, as the rest of this Pacification. And for the Remainder of their Rights and

Privileges, Ecclesiastical and Secular, which they enjoy'd before these Troubles, they shall be maintain'd therein; save, nevertheless the Rights of Sovereignty, and what depends thereon, for the Lords to whom they belong.

CXVIII. Finally, that the Troops and Armys of all those who are making War in the Empire, shall be disbanded and discharg'd; only each Party shall send to and keep up as many Men in his own Dominion, as he shall judge necessary for his Security.

CXIX. The Ambassadors and Plenipotentiarys of the Emperor, of the King, and the States of the Empire, promise respectively and the one to the other, to cause the Emperor, the most Christian King, the Electors of the Sacred Roman Empire, the Princes and States, to agree and ratify the Peace which has been concluded in this manner, and by general Consent; and so infallibly to order it, that the solemn Acts of Ratification be presented at Munster, and mutually and in good form exchang'd in the term of eight weeks, to reckon from the day of signing....

CXXI. That it never shall be alledg'd, allow'd, or admitted, that any Canonical or Civil Law, any general or particular Decrees of Councils, any Privi-

leges, any Indulgences, any Edicts, any Commissions, Inhibitions, Mandates, Decrees, Rescripts, Suspensions of Law, Judgments pronounc'd at any time, Adjudications, Capitulations of the Emperor, and other Rules and Exceptions of Religious Orders, past or future Protestations, Contradictions, Appeals, Investitures, Transactions, Oaths, Renunciations, Contracts, and much less the Edict of 1629 or the Transaction of Prague, with its Appendixes, or the Concordates with the Popes, or the Interims of the Year 1548. or any other politick Statutes, or Ecclesiastical Decrees, Dispensations, Absolutions, or any other Exceptions, under what pretence or colour they can be invented; shall take place against this Convention, or any of its Clauses and Articles neither shall any inhibitory or other Processes or Commissions be ever allow'd to the Plaintiff or Defendant.

CXXXII. That he who by his Assistance or Counsel shall contravene this Transaction or Publick Peace, or shall oppose its Execution and the abovesaid Restitution, or who shall have endeavour'd, after the Restitution has been lawfully made, and without exceeding the manner agreed on before, without a lawful Cog-

Glossary

Allodations	lands or estates held outright, with no ties of feudal obligation
Cessions and Alienations	territories ceded or otherwise conveyed to other parties
Diets of the Empire	qualified legislative bodies of the participating states
Edict of 1619 or the Transaction of Prague,...	attempts made during the war to reinstate Catholicism into formerly Protestant areas; their inclusion here is simply to state that the Treaty of Westphalia supersedes any and all previous such agreements
his most Christian Majesty	Louis XIV, king of France
his Sacred Imperial Majesty	Ferdinand III, ruler of the Holy Roman Empire and eldest son of Emperor Ferdinand II
Imperial Capitulation	approval of the treaty, a statement saying that the emperor will have to capitulate to the dictates of Westphalia
Laick	secular
renewing the Matricular-Book	renewal of imperial allegiance within the Holy Roman Empire
Moveables	personal property
regales	royal prerogatives

nizance of the Cause, and without the ordinary Course of Justice, to molest those that have been restor'd, whether Ecclesiasticks or Laymen; he shall incur the Punishment of being an Infringer of the publick Peace, and Sentence given against him according to the Constitutions of the Empire, so that the Restitution and Reparation may have its full effect.

CXXIII. That nevertheless the concluded Peace shall remain in force, and all Partys in this Transaction shall be oblig'd to defend and protect all and every Article of this Peace against any one, without distinction of Religion; and if it happens any point shall be violated, the Offended shall before all things exhort the Offender not to come to any Hostility, submitting the Cause to a friendly Composition, or the ordinary Proceedings of Justice....

CXXVI. And as often as any would march Troops thro' the other Territorys, this Passage shall be done at the charge of him whom the Troops belong to, and that without burdening or doing any harm or damage to those whole Countrys they march thro'. In a word, all that the Imperial Constitutions determine and ordain touching the Preservation of the publick Peace, shall be strictly observ'd....

CXXVIII. In Testimony of all and each of these things, and for their greater Validity, the Ambassadors of their Imperial and most Christian Majestys, and the Deputys, in the name of all the Electors, Princes, and States of the Empire, sent particularly for this end (by virtue of what has been concluded the 13th of October, in the Year hereafter mention'd, and has been deliver'd....

And that on condition that by the Subscription of the abovesaid Ambassadors and Deputys, all and every one of the other States who shall abstain from signing and ratifying the present Treaty, shall be no less oblig'd to maintain and observe what is contained in this present Treaty of Pacification, than if they had subscrib'd and ratify'd it; and no Protestation or Contradiction of the Council of Direction in the Roman Empire shall be valid, or receiv'd in respect to the Subscription and said Deputys have made.

Done, pass'd and concluded at Munster in Westphalia, the 24th Day of October, 1648.

ULOZHENIE, OR GREAT MUSCOVITE LAW CODE

1649

"Return fugitive peasants and landless peasants from flight ... to people of all ranks."

Overview

The Ulozhenie was Muscovite Russia's main legal code, and it was issued by Alexis I Mikhaylovich ("Alexei Mikhailovich" in the document) in 1649. Its full title, Sobornoe Ulozhenie, literally means "Collected Code of Laws." It is sometimes also referred to in English as the Great Muscovite Law Code of 1649. It replaced the Sudebniki (law codes) of Ivan III Vasilyevich (1497) and Ivan IV Vasilyevich (1550). These codes had promoted state centralization and the rise of state and legal bureaucracies. The Ulozhenie—a complex document running well over two hundred pages in modern printings—continued this process. It is primarily known, however, for its passages on serfdom, which take up only a few pages. The code represented the legal climax of a long historical process whereby Russia's once-free peasants (about 90 percent of the total population) had been reduced to a form of serfdom often compared to slavery. The new code terminated the few remaining rights of movement left to serfs from earlier legislation; ended time limitations on the return of runaways; eroded the differences between serf and slave classes (the two categories remained legally distinct until 1723, however); and pronounced the resulting system hereditary, permanent, and irrevocable. More generally, the Ulozhenie was a striking statement of political authority and social hierarchy, covering topics that included the relation of various social classes to the state and questions of authority within families.

Context

Several factors contributed to the creation and promulgation of the Ulozhenie. Ostensibly, it was an effort to bring order to a corpus of law that, owing to the issuance of numerous edicts over the previous two centuries, had become confusing, contradictory, and ineffective. A more specific trigger was a major riot that shook Moscow in 1648. The riot was in response to an unpopular salt tax and perceived corruption and abuses among state officials. More generally, the Ulozhenie was intended as a means of enforcing authority, order, and social hierarchy in a state that had suffered numerous major upheavals in the preceding decades, including foreign invasions, civil war, peasant uprisings, "false" czars, and mass migrations, many of them connected with the difficult interregnum of 1598 to 1613 known as the Time of Troubles. This traumatic period followed the death in 1598 of Fyodor I Ivanovich, son of Ivan IV (known as Ivan the Terrible). Fyodor was the last member of the seven-century-old Rurik Dynasty of Russian rulers. The Time of Troubles almost led to the complete collapse of Russia and the establishment of Polish Catholic rule in Moscow. Ultimately, however, it instead spawned a broad-based national movement for the regeneration of Muscovite and Orthodox Christian Russia as well as a deeply ingrained sense of the need for strong, central rule and clear lines of authority. The Ulozhenie addressed all these concerns.

As noted, some of the Ulozhenie's most important articles involve serfdom, specifically its transformation into virtual slavery. From the founding in 878 of Kievan Rus (the first ancestor state to both modern Russia and Ukraine, with its capital at Kiev), most peasants had enjoyed considerable freedom and independence. Typically organized in groups, they often entered voluntarily into agricultural communes, including on privately owned land, in order to produce and share food and other necessities. They left when they wished. Affairs changed little in this regard, even as Kiev's influence waned and Rus fragmented during the eleventh and twelfth centuries into an increasingly decentralized collection of principalities. The peasants' freedoms began seriously to erode, however, with the arrival of the Mongols, whose armies—primarily made up of Turkic Tatars under Mongol leadership—conquered most of the Rus from 1237 to 1241. The Mongol-Tatar hordes did not occupy their conquered areas but instead became absentee tax-collectors. They delegated to subordinate Rus princes the task of collecting payments from Russian peasant communes and other entities. Thus, the Rus princes came to wield considerable power over the communes and peasant constituents. Over the next two hundred years, one Russian principality, Moscow, increased its tax-collecting authority and political power prodigiously. By the end of the reign of Ivan III ("the

CA. 1019

- The Russkaia Pravda, or Justice of the Rus, the first secular Russian law code, is issued sometime during the reign of Yaroslav the Wise, Grand Prince of Kiev.

1497

- The first major rescript of Russian law, the Sudebnik of Grand Prince Ivan III, is promulgated. It promotes state centralization and peasant enserfment.

1533

- The reign of Ivan IV begins, ushering in more than fifty years of brutal struggles for personal power and state centralization that devastate many parts of Russia and cause major peasant flight; labor shortages result, leading to efforts to further limit peasant movement.

1550

- Ivan IV issues a new Sudebnik that advances the processes of state centralization and peasant enserfment.

1598

- **January 6**
  Fyodor I dies without an heir, ending over seven centuries of rule by the descendents of Rurik, the semilegendary first prince of the Rus. A chaotic interregnum known as the Time of Troubles follows.

Great"), in the first decade of sixteenth century the principality of Moscow had achieved two critical goals: the unification of most of the Russian lands under its own control and the end of Mongol-Tatar domination.

The resulting state was known as Muscovite Russia, or simply Muscovy, and its success and continued development was based in large part on the ever-increasing enserfment of the Russian peasantry. The reason for this lay in the importance of land grants. Church officials and nobles from many Russian lands had cooperated with power-hungry Muscovite princes primarily in return for permanent grants of land. Thereafter, during the fifteenth and sixteenth centuries, ever-more grants were made; increasingly, they went to the lower-ranking "service gentry" as revocable payment for ongoing state service, usually in civil administration or as military officers. Thus, there evolved two main types of land grant: permanent hereditary ones known as *votchiny* (held mainly by the nobility) and temporary service-related ones known as *pomestie* (held by the service gentry).

Regardless of type, the value of a land grant was determined almost entirely by the presence of peasants, who provided income in the form of labor and crops—the primary and often the only sources of revenue for the landlord. Until the late fifteenth century, it had remained common for landlords to negotiate terms of labor with peasants residing upon their lands. The two groups often had opposite interests, however. The landlords wanted permanent and reliable workers and ever-higher incomes. The peasants valued their freedom and independence, and they resented encroaching authority and rising taxation. Often, they simply moved on, leaving their landlords to face untended fields and economic hardship. The absence of natural boundaries and the lure of seemingly endless horizons to the east and south compounded the problem. Flight was especially common during the dislocations of the Time of Troubles.

Among landlords, however, the service gentry were especially vulnerable, since they faced the additional threat of having their peasants seized and transferred wholesale to the estates of higher-ranking and more powerful nobles. Thus, it was the service gentry who most actively pressured the state for help. Since Muscovy relied heavily on them for services and loyalty, as well as on military recruits from their lands, their pleas were taken to heart.

The state responded in stages. Ivan III's 1497 Sudebnik barred peasants from moving at any time of the year except during a two-week period at the end of the harvest, around Saint George's Day. Peasants also had to fulfill all contracted obligations to their landlords and pay a large contract-release fee. Continued peasant flight spurred ever-more repressive countermeasures. In 1570 in parts of the province of Novgorod, Ivan IV declared a one-off "prohibited year," during which peasants would not be able to move for any reason, even around Saint George's Day, regardless of their ability to pay all debts and release fees. Thereafter, the concept was applied more widely. By the 1580s prohibited years had become the norm throughout Muscovite Russia. Instead, the state designated occasional "free years." The last one was in 1602. Around the same time, the statute of limitations on recovery of a runaway peasant was increased, reaching fifteen years in the first part of the sixteenth century. The Ulozhenie abolished the limitation altogether, and subsequent legislation criminalized peasant flight.

The service gentry also lobbied the state for permanent possession of their service lands and for the right to pass them on as heritable property. The Ulozhenie reinforced the legal distinction between the two. In practice, however, service lands were treated increasingly as hereditary possessions as the sixteenth century progressed.

About the Author

The Ulozhenie was established at the order of Czar Alexis I. Alexis was born in March of 1629 and took the throne at the age of sixteen. His father and royal predecessor, Mikhail, was the founder of the Romanov Dynasty. Most historians consider Alexis to have been a pious and fairly effective ruler. Conservative rather than reactionary, he was cautiously favorable to reforms that appeared likely to strengthen or preserve tradition and authority, such as a new and more comprehensive law code. He was also distinguished by an ability to choose wise and talented advisers and to give them sufficient freedom of action. This latter trait is also clearly exemplified by the Ulozhenie, which Alexis authorized but did not compose. He died in 1676.

In the early summer of 1648, Alexis consulted with Patriarch Joseph of Moscow, church officials, boyars (nobles), and other prominent advisers. Then, on July 16, he appointed a five-person commission headed by the talented and prominent state servant Nikita Odoevsky and ordered them to compile a draft law. This was done by October 3. Odoevsky, a favorite also of the previous czar, was a minor noble who had already carved out successful careers for himself as a diplomat and military commander. Before being recruited for work on the Ulozhenie, he had proved himself in legal affairs, running the chancelleries of Kazan and Siberia. His commission drew on a wide body of existing legislation, including past legal cases, earlier Russian secular law codes, Orthodox ecclesiastical law, and Byzantine and Lithuanian codes. The draft was then amended and expanded by an "Assembly of the Land," comprising men from every rank of society (except the peasant masses) and two noblemen from each town. All these men were required to read and sign the finished product. The Ulozhenie was essentially a compilation and codification of existing laws, rather than an original composition. Nonetheless it is considered one of the great achievements of Russian literature prior to the nineteenth century.

Explanation and Analysis of the Document

The complete Ulozhenie is divided into twenty-five chapters, each dealing with a different general topic or leg-

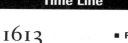

Time Line

1613

■ **February**
The Time of Troubles ends with the election of Mikhail Romanov as czar, beginning the Romanov Dynasty that rules Russia until 1917; at the same time the Russian state focuses increasingly on building social order and political authority.

1645

■ **July 12**
Alexis I, second czar of the Romanovs, takes the Russian throne.

1648

■ **June 2**
Crowds riot in Moscow, upset over high taxes and government corruption and demanding that the czar stem abuses and issue a new law code.

■ **July 16**
Alexis I appoints a commission to undertake the composition of the Ulozhenie.

1649

■ **January 29**
The Ulozhenie is officially approved. The enserfment of the Russian peasantry is now essentially complete. It will persist largely unchanged for more than two centuries.

islative area. They are presented in a specific order, corresponding to the importance or status accorded to each at the time, from the highest to the lowest. Thus, Chapter 1 considers the honor and authority of God and his church, the second chapter treats the personal honor of the czar, the third looks at matters of conduct in the czar's court, and so on. The final chapter (the "lowest," not excerpted here) treats unlawful taverns. The chapters between consider a wealth of issues, including the mint and currency, travel and foreigners, various ranks of service personnel, tolls and fees, the judicial process at various social levels, monasteries, different categories of landholding, social and political estates, slaves and serfs, robbery and theft, the death penalty, and palace musketeers. Some chapters are short—the one on palace musketeers has only three articles. Others are much longer. There are, for instance, 104 articles on robbery and theft and 119 on the judicial process regarding slaves. The longest of all, at 287 articles, considers the judicial process in general.

◆ Chapter 1: Blasphemers and Church Troublemakers

Chapter 1 begins with assertions of the supreme authority of God and of the one true faith (Russian Orthodoxy). Insults or offenses against either God or the church are especially serious crimes and are to be punished harshly. All aspects of the Russian Orthodox Church—its physical spaces, personnel, and rituals—are given special status. Crimes perpetrated within or against the church are to be treated separately from similar acts in other places. On the other hand, several articles call for the crime to be properly ascertained before punishment is meted out, thus suggesting the close connections between divinity and true justice. It should be noted that the law, while applicable in all churches, was written largely with the places of worship of the czar and elite classes in mind (especially places of worship within the Kremlin). This is evident in articles 8 and 9.

◆ Chapter 2: The Sovereign's Honor, and How to Safeguard His Royal Well-Being

Speaking generally, in Russian history, church and state were less antagonistic than is the case in the Catholic West. To some extent, this reflected the relative weakness of the Russian Orthodox Church, but it was also symptomatic of the mutually reinforcing role of each in the overall system of political power. Although the czar was not inferior to the Russian Orthodox Church, he was certainly inferior to God. Hence his powers and authorities are enumerated in Chapter 2, not Chapter 1. There is little here to distinguish the concept of the state from the person of the czar. Instead, the two are seen as more or less synonymous. Some of the clauses seem draconian. Articles 6 and 7 equate knowledge of treason with the act itself, for example. One senses a degree of paranoia also in the calls for "rigorous investigation" (article 9) and the like, although these are balanced to some degree by mercy for the innocent.

◆ Chapter 6: Travel Documents into Other States

This short chapter of six articles deals with foreign travel and clearly reflects state insecurities and xenophobia. Evidencing concern about possible connections between travel and treason, this chapter establishes a passport system. Unlike modern systems, however, permission was necessary for each separate trip. Such permissions were potentially available only to persons involved in commercial activity or others whose reasons for travel were deemed acceptable and useful to the state. The masses of peasants, tied irrevocably to their owners' estates by legislation elsewhere in the Ulozhenie, would not have been able to apply for permission. Note that this chapter tries to balance restrictions on travel with countervailing attempts not to hamper trade and commerce or to condemn people simply for living near an international border. The chapter focuses only on the czar's subjects and does not explicitly treat foreign nationals coming into Russia.

◆ Chapter 10: The Judicial Process

This chapter speaks to a basic goal of the Ulozhenie: the creation of a state of law, with all the apparatuses, offices, and procedures that might require. Alexis's concept of a state of law should not be misunderstood, however. In the Ulozhenie there is no concept of people as individuals, imbued with natural rights or equal before the law. Instead, the assumptions are that the law exists to serve the interests of the state (largely synonymous with the person and authority of the czar) and that persons will be treated collectively according to social order, religion, nationality, and other factors. As evidence of the high level of concern for creating a state of law, the chapter contains 287 articles, the most by far of any in the code. Only the first six are reproduced here; but they suggest the basic parameters of the overall system.

The czar emphasizes his own authority. The Ulozhenie and the legal system more generally are *his* possessions and expressions of *his* will—even if specific and important tasks must be delegated to boyars, *okol'nichie*, and others. Boyars were hereditary nobles in state service and held the highest rank in the Muscovite social hierarchy; *okol'nichie* were second in rank. There were at least eighteen different service ranks at the time. Beyond this initial statement, however, the czar calls for impartiality, honesty, and adherence to the principles and rulings of his code, both by the Muscovite court and in the provinces.

◆ Chapter 11: The Judicial Process for Peasants

This chapter includes thirty-four articles; about two-thirds of them are reproduced here. It is in this chapter that we find the legal basis for the full-fledged system of serfdom with which the social history of Russia from the seventeenth to nineteenth centuries is nearly synonymous.

Article 1 establishes the tone of the chapter. It takes as a reference point the cadastral books of 1626, which showed the place of registration of peasant families at that time. In some cases, a later census of 1646–1647 provided the reference point. The article calls for all runaway peasants and their descendants—along with their wives, children, and "movable property"—to be returned to their original estates "without any statute of limitations" regardless of where they currently reside. Article 1 deals specifically with peasants originally registered on crown lands (the "sovereign's peasants"); article 2 extends the ruling to all categories of landowners. According to the law, a peasant originally registered with a member of the service gentry (such as a *stol'nik* or *striapchii*) but now living elsewhere must also be returned to his place of registration as of 1626. Note that this rule applied even to peasants who had moved onto lands belonging directly to the czar. Thus, the first two articles establish a basic and draconian principle: Peasants have only one rightful and lawful place to live, the place at which they were properly and originally registered. They and their descendants were to be returned there no matter how long they had lived at some other place.

Article 3 establishes that the law would not be used to punish landlords who have previously held runaway peasants, only those landlords who would do so henceforth. This surely suggests the scale of the issue. No doubt "runaways" were extremely common. More generally, this article and numerous others throughout the code deal with the many problems, disputes, and uncertainties bound to arise as soon as efforts began to establish the "rightful" place of residence of any given peasant or peasant family. What should one do, for example, when marriages have been made among peasants not registered on the same estate in 1626? To which estate should the resulting family and any descendants properly belong? Should the larger family be broken up? And what about the "vacant houses" of runaway peasants (article 5)? On these and other similar issues, the Ulozhenie generally calls for proper investigations and trials, and it establishes that complications based on actions taken before passage of the law should be treated with some sympathy. Future actions, by contrast, are to be dealt with more legalistically. Article 10, for example, specifically calls for a fine of ten rubles per peasant per year to be levied against any landlord under whom fugitive peasants are living. Articles 12 to 19 and 33 to 34 cover a range of specific—and probably common—scenarios, such as first and second marriages, widows, and persons who cross the frontier or marry foreigners.

The law greatly affected not only peasants but also landowners. For the most part, the idea was to help them secure and retain labor for their landholdings. But the code could also cause them problems. Article 7, for example, treats the case of a landowner whose peasants are found after investigation to be the lawful property of another and therefore subject to removal. Articles 20 and 21 place upon landowners the responsibility of properly ascertaining the current legal status of persons wishing to settle on their estates. No doubt this would have presented a burden to landowners, and there was always the chance that a landlord, even one who intended to follow the law properly, might make a mistake or be deceived by his peasants. That landlord would still risk being levied a hefty fine.

Alexis I (© Bettmann/CORBIS)

◆ Chapter 16: Service Lands

Service lands (*pomestie*) were estates granted in return for state service and, at least originally, only for the duration of that service. These lands provided their holders with income and security. Article 1 lists various ranks of the service class along with the standard size of land grant for each. Articles 2 and 3 try to bring order and fairness to the process of land-grant swaps, which might occur if a member of the service gentry were to be transferred or moved or for other reasons. Although these lands were not hereditary possessions, they could, with government approval, be passed along to a relative or descendant, who would usually inherit the service obligation as well. As can be seen in articles 9 to 11 and 16, service lands also constituted a form of social insurance that provided income to retirees, widows, and unmarried daughters from the service class. A separate chapter of the Ulozhenie (not reproduced here) provided the legal framework for hereditary estates (*votchiny*).

◆ Chapter 19: Townsmen

This chapter establishes yet another social category: the "townsmen." Only the first article of a total of forty is reproduced here. It shows the czar's intent to exert his will, centralize control, and improve the collection of taxes from people and places either previously exempt under the authority of other high-ranking persons, such as the Russian Orthodox patriarch, or from whom it had otherwise been hard to collect taxes. By the seventeenth century,

> "If believers in non-Orthodox faiths, of whatever creed, or a Russian, casts abuse on the Lord God and our Savior Jesus Christ, or on the Lady Most Pure Who gave birth to Him, our Mother of God the Chaste Maiden Mary, or on the Holy Cross, or on His Holy Saints: rigorously investigate this by all methods of inquiry. If that is established conclusively: having convicted the blasphemer, execute him by burning him [in a cage]."
>
> (Chapter 1, Article 1)

> "Having hunted down those fugitive peasants and landless peasants of the sovereign, cart them [back] to the sovereign's court villages and to the rural taxpaying districts, to their old allotments as [registered in] the cadastral books, with their wives, and with their children, and with all their movable peasant property, without any statute of limitations."
>
> (Chapter 11, Article 1)

> "Return fugitive peasants and landless peasants from flight on the basis of the cadastral books to people of all ranks, without any statue of limitations."
>
> (Chapter 11, Article 2)

towns had become the loci of significant commercial activity and thus also of potential taxable wealth. When townsmen moved, those taxes, which generally were levied collectively rather than individually, often went uncollected. Beginning with the official approval of the Ulozhenie in 1649, townsmen were required to remain were they were, and they could, like serfs, be forcibly returned if they moved elsewhere without authorization. In return, they obtained certain monopolies on trade and commercial activities. In this article, a "limited service contract slave" is distinguished by possession of a contract stipulating the duration and nature of servitude. *"Deti boiarskie"* refers to a middle rank within the provincial, as opposed to the Muscovite, service class.

◆ **Chapter 21: Robbery and Theft Cases**

This chapter deals harsh justice to those found guilty of the offenses of robbery and theft. Note that articles 9 and 10 do not treat simply the crime at hand but prescribe routine torture to uncover other potential offenses. The underlying assumption is that a person who has been caught committing one crime likely committed others. Crime is thus understood as a symptom of a certain character type,

rather than as just an instance of illegal activity. Article 12 requires the death sentence for a third offense, except in the case of theft from a church (article 14), which is punishable by death for the first offense.

◆ **Chapter 22: Decree: For Which Offenses the Death Penalty Should Be Inflicted on Someone, and for Which Offenses the Penalty Should Not Be Death but [Another] Punishment Should Be Imposed**

This chapter contains twenty-six articles, half of which are reproduced here. Many of these articles exemplify the Ulozhenie's emphasis on clear hierarchy, unquestionable authority, and strict punishment. They are largely untempered by concerns for mitigating circumstances and possible exceptions. When reading the first articles, dealing with murders within families, it should be kept in mind that the law's authors imagined the nuclear family as a microcosm of the larger "state family." The authority given to parents, especially fathers, as heads of families mirrors that assumed by the czar over his larger "family"—the population of the Muscovite state. Similarly, the lack of power given to children represents in microcosm the subordination of all subjects to their social superiors and ultimately to the czar.

Thus, crimes committed by children against their parents are considered extremely serious, while crimes committed by parents against their children are reckoned to be minor. Following articles 5 and 6, any complaints made by children against their parents are to be ignored and even punished, but their responsibility to care for and feed their parents in old age is sacrosanct. Of course, one can also see in these articles the influence of some of the Ten Commandments, rather strictly and literally applied.

Returning to family themes, articles 14 to 16 reflect the harsh patriarchal culture of the time. A man's authority over his wife is considered absolute and sacred. A woman who violates this order by murdering her husband has committed a terrible crime. Whereas clauses treating the murder of a master by his slave (not reproduced here) simply call for the slave's death, article 14 goes so far as to prescribe the manner of the offending wife's execution. The seriousness of her action, as viewed by Muscovite culture, is further emphasized in the same article by the refusal to contemplate any mitigating circumstances or calls for leniency made by the children or other relatives. This stands in stark contrast to some other parts of the code, where a clear concern is indeed shown for mitigating circumstances and intent (see, for example, article 20 in this chapter). Note, however, that article 15 stipulates that the wife's crime, though unpardonable, is not to be paid for by the death of any innocent unborn child. The concern shown in article 16 for a woman's honor echoes the partriarchalism of article 14 in that it seeks primarily to protect the exclusive ownership of the wife by her husband. The use of the term "mistress of that house" speaks to the fact that the law had in mind primarily elite women and not the ordinary peasant, whose affairs were largely regulated by this time by their landlords. Articles 24 to 26 return to religious themes and freely mix elements of harsh legalism with Christian compassion.

Audience

As a general statement of state authority and social hierarchy, the Ulozhenie was intended ultimately for the entire Russian populace. It would, however, have been directly read or encountered only by a small literate minority, especially members of the service gentry, court officials, and the church hierarchy. Twelve hundred copies were made in the spring of 1649, and a further twelve hundred in the winter. Both quickly sold out, with the majority of copies probably going to courts and other government offices in Moscow and throughout provincial towns, where it henceforth provided the framework for legal cases and procedures (with the main exception of cases coming under church jurisdiction). It is unclear how well the document would have been known by litigants, at least in the first decades after publication. The illiterate masses of serfs would have come to know of the Ulozhenie only slowly, sporadically, and dimly. Parts of it might have been read to them by priests or landlords, perhaps as justification for their removal to another estate. Aspects of it would have spread by word of mouth. Generally, however, at this time and later, peasants tended to attribute their exploitation and suffering not to the czar or to any specific piece of legislation, but instead to landlords, local officials, and other persons of whom they had direct experience.

Impact

All classes of persons were affected by the Ulozhenie. The law's most enduring and significant consequences centered on its codification of serfdom, however. This system became the backbone of the economy and a fundamental determinant of the historical trajectory of the Russian state. Although serfdom had long provided both elites and the

---

Questions for Further Study

1. What was the impact of the Ulozhenie on the peasantry in Moscovite Russia? What role did land and land ownership play in the condition of the peasantry both before and after the promulgation of the new law code?

2. What social, political, and economic factors led to the formation of the Ulozhenie? What role did religion play in the process?

3. During this period in Russian history, considerable attention was given to the issue of unifying Russian territories under a central government. What historical and geographical factors might have prompted this concern?

4. Compare this law code with the eleventh-century Justice of the Rus. How are the codes similar? How do they differ? Does the Ulozhenie represent an evolution of law in Russia? What historical and cultural factors in Russia may have accounted for the differences?

5. What lasting effect did the Ulozhenie have on Russian society and its economy?

state with more or less stable sources of income, labor, and conscripts, it also fostered diverse and huge challenges that ultimately hampered the country's development. Under conditions of serf labor, for example, there was little incentive for investment in more productive or efficient farming methods and technologies, with the result that agriculture in Russia remained less efficient and productive than in many Western European regions. Russia's industrial and military development also lagged for similar reasons. Not surprisingly, the peasants themselves chafed under the burden of serfdom. After 1649, rebellions grew in frequency and scale. Peasant unrest, along with Russia's humiliating defeat in the Crimean War (1853–1856), which also could be traced to serfdom, eventually persuaded Alexander II to abolish the system "from above" in 1861, before the peasants abolished it themselves "from below." By 1861 serfdom was widely blamed for a stifling backwardness in many aspects of Russian society, whether in agriculture, industry, military effectiveness, or public morality.

Further Reading

■ Books

Hellie, Richard, ed. and trans. *The Muscovite Law Code (Ulozhenie) of 1649*. Irvine, Calif.: Charles Schlacks, Jr., 1988.

————. "Russian Law from Oleg to Peter the Great." Foreword to *The Laws of Rus': Tenth to Fifteenth Centuries*, ed. and trans. Daniel H. Kaiser. Salt Lake City, Utah: Charles Schlacks, Jr., 1992.

Longworth, Philip. *Alexis, Tsar of All the Russias*. London: Franklin Watts, 1984.

Pipes, Richard. *Russia under the Old Regime*. 2nd ed. London: Penguin, 1995.

Poe, Marshall T. *The Russian Elite in the Seventeenth Century*. Vol. 2: *A Quantitative Analysis of the "Duma Ranks," 1613–1713*. Helsinki: Finnish Academy of Science and Letters, 2004.

Wirtschafter, Elise Kimerling. *Russia's Age of Serfdom 1649–1861*. Malden, Mass.: Blackwell Publishers, 2008.

—Brian Bonhomme

Ulozhenie, or Great Muscovite Law Code

Chapter 1.—Blasphemers and Church Troublemakers. In It Are 9 Articles.

1. If believers in non-Orthodox faiths, of whatever creed, or a Russian, casts abuse on the Lord God and our Savior Jesus Christ, or on the Lady Most Pure Who gave birth to Him, our Mother of God the Chaste Maiden Mary, or on the Holy Cross, or on His Holy Saints: rigorously investigate this by all methods of inquiry. If that is established conclusively: having convicted the blasphemer, execute him by burning him [in a cage].

2. If a disorderly person, coming into God's church during the holy liturgy, by any action whatsoever does not permit the completion of the divine liturgy: having arrested him and investigated him rigorously [and having established] that he committed such a deed, punish him with death without any mercy.

3. If someone during the holy liturgy [or during] other church services, coming into God's church, proceeds to address indecent remarks to the patriarch, or a metropolitan, or archbishop and bishop, or archimandrite, or father superior and other member of the clerical order, and thereby in the church creates a disturbance for the divine liturgy, and this becomes known to the sovereign, and that is established conclusively: inflict on that disorderly person a beating [with the knout] in the market places for his offense.

4. If someone, coming into God's church, proceeds to assault anyone at all, and kills the person: after investigation, punish that killer himself with death.

5. If [the assailant] wounds someone, but does not kill him: inflict on him a beating [with the knout] in the market places without mercy, cast him in prison for a month, and the injured party shall collect from him a double dishonor compensation for the injury.

6. If such a disorderly person assaults anyone at all in God's church but does not wound [him]: for such an offense beat him with bastinadoes, and the person whom he struck shall collect his dishonor compensation from him.

7. If someone dishonors someone by word, but does not assault [him]: cast him in prison for a month for the offense. The person who was dishonored by him shall exact from him the dishonor com-pensation so that those looking on will not commit such offenses in God's church.

8. In church, during the church services, no one shall petition the Sovereign, Tsar, and Grand Prince of all Russia Aleksei Mikhailovich, or the great lord the most holy Iosif, Patriarch of Moscow and all Russia, or the metropolitans, and archbishops, and bishops about any personal affairs, so that, as a consequence, there will be no disruption of the church services in God's church because God's church is designed for prayer. It is fitting for Orthodox Christians to stand in God's church and pray with fear, and not to contemplate earthly matters.

9. If someone, forgetting the fear of God and disdaining the Tsar's order, proceeds to petition the sovereign, or patriarch, or any other high church officials about his personal affairs in God's church during the church services: cast that petitioner in prison for as long as the sovereign decrees.

Chapter 2.—The Sovereign's Honor, and How to Safeguard His Royal Well-Being. In It Are 22 Articles.

1. If someone by any intent proceeds to think up an evil deed against the sovereign's well-being, and someone denounces his evil intent, and after that denunciation that evil intent of his is established conclusively, that he conceived an evil deed against his tsarist majesty, and he intended to carry it out: after investigation, punish such a person with death.

2. Likewise, if in the realm of his tsarist majesty, someone, desiring to seize possessions of the Muscovite state and to become sovereign, begins to assemble an armed force to effect his evil intention; or, if someone proceeds to make friends with enemies of [his] tsarist majesty, and to establish secret relationships by [exchanging] advisory letters, and to render them aid in various ways so that those enemies of the sovereign, using his secret relationship with the enemy, may take possession of the Muscovite state, or commit any other bad deed; and someone denounces his activity; and after that denunciation his treason is established conclusively: punish such a traitor with death accordingly.

3. If a subject of his tsarist majesty surrenders a town to an enemy in an act of treason; or, a subject of his tsarist majesty receives into the towns foreigners from other states for the purpose of similarly committing treason; and that is established conclusively: punish such traitors with death also.

4. If someone premeditatedly, with treasonous intent, sets fire to a town, or to houses; and at that time, or later, the arsonist is arrested, and that felonious conduct of his is established conclusively: burn him [in a cage] himself without the slightest mercy.

5. Confiscate the service landholdings, and hereditary estates, and movable property of traitors for the sovereign.

6. If the wives and children of such traitors knew about their treason: similarly punish them with death.

7. If a wife did not know about the treason of her husband, or children [did not know] about the treason of their father, and it is established about that conclusively that they did not know about that treason: do not execute them for that, and inflict no punishment on them; [give] them a maintenance allotment from [the executed traitor's] hereditary estates and service landholdings that the sovereign grants.

8. If children remain after [the execution of] a traitor, and those children of his lived separately from him, and not with him [in the same household or on the same estate] prior to his treason, and those children of his did not know about his treason, and they had their own movable property and their hereditary estates were separate from his: do not confiscate from those children of his their movable property and hereditary estates.

9. If someone commits treason, and after him survive a father, or mother, or natural brothers, or half-brothers, or uncles, or any other member of his clan in the Muscovite state; and he lived together with them and they had common movable property and hereditary estates: conduct a rigorous investigation by all methods of inquiry about that traitor to determine whether his father, and mother, and clan knew about his treason. If it is established conclusively that they knew about the treason of that traitor: punish them with death also, and confiscate their hereditary estates, and service landholdings, and movable property for the sovereign.

10. If it is established conclusively about them that they did not know about the treason of that traitor: do not punish them with death, and do not confiscate the service landholdings, and hereditary estates, and movable property from them.

11. If a traitor, having been in another state, comes to the Muscovite state, and the sovereign bestows favor upon him, orders that he be forgiven his offenses: he shall have to earn service landholdings anew. The sovereign is free [to return or otherwise dispose of] his hereditary estates, but his former service landholdings shall not be returned to him.

12. If someone proceeds to denounce someone for a treasonous offense, but does not present any witnesses in support of his denunciation, and no other evidence is presented to convict [the accused], and there is no basis for initiating an investigation into such a treason case: compile a decree about such a treason case, upon rigorous review, as the sovereign decrees....

Chapter 6.—Travel Documents into Other States. In It Are 6 Articles.

1. If someone happens to leave the Muscovite state for a commercial enterprise, or for any other personal purpose, for another state, which state is at peace with the Muscovite state: that person in Moscow shall petition the sovereign, and in the provincial towns the governors, for a travel document. Without a travel document he shall not travel. In the provincial towns the governors shall issue them travel documents without any delay.

2. If governors do not proceed to issue people travel documents quickly, and thus cause people delay and losses, and there are petitioners against them for that, and that is established conclusively: the governors shall be in great disgrace with the sovereign for that. Concerning the fact that they cause people losses: exact [the value of the losses] from them two-fold and return it to the petitioners.

3. If someone travels to any [other] state without a travel document, and then, having been in another state, returns to the Muscovite state; and someone else proceeds to denounce him, [alleging] that he traveled on his own volition without a travel document for treasonous purposes, or for any other reprehensible purpose: on the basis of that denunciation, conduct a rigorous investigation by all methods of inquiry of that person who traveled to another state without the sovereign's travel document. If they say about him in the investigation that he indeed rode into another state without a travel document to commit treason, or for any other reprehensible purpose: after investigation, punish that person with death for treason.

4. If it is revealed during an investigation that he traveled to another state without a travel document on a trading enterprise, but not to commit treason: inflict punishment on him for that, beat him with the knout, so that others looking on will learn not to do that.

5. Concerning the fact that [some of the] sovereign's court villages, and rural taxpaying districts, and hereditary estates and service landholdings in the possession of people of various ranks of the border towns in the provinces are adjacent to Lithuanian and Swedish border land; and the sovereign's lands [in the past] have passed to the Lithuanian and Swedish side, and Lithuanian and Swedish land has passed to the sovereign's side; and the peasants [living in] the sovereign's court and rural taxpaying districts, and service landholders, and hereditary estate owners, and their slaves and peasants travel across those Lithuanian and Swedish frontier lands from town to town without travel documents, and they meet with Lithuanian and Swedish subjects: do not accuse them of any crime for that because they are living adjacent to Lithuanian and Swedish subjects on the frontier.

6. If service landholders and hereditary estate owners of the frontier towns learn of anything reprehensible, or of treason, among their slaves or peasants: they shall inform the sovereign about that, and in the provincial towns shall submit formal denunciations on the matter to the governors, and bring in their own slaves and peasants for arraignment. The governors shall interrogate those people against whom there is an accusation and shall conduct a rigorous investigation about them, concerning the accusation, by all methods of inquiry and shall write the sovereign about this; imprison those people against whom there is a denunciation until the sovereign [issues] a decree....

Chapter 10.—The Judicial Process. In It Are 287 Articles.

1. The judicial process of the Sovereign, Tsar, and Grand Prince of all Russia Aleksei Mikhailovich shall be directed by boyars, and okol'nichie, and counselors, and state secretaries, and various chancellery officials, and judges. All justice shall be meted out to all people of the Muscovite state, from the highest to the lowest rank, according to the law. Moreover, arriving foreigners and various people from elsewhere who are in the Muscovite state shall be tried by that same judicial process and rendered justice by the sovereign's decree according to the law. No one on his own initiative shall out of friendship or out of enmity add anything to or remove anything from judicial records. No one shall favor a friend nor wreak vengeance on an enemy in any matter. No one shall favor anyone in any matter for any reason. All of the sovereign's cases shall be processed without diffidence to the powerful. Deliver the wronged from the hand of the unjust.

2. Disputed cases which for any reason cannot be resolved in the chancelleries shall be transferred from the chancelleries in a report to the Sovereign, Tsar, and Grand Prince of all Russia Aleksei Mikhailovich and to his royal boyars, and okol'nichie, and counselors. The boyars, and okol'nichie, and counselors shall sit in the Palace [of Facets], and by the sovereign's decree shall handle the sovereign's various cases all together.

3. If a judge is an enemy of the plaintiff and a friend, or relative, of the defendant, and the plaintiff proceeds to petition the sovereign about that prior to the trial, [saying] that he is unable to bring a suit before that judge; or if a defendant proceeds to petition prior to a trial that the judge is a friend, or relative, or his plaintiff, and that he is unable to defend himself before that judge: that judge against whom there is such a petition shall not try that plaintiff and defendant. Another judge, whom the sovereign will appoint, shall try them.

4. But if a plaintiff or defendant proceeds to petition against a judge after a trial on grounds that the latter is a relative [of the opposing litigant], or was hostile: do not believe that petition, and do not transfer the case from chancellery to chancellery so that there will be no excessive delay for the plaintiff and defendant in this matter.

5. If a boyar, or okol'nichii, or counselor, or state secretary, or any other judge, in response to bribes of the plaintiff or defendant, or out of friendship or enmity convicts an innocent party and exculpates the guilty party, and that is established conclusively: collect from such judges the plaintiff's claim three-fold, and give it to the plaintiff. Collect the legal fees, and the judicial transaction fee, and the legal tenth for the sovereign from them as well. For that offense a boyar, and okol'nichii, and counselor shall be deprived of his rank. If a judge not of counselor rank commits such an injustice: inflict on those people a beating with the knout in the market place, and henceforth they shall not try judicial cases [i.e., they shall be deprived of their offices].

6. In the provincial towns, apply that same decree to governors, and state secretaries, and various chancellery officials for such injustices....

Chapter 11.—The Judicial Process for Peasants. In It Are 34 Articles.

1. Concerning the sovereign's peasants and landless peasants of court villages and rural taxpaying districts who, having fled from the sovereign's court villages and from the rural taxpaying districts, are now living under the patriarch, or under the metropolitans, and under the archbishops, and the bishop [sic]; or under monasteries; or under boyars, or under *okol'nichie*, and under counselors, and under chamberlains, and under *stol'niki*, and under *striapchie*, and under Moscow *dvoriane*, and under state secretaries, and under *zhil'tsy*, and under provincial *dvoriane* and *deti boiarskie*, and under foreigners, and under all hereditary estate owners and service landholders; and in the cadastral books, which books the census takers submitted to the Service Land Chancellery and to other chancelleries after the Moscow fire of the past year 1626, those fugitive peasants or their fathers were registered [as living] under the sovereign: having hunted down those fugitive peasants and landless peasants of the sovereign, cart them [back] to the sovereign's court villages and to the rural taxpaying districts, to their old allotments as [registered in] the cadastral books, with their wives, and with their children, and with all their movable peasant property, without any statute of limitations.

2. Similarly, if hereditary estate owners and service landholders proceed to petition the sovereign about their fugitive peasants and about landless peasants; and they testify that their peasants and landless peasants, having fled from them, are living in the sovereign's court villages, and in rural taxpaying districts, or as townsmen in the urban taxpaying districts, or as musketeers, or as cossacks, or as gunners, or as any other type of servicemen in the trans-Moscow or in the frontier towns; or under the patriarch, or under the metropolitans, or under the archbishops and bishops; or under monasteries; or under boyars, and under *okol'nichie*, and under counselors, and under chamberlains, and under *stol'niki*, and under *striapchie*, and under Moscow *dvoriane*, and under state secretaries, and under *zhil'tsy*, and under provincial *dvoriane* and *deti boiarskie*, and under foreigners, and under any hereditary estate owners and service landholders: return such peasants and landless peasants after trial and investigation on the basis of the cadastral books, which books the census takers submitted to the Service Land Chancellery after the Moscow fire of the past year 1626, if those fugitive peasants of theirs, or the fathers of those peasants of theirs, were recorded [as living] under them in those cadastral books, or [if] after those cadastral books [were compiled] those peasants, or their children, were recorded in new grants [as living] under someone in books allotting lands or in books registering land transfers. Return fugitive peasants and landless peasants from flight on the basis of the cadastral books to people of all ranks, without any statute of limitations.

3. If it becomes necessary to return fugitive peasants and landless peasants to someone after trial and investigation: return those peasants with their wives, and with their children, and with all their movable property, with their standing grain and with their threshed grain. Do not impose a fine for those peasants [on their current lords] for the years prior to this present Law Code.

Concerning peasants who, while fugitives, married off their unmarried daughters, or sisters, or kinswomen to peasants of those estate owners and service landholders under whom they were living, or elsewhere in another village or hamlet: do not fault that person and, on the basis of the status of those unmarried women, do not hand over the husbands to their former estate owners and service landholders because until the present sovereign's decree there was no rule by the sovereign that no one could receive peasants [to live] under him. [Only] statutes of limitations [on the recovery of] fugitive peasants were decreed and, moreover, in many years after the census takers [did their work], the hereditary estates and service landholdings of many hereditary estate owners and service landholders changed hands.

4. If fugitive peasants and landless peasants are returned to someone: chancellery officials of the sovereign's court villages and the rural taxpaying districts, and estate owners, and service landholders shall get from those people [to whom the fugitives are returned] inventory receipts, signed by them, for those peasants and landless peasants of theirs and their movable property in case of dispute in the future.

Order the town public square scribes to write the inventory receipts in Moscow and in the provincial towns; in villages and hamlets where there are no public square scribes, order the civil administration or church scribes of other villages to write such inventories. They shall issue such inventory receipts signed by their own hand.

Concerning people who are illiterate: those people shall order their own spiritual fathers, or people of the vicinity whom they trust, to sign those inventory receipts in their stead. No one shall order his own priests, and scribes, and slaves to write such inventories so that henceforth there will be no dispute by anybody or with anybody over such inventories.

5. Concerning the vacant houses of peasants and landless peasants, or [their] house lots, registered in the cadastral books with certain estate owners and service landholders; and in the cadastral books it is written about the peasants and landless peasants of those houses that those peasants and landless peasants fled from them in the years prior to [the compilation of] those cadastral books, but there was no petition from them against anyone about those peasants throughout this time: do not grant a trial for those peasants and landless peasants on the basis of those vacant houses and vacant lots because for many years they did not petition the sovereign against anyone about those peasants of theirs.

6. If fugitive peasants and landless peasants are returned from someone to plaintiffs after trial and investigation, and according to the cadastral books; or if someone returns [fugitives] without trial according to [this] Law Code: on the petition of those people under whom they had lived while fugitives, register those peasants in the Service Land Chancellery [as living] under those people to whom they are returned.

Concerning those people from whom they are taken: do not collect any of the sovereign's levies [due from the peasants] from such service landholders and hereditary estate owners on the basis of the census books. Collect all of the sovereign's levies from those estate owners and service landholders under whom they proceed to live as peasants upon their return.

7. If, after trial and investigation, and according to the cadastral books, peasants are taken away from any hereditary estate owners and returned to plaintiffs from their purchased estates; and they purchased those estates from estate owners with those peasants [living on them] after [the compilation of] the cadastres; and those peasants are registered on their lands in the purchase documents: those estate owners, in the stead of those returned peasants, shall take from the sellers similar peasants with all [their] movable property, and with [their] standing grain and with [their] threshed grain, from their other estates.

8. Concerning those estate owners and service landholders who in the past years had a trial about fugitive peasants and landless peasants; and at trial someone's [claims] to such fugitive peasants were rejected, prior to this decree of the sovereign, on the basis of the statute of limitations on the recovery of fugitive peasants in the prior decree of the great Sovereign, Tsar, and Grand Prince of all Russia Mikhail Fedorovich of blessed memory; and those fugitive peasants and landless peasants were ordered to live under those people under whom they lived out the years [of the] statute of limitations; or certain service landholders and hereditary estate owners arranged an amicable agreement in past years, prior to this decree of the sovereign, about fugitive peasants and landless peasants, and according to the amicable agreement someone ceded his peasants to someone else, and they confirmed it with registered documents, or they submitted reconciliation petitions [to settle court suits]: all those cases shall remain as those cases were resolved prior to this decree of the sovereign. Do not consider those cases anew and do not renegotiate [them].

9. Concerning peasants and landless peasants registered under someone in the census books of the past years 1645/46 and 1646/47; and after [the compilation of] those census books they fled from those people under whom they were registered in the census books, or they proceed to flee in the future: return those fugitive peasants and landless peasants, and their brothers, and children, and kinsmen, and grandchildren with [their] wives and with [their] children and with all [their] movable property, and with [their] standing grain and with threshed grain, from flight to those people from whom they fled, on the basis of the census books, without any statute of limitations. Henceforth no one ever shall receive others' peasants and shall not retain them under himself.

10. If someone after this royal Law Code proceeds to receive and retain under himself fugitive peasants, and landless peasants, and their children, and brothers, and kinsmen; and hereditary estate owners and service landholders demand those fugitive peasants of theirs from them [in a trial]: after trial and investigation, and according to the census books, return those fugitive peasants and landless peasants of theirs to them with [their] wives and with [their] children, and with all their movable property, and with [their] standing grain, and with [their] threshed grain, and with [their] grain still in the ground, without any statute of limitations.

Concerning the length of the time they live under someone as fugitives after this royal Law Code: collect from those under whom they proceed to live 10 rubles each for any peasant per year for the sovereign's taxes and the service landholder's incomes. Give [the money] to the plaintiffs whose peasants and landless peasants they are.

11. If someone proceeds to petition the sovereign against someone about such fugitive peasants and landless peasants; and those peasants and their fathers are not registered in the cadastral books under either the plaintiff or the defendant, but those peasants are registered under the plaintiff or the defendant in the census books of the past years 1645/46 and 1646/47: on the basis of the census books, return those peasants and landless peasants to that person under whom they are registered in the census books.

12. If a peasant's daughter of marriageable age flees from someone, from an hereditary estate or from a service landholding, after this royal decree; and while a fugitive she marries someone's limited service contract slave or a peasant; or after this royal decree someone entices a peasant's daughter of marriageable age, and having enticed [her], marries her to his own limited service contract slave, or peasant, or landless peasant; and that person from whom she fled proceeds to petition the sovereign about her; and it is established about that conclusively at trial and investigation that that unmarried young woman fled, or was enticed away: return her to that person from whom she fled, along with her husband and with her children, which children she bore by that husband. Do not return her husband's movable property with her.

13. If that fugitive unmarried young women marries someone's slave or peasant who is a widower; and prior [to his marriage] to her, that husband of hers had children by his first wife: do not return those first children of her husband to the plaintiff. They shall remain with that person in whose possession they were born into slavery or into peasantry.

14. If a plaintiff proceeds to sue for stolen property along with that fugitive unmarried young woman [which she allegedly stole when she fled]: grant him a trial for that. After trial compile the decree that is necessary.

15. If a peasant widow flees from someone; and her husband had been registered in the cadastral or allotment books, and in extracts [from them], or in any other documents among the peasants or the landless peasants [living] under that person from whom she fled; and having fled, that peasant woman marries someone's limited service contract slave or

peasant: return that peasant widow with her [new] husband to that service landholder under whom her first husband had been registered in the cadastral or census books, or in the extracts, and in any other documents.

16. If the first husband of that widow is not registered [as living] under that person from whom she fled in the cadastral and census books and in any other documents: that widow shall live under that person whose slave or peasant she marries.

17. If a peasant or landless peasant flees from someone; and in flight he marries his daughter of marriageable age or a widow to someone's limited service contract slave, or to a peasant, or to a landless peasant [living under] that person to whom he flees; and later on after trial it becomes necessary to return that fugitive peasant with [his] wife and with [his] children to that person from whom he fled: return that fugitive peasant or landless peasant to his former service landholder, together with his son-in-law to whom he had married his daughter [while] in flight. If that son-in-law of his has children by his first wife: do not hand over those first children of his to the plaintiff.

18. If such a fugitive peasant or landless peasant, while in flight marries his daughter to someone's limited service contract slave, or hereditary slave, or peasant, or landless peasant [registered under] another service landholder or hereditary estate owner: return that peasant's daughter who was married while in flight, along with her husband, to the plaintiff.

19. If a service landholder or estate owner proceeds to discharge from his service landholding or from his hereditary estate, or someone's bailiffs and elders proceed to discharge, peasant daughters of marriageable age or widows to marry someone's slaves or peasants: they shall give such peasant daughters, women of marriageable age and widows, manumission documents signed by their own hands, or by their spiritual fathers, in case of a future dispute.

Collect the fee for permitting such peasant daughters to marry peasants of another lord by mutual agreement. Concerning that which someone collects for the marriage departure fee: write that explicitly in the manumission documents.

20. If any people come to someone on [his] hereditary estate and service landholding and say about themselves that they are free; and those people desire to live under them as peasants or landless peasants: those people whom they approach shall

interrogate them – what kind of free people are they? And where is their birth place? And under whom did they live? And whence did they come? And are they not someone's fugitive slaves, and peasants, and landless peasants? And do they have manumission documents?

If they say that they do not have manumission documents on their person: service landholders and hereditary estate owners shall find out about such people accurately, whether they really are free people. Having investigated accurately, bring them in the same year for registration to the Service Land Chancellery in Moscow; Kazan'-area residents and residents of Kazan' by-towns shall bring them to Kazan'; Novgorodians and residents of the Novgorodian by-towns shall bring them to Novgorod; Pskovians and residents of the Pskov by-towns shall bring them to Pskov. [Chancellery officials] in the Service Land Chancellery and governors in the provincial towns shall interrogate such free people on that subject and shall record their testimonies accurately.

If it becomes necessary to give those people who are brought in for registration, on the basis of their testimony under interrogation, as peasants to those people who brought them in for registration: order those people to whom they will be given as peasants to affix their signatures to the testimonies of those people after they have been taken.

21. If an estate owner or a service landholder brings in for registration the person who approached him without having checked accurately, and they proceed to take such people in as peasants: return such people as peasants to plaintiffs after trial and investigation, and according to the census book, along with [their] wives, and with [their] children, and with [their] movable property.

Concerning [what shall be exacted] from those people who take in someone else's peasant or landless peasant without checking accurately: collect for those years, however many [the peasant] lived under someone, 10 rubles per year for the sovereign's taxes and for the incomes of the hereditary estate owner and service landholder because [of this rule]: without checking accurately, do not receive someone else's [peasant]....

33. Concerning slaves and peasants who flee across the frontier from service landholders and from hereditary estate owners of all ranks and from the border towns; and, having been across the frontier and returning from across the frontier, they do not want to live with their own old service landholders and hereditary estate owners, [and] they proceed to request their freedom: having interrogated those

fugitive slaves and peasants, return them to their old service landholders and hereditary estate owners from whom they fled. Do not grant them freedom.

34. Concerning slaves and peasants who flee across the frontier to the Swedish and [Polish-] Lithuanian side from any hereditary estate owners and service landholders who have been granted service landholdings in the frontier towns; and across the frontier they marry similarly fugitive older women and young women of marriageable age [who belong to] different service landholders; and having gotten married, they return from across the frontier to their own old service landholders and hereditary estate owners; and, when they return, those old service landholders of theirs proceed to petition the sovereign, one about the young woman of marriageable age or about the older woman, [stating] that his peasant woman married that fugitive peasant; and his defendant proceeds to testify that his peasant married that fugitive young woman or the older woman across the frontier while a fugitive: at trial and investigation, grant them lots on the question of those fugitive slaves and peasants of theirs. Whoever gets the lot, that one [shall get the couple and] shall pay a 5-ruble marriage departure fee for the young woman, or for the older woman, or for the man because they were both fugitives across the frontier....

Chapter 16.—Service Lands. In It Are 69 Articles.

1. [The following size] service landholdings shall be in Moscow province: For boyars, 260 acres per man.

For *okol'nichie* and for counselor state secretaries, 195 acres per man.

For *stol'niki*, and for *striapchie*, and for Moscow *dvoriane*, and for state secretaries, and for commanders of Moscow musketeers, and for senior stewards of the Palace Chancellery, and for stewards responsible for managing various parts of the palace economy, 130 acres per man.

For provincial *dvoriane* who are serving by selection in Moscow, 91 acres per man.

For *zhil'tsy*, and for mounted grooms, and for centurions of the Moscow musketeers, 65 acres per man.

For palace court officials, and for *striapchie*, and for provisioned, and for officials working for the tsaritsa, and for *deti boiarskie*, 13 acres per each 130 acres of their service land compensation entitlements.

2. Concerning service landholders of all ranks who desire to exchange their service landholdings

among themselves: they shall petition the sovereign about registering those exchanged service landholdings of theirs. They shall submit signed petitions on that matter to the Service Land Chancellery.

3. Moscow people of all ranks shall exchange service landholdings with [other] Moscow people of all ranks, and with provincial *dvoriane* and *deti boiarskie*, [and] with foreigners, acre for acre, and inhabited land for inhabited land, and waste land for waste land, and [also] uninhabited land for waste land. In response to their joint petition and the signed petitions, record those service landholdings of theirs [which] they exchanged among themselves.

Where someone in an exchange received a few extra acres above an equal exchange: in response to their joint petition about that transaction, record those few [extra] acres for them....

9. If anyone surrenders a service landholding because of superannuation – an uncle to a nephew, or a brother to a brother; and in the document recording the surrender of the land and in the petition about registration he writes that the nephew is to feed the uncle, or the brother his brother, until his death; and subsequently the uncle proceeds to petition against the nephew, or the brother against the brother, [alleging] that he is not feeding him, is driving him off the service landholding, and is ordering the peasants not to obey him: take away such surrendered service landholdings from such nephews and brothers and return them to those to whom they belonged previously. Whatever documents they gave on themselves [surrendering the service landholdings] are void.

10. If widows or unmarried young women proceed to surrender their maintenance service landholdings to anyone so that those people to whom they surrender those service landholdings of theirs will feed them and find them a husband: they shall get signed registration documents from those people to whom they surrender those service landholdings of theirs [promising] that such people will feed them and marry them off.

If a widow or unmarried young woman, having surrendered her service landholding, proceed [sic] to petition the sovereign that those people to whom they surrendered those service landholdings of theirs are not feeding them, and are not marrying them off, and are driving them out from those maintenance service landholdings of theirs: compile a decree on the matter of that petition of theirs. Having taken [back] their widows' and unmarried young women's maintenance service landholdings, return them to those widows and unmarried young women for

[their] maintenance as previously. Whatever documents they gave are void.

11. Unmarried young women [may] surrender their own maintenance service landholdings when the unmarried young woman is of age, 15 years old.

If someone proceeds to petition the sovereign about an unmarried young woman's maintenance service landholding and says that an unmarried young woman surrendered her maintenance service landholding to him, but if the unmarried young woman at that time is a minor, less than 15 years of age: do not believe such petitioners, and do not register the unmarried young women's maintenance service landholdings as theirs....

16. If women remain childless after [the death] of people of Moscow ranks, and provincial *dvoriane* and *deti boiarskie*, and foreigners; and there are no service landholdings and purchased hereditary estates remaining after [the death of] their husbands, and there is nothing from which to give them a maintenance allotment, but their husbands' estates granted for service and clan estates do remain: after review, grant the wives of such deceased [servicemen] a maintenance allotment from their husbands' estates granted for service for the duration of their lives.

Those widows shall not sell, and shall not mortgage, and shall not give away [to religious establishments for prayers] for their soul, and shall not register for themselves as a dowry those estates granted for service.

If [a widow with a maintenance allotment] marries, or becomes a nun, or dies: grant those estates to the hereditary estate owners in the [husband's] clan who are most closely related [to him]....

Chapter 19.—Townsmen. In It Are 40 Articles.

1. Concerning the [tax-exempt] settlements in Moscow belonging to the patriarch, and metropolitans, and other high church officials, and monasteries, and boyars, and *okol'nichie*, and counselors, and [tsar's] intimates, and people of all ranks; and in those settlements are living merchants and artisans who pursue various trading enterprises and own shops, but are not paying the sovereign's taxes and are not rendering service: confiscate all of those settlements, with all the people who are living in those settlements, for the sovereign [and place them] all on the tax rolls [and force them to render] service without any statute of limitations and irrevocably, except for limited service contract slaves.

If it is said in an inquiry that the limited service contract slaves are their perpetual slaves, return them to those people to whom they belong. Order them moved back to their houses. Concerning those limited service contract slaves whose fathers and whose clan ancestors were townsmen, or from the sovereign's rural districts: take those [people] to live in the urban taxpaying districts.

Henceforth, except for the sovereign's settlements, no one shall have [tax-exempt] settlements in Moscow or in the provincial towns.

Confiscate the patriarch's settlements completely, excepting those palace court officials who for a long time lived under former patriarchs in their patriarchal ranks as *deti boiarskie*, singers, secretaries, scribes, furnace tenders, guards, cooks and bakers, grooms, and as his palace court officials of other ranks who are given an annual salary and grain....

Chapter 21.—Robbery and Theft Cases. In It Are 104 Articles.

9. If a thief is brought in, and one theft is attributed to him: torture that thief about other thefts and homicide. If he does not confess under torture to other thefts and homicide, but testifies that he stole for the first time, and did not commit a homicide: beat that thief with the knout for the first theft, cut off his left ear, and imprison him for two years, and give out his property in shares to the plaintiffs. Having taken him out of prison, send him in chains to work as a slave on various forced labor projects wherever the sovereign decrees.

When he has sat out the two years in prison, send him to the southern frontier towns, wherever the sovereign decrees. Order him to remain in the southern frontier towns, in the rank befitting him.

Issue him a letter over the signature of a state secretary [stating] that he sat out the sentence in prison for his felony and has been released from prison.

10. If that same thief is apprehended in a second theft: torture him about other thefts accordingly. If he confesses only to two thefts, and [says] that he did not commit a homicide: after the torturing, beat him with the knout and, having cut off his right ear, imprison him for four years. Having taken him out of prison, send him to [work] on the sovereign's various forced labor projects, accordingly in chains.

When he has sat out the sentence in prison: exile him to the frontier towns, wherever the sovereign decrees.

Issue him a letter [stating] that he sat out the sentence in prison for the second theft and has been released from prison....

12. If a thief is brought in, and three, or four, or more thefts are attributed to him: having tortured that thief, punish him with death, even though he did not commit a homicide. Distribute his movable property to the plaintiffs in shares.

13. If a thief commits a homicide at the first theft, punish him with death.

14. Punish church thieves also with death without the slightest mercy. Give back their movable property [to compensate for] the church thefts....

Chapter 22.—Decree: For Which Offenses the Death Penalty Should Be Inflicted on Someone, and for Which Offenses the Penalty Should Not Be Death, But [Another] Punishment Should Be Imposed. In It Are 26 Articles.

1. If any son or daughter kills his father or mother: for patricide or matricide, punish them also with death, without the slightest mercy.

2. If any son or daughter kills his or her father or mother with some other people, and that is established conclusively: after investigation, also punish with death, without the slightest mercy, those who committed such a deed with them.

3. If a father or mother kills a son or daughter: imprison them for a year after that. After having sat in prison for a year, they shall go to God's church, and in God's church they shall declare aloud that sin of theirs to all the people. Do not punish a father or mother with death for [killing] a son or daughter.

4. If someone, a son or a daughter, forgetting Christian law, proceeds to utter coarse speeches to a father or mother, or out of impudence strikes a father or mother, and the father or mother proceeds to petition against them for that: beat such forgetters of Christian law with the knout for the father and mother.

5. If any son or daughter plunder[s] a father's or mother's movable property by force; or not honoring the father and mother and [attempting] to drive them out, proceed[s] to denounce them for some evil deeds; or a son or daughter does not proceed to respect and feed a father and mother in their old age, does not proceed to support them materially in any way, and the father or mother proceed[s] to petition the sovereign against him or her about that: inflict a severe punishment on such children for such deeds of theirs, beat them mercilessly with the knout, and

command them to attend to their father and mother in all obedience without any back-talk. Do not believe their denunciation.

6. If any son or daughter proceed[s] to petition for a trial against a father or mother: do not grant them a trial in any matter against a father or mother. Beat them with the knout for such a petition and return them to the father and mother....

14. If a wife kills her husband, or feeds him poison, and that is established conclusively: punish her for that, bury her alive in the ground and punish her with that punishment without any mercy, even if the children of the killed [husband], or any other close relatives of his, do not desire that she be executed. Do not show her the slightest mercy, and keep her in the ground until that time when she dies.

15. If a woman is sentenced to the death penalty and she is pregnant at that time: do not punish that woman with death until she gives birth, and execute her at the time when she has given birth. Until that time, keep her in prison, or in the custody of reliable bailiffs, so that she will not depart.

16. If someone with felonious intent comes into someone's house, and desires to do something shameful to the mistress of that house, or desires to carry her away somewhere out of that house; and her slaves do not defend her against that felon, and proceed to assist those people who have come for her in the commission [of the crime]; and subsequently such a deed of theirs is discovered: punish with death all those felons who with such intent come into another's house and those slaves who assist them in the commission of such a felony....

20. If someone shoot[s] from a handgun or from a bow at a wild animal, or at a bird, or at a target; and the arrow or bullet goes astray and kills someone over a hill or beyond a fence; or if someone by any chance kills someone with a piece of wood, or a rock, or anything else in a non-deliberate act; and previously there was no enmity or other animosity between that person who killed and that [person] he killed; and it is established about that conclusively that such a homicide occurred without deliberation and without intent: do not punish anyone with death for such a homicide and do not incarcerate anyone in prison because that event occurred accidently, without intent....

24. If a Muslim by any means whatsoever, by force or by deceit, compels a Russian [to convert] to his Islamic faith; and he circumcises that Russian according to his Islamic faith; and that is established conclusively: punish that Muslim after investigation, burn him with fire without any mercy.

Concerning the Russian whom he converted to Islam: send that Russian to the patriarch, or to another high ecclesiastical figure, and order him to compile a decree according to the canons of the Holy Apostles and the Holy Fathers.

25. If someone of the male gender, or the female gender, having forgotten the wrath of God and Christian law, proceeds to procure adult women and mature girls for fornication, and that is established conclusively: inflict a severe punishment on them for such a lawless and vile business, beat them with the knout.

26. If a woman proceeds to live in fornication and vileness, and in fornication begets children with someone; and she herself, or someone else at her command, destroys those children; and that is established conclusively: punish with death without any mercy such lawless women and that person who destroyed her children at her order so that others looking on will not commit such a lawless and vile deed and will refrain from fornication.

Glossary

manumission documents	official papers stating that the bearer, a former slave, has been freed
Mikhail Fedorovich	Mikhail Fedorovich Romanov (1596–1645)
service landholding	rented land whose tenant was required to serve the state lifelong or until too infirm to continue his duties (that is, until superannuated)
spiritual fathers	Orthodox clergy and other personnel
stol'niki,..., ***striapchie,...***, ***dvoriane,...***, ***zhil'tsy***	specific ranks or titles within the service gentry, with *dvoriane* referring to nobles and gentry in state service

HABEAS CORPUS ACT OF THE RESTORATION

"Great delays have been used by sheriffs ... to whose custody any of the King's subjects have been committed for ... criminal matters."

Overview

The Habeas Corpus Act, based on the common-law writ of *habeas corpus ad subjiciendum* (Latin for "you shall have the body for submitting") was enacted in England on May 27, 1679. The act was and, with amendments, continues to be in modern times a key piece of legislation that protects the rights of individuals against arbitrary and unlawful detention by the king or the executive and against abuses of procedure by the judiciary and state custodians. The concept of habeas corpus was not born with the 1679 act, having origins predating the Magna Carta. A cornerstone of the English constitution, the Magna Carta, or Great Charter, which was written in Latin and first issued in 1215, established that the will of the monarch, King John, was bound by the law. It specifically set out particular rights to be enjoyed by all subjects, whether free or imprisoned, which supported appeals against unlawful detention. The Habeas Corpus Act of 1679 is held to be of similar constitutional importance to the U.S. Bill of Rights and even the Magna Carta itself.

The Habeas Corpus Act outlines in concrete terms the duties of judges and custodians, including the legally binding procedures to be followed, details of the time frames to work within, and remedies and punishments for failure to comply with these terms. Above all, it confirms that every English subject has the legal right to be presented before a judge, even when the courts are not in session; to obtain the reason for detention; and to ascertain whether the custodian has legal authority to detain him or her. The act obligates the lord chancellor and judges of the three common-law courts to issue a writ of habeas corpus on the first request, to be served on the custodian in question; the writ forces the custodian to appear in court, with the detainee present and a copy of the warrant or other documents detailing the reason for arrest, within three days of the writ's being served. The act provides for a longer period for compliance when prisoners are interned more than twenty miles from the court that issued the writ. Notably, cases of treason and felony are excluded from this aspect of the writ, and detentions made by either houses of Parliament are not subject to the act.

Since the Habeas Corpus Act was first enacted, it has been suspended on several occasions, most notably in 1689, when the threat of Catholic-leaning counter-revolutionary forces loyal to James II threatened to destabilize the monarchy of the recently installed Protestant monarchs William III and Mary II. Another notable suspension was in the immediate aftermath of the French Revolution (1794–1795), when England was embroiled in a series of wars with France and concern about French spies was heightened by the activities of pro-revolutionary radical thinkers such as Thomas Paine. In 1817 the act was suspended to help control outbreaks of civil unrest caused by falling grain prices and unemployment following the end of the Napoleonic Wars in 1815.

Context

The Habeas Corpus Act did not emerge and crystallize overnight. Versions of the bill containing all the key elements of the 1679 act passed through the House of Commons with little difficulty in 1668, 1674, 1675, and 1677 before stalling in the House of Lords. The preexistence of the common-law writ, a well-established legal principle, raised questions about why an act securing it was really necessary. The foremost reason was that the early years of the Restoration—which commenced when Charles II's enthronement reinstated the monarchies of England, Scotland, and Ireland in 1660—were years in which the Stuart monarchs sought to reestablish the royal prerogative, including the detention of people for seditious libel under the king's name simply on the ground of suspicion. Thus, protecting the basic rights of individuals under these conditions came to be considered of fundamental importance by many members of Parliament. There already existed statute legislation from the reign of Charles I that, to some extent, protected the subject's right to habeas corpus, but it was ineffective because it did not provide full guidance regarding the duties and responsibilities of the judges or custodians nor did it set out punishment for breaches.

Throughout the 1660s, there were vast disparities concerning the duration of a prisoner's detention without trial. However, a wait of a year was not considered uncommon. In

1666

■ **December**
John Mordaunt, 1st Viscount Mordaunt of Avalon, is impeached by Parliament for the unlawful imprisonment of William Taylor.

1667

■ **October**
Impeachment proceedings begin in the House of Commons against Edward Hyde, 1st Earl of Clarendon, in part, for sending prisoners to Jersey in gross breach of the principle of habeas corpus.

1668

■ **April**
Charles Paulet, Lord St. John, is given permission to propose a bill to ensure that habeas corpus is respected; the bill passes through the House of Commons but stalls in the House of Lords.

1674

■ The second habeas corpus bill passes through the House of Commons but gets no further.

1677

■ A third attempt to pass the habeas corpus bill, virtually identical to the second habeas corpus bill, once more stalls in the House of Lords.

addition, during this decade there was a substantial increase in the number of unlawful detentions of subjects even after a writ of habeas corpus had been served. Four famous cases in 1666 and 1667 offer real evidence of the prevailing and often ambivalent attitude of judges and custodians toward the writ before enactment of the act securing it. The case of William Taylor, surveyor of Windsor Castle, who was unlawfully detained by John Mordaunt, 1st Viscount Mordaunt of Avalon, and whose appeal for issue of a writ of habeas corpus was turned down on arbitrary grounds (while his daughter was allegedly raped by Mordaunt) is often cited as one of the more notorious infractions. The case of Samuel Moyer, who was imprisoned for five years without trial, caused a scandal when his five-hundred-pound bribe to his two jailers to obtain his release became the subject of a quarrel between them. The third case involved Edward Hyde, 1st Earl of Clarendon, who was alleged to have advocated that prisoners should be sent to outlying dominions to avoid the serving of a writ of habeas corpus. Finally, Lord Chief Justice Sir John Kelynge was charged with refusing to issue a writ of habeas corpus and forcing the detainee concerned to appeal directly to the king.

These four cases contributed to the persuading of some in the House of Lords that a habeas corpus act was really necessary. In addition, it became apparent that even if a writ was speedily issued, executing the writ was still sometimes problematic. Under the common law as it stood, jailers or custodians were under no legal obligation to accept the first or second (*alias*) writs, and only on the third (*pluries*) writ were they obligated to take action. This could mean a delay of weeks or even months before a writ would be enforced. The Whig-inclined Sir Henry Care, in his much cited work *English Liberties; or, The Free-Born Subject's Inheritance* (1680), attributed the bill primarily to the abuses of jailers whose efforts to extort money to accept the writ, or in many cases simple negligence, caused the common law to be ineffective. Custodial and judicial indiscretion alike therefore contributed greatly to the need for a statute.

Yet abuse of the common law was not the only motive force behind the habeas corpus bill. Alongside the high-profile cases of abuse, the bill was very much influenced by the politics of Anthony Ashley Cooper, 1st Earl of Shaftesbury, and his coterie of followers, who sought to weaken the royal prerogative and bolster parliamentary sovereignty. Individual liberties, they argued, could not be guaranteed under existing laws. The habeas corpus bill was framed at the height of Shaftesbury's politically incendiary "exclusion bill" campaign, which sought to prevent James, Charles II's Catholic brother, from acceding to the throne upon Charles's death. It was popularly believed that James would use the royal prerogative much more widely and arbitrarily. However, despite significant support in the House of Commons, many in the House of Lords and among Country Whigs felt that the habeas corpus bill encroached too far on the royal prerogative, which was the basis of the Lords' continued rejection of the bill as passed by the Commons on four separate occasions. In turn, the bill was very unfavorably received by the king himself.

After so many readings of the bill over several years, the need to buttress the broad principle of habeas corpus with statutory force was largely ingrained within members of the House of Commons. In order to gain more traction in the House of Lords, members of the Commons saw fit to redraft the bill. The long Shaftesburian preamble, which many lords found offensive, was dropped, making the bill much leaner and more palatable. Throughout the mid-1670s there had actually been two proposed bills relating to detainees' rights: the habeas corpus bill and the transportation bill. The latter was proposed as a specific remedy to prevent those detained without trial from being deported to the colonies, at a time when deportations to Jamaica were at their peak. The decision to make this a separate bill was based on the political calculation that it would overload the habeas corpus bill and potentially jeopardize it. However, those in the Commons opted to amalgamate the two for the bill of 1679.

In April 1679 the redrafted habeas corpus bill passed through the Commons and up to the House of Lords. After two readings to the house, the bill was read to the whole house sitting in committee, a procedure that allowed greater scrutiny and the opportunity for individual members to pass comment before the bill was subjected to examination by a smaller select committee. The select committee made several important amendments before sending it back to the Commons on May 2. These amendments were finally accepted by the House of Commons, more or less verbatim, in a compromise to ensure that the bill became law before the end of the parliamentary session. The amendments by the Lords appear in the final act as clauses IV, VIII, XIII, XVIII, XX, and XXI. The Commons did add its own amendment to one of the Lords' amendments—clause XIX—and the bill finally became law on May 27, 1679, although the provisions of the act would not take force until June 1 and were not retroactive.

There have been persistent rumors, first attributed to the historian Gilbert Burnet soon after the passage of the act, that it was not legally passed into law owing to a deliberate miscount of votes by Ford Grey, 3rd Baron Grey of Warke, who counted in a very rotund member of Parliament as ten votes—a jest not picked up by the second teller, James Bertie, 1st Earl of Abingdon (Lord Norreys), and allowed to stand. Fueling this rumor, the minutes of the session state that 112 votes were cast in total, while the official attendance list records only 107 House of Lords members present. However, recent scholarship has explained this discrepancy and shown that attendance lists of this period were notoriously unreliable. There is now broad consent that the story has no foundation in fact.

The cause of the favorable change of attitude toward the habeas corpus legislation by members of the House of Lords has been the subject of some debate. Helen A. Nutting has attributed the shift to the lessening of post-Restoration paranoia and, more important, has suggested that the courts, especially the King's Bench Division—where the common-law writ of habeas corpus was most applied for—had made significant improvements to the efficiency of the

judicial system and records, such that there was less resistance on the part of justices. In fact, in the years immediately prior to the passing of the act, the long pretrial detentions typical of the 1660s were uncommon.

About the Author

The initiator of the legislation was Charles Paulet, 1st Duke of Bolton (Lord St. John), who was first granted permission to introduce a bill in April 1668. Lord St. John (1631–1699) began his parliamentary career as a support-

1679

- **April**
  The habeas corpus bill passes through the House of Commons and is read in the House of Lords and subjected to a select committee's examination.

- **May 2**
  The House of Commons considers six amendments to the bill by the House of Lords.

- **May 2–26**
  Members of the Commons and Lords hold a series of meetings to discuss the Lords' six amendments; members of the Lords remain resolute.

- **May 27**
  The bill passes in the House of Lords by a vote of fifty-seven to fifty-five, and the Habeas Corpus Act is given royal assent.

1689

- **March 16**
  The Habeas Corpus Act is suspended for the first time in the wake of the Revolution of 1688.

er of Charles II, but during the 1670s moved to the ranks of the opposition. He participated in various important parliamentary committees, most notably investigating the conduct of Thomas Osborne, known as the Earl of Danby, who was impeached on charges of high treason for negotiating with France on matters of peace and war without the knowledge of the Privy Council. He also participated in an inquiry concerning the "Popish plot," a supposed (but fictitious) Catholic conspiracy to murder Charles II.

Anthony Ashley Cooper, 1st Earl of Shaftesbury, a prominent Whig, had significant input into the bill, although the extent of his role has been called into question in recent years. Shaftesbury (1621–1683) had a rich and varied career and became one of the most influential politicians of his generation. At the beginning of the English Civil War in 1641, he supported the Royalist cause but defected to the Parliamentarians in 1644. Never completely supportive of Oliver Cromwell's Protectorate (the period after the Civil War during which England was ruled by a Lord Protector), by 1660 his political sentiments placed him on the commission to recall Charles II to the throne. During the 1670s his previously tolerant position toward Catholics hardened, and this attitude placed him at odds with the Crown. His vehement attacks against the administration for what he perceived as tolerance to Catholics led to his imprisonment in 1677. He was released in 1678 and continued to play a leading role in Whig circles.

Significant alterations and additions to the bill were made during its final passage through Parliament, and the work of Frances North, 1st Baron Guilford, relating to the six amendments made by the House of Lords are worthy of particular note. Lord North and the Earl of Shaftesbury had clashed on the issue of the impeachment of Thomas Osborne, Lord Danby. The Earl of Shaftesbury had long been in opposition to Danby's strict interpretation of penal laws against Catholics and what he suspected was his support for absolute monarchy. In some sense, the act was therefore a remarkable compromise between two men who had long been fiercely opposed to each other. Lord North (1637–1685) had a long career as a judge, having been called to the bar in 1661. A prodigious early legal career culminated in his appointment as solicitor-general in 1671, from which point his focus turned to politics. In 1673 he became attorney-general and in 1675 lord chief justice. In 1679 he became a member of the Privy Council, a role that further entangled him in political affairs. His support and protection of the royal prerogative helped him gain the position of lord keeper of the great seal in 1682, which put him in charge of the Court of Chancery.

Explanation and Analysis of the Document

The final Habeas Corpus Act passed in 1679 contains twenty-one separate clauses. The clauses can be broadly grouped into three categories: those outlining the procedures, duties, and responsibilities for compliance with the act by all parties involved as well as penalties for noncom-pliance; those relating to the transportation of detainees pretrial or of those convicted of crimes after sentencing; and those supplied as amendments to the bill by the House of Lords.

◆ **Procedures, Duties, and Responsibilities and Penalties for Noncompliance**

Since the purpose of giving statutory force to the preexisting common-law writ was largely to ensure the establishment of clear procedures for observing habeas corpus, the most important clauses relate to duties of compliance, as well as to remedies for noncompliance with the measures of the act. The act stipulates in clause III that upon receiving a witnessed written request for the writ of habeas corpus by a detainee or his agents, judges are "authorized and required" to issue a writ of habeas corpus signed by them. From clause X, failure to comply with this clause during "vacation time" would result in a £500 fine. Detainees could request the writ at the High Court of Chancery, the Court of Exchequer, the King's Bench, or the Court of Common Pleas. The act requires in clause II that upon receiving the writ, the custodian or warder must bring the prisoner before the court within three days if he or she is held within twenty miles of the issuing court, within ten days if within one hundred miles, and within a maximum of twenty days for still greater distances.

Furthermore, as noted in clause V, the custodian or police officer to whom the request for a warrant of arrest was made had to issue one to the detainee within six hours of the request, and the custodian could not shift the custody of the prisoner. Failure to comply with this part of the act was punishable for the first offense by a £100 fine (payable to the detainee) and, for the second offense, by a £200 fine and ineligibility to hold "his said office" any longer. After the prisoner appeared before the court, the reason for his detention was to be considered by the judge if submitted by the custodian; otherwise the detainee had to be released. Where a warrant attended the prisoner, the judge had three options: to release the prisoner on the ground of insufficient cause, to bail the prisoner to appear at a later date, or to remand the prisoner in custody. If the custodian neglected or refused to bring the prisoner before the court, it was also punishable by a £100 fine. Clause VI adds that no person could be detained twice for the same offense, including through "colourable pretence or variation"—that is, slightly changing the charge to avoid the spirit of the act—with a breach punishable by a £500 fine. The penalties were, in general, considered by the Lords as harsh, but there is not much evidence of serious breaches of the act before its first suspension in 1689.

◆ **Transportation of Detainees and Prisoners**

Clauses XI–XVI of the act relate to the practice of pretrial transportation of detainees to English colonies such as Jamaica or English territories such as Jersey and Guernsey in deliberate maneuvers to avoid the possibility of habeas corpus. Clauses XI, XII, and XIV had been the central features of the transportation bill that never passed separate-

Restoration commemorative caudle cup, featuring portrait of Charles II (© Museum of London)

ly. The practice of what amounted to extraterritorial rendition was notoriously highlighted by Edward Hyde, 1st Earl of Clarendon, who was impeached by the House of Commons in 1667 and forced to flee to France for flagrantly flouting the principle of habeas corpus by sending prisoners to Jersey and then to places farther afield. The problem was that the legal status of the common-law writ within Crown colonies was not altogether clear, and while it was thought to apply, the practical difficulties of applying for writs from afar and having them properly served effectively denied the detainees habeas corpus. It is important, however, to distinguish the illegal transportation of prisoners covered by the act from the legal transportation of those sentenced to penal servitude having been through the due process of law. For example, in 1686, 306 individuals who had taken part in the failed Monmouth Rebellion to overthrow James II were sent to Barbados, while another 159 were sent to Jamaica, all without infringing upon the provisions of the Habeas Corpus Act.

Clause XI declares that the act was to be enforceable in all places within the kingdom of England and the dominion of Wales, including places with unusual legal and constitutional statuses, "privileged places" such as the Cinque Ports (coastal towns in Kent and Sussex on the English Channel), the border town Berwick-upon-Tweed (for which English or Scottish jurisdiction had not been settled), and the Channel Islands of Jersey and Guernsey. Clause XII addresses the issue of unlawful transportation to and detention in places overseas, such as in the plantation colonies of the Caribbean. The act forbids all residents of England, Wales, and Berwick-upon-Tweed from being sent as prisoners to Scotland, Ireland, Jersey, Guernsey, or Tangier or any other of his majesty's dominions and territories. The act also states that breaches of the act would allow the plaintiff to bring an action of false imprisonment and to recover treble costs and at least £500 damages.

Clauses XIII (added by the Lords) and XIV protect against abuse of the act by detainees in the event that they consent

> "*Great delays have been used by sheriffs, gaolers and other officers, to whose custody any of the King's subjects have been committed for criminal or supposed criminal matters, in making returns of writs of* habeas corpus *... to avoid their yielding obedience to such writs, contrary to their duty and the known laws of the land.*"
>
> (Clause I)

> "*Whensoever any person ... shall bring any* habeas corpus *... the said officer ... shall within three days after the service thereof ... bring ... the body of the party ... unto or before the lord chancellor, or lord keeper of the great seal of* England *for the time being, or the judges or barons of the said court from whence the said writ shall issue.*"
>
> (Clause II)

> "*The said lord chancellor, lord keeper, justices or barons or any of them, upon view of the copy or copies of the warrant or warrants of commitment and detainer, or otherwise upon oath made that such copy or copies were denied to be given ... are herby authorized and required, upon request made in writing ... to award and grant an* habeas corpus.*"
>
> (Clause III)

to being sent to the colonies pretrial or after sentencing but then renege and try to bring an action of unlawful imprisonment under habeas corpus. Finally, clause XVI clarifies that the Habeas Corpus Act does not interfere with the ancient principle of judicial jurisdiction, by which any subject charged with a capital offense committed within the king's realm could be sent to the place where the crime was committed to face trial. This principle is still broadly in force.

◆ **Amendments by the House of Lords**

During the Easter parliamentary recess of 1679, a small select committee of the House of Lords set to work drafting amendments to the habeas corpus bill. Lord North, long the most outspoken and eloquent opponent of the bill, was the motive force behind many of the amendments. The main revisions form the substantial parts of clauses IV, VIII, XIII, XVIII, XX, and XXI. It has been suggested that these clauses significantly weaken the act, but they mainly provide safeguards against abuse of the act by detainees or potential conflicts of interest with other laws and judicial proceedings.

Although ordinarily application for the writ of habeas corpus could be made at any time, including during vacation time or parliamentary recess, clause IV adds the caveat that if a prisoner had neglected to seek the writ within two terms of detention, habeas corpus would not be granted during vacation time. Clause VIII makes clear that the act only applied in criminal cases and could not be extended to civil cases or debtors, while the aforementioned clause XIII protects merchants who had contractual agreements for immigration.

Perhaps the most important amendment is clause XVIII, which anticipated potential abuse of the law by detainees seeking to use its provisions to evade or preempt trial at the scheduled assizes, The assizes were criminal courts that moved around the country periodically to try more serious cases referred to them by the Quarter Sessions. They were abolished along with the Quarter Sessions by the Courts Act of 1791. Once the date of the assizes was announced, no habeas corpus writs could be served, but the detainee could present the writ at the assizes when they were in session. This amendment solicited a further amendment by the House of Commons, clause XIX, which allowed habeas corpus to be served after the assizes, presumably if the assizes did not make the writ redundant.

The penultimate amendment, clause XX, secured the right of a general plea against any accusation of an infraction or breach of the act. This was a vital check on unwarranted accusations. The final amendment, clause XXI, relates to detentions based on the suspicion of felony or treason; it confirmed that these were still detainable offenses and that the act itself should not induce courts to release on bail such detainees who would not have been bailed prior to the act.

Audience

The Habeas Corpus Act of 1679 was directed at three main groups: all those detained; those responsible for the procedures of detention, namely, the justices and custodians; and the originators of the detention, as answerable to the king and ministers of the executive. Following the act, English subjects were safeguarded from lengthy unlawful detention and intermittent periods of incarceration without trial (excluding under treason and felony charges). As directed toward the originators of detention, the act made clear that in all criminal cases except treason and felony (which carried longer periods of detention but not total exemption from the principle of habeas corpus), clear charges substantiated with evidence would have to be brought before the detainee in a timely manner. This was not necessarily expected to reduce the number of detentions, but it was expected to reduce their arbitrary and uncertain nature. Finally, from the procedural point of view, those responsible for the execution of justice were given clear duties and responsibilities, which went a long way toward standardizing the way habeas corpus writs were dealt with.

Impact

The contemporary impact of the Habeas Corpus Act on English society has been considered by some historians to have been rather muted. However, its codification of the ancient common-law writ of habeas corpus had a significant impact on the expediency of justice and significantly curbed the royal prerogative. In combination with the English Bill of Rights, enacted a decade later, which curbed unreasonable bail demands and "cruel and unusual punishments," the right of individuals to be protected against procedural abuse and arbitrary interference with the administration of justice was supported as never before. The principle of habeas corpus was transposed to the American colonies and eventually enshrined in the U.S. Constitution; Article I, Section 9, significantly states that "the privilege of the writ of habeas corpus shall not be suspended" unless in times of rebellion or invasion or for the purpose of ensuring public safety. The common-law concept of habeas corpus was adopted by many U.S. states in the framing of their individual constitutions. For example, Article LX of the Georgia Constitution of 1777 states, "The principles of the habeas-corpus act shall be a part of this constitution." In 2005 the United Kingdom's Prevention of Terrorism Act, passed in the wake of the attacks of September 11, 2001, allowed terror suspects to be detained without charge for a longer period than that stipulated in the 1984 Police and

Questions for Further Study

1. Imagine that you and a friend are watching a movie or television program and that one of the characters, an attorney or judge, makes reference to "habeas corpus." Explain to your friend just what that term means and why it is an important civil right.

2. Compare this document with a much earlier document, the Constitutions of Clarendon (1164). How had concepts of judicial responsibility changed—or perhaps remained the same—between the twelfth and the seventeenth centuries?

3. Define "common law." If the concept of habeas corpus was ingrained in common law, why was a parliamentary act necessary?

4. During the U.S. Civil War, President Abraham Lincoln suspended habeas corpus. So did President Woodrow Wilson during World War I. More recently, issues surrounding habeas corpus have arisen in connection with U.S. and British detention of suspected terrorists. Do you think these measures are ever justifiable? Explain.

5. What political issues in England surrounding the restoration of the monarchy gave rise to the Habeas Corpus Act?

Criminal Evidence Act. This has been seen as an infringement on the principle of habeas corpus and proves the continuing relevance of the Habeas Corpus Act of 1679.

Further Reading

■ Articles

Crawford, Clarence C. "The Suspension of the Habeas Corpus Act and the Revolution of 1689." *English Historical Review* 30, no. 120 (October 1915): 613–630.

Davies, Godfrey, and Klotz, Edith L. "The Habeas Corpus Act of 1679 in the House of Lords." *Huntington Library Quarterly* 3, no. 4 (July 1940): 469–470.

Nutting, Helen A. "The Most Wholesome Law—The Habeas Corpus Act of 1679." *American Historical Review* 65, no. 3 (April 1960): 527–543.

■ Books

Antieau, Chester J. *The Practice of Extraordinary Remedies: Habeas Corpus and the Other Common Law Writs*, vol. 1. London: Oceana Publications, 1987.

Care, Henry. *English Liberties; or, The Free-Born Subject's Inheritance*. London: G. Larkin, 1680.

Sharpe, Robert J. *The Law of Habeas Corpus*. Oxford, U.K.: Clarendon Press, 1989.

■ Web Sites

"Article 1, Section 9, Clause 2: Opinion on the Writ of Habeas Corpus." The Founders' Constitution, University of Chicago Press Web site.

   http://press-pubs.uchicago.edu/founders/documents/a1_9_2-s3.html.

"Article 1, Section 9, Clause 2: William Blackstone, Commentaries." The Founders' Constitution, University of Chicago Press Web site.

   http://press-pubs.uchicago.edu/founders/documents/a1_9_2-s4.html.

—Peter Robinson

HABEAS CORPUS ACT OF THE RESTORATION

Whereas great delays have been used by sheriffs, gaolers and other officers, to whose custody any of the King's subjects have been committed for criminal or supposed criminal matters, in making returns of writs of *habeas corpus* to them directed, by standing out an *alias* and *pluries habeas corpus*, and sometimes more, and by other shifts to avoid their yielding obedience to such writs, contrary to their duty and the known laws of the land, whereby many of the King's subjects have been and hereafter may be long detained in prison, in such cases where by law they are bailable, to their great charges and vexation:

II. For the prevention whereof, and the more speedy relief of all persons imprisoned for any such criminal or supposed criminal matters; (2) be it enacted by the King's most excellent majesty, by and with the advice and consent of the lords spiritual and temporal, and commons, in this present parliament assembled, and by the authority thereof, That whensoever any person or persons shall bring any *habeas corpus* directed unto any sheriff or sheriffs, gaoler, minister or other person whatsoever, for any person in his or her custody, and the said writ shall be served upon the said officer, or left at the gaol or prison with any of the under-officers, under-keepers or deputy of the said officers or keepers, that the said officer or officers, his or their under-officers, under-keepers or deputies, shall within three days after the service thereof as aforesaid (unless the commitment aforesaid were for treason or felony, plainly and specially expressed in the warrant of commitment) upon payment or tender of the charges of bringing the said prisoner, to be ascertained by the judge or court that awarded the same, and endorsed upon the said writ, not exceeding twelve pence per mile, and upon security given by his own bond to pay the charges of carrying back the prisoner, if he shall be remanded by the court or judge to which he shall be brought according to the true intent of this present act, and that he will not make any escape by the way, make return of such writ; (3) and bring or cause to be brought the body of the party so committed or restrained, unto or before the lord chancellor, or lord keeper of the great seal of England for the time being, or the judges or barons of the said court from whence the said writ shall issue, or unto and before

such other person or persons before whom the said writ is made returnable, according to the command thereof; (4) and shall then likewise certify the true causes of his detainer or imprisonment, unless the commitment of the said party be in any place beyond the distance of twenty miles from the place or places where such court or person is or shall be residing; and if beyond the distance of twenty miles, and not above one hundred miles, then within the space of ten days, and if beyond the distance of one hundred miles, then within the space of twenty days, after such delivery aforesaid, and not longer.

III. And to the intent that no sheriff, gaoler or other officer may pretend ignorance of the import of any such writ; (2) be it enacted by the authority aforesaid, That all such writs shall be marked in this manner, *Per statutum tricesimo primo Caroli secundi Regi*, and shall be signed by the person that awards the same; (3) and if any person or persons shall be or stand committed or detained as aforesaid, for any crime, unless for felony or treason plainly expressed in the warrant of commitment, in the vacation-time, and out of term, it shall and may be lawful to and for the person or persons so committed or detained (other than persons convict or in execution by legal process) or any one on his or their behalf, to appeal or complain to the lord chancellor or lord keeper, or any one of his Majesty's justices, either of the one bench or of the other, or the barons of the exchequer of the degree of the coif; (4) and the said lord chancellor, lord keeper, justices or barons or any of them, upon view of the copy or copies of the warrant or warrants of commitment and detainer, or otherwise upon oath made that such copy or copies were denied to be given by such person or persons in whose custody the prisoner or prisoners is or are detained, are hereby authorized and required, upon request made in writing by such person or persons, or any on his, her or their behalf, attested and subscribed by two witnesses who were present at the delivery of the same, to award and grant an *habeas corpus* under the seal of such court whereof he shall then be one of the judges, (5) to be directed to the officer or officers in whose custody the party so committed or detained shall be, returnable immediate before the said lord chancellor or lord keeper, or such justice, baron or any other justice or baron of the degree of the coif of any of the said courts; (6) and upon service thereof as aforesaid, the officer or officers, his or their under-officer or under-officers, under-keeper or under-keepers, or their deputy, in whose custody the party is so committed or detained, shall within the times respectively before limited, bring such prisoner or prisoners before the said lord chancellor or lord keeper, or such justices, barons or one of them, before whom the said writ is made returnable, and in case of his absence before any other of them, with the return of such writ, and the true causes of the commitment and detainer; (7) and thereupon within two days after the party shall be brought before them, the said lord chancellor or lord keeper, or such justice or baron before whom the prisoner shall be brought as aforesaid, shall discharge the said prisoner from his imprisonment, taking his or their recognizance, with one or more surety or sureties, in any sum according to their discretions, having regard to the quality of the prisoner and nature of the offence, for his or their appearance in the court of King's bench the term following, or at the next assizes, sessions or general gaol-delivery of and for such county, city or place where the commitment was, or where the offence was committed, or in such other court where the said offence is properly cognizable, as the case shall require, and then shall certify the said writ with the return thereof, and the said recognizance or recognizances into the said court where such appearance is to be made; (8) unless it shall appear unto the said lord chancellor or lord keeper, or justice or justices, or baron or barons, that the party so committed is detained upon a legal process, order or warrant, out of some court that hath jurisdiction of criminal matters, or by some warrant signed and sealed with the hand and seal of any of the said justices or barons, or some justice or justices of the peace, for such matters or offences for the which by the law the prisoner is not bailable.

IV. Provided always, and be it enacted, That if any person shall have wilfully neglected by the space of two whole terms after his imprisonment, to pray a *habeas corpus* for his enlargement, such person so wilfully neglecting shall not have any *habeas corpus* to be granted in vacation-time, in pursuance of this act.

V. And be it further enacted by the authority aforesaid, That if any officer or officers, his or their under-officer or under-officers, under-keeper or under-keepers, or deputy, shall neglect or refuse to make the returns aforesaid, or to bring the body or bodies of the prisoner or prisoners according to the command of the said writ, within the respective times aforesaid, or upon demand made by the prisoner or person in his behalf, shall refuse to deliver, or within the space of six hours after demand shall not deliver, to the person so demanding, a true copy of the warrant or warrants of commitment and detainer of such prisoner, which he and they are hereby required to deliver accordingly, all and every the head gaolers and keepers of such prisons, and such other person in whose custody the prisoner shall be detained, shall for the first offence forfeit to the prisoner or party grieved the sum of one hundred pounds; (2) and for the second offence the sum of two hundred pounds, and shall and is hereby made incapable to hold or execute his said office; (3) the said penalties to be recovered by the prisoner or party grieved, his executors or administrators, against such offender, his executors or administrators, by any action of debt, suit, bill, plaint or information, in any of the King's courts at Westminster, wherein no essoin, protection, privilege, injunction, wager of law, or stay of prosecution by *Non vult ulterius prosequi*, or otherwise, shall be admitted or allowed, or any more than one imparlance; (4) and any recovery or judgment at the suit of any party grieved, shall be a sufficient conviction for the first offence; and any after recovery or judgment at the suit of a party grieved for any offence after the first judgment, shall be a sufficient conviction to bring the officers or person within the said penalty for the second offence.

VI. And for the prevention of unjust vexation by reiterated commitments for the same offence; (2) be it enacted by the authority aforesaid, That no person or persons which shall be delivered or set at large upon any *habeas corpus*, shall at any time hereafter be again imprisoned or committed for the same offence by any person or persons whatsoever, other than by the legal order and process of such court wherein he or they shall be bound by recognizance to appear, or other court having jurisdiction of the cause; (3) and if any other person or persons shall knowingly contrary to this act recommit or imprison, or knowingly procure or cause to be recommitted or imprisoned, for the same offence or pretended offence, any person or persons delivered or set at large as aforesaid, or be knowingly aiding or assisting therein, then he or they shall forfeit to the prisoner or party grieved the sum of five hundred pounds; any colourable pretence or variation in the warrant or warrants of commitment notwithstanding, to be recovered as aforesaid.

VII. Provided always, and be it further enacted, That if any person or persons shall be committed for high treason or felony, plainly and specially expressed in the warrant of commitment, upon his prayer or petition in open court the first week of the term, or first day of the sessions of *oyer* and *terminer* or general gaol-delivery, to be brought to his trial, shall not be indicted some time in the next term, sessions of *oyer* and *terminer* or general gaol-delivery, after such commitment; it shall and may be lawful to and for the judges of the court of King's bench and justices of *oyer* and *terminer* or general gaol-delivery, and they are hereby required, upon motion to them made in open court the last day of the term, sessions or gaol-delivery, either by the prisoner or any one in his behalf, to set at liberty the prisoner upon bail, unless it appear to the judges and justices upon oath made, that the witnesses for the King could not be produced the same term, sessions or general gaol-delivery; (2) and if any person or persons committed as aforesaid, upon his prayer or petition in open court the first week of the term or first day of the sessions of *oyer* and *terminer* and general gaol-delivery, to be brought to his trial, shall not be indicted and tried the second term, sessions of *oyer* and *terminer* or general gaol-delivery, after his commitment, or upon his trial shall be acquitted, he shall be discharged from his imprisonment.

VIII. Provided always, That nothing in this act shall extend to discharge out of prison any person charged in debt, or other action, or with process in any civil cause, but that after he shall be discharged of his imprisonment for such his criminal offence, he shall be kept in custody according to the law, for such other suit.

IX. Provided always, and be it enacted by the authority aforesaid, That if any person or persons, subjects of this realm, shall be committed to any prison or in custody of any officer or officers whatsoever, for any criminal or supposed criminal matter, that the said person shall not be removed from the said prison and custody into the custody of any other officer or officers; (2) unless it be by *habeas corpus* or some other legal writ; or where the prisoner is delivered to the constable or other inferior officer to carry such prisoner to some common gaol; (3) or where any person is sent by order of any judge or assize or justice of the peace, to any common workhouse or house of correction; (4) or where the prisoner is removed from one prison or place to another within the same county, in order to his or her trial or discharge in due course of law; (5) or in case of sudden fire or infection, or other necessity; (6) and if any person or persons shall after such commitment

aforesaid make out and sign, or countersign any warrant or warrants for such removal aforesaid, contrary to this act; as well he that makes or signs, or countersigns such warrant or warrants, as the officer or officers that obey or execute the same, shall suffer and incur the pains and forfeitures in this act before mentioned, both for the first and second offence respectively, to be recovered in manner aforesaid by the party grieved.

X. Provided also, and be it further enacted by the authority aforesaid, That it shall and may be lawful to and for any prisoner and prisoners as aforesaid, to move and obtain his or their *habeas corpus* as well out of the high court of chancery or court of exchequer, as out of the courts of King's bench or common pleas, or either of them; (2) and if the said lord chancellor or lord keeper, or any judge or judges, baron or barons for the time being, of the degree of the coif, of any of the courts aforesaid, in the vacation time, upon view of the copy or copies of the warrant or warrants of commitment or detainer, or upon oath made that such copy or copies were denied as aforesaid, shall deny any writ of *habeas corpus* by this act required to be granted, being moved for as aforesaid, they shall severally forfeit to the prisoner or party grieved the sum of five hundred pounds, to be recovered in manner aforesaid.

XI. And be it declared and enacted by the authority aforesaid, That an *habeas corpus* according to the true intent and meaning of this act, may be directed and run into any county palatine, the cinque-ports, or other privileged places within the kingdom of England, dominion of Wales, or town of Berwick upon Tweed, and the islands of Jersey or Guernsey; any law or usage to the contrary notwithstanding.

XII. And for preventing illegal imprisonments in prisons beyond the seas; (2) be it further enacted by the authority aforesaid, That no subject of this realm that now is, or hereafter shall be an inhabitant or resiant of this kingdom of England, dominion of Wales, or town of Berwick upon Tweed, shall or may be sent prisoner into Scotland, Ireland, Jersey, Guernsey, Tangier, or into parts, garrisons, islands or places beyond the seas, which are or at any time hereafter shall be within or without the dominions of his Majesty, his heirs or successors; (3) and that every such imprisonment is hereby enacted and adjudged to be illegal; (4) and that if any of the said subjects now is or hereafter shall be so imprisoned, every such person and persons so imprisoned, shall and may for every such imprisonment maintain by virtue of this act an action or actions of false imprisonment, in any of his Majesty's courts of record, against the person or persons by whom he or she shall be so committed, detained, imprisoned, sent prisoner or transported, contrary to the true meaning of this act, and against all or any person or persons that shall frame, contrive, write, seal or countersign any warrant or writing for such commitment, detainer, imprisonment or transportation, or shall be advising, aiding or assisting, in the same, or any of them; (5) and the plaintiff in every such action shall have judgment to recover his treble costs, besides damages, which damages so to be given, shall not be less than five hundred pounds; (6) in which action no delay stay or stop of proceeding by rule, order or command, nor no injunction, protection or privilege whatsoever, nor any more than one imparlance shall be allowed, excepting such rule of the court wherein the action shall depend, made in open court, as shall be thought in justice necessary, for special cause to be expressed in the said rule; (7) and the person or persons who shall knowingly frame, contrive, write, seal or countersign any warrant for such commitment, detainer or transportation, or shall so commit, detain, imprison or transport any person or persons contrary to this act, or be any ways advising, aiding or assisting therein, being lawfully convicted thereof, shall be disabled from thenceforth to bear any office of trust or profit within the said realm of England, dominion of Wales, or town of Berwick upon Tweed, or any of the islands, territories or dominions thereunto belonging; (8) and shall incur and sustain the pains, penalties and forfeitures limited, ordained and provided in and by the statute of provision and praemunire made in the sixteenth year of King Richard the Second; (9) and be incapable of any pardon from the King, his heirs or successors, of the said forfeitures, losses or disabilities, or any of them.

XIII. Provided always, That nothing in this act shall extend to give benefit to any person who shall by contract in writing agree with any merchant or owner of any plantation, or other person whatsoever, to be transported to any parts beyond the seas, and receive earnest upon such agreement, although that afterwards such person shall renounce such contract.

XIV. Provided always, and be it enacted, That if any person or persons lawfully convicted of any felony, shall in open court pray to be transported beyond the seas, and the court shall think fit to leave him or them in prison for that purpose, such person or persons may be transported into any parts beyond the seas, this act or any thing therein contained to the contrary notwithstanding.

XV. Provided also, and be it enacted, That nothing herein contained shall be deemed, construed or taken, to extend to the imprisonment of any person before the first day of June one thousand six hundred seventy and nine, or to any thing advised, procured, or otherwise done, relating to such imprisonment; any thing herein contained to the contrary notwithstanding.

XVI. Provided also, That if any person or persons at any time resident in this realm, shall have committed any capital offence in Scotland or Ireland, or any of the islands, or foreign plantations of the King, his heirs or successors, where he or she ought to be tried for such offence, such person or persons may be sent to such place, there to receive such trial, in such manner as the same might have been used before the making of this act; any thing herein contained to the contrary notwithstanding.

XVII. Provided also, and be it enacted, That no person or persons shall be sued, impleaded, molested, or troubled for any offence against this act, unless the party offending be sued or impleaded for the same within two years at the most after such time wherein the offence shall be committed, in case the party grieved shall not be then in prison; and if he shall be in prison, then within the space of two years after the decease of the person imprisoned, or his or her delivery out of prison, which shall first happen.

XVIII. And to the intent no person may avoid his trial at the assizes or general gaol-delivery, by procuring his removal before the assizes, at such time as he cannot be brought back to receive his trial there; (2) be it enacted, That after the assizes proclaimed for that county where the prisoner is detained, no person shall be removed from the common gaol upon any *habeas corpus* granted in pursuance of this act, but upon any such *habeas corpus* shall be brought before the judge of assize in open court, who is thereupon to do what to justice shall appertain.

XIX. Provided nevertheless, That after the assizes are ended, any person or persons detained, may have his or her *habeas corpus* according to the direction and intention of this act.

XX. And be it also enacted by the authority aforesaid, That if any information, suit or action shall be brought or exhibited against any person or persons for any offence committed or to be committed against the form of this law, it shall be lawful for such defendants to plead the general issue, that they are not guilty, or that they owe nothing, and to give such special matter in evidence to the jury that shall try the same, which matter being pleaded had been good and sufficient matter in law to have discharged the said defendant or defendants against the said information, suit or action, and the said matter shall be then as available to him or them, to all intents and purposes, as if he or they had sufficiently pleaded, set forth or alleged the same matter in bar or discharge of such information suit or action.

XXI. And because many times persons charged with petty treason or felony, or as accessories thereunto, are committed upon suspicion only, whereupon they are bailable, or not, according as the circumstances making out that suspicion are more or less weighty, which are best known to the justices of peace that committed the persons, and have the examinations before them, or to other justices of the peace in the county; (2) be it therefore enacted, That where any person shall appear to be committed by any judge or justice of the peace and charged as accessory before the fact, to any petty treason or felony, or upon suspicion thereof, or with suspicion of petty treason or felony, which petty treason or felony shall be plainly and specially expressed in the warrant of commitment, that such person shall not be removed or bailed by virtue of this act, or in any other manner than they might have been before the making of this act.

Glossary

Berwick upon Tweed	the northernmost town in England, scene of many battles in the border wars between the kingdoms of England and Scotland
barons … degree of the coif	relating to the Order of the Coif, a group of sergeants-at-law whose members became judges in the Court of Common Pleas and later the King's Bench
cinque-ports	in southeastern England, the coastal towns located where the distance across the channel is the shortest
colourable	seemingly valid
enlargement	setting free
general gaol-delivery	a legal commission by which prisoners are quickly brought to trial before a court
lords spiritual and temporal, and commons	members of Parliament. At the time of the act, the lords spiritual were bishops of the Church of England, and the lords temporal were members of the hereditary peerage; they comprised the House of Lords. "Commons," representatives of the towns and cities, sat in the House of Commons.
Non vult ulterius prosequi	a plea of not wishing to pursue a prosecution further
Per statutum tricesimo primo Caroli secundi Regi	in accordance with the thirty-first statute of the reign of King Charles the Second
returnable	required by law to be delivered
vacation-time	a parliamentary recess

"It is inconsistent with the safety and welfare of this Protestant kingdom to be governed by a popish prince."

Overview

The English Bill of Rights is a statute law that was passed by Parliament and given royal assent on December 16, 1689. Along with the Magna Carta (1215), the Petition of Right (1628), the Act of Habeas Corpus (1679), and the Act of Settlement (1701), it is considered one of the most important documents that make up the uncodified constitution of England. The constitution is said to be uncodified because it is not recorded in a single document but is rather a collection of documents written at different times. Developments in the late twentieth century, such as the United Kingdom's entry into the European Union and the process of devolution in Scotland and Wales, have cast doubt on the continuing relevance of the Bill of Rights. However, its passage into law is still regarded as a significant legal and constitutional watershed.

The Bill of Rights was closely modeled on the Declaration of Rights, to which William and Mary, Prince and Princess of Orange, assented on February 13, 1689, before their declaration as King William III and Queen Mary II. The bill defined the relationship between the English monarch and Parliament, consisting of the House of Commons and House of Lords, and it firmly placed sovereignty with Parliament and by extension the people of England. Although whether the bill technically constituted the establishment of a constitutional monarchy is debatable, at the very least it formally heralded the end in England of the "divine right" of kings. It also halted the drift toward absolutism that had been characteristic of the Stuart dynasty, in particular King Charles I (r. 1625–1649) and King James II (r. 1685–1688). In short, the bill provided the framework for establishing a constitutional monarchy, and that framework consisted of wide-ranging provisions pertaining to three main concerns: defining the relationship between Parliament and the Crown, clarifying the rules of royal succession, and giving statutory protection to the rights of individuals.

The Bill of Rights was composed amid the turbulence of the Glorious Revolution of 1688–1689, during which James II fled to France and the throne was offered to William and Mary. Many of the bill's provisions were left deliberately and necessarily vague; the intention was that they would be "worked up" in subsequent decades. In fact, many were, most notably as the Triennial Act (1694), which ensured regular parliamentary meetings and elections; the Civil List Act (1697), which made Parliament, rather than the king, directly responsible for the payment of people on the Civil List (made up of officials charged with carrying out duties associated with the maintenance of the royal household); and the Act of Settlement (1701), which settled the succession to the English throne.

Context

The English Bill of Rights owes its existence to events that led up to the Glorious Revolution, also known as the English Revolution. Many of the bill's provisions directly address contentious political issues of this tumultuous period.

Following the death of King Charles II on February 6, 1685, his brother, James, a staunch Catholic, ascended the British throne and became James II of England and Ireland as well as James VII of Scotland. James's Catholicism immediately posed several problems, since England had been confirmed as a Protestant Anglican nation over a century earlier by the Second Act of Supremacy and the Act of Uniformity. These acts formed the basis of the Elizabethan Religious Settlement of 1559, which established the sovereign as "supreme governor" of the Anglican Church and compelled the English people to attend Anglican Sunday services. However, despite England's Anglicanism, James was crowned amid objections that were muted for a number of reasons. First, only twenty-five years had passed since the English monarchy had been restored in 1660 after the collapse of the Protectorate, the period of Oliver Cromwell's direct personal rule as lord protector. Supporters of the monarchy and royal prerogative feared that the legitimacy of the Restoration itself might be threatened if James were denied the throne. Second, aristocratic families, notably Tory, held sacrosanct the principle of lineage and hereditary succession because it supported their own hereditary titles. Third, widespread aversion to reviving the turmoil associated with the English Civil War (1642–1651), which for many

1559

- **April**
Act of
Supremacy
and Act of
Uniformity are
passed, making
Elizabeth I
"supreme
governor"
of the Church
of England.

1625

- **March 27**
Charles I, a
staunch believer
in the "divine
right of kings,"
begins his reign.

- **May 11**
Charles I marries
Henrietta Maria, a
Catholic, against
the wishes of
Parliament, sowing
the seeds for
religious conflict.

1641

- **December 1**
The "Grand
Remonstrance"
is handed to
Charles I,
outlining a list
of Parliament's
grievances with
his foreign,
financial, and
religious policies
and helping to
precipitate the
English Civil
War.

1653

- **December 16**
Oliver Cromwell
is sworn in as
Lord Protector,
ruling until
1658.

1661

- **April 23**
Charles II is
crowned at
Westminster
Abbey,
completing the
Restoration of
the monarchy.

English was still within living memory, restrained the likelihood of dissent.

Perhaps those memories were stirred during the summer of 1685, less than five months after James became king, when the illegitimate Protestant son of Charles II, the Duke of Monmouth, James Scott, failed in his violent attempt to usurp the throne. Therefore, initial reticence toward challenging James' succession was not altogether surprising, despite worries that he might later use his royal prerogative to grant greater tolerance to Catholics and reintegrate them into civic life in defiance of the Corporation Act of 1661, which made membership of town corporations dependent upon taking of the sacrament according to the rites of the Church of England, and the Test Act of 1673, which imposed a similar test on public and military officeholders.

In addition to signaling the possibility of religious strife, the reign of James II commenced amid profound constitutional debate regarding the precise status of the monarch in relation to Parliament and the people whom its members represented. The supremacy of Parliament as the sovereign decision-making body over the king had been debated during the reign of Charles I. Some members of Parliament, especially those who were Whigs, had already detected absolutist traits in James II's behavior and wanted to safeguard the sovereignty of Parliament with statutory force. Initially, though, most members of Parliament and leading lights of the aristocracy adopted a wait-and-see policy, provided that James would not overstep his powers as king. Also, James did not yet have a male heir, and many believed that the Crown would eventually revert to a Protestant, in particular, James's oldest daughter, Anne, who had been raised as an Anglican rather than a Catholic.

A number of James's actions, however, soon showed that he shared the Stuart penchant for absolutist rule—in particular, by using his dispensing power to exempt subjects from the force of statute laws. He also actively promoted Catholic participation in civil life, which could have led to a "Catholic Restoration." He began filling his court with Catholics, including his private Jesuit confessor, Sir Edward Petre, and a representative from the papacy, Ferdinando d'Adda. Further, on April 4, 1687, James exercised his dispensing power by issuing the Declaration of Indulgence, which circumvented penal laws against Catholics and Protestant dissenters. James then issued a revised Declaration of Indulgence on April 27, 1688, and ordered Anglican clergymen to read it aloud in their churches. William Sancroft, the Archbishop of Canterbury, and six other bishops—together known as the "Seven Bishops"—refused to read the declaration to their congregations. Because they petitioned the king to rescind the order to have the declaration read, they were quickly arrested and tried for seditious libel. In June they were acquitted to rapturous celebration by largely Anglican crowds.

The "Seven Bishops" case alienated James's Tory supporters, who came to fear a Catholic rebellion, especially in light of the fact that the hysteria surrounding false allegations of a "Popish plot" in 1678 to assassinate Charles II, involving Jesuit priests and numerous Catholic nobles, had still not fully subsided. Furthermore, the effects of King Louis XIV's revocation of the Edict of Nantes in 1685, ending toleration of French Protestants in his kingdom, added to the climate of suspicion and fear. Thus, James's use of his dispensing power to promote Catholics against existing statutory law, his persecution of prominent Anglican clergymen, and his desire for a large standing army, combined with events abroad, united two opposing political factions, the Whigs and Tories, against him. The spark that triggered the sequence of events culminating in the deposal of James and the installation of William and Mary came on June 10, 1688, when James's wife, Mary of Modena, gave birth to a male heir, James Edward. The possibility of a Catholic succession to the British throne was, for most English Protestants, simply untenable.

In response to the threat of a Catholic royal succession, seven representatives of England's leading Protestant families, nicknamed the "Immortal Seven," with tacit support from the Anglican Church, made a direct appeal to Prince William of Orange. William was James II's Protestant son-in-law; he was married to James's younger daughter, Mary, who like her sister, Anne, had been raised a Protestant. Mary was also William's cousin, since William's mother was the daughter of Charles I. The letter, dated June 30, 1688, signaled the beginning of a new chapter in English political history. As stadtholder ("head of state") of five of the United Provinces of the Netherlands, William of Orange was fiercely Protestant and keenly interested in maintaining war with the absolutist Catholic French monarch, Louis XIV, in order to defend Dutch interests.

On November 5, 1688, William landed at Brixham on Tor Bay in southwestern England with a vast armada of ships. Ahead of his arrival, he had dispatched agents to distribute leaflets written in English that stated his intention to rescue England for the Protestant cause. Bad weather had impeded James II's fleet in the Thames estuary, and after the defection to William of several high-profile commanders, James's army gradually lost confidence. William's forces proceeded toward London with little resistance; meanwhile, James himself was captured. On December 23, 1688, James was allowed to flee to France. The peers of the realm suggested recalling all members of Parliament from the reign of Charles II to decide how to deal with what amounted to an interregnum. On February 13, 1689, the Declaration of Rights was read aloud to William and Mary, who swore oaths in support of it, and they were crowned King William III and Queen Mary II on April 11, 1689. Following the coronation, the declaration was reworked and renamed the Bill of Rights. Finally, after much negotiation in the House of Commons and House of Lords, especially over the monarch's dispensing power, the bill was given royal assent on December 16, 1689.

About the Author

The Bill of Rights was by its very nature a collectively authored document. Since it was based on the Declaration

Time Line

1687

- **April 4**
  James II issues his first Declaration of Indulgence, which calls for official tolerance of Roman Catholics and Protestant dissenters such as Presbyterians.

1688

- **April 27**
  James II issues a revised Declaration of Indulgence. The case of the "Seven Bishops" ensues, making James deeply unpopular among the Anglican clergy.

- **June 10**
  James II's male heir to the throne, James Edward, is born, threatening the prospect of a Catholic dynasty.

- **June 30**
  A group of English nobles nicknamed the "Immortal Seven" send a letter to the Dutch stadtholder, Prince William of Orange, in which they request him to restore the supremacy of Protestant Anglicanism within the English realm.

- **November 5**
  William of Orange lands at Brixham on Tor Bay in southwestern England with a large army; in the following weeks, his forces remain largely unopposed as they proceed toward London.

- **December 23**
  Having abdicated earlier in the month, James II flees to Saint-Germain-en-Laye, France.

Time Line

1689

■ **February 13**
The Declaration of Rights, having been drawn up by the Convention Parliament, is read aloud to William and Mary; after they swear oaths in its support, they are officially proclaimed King William III and Queen Mary II.

■ **December 16**
After passage by Parliament, the Bill of Rights is given royal assent.

of Rights, authorship can be attributed to the Convention Parliament, which was the first parliament convened following the arrival of William of Orange in England. The Convention Parliament comprised members who had been in Charles II's last Parliament, which he had dissolved in 1681. A small commission made up of Convention Parliament members drafted the declaration. Individual contributions of commission members, however, are difficult to determine. Many constitutional historians have argued that the political philosophy of John Locke was the intellectual foundation of the Bill of Rights. Locke had been in exile in Holland throughout much of James II's reign and had returned to England with William of Orange's wife in 1688. However, only an indirect connection can be made, since most of Locke's important works, such as *Two Treatises of Government*, which emphasized the concept of a separation of powers, were published after his return to England.

Explanation and Analysis of the Document

The Bill of Rights can be broken into two distinct parts. The first part contains a list of "abuses" committed by James II, which are then followed by articles that restate the substance of each of these abuses in the negative and declare each of them either "illegal," "pernicious," "against law," or "void." The second part comprises thirteen articles designed to safeguard the Protestant succession to the throne, to establish that both Houses of Parliament give their assent to the succession and bill, and, finally, to secure the permanence of the document.

◆ First Part: Abuses and Restatements

James's twelve abuses are restated as thirteen articles declaring what are more accurately described as wrongs rather than rights. This was a rhetorical ploy by the framers of the bill to secure its passage in Parliament. By reviewing and assenting to the criminality of James II's actions, it was difficult to deny the correctness of the subsequent generalized restatements, which were more controversial. For example, the second abuse, regarding the prosecution of "worthy prelates" for petitioning the king, is restated as "it is the right of the subjects to petition the king." The preamble is important in determining the bill's legality and emphasizes the lawful, full, and free nature of the Convention Parliament and the circumstances under which the Declaration of Rights, on which the Bill of Rights was based, was read aloud.

The twelve abuses of James II and the articles restating them are separated by an important passage that is a de facto declaration that James II had abdicated and placed himself in exile in France. By contrast, in the same paragraph, William of Orange is praised as "the glorious instrument of delivering this kingdom from popery and arbitrary power." It is made clear that a Convention Parliament was lawfully convened upon the advice and consent of "the Lords Spiritual and Temporal" and leaders in the House of Commons and that it was entrusted with the task of ensuring that "laws and liberties might not again be in danger of being subverted."

The first and second articles, which refer to the first abuse of James II, deal with the king's power to suspend or temporarily dispense with the law, or the execution of the law, without prior approval of Parliament. In reality, kings had seldom invoked the so-called suspending power. The first article, therefore, found broad agreement within the Convention Parliament. The second article, relating to the dispensing power of the Crown, was far more controversial. This concerned the monarch's ability to exempt people or groups from laws under certain conditions. Both Charles II and James II had regularly invoked the dispensing power to give greater freedom to Catholics and Protestant dissenters. The phrase "of late" makes explicit reference to the actions of James II; it was designed to circumvent claims of historical precedent for monarchs using the dispensing power. Historical precedent, however, was perhaps not so easily dismissed. The concept of dispensing power had existed since the thirteenth century, when Henry II had used it in imitation of papal dispensations. Elizabeth I also widely used the dispensing power, though seldom controversially. Many Tories argued that the monarch's dispensing power was necessary because laws were seldom revised and often became outdated. Therefore, it was right that the king could, as one member of Parliament put it, "Supply [the law's] defects, pardoning a condemned Innocent" (qtd. in Edie, p. 435). The clause was left in the bill because the majority of Convention Parliament members felt that the dispensing power was a major hurdle to the establishment of a constitutional monarchy.

The second and third abuses also had direct relevance to the events preceding the Glorious Revolution. The second abuse, corresponding to the fifth restatement, mentions "worthy prelates" who had petitioned the king. These were

Cufflinks decorated with portraits of William and Mary (© Museum of London)

the "Seven Bishops" who had been prosecuted for having petitioned James II, after they had refused to read the Declaration of Indulgence aloud in their churches. The right to petition the king originated in Saxon times and has since been considered one of the ancient rights of English subjects. The third abuse corresponds to the third restatement, which outlaws the Court of Commissioners for Ecclesiastical Causes. James II had established this court in 1686 to assist Catholics and to monitor universities and the Anglican Church. The measure was deeply unpopular, especially because such commissions had been outlawed in 1661.

Rising levels of taxation, which also related to control over revenue, had long created conflict between Parliament and the monarchy. According to the fourth charge of abuse, James II had levied money for use by the Crown in ways other than those stipulated by Parliament. Charles I had also antagonized Parliament with his unsanctioned revival of the ship tax and other ancient laws. Revenue was important for the monarch for three main reasons: first, for maintaining the Civil List and his own court; second, to pay for a standing army and defense of the realm; and third, to bribe secret service agents, influence elections, and secure loyalty. The bill covers all three of these reasons and limits the monarch's power to raise revenue.

The Civil List was of great importance, since it funded officials working for the royal family, offices known as sinecures (which required little or no real work but which were often accompanied by titles and salaries and were designed as a way of distributing royal patronage), and the pensions of courtiers and servants of the Crown upon retirement from active service. All were skillfully distrib-

uted to ensure support for the king. If Parliament could not control the revenue used for these purposes, then it would be ineffective and cede more power to the king. The fourth article states that revenue may not be collected for use of the Crown "without grant of Parliament." However, control over revenue would remain a source of contention during William III's rule. In the early years of his reign, William frequently tussled with Parliament over revenue for the Civil List and payment for the war with France. Gradually, later Parliaments took greater control over revenue.

The sixth article, corresponding to the fifth abuse of James II, bans the king from keeping a standing army without the support of Parliament. James's decision to maintain a standing army in times of peace without the consent of Parliament not only had drained revenue but also had been extremely menacing and against English tradition. Furthermore, the armies of Charles II and James II were composed mainly of Catholics, and many leading generals were Catholic. Debates about a standing army would resurface in the late eighteenth century during the American Revolution. In James's time, it is unlikely that Parliament would have endorsed the creation of a standing army. The Catholic threat is also reflected in the seventh article (corresponding to the sixth abuse), which states that Protestants are allowed to bear arms. This article has relevance to the Second Amendment to the U.S. Constitution, where the right to bear arms is guaranteed in the context of maintaining the security of the state. Significantly, however, the English Bill of Rights does not justify this right.

The eighth, ninth, and thirteenth articles concern elections and parliamentary procedure. The eighth article, cor-

Engraving of the flight of James II to France (© Bettmann/CORBIS)

has perhaps the most contemporary significance, since it limits excessive bail, fines, and "cruel and unusual punishments." Judicial discretion was considerable during this period, and this article sought to prevent arbitrary abuse by judges. While judges rarely issued punishments outside the bounds of the law, they often set disproportionate and prohibitive bail, an amount of money paid as a guarantee of returning to court for judgment. This article was designed to ensure that all subjects had the same standing before the court. The words "cruel and unusual punishments" have a somewhat different meaning than what normally would be assumed today. In Restoration England, cruelty was defined not in terms of suffering but whether the punishment was commensurate with the crime. The eleventh article describes the process for selecting jury panels and specifies that a jury for a treason trial must be composed of "freeholders," subjects who owned land or property. This meant that juries were composed of wealthier members of society and excluded leaseholders or people who rented land and dwellings. The twelfth article, corresponding to the twelfth abuse of James II, prohibits the practice of promising to others the fines and lands of defendants prior to trial, which blatantly presupposed guilt and was contrary to the basic tenets of jurisprudence.

◆ **Second Part: Safeguarding the Succession and the Bill of Rights**

The second part of the Bill of Rights is more typical of a seventeenth-century legal document, both in style and language. The three most important features include a precise description of the royal succession (covered by articles II, VIII, IX, and X), a determination that there shall not be a Catholic monarch or a monarch married to a Catholic (article IX), and a provision that safeguarded the bill and subsequent acts passed by the Convention Parliament from being dispensed *non obstante*—dispensed by the monarch, that is—unless a particular act itself would allow dispensation (the substance of articles XI and XII). The bill further emphasizes that the enthronement of William and Mary has the authority and support of both Houses of Parliament (articles I, II, VI, and VIII), that James II abdicated his throne (article VII), and that with their majesties' consent, Parliament participates in the governance of the realm (article V). Article IV is a statement of William and Mary's acceptance of the crown, while article III contains oaths of allegiance to the crown.

Guaranteeing the royal succession is a problem for all monarchies. Indeed, the establishment of the Church of England had stemmed from Henry VIII's desire for a male heir. The unexpected birth of a male heir to James II and Mary of Modena had triggered the Glorious Revolution. The Bill of Rights established the following succession: William III and Mary II were to continue as lawful king and queen during their lifetimes. Upon the death of either one, the other would become sole ruler. After the deaths of both monarchs, the rightful line of kingship would pass to the "heirs of the body" of Mary II. If for any reason there was no royal issue, the throne would revert to Queen Anne of

responding to the seventh abuse, declares that elections should be free. This was a direct attack on royal interference in elections in ways that had included designating candidates, excluding people from office, and voiding election results. It is important to note, however, that this provision focuses on the candidates, not the voters. The ninth article (corresponding to the eighth abuse) requires that speech in Parliament be free and that verbal exchanges between members of Parliament shall not be subject to court proceedings. This basic tenet of parliamentary privilege is still practiced today. The thirteenth and final article, without a directly corresponding abuse, maintains that Parliament shall be convened frequently. In the seventeenth century, the king's prerogative to govern without Parliament sitting—a prorogued Parliament—had been invoked several times, most notably by Charles I in 1629 in what became known as the Eleven Years' Tyranny. The frequency of parliamentary gathering was also related to counteracting a strong argument in favor of the monarch's dispensing power: the need to amend and update legislation.

The tenth, eleventh, and twelfth articles (corresponding to the ninth through twelfth abuses) all focus on judicial procedure and the rights of individuals. The tenth clause

"*King James the Second, by the assistance of divers evil counsellors, judges and ministers employed by him, did endeavour to subvert and extirpate the Protestant religion and the laws and liberties of this kingdom.*"

(Preamble)

"*The pretended power of suspending the laws or the execution of laws by regal authority without consent of Parliament is illegal.*"

(Abuse I)

"*Election of members of Parliament ought to be free.*"

(Restatement VIII)

"*The said Lords Spiritual and Temporal and Commons assembled at Westminster do resolve that William and Mary, Prince and Princess of Orange, be and be declared king and queen of England, France and Ireland.*"

(Second Part: II)

"*The rights and liberties asserted and claimed in the said declaration are the true, ancient and indubitable rights and liberties of the people of this kingdom.*"

(Second Part: VI)

"*It hath been found by experience that it is inconsistent with the safety and welfare of this Protestant kingdom to be governed by a popish prince.*"

(Second Part: IX)

Denmark, Mary II's sister, and in the event of her death to her progeny. In the event that none of these successions were possible, then the heirs of William III would have the royal title. The framers of the bill were anxious to settle the succession quickly, although further stipulations would have to be made in the Act of Settlement of 1701. In the end Queen Anne outlived her only progeny, Prince William, Duke of Gloucester, who died of smallpox in July of 1700 at the age of eleven. This tested the new rules of succession and reset the line to the Hanoverian descendants of King James I, the heirs of Sophia, the duchess of Hanover.

Sophia was the daughter of the German elector Palatine Frederick V and Princess Elizabeth, who was the daughter of King James I. Her son was the first Hanoverian English king, George I.

The succession was drawn up to ensure a Protestant successor. The bill states that henceforth there shall be no Catholic monarch of England nor any monarch married to a Catholic. This law is still in force today, and the rationale behind this determination is obvious. A Catholic monarch such as James II could have sought rapprochement with the pontiff in Rome, interfered with the Anglican Church, or otherwise compromised the "safety and welfare" of Protestant England.

Audience

Although it is very similar to the Declaration of Rights in content, the Bill of Rights was directed at a somewhat different audience. The declaration had itself been preceded by William of Orange's own Declaration of the Hague, which William's close adviser, Gilbert Burnet, had translated into English and then distributed when William landed at Tor Bay in November 1688. The audience for the Declaration of the Hague was very broad, since the document was aimed at garnering on-the-ground support for William. The Declaration of Rights, however, sought to appease the Anglican clergy and Protestant royalist supporters of James II; it was also directed at William and Mary themselves, who had threatened to leave England if they were not crowned or voted sufficient revenue to continue the Dutch war with France.

The Bill of Rights had four different audiences. First, for William and Mary, the bill was a clear statement of the extent and limitations of their royal prerogative. Second, for James II and his Catholic, Irish, and French supporters, it proclaimed that the settlement about succession to the English throne was legal, final, and irreversible. Third, the bill was directed at all members of Parliament, the very body that had drafted it, in their capacity as representatives of the English people. It set out in clear language certain rights that all English subjects were entitled to within the framework of seventeenth-century constitutional thought, such as freedom to petition the monarch regarding grievances. Finally, the bill functioned as a broader statement to European powers that England was a constitutional monarchy and remained a Protestant nation ruled by Parliament.

Impact

The Bill of Rights has had a lasting impact on England's constitutional development and political history as well as on the formulation of comprehensive bills of rights in other countries. Much of its content was the product of its time, especially of the political upheaval and dramatic events of the Glorious Revolution. As a testament to the bill's definitive nature, however, it is still widely cited today, and it retains statutory force and is considered a pillar of the Revolution Settlement, encompassing a series of acts beginning with the Bill of Rights (1689) and ending with the Act of Settlement (1701), which secured a Protestant succession to the English throne.

The importance of the Bill of Rights as a focal point for individual rights and free and fair government reemerged in the late eighteenth century, when it was widely discussed during the American and French revolutions. The Revolution Society, founded to celebrate the Glorious Revolution of 1688 and chaired by Charles Stanhope, 3rd Earl Stanhope, reprinted the Bill of Rights in its entirety to raise awareness of its constitutional importance and as an example of English liberties during the formulation of a new French Constitution in the early 1790s. However, interpretations of the process that led up to the bill's enactment have been continually debated. The conservative historian

Questions for Further Study

1. At about the same time as the English Bill of Rights came out, John Locke published the *Second Treatise on Civil Government*. Read the two documents in conjunction with each other. How do they each reflect prevailing attitudes toward civil rights, the position of the monarchy, and similar issues?

2. Summarize the political events in England that gave rise to the English Bill of Rights.

3. Examine the Time Line associated with the English Bill of Rights. As an exercise in "what if," imagine that one of the events leading up to the passage of the Bill of Rights had not taken place or had turned out radically different. What impact do you think this change in historical circumstances might have had on the development of civil rights in England?

4. Trace the development of Western concepts of civil rights from the Magna Carta through the Habeas Corpus Act of the Restoration and the English Bill of Rights to the UN Declaration of Human Rights. Have concepts of civil rights changed? Have they remained consistent? Explain.

5. What impact did the English Bill of Rights have on the U.S. Constitution?

J. C. D. Clark has argued that the significance of the bill has been exaggerated and that it did little more than put rights and freedoms that had long existed into written form. Nonetheless, in its historical context the Bill of Rights represented a decisive step in favor of parliamentary sovereignty. The sections on cruel and unusual punishment and free and fair elections anticipate many of the key legal documents of the twentieth century.

In addition to its historical importance, the bill has had a huge political, philosophical, and linguistic influence worldwide by setting forth a precedent upon which framers of later constitutions and declarations have drawn. Most notably, the U.S. Bill of Rights and the United Nation's Universal Declaration of Human Rights, while different in scope and tenor, are clearly indebted to the English Bill of Rights.

Further Reading

■ Articles

Colls, R. "The Constitution of the English." *History Workshop Journal* 46 (Autumn 1998): 97–127.

Edie, C. A. "Revolution and the Rule of Law: The End of the Dispensing Power, 1689." *Eighteenth-Century Studies* 10, no. 4 (Spring 1977): 434–450.

Reitan, E. A. "From Revenue to Civil List, 1689–1702: The Revolution Settlement and the 'Mixed and Balanced' Constitution." *Historical Journal* 13, no. 4 (December 1970): 571–588.

Schwoerer, L. G. "Celebrating the Glorious Revolution, 1689–1989: 1989 Presidential Address to the North American Conference on British Studies." *Albion: A Quarterly Journal Concerned with British Studies* 22, no. 1 (Spring 1990): 1–20.

■ Books

Ball, Terence, and J. G. A. Pocock, eds. *Conceptual Change and the Constitution.* Lawrence: University of Kansas Press, 1988.

Clark, J. C. D. *English Society, 1660–1832: Religion, Ideology, and Politics during the Ancien Regime.* New York: Cambridge University Press, 2000.

Jones, J. R., ed. *Liberty Secured? Britain before and after 1688.* Stanford: Stanford University Press, 1992.

Pincus, C. A. *England's Glorious Revolution, 1688–1689: A Brief History with Documents.* New York: Palgrave Macmillan, 2006.

Pocock, J. G. A. *The Ancient Constitution and the Feudal Law: A Study of English Historical Thought in the Seventeenth Century.* Cambridge, U.K.: Cambridge University Press, 1987.

■ Web Sites

Maer, Lucinda, and Oonagh Gay. "Bill of Rights 1689." U.K. Parliament and Constitution Centre Web site. http://www.parliament.uk/commons/lib/research/briefings/snpc -00293.pdf.

—Peter Robinson

ENGLISH BILL OF RIGHTS

An Act Declaring the Rights and Liberties of the Subject and Settling the Succession of the Crown

Whereas the Lords Spiritual and Temporal and Commons assembled at Westminster, lawfully, fully and freely representing all the estates of the people of this realm, did upon the thirteenth day of February in the year of our Lord one thousand six hundred eighty-eight [old style date] present unto their Majesties, then called and known by the names and style of William and Mary, prince and princess of Orange, being present in their proper persons, a certain declaration in writing made by the said Lords and Commons in the words following, viz.:

Whereas the late King James the Second, by the assistance of divers evil counsellors, judges and ministers employed by him, did endeavour to subvert and extirpate the Protestant religion and the laws and liberties of this kingdom;

I. By assuming and exercising a power of dispensing with and suspending of laws and the execution of laws without consent of Parliament;

II. By committing and prosecuting divers worthy prelates for humbly petitioning to be excused from concurring to the said assumed power;

III. By issuing and causing to be executed a commission under the great seal for erecting a court called the Court of Commissioners for Ecclesiastical Causes;

IV. By levying money for and to the use of the Crown by pretence of prerogative for other time and in other manner than the same was granted by Parliament;

V. By raising and keeping a standing army within this kingdom in time of peace without consent of Parliament, and quartering soldiers contrary to law;

VI. By causing several good subjects being Protestants to be disarmed at the same time when papists were both armed and employed contrary to law;

VII. By violating the freedom of election of members to serve in Parliament;

VIII. By prosecutions in the Court of King's Bench for matters and causes cognizable only in Parliament, and by divers other arbitrary and illegal courses;

IX. And whereas of late years partial corrupt and unqualified persons have been returned and served on juries in trials, and particularly divers jurors in trials for high treason which were not freeholders;

X. And excessive bail hath been required of persons committed in criminal cases to elude the benefit of the laws made for the liberty of the subjects;

XI. And excessive fines have been imposed; And illegal and cruel punishments inflicted;

XII. And several grants and promises made of fines and forfeitures before any conviction or judgment against the persons upon whom the same were to be levied;

All which are utterly and directly contrary to the known laws and statutes and freedom of this realm;

And whereas the said late King James the Second having abdicated the government and the throne being thereby vacant, his Highness the prince of Orange (whom it hath pleased Almighty God to make the glorious instrument of delivering this kingdom from popery and arbitrary power) did (by the advice of the Lords Spiritual and Temporal and divers principal persons of the Commons) cause letters to be written to the Lords Spiritual and Temporal being Protestants, and other letters to the several counties, cities, universities, boroughs and cinque ports, for the choosing of such persons to represent them as were of right to be sent to Parliament, to meet and sit at Westminster upon the two and twentieth day of January in this year one thousand six hundred eighty and eight [old style date], in order to such an establishment as that their religion, laws and liberties might not again be in danger of being subverted, upon which letters elections having been accordingly made;

And thereupon the said Lords Spiritual and Temporal and Commons, pursuant to their respective letters and elections, being now assembled in a full and free representative of this nation, taking into their most serious consideration the best means for attaining the ends aforesaid, do in the first place (as their ancestors in like case have usually done) for the vindicating and asserting their ancient rights and liberties declare:

I. That the pretended power of suspending the laws or the execution of laws by regal authority without consent of Parliament is illegal;

II. That the pretended power of dispensing with laws or the execution of laws by regal authority, as it hath been assumed and exercised of late, is illegal;

III. That the commission for erecting the late Court of Commissioners for Ecclesiastical Causes, and all other commissions and courts of like nature, are illegal and pernicious;

IV. That levying money for or to the use of the Crown by pretence of prerogative, without grant of Parliament, for longer time, or in other manner than the same is or shall be granted, is illegal;

V. That it is the right of the subjects to petition the king, and all commitments and prosecutions for such petitioning are illegal;

VI. That the raising or keeping a standing army within the kingdom in time of peace, unless it be with consent of Parliament, is against law;

VII. That the subjects which are Protestants may have arms for their defence suitable to their conditions and as allowed by law;

VIII. That election of members of Parliament ought to be free;

IX. That the freedom of speech and debates or proceedings in Parliament ought not to be impeached or questioned in any court or place out of Parliament;

X. That excessive bail ought not to be required, nor excessive fines imposed, nor cruel and unusual punishments inflicted;

XI. That jurors ought to be duly impanelled and returned, and jurors which pass upon men in trials for high treason ought to be freeholders;

XII. That all grants and promises of fines and forfeitures of particular persons before conviction are illegal and void;

XIII. And that for redress of all grievances, and for the amending, strengthening and preserving of the laws, Parliaments ought to be held frequently. And they do claim, demand and insist upon all and singular the premises as their undoubted rights and liberties, and that no declarations, judgments, doings or proceedings to the prejudice of the people in any of the said premises ought in any wise to be drawn hereafter into consequence or example.

I. To which demand of their rights they are particularly encouraged by the declaration of his Highness the prince of Orange as being the only means for obtaining a full redress and remedy therein. Having therefore an entire confidence that his said Highness the prince of Orange will perfect the deliverance so far advanced by him, and will still preserve them from the violation of their rights which they have here asserted, and from all other attempts upon their religion, rights and liberties:

II. The said Lords Spiritual and Temporal and Commons assembled at Westminster do resolve that William and Mary, prince and princess of Orange, be and be declared king and queen of England, France and Ireland and the dominions thereunto belonging, to hold the crown and royal dignity of the said kingdoms and dominions to them, the said prince and princess, during their lives and the life of the survivor to them, and that the sole and full exercise of the regal power be only in and executed by the said prince of Orange in the names of the said prince and princess during their joint lives, and after their deceases the said crown and royal dignity of the same kingdoms and dominions to be to the heirs of the body of the said princess, and for default of such issue to the Princess Anne of Denmark and the heirs of her body, and for default of such issue to the heirs of the body of the said prince of Orange. And the Lords Spiritual and Temporal and Commons do pray the said prince and princess to accept the same accordingly.

III. And that the oaths hereafter mentioned be taken by all persons of whom the oaths have allegiance and supremacy might be required by law, instead of them; and that the said oaths of allegiance and supremacy be abrogated.

I, A.B., do sincerely promise and swear that I will be faithful and bear true allegiance to their Majesties King William and Queen Mary. So help me God.

I, A.B., do swear that I do from my heart abhor, detest and abjure as impious and heretical this damnable doctrine and position, that princes excommunicated or deprived by the Pope or any authority of the see of Rome may be deposed or murdered by their subjects or any other whatsoever. And I do declare that no foreign prince, person, prelate, state or potentate hath or ought to have any jurisdiction, power, superiority, pre-eminence or authority, ecclesiastical or spiritual, within this realm. So help me God.

IV. Upon which their said Majesties did accept the crown and royal dignity of the kingdoms of England, France and Ireland, and the dominions thereunto belonging, according to the resolution and desire of the said Lords and Commons contained in the said declaration.

V. And thereupon their Majesties were pleased that the said Lords Spiritual and Temporal and Commons, being the two Houses of Parliament, should continue to sit, and with their Majesties' royal concurrence make effectual provision for the settlement of the religion, laws and liberties of this kingdom, so that the same for the future might not be in danger again of being subverted, to which the said Lords Spiritual and Temporal and Commons did agree, and proceed to act accordingly.

VI. Now in pursuance of the premises the said Lords Spiritual and Temporal and Commons in Parliament assembled, for the ratifying, confirming and establishing the said declaration and the articles, clauses, matters and things therein contained by the force of law made in due form by authority of Parliament, do pray that it may be declared and enacted that all and singular the rights and liberties asserted and claimed in the said declaration are the true, ancient and indubitable rights and liberties of the people of this kingdom, and so shall be esteemed, allowed, adjudged, deemed and taken to be; and that all and every the particulars aforesaid shall be firmly and strictly holden and observed as they are expressed in the said declaration, and all officers and ministers whatsoever shall serve their Majesties and their successors according to the same in all time to come.

VII. And the said Lords Spiritual and Temporal and Commons, seriously considering how it hath pleased Almighty God in his marvellous providence and merciful goodness to this nation to provide and preserve their said Majesties' royal persons most happily to reign over us upon the throne of their ancestors, for which they render unto him from the bottom of their hearts their humblest thanks and praises, do truly, firmly, assuredly and in the sincerity of their hearts think, and do hereby recognize, acknowledge and declare, that King James the Second having abdicated the government, and their Majesties having accepted the crown and royal dignity as aforesaid, their said Majesties did become, were, are and of right ought to be by the laws of this realm our sovereign liege lord and lady, king and queen of England, France and Ireland and the dominions thereunto belonging, in and to whose princely persons the royal state, crown and dignity of the said realms with all honours, styles, titles, regalities, prerogatives, powers, jurisdictions and authorities to the same belonging and appertaining are most fully, rightfully and entirely invested and incorporated, united and annexed.

VIII. And for preventing all questions and divisions in this realm by reason of any pretended titles to the crown, and for preserving a certainty in the succession thereof, in and upon which the unity, peace, tranquility and safety of this nation doth under God wholly consist and depend, the said Lords Spiritual and Temporal and Commons do beseech their Majesties that it may be enacted, established and declared, that the crown and regal government of the said kingdoms and dominions, with all and singular the premises thereunto belonging and appertaining, shall be and continue to their said Majesties and the survivor of them during their lives and the life of the survivor of them, and that the entire, perfect and full exercise of the regal power and government be only in and executed by his Majesty in the names of both their Majesties during their joint lives; and after their deceases the said crown and premises shall be and remain to the heirs of the body of her Majesty, and for default of such issue to her Royal Highness the Princess Anne of Denmark and the heirs of the body of his said Majesty; and thereunto the said Lords Spiritual and Temporal and Commons do in the name of all the people aforesaid most humbly and faithfully submit themselves, their heirs and posterities for ever, and do faithfully promise that they will stand to, maintain and defend their said Majesties, and also the limitation and succession of the crown herein specified and contained, to the utmost of their powers with their lives and estates against all persons whatsoever that shall attempt anything to the contrary.

IX. And whereas it hath been found by experience that it is inconsistent with the safety and welfare of this Protestant kingdom to be governed by a popish prince, or by any king or queen marrying a papist, the said Lords Spiritual and Temporal and Commons do further pray that it may be enacted, that all and every person and persons that is, are or shall be reconciled to or shall hold communion with the see or Church of Rome, or shall profess the popish religion, or shall marry a papist, shall be excluded and be for ever incapable to inherit, possess or enjoy the crown and government of this realm and Ireland and the dominions thereunto belonging or any part of the same, or to have, use or exercise any regal power, authority or jurisdiction within the same; and in all and every such case or cases the people of these realms shall be and are hereby absolved of their allegiance; and the said crown and government shall from time to time descend to and be enjoyed by such person or persons being Protestants as should have inherited and enjoyed the same in case the said person or persons so reconciled, holding communion or professing or marrying as aforesaid were naturally dead.

X. And that every king and queen of this realm who at any time hereafter shall come to and succeed in the imperial crown of this kingdom shall on the first day of the meeting of the first Parliament next after his or her coming to the crown, sitting in his or her throne in the House of Peers in the presence of the Lords and Commons therein assembled, or at his or her coronation before such person or persons who shall administer the coronation oath to him or her at the time of his or her taking the said oath (which shall first happen), make, subscribe and audibly repeat the declaration mentioned in the statute made in the thirtieth year of the reign of King Charles the Second entitled, "An Act for the more effectual preserving the king's person and government by disabling papists from sitting in either House of Parliament." But if it shall happen that such king or queen upon his or her succession to the crown of this realm shall be under the age of twelve years, then every such king or queen shall make, subscribe and audibly repeat the same declaration at his or her coronation or the first day of the meeting of the first Parliament as aforesaid which shall first happen after such king or queen shall have attained the said age of twelve years.

XI. All which their Majesties are contented and pleased shall be declared, enacted and established by authority of this present Parliament, and shall stand, remain and be the law of this realm for ever; and the same are by their said Majesties, by and with the advice and consent of the Lords Spiritual and Temporal and Commons in Parliament assembled and by the authority of the same, declared, enacted and established accordingly.

XII. And be it further declared and enacted by the authority aforesaid, that from and after this present session of Parliament no dispensation by *non obstante* of or to any statute or any part thereof shall be allowed, but that the same shall be held void and of no effect, except a dispensation be allowed of in such statute, and except in such cases as shall be specially provided for by one or more bill or bills to be passed during this present session of Parliament.

XIII. Provided that no charter or grant or pardon granted before the three and twentieth day of October in the year of our Lord one thousand six hundred eighty-nine shall be any ways impeached or invalidated by this Act, but that the same shall be and remain of the same force and effect in law and no other than as if this Act had never been made.

Glossary

cinque ports	in southeastern England, the coastal towns located where the distance across the channel is the shortest
Lords Spiritual and Temporal, and Commons	members of Parliament. At the time of the act, the Lords Spiritual were bishops of the Church of England, and the Lords Temporal were members of the hereditary peerage; they comprised the House of Lords. "Commons," representatives of the towns and cities, sat in the House of Commons
[old style date]	date according to the Julian calendar, not the Gregorian [new style] calendar, which had been in use in continental Europe since 1582

John Locke (Library of Congress)

"The natural liberty of man is to be free from any superior power on earth."

Overview

John Locke, one of the most influential philosophers and political theorists of seventeenth-century England, was the author of the *Second Treatise on Civil Government*. This treatise was part of a larger work titled *Two Treatises of Government*, which Locke published anonymously in 1690. The first treatise consisted of Locke's refutation of views that had been published by another political theorist, Robert Filmer, who argued that monarchs had a divine right to rule. The second, and more famous, treatise was identified on the volume's cover as "an Essay Concerning the True Original, Extent, and End of Civil Government." Thus it came to be called the *Second Treatise on Civil Government*.

The second volume of the greater work was written with two purposes in mind. The first was to justify resistance to King Charles II, who proved unpopular after being restored to the British throne in 1660 because of his Catholic leanings. The second purpose was to justify the so-called Glorious Revolution, which brought William of Orange and Mary from Holland to England in 1688 to claim the throne, in the process driving Charles II's successor (and Mary's father), James II, into exile—although Locke had been at work on the treatise years before the Glorious Revolution took place. The text stands as a key document in the history of Western political thought. In fact, the treatise provided an intellectual foundation for the future rejection of absolute monarchies—a process that began in Western culture in the eighteenth century, most notably with the French and American revolutions, and continued into the nineteenth century. Furthermore, the corpus of Locke's work, including the *Second Treatise*, was crucial in the history of rationalism, itself a key component of the eighteenth century's Enlightenment. The views expressed by Locke found their way into such pivotal documents as the American Declaration of Independence.

Context

The context of the *Second Treatise on Civil Government* was the Glorious Revolution of 1688, an event whose roots stretched back at least to the reign of King Henry VIII in the early sixteenth century. Henry's rejection of Roman Catholicism and his reformation of the church in England coincided with the greater Protestant Reformation, launched by Martin Luther in Germany in 1517 with the publication of his *Ninety-five Theses*. Henry's reforms, however, did not go far enough for those who wanted to see the church fully purified. Out of this discontent rose the Puritans, who became the party of radical reform. Pitted against them was the Church of England (Anglican) establishment, which sought to impose national unity of religion in England. The ensuing struggle reached a climax of armed conflict in the mid-seventeenth century under King Charles I: the three-stage English Civil War took place through the 1640s between the Royalists (supporters of the king) and a Parliament dominated by Puritans. In 1649 the defeated Charles I was convicted of treason by Parliament and executed.

The Puritans, led by Oliver Cromwell and later his son Richard, ruled England for about seven years; during this period, called the Interregnum, the state was variously called the Commonwealth or the Protectorate. Under the Puritans, strict standards of morality were enforced, with holidays, the theater, gambling, and other amusements suppressed. Richard succeeded his father to the position of lord protector on the latter's death, but after Richard abdicated in 1659, the monarchy was restored, and Charles II was crowned in 1660, an event called the Restoration. The Restoration was a period of reaction to the strict morality enforced during the Commonwealth, as people indulged their pent-up desires for theater, art, fashion, and pleasure. Charles's own hedonistic way of life was almost a relief to the English people. At the same time, efforts were made to impose religious uniformity in England. The Anglicans were able to expel Presbyterian and other "dissenting" Protestant ministers from their pulpits, pushing them to the fringes of society along with Catholics. Charles II, though, was sympathetic to Catholicism and sought to grant legal relief to Catholics, as well as to Dissenters.

Charles personally favored a policy of religious tolerance, but he bowed to Parliament's desire to restore the supremacy of the Church of England by agreeing to the Clarendon Code. This code was a series of laws that

1642

- The English Civil War between the Puritans, operating through Parliament, and the Crown begins.

1649

- **January 30** King Charles I is executed, and England becomes the Commonwealth.

1660

- The monarchy is restored under Charles II.

1666

- John Locke meets Lord Anthony Ashley Cooper (later the First Earl of Shaftesbury).

1668

- The Royal Society elects Locke to be a fellow.

1679

- The Earl of Shaftesbury champions a bill to exclude James, Duke of York, Charles's Catholic brother, from the throne.

1683

- The Rye House Plot, a plot to kill Charles II and his brother James, is exposed; Locke flees to Holland, and Whig leaders are arrested.

enforced religious conformity and made "meeting houses" and dissenting or nonconformist worship illegal. Yet in 1672 he issued the Royal Declaration of Indulgence, which extended tolerance to Nonconformists and Catholics. Later, though, he rescinded the declaration under pressure from Parliament. Then, in the late 1670s, the purported "Popish Plot" provoked fear after it was revealed that Charles's brother and heir, James, was a Catholic. This discovery led to a split between the Whig Party, which advocated the exclusion of Catholics and Dissenters from public office, and the Tory Party, which opposed exclusion. When a 1683 plot to assassinate both Charles and James, the Rye House Plot, was exposed, numerous Whig leaders were forced into exile or even killed.

Charles meanwhile had dissolved Parliament in 1679 when it attempted to remove James from the line of succession, and he ruled without Parliament until he died in 1685—on his deathbed converting to Catholicism. When the Catholic James II's wife gave birth to a son, the nobility decided that the time had come to extirpate Catholic rule once and for all by inviting William, Prince of Orange, a Protestant, to assume the throne of England. (Orange was a principality in Holland; it is now part of France.) William had some legitimate claim to the throne as the husband of James II's daughter, Mary, by his deceased first wife. William invaded England in 1688, met with no meaningful resistance, and was crowned on April 11, 1689. With James II in exile, the establishment of Protestantism in England was made permanent. This change in the monarchy was named the Glorious Revolution because in the main it was accomplished without bloodshed. Such a major step, however, required justification. John Locke provided that justification in his *Second Treatise*, at the same time outlining a theory and philosophy of government. It is believed, too, that a goal of his was to refute the views of Thomas Hobbes's influential book *Leviathan*, an argument in favor of absolutist governments published in 1651 and translated into Latin in 1668.

About the Author

Locke was born in Wrington, England, on August 29, 1632, to Puritan parents. During the English Civil War in the 1640s his father fought for the Parliamentarians. He attended the Westminster School in London and was made a King's Scholar. In 1652 he entered the Christ Church college at Oxford University, earning a bachelor's degree in 1656 and a master's in 1658. He discovered, however, that his interest lay less with the classical subjects taught at Oxford and more with newly emerging experimental sciences and medicine. Inspired by the empirical views of such thinkers as Sir Francis Bacon and René Descartes, he began to investigate natural science subjects, eventually joining England's Royal Society in 1668. In the 1660s he collaborated on experiments with Robert Boyle, considered the father of modern chemistry. In his journals and correspondence between 1656 and 1666 are repeated references to his interests in natural science and in the study of society, politics, and moral philosophy.

In 1666 Locke met Lord Anthony Ashley Cooper and became his personal adviser on general affairs—an important relationship because Baron Ashley was an active politician who supported a constitutional monarchy, Protestant succession, civil liberties, toleration of religion, the rule of Parliament, and the expansion of the British Empire for trade. Ashley, later the First Earl of Shaftesbury, was one of the sponsors of the bill to exclude James II from succeeding to the throne, and in the aftermath he was tried for treason but was acquitted. After the Rye House Plot was uncovered, Locke fled to Holland, fearing that he would be tainted by his association with Lord Shaftesbury. Meanwhile, throughout the late 1660s and 1670s he was intimately involved with issues of trade and colonization while continuing his studies and gathering ideas for one of his most famous works, *An Essay Concerning Human Understanding*. This book, published in 1689, proved to be a cornerstone of Enlightenment views about perception, sensation, reason, knowledge, and the relationship between knowledge and faith. In 1690 he published his political masterpiece, *Two Treatises of Government*. After a stint at the newly created Board of Trade, he retired to a country estate in Essex called Oates, where he died on October 28, 1704.

Explanation and Analysis of the Document

The excerpts from the *Second Treatise on Civil Government* are taken from four chapters: Chapter II, "Of the State of Nature"; Chapter III, "Of the State of War"; Chapter IV, "Of Slavery"; and Chapter V, "Of Property." These excerpts deal with fundamental questions about government, including the origin of government and what makes the authority of government legitimate.

◆ Chapter II: "Of the State of Nature"

Locke's *Second Treatise* argues that governments originated from a primal social contract. Locke, like other social contract theorists, posited a fictive political environment called the "state of nature," a kind of theoretical state in which people enjoy absolute freedom, without the constraints of society and government. He begins with the premise that originally people lived in a primitive state of nature without any government and in accordance with the "law of nature." In support of his view he quotes Richard Hooker, an Anglican theologian and the author of the multivolume work *Of the Lawes of Ecclesiastical Politie*, first published in the 1590s. The essence of Hooker's view, according to Locke, is that equality is "the foundation of that obligation to mutual love amongst men." Freedom, however, does not mean unfettered license—that is, license for people to do wrong or to do whatever they want. While people live in a state of nature, they are obligated to follow the law of nature, which dictates that a person may not "take away, or impair the life, or what tends to the preservation of the life, the liberty, health, limb, or goods of

Time Line

1685

- **February 6**
  Charles II dies.

- **April 23**
  James II is crowned king.

1688

- William, Prince of Orange, invades England and overthrows James II in the Glorious Revolution.

1689

- **February 13**
  William III takes the throne as king of England; he is crowned on April 11.

- Locke's work *An Essay Concerning Human Understanding* is published.

1690

- Locke's *Two Treatises of Government*, containing the *Second Treatise on Civil Government*, is published.

1704

- **October 28**
  Locke dies at Oates, a country estate in Essex.

another." Still, in the state of nature some people violate the natural rights of others. Thus, to protect their rights, people join together to create government. This is accomplished by means of a "social contract" by which each person agrees to give up certain rights, such as the right to exact vengeance, in order to better protect the more fundamental rights of life, liberty, and property.

Much of the discussion in this chapter is given over to such matters as vengeance, criminals, and violations of natural law. Locke argues that if there is no means of enforcing natural law, then people can violate it at will. In a pure state of nature, an individual who has been harmed by another possesses a natural right to seek retribution. In so doing, that person achieves power over another, and this power is essentially the beginnings of government. The person who has harmed another has broken the tie ("tye," as Locke spells it) that binds people to one another. In breaking the tie, the offender has harmed not just an individual but, indeed, the entire human species. The social contract creates a government that is assigned the duty of protecting natural rights. Laws are made legitimate by the fact that the government is created by the will of the people; by consenting to the social contract, each person is obeying himself or herself, because the law is really each person's will. This is the case even if someone has not expressly agreed to the social contract. By staying within a society, a person tacitly accepts the terms of the social contract. The social contract then makes government legitimate; its laws are morally binding because they are the laws created by personal consent of the governed.

Locke goes into some detail in discussing particular instances. He argues that a national government does not have jurisdiction over aliens. More important, he takes up the issues of punishment, deterrence of crime, and retribution. Again, in a state of nature, each person is the executor of his or her right to self-preservation and therefore of the right to seek retribution against a criminal. The problem, of course, noted in section 13, is that in the state of nature, every person is, in effect, prosecutor, judge, jury, and potential executioner with respect to his or her own concerns and grievances. Nevertheless, a person in a state of nature at least has the right to seek justice when the laws of nature have been violated—and as a check, that person's justice is then subject to the sense of justice of "the rest of mankind" and to potential further retribution. A larger problem is that a king or prince as head of a government, "commanding a multitude," can likewise function as prosecutor, judge, jury, and executioner, but without any means of retribution available to the masses in the case of royal injustice. The paradox for Locke is that government, while restraining vengeance and retribution, can be yet another form of subjecting people to the potentially unjust will of another.

◆ Chapter III: "Of the State of War"

Locke begins this chapter by defining war—which in this discussion is considered more in the context of conflict between individuals—as a state of "enmity and destruction" that comes about when one person makes a premeditated assault on another's life. But a crucial part of the law of self-preservation is that one person may take another's life in self-defense, since any aggression on the part of one person challenges the victim's essential freedom. In the author's words, "I should have a right to destroy that which threatens me with destruction: for, by the fundamental law of nature, man being to be preserved as much as possible, when all cannot be preserved, the safety of the innocent is to be preferred." From this premise Locke argues that one can kill a thief because any attack on a person's property is an attack on his or her freedom. Further, anyone who attempts to put himself in a position of absolute power over

another is essentially making war—clearly an argument against absolute monarchies and the presumed divine right of monarchs to rule.

Locke proceeds by delineating how the state of war and the state of nature are not the same. In the state of nature, people live together and are governed by reason. They have no common superiors in the form of persons. War, on the other hand, is a state in which people exert force on others. Facing force or the threat of force, a person under attack has the right to fight back—to make war. The defining characteristic of the state of nature, Locke argues, is the lack of a common judge or authority. By reason rather than through any personal authority, then, force directed against a person is considered a violation of the natural law that prevails in the state of nature and thus forms a sufficient basis for waging war.

War, however, can take place both in the state of nature and in society. The difference between the two, noted in section 19, has to do with the conclusion of the conflict. In the state of nature, war does not come to an end unless the aggressor makes peace and offers reparations for any damage done. Until that time comes, the injured party has the right to try to destroy his adversary. In society, on the other hand, both the aggressor and the victim can appeal to authority to resolve the conflict. A chief problem that can occur is that the authorities can fail to act with justice. When such is the case, the state of war will persist, for "wherever violence is used, and injury done, though by hands appointed to administer justice, it is still violence and injury, however coloured with the name, pretences, or forms of law" (section 20).

Again, such passages can be viewed as offering justification not only for the regicide of 1649 but also for the Glorious Revolution. Other writers, such as Robert Filmer (whose arguments are addressed by Locke primarily in the *First Treatise*) and Thomas Hobbes (in *Leviathan*) had argued that monarchs held supreme authority; in Filmer's view, they have a divine right to rule, while in Hobbes's view, supreme monarchs are necessary to protect people from their own baseness and destructiveness. The essence of Locke's argument is that people have the same right to oppose unjust leadership as they do to oppose attacks on their persons or property in a state of nature. Locke concludes the discussion by maintaining that people enter into society principally to avoid the state of war, for the existence of authority increases stability and personal security and reduces the need for war.

◆ Chapter IV: "Of Slavery"

This chapter does not deal with slavery as the word is traditionally understood. Rather, it deals more generally with the concept of one person having absolute power over another. Thus, a person under a despotic government is just as much a slave as someone engaged in forced labor for another. Locke states his fundamental view in the chapter's opening sentence: "The natural liberty of man is to be free from any superior power on earth, and not to be under the will or legislative authority of man, but to have only the law of nature for his rule." He goes on to distinguish natural liberty from social liberty. Natural liberty is a state in which one is guided by the law of nature; social liberty is a state in which people have the right to be subject to no legislative power other than that created by the consent of the governed. A commonwealth is established only "by consent." The commonwealth's authorities can act only "according to the trust" put in them.

Locke's view is that freedom from power that is absolute or arbitrary is fundamental—so much so that a person cannot give it up, even if one wanted to do so. Further, slavery represents an extension of the state of war discussed in Chapter III. In section 24, Locke cites the example of the Jews in the Old Testament book of Exodus, who sold themselves not into slavery but into drudgery, for their conquerors did not have absolute power over them.

◆ Chapter V: "Of Property"

A central portion of the *Second Treatise* is Locke's discussion of property. He begins with the notion that both the Bible and natural reason sanction the right of people to use the earth for their survival and comfort. The important question is that if the earth exists for humankind in general, how does one acquire individual property? Locke's answer is to begin by noting that one's body is property. But a person owns not only the physical object of one's body but also the labor one performs with that body. Labor, then, is a type of property, so when people add their labor to some item, they now own the item (or at least a share of the item). Locke provides a simple example in section 28: An apple on a tree exists for the benefit of humankind. However, when the apple is picked, a person has added labor to the apple, and the apple now belongs to the person. A person can do this without obtaining the consent of humankind.

Locke argues, however, that this type of economic activity has boundaries. A person can fairly acquire only as much goods as he or she can reasonably use. If a person picks more apples than needed, the surplus will rot and go to waste. Similarly, in the case of land, a person is entitled only to as much land as he or she can reasonably use—to build a house on, for example, or to farm. In summary, what determines the value of a commodity is the labor invested in it, and it is labor that people use to make their world inhabitable.

Audience

Locke's intended audience for the *Two Treatises of Government* has been a matter of considerable scholarly debate. The orthodox view is that his primary audience was the aristocracy of England. The aristocracy had been the motive force behind the Glorious Revolution, and the views expressed in the *Second Treatise* seem to provide a justification for that revolution. However, the aristocracy never really accepted Locke's views, regarding them as too radical. Other scholars have argued that Locke's primary audience

was the landed gentry, yet this class also regarded Locke as too radical, even though Locke was outlining a theory of government that would have provided stability for the landed class, particularly in his defense of private property. Still other scholars contend that Locke's true audience consisted of such people as city merchants, tradespeople, artisans, and minor gentry. These classes would have found Locke's views congenial, for his essential argument is that people possess natural rights as free men and women regardless of the amount of property they own. Locke effectively advocates the inclusion of these classes in the process of choosing a nation's leaders and form of government.

Impact

Locke's influence on thinkers and political actors in the eighteenth century was varied. Often that influence was indirect, as those who followed him, rather than forming a cohesive group of philosophical disciples, were attracted to different aspects of his views. Some built upon his epistemology, the philosophical line of inquiry that examines what can be known and the process of knowing. Others were attracted to his advocacy of religious toleration, while still others saw his quiet reasoning style as a model for thinking in the Age of Reason and the Enlightenment.

What can be said with some assurance is that Locke in general and the *Second Treatise on Civil Government* in particular had a profound impact on the American colonists—although a minority of scholars dispute this view. The Declaration of Independence, which Thomas Jefferson said was an expression of American sentiment, is a very Lockean document, for the principles embodied in the declaration can trace their origins back to the *Second Treatise* and its treatment of the inalienable natural rights of the people. Indeed, in the preamble to the Declaration of Independence, the authors refer to the "the separate and equal station to which the laws of nature and of nature's God entitle them." The document famously goes on to state, "We hold these truths to be self-evident, that all men are created equal, that they are endowed by their Creator with certain unalienable rights, that among these are life, liberty, and the pursuit of happiness." These are words that could almost have been written by Locke himself. Later, after the American Revolution, the delegates to the Constitutional Convention in 1787 demonstrated knowledge of Locke's philosophy and embodied his principle of political compacts in such documents as the Federalist Papers. The Fifth and Fourteenth Amendments to the Constitution derive from Locke, and his *Second Treatise* is quoted directly where it says that no one shall be deprived of "life, liberty, or property" without due process of law.

Ironically—given that Locke is now considered a major Enlightenment thinker—the *Second Treatise* was not widely read in the eighteenth and nineteenth centuries, and while many intellectuals saw his theories as important, many others dismissed them. Only in the twentieth century did inter-

"To understand political power right, and derive it from its original, we must consider, what state all men are naturally in, and that is, a state of perfect freedom to order their actions, and dispose of their possessions and persons, as they think fit, within the bounds of the law of nature, without asking leave, or depending upon the will of any other man."

(Chapter II, Section 4)

"But though this be a state of liberty yet it is not a state of licence: though man in that state have an uncontroulable liberty to dispose of his person or possessions, yet he has not liberty to destroy himself, or so much as any creature in his possession, but where some nobler use than its bare preservation calls for it."

(Chapter II, Section 6)

"And thus, in the state of nature, one man comes by a power over another; but yet no absolute or arbitrary power, to use a criminal, when he has got him in his hands, according to the passionate heats, or boundless extravagancy of his own will; but only to retribute to him, so far as calm reason and conscience dictate, what is proportionate to his transgression."

(Chapter II, Section 8)

"It is not every compact that puts an end to the state of nature between men, but only this one of agreeing together mutually to enter into one community, and make one body politic; other promises, and compacts, men may make one with another, and yet still be in the state of nature."

(Chapter II, Section 14)

"He who attempts to get another man into his absolute power, does thereby put himself into a state of war with him."

(Chapter III, Section 17)

"The natural liberty of man is to be free from any superior power on earth, and not to be under the will or legislative authority of man, but to have only the law of nature for his rule."

(Chapter IV, Section 22)

est in Locke revive, and his work is now considered foundational in the history of constitutional government.

Further Reading

■ Books

Aaron, Richard I. *John Locke*. 2nd ed. New York: Oxford University Press, 1955.

Chappell, Vere, ed. *The Cambridge Companion to Locke*. Cambridge, U.K.: Cambridge University Press, 1994.

Cranston, Maurice W. *John Locke: A Biography*. Oxford, U.K.: Oxford University Press, 1985.

Czajkowski, Casimir J. *The Theory of Private Property in John Locke's Political Philosophy*. Notre Dame, Ind.: University of Notre Dame Press, 1941.

Johnson, Merwyn S. *Locke on Freedom: An Incisive Study of the Thought of John Locke*. Austin, Tex.: Best Printing, 1978.

Sabine, George H. *A History of Political Theory*. 3rd ed. New York: Holt, Rinehart and Winston, 1961.

Yolton, John W. *John Locke: An Introduction*. Oxford, U.K.: Oxford University Press, 1985.

■ Web Sites

"The Digital Locke Project." Digital Locke Project Web site. http://www.digitallockeproject.nl/.

"Timeline: The Life and Work of John Locke (1632–1704)." The Forum at the Online Library of Liberty Web site. http://oll.libertyfund.org/index.php?option=com_content&task=view&id=1181&Itemid=273.

—Andrew J. Waskey

Questions for Further Study

1. Define such phrases as *law of nature* and *state of nature* as Locke used them. In what sense is it possible for people in more modern historical times to live in a state of nature?

2. One of the chief beliefs that came from the Enlightenment was that absolute monarchy and hereditary rule were illegitimate. How did Locke contribute to the intellectual underpinnings of this belief?

3. Based on what you have read, how do you think Locke would have responded to a document such as the Constitutions of Clarendon (1164), written by King Henry II in an effort to reassert his rights as king? How do you think Henry would have reacted to Locke's *Second Treatise* if he could have read it?

4. The so-called Popish plot of 1678—an entirely fictitious conspiracy—whipped up anti-Catholic hysteria in England and played an important role in the religious controversies of the time. Why do you think Catholicism was feared in seventeenth-century England? What would Locke's position have been on Catholicism as an institution in England?

5. The term *social contract* is one that is still used in discussions of people's obligations to and rights within the social order. What did Locke mean by the phrase "social contract"? Has his notion of the social contract changed in the modern world?

JOHN LOCKE'S SECOND TREATISE ON CIVIL GOVERNMENT

Chapter II. Of the State of Nature.

Sect. 4. To understand political power right, and derive it from its original, we must consider, what state all men are naturally in, and that is, a state of perfect freedom to order their actions, and dispose of their possessions and persons, as they think fit, within the bounds of the law of nature, without asking leave, or depending upon the will of any other man.—A state also of equality wherein all the power and jurisdiction is reciprocal, no one having more than another; there being nothing more evident, than that the creatures of the same species and rank, promiscuously born to all the same advantages of nature, and the use of the same faculties, should also be equal one amongst another without subordination or subjection, unless the lord and master of them all should, by any manifest declaration of his will, set one above another, and confer on him, by an evident and clear appointment, an undoubted right to dominion and sovereignty.

Sect. 5. This equality of men by nature, the judicious Hooker looks upon as so evident in itself, and beyond all question, that he makes it the foundation of that obligation to mutual love amongst men, on which he builds the duties they owe one another, and from whence he derives the great maxims of justice and charity. His words are,

—The like natural inducement hath brought men to know that it is no less their duty, to love others than themselves; for seeing those things which are equal, must needs all have one measure; if I cannot but wish to receive good, even as much at every man's hands, as any man can wish unto his own soul, how should I look to have any part of my desire herein satisfied, unless myself be careful to satisfy the like desire, which is undoubtedly in other men, being of one and the same nature? To have any thing offered them repugnant to this desire, must needs in all respects grieve them as much as me; so that if I do harm, I must look to suffer, there being no reason that others should shew greater measure of love to me, than they have by me shewed unto them: my desire therefore to be loved of my equals in nature as much as possible may be, imposeth upon me a natural duty of bearing to them-ward fully the like affection; from which rela-

tion of equality between ourselves and them that are as ourselves, what several rules and canons natural reason hath drawn, for direction of life, no man is ignorant, Eccl. Pol. lib. i.

Sect. 6. But though this be a state of liberty, yet it is not a state of licence: though man in that state have an uncontroulable liberty to dispose of his person or possessions, yet he has not liberty to destroy himself, or so much as any creature in his possession, but where some nobler use than its bare preservation calls for it. The state of nature has a law of nature to govern it, which obliges every one: and reason, which is that law, teaches all mankind, who will but consult it, that being all equal and independent, no one ought to harm another in his life, health, liberty, or possessions: for men being all the workmanship of one omnipotent, and infinitely wise maker; all the servants of one sovereign master, sent into the world by his order, and about his business; they are his property, whose workmanship they are, made to last during his, not one another's pleasure: and being furnished with like faculties, sharing all in one community of nature, there cannot be supposed any such subordination among us, that may authorize us to destroy one another, as if we were made for one another's uses, as the inferior ranks of creatures are for our's. Every one, as he is bound to preserve himself, and not to quit his station wilfully, so by the like reason, when his own preservation comes not in competition, ought he, as much as he can, to preserve the rest of mankind, and may not, unless it be to do justice on an offender, take away, or impair the life, or what tends to the preservation of the life, the liberty, health, limb, or goods of another.

Sect. 7. And that all men may be restrained from invading others rights, and from doing hurt to one another, and the law of nature be observed, which willeth the peace and preservation of all mankind, the execution of the law of nature is, in that state, put into every man's hands, whereby every one has a right to punish the transgressors of that law to such a degree, as may hinder its violation: for the law of nature would, as all other laws that concern men in this world be in vain, if there were no body that in the state of nature had a power to execute that law, and thereby preserve the innocent and restrain offenders. And if any one in the state of nature may punish another for any evil he has done, every one may do so: for in that state of perfect equality, where naturally there is no superiority or jurisdiction of one over another, what any may do in prosecution of that law, every one must needs have a right to do.

Sect. 8. And thus, in the state of nature, one man comes by a power over another; but yet no absolute or arbitrary power, to use a criminal, when he has got him in his hands, according to the passionate heats, or boundless extravagancy of his own will; but only to retribute to him, so far as calm reason and conscience dictate, what is proportionate to his transgression, which is so much as may serve for reparation and restraint: for these two are the only reasons, why one man may lawfully do harm to another, which is that we call punishment. In transgressing the law of nature, the offender declares himself to live by another rule than that of reason and common equity, which is that measure God has set to the actions of men, for their mutual security; and so he becomes dangerous to mankind, the tye, which is to secure them from injury and violence, being slighted and broken by him. Which being a trespass against the whole species, and the peace and safety of it, provided for by the law of nature, every man upon this score, by the right he hath to preserve mankind in general, may restrain, or where it is necessary, destroy things noxious to them, and so may bring such evil on any one, who hath transgressed that law, as may make him repent the doing of it, and thereby deter him, and by his example others, from doing the like mischief. And in the case, and upon this ground, every man hath a right to punish the offender, and be executioner of the law of nature.

Sect. 9. 1 doubt not but this will seem a very strange doctrine to some men: but before they condemn it, I desire them to resolve me, by what right any prince or state can put to death, or punish an alien, for any crime he commits in their country. It is certain their laws, by virtue of any sanction they receive from the promulgated will of the legislative, reach not a stranger: they speak not to him, nor, if they did, is he bound to hearken to them. The legislative authority, by which they are in force over the subjects of that commonwealth, hath no power over him. Those who have the supreme power of making laws in England, France or Holland, are to an Indian, but like the rest of the world, men without authority: and therefore, if by the law of nature every man hath not a power to punish offences against it, as he soberly judges the case to require, I see not how the magistrates of any community can punish an alien of another country; since, in reference to him, they can have no more power than what every man naturally may have over another.

Sect. 10. Besides the crime which consists in violating the law, and varying from the right rule of reason, whereby a man so far becomes degenerate, and declares himself to quit the principles of human nature, and to be a noxious creature, there is commonly injury done to some person or other, and some other man receives damage by his transgression: in which case he who hath received any damage, has, besides the right of punishment common to him with other men, a particular right to seek reparation from him that has done it: and any other person, who finds it just, may also join with him that is injured, and assist him in recovering from the offender so much as may make satisfaction for the harm he has suffered.

Sect. 11. From these two distinct rights, the one of punishing the crime for restraint, and preventing the like offence, which right of punishing is in every body; the other of taking reparation, which belongs only to the injured party, comes it to pass that the magistrate, who by being magistrate hath the common right of punishing put into his hands, can often, where the public good demands not the execution of the law, remit the punishment of criminal offences by his own authority, but yet cannot remit the satisfaction due to any private man for the damage he has received. That, he who has suffered the damage has a right to demand in his own name, and he alone can remit: the damnified person has this power of appropriating to himself the goods or service of the offender, by right of self-preservation, as every man has a power to punish the crime, to prevent its being committed again, by the right he has of preserving all mankind, and doing all reasonable things he can in order to that end: and thus it is, that every man, in the state of nature, has a power to kill a murderer, both to deter others from doing the like injury, which no reparation can compensate, by the example of the punishment that attends it from every body, and also to secure men from the attempts of a criminal, who having renounced reason, the common rule and measure God hath given to mankind, hath, by the unjust violence and slaughter he hath committed upon one, declared war against all mankind, and therefore may be destroyed as a lion or a tyger, one of those wild savage beasts, with whom men can have no society nor security: and upon this is grounded that great law of nature, Whoso sheddeth man's blood, by man shall his blood be shed. And Cain was so fully convinced, that every one had a right to destroy such a criminal, that after the murder of his brother, he cries out, Every one that findeth me, shall slay me; so plain was it writ in the hearts of all mankind.

Sect. 12. By the same reason may a man in the state of nature punish the lesser breaches of that law. It will perhaps be demanded, with death? I answer, each transgression may be punished to that degree, and with so much severity, as will suffice to make it an ill bargain to the offender, give him cause to repent, and terrify others from doing the like. Every offence, that can be committed in the state of nature, may in the state of nature be also punished equally, and as far forth as it may, in a commonwealth: for though it would be besides my present purpose, to enter here into the particulars of the law of nature, or its measures of punishment; yet, it is certain there is such a law, and that too, as intelligible and plain to a rational creature, and a studier of that law, as the positive laws of commonwealths; nay, possibly plainer; as much as reason is easier to be understood, than the fancies and intricate contrivances of men, following contrary and hidden interests put into words; for so truly are a great part of the municipal laws of countries, which are only so far right, as they are founded on the law of nature, by which they are to be regulated and interpreted.

Sect. 13. To this strange doctrine, viz. That in the state of nature every one has the executive power of the law of nature, I doubt not but it will be objected, that it is unreasonable for men to be judges in their own cases, that self-love will make men partial to themselves and their friends: and on the other side, that ill nature, passion and revenge will carry them too far in punishing others; and hence nothing but confusion and disorder will follow, and that therefore God hath certainly appointed government to restrain the partiality and violence of men. I easily grant, that civil government is the proper remedy for the inconveniencies of the state of nature, which must certainly be great, where men may be judges in their own case, since it is easy to be imagined, that he who was so unjust as to do his brother an injury, will scarce be so just as to condemn himself for it: but I shall desire those who make this objection, to remember, that absolute monarchs are but men; and if government is to be the remedy of those evils, which necessarily follow from men's being judges in their own cases, and the state of nature is therefore not to be endured, I desire to know how much better it is than the state of nature, where one man, commanding a multitude, has the liberty to be judge in his own case, and may do to all his subjects whatev-

er he pleases, without the least liberty to any one to question or controul those who execute his pleasure? and in whatsoever he doth, whether led by reason, mistake or passion, must be submitted to? much better it is in the state of nature, wherein men are not bound to submit to the unjust will of another: and if he that judges, judges amiss in his own, or any other case, he is answerable for it to the rest of mankind.

Sect. 14. It is often asked as a mighty objection, where are, or ever were there any men in such a state of nature? To which it may suffice as an answer at present, that since all princes and rulers of independent governments all through the world, are in a state of nature, it is plain the world never was, nor ever will be, without numbers of men in that state. I have named all governors of independent communities, whether they are, or are not, in league with others: for it is not every compact that puts an end to the state of nature between men, but only this one of agreeing together mutually to enter into one community, and make one body politic; other promises, and compacts, men may make one with another, and yet still be in the state of nature. The promises and bargains for truck, &c; between the two men in the desert island, mentioned by Garcilasso de la Vega, in his history of Peru; or between a Swiss and an Indian, in the woods of America, are binding to them, though they are perfectly in a state of nature, in reference to one another: for truth and keeping of faith belongs to men, as men, and not as members of society.

Sect. 15. To those that say, there were never any men in the state of nature, I will not only oppose the authority of the judicious Hooker, Eccl. Pol. lib. i. sect. 10, where he says, The laws which have been hitherto mentioned, i.e. the laws of nature, do bind men absolutely, even as they are men, although they have never any settled fellowship, never any solemn agreement amongst themselves what to do, or not to do: but forasmuch as we are not by ourselves sufficient to furnish ourselves with competent store of things, needful for such a life as our nature doth desire, a life fit for the dignity of man; therefore to supply those defects and imperfections which are in us, as living single and solely by ourselves, we are naturally induced to seek communion and fellowship with others: this was the cause of men's uniting themselves at first in politic societies. But I moreover affirm, that all men are naturally in that state, and remain so, till by their own consents they make themselves members of some politic society; and I doubt not in the sequel of this discourse, to make it very clear.

Chapter III. Of the State of War.

Sect. 16. THE state of war is a state of enmity and destruction: and therefore declaring by word or action, not a passionate and hasty, but a sedate settled design upon another man's life, puts him in a state of war with him against whom he has declared such an intention, and so has exposed his life to the other's power to be taken away by him, or any one that joins with him in his defence, and espouses his quarrel; it being reasonable and just, I should have a right to destroy that which threatens me with destruction: for, by the fundamental law of nature, man being to be preserved as much as possible, when all cannot be preserved, the safety of the innocent is to be preferred: and one may destroy a man who makes war upon him, or has discovered an enmity to his being, for the same reason that he may kill a wolf or a lion; because such men are not under the ties of the commonlaw of reason, have no other rule, but that of force and violence, and so may be treated as beasts of prey, those dangerous and noxious creatures, that will be sure to destroy him whenever he falls into their power.

Sect. 17. And hence it is, that he who attempts to get another man into his absolute power, does thereby put himself into a state of war with him; it being to be understood as a declaration of a design upon his life: for I have reason to conclude, that he who would get me into his power without my consent, would use me as he pleased when he had got me there, and destroy me too when he had a fancy to it; for no body can desire to have me in his absolute power, unless it be to compel me by force to that which is against the right of my freedom, i.e. make me a slave. To be free from such force is the only security of my preservation; and reason bids me look on him, as an enemy to my preservation, who would take away that freedom which is the fence to it; so that he who makes an attempt to enslave me, thereby puts himself into a state of war with me. He that, in the state of nature, would take away the freedom that belongs to any one in that state, must necessarily be supposed to have a design to take away every thing else, that freedom being the foundation of all the rest; as he that, in the state of society, would take away the freedom belonging to those of that society or commonwealth, must be supposed to design to take away from them every thing else, and so be looked on as in a state of war.

Sect. 18. This makes it lawful for a man to kill a thief, who has not in the least hurt him, nor declared any design upon his life, any farther than, by the use of force, so to get him in his power, as to take away his money, or what he pleases, from him; because using force, where he has no right, to get me into his power, let his pretence be what it will, I have no reason to suppose, that he, who would take away my liberty, would not, when he had me in his power, take away every thing else. And therefore it is lawful for me to treat him as one who has put himself into a state of war with me, i.e. kill him if I can; for to that hazard does he justly expose himself, whoever introduces a state of war, and is aggressor in it.

Sect. 19. And here we have the plain difference between the state of nature and the state of war, which however some men have confounded, are as far distant, as a state of peace, good will, mutual assistance and preservation, and a state of enmity, malice, violence and mutual destruction, are one from another. Men living together according to reason, without a common superior on earth, with authority to judge between them, is properly the state of nature. But force, or a declared design of force, upon the person of another, where there is no common superior on earth to appeal to for relief, is the state of war: and it is the want of such an appeal gives a man the right of war even against an aggressor, tho' he be in society and a fellow subject. Thus a thief, whom I cannot harm, but by appeal to the law, for having stolen all that I am worth, I may kill, when he sets on me to rob me but of my horse or coat; because the law, which was made for my preservation, where it cannot interpose to secure my life from present force, which, if lost, is capable of no reparation, permits me my own defence, and the right of war, a liberty to kill the aggressor, because the aggressor allows not time to appeal to our common judge, nor the decision of the law, for remedy in a case where the mischief may be irreparable. Want of a common judge with authority, puts all men in a state of nature: force without right, upon a man's person, makes a state of war, both where there is, and is not, a common judge.

Sect. 20. But when the actual force is over, the state of war ceases between those that are in society, and are equally on both sides subjected to the fair determination of the law; because then there lies open the remedy of appeal for the past injury, and to prevent future harm: but where no such appeal is, as in the state of nature, for want of positive laws, and judges with authority to appeal to, the state of war once begun, continues, with a right to the innocent party to destroy the other whenever he can, until the aggressor offers peace, and desires reconciliation on such terms as may repair any wrongs he has already done, and secure the innocent for the future; nay, where an appeal to the law, and constituted judges, lies open, but the remedy is denied by a manifest perverting of justice, and a barefaced wresting of the laws to protect or indemnify the violence or injuries of some men, or party of men, there it is hard to imagine any thing but a state of war: for wherever violence is used, and injury done, though by hands appointed to administer justice, it is still violence and injury, however coloured with the name, pretences, or forms of law, the end whereof being to protect and redress the innocent, by an unbiassed application of it, to all who are under it; wherever that is not bona fide done, war is made upon the sufferers, who having no appeal on earth to right them, they are left to the only remedy in such cases, an appeal to heaven.

Sect. 21. To avoid this state of war (wherein there is no appeal but to heaven, and wherein every the least difference is apt to end, where there is no authority to decide between the contenders) is one great reason of men's putting themselves into society, and quitting the state of nature: for where there is an authority, a power on earth, from which relief can be had by appeal, there the continuance of the state of war is excluded, and the controversy is decided by that power. Had there been any such court, any superior jurisdiction on earth, to determine the right between Jephtha and the Ammonites, they had never come to a state of war: but we see he was forced to appeal to heaven. The Lord the Judge (says he) be judge this day between the children of Israel and the children of Ammon, Judg. xi. 27. and then prosecuting, and relying on his appeal, he leads out his army to battle: and therefore in such controversies, where the question is put, who shall be judge? It cannot be meant, who shall decide the controversy; every one knows what Jephtha here tells us, that the Lord the Judge shall judge. Where there is no judge on earth, the appeal lies to God in heaven. That question then cannot mean, who shall judge, whether another hath put himself in a state of war with me, and whether I may, as Jephtha did, appeal to heaven in it? of that I myself can only be judge in my own conscience, as I will answer it, at the great day, to the supreme judge of all men.

Chapter IV. Of Slavery.

Sect. 22. The natural liberty of man is to be free from any superior power on earth, and not to be under the will or legislative authority of man, but to have only the law of nature for his rule. The liberty of man, in society, is to be under no other legislative power, but that established, by consent, in the commonwealth; nor under the dominion of any will, or restraint of any law, but what that legislative shall enact, according to the trust put in it. Freedom then is not what Sir Robert Filmer tells us, Observations, A. 55. a liberty for every one to do what he lists, to live as he pleases, and not to be tied by any laws: but freedom of men under government is, to have a standing rule to live by, common to every one of that society, and made by the legislative power erected in it; a liberty to follow my own will in all things, where the rule prescribes not; and not to be subject to the inconstant, uncertain, unknown, arbitrary will of another man: as freedom of nature is, to be under no other restraint but the law of nature.

Sect. 23. This freedom from absolute, arbitrary power, is so necessary to, and closely joined with a man's preservation, that he cannot part with it, but by what forfeits his preservation and life together: for a man, not having the power of his own life, cannot, by compact, or his own consent, enslave himself to any one, nor put himself under the absolute, arbitrary power of another, to take away his life, when he pleases. No body can give more power than he has himself; and he that cannot take away his own life, cannot give another power over it. Indeed, having by his fault forfeited his own life, by some act that deserves death; he, to whom he has forfeited it, may (when he has him in his power) delay to take it, and make use of him to his own service, and he does him no injury by it: for, whenever he finds the hardship of his slavery outweigh the value of his life, it is in his power, by resisting the will of his master, to draw on himself the death he desires.

Sect. 24. This is the perfect condition of slavery, which is nothing else, but the state of war continued between a lawful conqueror and a captive: for, if once compact enter between them, and make an agreement for a limited power on the one side, and obedience on the other, the state of war and slavery ceases, as long as the compact endures: for, as has been said, no man can, by agreement, pass over to another that which he hath not in himself, a power over his own life. I confess, we find among the Jews, as well as other nations, that men did sell themselves; but, it is plain, this was only to drudgery, not to slavery: for, it is evident, the person sold was not under an absolute, arbitrary, despotical power: for the master could not have power to kill him, at any time, whom, at a certain time, he was obliged to let go free out of his service; and the master of such a servant was so far from having an arbitrary power over his life, that he could not, at pleasure, so much as maim him, but the loss of an eye, or tooth, set him free, Exod. xxi.

Chapter V. Of Property.

Sect. 25. Whether we consider natural reason, which tells us, that men, being once born, have a right to their preservation, and consequently to meat and drink, and such other things as nature affords for their subsistence: or revelation, which gives us an account of those grants God made of the world to Adam, and to Noah, and his sons, it is very clear, that God, as king David says, Psal. cxv. 16. has given the earth to the children of men; given it to mankind in common. But this being supposed, it seems to some a very great difficulty, how any one should ever come to have a property in any thing: I will not content myself to answer, that if it be difficult to make out property, upon a supposition that God gave the world to Adam, and his posterity in common, it is impossible that any man, but one universal monarch, should have any property upon a supposition, that God gave the world to Adam, and his heirs in succession, exclusive of all the rest of his posterity. But I shall endeavour to shew, how men might come to have a property in several parts of that which God gave to mankind in common, and that without any express compact of all the commoners.

Sect. 26. God, who hath given the world to men in common, hath also given them reason to make use of it to the best advantage of life, and convenience. The earth, and all that is therein, is given to men for the support and comfort of their being. And tho' all the fruits it naturally produces, and beasts it feeds, belong to mankind in common, as they are produced by the spontaneous hand of nature; and no body has originally a private dominion, exclusive of the rest of mankind, in any of them, as they are thus in their natural state: yet being given for the use of men, there must of necessity be a means to appropriate them some way or other, before they can be of any use, or at all beneficial to any particular man. The fruit, or venison, which nourishes the wild Indian, who knows no enclosure, and is still a tenant in common, must be his, and so his, i.e. a part of him, that another can no longer have any right to it, before it can do him any good for the support of his life.

Sect. 27. Though the earth, and all inferior creatures, be common to all men, yet every man has a property in his own person: this no body has any right to but himself. The labour of his body, and the work of his hands, we may say, are properly his. Whatsoever then he removes out of the state that nature hath provided, and left it in, he hath mixed his labour with, and joined to it something that is his own, and thereby makes it his property. It being by him removed from the common state nature hath placed it in, it hath by this labour something annexed to it, that excludes the common right of other men: for this labour being the unquestionable property of the labourer, no man but he can have a right to what that is once joined to, at least where there is enough, and as good, left in common for others.

Sect. 28. He that is nourished by the acorns he picked up under an oak, or the apples he gathered from the trees in the wood, has certainly appropriated them to himself. No body can deny but the nourishment is his. I ask then, when did they begin to be his? when he digested? or when he eat? or when he boiled? or when he brought them home? or when he picked them up? and it is plain, if the first gathering made them not his, nothing else could. That labour put a distinction between them and common: that added something to them more than nature, the common mother of all, had done; and so they became his private right. And will any one say, he had no right to those acorns or apples, he thus appropriated, because he had not the consent of all mankind to make them his? Was it a robbery thus to assume to himself what belonged to all in common? If such a consent as that was necessary, man had starved, notwithstanding the plenty God had given him. We see in commons, which remain so by compact, that it is the taking any part of what is common, and removing it out of the state nature leaves it in, which begins the property; without which the common is of no use. And the taking of this or that part, does not depend on the express consent of all the commoners. Thus the grass my horse has bit; the turfs my servant has cut; and the ore I have digged in any place, where I have a right to them in common with others, become my property, without the assignation or consent of any body. The labour that was mine, removing them out of that common state they were in, hath fixed my property in them.

Sect. 29. By making an explicit consent of every commoner, necessary to any one's appropriating to himself any part of what is given in common, children or servants could not cut the meat, which their father or master had provided for them in common, without assigning to every one his peculiar part. Though the water running in the fountain be every one's, yet who can doubt, but that in the pitcher is his only who drew it out? His labour hath taken it out of the hands of nature, where it was common, and belonged equally to all her children, and hath thereby appropriated it to himself.

Sect. 30. Thus this law of reason makes the deer that Indian's who hath killed it; it is allowed to be his goods, who hath bestowed his labour upon it, though before it was the common right of every one. And amongst those who are counted the civilized part of mankind, who have made and multiplied positive laws to determine property, this original law of nature, for the beginning of property, in what was before common, still takes place; and by virtue thereof, what fish any one catches in the ocean, that great and still remaining common of mankind; or what ambergrise any one takes up here, is by the labour that removes it out of that common state nature left it in, made his property, who takes that pains about it. And even amongst us, the hare that any one is hunting, is thought his who pursues her during the chase: for being a beast that is still looked upon as common, and no man's private possession; whoever has employed so much labour about any of that kind, as to find and pursue her, has thereby removed her from the state of nature, wherein she was common, and hath begun a property.

Glossary

Eccl. Pol. lib. i	a reference to Volume 1 of Richard Hooker's *Of the Lawes of Ecclesiastical Politie*

BRITISH REGULATING ACT

"For the better Management of the said United Company's Affairs in India, ... the Government [shall appoint] a Governor General."

Overview

The British Regulating Act was passed in the British House of Commons in 1773 in response to severe financial crisis within and public scandal surrounding the East India Company. The act generally can be considered as the first foray of the British government into the control of the Indian Subcontinent. While later measures would more clearly define the British imperial project in India, the Regulating Act established overt parliamentary oversight over activities in the region for the first time. Parliament's investigation into the actions of individual East India Company members and the company in general concluded that the company had become so corrupt and was so badly mismanaged that it could no longer operate as an independent company and had to be put under the oversight of Parliament.

In addition to establishing oversight of the East India Company in the region, the act ordered that the governor of Bengal was to be assigned as the governor-general of India, and a governing council was to be established in Bengal, Bombay, and Madras. This requirement set the precedent for future involvement by the British in designating chief officials in India. The structure of governance initiated in this act would remain largely intact until the end of the East India Company era of control in 1857. The act also established a British supreme judiciary and called for British judges to be sent to India to administer the British judicial system in India. The court's jurisdiction included all British subjects and their servants in India. The act also set the salaries of the various officials and judges in India, determined terms and processes for removal, and placed limitations on the activities of East India Company employees and contractors.

Context

The great wealth of the Indian Subcontinent had attracted European interest for centuries before the Regulating Act of 1773. The arrival of the Portuguese at Calicut, in southern India, in 1498 gave rise to a long and sustained European presence in the region. However, the Portuguese were short-lived as the dominant trading power on the subcontinent. By 1600 the Dutch had clearly established themselves as the prevailing European power with regard to the Indian Ocean trade of textiles and spices. This trade zone encompassed much of Southeast Asia and the Indian Subcontinent.

The East India Company was granted a charter to conduct business in India by Queen Elizabeth I in 1600. The objectives of the company were to gain access to the lucrative spice trade and to find new markets for British textile exports. Initially, the British company was unable to compete with the massive Dutch trading company and was forced to focus its trading interest on India while the Dutch company controlled the lucrative islands of present-day Indonesia.

In the late seventeenth century and into the eighteenth century, European trading companies began organizing more permanent enclaves to facilitate trade in the region. The East India Company established factories on the east and west coasts of the subcontinent, in Bombay, Madras, and Bengal. The company operated in India through a combination of diplomacy and force, building important alliances with Mogul rulers and local elites. Competition between French and British companies in India also led the outposts to assume a more and more military character. The East India Company established sepoy armies, that is, armies that consisted of local soldiers led by British company officials.

The East India Company grew increasingly powerful and faced resistance from local authorities and nabobs (provincial governors) as they expanded operations. Fort William was established in Bengal under the British, and in 1756 it became the site of conflict between the local ruler, Sirājud-Dawlah, and the East India Company. On June 19, 1756, the fort was captured by the nabob's forces. According to the British commander of the fort, John Holwell, the nabob's troops took 146 prisoners of war, including civilian women and children, crowding them into a single holding room and keeping them there overnight. The conditions were so terrible, he claimed, that 123 of the prisoners suffocated from the confinement and heat. This incident became highly sensationalized in the British press, which

1600

- **December 31**
  The English East India Company is formed, and Queen Elizabeth I gives a charter to the company.

1756

- **June 20**
  The takeover of Fort Williams and the holding of prisoners in a guard room later dubbed the "Black Hole of Calcutta" takes place. This event is highly sensationalized in the British press and is frequently cited as a means of legitimating the imperial presence in India.

1757

- **June 23**
  The East India Company's sepoy army defeats the nabob of Bengal in the Battle of Plassey, giving the British political control of Calcutta.

1765

- **August 16**
  The Treaty of Allahabad grants the right of revenue collection in the Mogul provinces of Bengal, Bihar, and Orissa to the East India Company in return for military support and an annual payment of £300,000 to the emperor.

gave the name "Black Hole of Calcutta" to the guard room of the fort.

While no British survivors countered Holwell's depiction, the circumstances of the event remain highly controversial. No evidence was found to support the story, and later investigation raised issue with whether the terms of Howell's description were even physically possible. Some historians believe that Holwell's account must have been exaggerated, while others doubt the occurrence at all. Regardless, following the event in Britain, many tabloids and newspapers ran serial accounts of the episode, emphasizing the civilian deaths and referencing the event as evidence of the need for greater governmental and military control in India. The "Black Hole of Calcutta" became a regular reference throughout the imperial presence in India as a coded symbol of the "uncivilized" nature of the Indian people under rule.

Within a year the Battle of Plassey occurred (1757), in which a sepoy army controlled by the East India Company defeated the troops of the local nabob to regain political control of Calcutta. By then the British had made several inroads into establishing influence in different regions of the subcontinent. The results of the Battle of Plassey were wide ranging; among the important consequences was the granting, in 1765, of *diwan* by the Mogul emperor to the East India Company for the provinces of Bengal, Bihar, and Orissa. The right of *diwan* was essentially the right to collect revenue, but as the power of the Mogul throne and of the local nabobs declined, the East India Company gained increasing control of the overall administration of the provinces, and the Mogul emperor became virtually dependent on the company.

The revenue collected, however, was soon realized to be grossly inadequate to maintain the costs of the East India Company presence in the provinces. In addition to massive famine, the provinces were undergoing significant environmental and political changes that led to unrest and conflict in various areas throughout the region. Company officials were frequently discovered to be abusing their power and funneling revenue toward their personal interests. The British government and public were growing more aware that company officials were not qualified to operate in such a political capacity. In 1772, John Burgoyne, chairman of a select committee of the House of Commons, brought forward three separate motions accusing East India Company officials of abuse of power. Other members of the House came to the defense of the company officials, and no punitive action was taken. One particularly outspoken defender of the East India Company was Alexander Wedderburn, who was highly influenced by a former company official, Robert Clive, and had even put forth a motion defending Clive in the face of Burgoyne's 1772 charges of abuse. In effect, two camps emerged in the House of Commons with one highly critical of the East India Company and one highly defensive.

In 1773, however, the East India Company came under scrutiny again by two separate house committees, one of which was a secret committee investigating the behavior of the company's highest officials. By 1773 the East India Company was in financial ruin and was considering bankruptcy. The most recent version of the charter granted to the company stipulated that the company was required to pay £400,000 annually to the British government in order to maintain the monopoly, but it had not been able to pay since 1768. The British government had extended several loans to the company, and all were in danger of default. In addition, there was significant public dissatisfaction over the scandals associated with the conduct of company officials in India. The Secret Committee of the House of Commons was charged with investigating the mismanagement of a national asset, and the report of their findings served as the basis for the institutional reform of the British Regulating Act of 1773. The act maintained the same sentiment as the investigation of the special committee but represents the compromise of an act negotiated through a political body that was highly polarized. Straddling the faction was the prime minister, Frederick North, 2nd Earl of Guilford, known as Lord North, who agreed with the recommendations of the investigation but was also influenced by members of Parliament with substantial financial stakes in the East India Company.

About the Author

The British Regulating Act was the product of a select committee appointed by the British House of Commons. John Burgoyne was a particularly outspoken critic of the East India Company and the head of the select committee. Burgoyne was born in Sutton, Bedfordshire, England, on February 24, 1722. After completing his education at the Westminster School, he purchased an army commission, and for the next eighteen years he served in the British military, gaining a reputation as a bold, fashionable officer and acquiring the nickname Gentleman Johnny. In 1768 he turned full time to politics and entered Parliament (though he had held a parliamentary seat earlier), where his most notable contribution was his opposition to the East India Company. With the outbreak of the American Revolution, he again assumed military command but fell into some disgrace as a result of the disastrous Saratoga (New York) campaign, for he surrendered his forces on October 17, 1777. Blamed for the defeat, he returned to England and private life, though he held minor administrative posts before his death on August 4, 1792. Burgoyne was also a talented playwright. Two of his plays, *The Maid of the Oaks* and *The Heiress*, continue to be regarded as accomplished dramatic works.

At the time the act was passed, the prime minister of Great Britain was Frederick North, 2nd Earl of Guilford, known as Lord North. Lord North was born on April 13, 1732. After attending Eton and Trinity College, he entered politics, winning a seat in Parliament, where he was known for his booming voice and acerbic wit in parliamentary debates. On January 30, 1770, King George III appointed him prime minister. He also served as home secretary and chancellor of the exchequer. North unwittingly played a

Time Line

1769–1773
- The Bengal famine results in the death of more than fifteen million people.

1772
- **May 10**
  John Burgoyne makes three motions before the House of Commons charging East India Company officials with abuse of power and improper appropriation of money in Bengal.

1773
- The British Regulating Act is passed, and the British government assumes greater responsibility for the activities of the East India Company and for British subjects in India.

1784
- Pitt's India Act is passed in an attempt to address some of the British Regulating Act's shortcomings in implementation and to clarify the dual system of control between the British government and the East India Company.

1857
- **May 10**
  Indian sepoy troops rise up in several areas of India in what is called both the Mutiny of 1857 and the Rebellion of 1857. This rebellion would lead the British Crown to abolish East India Company control of India and establish direct colonial rule.

significant role in the American Revolution. In an effort to rescue the financially distressed East India Company, he ordered that the company's surplus inventories of tea be shipped to the colonies. He opposed efforts to have the import duty on tea removed, so it was retained under the terms of the Tea Act of 1773. The consequence was the Boston Tea Party when, on the night of December 16, 1773, revolutionaries in Boston dumped British tea into Boston Harbor. To punish the colonies, North drafted several pieces of legislation, including the so-called Coercive Acts, that had the effect of rousing revolutionary fervor in the colonies. The war went badly; after the British surrender at Yorktown and after losing a vote of no-confidence, he resigned as prime minister on March 20, 1882. He retained his seat in Parliament until 1790, and he died on August 5, 1792. North's name survives in Great Britain as the prime minister who "lost the American colonies."

Explanation and Analysis of the Document

The British Regulating Act of 1773 marks the first instance in British history of a parliamentary act in response to the shortcomings of a Crown charter. The act is described in its title as "A Bill [With the Amendments] for Establishing certain Regulations for the better Management of the Affairs of the East India Company, as well in India as in Europe." This description suggests important issues. First, the bill explicitly states that its purpose was to create "better management" of the East India Company, pointing to the dissatisfaction of the government with the company's state of affairs. The phrase "in India as in Europe" is particularly important, as it makes immediately clear that the jurisdiction of the government does not exist only within Britain and that the bill intends to regulate the actions of officials in India as well. This act marks the first instance of such overt British governmental involvement in the activities on the subcontinent.

◆ Paragraphs 1 and 2

The British government's dissatisfaction with the management of the East India Company is revealed in the opening lines of the bill. The East India Company had previously operated in relative sovereignty under various charters granted by the Crown. These charters placed very limited regulation on the company. Thus, the bill begins by declaring that the former charters granted insufficient power to address the widespread instances of fraud and other forms of abuse and mishandling on the part of the company. It further notes that this state of affairs had led to the "Scandal" and "Dishonour" of the nation. The East India Company had become an embarrassment to the British (particularly within the increasingly competitive era of European colonial expansion) and was financially unable to meet its obligations to the nation. The document's forceful, and even at times harsh, tone reflects the frustration and, in some corners of government, outrage at the actions of the company. The opening paragraph acknowledges that there is not sufficient governmental control in the charter agreements and that the present circumstances of the company (widespread scandal and virtual bankruptcy) required increased governmental involvement. Paragraph 2 indicates that the governmental structure of India "has not answered the good Purposes intended thereby."

◆ Paragraphs 3–5

While the act stipulates many specific requirements pertaining to the operation of the company, two key requirements position the Regulating Act as an important historical document. The first is the establishment of a governor-general of India based in Bengal and presidential councils for Madras, Bengal, and Bombay. The second is the establishment of a supreme court in India. These two key aspects of the documents marked the first substantial move toward British control in India. Paragraphs 3 through 5 outline the new governmental structure of India.

The governor-general was established alongside the presidential councils "for the better Management of the said United Company's Affairs in India." The act declares that at Fort William in Bengal, a governor-general and four councilors will be appointed. This directive effectively established the position of governor-general and positioned Bengal firmly as the seat of the British imperial presence because the new governor-general would be based there. The governor-general would have control of the "Ordering, Management, and Government, of all the Territorial Acquisitions and Revenues." He would have the "Power of superintending and controuling the Government and Management" of regions such as Madras, Bombay, and Bencoolen. He would have military power to defend British interests and to negotiate with "Indian Princes or Powers," a reference to the so-called Princely States that remained under the nominal control of local rulers. The act specifies that "all Transactions and Matters whatsoever, that shall come to their Knowlege, relating to the Government, Revenues, or Interest, of the said United Company" are to be communicated to the governor-general. Further, the act mandates frequent and detailed communication of all matters pertaining to India to the Crown and the ministries in England.

The intention of this part of the act was to alleviate the corruption and personal profiteering that had been taking place by creating a more clearly accountable political figure in the region and outlining the terms of office and service. This part of the act also specifies that the governor-general's and councilors' term of office would be five years and stipulates the process by which they could be removed. Notably, the governor-general could be fired by the East India Company, but the directors could ask the king to remove the governor or a councilor. This stipulation is important because it openly illustrates the new, more assertive role of the British government in the affairs of the East India Company.

◆ Paragraphs 6 and 7

Following the establishment of the political and administrative offices of governor-general and the councils in

India, the act addresses the other key issue at hand. The act set up a court system in India for the members of the East India Company and related individuals. While some versions of British courts had been operating in the outpost regions prior to the passage of the act, the courts were not unified, and their authority was ambiguously defined. This act's definition of the British courts and the role of British law in the region came in response to the corruption and abuses of company officials. The act not only made East India Company officials accountable to British law but also provided sweeping authority to the court in the region.

The act establishes a "Supreme Court of Judicature" at Fort William. The court was to consist of a chief justice and three additional justices. The court would have "full Power" to "do all such other Things as shall be found necessary for the Administration of Justice." Notably, again, the court was seated in Bengal at Fort William, further designating Bengal as the center of British power in the region. The phrase "to do all such other Things as shall be found necessary for the Administration of Justice" is particularly vague in this section of the document and led to wide interpretation of the actual limits of the court's power. Furthermore, the majority of clerks and officers of the court were to be appointed by the judges, giving them complete control over who had access to the positions. This is an issue that was revisited with Pitt's India Act of 1784.

The document goes on to state that the jurisdiction of the court extended not only to employees of the East India Company but also to any natives of India making complaints against anyone related to the company. While this stipulation was presented as a way to establish British governmental responsibility for the actions of East India Company officials, it also placed British subjects under the British judicial system and alleviated the threat of local justice systems that might not be sympathetic to the British presence. The establishment of the superiority of British law and order on the subcontinent is a profoundly important aspect of the document, even though full, overt British control of the region would come later.

◆ **Paragraph 8**

Another significant provision of the act is contained in the eighth paragraph, which states that it will be unlawful for persons who have been dismissed from or resigned from the East India Company to carry on trade in India. It also states that it would be unlawful for "any free Merchant, free Mariner, or other Person" whose agreements with the East India Company to engage in trade have expired to "carry on, or be in any wise concerned in any Trade, Traffick, Merchandize, or Commerce" in the East Indies. This provision reconfirms the East India Company's monopoly in the region. Anyone who had ever worked for the East India Company was forbidden to work for, or even contract for, any other trading entity in the region.

◆ **Paragraphs 9 and 10**

Finally, the last major section of the act declares that the governor-general and councils could establish "Rules,

Colonial governor Warren Hastings (© Bettmann/CORBIS)

Ordinances, and Regulations" as they saw fit. The supreme court had to approve and confirm these regulations as legal, and they could not run contradictory to local laws, but fines could be assessed in cases of noncompliance. This step was important in the imposition of British authority on the Indian Subcontinent as it set the foundation for British lawmaking in the region. Paragraph 9 specifies procedures for enacting and promulgating these rules, ordinances, and regulations, and for repealing them. Paragraph 10 gives the governor-general and council "full Power and Authority to act as Justices of the Peace" in the Indian settlements and "to do and transact all Matters and Things which to the Office of a Justice or Justices of the Peace do belong."

Audience

There are four clear audiences for the British Regulating Act, one that the British most likely overlooked The act is a legal document, so the first and most direct audience consisted of the members of the House of Commons and Lord North himself. Within this body, however, were members who were also part of the second audience: officials and shareholders and defenders of the East India Company. Many members of the House of Commons were influenced either directly by their personal stake in the company or by the powerful lobby that the company operated. The document addressed this audience in two ways.

"To prevent ... various [frauds] Abuses, [and Oppressions] ... , as well at home as in India, ... it is therefore become highly expedient that certain further Regulations, better adapted to their present Circumstances and Condition, should be provided."

(Paragraph 1)

"And for the better Management of the said United Company's Affairs in India, Be it further Enacted by the Authority aforesaid, That [from and after] [for] the Government [or] [of the] Presidency of [Fort William in] Bengal, [there] shall [consist of] [be appointed] a Governor General, and [Four] Councillors."

(Paragraph 3)

"That it shall and may be lawful for His Majesty, by Charter, or Letters Patents under the Great Seal of Great Britain, to erect and establish a Supreme Court of Judicature at Fort William."

(Paragraph 6)

"It shall not be lawful for any Person or Persons whatsoever, who shall have been dismissed from, or shall have voluntarily resigned, the Service of said United Company ... from thenceforth to carry on, or be in any wise concerned in any Trade, Traffick, Merchandize, or Commerce whatsoever, in the East Indies, ... without the Licence of the said United Company."

(Paragraph 8)

"And be it further Enacted by the Authority aforesaid, That the Governor General and Council for the Time being of the said United Company's Settlement at Fort William aforesaid, and the Chief Justice and other Judges of the said Supreme Court of Judicature, shall and may, and they are hereby respectively declared to be and to have full Power and Authority to act as Justices of the Peace for the said Settlement."

(Paragraph 10)

First, the language of the document is stern when discussing the current conditions of the East India Company, and it reads at points much more like a prosecutorial document than a regulating act. This is an attempt by the authors to make the case for corruption to members of Parliament sympathetic to the company and to preempt any defense of the company's actions those defenders might raise. Second, the East India Company itself exerted influence over the shape of the act by taking part in negotiations over the final document. The committee report on which the Regulating Act was based advocated stronger control and harsh punishment for prior company abuses, but the Regulating Act of 1773 reflects a compromise on the part of both sides. The faction of the House of Commons opposed to the East India Company had to lighten their punitive approach, and the faction that supported the company had to accept increased regulation of the company.

The third audience for the act was the general public, both within Britain and among the European colonial powers. The British public was upset by tales of various abuses by company officials, and the act was designed to address these grievances (or give the appearance of addressing them). The behavior of the East India Company was also an embarrassment to the British colonial project, and the act was certainly intended to be read by other colonial powers in the region, such as the French and the Dutch. These powers would learn that Britain was reining in the abuses

of the East India Company while at the same time preserving the company's monopoly in the region.

A fourth important audience of the document is never addressed in the text, nor did this audience have any input into the contents of the Act. This audience is the entire local population of India. The British Regulating Act is regularly seen as the opening of formal colonial power on the subcontinent, and it is notable that any discussion or consideration of the desires of the local population is completely absent from the act.

Impact

The impact of the British Regulating Act would be felt by millions. The act represented a turning point in the establishment of formal British colonialism in India. The act also opened an unprecedented door for governmental regulation in the affairs of a specific company. This regulation would lead to further regulation of the company's activities, the end of the company's monopoly in India, and ultimately the British government's assumption of control over its Indian colony.

Warren Hastings, India's first governor-general, spent virtually his entire professional life as a member of the East India Company. Among the first four councilors was Richard Barwell, who had long worked for the company.

Questions for Further Study

1. Read this document in conjunction with Queen Victoria's Proclamation concerning India and with the Government of India Act of 1919. How did Britain's governance of its colonies in India evolve over time? What steps did the people of India take to grow more independent of Britain?

2. In large part, the British Regulating Act was not entirely successful in achieving its ends. Why do you think this was so? What provisions of the act were inadequate to solving the problems Britain faced in India?

3. In discussions of the British East India Company, the company is frequently referred to almost as if it were a person. Yet the "company" was an abstract entity made of up individuals who took actions or made decisions that reflected badly on England. What conditions allowed, encouraged, or enabled the members of the East India Company to abuse their privileges? How did Parliament attempt to change those conditions?

4. Read the British Regulating Act in connection with the Constitution Act of Canada. During roughly the same time periods, England maintained colonies in North America, including those that would become the nation of Canada. Yet Britain administered the colonies in North America and India in very different manners. Why do you think this was the case? What were the effects of these differences?

5. During the twentieth century, Britain extended its reach into the Middle East, as exemplified by the D'Arcy Concession. Read that document and explain what, if anything, Britain learned from its experiences in India in its dealings with Persia over oil.

The other three, though— John Clavering, George Monson, and Philip Francis—were company outsiders sent from England. This group seemed determine to undermine Hastings, frustrating his plans and accusing him of corruption and maladministration. One particularly notorious charge was that after an Indian opponent accused Hastings of trading favors for his own advantage, Hastings accused the Indian of forgery and used his influence to have him tried and hanged. In 1785 Hastings returned to England and was impeached for corruption, but after a seven-year trial, he was found not guilty. Similarly, the judges of the supreme court were unable to work amicably, and they interpreted their power in the widest sense. Many local accusations were made that judges and administrators were abusing their privileges, and the seeds of dissatisfaction were planted among local populations.

Many of the act's provisions were vaguely laid out and difficult to enforce. As a result, several subsequent acts were passed over the next decades in efforts to clarify the administration and processes stipulated in the Regulating Act. In addition, corruption and profiteering remained endemic in the East India Company. In 1784 Pitt's India Act attempted to revise the Regulating Act in a way that would more forcefully deal with the still widespread corruption taking place. This act attempted to resolve the problem of infighting between the governor-general and the council by significantly increasing the authority of the governor-general.

Overall, the British Regulating Act set the tone for British colonialism on the Indian Subcontinent. It established that the East India Company was still a sovereign company but that it was wholly accountable to the British government. The basic premises laid out in the British Regulating Act would remain in place until the era of East India Company rule ended following the uprisings of 1857.

Further Reading

■ Articles

Elofson, W. M. "The Rockingham Whigs in Transition: The East India Company Issue 1772–1773." *English Historical Review* 104, no. 413 (October 1989): 947–974.

■ Books

Bowen, H. V. *Revenue and Reform: The Indian Problem in British Politics, 1757–1773*. Cambridge, U.K.: Cambridge University Press, 1991.

Grant, Robert. *A Sketch of the History of the East-India Company from Its First Formation to the Passing of the Regulating Act of 1773, with a Summary View of the Changes Which Have Taken Place since That Period in the Internal Administration of British India*. London: Black, Parry, and Co., 1813.

Peers, Douglas M. *India under Colonial Rule: 1700–1885*. New York: Pearson Education, 2006.

Travers, Robert. *Ideology and Empire in Eighteenth-Century India: The British in Bengal*. New York: Cambridge University Press, 2007.

■ Web Sites

"The Age of George III." Web of English History Web site.
   http://www.historyhome.co.uk/c-eight/18chome.htm.

"Manas: India and Its Neighbors." University of California, Los Angeles, Web site.
   http://www.sscnet.ucla.edu/southasia/index.html.

—Samantha Christiansen

BRITISH REGULATING ACT

A Bill [With the Amendments] for Establishing certain Regulations for the better Management of the Affairs of the East India Company, as well in India as in Europe.

Whereas the several Powers and Authorities granted by Charters to the United Company of Merchants of England trading to the East Indies, have been found by Experience not to have sufficient Force and Efficacy to prevent [or restrain the practice of] various [frauds] Abuses, [and Oppressions] which [has too long] [*have*] prevailed in the Government and Administration of the Affairs of the said United Company, as well at Home as in India [to the great Scandal and Dishonour of this Nation, and] to the manifest Injury of the public Credit, and of the Commercial Interests of the said Company, and it is therefore become highly expedient that certain further Regulations, better adapted to their present Circumstances and Condition, should be provided and established:

And whereas the electing and choosing of Directors of the said United Company every Year, in such Manner as at present prescribed by Charter, has not answered the good Purposes intended thereby, but on the contrary, by limiting the Duration of their Office to so short a Time, evidently tends to weaken the Authority of the Court of Directors, and to produce Instability in the Councils and Measures of the said Company: …

And for the better Management of the said United Company's Affairs in India, Be it further Enacted by the Authority aforesaid, That [from and after] [*for*] the Government [or] [*of the*] Presidency of [*Fort William, in*] Bengal, [*there*] shall [consist of] [*be appointed*] a Governor General, and [*Four*] Councillors; and that the Whole Civil and Military Government of the said [United Company's] Presidency [of Bengal] and also the Ordering, Management, and Government, of all the Territorial Acquisitions and Revenues in the Kingdoms of Bengal, Bahar, and Orissa, [*shall*] during such Time as the [same] [*Territorial Acquisitions and Revenues*] shall remain in the Possession of the said United Company [shall] be and are hereby vested in the said Governor General and Council of the said Presidency of [*Fort William, in*] Bengal [*in like Manner, to all Intents and Purposes whatsosever, as the same now*

are, or at any Time heretofore might have been, exercised by the President and Council, or Select Committee, in the said Kingdoms].

And be it further Enacted by the Authority aforesaid, That the said Governor General and Council, or any [*Three*] of them, shall have, and they are hereby authorized to have, Power of superintending and controuling the Government and Management of the Presidencies of Madrass [and] Bombay, [*and Bencoolen*] respectively, so far and insomuch as that it shall not be lawful, [from and after the] for any [Governor] [*President*] and Council of Madrass, [or] Bombay, [*or Bencoolen*] for the Time being, to make any Orders for commencing Hostilities, or declaring or making War against any Indian Princes or Powers [except in the cases of imminent necessity, for the Defence of the Presidency under their respective Government or Command] or for negociating or concluding any Treaty of Peace, or other Treaty, with any such Indian Princes or Powers, without the Consent and Approbation of the said Governor General and Council [of Bengal, or any of them] first had and obtained [*except in such Cases of imminent Necessity as would render it dangerous to postpone such Hostilities or Treaties until the Orders from the Governor General and Council might arrive and except in such Cases where the said Presidents and Councils respectively shall have received special Orders from the said United Company*] and any [Governor] [*President*] and Council of Madrass [or] Bombay [*or Bencoolen*] who shall offend in any of the Cases aforesaid, shall [*be liable to be suspended from his Office, by the Order of the said Governor General and Council*] And every [Governor] [*President*] and Council of Madrass [and] Bombay [*and Bencoolen*] for the Time being, shall, and they are hereby respectively directed and required to pay due Obedience to such Orders as they shall receive touching the Premises from the said Governor General and Council [of Bengal,] for the Time being, and constantly and diligently to transmit to the said Governor [*General*] and Council [as often as the same shall be by them required] Advice and Intelligence of all Transactions and Matters whatsoever, that shall come to their Knowlege, relating to the Government, Revenues, or Interest, of the said United Company; and the said Governor General and

Council [of Bengal] for the Time being, shall, and they are hereby directed and required to pay due Obedience to all such Orders as they shall receive from the Court of Directors of the said United Company, and to correspond from Time to Time, and constantly and diligently transmit to the said Court an exact Particular of all Advices or Intelligence, and of all Transactions and Matters whatsoever, that shall come to their Knowlege, relating to the Government, Commerce, Revenues, or Interest, of the said United Company; and the Court of Directors of the said Company, or their Successors, shall, and they are hereby directed and required, from Time to Time, before the Expiration of [*Fourteen*] Days after the receiving any such Letters or Advices, to give in and deliver unto the High Treasurer, or Commissioners of His Majesty's Treasury for the Time being, a true and exact Copy of such Parts of the said Letters or Advices as shall any Way relate to the Management of the Revenues of the said Company; and in like Manner to give in and deliver to One of His Majesty's Principal Secretaries of State, for the Time being, a true and exact Copy of all such Parts of the said Letters or Advices as shall any Way relate to the Civil or Military Affairs and Government of the said Company; all which Copies shall be fairly written, and shall be signed by [*Two*] or more of the Directors of the said Company [and Oath shall be made of the Truth of every such Copy, according to the true Intent and Meaning of this act, by the proper Officers or Servents of the said Company, before any One Justice of the Peace, which Oath such Justice is hereby authorised and required to administer].

And it is hereby further Enacted, That _____ shall be the First Governor General, and that _____ shall be the [*Four*] First Councillors; and they and each of them shall hold and continue in his and their respective Offices for and during the Term of [*Five*] Years [*from the Time of their Arrival at Fort William in Bengal, and taking upon them the Government of the said Presidency*] and shall not be removeable in the mean Time, except by His Majesty [in Council] [*His Heirs and Successors*] upon [Complaint] [*Representation*] made by the Court of Directors of the United Company for the Time being [*and in Case of the Avoidance of the Office of such Governor General by Death, Resignation, or Removal, his Place shall, during the Remainder of the Term aforesaid, as often as the Case shall happen, be supplied by the Person of the Council who stands next in Rank to such Governor General*] and in Case of the Death [or] Removal [*or Promotion*] of [the said Governor General, or of] any or the

said Council [his majesty is] [*the Directors of the said United Company are*] hereby impowered, for and during the *Remainder of the*] said Term of [*Five Years*] to nominate and appoint [such] [*by and with the Consent of His Majesty, his Heirs and Successors, to be signified under his or their Sign Manual, a* Person [or Persons as he shall judge most fit and proper] to succeed to [such] [*the*] Office [or Offices] so become vacant [*in the said Council*] and [in the mean Time] [*until such Appointment shall be made*] all the powers and Authorities vested in the Governor General and Council, shall rest and continue in, and be exercised and executed by, the Governor [*General*] and Council [or by the Council, as the Case shall happen] remaining and surviving. [and be it further Enacted, That in Case of the avoidance of the Office of such Governor General, by Death or Removal, his Place shall be supplied by the Person of the Council who stands next in Rank to such Governor General, until another Governor General shall be appointed by His Majesty as aforesaid] and moreover, if it shall happen that after the Death or Removal, or during the Absence, of any One of the Members of the said Council, a Difference of Opinion should arise upon any Question proposed in any Consultation, and such Council should happen to be equally divided, then and in every such Case the said Governor General [or the Person who shall supply his Place as aforesaid] shall have a Casting Voice, and his Opinion shall be decisive and conclusive [*and from and after the Expiration of the said Term of Five Years, the Power of nominating and removing the succeeding Governor General and Council shall be vested in the Directors of the said United Company*]....

And whereas his late Majesty King George the Second did, by his Letters Patent, bearing Date at Westminster the Eighth Day of January, in the Twenty-sixth Year of his Reign, grant unto the said United Company of Merchants of England trading to the East Indies, His Royal Charter, thereby, amongst other Things, constituting and establishing Courts of Civil, Criminal, and Ecclesiastical Jurisdiction at the said United Company's respective Settlements at Madrass, Patnam, Bombay, on the Island of Bombay, Fort William, in Bengal, which said Charter does not sufficiently provide for the due Administration of Justice, in such Manner as the present State and Condition of the Company's Presidency of [*Fort William, in*] Bengal, do require; Be it. therefore Enacted by the Authority aforesaid, That it shall and may be lawful for His Majesty, by Charter, or Letters Patents under the Great Seal of Great Britain, to erect and establish a Supreme Court of Judicature at Fort William aforesaid, to consist of a Chief Justice and [*Three*] other Judges [*being Barristers of not less than Five Years standing*] to be named from Time to Time, by His Majesty, His Heirs and Successors; which said Supreme Court of Judicature shall have, and the same Court is hereby declared to have, full Power and Authority to exercise and perform all Civil, Criminal, Admiralty, and Ecclesiastical Jurisdiction, and to appoint such Clerks and other Ministerial Officers of the said Court, with [such] reasonable Salaries [*as shall be approved of by the said Governor General and Council*] and to form and establish such Rules of Practice, and such Rules for the Process of the said Court; and to do all such other Things as shall be found necessary for the Administration of Justice, and the due Execution of all or any of the Powers which by the said Charter shall or may be granted and committed to the said Court, and also shall be at all Times a Court of Record, and shall be a Court of Oyer and Terminer and Gaol Delivery in and for the said Town of Calcutta, and Factory of Fort William, in Bengal aforesaid, and the Limits thereof, and the Factories subordinate thereto.

Provided nevertheless, and be it further Enacted by the Authority aforesaid, That the said new Charter, which His Majesty is herein before impowered to grant, and the Jurisdiction, Powers, and Authorities, to be thereby established, shall and may extend to all British Subjects who shall reside in the Kingdoms or Provinces of Bengal, Bahar, and Orissa, or any of them, under the Protection of the said United Company; and the same Charter shall be competent and effectual, and the Supreme Court of Judicature therein and thereby to be established shall have full Power and Authority to hear and determine all Complaints [of the natives of India] against any of His Majesty's Subjects, for any Crimes, Misdemeanors, or Oppressions, committed or to be committed; and also to entertain, hear, and determine, any Suits or Actions whatsoever against any of His Majesty's Subjects in [India] [*Bengal, Bahar, and Orissa,*] and any Suit, Action, or Complaint [of any native of India] against any [other native of India] [*Person*] who shall, at the Time when such Debt or Cause of Action or Complaint shall have arisen, have been employed by, or shall then have been, directly or indirectly, in the Service of the said United Company, or of any of His Majesty's Subjects: Provided also, That the said Court shall not be competent to hear, try, or determine, any Indictment or Information against the said Governor General, of any of the said Council; for the

Time being, for any [Crime or Misdemeanor] [*Offence, not being Treason or Felony*] which such Governor General, or any of the said Council, shall or may be charged with having committed in [India] [*Bengal, Bahar, and Orissa.*]…

And be it further Enacted, by the Authority aforesaid, That from and after [*the said First Day of August One thousand Seven hundred and Seventy-four*] it shall not be lawful for any Person or Persons whatsoever, who shall have been dismissed from, or shall have voluntarily resigned, the Service of the said United Company, or for any free Merchant, free Mariner, or other Person, whose Covenants or Agreements with the said United Company, for residing or trading in India, shall be expired, from thenceforth to carry on, or be in any wise concerned in any Trade, Traffick, Merchandize, or Commerce whatsoever, in the East Indies, other than for the Disposal of his or their Stock in Hand, without the Licence of the said United Company, or [their] [*the*] Governor [*General and Council of the Presidency of Fort William, in Bengal*] or [*the*] President and Council at the Place or Settlement where such Person or Persons shall reside, for that Purpose first had and obtained.…

And be it further Enacted by the Authority aforesaid, That it shall and may be lawful for the Governor General and Council of the said United Company's Settlement at Fort William, in Bengal, from Time to Time, to make and issue such Rules, Ordinances, and Regulations, for the good Order and Civil Government of the said United Company's Settlement at Fort William aforesaid, and other Factories and Places subordinate or to be subordinate thereto, as shall be deemed just and reasonable (such Rules, Ordinances, and Regulations not being repugnant to the Laws of this Realm) [and also to impose and levy all necessary and reasonable Imposts and Duties on Commerce and Trade, for the Support of the said United Company's Civil Government in Bengal] and to set, impose, inflict, and levy reasonable Fines and Forfeitures for the Breach or Non Observance of such Rules, Ordinances [*and*] Regulations [Rates and Duties] but, nevertheless, the same or any of them shall not be valid, or of any Force or Effect, until the same shall be duly registered and published in the said Supreme Court of Judicature, which shall be by the said new Charter established, with the Consent and Approbation of the said Court, which Registry shall not be made until the Expiration of [*Twenty*] Days after the same shall be openly published, and a Copy thereof affixed in some conspicuous Part of the Court House, or Place where the said Supreme Court shall be held; and from and immediately after such Registry as aforesaid, the same shall be good and valid in Law; but, nevertheless, it shall be lawful for any Person or Persons in India to appeal therefrom to His Majesty, His Heirs or Successors, in Council, who are hereby impowered, if they think fit, to set aside and repeal any such Rules, Ordinances [*and*] Regulations [Rates and Duties] respectively, so as such Appeal, or Notice thereof, be lodged in the said new Court of Judicature within the Space of [*Sixty*] Days after the Time of the registering and publishing the same; and it shall be lawful for any Person or Persons in England to appeal therefrom, in like Manner, within [*Sixty*] Days after the publishing the same in England; and it is hereby directed and required, that a Copy of all such Rules, Ordinances [*and*] Regulations [Rates and Duties] shall be affixed in some conspicuous and public Place in the India House, there to remain and be resorted to as Occasion shall require; yet nevertheless such Appeal shall not obstruct, impede, or hinder the immediate Execution of any Rule, Ordinance [*or*]

Regulation [Rate or Duty] so made and registered as aforesaid, until the same shall appear to have been set aside or repealed, upon the Hearing and Determination of such Appeal.

And be it further Enacted by the Authority aforesaid, That the Governor General and Council for the Time being of the said United Company's Settlement at Fort William aforesaid, and the Chief Justice and other Judges of the said Supreme Court of Judicature, shall and may, and they are hereby respectively declared to be and to have full Power and Authority to act as Justices of the Peace for the said Settlement, and for the several Settlements and Factories subordinate thereto, and to do and transact all Matters and Things which to the Office of a Justice or Justices of the Peace do belong and appertain; and for that Purpose the said Governor General and Council are hereby authorized and impowered to hold Quarter Sessions, within the said Settlement of Fort William aforesaid [*Four Times*] in every Year, and the same shall be at all Times a Court of Record.

Glossary

avoidance	becoming vacant
Court of Oyer and Terminer and Gaol Delivery	court for the prompt trying and sentencing of prisoners held in jail
Sign Manual	the handwritten signature of the British monarch

LE GÉNÉRAL LA FAYETTE

Marquis de Lafayette (Library of Congress)

DECLARATION OF THE RIGHTS OF MAN AND OF THE CITIZEN AND DECLARATION OF THE RIGHTS OF WOMAN AND OF THE FEMALE CITIZEN

"All citizens, being equal in the eyes of the law, are equally eligible to all dignities and to all public positions and occupations."

Overview

On August 26, 1789, the National Assembly of France approved the Declaration of the Rights of Man and of the Citizen, a document that ended the ancien régime in France. The term ancien régime refers to the old society before the outbreak of the French Revolution that year. As a society, it was characterized by an absolute monarch as ruler, a hierarchical social structure with each social class having a set of privileges, and a restrictive labor system controlled by the guilds (associations of tradesmen). The representatives of the French people organized as the National Assembly borrowed heavily on the writings of Marie-Joseph du Motier, marquis de Lafayette. In July 1789 Lafayette wrote a preamble to a future constitution of France, proclaiming that the principle of all sovereignty resided in the nation. This preamble provided a model for the version of the preamble written by the liberal Emmanuel Joseph Sieyès, also known as Abbé Sieyès. This later preamble, expanded in August 1789, was based on the motto of the French Revolution—"liberty, equality, and fraternity"—and was inspired by the U.S. Declaration of Independence (1776). Strongly influenced by Enlightenment ideas, the declaration was accepted by the French king Louis XVI on October 5, 1789, and was promulgated on November 3, 1789.

In September 1791, Marie Gouze wrote the Declaration of the Rights of Woman and of the Female Citizen. A self-educated butcher's daughter from the south of France, she wrote a number of pamphlets, plays, and speeches under the name Olympe de Gouges. Her preamble was a call to arms to all women, including the queen of France, Marie-Antoinette. Calling on the Supreme Being for guidance, she lists seventeen rights of women and female citizens. Ending with a sample marriage contract designed to ensure more equitable treatment of women, Gouges's declaration was never accepted or promulgated.

Context

At the beginning of the eighteenth century, France experienced a period of expansion, population growth, and increased urbanization, and the newer colonial empires of France began to pay off. By the end of the century, the population surge had begun to press against the food supply. Land hunger and food shortages went hand in hand with increasing social dissatisfactions in the country. France was experiencing growing pains. Although France was changing, the structure of French society, a system of privilege, was not. The social structure was more than one hundred years old. The population was divided into three "estates," each with its own set of privileges, although the privileges were not equal. The First Estate was the clergy, the Second Estate consisted of the nobility, and the Third Estate included everyone else. The economic crises of 1787, 1788, and 1789 showed the weakness of the social order. This situation stimulated suspicions between the lower and the upper classes and between all classes and the government; it gave rise to an indefinite fear of complacency. Moreover, there was a general lack of confidence in the established social and political order.

The response of King Louis XVI was to call an Assembly of Notables, a meeting of select members of the nobility. In 1788 he invited them to come to his palace, Versailles, in the hope that the nobility would agree to gifts to the crown and to a new taxation structure. Thus the nobility, by acting in concert with the crown, would relieve the fiscal crisis faced by Louis XVI and the government. The assembly failed to produce the desired results, however, and Louis was forced to call a meeting of the Estates-General of France in 1789. This medieval representative institution in France had not met for 175 years before Louis XVI reconvened it on May 5, 1789, to deal with the looming financial crisis. France was on the verge of bankruptcy.

The meeting of the Estates-General provided those elected to it with the opportunity to present their grievances. On June 20, 1789, the members of the newly formed National Assembly took the Tennis Court Oath, pledging to remain together until they had drafted and passed a new constitution. The National Assembly, also called the Constituent Assembly, is what the Third Estate's delegation to the Estates-General decided to call itself when, on June 16, 1789, it proclaimed itself the sole legitimate representative of the French nation. The name stuck when, after a failed attempt to undo this clear usurpation

1788

- **August 8**
  King Louis XVI agrees to convoke the Estates-General, a general assembly representing the French people, for 1789.

- **August 16**
  The Treasury suspends repayments on government loans, effectively declaring bankruptcy.

- **November**
  The second Assembly of Notables, consisting of members of the ruling elite, meets at Versailles to discuss the Estates-General.

- **December 27**
  The representation of the Third Estate is doubled as a result of public outcry.

1789

- **January**
  Emmanuel-Joseph Sieyès's pamphlet *What Is the Third Estate?* appears.

- **February–June**
  Elections to the Estates-General are held to select members from all provinces in France and from each of the three estates—the clergy, the nobility, and the rest of the population.

- **May 5**
  The Estates-General is convened.

of royal authority, Louis XVI ordered the noble and clerical delegations to join the National Assembly on June 27, 1789. (The National Assembly differed greatly from the Estates-General. The latter organization, which dated to the fourteenth century, was primarily a consultative assembly, convoked at the pleasure of the king.) These events marked the birth of the Patriot Party, resulting in part from the success of a small pamphlet published by Emmanuel-Joseph Sieyès in January 1789 titled "What Is the Third Estate?" It contains these stirring lines: "What is the Third Estate? *Everything*. What has it been until now in the political order? *Nothing*. What does it want to be? *Something*" (qtd. in Baker, p. 154). Sieyès's argument was based on the concepts of utility and nationalism. The Third Estate was the most useful class to the nation. The nobles constituted an *imperium in imperio*, or empire within an empire. The Third Estate's demands for equality were moderate. It was by itself the National Assembly and therefore should create a system that eliminated class privilege.

To put all of these events in context, a thumbnail summary of the key events of the French Revolution is necessary. The French Revolution actually began in the spring and summer of 1789, when food riots erupted throughout France. However, the traditional date marking the start of the Revolution is July 14, 1789, when revolutionaries stormed and seized the royal prison, the Bastille, in Paris. The next month, the National Assembly issued the Decrees Abolishing the Feudal System and the Declaration of the Rights of Man and of the Citizen. In October of that year, Parisian women marched on the king's palace at Versailles and forced him to return to Paris. But in June 1791 the royal family, fearing for their lives, attempted to flee France and were arrested at Varennes, France (the so-called "flight to Varennes"). Later, in October, the new Legislative Assembly met for the first time. By 1792 counterrevolutionary movements were forming, though in August of that year the king was imprisoned; that same month, the National Convention replaced the Legislative Assembly. The Revolution began to turn violent when prisoners, most of them aristocrats, were killed during the so-called September Massacres of 1792. In 1792 the monarchy was abolished, and the First French Republic was proclaimed. Louis XVI was executed on January 21, 1793, and in March the Revolutionary Tribunal was created, leading to the Reign of Terror under Maximilien de Robespierre and the radical Jacobins. Then, on October 16, 1793, Marie-Antoinette was executed. Further violence took place when Robespierre and other radicals were executed by moderates. By 1794 the Reign of Terror had come to an end.

The storming of the Bastille had few practical consequences, but symbolically it was of enormous significance. It represented the Revolution-inspired attack on the ancien régime. Today it is celebrated as Bastille Day, or French Independence Day. Shortly after the fall of the Bastille, in a series of disturbances in the countryside of France, rural peasants revolted against their feudal overlords during July and August 1789, a period known as the Great Fear. These revolts were occasioned by rumors of an aristocratic plot to hoard grain and drive up prices while sending gangs of bandits to ruin the peasants' crops in the countryside. France's economic crisis reached a peak in 1788 and 1789. The harvest of 1788 was terrible, leading to food shortages, high prices, and famine in 1789. Fearful that the peasants would next begin to attack the property of the bourgeois, or middle class, the National Assembly in August issued a series of decrees that, in effect, destroyed the ancien régime. Once they had agreed on the importance of drafting a declaration of rights, the deputies in the National Assembly faced the more difficult task of crafting a declaration that a majority could accept. They agreed on seventeen articles that laid out a new vision of government; the protection of natural rights replaced the will of the king as the justification for authority. The National Assembly deliberated carefully and on August 4, 1789, granted France the equality demanded by the bourgeois as Armand II, duke of Aiguillon, a liberal nobleman, renounced his rights, prerogatives, and dues in order to satisfy the peasants and restore order to the countryside. Effectively, this act ended the feudal system in France. On August 26, 1789, the assembly approved the Declaration of the Rights of Man and of the Citizen.

The declaration expresses the liberal and universal goal of the philosophes, the general term for those academics and intellectuals who became the leading voices of the French Enlightenment during the eighteenth century. The most important of these men were Voltaire, Jean-Jacques Rousseau, Denis Diderot, and Charles-Louis de Secondat, baron of Montesquieu. The two fundamental ideas of the Enlightenment were rationalism and relativism. Rationalism was the belief that through the power of reason, humans could arrive at truth and improve human society. The philosophes were eager to demonstrate that human reason was the best guide for organizing society and government. Relativism, a philosophy that different ideas, cultures, and beliefs had equal worth, gripped the European mind as the impact of the Age of Exploration demonstrated that adherence to this philosophy had practical and intellectual value in any societal program for reform. Europeans were exposed to a variety of cultures and peoples worldwide. The Declaration of the Rights of Man and of the Citizen also addressed the interests of the bourgeois, including their demands for government by the people and the idea that the aim of the government is to preserve the natural rights of the individual. The political ideas of John Locke and Montesquieu and Rousseau's work *The Social Contract*, along with Voltaire's thoughts on equality and an end to government censorship, spring from the pages of the document. In addition, the National Assembly helped businesses stop tariffs, ended the guild system, and decreed that French colonies trade only with France.

Following August 26, 1789, the National Assembly got the breathing space it needed and proceeded to rebuild France from the ground up. The Great Reforms of 1789–1791, all rooted in the ideological foundations of the declaration and the writings of the philosophes, fall roughly into three categories. First, the Patriots wanted to limit

Time Line

1789

- **June 17**
  Members of the Third Estate declare themselves to be the National Assembly, claiming sovereign powers over taxation and stating their intention to frame a constitution that would limit the power of the king.

- **June 20**
  The National Assembly is locked out of its meeting room; members go to a nearby tennis court and take the Tennis Court Oath, pledging not to disband until they give France a constitution.

- **July**
  Sieyès writes a preamble to the French Constitution, later expanding it and basing it on a model provided by the Marquis de Lafayette.

- **August 26**
  The Declaration of the Rights of Man and of the Citizen is accepted by the National Assembly.

1791

- **September 14**
  On the day that Louis XVI accepts the new constitution, Olympe de Gouges presents the Declaration of the Rights of Woman and of the Female Citizen.

- **September 30**
  The National Assembly is dissolved.

- **October 1**
  The Legislative Assembly, a revolutionary body legislated under the Constitution of 1791, is convened.

1792

■ **June**
Overthrow of
the monarchy
ends the
government of
Louis XVI.

■ **September**
The National
Convention, elected
to draw up a
constitution for the
French Republic,
meets and
proclaims a
republic.

■ **December**
The trial of Louis
XVI takes place.

1793

■ **January 16**
Louis XVI is
condemned to
death; he is
executed five
days later.

the government by decentralizing the administration and the judiciary. On December 14, 1789, the National Assembly established a structure for municipal governments throughout France. For this purpose it created a distinction between active citizens (men who paid yearly taxes equal to three days' wages) who could vote and passive citizens who could not vote. On December 22, 1789, the assembly established a structure for new departmental administration. The number of departments throughout France was reduced. The departments were subdivided into districts and cantons. In the cantons only active citizens could vote and then only for electors who would choose deputies to the National Assembly and district officials who had to pay yearly taxes equal to ten days' wages. Deputies to the National Assembly had to pay yearly taxes equal to a silver mark. On August 16, 1790, cantons, districts, and departments were given courts staffed by elected judges.

Second, to deal further with the bankruptcy problem, the National Assembly on December 19, 1789, authorized the issuance of paper money (assignats) to be backed by church lands and to be redeemable when they were sold. On February 13, 1790, the National Assembly suppressed the monastic orders, thus creating a supply of salable land. Members of the National Assembly did not wish to destroy the church, which they considered to be a useful source of popular moral inspiration. On July 12, 1790, they issued the Civil Constitution of the Clergy, making departments and dioceses coterminous. Bishops and priests were to be elected in the same fashion as other departmental and dis-

trict officials; they were paid by the state. Moreover, they were required to pledge allegiance to the constitution of the nation. Only a few members of the clergy did so; most clergy became refractory, or nonaccepting, clergy. Many left France or went into hiding.

Finally, in more general financial and economic reforms, the National Assembly was strongly influenced by physiocratic doctrines (doctrines of utility or usefulness). In October 1790 it established a unified tariff for France. In November 1790 it set up two basic taxes—a contribution on land and a contribution on personal property. Also, on June 14, 1791, the National Assembly passed the Le Chapelier Law, which prohibited industrial and labor strikes. On May 21, 1791, the assembly established the metric system. The reorganization of France from the ground up was complete.

From the outset of the Revolution, there were scattered demands for women's rights. These demands were often rejected by revolutionary legislators, the vast majority of whom insisted that women were not fit to exercise political rights. Basing their rejection of women's rights on the very nature of woman herself, these legislators proclaimed that neither men nor women would receive any benefit from equality and full active participation on the part of women in the newly envisioned government of France. Clearly the idea of women's rights was constructed in disparaging and unequal terms in the revolutionary political discourse. Nevertheless, Gouges steadfastly appealed to women of all ranks to unite around her leadership in order to exert political power in the common interest for the common good. In order to redress the exclusion of women from the Declaration of the Rights of Man and of the Citizen, Gouges issued the Declaration of Rights of Woman and of the Female Citizen in September 1791. She was hopeful that the Legislative Assembly of 1791 would ratify the document.

About the Author

The Declaration of the Rights of Man and of the Citizen sought to define natural and civil rights for the citizens of France. Much of the document was taken from a draft done by General Lafayette, a liberal and a heroic participant in the American Revolution, at the request of the National Assembly during the summer of 1789.

Born to the Motier family in the Auvergne on September 6, 1757, Lafayette studied at the prestigious Collège du Plessis in Paris before joining the French army in 1771. Leaving France for America, he participated in the American War of Independence. He then fought in the French Revolutionary Wars, a series of conflicts (1792–1802) fought between the French Revolutionary government and several European states. Thus he became a hero on both sides of the Atlantic. Politically liberal, Lafayette rose to leadership as early as 1788, favoring a parliamentary monarchy like England's but one based on a formal written constitution like that of the United States. Increasingly, Lafayette's efforts to hold the Revolution to a more moderate course grew difficult. Given the position of commander of the National Guard, Lafayette unwisely ordered the guard to fire on a crowd gathered in the Champs de Mars in 1791. The general refused to support Napoléon's Imperial France and returned to political life in France only after Napoléon's final abdication in 1815. Strongly opposing Louis XVIII and Charles X, Lafayette sat in the Chamber of Deputies as a member of the opposition party from 1818 to 1824. He died on May 20, 1834, in Paris.

The modifications of the Declaration of the Rights of Man and of the Citizen took place through a series of debates held from August 1 through August 4, 1789. The principal proponent of a declaration was Mathieu de Montmorency, duke of Montmorency-Laval. Montmorency was born in 1767 and, as an adolescent, had served along with his father in the American Revolution. He returned from that war imbued with democratic ideals. In 1789 he was elected deputy to the Estates-General, becoming closely allied with Lafayette and the reforming faction of nobles.

Marie Gouze, the author of the Declaration of the Rights of Woman and of the Female Citizen, was a French author and activist. She was born in Montauban in southern France on December 31, 1748, to a modest family—her father was a butcher. Her mother was rumored to have had an affair with Jean-Jacques Lefranc, marquis de Pompignan, who some claimed was Marie's real father. A rebellious young woman, she married a French officer, Louis Aubrey, at age seventeen. Together they had a son. Louis Aubrey, who was much older than Marie, died three years into the marriage. Vowing never to abandon her son, she went to Paris seeking fame as a writer and taking the pen name Olympe de Gouges. Her career as a playwright brought her only modest success. Swept up in the political events of the 1780s in France, she initially took a somewhat moderate stance, arguing that reforms were intended to bring about change without sacrificing social stability. At first a supporter of the monarchy, she became impatient with the inaction of Louis XVI and Marie-Antoinette. She encouraged Louis to leave his throne and put in its place a regency government. The flight to Varennes in 1791 by the royal family forced her to break with Louis and side completely with the revolutionaries. Olympe de Gouges is best known for her Declaration of the Rights of Woman and of the Female Citizen, published in September 1791. She is considered a feminist pioneer, and her bold personality emerges strongly in her writings. Through the declaration she challenged the notion of male-female inequality. She used powerful language that was dangerous for her at the time; on November 3, 1793, she was executed for crimes against the government.

Explanation and Analysis of the Document

On the August 4, 1789, Armand II, the duke of Aiguillon, a liberal nobleman, renounced rights, prerogatives, and dues in order to satisfy the peasants and restore order to the countryside. Effectively, this action ended the feudal system in France. On August 26, 1789, the National Assembly deputies faced the difficult task of composing a bill of rights that a majority of the deputies could accept. A lengthy debate ensued, with the following questions raised: Should the declaration be short and limited to general principles, or should it include a long explanation of the significance of each article? Should the declaration include a list of duties or only rights? What precisely were "the natural, inalienable, and sacred rights of man"? After several days of debate and voting, the deputies suspended their deliberations on the declaration, having agreed on seventeen articles that laid out a new vision of government. The basis of authority was no longer the king but the will of the people. The duty of the government was to protect the natural rights of its citizens.

The document embodies the political ideas of Locke and Rousseau with regard to the idea of the social contract and the general will, as well as Montesquieu's work *The Spirit of the Laws*, which calls for a separation of powers. Montesquieu argues that the power of the government should be divided into separate branches, usually legislative, judicial, and executive, so that no one branch of government could gain too much authority. The ideas expressed in the Declaration of the Rights of Man and of the Citizen were influenced by the preamble to the U.S. Constitution. In his preamble to the French Constitution, Sieyès wrote in August 1789 that after having set forth the natural and civil rights of citizens, political rights would follow. He believed that all inhabitants of France were entitled to the right of protection of their person, their property, and their liberty; however, all did not have the right to take an active part in the formation of the public authorities—including women, children, foreigners, and those who contributed nothing to maintaining the public establishment. All could enjoy the benefits of society, but only those who contributed to the public establishment could declare themselves to be true active citizens, true members of the association.

The Declaration of the Rights of Woman and of the Female Citizen, written by Olympe de Gouges, appeared as a pamphlet on September 14, 1791, and it, too, embodied the ideas of the philosophes. Especially prevalent was the notion of the general will of Rousseau's *Social Contract*. Many concepts were likewise taken from the Cercle Social, a small band of supporters of women's rights. They launched a campaign for women's rights in 1790 and again in 1791, denouncing the prejudices against women that denied them equal rights in marriage and in education. While this group of women activists never formulated a specific plan, they published newspapers and pamphlets in order to foster a more egalitarian atmosphere for women and argued for more liberal divorce laws and reforms in inheritance laws. In her pamphlet Olympe de Gouges sought to redress the exclusion of women from political participation and from the guarantee of civil rights.

◆ Declaration of the Rights of Man and of the Citizen

PARAGRAPH 1 "The representatives of the French people constituted as a National Assembly … have resolved to set

Death of Louis XVI (Library of Congress)

forth in a solemn declaration the natural, inalienable, and sacred rights of Man." Rather than ending debate about rights, the vote on the declaration opened it up in new ways. The people of France now possessed an official document based on universal principles; this document encouraged further discussion of human rights and, in fact, demanded clarification concerning who was included in the definition of "man and citizen." Should the definition include the poor, those without property, the religious minority, blacks, mulattoes (people of mixed race), or even women? Where should the lines defining citizenship be drawn? The question of citizenship helped drive the Revolution into increasingly radical directions after 1789. Each group excluded in 1789 began to assert its claims to the right to be citizens of France. French legislators approached the question of citizenship step by step over a period of five years after 1789. France was in flux, the Patriot Party walked a tightrope, and the Revolution was never on solid ground.

ARTICLES 1–4 In proclaiming the Declaration of the Rights of Man and of the Citizen, the National Assembly defined liberty in broad terms in order to provide essential freedoms and liberties with few restrictions. This is evident in Article 1, which states that men are born and remain free and equal in rights. Article 2 provides a definition of the social contract theory's idea of natural rights: These rights are liberty, property, security, and resistance to oppression. Article 3 states the radical notions that the sovereignty of the nation resides in the nation; the nation is defined as the only source from which authority is deliv-

ered. This statement constituted an attack on the ancien régime concept of absolute monarchs ruling by divine right; the power of royalty was to be taken by the National Assembly, "the nation assembled." Article 4 offers an explanation of the limits of freedom and liberty and clearly puts all freedoms and protections under the written law.

ARTICLES 5–9 Articles 5–8 of the declaration deal with the establishment of new laws of the nation. These laws protect citizens from arbitrary arrest and imprisonment and grant equality to all citizens, especially in the eyes of the law. Article 5 is closely tied to the principles asserted in the previous article. Article 6 provides a direct statement of an important element in Jean-Jacques Rousseau's work *The Social Contract*. Here the idea that the general will expresses the law of the land provides for citizen political participation, whether directly or through elected representatives. Being equal before the law, every citizen is likewise entitled to all dignities and public positions—a strong statement that suggests the revolutionary principle that careers should be open only to those with talent. Articles 7–9 address the legal system. Under the ancien régime, each order had its own law courts, and certain provinces had their own courts. With enough influence one could have one's case transferred to the king's court. No member of the clergy could be tried in any court other than an ecclesiastical court. Taken together, these articles establish equality under the law and a more humane penal code. The importance of the written law as the foundation of these rights is evident.

ARTICLES 10 AND 11 Article 10 addresses the ancien régime's practice of censorship and the lack of "free speech." The written law is held up as the determinant of limits—citizens are free to communicate ideas and opinions, including speech related to religious beliefs, "provided their manifestation [speech] does not disturb the public order established by law." Article 11 makes clear that the right of free speech is "one of the most precious rights of man."

ARTICLES 12–14 Article 12 addresses the need for public military forces—a national army, not the private army of the monarch—to be gathered by conscription, or the *levee en masse*. Article 13 redresses the ancien régime's secrecy in accounts—that is, how public funds are spent—and proposes an equitable distribution for the costs of administering the government, stating that citizens must be told exactly what their share of this cost would be. Article 14 takes the power of taxation out of the hands of the king and the Estates-General, reserving these decisions to either direct action by the individual or action through elected representatives. Included in this article is the right to determine not only the mode of assessment but the duration of the taxation.

ARTICLES 15–17 Article 16 makes every civil servant, administrator, and public agent accountable for his administration. This article redresses the practice of venality under the ancien régime, where government offices were bought and accountability was owed only to the king. Article 16 demands that the written law be placed above everything in creating a new society, for the written law legitimizes society. Clearly, this article makes the legislative separation of powers—the idea of the philosophe Montesquieu—and a written law governing all elements of this society the necessary foundation for a constitutional society. Finally, Article 17 establishes the right to own property, as described by John Locke. The article also sets forth the principle of eminent domain, or the right of the state to seize property in cases of necessity.

◆ **Declaration of the Rights of Woman and of the Female Citizen**

PREAMBLE In her preamble, Olympe de Gouges makes an impassioned plea to all women to join her in demanding to be constituted as a national assembly. Further asking for the rights afforded to men, her opening words embody the injustice felt by women as they clearly perceived the pain of exclusion: "Man are you capable of being just?" The preamble makes a positive statement of the need for women and men to be treated equally under the new laws of the New France. Until all were freed from oppression, none would truly have the freedoms set out in the Declaration of the Rights of Man and of the Citizen; Gouges provided the antidote, demanding a bill of rights for women.

ARTICLES I–XVII Divided into seventeen articles, the document follows closely the Declaration of the Rights of Man and of the Citizen. One notable exception is the first article, echoing and paraphrasing the words of Rousseau in the *Discourse on the Origin and Basis of Inequality among Men*, modified for the female plea for equal rights: "Woman is born free and lives equal to man in her rights.

Social distinctions can be based only on the common utility." This article, along with Article IV, articulates the feminist position of 1789–1791 that the only limits on the exercise of the natural rights of women were perpetual male tyranny. Gouges calls for a reform of this tyranny by employing natural law and reason, an embodiment of the two major themes of the French Enlightenment. The sixth article reiterates Rousseau's idea of the general will as the highest authority in the nation, adding that women and men must participate fully, and thus they must equally be allowed all honors, positions, and public employment. Carefully noting that an individual's capacity figures into the equation, de Gouges wants only virtues and talents to be used for making distinctions. There are no major diversions from the Declaration of the Rights of Man and of the Citizen from Article VI until Article XVII; here Gouges establishes the basis for a new set of inheritance laws and equal access to property.

POSTSCRIPT: In her powerful postscript, Gouges addresses the plight of women in eighteenth-century society, calling on women to stand up for their rights and to protest the structure of the patriarchal society enslaving all French women. Drawing on prefeminist rhetoric, she tackles the political issues of divorce, child custody, property division, and women's participation in the political process, stating that "regardless of what barriers confront you, it is in your power to free yourselves; you have only to want to." Additionally, in this postscript she calls for an education act for women, to be supported and funded by the legislature. Further, she pleads for the recognition of the unmarried woman's right to the claim the "name and the wealth of their father" for her children. Thus, she addresses the status of women in domestic relations, property laws—equally dividing the family fortunes—conjugal agreements, and education. Her passion here for promulgating women's rights in eighteenth-century France earned her the title "rebel daughter."

SOCIAL CONTRACT BETWEEN MAN AND WOMAN Appended to the declaration is a social contract between man and woman, designed to determine the equitable division of their property if one dies. Gouges calls for the fair treatment of children and for a fair law to "assist widows and young girls deceived … by an inconstant man to hold to his obligations or at least [to pay] an indemnity equal to his wealth." Gouges concludes her contract by forcefully asserting that she has indeed "a foolproof way to elevate the soul of women; it is to join them to all the activities of man." She goes on to say that "if man persists in finding this way impractical, let him share his fortune with woman, not at his caprice, but by the wisdom of laws." Here Gouges is attempting to give a sort of social security to women in order to remove them from the uncertainty of subjection to the whims of men. In a radical last sentence, she advocates for "the marriage of priests and the strengthening of the king on his throne" (here revealing herself to be a constitutional monarchist), declaring that with these changes, along with the implementation of the Declaration of the Rights of Woman and of the Female Citizen, the government of France "cannot fail."

"The representatives of the French people, organized as a National Assembly, believing that the ignorance, neglect, or contempt of the rights of man are the sole cause of public calamities and of the corruption of governments, have determined to set forth in a solemn declaration the natural, unalienable, and sacred rights of man."

(Declaration of the Rights of Man and of the Citizen, Paragraph 1)

"Law is the expression of the general will. Every citizen has a right to participate personally, or through his representative, in its foundation. It must be the same for all, whether it protects or punishes. All citizens, being equal in the eyes of the law, are equally eligible to all dignities and to all public positions and occupations, according to their abilities, and without distinction except that of their virtues and talents."

(Declaration of the Rights of Man and of the Citizen, Article 6)

"The free communication of ideas and opinions is one of the most precious of the rights of man. Every citizen may, accordingly, speak, write, and print with freedom, but shall be responsible for such abuses of this freedom as shall be defined by law."

(Declaration of the Rights of Man and of the Citizen, Article 11)

"Believing that ignorance, omission, or scorn for the rights of women are the only causes of public misfortune and of the corruption of governments, [the women] have resolved to set forth a solemn declaration the natural inalienable, and sacred rights of woman in order that this declaration, constantly exposed before all members of the society, will ceaselessly remind them of their rights and duties."

(Declaration of the Rights of Woman and of the Female Citizen, Preamble)

"Consequently, the sex that is as superior in beauty as it is in courage during the sufferings of maternity recognizes and declares in the presence and under the auspices of the Supreme Being, the following Rights of Woman and of Female Citizens."

(Declaration of the Rights of Woman and of the Female Citizen, Preamble)

Audience

The audience of the Declaration of the Rights of Man and of the Citizen included the upper-middle class, liberal nobles, liberal clergy, and white men over the age of twenty-five who paid a certain amount of taxes per year. The declaration attempted to include other citizens but excluded women, children, and people of color from participation in the political process.

The Declaration of the Rights of Woman and of the Female Citizen was addressed to the nobility, including the queen, Marie-Antoinette, to married and unmarried women of all social ranks, and to revolutionaries who favored the implementation of rights for women.

Impact

The reforms of the National Assembly dismantled the ancien régime in France. The instrument by which this was done was the Declaration of the Rights of Man and of the Citizen. With the National Assembly's decrees of August 4, 1789, the equality demanded by the bourgeois was achieved. The declaration expressed the liberal and universal goal of Enlightenment philosophers and the middle class—government by the people—with the aim of ensuring that government would exist to preserve the natural rights of the individual. The declaration struck at the Roman Catholic Church in France by ending tithes, taking church lands, and resulting in passage of the Civil Constitution of the Clergy in 1790, making the clergy civil servants elected by the people and paid by the state. This issue divided the French people.

The 1791 constitution upheld the principles of the Declaration of the Rights of Man and of the Citizen by limiting the power of the king and guaranteeing equal taxation under the law. The provincial units in France were replaced with eighty-three departments, bishoprics were reduced to the same number, a standardized system of courts and a uniform law code were introduced, and the sale of judicial offices was ended. The declaration also introduced a more humane penal code. The National Assembly aided businesses by ending tariffs and the guild system, instituting a uniform system of weights and measures, decreeing that French colonies trade only with France, and implementing an external tariff to protect French manufacturers. In effect, the Declaration of the Rights of Man and of the Citizen ended the ancien régime in France. People had entered a stage in human history characterized by emancipation from superstition, prejudice, cruelty, and enthusiasm. Liberty had triumphed over tyranny.

The Declaration of the Rights of Woman and of the Female Citizen was never put into law, yet this should not deter an examination of its impact. Olympe de Gouges identified "woman as the other"; pled for women's rights, including sexual rights; decried the lack of political power of women; and created a feminist rhetoric to address the inequality between women and men. For women, the legacy of the French Revolution was contradictory. On the one hand, the unit of national sovereignty was declared to be a universal, abstract, rights-bearing individual; on the other hand, this human individual was almost immediately represented as a man. Gouges saw clearly that the attribution of citizenship to white male subjects complicated the project of claiming equal rights when these rights depended on physical characteristics.

Questions for Further Study

1. Concepts of natural rights were current in the Age of Enlightenment. Using these declarations, alongside the English Bill of Rights, the Dutch Declaration of Independence, and John Locke's *Second Treatise on Civil Government*, define the concept of natural rights as it was understood at the time.

2. What was the Third Estate in revolutionary France? Why was this group important? What contribution did it make to the French Revolution?

3. It is popularly believed that the French Revolution was purely the result of the license of the aristocracy and its cruelty to the lower classes. While these were important factors, what other factors contributed to the French Revolution? How did the declarations try to address these issues?

4. Why do you think that the Declaration of the Rights of Woman and of the Female Citizen received little in the way of a hearing in revolutionary France?

5. Compare the Declaration of the Rights of Man and of the Citizen with the Constitution of Haiti. What impact did the declaration have on events in Haiti in the early nineteenth century?

Further Reading

■ Books

Baker, Keith Michael. *The Old Regime and the French Revolution.* Chicago: University of Chicago Press, 1987.

Best, Geoffrey, ed. *The Permanent Revolution: The French Revolution and Its Legacy, 1789–1989.* London: Fontana Press, 1988.

Doyle, William.*The French Revolution: A Very Short Introduction.* Oxford, U.K.: Oxford University Press, 2001.

Hunt, Lynn. *The French Revolution and Human Rights: A Brief Documentary History.* New York: Bedford Books, 1996.

Mason, Laura, and Tracey Rizzo. *The French Revolution: A Document Collection.* Boston: Houghton Mifflin, 1999.

Popkin, Jeremy. *A Short History of the French Revolution*, 5th ed. Englewood Cliffs, N.J.: Prentice Hall, 2009.

Roberts, J. M. *The French Revolution*, 2nd ed. Oxford, U.K.: Oxford University Press, 1997.

■ Web Sites

"Liberty, Equality, Fraternity: Exploring the French Revolution." George Mason University Web site.
   http://chnm.gmu.edu/revolution.

—Anne York

DECLARATION OF THE RIGHTS OF MAN AND OF THE CITIZEN

The representatives of the French people, organized as a National Assembly, believing that the ignorance, neglect, or contempt of the rights of man are the sole cause of public calamities and of the corruption of governments, have determined to set forth in a solemn declaration the natural, unalienable, and sacred rights of man, in order that this declaration, being constantly before all the members of the Social body, shall remind them continually of their rights and duties; in order that the acts of the legislative power, as well as those of the executive power, may be compared at any moment with the objects and purposes of all political institutions and may thus be more respected, and, lastly, in order that the grievances of the citizens, based hereafter upon simple and incontestable principles, shall tend to the maintenance of the constitution and redound to the happiness of all. Therefore the National Assembly recognizes and proclaims, in the presence and under the auspices of the Supreme Being, the following rights of man and of the citizen:

Articles:

1. Men are born and remain free and equal in rights. Social distinctions may be founded only upon the general good.

2. The aim of all political association is the preservation of the natural and imprescriptible rights of man. These rights are liberty, property, security, and resistance to oppression.

3. The principle of all sovereignty resides essentially in the nation. No body nor individual may exercise any authority which does not proceed directly from the nation.

4. Liberty consists in the freedom to do everything which injures no one else; hence the exercise of the natural rights of each man has no limits except those which assure to the other members of the society the enjoyment of the same rights. These limits can only be determined by law.

5. Law can only prohibit such actions as are hurtful to society. Nothing may be prevented which is not forbidden by law, and no one may be forced to do anything not provided for by law.

6. Law is the expression of the general will. Every citizen has a right to participate personally, or through his representative, in its foundation. It must be the same for all, whether it protects or punishes. All citizens, being equal in the eyes of the law, are equally eligible to all dignities and to all public positions and occupations, according to their abilities, and without distinction except that of their virtues and talents.

7. No person shall be accused, arrested, or imprisoned except in the cases and according to the forms prescribed by law. Any one soliciting, transmitting, executing, or causing to be executed, any arbitrary order, shall be punished. But any citizen summoned or arrested in virtue of the law shall submit without delay, as resistance constitutes an offense.

8. The law shall provide for such punishments only as are strictly and obviously necessary, and no one shall suffer punishment except it be legally inflicted in virtue of a law passed and promulgated before the commission of the offense.

9. As all persons are held innocent until they shall have been declared guilty, if arrest shall be deemed indispensable, all harshness not essential to the securing of the prisoner's person shall be severely repressed by law.

10. No one shall be disquieted on account of his opinions, including his religious views, provided their manifestation does not disturb the public order established by law.

11. The free communication of ideas and opinions is one of the most precious of the rights of man. Every citizen may, accordingly, speak, write, and print with freedom, but shall be responsible for such abuses of this freedom as shall be defined by law.

12. The security of the rights of man and of the citizen requires public military forces. These forces are, therefore, established for the good of all and not for the personal advantage of those to whom they shall be intrusted.

13. A common contribution is essential for the maintenance of the public forces and for the cost of administration. This should be equitably distributed among all the citizens in proportion to their means.

14. All the citizens have a right to decide, either personally or by their representatives, as to the necessity of the public contribution; to grant this freely; to know to what uses it is put; and to fix the proportion, the mode of assessment and of collection and the duration of the taxes.

15. Society has the right to require of every public agent an account of his administration.

16. A society in which the observance of the law is not assured, nor the separation of powers defined, has no constitution at all.

17. Since property is an inviolable and sacred right, no one shall be deprived thereof except where public necessity, legally determined, shall clearly demand it, and then only on condition that the owner shall have been previously and equitably indemnified.

Declaration of the Rights of Woman and of the Female Citizen

Man, are you capable of being just? It is a woman who poses the question; you will not deprive her of that right at least. Tell me, what gives you sovereign empire to oppress my sex? Your strength? Your talents? Observe the Creator in his wisdom; survey in all her grandeur that nature with whom you seem to want to be in harmony, and give me, if you dare, an example of this tyrannical empire. Go back to animals, consult the elements, study plants, finally glance at all the modifications of organic matter, and surrender to the evidence when I offer you the means; search, probe, and distinguish, if you can, the sexes in the administration of nature. Everywhere you will find them mingled; everywhere they cooperate in harmonious togetherness in this immortal masterpiece.

Man alone has raised his exceptional circumstances to a principle. Bizarre, blind, bloated with science and degenerated—in a century of enlightenment and wisdom—into the crassest ignorance, he wants to command as a despot a sex which is in full possession of its intellectual faculties; he pretends to enjoy the Revolution and to claim his rights to equality in order to say nothing more about it.

For the National Assembly to decree in its last sessions, or in those of the next legislature:

◆ Preamble

Mothers, daughters, sisters [and] representatives of the nation demand to be constituted into a national assembly. Believing that ignorance, omission, or scorn for the rights of woman are the only causes of public misfortunes and of the corruption of governments, [the women] have resolved to set forth a solemn declaration the natural, inalienable, and sacred rights of woman in order that this declaration, constantly exposed before all members of the society, will ceaselessly remind them of their rights and duties; in order that the authoritative acts of women and the authoritative acts of men may be at any moment compared with and respectful of the purpose of all political institutions; and in order that citizens' demands, henceforth based on simple and incontestable principles, will always support the constitution, good morals, and the happiness of all.

Consequently, the sex that is as superior in beauty as it is in courage during the sufferings of maternity recognizes and declares in the presence and under the auspices of the Supreme Being, the following Rights of Woman and of Female Citizens.

Article I. Woman is born free and lives equal to man in her rights. Social distinctions can be based only on the common utility.

Article II. The purpose of any political association is the conservation of the natural and imprescriptible rights of woman and man; these rights are liberty property, security, and especially resistance to oppression.

Article III. The principle of all sovereignty rests essentially with the nation, which is nothing but the union of woman and man; no body and no individual can exercise any authority which does not come expressly from it (the nation).

Article IV. Liberty and justice consist of restoring all that belongs to others; thus, the only limits on the exercise of the natural rights of woman are perpetual male tyranny; these limits are to be reformed by the laws of nature and reason.

Article V. Laws of nature and reason proscribe all acts harmful to society; everything which is not prohibited by these wise and divine laws cannot be prevented, and no one can be constrained to do what they do not command.

Article VI. The law must be the expression of the general will; all female and male citizens must contribute either personally or through their representatives to its formation; it must be the same for all: male and female citizens, being equal in the eyes of the law, must be equally admitted to all honors, positions, and public employment according to their capacity and without other distinctions besides those of their virtues and talents.

Article VII. No woman is an exception; she is accused, arrested, and detained in cases determined by law. Women, like men, obey this rigorous law.

Article VIII. The law must establish only those penalties that are strictly and obviously necessary....

Article IX. Once any woman is declared guilty, complete rigor is exercised by law.

Article X. No one is to be disquieted for his very basic opinions; woman has the right to mount the scaffold; she must equally have the right to mount the rostrum, provided that her demonstrations do not disturb the legally established public order.

Article XI. The free communication of thoughts and opinions is one of the most precious rights of woman, since that liberty assures recognition of children by their fathers. Any female citizen thus may say freely, I am the mother of a child which belongs to you, without being forced by a barbarous prejudice to hide the truth; (an exception may be made) to respond to the abuse of this liberty in cases determined by law.

Article XII. The guarantee of the rights of woman and the female citizen implies a major benefit; this guarantee must be instituted for the advantage of all, and not for the particular benefit of those to whom it is entrusted.

Article XIII. For the support of the public force and the expenses of administration, the contributions of woman and man are equal; she shares all the duties and all the painful tasks; therefore, we must have the same share in the distribution of positions, employment, offices, honors, and jobs.

Article XIV. Female and male citizens have the right to verify, either by themselves of through their representatives, the necessity of the public contribution. This can only apply to women if they are granted an equal share, not only of wealth, but also of public administration, and in the determination of the proportion, the base, the collection, and the duration of the tax.

Article XV. The collectivity of women, joined for tax purposes to the aggregate of men, has the right to demand an accounting of his administration from any public agent.

Article XVI. No society has a constitution without the guarantee of rights and the separation of powers; the constitution is null if the majority of individuals comprising the nation have not cooperated in drafting it.

Article XVII. Property belongs to both sexes whether united or separate; for each it is an inviolable and sacred right; no one can be deprived of it, since it is the true patrimony of nature, unless the legally determined public need obviously dictates it, and then only with a just and prior indemnity.

♦ **Postscript**

Woman, wake up; the tocsin of reason is being heard throughout the whole universe; discover your rights. The powerful empire of nature is no longer surrounded by prejudice, fanaticism, superstition, and lies. The flame of truth has dispersed all the clouds of folly and usurpation. Enslaved man has multiplied his strength and needs recourse to yours to break his chains. Having become free, he has become unjust to his companion. Oh, women, women! When will you cease to be blind? What advantage have you received from the Revolution? A more pronounced scorn, a more marked disdain. In the centuries of corruption you ruled only over the weakness of men. The reclamation of your patrimony, based on the wise decrees of nature-what have you to dread from such a fine undertaking? The bon mot of the legislator of the marriage of Cana? Do you fear that our French legislators, correctors of that morality, long ensnared by political practices now out of date, will only say again to you: women, what is there in common between you and us? Everything, you will have to answer. If they persist in their weakness in putting this non sequitur in contradiction to their principles, courageously oppose the force of reason to the empty pretentions of superiority; unite yourselves beneath the standards of philosophy; deploy all the energy of your character, and you will soon see these haughty men, not groveling at your feet as servile adorers, but proud to share with you the treasures of the Supreme Being. Regardless of what barriers confront you, it is in your power to free yourselves; you have only to want to.

Marriage is the tomb of trust and love. The married woman can with impunity give bastards to her husband and also give them the wealth which does not belong to them. The woman who is unmarried has only one feeble right; ancient and inhuman laws refuse to her for her children the right to the name and the wealth of their father; no new laws have been made in this matter. If it is considered a paradox and an impossibility on my part to try to give my sex an honorable and just consistency, I leave it to men to attain glory for dealing with this matter; but while we wait, the way can be prepared through national education, the restoration of morals, and conjugal conventions.

Form for a Social Contract between Man and Woman

We, _____ and _____, moved by our own will, unite ourselves for the duration of our lives, and for the duration of our mutual inclinations, under the following conditions: We intend and wish to make our wealth communal, meanwhile reserving to ourselves the right to divide it in favor of our children and of those toward whom we might have a particular inclination, mutually recognizing that our property belongs directly to our children, from whatever bed they come, and that all of them without distinction have the right to bear the name of the fathers and mothers who have acknowledged them, and we are charged to subscribe to the law which punishes the renunciation of one's own blood. We likewise obligate ourselves, in case of separation, to divide our wealth and to set aside in advance the portion the law indicates for our children, and in the event of a perfect union, the one who dies will divest himself of half his property in his children's favor, and if one dies childless, the survivor will inherit by right, unless the dying person has disposed of half the common property in favor of one whom he judged deserving.

That is approximately the formula for the marriage act I propose for execution. Upon reading this strange document, I see rising up against me the hypocrites, the prudes, the clergy, and the whole infernal sequence. But how it [my proposal] offers to the wise the moral means of achieving the perfection of a happy government! ...

Moreover, I would like a law which would assist widows and young girls deceived by the false promises of a man to whom they were attached; I would like, I say, this law to force an inconstant man to hold to his obligations or at least [to pay] an indemnity equal to his wealth. Again, I would like this law to be rigorous against women, at least those who have the effrontery to have recourse to a law which they themselves had violated by their misconduct, if proof of that were given. At the same time, as I showed in *Le Bonheur primitif de l'homme* in 1788, that prostitutes should be placed in designated quarters. It is not prostitutes who contribute the most to the depravity of morals, it is the women of society. In regenerating the latter, the former are changed. This link of fraternal union will first bring disorder, but in consequence it will produce at the end a perfect harmony.

I offer a foolproof way to elevate the soul of women; it is to join them to all the activities of man; if man persists in finding this way impractical, let him share his fortune with woman, not at his caprice, but by the wisdom of laws. Prejudice falls, morals are purified, and nature regains all her rights. Add to this the marriage of priests and the strengthening of the king on his throne, and the French government cannot fail.

bon mot of the legislator of the marriage of Cana	a sarcastic allusion to the story in John 2:1–12; a connection between Jesus (the "legislator") to the author's point about women's rights entails an unsustainable stretch of reasoning
imprescriptible	not subject to loss or diminution for any reason
Le Bonheur primitif de l'homme	title of a pamphlet (English: *The Primitive Happiness of Man*) by Olympe de Gouges

King George III (AP/Wide World Photos)

"My capital is the hub and centre about which all quarters of the globe revolve."

Overview

Arguably the earliest communication between a monarch of China and the ruler of a European country, Qianlong's letter to George III was the official response to Lord George Macartney's mission, sponsored by the British East India Company in cooperation with the British government, to secure diplomatic relations and improved trade conditions with the Qing Dynasty. From its establishment in 1600, the British East India Company was a major exporter of silk, tea, porcelain, and lacquerware from China to England and the rest of Europe. Beginning in the mid-eighteenth century, the East India Company also attempted to sell English and European goods, most of them manufactured products, to China in order to offset a mounting trade deficit. Before the Macartney embassy, the company had sent emissaries to China, hoping to broaden trade relations and gain better access to the Chinese market. None of them was successful.

It was in this context that Lord Macartney undertook his mission. Unlike his predecessors, he was permitted to enter the Qing palaces in Beijing and elsewhere, have an audience with the Qing emperor Qianlong and his confident Heshen, and present George III's letter to the emperor. None of this had been achieved before. But in the end Macartney failed to realize the goals set by the government and the East India Company for his embassy. Considering himself to be the ruler of the "central country," at the time the richest and most powerful in the world, Emperor Qianlong rejected all of Macartney's requests. Nor did the emperor think that a small maritime kingdom located several thousand miles away was a force deserving his attention and concern. Little did he know that all this was to change in about a half century.

Context

Several factors prompted the British East India Company and the British government to launch the Macartney embassy to seek diplomatic contact with Qing China, occa-

sioning the letter exchange between George III and Emperor Qianlong. First, during the second half of the eighteenth century the Industrial Revolution was well under way and was playing an increasingly important role in shaping British foreign policy. Propelled by the British desire for raw materials and new markets, British foreign policy became more and more colonialist and expansionist. Having won the Seven Years' War (1756–1763), the British began to establish their colonial empire around the world—a drive that continued despite the later loss of the North American colonies in the American Revolution. Indeed, to some extent, this loss may have served to deepen the English craving to seek compensations elsewhere. Second, the eighteenth century was an era of exploration and discovery. Even as Britain was dispatching the Macartney mission to China, it was beginning to expand its holdings in Canada, India, and Australia. Little wonder, then, that among Macartney's retinue were botanists, artists, and cartographers. The embassy thus was both a diplomatic mission and a voyage of discovery; as the former realized an economic interest, the latter showed a curiosity for first-hand knowledge of the mysterious Far East. Born and raised in Northern Ireland, George Macartney, who was created Viscount Macartney of Dervock right before his departure, was regarded as the best available diplomat and administrator to fill the post, because he had had experience dealing with Catherine the Great of Russia, another despotic ruler.

The third and perhaps most immediate reason for Britain's desire to secure diplomatic relations with China was that though the English trade with China would not be formally established until the early eighteenth century, that trade was nevertheless quickly increasing in importance. Throughout the seventeenth century, for example, tea drinking had gradually become a national habit in England, generating a strong demand for expanded trade with China. Indeed, according to Jonathan Spence, "by 1800, the East India Company was buying over 23 million pounds of China tea at a cost of £3.6 million" (p. 122). Between 1660 and 1700 the East India Company had made attempts to establish a factory in the provincial capital of Guangzhou (known in English as Canton) and elsewhere, but to no avail. By 1710 English merchants were trading regularly in

1600

- **December 31**
The East India Company is established by charter and soon becomes a major trader with the Indian Subcontinent and the Orient.

1644

- The Manchus found the Qing Dynasty, or Empire of the Great Qing.

1683

- The Qing, under Emperor Kangxi, unify the whole country by defeating various forces in South China, Tibet, and Taiwan.

1736

- Emperor Qianlong ascends the throne.

1760

- The Qing Dynasty imposes the Canton System to control trade in China.

- **October 25**
King George III ascends the throne of England.

1763

- **February 10**
The Treaty of Paris is signed, ending the Seven Years' War and establishing Britain's dominance of most colonies outside Europe.

Guangzhou, but their activities were straitjacketed by the Canton System imposed by the Qing Dynasty in 1760. By sponsoring the Macartney embassy, the company hoped, through diplomacy, to circumvent the Canton System and other Qing governmental regulations and gain direct access to Chinese goods.

The Qing Dynasty was not completely disinterested in foreign trade and the profit it generated. Although Emperor Qianlong forcefully rejected Macartney's requests for expanded trade, the Qing court reaped handsome customs revenue from seaborne foreign commerce in certain ports along the coast. This stood in stark contrast to the policy of its predecessor, the Ming Dynasty (1368–1644), which during the early fifteenth century was known for launching stupendous maritime expeditions that reached the eastern and southeastern coasts of Africa. But from the time of the mid-Ming, troubled by piracy, the dynasty resumed its policy of *haijin*, or "coastal clearance," forbidding the Chinese to sail into the sea and foreign merchants to come ashore. The Qing rulers continued this "sea ban" policy, though for a different reason—to prevent the recuperation of the remaining Ming forces that had been active along the coast and in Taiwan. After Emperor Kang Xi, the dynasty's second and perhaps most able ruler, had pacified the coastal regions in 1683, he lifted the ban on overseas trade. Ironically, it was during Emperor Qianlong's reign that the sea ban was greatly relaxed, giving rise to the Cohong, a merchant guild that gradually gained a monopoly, authorized by the Qing government, on trading with Western merchants. The Cohong thus became a core agency in the Canton System, which helped put overseas trade under the direct control of both the provincial government and the central government's Ministry of Revenue. The Canton System was aimed at delimiting foreign trade and exploiting its income for the Qing court.

While Emperor Qianlong showed interest in foreign trade, he was clearly not ready to expand it to the extent desired by the British. The Qing was founded by the Manchus, a nomadic group and an ethnic minority that had arisen originally in Manchuria, today's Northeast China. After replacing the Ming Dynasty, the Manchu rulers quickly adopted a policy of presenting themselves as the legitimate successors of the Ming imperial realm. In economic terms, this meant that the Qing continued the traditional emphasis on agricultural development, one that had been in place for two millennia. Like the Ming and most of its predecessors, the Qing considered itself politically and ideologically the owner of the Central Country (Zhongguo, or "Middle Kingdom"), an undisputed center of civilization in the world and one that radiated its cultural influence to the surrounding regions. All this was reflected in the practice of the entrenched "tributary system" that the Qing had inherited from its predecessors in managing relations with its neighbors. Under this system, it was assumed that uncultured neighboring barbarians would be attracted to China and would be transformed by Chinese culture. The Chinese ruler would show compassion for foreign emissaries. In Emperor Qianlong's era, these "tributary states" could be found not only in today's Korea, Vietnam, Burma, and Thailand but also in parts of Russia, the Netherlands, and Portugal.

Compared with the Russians, who had established an ecclesiastical mission in Beijing, and the Portuguese, who had held Macao as their enclave, the British were latecomers in seeking a relationship with Qing China. However, powered by the raging Industrial Revolution, this nation of just eight million—compared with 330 million in Qing China—began to sense that they represented the burgeoning great power in the world. This sentiment was evident in the instructions given by Henry Dundas, the home secretary of the British Government, to Lord Macartney:

1. to negotiate a treaty of commerce and friendship and to establish a resident minister at the court of Qianlong;

2. to extend British trade in China by opening new ports where British woolens might be sold;

3. to obtain from China the cession of a piece of land or an island nearer to the tea- and silk-producing area than Guangzhou, where British merchants might reside the whole year and where British jurisdiction could be exercised;

4. to abolish the existing abuses in the Canton System and to obtain assurances that they would not be revived;

5. to create new markets in China for British products hitherto unknown, such as hardware; and

6. to open Japan and Vietnam to British trade by means of treaties.

The nature and scope of these charges suggest that the British government hoped to attain much more from their contact with the Chinese than had been accomplished by other Europeans. Most important, they wanted their country to be treated as an equal by the Qing ruler. Lord Macartney intended to show the Chinese that a new power had been born in the West.

Steam-driven vessels would indeed bring the English close to the Chinese shore and deliver a serious blow to their empire in the mid-nineteenth century. But Emperor Qianlong did not foresee this. After all, the Qing Dynasty, from the time of its founding in the mid-seventeenth century and until the time of Qianlong, had stood undefeated in all the wars it had fought with its enemies. The emperor was willing to show his compassion for, or even "cherish," the visit of an embassy from afar, especially one offering belated congratulations for his eightieth birthday and presenting tribute to his Celestial Empire. But he was uninterested in anything beyond that, let alone in any notion of treating the British as equals.

On September 14, 1793, a year after departing from London, Macartney and his retinue were received by the emperor at Rehe, a Qing summer palace north of Beijing. As he presented King George III's letter to Qianlong, Macartney is said to have knelt on one knee, as if he were being received by his king, though he omitted kissing the emperor's hand. Macartney and his associates denied that they ever performed kowtow (which required bending both knees) at the Qing court, but new scholarship reveals that while the Chinese ministers were performing the kowtow on one or two other occasions, prostrating their bodies and

Time Line

1760s

- A series of inventions in cotton spinning are patented in Britain, propelling the expansion of its textile industry and sparking interest in acquiring silk and other fabrics from China.

1780s

- James Watts improves the design of the steam engine, a landmark event in the Industrial Revolution and one that led to advances in oceangoing vessels.

1792

- **September** The British East India Company and British government dispatch Lord George Macartney as ambassador to China for developing trade and diplomatic relations with the Qing Empire, where he remains until 1794.

1793

- **September 14** Macartney presents a letter from George III to Emperor Qianlong, seeking to secure diplomatic relations and improved trade conditions with Qing China.

- **October 3** Emperor Qianlong summons Macartney to his court and tenders his reply to King George's letter.

1796 ■ Emperor Jiaqing ascends the throne.

1799 ■ Emperor Qianlong dies.

1820 ■ **January 29** George III dies.

1839 ■ The First Opium War begins.

knocking their foreheads on the ground, the British also knelt on both knees and bowed their heads to the ground. Thus, scholars differ in their reading and interpretation of the sources regarding the kowtow ritual. Despite this, most of them seem to agree that even if the English, or Macartney, had followed the usual ritual in meeting Emperor Qianlong, it would not have altered their mission's outcome—the emperor would still have rejected their requests. For though the Qing court delighted in profiting from tea, silk, lacquer, and porcelain exports to Europe, such things remained luxurious and therefore peripheral to their agriculture-based economy.

About the Author

Emperor Qianlong was born Hongli, the fourth son of Emperor Yongzheng, in 1711. Qianlong was his reign name, and he would not take it until he assumed the throne of the empire. In imperial China, members of the upper class usually had several names for difference occasions. The name given by the parents was used strictly within the family. Emperors had a reign name because, out of deference, no one outside the family was supposed to use his given name. Qianlong was the fourth emperor of the Qing Dynasty, and his reign—which began in 1736 and ended officially in 1795 (though he remained in power until his death in 1799)—was the longest in the dynasty, representing its heyday. Among the emperor's many accomplishments was the acquisition of a huge territory in the northwest, known as Xinjiang, or "New Territory," which doubled what was then China's territory. Under Qianlong's rule, the population experienced a boom, attesting to the vibrancy of the economy.

Besides being an able administrator, Emperor Qianlong was a cultural dilettante. He penned a great number of poems and essays in Chinese and was a patron of an ambitious ten-year bibliographic project known as the Four Treasuries (*Siku quanshu*), the avowed aim of which was to cull, catalog, and abstract all existing books. The study of Chinese Confucian culture, in the form of "evidential learning"— an intellectual trend of the Qing period that emphasized an empirical approach to the understanding of Confucian classics—flourished.

Explanation and Analysis of the Document

After he presented King George III's letter to Emperor Qianlong on September 14, 1793, Lord Macartney did not receive a reply until October 3, when he and his assistant were ushered into Beijing's Forbidden City and asked to genuflect before the scroll that represented the emperor's rejoinder. In fact, Qianlong's response had been ready since September 22. Indeed, Qing court documents reveal that the letter had been drafted as early as July 30 and had been submitted to Emperor Qianlong on August 3, more than six weeks before King George III's letter was even delivered. In other words, the failure of the British mission to establish trade and diplomatic relations was "inevitable from the outset" (Peyrefitte, p. 288). Nevertheless, Macartney's omitting to kneel on both knees when he delivered his king's requests to the emperor apparently had served to toughen the letter's tone in rejecting these requests. As an imperial edict, Qianlong's response was written in classical Chinese and rendered into Latin by Jesuit missionaries. Next, the embassy drafted an English summary of the Latin translation, erasing any trace of offensive and condescending phrases. Neither of these texts has survived. The letter exists today only in abridged versions.

◆ **Paragraphs 1–6**

In the first two paragraphs, Emperor Qianlong politely acknowledges the effort by King George III to send a diplomatic mission, which he interprets as a "desire to partake of the benefits of our civilisation." He delights in the fact that the mission was sent to congratulate him on the anniversary of his birthday. In return for this friendly gesture and for the mission's gifts (which he regards as tributes), the emperor informs King George that he has shown his generosity by personally meeting the embassy and treating them with presents and banquets.

In the next four paragraphs, the emperor proceeds to the first important issue: rejecting the embassy's request to establish a diplomatic residency in Beijing and denying English merchants permission to travel and trade freely in the country. His reasons are three: First, drawing perhaps on the experience of the Jesuit missions, the emperor cites the historical precedent that once a European was permitted to live in China, he then would be expected to adopt the Chinese way of life and would be forbidden to return home. This would not suit the goal that the diplomatic residency hoped to achieve. Second, the emperor suggests that there is nothing wrong with the Canton System of managing and

Seals belonging to the Qianlong Emperor (Freer Gallery of Art, Smithsonian Institution, Washington, D.C.: Anonymous gift, F1978.51a-f)

controlling trade with the Europeans, and he refuses to alter it to accommodate the English request that a resident diplomat be allowed to direct English trade with China. He asks, "If each and all [Europeans] demanded to be represented at our Court, how could we possibly consent?"— a reflection of the historical reality that tributary missions from foreign lands would remain in China for no more than several months. It likewise suggests that although the emperor was aware that Europe comprised many nations, he did not know that diplomatic residence had become a

common practice among them. Of course, knowing would almost certainly not have altered his judgment: Qianlong was quite confident that China's "ceremonies and code of laws" were superior to those of the Europeans.

This sense of cultural superiority stands as Qianlong's third reason for dismissing the English request. He tells the king that he believes that even if the English envoy "were able to acquire the rudiments of our civilisation, you could not possibly transplant our manners and customs to your alien soil." Considering himself to be the ruler of a superior civilization occupying the center of the universe, the emperor makes it clear to King George that if he permits certain trade with the English, it is because he wants to bestow grace and extend friendship to a foreign nation, for "we possess all things. I set no value on objects strange or ingenious, and have no use for your country's manufactures."

◆ Paragraphs 7 and 8

These paragraphs explain the emperor's refusal to expand trade with the English. They begin with a similar acknowledgment, only now in a somewhat more condescending tone. Noting King George's interest in seeking to "come into touch with our converting influence" and his "respectful spirit of submission," the emperor informs the king that he has reciprocated with "the bestowal of valuable presents."

The emperor continues to explain somewhat haughtily to the English king why he is forced to reject his emissary's requests. The emperor sees the proposal to expand trade and bypass the Cohong as a violation of the existent practice, which he considers impeccable. Such a request, if granted, would set a "bad example" for other nations. Thus, he not only wanted his ministers to educate the embassy about the rules of his empire but also ordered them to arrange departure for the embassy.

◆ Paragraphs 9–12

The next four paragraphs address Macartney's detailed requests for gaining access to the Chinese market, which include setting facilities for assisting English ships in port cities other than Xiamen ("Aomen" in the document); establishing a merchant repository in Beijing, the Qing capital; allowing English merchants to reside on a small island near Zhoushan ("Chusan"); and gaining them a residential compound in the city of Guangzhou ("Canton"). The emperor rejects all of these requests because he considers the established Cohong system the best way to handle foreign trade. Specifically, he states that the port city Xiamen, located in southeastern China, is the most ideal geographic location for a merchant repository because it is "near to the sea." More important, it was where the Cohong ran its operation by which the Qing Dynasty controlled and contained trade with the West. The emperor regards the request for merchant residence and repository as an infringement on the empire's territorial integrity. But in doing so, he has to explain why the Russians were granted such a facility in Beijing. Although his answer is hardly persuasive, it is nevertheless unequivocal: "The accommodation furnished to them [the Russians] was only temporary." He underscores the fact that his dynasty restricts the movement of foreigners when he says that they have never been allowed "to cross the Empire's barriers and settle at will amongst the Chinese people."

In responding to the request for an island near Zhoushan where merchants could reside and warehouse goods, the emperor is unequivocal that it would set up an "evil example." He asks how he could comply with such requests from other nations. The same argument is applied to the request for a site in Guangzhou. If he allows the English to gain such a privilege, then other European nations would seek the same, which he regards as dangerous, for "friction would inevitably occur between the Chinese and your barbarian subjects." In the same spirit, he sees that this permission would invariably expand their contacts with the Chinese people.

◆ Paragraphs 13 and 14

The next two paragraphs deal with issues related to tax and tariff. One of the major reasons for the English government to send the Macartney mission to China was to seek, in modern language, a "most favored nation status" for Britain. This status would reduce duties and tariffs levied by Qing China on English merchandise. Emperor Qianlong also rejects these requests. As before, he does so by stressing the issue of equality. As he puts it, he does not want to "make an exception in your case" lest the principle of equality exercised by the Qing court in managing foreign trade be violated. Yet what lurks beneath this seemingly grand reason is his refusal to make any changes to the existing Cohong system.

◆ Paragraph 15

The next paragraph, denying the request to conduct missionary activities in China, offers a glimpse into the emperor's mindset regarding cultural exchange in general and his recalcitrant attitude toward managing overseas trade in particular. Although he does not denigrate Christianity, he clearly regards the Chinese moral system as superior. He describes how this system was established from time immemorial and how it has been religiously observed by generations of Chinese. He reminds the king that Europeans present in China are prohibited from preaching their religion to his subjects. This explanation was consistent with the policy instituted in the early eighteenth century by Emperor Kangxi—Emperor Qianlong's much-loved grandfather—in the wake of the Rites Controversy, which essentially forbade Christian missionaries from proselytizing the Chinese.

◆ Paragraph 16

Having rejected all of the requests "wantonly" made by the Macartney embassy on behalf of King George III, Emperor Qianlong concludes his letter by blaming Lord Macartney and not the king himself for entertaining and presenting such "wild ideas and hopes." Even if the king were somewhat involved, the emperor writes, it was out of ignorance and innocence; he assumes that King George III "had no intention of transgressing [Qing dynasty regulations]." He goes on to deliver a stern warning to King George III: If the British government persists in pursuing those proposals, it and its emissaries will face severe punishments. "Tremblingly obey and show no negligence!" he tells the king.

Audience

Emperor Qianlong's letter was, first and foremost, addressed to the king of England, George III. Although he wrote as one monarch to another, Qianlong was issuing a response in the form of an "imperial edict." He was placing

"As to your entreaty to send one of your nationals to be accredited to my Celestial Court and to be in control of your country's trade with China, this request is contrary to all usage of my dynasty and cannot possibly be entertained."

(Paragraph 3)

"How can our dynasty alter its whole procedure and system of etiquette, established for more than a century, in order to meet your individual views?"

(Paragraph 4)

"Swaying the wide world, I have but one aim in view, namely, to maintain a perfect governance and to fulfil the duties of the State: strange and costly objects do not interest me."

(Paragraph 5)

"My capital is the hub and centre about which all quarters of the globe revolve."

(Paragraph 10)

"Ever since the beginning of history, sage Emperors and wise rulers have bestowed on China a moral system and inculcated a code, which from time immemorial has been religiously observed by the myriads of my subjects. That has no hankering after heterodox doctrines."

(Paragraph 15)

himself on a quite different footing. Although Qianlong was, in a sense, having his own "audience" with the British king, his condescending tone was that of a superior. King George, as the intended recipient, would have been unlikely to have received the letter in the spirit in which it was offered. We do not know, however, whether the letter was ever delivered.

The more immediate audience for the emperor's letter was Lord McCartney and his embassy. Written in classical Chinese, the letter had first to be translated by Jesuit missionaries into Latin and then by the embassy into English. The embassy was concerned enough about the language to erase any trace of offensive and condescending phrases. Macartney wrote of the event in his journal, where he describes being received at the palace by the First Minister,

but without the usual graciousness and with a certain constraint. Later, when high officials of the court delivered the letter itself to him at home, Macartney comments that from their manner it had become clear that the Chinese wanted the British embassy to leave. He does not remark on the contents of the letter itself. In early 1794 Macartney sailed for home, disappointed that his mission had failed.

Impact

In response to King George's request for broadening trade and bettering diplomatic relations, Emperor Qianlong wrote his letter in the form of an imperial edict, explaining in detail how and why he would not grant such a request. The emperor wanted to tell the English king how ignorant he was about the magnificence of the Chinese Empire and how improper his request was. However, we are unsure whether Lord Macartney actually delivered Emperor Qianlong's letter to King George. Hence, we do not know King George's reaction. In other words, whatever the emperor's intention was in writing the letter, it did not have the intended impact.

This first communication between the Qing emperor of China and the king of England was not entirely fruitless. Although George Macartney failed in his diplomatic mission to open the door to British trade with China, he was more successful in his voyage of discovery. During his six-month sojourn in China he made careful and detailed observations of the country in his journal, as did some of other members in the embassy. Their portrayal of the Chinese as a stubborn and superstitious people and the Qing Dynasty as a backward-looking empire, uninterested in change and novelty, eventually altered the more positive image of China in the European mind generated by the Jesuits' writings and by the *philosophes*. Instead, Macartney and his assistants were convinced that to change China "the effort required would be superhuman and that violence could someday be necessary" (Peyrefitte, p. 541). Violence was indeed used in the First Opium War of 1839–1842.

Further Reading

■ Articles
Esherick, Joseph. "Cherishing Sources from Afar." *Modern China* 24, no. 2 (April 1998): 135–161.

—. "Tradutore, Traditure, A Reply to James Hevia." *Modern China* 24, no. 3 (July 1998): 328–332.

Gillingham, Paul, "The Macartney Embassy to China." *History Today* 43, no. 11 (November 1993): 28–34.

Hevia, James H. "Postpolemical Historiography: A Response to Joseph W. Esherick," *Modern China* 24, no. 3 (July 1998): 319–327.

■ Books
Cranmer-Byng, J. L., ed. *An Embassy to China: Being the Journal Kept by Lord Macartney during his Embassy to the Emperor Ch'ien-lung, 1793–1794.* St. Claire Shores, Mich.: Scholarly Press, 1972.

Hevia, James H. *Cherishing Men from Afar: Qing Guest Ritual and the Macartney Embassy of 1793.* Durham, N.C.: Duke University Press, 1995.

Peyrefitte, Alain. *The Collision of Two Civilizations: The British Expedition to China in 1792–4,* trans. Jon Rothschild. Hammersmith, U.K.: Harvill, 1993.

Spence, Jonathan. *The Search for Modern China.* New York: W. W. Norton, 1990.

—Q. Edward Wang

Questions for Further Study

1. The British East India Company was a private corporation, but during the eighteenth century and into the nineteenth century it represented a projection of British imperial power in Asia and thus became a governing power. How and to what extent was the company able to achieve this goal?

2. Why was China such an important market for Great Britain? What economic reasons did Great Britain have for strengthening trade relations with China?

3. To what extent did cultural differences between China and England lead to the Chinese emperor's rejection of King George III's proposal? What specific cultural practices in China influenced Qianlong's response to King George?

4. Qianlong rejected out of hand every one of Britain's proposals. What do you believe was the underlying reason for his refusal even to entertain the possibility of agreeing to any of these proposals?

5. Compare and contrast Qianlong's Letter to King George III with Lin Zexu's "Moral Advice to Queen Victoria," written less than four decades later in 1839. Did the later letter suggest any advances in relations between Great Britain and China, or was China still "closed" to Britain and its trading goals?

QIANLONG'S LETTER TO GEORGE III

You, O King, live beyond the confines of many seas, nevertheless, impelled by your humble desire to partake of the benefits of our civilisation, you have dispatched a mission respectfully bearing your memorial. Your Envoy has crossed the seas and paid his respects at my Court on the anniversary of my birthday. To show your devotion, you have also sent offerings of your country's produce.

I have perused your memorial: the earnest terms in which it is couched reveal a respectful humility on your part, which is highly praiseworthy. In consideration of the fact that your Ambassador and his deputy have come a long way with your memorial and tribute, I have shown them high favour and have allowed them to be introduced into my presence. To manifest my indulgence, I have entertained them at a banquet and made them numerous gifts. I have also caused presents to be forwarded to the Naval Commander and six hundred of his officers and men, although they did not come to Peking, so that they too may share in my all-embracing kindness.

As to your entreaty to send one of your nationals to be accredited to my Celestial Court and to be in control of your country's trade with China, this request is contrary to all usage of my dynasty and cannot possibly be entertained. It is true that Europeans, in the service of the dynasty, have been permitted to live at Peking, but they are compelled to adopt Chinese dress, they are strictly confined to their own precincts and are never permitted to return home. You are presumably familiar with our dynastic regulations. Your proposed Envoy to my Court could not be placed in a position similar to that of European officials in Peking who are forbidden to leave China, nor could he, on the other hand, be allowed liberty of movement and the privilege of corresponding with his own country; so that you would gain nothing by his residence in our midst.

Moreover, our Celestial dynasty possesses vast territories, and tribute missions from the dependencies are provided for by the Department for Tributary States, which ministers to their wants and exercises strict control over their movements. It would be quite impossible to leave them to their own devices. Supposing that your Envoy should come to our Court, his language and national dress differ from that of our people, and there would be no place in which to bestow him. It may be suggested that he might imitate the Europeans permanently resident in Peking and adopt the dress and customs of China, but, it has never been our dynasty's wish to force people to do things unseemly and inconvenient. Besides, supposing I sent an Ambassador to reside in your country, how could you possibly make for him the requisite arrangements? Europe consists of many other nations besides your own: if each and all demanded to be represented at our Court, how could we possibly consent? The thing is utterly impracticable. How can our dynasty alter its whole procedure and system of etiquette, established for more than a century, in order to meet your individual views? If it be said that your object is to exercise control over your country's trade, your nationals have had full liberty to trade at Canton for many a year, and have received the greatest consideration at our hands. Missions have been sent by Portugal and Italy, preferring similar requests. The Throne appreciated their sincerity and loaded them with favours, besides authorising measures to facilitate their trade with China. You are no doubt aware that, when my Canton merchant, Wu Chao-ping, was in debt to the foreign ships, I made the Viceroy advance the monies due, out of the provincial treasury, and ordered him to punish the culprit severely. Why then should foreign nations advance this utterly unreasonable request to be represented at my Court? Peking is nearly two thousand miles from Canton, and at such a distance what possible control could any British representative exercise?

If you assert that your reverence for Our Celestial dynasty fills you with a desire to acquire our civilisation, our ceremonies and code of laws differ so completely from your own that, even if your Envoy were able to acquire the rudiments of our civilisation, you could not possibly transplant our manners and customs to your alien soil. Therefore, however adept the Envoy might become, nothing would be gained thereby.

Swaying the wide world, I have but one aim in view, namely, to maintain a perfect governance and to fulfil the duties of the State: strange and costly objects do not interest me. If I have commanded that the tribute offerings sent by you, O King, are to be accepted, this was solely in consideration for the spirit which prompted you to dispatch them from afar. Our dynasty's majestic virtue has penetrated unto every country under Heaven, and Kings of all nations have offered their costly tribute by land and sea. As your Ambassador can see for himself, we possess all things. I set no value on objects strange or ingenious, and have no use for your country's manufactures. This then is my answer to your request to appoint a representative at my Court, a request contrary to our dynastic usage, which would only result in inconvenience to yourself. I have expounded my wishes in detail and have commanded your tribute Envoys to leave in peace on their homeward journey. It behoves you, O King, to respect my sentiments and to display even greater devotion and loyalty in future, so that, by perpetual submission to our Throne, you may secure peace and prosperity for your country hereafter. Besides making gifts (of which I enclose an inventory) to each member of your Mission, I confer upon you, O King, valuable presents in excess of the number usually bestowed on such occasions, including silks and curios—a list of which is likewise enclosed. Do you reverently receive them and take note of my tender goodwill towards you! A special mandate.

You, O King, from afar have yearned after the blessings of our civilisation, and in your eagerness to come into touch with our converting influence have sent an Embassy across the sea bearing a memorial. I have already taken note of your respectful spirit of submission, have treated your mission with extreme favour and loaded it with gifts, besides issuing a mandate to you, O King, and honouring you with the bestowal of valuable presents. Thus has my indulgence been manifested.

Yesterday your Ambassador petitioned my Ministers to memorialise me regarding your trade with China, but his proposal is not consistent with our dynastic usage and cannot be entertained. Hitherto, all European nations, including your own country's barbarian merchants, have carried on their trade with our Celestial Empire at Canton. Such has been the procedure for many years, although our Celestial Empire possesses all things in prolific abundance and lacks no product within its own borders. There was therefore no need to import the manufactures of outside barbarians in exchange for our own produce. But as the tea, silk and porcelain which the Celestial Empire produces, are absolute necessities to European nations and to yourselves, we have permitted, as a signal mark of favour, that foreign *hongs* should be established at Canton, so that your wants might be supplied and your country thus participate in our beneficence. But your Ambassador has now put forward new requests which completely fail to recognise the Throne's principle to 'treat strangers from afar with indulgence,' and to exercise a pacifying control over barbarian tribes, the world over. Moreover, our dynasty, swaying the myriad races of the globe, extends the same benevolence towards all. Your England is not the only nation trading at Canton. If other nations, following your bad example, wrongfully importune my ear with further impossible requests, how will it be possible for me to treat them with easy indulgence? Nevertheless, I do not forget the lonely remoteness of your island, cut off from the world by intervening wastes of sea, nor do I overlook your excusable ignorance of the usages of our Celestial Empire. I have consequently commanded my Ministers to enlighten your Ambassador on the subject, and have ordered the departure of the mission. But I have doubts that, after your Envoy's return he may fail to acquaint you with my view in detail or that he may be lacking in lucidity, so that I shall now proceed to take your requests *seriatim* and to issue my mandate on each question separately. In this way you will, I trust, comprehend my meaning.

(1) Your Ambassador requests facilities for ships of your nation to call at Ningpo, Chusan, Tientsin and other places for purposes of trade. Until now trade with European nations has always been conducted at Aomen, where the foreign *hongs* are established to store and sell foreign merchandise. Your nation has obediently complied with this regulation for years past without raising any objection. In none of the other ports named have *hongs* been established, so that even if your vessels were to proceed thither, they would have no means of disposing of their cargoes. Furthermore, no interpreters are available, so you would have no means of explaining your wants, and nothing but general inconvenience would result. For the future, as in the past, I decree that your request is refused and that the trade shall be limited to Aomen.

(2) The request that your merchants may establish a repository in the capital of my Empire for the storing and sale of your produce, in accordance with the precedent granted to Russia, is even more impracticable than the last. My capital is the hub and centre about which all quarters of the globe revolve. Its ordinances are most august and its laws are strict in the extreme. The subjects of our dependencies have never been allowed to open places of business in

Peking. Foreign trade has hitherto been conducted at Aomen, because it is conveniently near to the sea, and therefore an important gathering place for the ships of all nations sailing to and fro. If warehouses were established in Peking, the remoteness of your country, lying far to the north-west of my capital, would render transport extremely difficult.

Before Kiakhta was opened, the Russians were permitted to trade at Peking, but the accommodation furnished to them was only temporary. As soon as Kiakhta was available, they were compelled to withdraw from Peking, which has been closed to their trade these many years. Their frontier trade at Kiakhta is on all fours with your trade at Aomen. Possessing facilities at the latter place, you now ask for further privileges at Peking, although our dynasty observes the severest restrictions respecting the admission of foreigners within its boundaries, and has never permitted the subjects of dependencies to cross the Empire's barriers and settle at will amongst the Chinese people. This request is also refused.

(3) Your request for a small island near Chusan, where your merchants may reside and goods be warehoused, arises from your desire to develop trade. As there are neither foreign *hongs* nor interpreters in or near Chusan, where none of your ships have ever called, such an island would be utterly useless for your purposes. Every inch of the territory of our Empire is marked on the map and the strictest vigilance is exercised over it all: even tiny islets and far-lying sand-banks are clearly defined as part of the provinces to which they belong. Consider, moreover, that England is not the only barbarian land which wishes to establish relations with our civilisation and trade with our Empire: supposing that other nations were all to imitate your evil example and beseech me to present them each and all with a site for trading purposes, how could I possibly comply? This also is a flagrant infringement of the usage of my Empire and cannot possibly be entertained.

(4) The next request, for a small site in the vicinity of Canton city, where your barbarian merchants may lodge or, alternatively, that there be no longer any restrictions over their movements at Aomen, has arisen from the following causes. Hitherto, the barbarian merchants of Europe have had a definite locality assigned to them at Aomen for residence and trade, and have been forbidden to encroach an inch beyond the limits assigned to that locality. Barbarian merchants having business with the *hongs* have never been allowed to enter the city of Canton; by these measures, disputes between Chinese and barbarians

are prevented, and a firm barrier is raised between my subjects and those of other nations. The present request is quite contrary to precedent; furthermore, European nations have been trading with Canton for a number of years and, as they make large profits, the number of traders is constantly increasing. How would it be possible to grant such a site to each country? The merchants of the foreign *hongs* are responsible to the local officials for the proceedings of barbarian merchants and they carry out periodical inspections. If these restrictions were withdrawn, friction would inevitably occur between the Chinese and your barbarian subjects, and the results would militate against tile benevolent regard that I feel towards you. From every point of view, therefore, it is best that the regulations now in force should continue unchanged.

(5) Regarding your request for remission or reduction of duties on merchandise discharged by your British barbarian merchants at Aomen and distributed throughout the interior, there is a regular tariff in force for barbarian merchants' goods, which applies equally to all European nations. It would be as wrong to increase the duty imposed on your nation's merchandise on the ground that the bulk of foreign trade is in your hands, as to make an exception in your case in the shape of specially reduced duties. In future, duties shall be levied equitably without discrimination between your nation and any other, and, in order to manifest my regard, your barbarian merchants shall continue to be shown every consideration at Aomen.

(6) As to your request that your ships shall pay the duties leviable by tariff, there are regular rules in force at the Canton Custom house respecting the amounts payable, and since I have refused your request to be allowed to trade at other ports, this duty will naturally continue to be paid at Canton as heretofore.

(7) Regarding your nation's worship of the Lord of Heaven, it is the same religion as that of other European nations. Ever since the beginning of history, sage Emperors and wise rulers have bestowed on China a moral system and inculcated a code, which from time immemorial has been religiously observed by the myriads of my subjects. There has been no hankering after heterodox doctrines. Even the European (missionary) officials in my capital are forbidden to hold intercourse with Chinese subjects; they are restricted within the limits of their appointed residences, and may not go about propagating their religion. The distinction between Chinese and barbarian is most strict, and your Ambassador's request that

barbarians shall be given full liberty to disseminate their religion is utterly unreasonable.

It may be, O King, that the above proposals have been wantonly made by your Ambassador on his own responsibility, or peradventure you yourself are ignorant of our dynastic regulations and had no intention of transgressing them when you expressed these wild ideas and hopes. I have ever shown the greatest condescension to the tribute missions of all States which sincerely yearn after the blessings of civilisation, so as to manifest my kindly indulgence. I have even gone out of my way to grant any requests which were in any way consistent with Chinese usage. Above all, upon you, who live in a remote and inaccessible region, far across the spaces of ocean, but who have shown your submissive loyalty by sending this tribute mission, I have heaped benefits far in excess of those accorded to other nations. But the demands presented by your Embassy are not only a contravention of dynastic tradition, but would be utterly improductive

of good result to yourself, besides being quite impracticable. I have accordingly stated the facts to you in detail, and it is your bounden duty reverently to appreciate my feelings and to obey these instructions henceforward for all time, so that you may enjoy the blessings of perpetual peace. If, after the receipt of this explicit decree, you lightly give ear to the representations of your subordinates and allow your barbarian merchants to proceed to Chêkiang and Tientsin, with the object of landing and trading there, the ordinances of my Celestial Empire are strict in the extreme, and the local officials, both civil and military, are bound reverently to obey the law of the land. Should your vessels touch the shore, your merchants will assuredly never be permitted to land or to reside there, but will be subject to instant expulsion. In that event your barbarian merchants will have had a long journey for nothing. Do not say that you were not warned in due time! Tremblingly obey and show no negligence! A special mandate!

tribute missions	persons representing dependent states who appeared before the emperor bearing rare and valuable items as evidence of submission to the Qing Dynasty
Swaying the wide world	a reflection of the emperor's belief his geopolitical importance far outweighed that of Great Britain, continental Europe, and the rest of the known world

Toussaint Louverture (Library of Congress)

CONSTITUTION OF HAITI

"There can be no slaves on this territory; servitude has been forever abolished."

Overview

The 1801 Constitution of Haiti, promulgated in the wake of the Haitian Revolution that had begun in 1791, was the first in a series of some twenty-three constitutions that have been adopted in that nation. Haiti, at the time called Saint Domingue, had been a French colony since the late seventeenth century; the name Haiti, from the indigenous name Ayiti ("mountainous land") was adopted at independence in 1804. Along with Jamaica, Haiti produced the bulk of the world's sugar in a plantation economy built on the backs of slaves imported from Africa. The Haitian Revolution was essentially a slave revolt, the only successful slave revolt in modern history. As a result of the revolt, Haiti became the first independent nation in Latin America, the second in the Western Hemisphere (after the United States), and the first postcolonial nation led by blacks.

The constitution, sometimes called the Saint Domingue Constitution, was written by a ten-member committee, though the document the committee produced embodied the thinking of François-Dominique Toussaint-Louverture, a former slave who became a prominent leader of the revolution. In the 1790s he was able to expel Europeans from Haiti and establish Haiti as a self-governing polity with himself as governor. The 1801 constitution abolished slavery and named him governor for life, though his administration was brief, for in response to the constitution the French reasserted control over its colony. Nevertheless, Toussaint-Louverture and the 1801 constitution were of immense significance, for they launched the process of overthrowing European colonial rule in the Americas—rule that extended back some three centuries to the decades after Christopher Columbus's historic voyage to the New World.

Context

As a French colony, Haiti was a leading supplier of sugar and, as such, was France's most lucrative colony—and, in fact, the most lucrative European colony in the world. It had been under the firm control of the French since 1697,

when the Treaty of Ryswick divided the island of Hispaniola between France, which controlled Saint Domingue (the western third of the island), and Spain, which controlled the Dominican Republic. White landowners developed immense plantations for the raising of sugarcane, coffee, indigo, and other crops for export, all labor-intensive industries that depended on slave labor. Because they were vastly outnumbered, plantation owners lived in fear of slave rebellions. They passed repressive laws that had the effect of creating a caste system. At the top of the system, of course, were *blancs*, or the white planters, who in turn were divided into *grand blancs*, or wealthy, aristocratic planters, and *petit blancs*, a class consisting of shopkeepers, artisans, and free day laborers. Occupying a middle tier were free blacks and mixed-race people (often the offspring of white planters and slave mothers), frequently referred to as mulattoes or *gens de couleur*. Members of this tier were typically educated and either worked as overseers on the plantations or served in the army; most had formerly been slaves. The lowest caste, of course, were black slaves.

Throughout the middle and late 1700s, whites and blacks engaged in a series of violent clashes. Large numbers of escaped slaves, called Maroons, formed gangs that lived in the forests. These gangs, which were generally small but sometimes grew to thousands of men, repeatedly attacked French plantations. Their efforts tended to be disorganized, however, until the emergence of François Mackandal, a Maroon and reputed Vodou priest who in 1751 succeeded in organizing the groups in a rebellion that lasted until 1757, when the French captured Mackandal, who was executed in 1758. (Vodou, popularly spelled "voodoo," is an indigenous religion that blends traditional West African religious beliefs and Christianity.) But despite the loss of Mackandal, the spirit of rebellion continued to grow and spread.

By the late 1700s, Haiti was riven by caste, racial, and national rivalries. The *petit blancs* resented the *grand blancs* because of their wealth and power. The *grand blancs* resented the French government's restrictions on their trade and supported the concept of an independent Haiti. The white colonists numbered about forty thousand, while the *gens de couleur* numbered about twenty-eight thousand. Meanwhile, the number of slaves was at least a half

1697
- The Treaty of Ryswick divides the island of Hispaniola between France and Spain.

1743
- **May 20** Toussaint-Louverture is born.

1758
- François Mackandal is executed for organizing a rebellion.

1777
- **June 3** The Treaty of Aranjuez between France and Spain recognizes the French colony of Saint Domingue.

1789
- **July 14** The storming of the Bastille in Paris launches the French Revolution.

1791
- **May 15** The French General Assembly grants full political rights to mulattos and free blacks.
- **August 22** The Haitian Revolution begins.

1792
- **April 4** The French General Assembly enfranchises free blacks and free mulattoes but does not emancipate the slaves.

million, and the slaves resented not only the abuses of their masters but also the privileges of free blacks. Complicating matters was competition for control of the lucrative colony among the French, Spanish, and British. Throughout the colony could be found advocates for independence, French loyalists, those who were loyal to Spain, and those who saw the British as their allies and liberators. On top of that, there were strong regional rivalries, with the colony's southern and western regions vying for economic supremacy against the more fertile and profitable northern coast.

While this complex stew was brewing in the New World, back in Europe, 1789 saw the beginning of the French Revolution. Haitians of all classes and colors watched the revolution with interest. Free people of color were emboldened by the revolutionary government's 1789 Declaration of the Rights of Man and consequently were often called Black Jacobins, a reference to political radicals in revolutionary France. The people of color agitated for civil rights, particularly the right to vote, sending emissaries to Paris to lobby for their cause. Whites supported the revolution, believing that it would lead to Haitian independence and that independence would give them a free hand in world trade. When the French government granted French citizenship and civil rights to free people of color in May 1791, white colonists refused to recognize the decision (which was later revoked). The result was a state of high tension between Haiti's former slaves and whites, particularly the *grand blancs*. Developments in France, where power after the revolution rapidly changed hands, added to the air of uncertainty.

The fuse was lit, and the explosion occurred on August 22, 1791, when the Haitian Revolution began at the instigation of Dutty Boukman, a Vodou priest and Maroon leader. Events over the next three years unfolded rapidly. In the early months, some hundred thousand slaves joined the revolt and embarked on a campaign of retaliation that killed two thousand whites and burned nearly two hundred plantations (out of a total of about eight thousand). Alarmed, the French dispatched six thousand troops to the island to quell the revolt. After the French declared war on England in 1793, white planters signed treaties with the British, intending for the British to gain sovereignty over the island. Meanwhile, the Spanish still occupied the Dominican Republic. Sensing an opportunity to expand their sphere of influence, the Spanish invaded Saint Domingue with the support of Saint Domingue's slaves.

By the time hostilities had been suspended in 1794, a hundred thousand blacks and twenty-four thousand whites had been killed. That year, the French National Convention abolished slavery and granted full civil and political rights to all blacks in Haiti. Napoléon Bonaparte issued the Proclamation on Saint Domingue in December 1799. In it, he asserted that he and the French government supported the colony's blacks: "The Consuls of the Republic, in announcing to you the new social pact, declare to you that the sacred principles of the freedom and equality of blacks will never suffer among you the least attack or modification" [qtd. at http:// thelouvertureproject.org/index.php?title=Napol%C3%A9on _Bonaparte_Proclamation_on_Saint-Domingue_(1799)].

Amid this chaos, Toussaint-Louverture emerged as the most dominant figure in Saint Domingue. A skilled, if untutored military commander, he initially fought on the side of the Spanish. In response to the arrival of British troops, he agreed to fight for France on the condition that slaves would be freed. Under his leadership, the Spanish were driven out of Saint Domingue. He subdued local rivals for preeminence, defeated a British contingent of forces in 1798, and in 1801 freed the slaves in Santo Domingo, the capital of the Dominican Republic. (That city changed hands from the Spanish, to the French, to the Haitians, back to the French, then to the Spanish, and then again to the Haitians, all in a span of about twenty years.) By this time he was the de facto ruler of an autonomous Haiti. He issued the constitution on May 9, 1801, and the constitution took effect on July 8 of that year.

About the Author

Toussaint-Louverture called for a constitutional assembly to write a constitution for Saint Domingue, even though it was still technically a colony of France. The assembly, whose members' names are listed at the end of the document, was composed of three mulattoes and seven whites. Their deliberations were directed by Bernard Borgella, the mayor of Port-au-Prince and formerly a barrister in the French city of Bordeaux. Chief among the members was Julien Raimond, a free man of color who was born in 1744 on the island of Martinique. His mother was a mulatto, and his father, a French colonist, was a planter. Raimond achieved wealth as an indigo planter, and by the 1780s he owned about a hundred slaves. He gained fame in the history of Haiti, however, for his ultimate opposition to slavery. He moved to Paris, where he petitioned the colonial ministry for the end of slavery and full equality for blacks in France's colonies. Working with an abolitionist group called Société des Amis des Noirs, or Society of Friends of the Blacks, he presented his case so effectively that the French General Assembly took up the issue in 1790 and in 1792 granted political rights to mulattos and free blacks. He died in 1801, shortly after the constitution he helped write took effect.

The motive force behind the constitution, however, was Toussaint-Louverture. He was born into slavery on May 20, 1743, as Toussaint Bréda near Le Cap in northern Haiti. Legend holds that his father had been an African chieftain, but it is likely that his father was actually the man whom others have often called his godfather and whom Toussaint-Louverture claimed as his father: Pierre Baptiste Simon, an educated black slave. Toussaint-Louverture was somewhat fortunate in that the owners of the Bréda plantation treated their slaves with kindness, and Toussaint was able to acquire an informal education. He was granted his freedom in 1776 when he married, and in the ensuing years he would rent and work a farm.

Toussaint may have been involved in planning the 1791 revolt, though it is uncertain. What is certain is that he joined the military, serving initially as a doctor but rising to the rank of commander. Throughout the 1790s he demonstrated his

Time Line

1793

- **February 1**
  France declares war on England.

1794

- **February 4**
  The French National Assembly abolishes slavery in the colonies.

1799

- **November 9**
  Napoléon overthrows the failing French Directory in a coup d'état; he later declares himself consul for life.

- **December 25**
  Napoléon issues the Proclamation on Saint Domingue.

1801

- **January 28**
  Toussaint-Louverture conquers Santo Domingo, putting him in control of all of Hispaniola; he abolishes slavery throughout the island.

- **May 9**
  Toussaint-Louverture issues a constitution.

- **July 8**
  The Haitian constitution takes effect.

1802

- **May 7**
  Toussaint Louverture signs a treaty with the French.

1802

- **May 20**
  Napoléon reestablishes slavery in the French colonies.

- **June 7**
  Toussaint-Louverture is captured by the French.

1803

- **April 7**
  Toussaint-Louverture dies of pneumonia in a French prison.

- **November 18**
  The French are defeated at the Battle of Vertières by the rebel general Jean-Jacques Dessalines.

1804

- **January 1**
  Dessalines proclaims Saint Domingue's independence; the nation is called the Republic of Hayti (later Haiti).

skill as a military leader and as a diplomat. In 1793 he added "Louverture" (often spelled L'Ouverture), meaning "the opener of the way," to his name. By the turn of the century he had consolidated his position as governor not just of Saint Domingue but, indeed, of the entire island of Hispaniola. In response to Toussaint-Louverture's constitution, Napoléon dispatched troops to the island under the command of his brother-in-law, General Victor Emmanuel Leclerc. Toussaint-Louverture put up resistance as long as he could, but the numbers were overwhelming, and he surrendered, signing a treaty with the French on May 7, 1802. He believed that he would be able to retire to his farm, but just a month later Leclerc had him arrested. He was taken to France, where he died in the Fort de Joux prison on April 7, 1803.

Explanation and Analysis of the Document

The language of the constitution of 1801 is simple and straightforward. It resembles other constitutions in that it establishes a system of laws and government for the colony in thirteen titles and seventy-seven articles. At the same time, it vests considerable authority in the hands of the colony's governor.

◆ Title I: On the Territory

Title I, consisting of two articles, defines the extent of Saint Domingue, which included the mainland and several islands. This title also indicates that the colony was to be divided into departments, *arrondisements*, and parishes. These terms reflect the administrative organization of France. A department was analogous to a state, a parish was analogous to a county (the same designation used in Louisiana, where it is likewise an indication of past French control), and an *arrondisement* was analogous to a precinct or district in a city. All were administrative subdivisions. Particularly noteworthy is that the constitution does not proclaim complete independence. It defines Saint Domingue as a colony and part of the French Empire.

◆ Title II: On Its Inhabitants

Article 3 is a core element of the constitution, declaring that there could be no slaves in the territory. The title goes on to grant freedom of employment and to eliminate distinctions based on skin color. All persons living in the colony were not only "free" but also "French." Again, the constitution does not declare independence from France.

◆ Title III: On Religion

Toussaint-Louverture was a lifelong Catholic, and since he identified himself as a Frenchman, it is not entirely surprising that he would impose Catholicism—specifically Roman Catholicism—on the colony. He was also opposed to Vodou. (In Haitian Vodou, various deities, called *loa*, are subordinate to Bondyè, a greater god who does not intervene in human affairs. Worship is therefore directed to the *loa*. Vodou also places great value on ancestor worship and avoidance of evil witchcraft.) The constitution calls for the maintenance of the Catholic Church in each parish and notes that resources would be directed to its support.

◆ Title IV: On Morals

This title addresses marriage and children. It promotes marriage, which "tends to the purity of morals." Consistent with Catholicism, the constitution forbids divorce. It also provides for the passage of laws designed to protect the welfare of children and family ties. The constitution specifies children "born through marriage," suggesting that different laws could apply to children born as a result of sexual misconduct (for example, involving white planters and their black or mulatto employees).

◆ Title V: On Men in Society

Title V, along with Titles IX and XIII, is as close as the constitution comes to issuing a bill of rights. Two essential rights are recognized. Article 12 "guarantees individual freedom and safety" and states that a person could be arrested only "by virtue of a formally expressed order, issued by a functionary who the law gives the right to arrest and detain." Article 13 protects property rights, calling property "sacred and inviolable." This provision protected landowners from having their land seized illegally by the government, and it had the effect of protecting the rights of plantation owners to their property.

◆ Title VI: On Cultivation and Commerce

A chief reason why Toussaint-Louverture wanted to protect property rights was that he wanted to protect commerce. He recognized that Saint Domingue depended on agricultural production and trade, and for that reason, he did not wish to permit "the least interruption in its labor and cultivation." The constitution goes on to note that "every habitation is a manufactory that demands a gathering together of cultivators and workers." It also asserts that changes in the habitation of cultivators would bring the ruin of farming, and it refers to the "introduction of cultivators indispensable to the reestablishment of planting." These are key provisions of the constitution, for essentially they tied black workers to the plantations where they worked. Toussaint-Louverture opposed slavery and mandated its abolition, but these provisions in the constitution limited the mobility of black workers in an attempt to ensure that Saint Domingue would remain a profitable French colony. Title VI shows other evidence of the constitution's authors' desire to assert their connection with France as well: It uses French revolutionary dating ("20 Vendémiaire" rather than October 11 and "19 Pluviôse" ["Pluviose" in the document]" rather than February 7).

◆ Title VII: On Legislation and Legislative Authority

Title VII turns to the specifics of government. It provides for an assembly and specifies rules for membership in the assembly, election procedures, meetings of the assembly, and similar practical matters. It is noteworthy that all bills passed by the assembly have to have been proposed by the governor. Further, the assembly functions largely in an advisory capacity: "It expresses its wishes on the regulations made and on the application of laws already made, on the abuses to be corrected, on the improvements to be undertaken."

◆ Title VIII: On Government

The constitution places control of the colony firmly in the hands of Toussaint-Louverture and his successors. The governor "directly corresponds with the government of the metropole," a word used in France, England, and other European countries to refer to the mother country, independent of its colonies. The title goes on to praise Toussaint-Louverture for his services to the colony and to lay out provisions for him to name his successor. The constitution mandates that succeeding governors remain loyal to the French government. It puts the governorship in the hands of the highest-ranking general in the event that a governor died without naming a successor. Articles 34 through 40 specify the powers of the governor, giving him command of the military, oversight of the colony's finances, censorship authority, command of the colony's agricultural activities, and other authority as well. Historians have noted that the constitution was not a particularly democratic document, for it vested considerable control in the governor, particularly Toussaint-Louverture.

◆ Title IX: On Tribunals

Title IX protects the right to a fair trial. It reflects the French judicial system by establishing *tribunaux de première instance*, meaning "courts of first instance," or trial courts, and also appeals courts. Additionally, it provides for a *tribunal de cassation*, otherwise known as a "court of error." This court—a court of final appeal—was analogous to the U.S. Supreme Court and to the *tribunal de cassation* established in France in 1790. Military tribunals were to be under the authority of the island's governor.

◆ Title X: On Municipal Administration

Title X turns to practical matters of administration in the cities, specifying that each was to have a mayor and administrators. The municipal administration was to be responsible for policing the area under its jurisdiction, administering funds, and similar basic functions.

◆ Title XI: On the Armed Force

The constitution places the armed forces under the command of the governor. It divides the armed forces into a paid regular army and an unpaid "national guard." The latter could operate only within its parish except in cases of emergency. The constitution specifies that the police (*gendarmerie*) were to be considered part of the armed forces.

◆ Title XII: On Finances and Goods Seized from Vacant Domains

After specifying the colony's sources of revenue, the constitution turns to one of the problems that arose from the Haitian Revolution: what to do about the properties of landowners who had lost their lives during the conflict and what to do about the contracts (*fermages*) between landowners and tenants. While the language of Title XII is in places obscure, essentially it grants the colonial administration power to seize goods and vacant lands but also obligates the administration to return those goods and lands with the restoration of peace between France and its adversaries.

◆ Title XIII: General Dispositions

As "General Dispositions" suggests, this title addresses a number of miscellaneous matters. It functions in part as a bill of rights by stating that "every person's home is an inviolable asylum," that citizens were protected from arbitrary arrest, and that they could petition the government. Patent rights are protected, as is the right to form schools. A uniform system of weights and measures is mandated. Citizens had the obligation to come to the defense of the colony. The obligations of leases are protected. The general dispositions also provide for the payment of "warriors" and forbid "seditious gatherings."

"There can be no slaves on this territory; servitude has been forever abolished. All men are born, live and die there free and French."

(Title II, Article 3)

"The Catholic religion, Apostolic and Roman, is the only one publicly professed."

(Title III, Article 6)

"The Constitution guarantees individual freedom and safety. No one can be arrested except by virtue of a formally expressed order, issued by a functionary who the law gives the right to arrest and detain in a publicly designated place."

(Title V, Article 16)

"Any change in domicile on the part of cultivators brings with it the ruin of farming."

(Title VI, Article 16)

"The Constitution names as governor Citizen Toussaint Louverture, General-in-Chief of the army of Saint-Domingue and, in consideration of the important services that the general has rendered to the colony in the most critical circumstances of the revolution, and per the wishes of the grateful inhabitants, the reins are confided to him for the rest of his glorious life."

(Title VIII, Article 28)

"Every citizen owes his services to the land that nourishes him and that saw him born; to the maintenance of liberty equality and property every time the law calls him to defend them."

(Title XIII, Article 76)

The constitution concludes with a statement from Toussaint-Louverture, who approves it after—as he somewhat disingenuously claims—having learned of it. He also states, perhaps naively, that he has passed it on to the French government for its approval. Napoléon declined to approve the constitution and invaded the colony.

Audience

The constitution's chief audience was, of course, the Haitian people. Like any constitution, this one laid out principles of governance, the structure of the government, and similar matters. Historians generally focus on three elements of the constitution that are noteworthy: its abolition of slavery, its establishment of Catholicism as the nation's religion, and its naming of Toussaint-Louverture as governor for life.

A second audience was Napoléon Bonaparte, the first consul of France. Toussaint-Louverture sent the constitution to Napoléon with a letter that is said to have begun with the words, "From the first of the blacks to the first of the whites" (qtd. in Hochschild, p. 291). Napoléon, despite the 1799 Proclamation on Saint Domingue, was not amused and in response dispatched an expeditionary force—the largest overseas force in French history to that time—to reclaim the colony and reinstitute slavery.

A third audience was the people of the Western Hemisphere, including the United States. Just a generation earlier, the American colonies revolted against Great Britain, establishing the first modern independent nation in the Western Hemisphere; Haiti was the second. Americans watched events in Haiti with great interest, for the rebellion and consequent constitution abolished slavery—an ongoing institution in the United States. It was Alexander Hamilton who recommended that Toussaint-Louverture be named governor-general for life. At the time, the French maintained colonies in North America, and Americans were interested in the effects that Haiti's break with France would have in those colonies—with good reason, for Napoléon concluded that he was unable to defend France's interests in North America. The result was the Louisiana Purchase under President Thomas Jefferson, who, at a cost of about three cents an acre, doubled the size of the United States.

Impact

The 1801 Constitution of Haiti was a short-lived document. In the estimation of Napoléon, Toussaint-Louverture had gone too far in writing a constitution for what was still a French colony. By 1801 Napoléon had signed peace treaties with many of his adversaries in the Napoleonic Wars, so he was able to turn his attention to internal problems—and to Haiti. Accordingly, he dispatched a fleet to the island, and by the end of February 1802 these forces had taken control of most of Haiti's cities and ports. Toussaint-Louverture and his generals, notably Jean-Jacques Dessalines, put up resistance, but the numbers were against them. Their only weapons were the large number of white hostages they held and Haiti's terrain, which forced the French to fight in jungles and to find their way around mountain gorges, where ambushes were a constant threat. The French, however, held a weapon of their own in the form of Toussaint-Louverture's two sons, who had been studying in France but who were in effect hostages. Running out of resources and with morale low among his troops, Toussant-Louverture surrendered and, on May 7, 1802, signed a peace agreement with the French. On May 20, 1802, Napoléon reestablished slavery in the French colonies.

Toussaint-Louverture retired to his farm, under house arrest. He continued to correspond with rebels and made plans for a new offensive against the French. At this point, an ally came to his aid: yellow fever. The illness devastated the French forces, reducing their numbers to fewer than ten thousand; General Leclerc died of the disease in November 1802. Meanwhile, news of Napoléon's reinstatement of slavery spread. Hostilities resumed and continued until November 18, 1803, when the rebels, led by General Dessalines, defeated the French at the Battle of Vertières. By the end of the year, all French troops had departed.

General Dessalines proclaimed Haitian independence on the first day of 1804. He, like Toussaint-Louverture, named himself governor-general for life, though on October 6 of that year he was crowned emperor as Jacques I. After massacring the French colonists who remained on the island, he instituted a system of serfdom to keep the sugar plantations running. Dessalines was assassinated on October 17, 1806, and at that point the country split. In the north, Henri Christophe, one of Toussaint-Louverture's generals, was elected president and, on March 26, 1811, was crowned King Henri I. The south proclaimed itself a republic under the presidency of Alexandre Pétion, another of Toussaint-Louverture's generals and Christophe's rival for power. Some observers alleged the Pétion may have been complicit in the assassination of Dessalines, but this charge was never proved. Still, power appears to have corrupted Pétion, who came to find his earlier democratic ideals restrictive and who suspended the legislature in 1816 until his death in 1818. Meanwhile, Haiti—or parts of it—had been governed by constitutions promulgated in 1804, 1805, 1806, 1807, 1811, and 1816. Numerous other constitutions followed throughout the nineteenth and twentieth centuries. As of this writing, Haiti is ruled by its constitution of 1987.

Although Toussaint-Louverture's vision of Haiti did not last, at least not in its entirety, the rebellion he helped lead and the constitution he wrote had profound significance. In the words of Michel-Rolph Trouillot (p. 83), "The Haitian revolution was unthinkable in its time: it challenged the very framework within which proponents and opponents had examined race, colonialism, and slavery in the Americas."

Further Reading

■ Books

Bell, Madison Smartt. *Toussaint Louverture: A Biography*. New York: Pantheon, 2007.

Dubois, Laurent, and John D. Garrigus. *Slave Revolution in the Caribbean, 1789–1804: A Brief History with Documents*. Boston: Bedford/St. Martin's Press, 2006.

DuPuy, Alex. *Haiti in the World Economy: Class, Race, and Underdevelopment since 1700*. Boulder, Colo.: Westview Press, 1989.

Hochschild, Adam. *Bury the Chains: Prophets and Rebels in the Fight to Free an Empire's Slaves*. Boston: Houghton Mifflin, 2005.

Hunt, Alfred N. *Haiti's Influence on Antebellum America: Slumbering Volcano in the Caribbean*. Baton Rouge: Louisiana State University Press, 1988.

Ott, Thomas. *The Haitian Revolution: 1789–1804*. Knoxville: University of Tennessee Press, 1973.

Rodriguez, Junius P., ed. *Encyclopedia of Slave Resistance and Rebellion*. Westport, Conn.: Greenwood, 2007.

Ros, Martin. *Night of Fire: The Black Napoleon and the Battle for Haiti*. Kent, U.K.: Spellmount Publishers, 1994.

Toussaint L'Ouverture. *The Haitian Revolution*, ed. Nick Nesbitt. New York: Verso, 2008.

Trouillot, Michel-Rolph. *Silencing the Past: Power and the Production of History*. Boston: Beacon Press, 1995.

■ Web Sites

Asté, Patricia. "Égalité for All: Toussaint Louverture and the Haitian Revolution." Public Broadcasting Service Web site.
http://www.pbs.org/egaliteforall.

Beard, J. R. *Toussaint L'Ouverture: A Biography and Autobiography*. University of North Carolina at Chapel Hill "Documenting the American South" Web site.
http://docsouth.unc.edu/neh/beard63/beard63.html.

The Louverture Project Web site.
http://thelouvertureproject.org/index.php?title=Main_Page.

—Michael J. O'Neal

Questions for Further Study

1. Toussaint-Louverture is regarded as a major figure in the quest to end slavery and the exploitation of colonies in the New World. Yet the constitution that appeared over his name is in many ways not a very democratic document. Additionally, it was a very short-lived document. How would you resolve this apparent inconsistency?

2. Repeatedly, historians note that early cultures were marked by a system of social class or caste. Describe the caste system as it existed in Haiti in the eighteenth century. Why does it seem to have been inevitable that caste systems developed in cultures throughout the world?

3. What role did the faraway French Revolution play in political developments in Haiti?

4. In a document such as the Requerimiento of 1513, Catholicism was imposed on the native peoples of the New World. Interestingly, though, Catholicism seems to have taken root in Central and South America to the extent that nearly three hundred years later, Toussaint-Louverture constitutionally mandated that Catholicism would be Haiti's official religion. Why do you think Catholicism largely supplanted native religious beliefs in the New World?

5. Compare this document with a document such as the Closed Country Edict, issued in Japan in 1635. How do the two documents illustrate how issues involving foreign trade could dominate politics in earlier centuries? What commodities continue to dominate political discussion between nations in the twenty-first century?

CONSTITUTION OF HAITI

First Title. On the Territory

Art 1—The entire extent of Saint-Domingue, and Samana, Tortuga, Gonave, the Cayemites, Ile-a-Vache, the Saone and other adjacent islands, form the territory of one colony, that is part of the French Empire, but is subject to particular laws.

Art 2—The territory of this colony is divided into departments, *arrondisements*, and parishes.

Title II. On Its Inhabitants

Art 3—There can be no slaves on this territory; servitude has been forever abolished. All men are born, live and die there free and French.

Art 4—All men can work at all forms of employment, whatever their color.

Art 5—No other distinctions exist than those of virtues and talents, nor any other superiority than that granted by the law in the exercise of a public charge. The law is the same for all, whether it punishes or protects.

Title III. On Religion

Art 6—The Catholic religion, Apostolic and Roman, is the only one publicly professed.

Art 7—Every parish provides for the maintenance of the religious cult and its ministers. Manufactured goods are especially destined for this expense and for presbyteries and the lodging of ministers.

Art 8—The governor of the colony assigns to each minister of the religion the scope of his spiritual administration, and these ministers can never, under any pretext, form a body within the colony.

Title IV. On Morals

Art 9—Since marriage, by its civil and religious institution, tends to the purity of morals, those spouses who practice the virtues demanded by their state, will always be distinguished and specially protected by the government.

Art 10—Divorce will not take place in the colony.

Art 11—The state of the rights of children born through marriage will be fixed by laws that will tend to spread and maintain social virtues, and to encourage and solidify family ties.

Title V. On Men in Society

Art 12—The Constitution guarantees individual freedom and safety. No one can be arrested except by virtue of a formally expressed order, issued by a functionary who the law gives the right to arrest and detain in a publicly designated place.

Art 13—Property is sacred and inviolable. Every person, either by himself or his representatives, has the free disposal and administration of that which is recognized as belonging to him. Whoever infringes upon this right renders himself criminal towards society and responsible as concerns the person troubled in his property.

Title VI. On Cultivation and Commerce

Art 14—The colony, being essentially agricultural, cannot allow the least interruption in its labor and cultivation.

Art 15—Every habitation is a manufactory that demands a gathering together of cultivators and workers; it's the tranquil asylum of an active and constant family, of which the owner of the land or his representative is necessarily the father.

Art 16—Every cultivator and worker is a member of the family and a shareholder in its revenues.

Any change in domicile on the part of cultivators brings with it the ruin of farming.

In order to do away with a vice so disastrous for the colony and contrary to public order, the governor makes all the police regulations that the circumstances render necessary in conformity with the bases of the police regulation of 20 Vendémiaire of the year 9, and the proclamation of General-in-Chief Toussaint Louverture of the following 19 Pluviose.

Art 17—The introduction of the cultivators indispensable to the re-establishment and the growth of planting will take place in Saint-Domingue. The Constitution charges the governor to take the appropriate measures to encourage and favor this increase in arms, stipulate and balance the diverse interests, and assure and guarantee the carrying out of the respective engagements resulting from this introduction.

Art 18—The commerce of the colony consists only in the exchange of the goods and products of its territory; consequently the introduction of those of the same nature as its own is and remains prohibited.

Title VII. On Legislation and Legislative Authority

Art 19—The regime of the colony is determined by the laws proposed by the governor and rendered by an assembly of inhabitants who gather at fixed periods in the center of the colony under the title of Central Assembly of Saint-Domingue.

Art 20—No law relative to the internal administration of the colony can be promulgated unless it bears the following formula: the Central Assembly of Saint-Domingue, on the proposition of the Governor, renders the following law.

Art 21—Laws will only be obligatory for citizens from the day of their promulgation in the departmental capitals. The promulgation of a law occurs in the following fashion: in the name of the French colony of Saint-Domingue, the governor orders that the above law be sealed, promulgated, and executed in the whole colony.

Art 22—The Central Assembly of Saint-Domingue is composed of two deputies per department who, in order to be eligible, must be at least 30 years old and have resided in the colony five years.

Art 23—The Assembly is renewed every two years by half; no one can be a member six consecutive years. The election takes place thusly: the municipal administrations every two years name on 10 Ventose (March 1), each one with one deputy, who will meet ten days later in the capitals of their respective departments where they form as many departmental electoral assemblies, who will each name a deputy to the Central Assembly. The next election will take place the 10 Ventose of the eleventh year of the French republic (March 1, 1803). In case of death, resignation or otherwise of one or several members of the Assembly, the Governor will see to their replacement. He also designates the members of the current Central Assembly who, at the period of the first renewal, shall remain members of the Assembly for two more years.

Art 24—The Central Assembly votes on the adoption or rejection of laws proposed to it by the Governor. It expresses its wishes on the regulations made and on the application of laws already made, on the abuses to be corrected, on the improvements to be undertaken, on all parts of service of the colony.

Art 25—Its session begins every year the first of Germinal (March 22) and cannot exceed a duration of three months. The governor can convoke it extraordinarily. The sessions are not public.

Art 26—If need be, the Central Assembly determines the basis, the amount, the duration and the mode of collection of taxes based on the state of the receipts and expenses presented to it, and on their increase or decrease. These states will be summarily published.

Title VIII. On Government

Art 27—The administrative reins of the colony are confided to a Governor, who directly corresponds with the government of the metropole in all matters relating to the colony.

Art 28—The Constitution names as governor Citizen Toussaint Louverture, General-in-Chief of the army of Saint-Domingue and, in consideration of the important services that the general has rendered to the colony in the most critical circumstances of the revolution, and per the wishes of the grateful inhabitants, the reins are confided to him for the rest of his glorious life.

Art 29—In the future each governor will be named for five years, and can be continued every five years for reason of good administration.

Art 30—In order to consolidate the tranquility that the colony owes to the firmness, the activity, the indefatigable zeal, and the rare virtues of General Toussaint Louverture, and as a sign of the unlimited confidence of the inhabitants of Saint-Domingue, the Constitution attributes exclusively to this general the right to choose the citizen who, in the unhappy instance of his death, shall immediately replace him. This choice shall be secret. It will be consigned in a sealed packet that can only be opened by the Central Assembly in the presence of all the generals of the army of Saint-Domingue in active service and the commanders-in-chief of the departments.

General Toussaint Louverture will take all the precautionary measures necessary to make known to the Central Assembly the place this important packet has been deposited.

Art 31—The citizen who will have been chosen by General Toussaint Louverture to take the reins of government upon his death, will take a vow to the Central Assembly to execute the Constitution of Sant-Domingue and to remain attached to the French government, and will be immediately installed in his functions, all of this in the presence of the army generals in active service and the commanders-in-chief of the departments who will all, individually and without cease will pledge to the new governor the vow of obedience to his orders.

Art 32—No more than one month before the expiration of the five years set for the administration of each sitting governor, he will convoke the Central Assembly, the meeting of army generals in active service and the commanders- in- chief of the departments at the ordinary place of the meetings of the Central Assembly in order to name, along with the members of that Assembly, the new governor, or to maintain the sitting one in office.

Art 33—Any failure in convocation on the part of the sitting governor is a manifest infraction of the constitution. In this case the highest ranking general, or the one with the most seniority of the same rank, who is on active duty in the colony shall take, by right and provisionally, the reins of government. This general will immediately convoke the other active duty generals, the commanders-in-chief of the departments and the members of the Central Assembly, all of who must obey the convocation in order to proceed with the nomination of a new governor.

In case of death, resignation or otherwise of a governor before the expiration of his functions, the government in the same way passes into the hands of the highest ranking general or the one with the most seniority of the same rank, who will convoke to the same ends as above the members of the Central Assembly, the generals in active service and the commanders-in-chief of departments.

Art 34—The Governor seals and promulgates the laws; he names to all civil and military posts. He commands in chief the armed forces and is charged with its organization, the ships of State docked in the ports of the colony receive his orders. He determines the division of the territory in the manner most in conformity with internal relations. According to the law, he watches over and provides for the internal and external security of the colony, and given that the state of war is a state of abandonment, malaise and nullity for the colony, the governor is charged in that circumstance to take the measures necessary to assure the colony subsistence and provisioning of all kinds.

Art 35—He influences the general policies of the inhabitants and manufactories, and ensures that owners, farmers and their representatives observe their obligations towards the cultivators and workers, and the obligations of cultivators and workers towards the owners, farmers and their representatives.

Art 36—He proposes to the Central Assembly the propositions of law as well as those changes in the Constitution that experience can render necessary.

Art 37—He directs the collection, the payment and the use of the finances of the colony and, to this effect, gives all orders.

Art 38—Every two years he presents at the Central Assembly the state of the receipts and expenses of each department, year by year.

Art 39—He oversees and censors, via commissioners, every writing meant for publication on the island. He suppresses all those coming from foreign countries that will tend to corrupt the morals or again trouble the colony. He punishes the authors or sellers, according to the seriousness of the case.

Art 40—If the Governor is informed that there is in the works some conspiracy against the tranquility of the colony, he has immediately arrested the persons presumed to be its authors, executors or accomplices. After having had them submit to an extra-judiciary interrogation if it is called for he has them brought before a competent tribunal.

Art 41—The salary of the Governor is fixed at present at three hundred thousand francs. His guard of honor is paid for by the colony.

Title IX. On Tribunals

Art 42—The right of citizens to be amicably judged by arbitrators of their choice cannot be infringed.

Art 43—No authority can suspend or hinder the execution of decisions rendered by the tribunals.

Art 44—Justice is administered in the colony by *tribunaux de premiÉre instance* and appeal tribunals. The law determines the organization of the one and the other, their number, their competency, and the territory forming the field of each. These tribunals, according to their degree of jurisdiction, handle all civil and criminal affairs.

Art 45—The colony has a *tribunal de cassation*, which pronounces on all requests for appeals against the decisions rendered by appeals courts, and complaints against an entire tribunal. This tribunal has no knowledge of the essence of affairs, but it reverses decisions rendered on procedures in which form was violated, or that contain some kind of evident contravention of the law, and sends the essence of the trial to the tribunal that must deal with it.

Art 46—The judges of these diverse tribunals preserve their functions all their lives, unless condemned for heinous crimes. The government commissioners can be revoked.

Art 47—Crimes by those in the military are subject to special tribunals and particular forms of judgement. These tribunals also know all kinds of theft, the violation of asylum, assassinations, murders, arson, rape, conspiracy and revolt. Their organization belongs to the governor of the colony.

Title X. On Municipal Administration

Art 48—There is a municipal administration in every parish of the colony; in that in which is placed a *tribunal de premiÊre instance* the municipal administration is composed of a mayor and four administrators. The government commissioner attached to the tribunal fulfills the functions of commissioner attached to the municipal administration without pay. In the other parishes the municipal administrations are composed of a mayor and two administrators, and the functions of commissioner attached to them are filled without pay by substitute commissioners attached to the tribunal that are responsible for these parishes.

Art 49—The members of municipal administrations are named for two years, but they can be continued in office. Their nomination falls upon the government that, from a list of at least sixteen persons presented to it by each municipal administration, chooses those persons most apt to guide the affairs of each parish.

Art 50—The functions of the municipal administrations consist in the simple exercise of policing cities and towns, in the administration of funds, assuring the revenues of manufactured goods and the additional impositions of the parishes. In addition, they are especially charged with the keeping of registers of births, marriages and deaths.

Art 51—Mayors exercise particular functions determined by the law.

Title XI. On the Armed Force

Art 52—The armed force is essentially obedient; it can never deliberate. It is at the disposition of the Governor, who can only set it in motion for the maintenance of public order, the protection due to all citizens, and the defense of the colony.

Art 53—It is divided into paid colonial guard and unpaid colonial guard.

Art 54—The unpaid colonial guard does not leave the limits of its parish except in cases of imminent danger, and under orders from, and under the personal responsibility of, the military commander or his place. Outside the limits of its parish it becomes paid and is subject in this case to military discipline; in any other it is subject only to the law.

Art 55—The colonial gendarmerie is part of the armed force. It is divided into horseback and foot gendarmerie. The horseback gendarmerie is instituted for high police matters and the safety of the countryside. It is paid for from the colonial treasury. The foot gendarmerie is instituted for the police functions in cities and towns. It is paid for by the cities and towns where it accomplishes its service.

Art 56—The army recruits upon the proposal made by the Governor to the Central Assembly, and following the mode established by law.

Title XII. On Finances and Goods from Seized and Vacant Domains

Art 57—The finances of the colony are composed of:

> Rights on imported goods, weights and measures
> Rights on the rental value of houses in cities and towns, of those that produce manufactured goods other than those of cultivation, and salt
> Revenue from ferries and post
> Fines, confiscations, wrecks
> Rights from the saving of shipwrecked ships
> Revenue from colonial domains

Art 58—The product of the *fermage* of goods seized from absentee owners without representatives are provisionally part of the public revenue of the colony, and are applied to administrative expenses. Circumstances will determine the laws that can be made relative to the overdue public debt and the *fermage* of goods seized by the administration at a period prior to the promulgation of the current Constitution, and towards those that will have been collected in a later time; they can be demanded and reimbursed in the year following the lifting of the seizure of the good.

Art 59—The funds coming from the sale of movable goods and the price of vacant successions, open in the colony under the French government since 1789, will be deposited in a special cashbox and will only be available, along with the real estate combined in colonial domains, two years after the publication on the island of peace between France and the maritime powers. Of course, this time span is only relative to those successions whose delay of five years—fixed by the edict of 1781—will have expired; and as relates to those opened at eras closer to peace, they can only be available and combined at the expiration of seven years.

Art 60—Foreigners inheriting in France from their foreign or French relatives will also inherit in Saint-Domingue. They can contract, acquire, and receive goods situated in the colony and can dispose of them just like Frenchmen by all the means authorized by the law.

Art 61—The mode of collection and administration of goods from seized and vacant domains will be determined by law.

Art 62—A temporary accounting commission regulates and verifies the accounting of receipts and expenses of the colony. This commission is composed of three members, chosen and named by the governor.

Title XIII. General Dispositions

Art 63—Every person's home is an inviolable asylum. During the night, no one has the right to enter there except in case of fire, flood or appeal from within. During the day it can be entered for a specially determined objective, or by a law or an order emanating from a public authority.

Art 64—In order for an act ordering the arrest of a person to be executed it is necessary that it:

Formally express the motive for the arrest and the law in execution of which it is ordered;

Emanate from a functionary who the law had formally given the power to do so;

The person arrested be given a copy of the order.

Art 65—All those who, not having been given by the law the power to arrest, will give, sign, execute, or have executed the arrest of a person will be guilty of the crime of arbitrary detention.

Art 66—All persons have the right to address individual petitions to any constituted authority, and especially to the governor.

Art 67—No corporation or association contrary to public order can be formed in the colony.

No assembly of citizens can qualify itself as popular society. Any seditious gathering shall be immediately broken up at first by verbal order and, if necessary, by the development of armed force.

Art 68—Every person has the right to form private establishments for the education and instruction of youth, with the authorization and under the surveillance of municipal administrations.

Art 69—The law particularly watches over those professions that deal with public morality, the safety, the health and the fortunes of citizens.

Art 70—The law provides for the recompense of inventors of rural machinery, or the maintenance of the exclusive property in their discoveries.

Art 71—In the entire colony there is a uniformity in weights and measures.

Art 72—The governor will distribute, in the name of the colony, recompense to warriors who have rendered striking service in fighting for the common defense.

Art 73—Absent owners, for whatever cause, preserve their rights over the goods belonging to them situated in the colony. In order to have the seizure lifted, it will suffice for them to present their titles of ownership or, lacking titles, supplicative acts whose formula the law determines. Nevertheless, those inscribed and maintained on the general list of émigrés from France are excepted from this disposition. In this case their goods will continue to be administered as colonial domains until they have been taken from the lists.

Art 74—As a guarantee of the public law, the colony proclaims that all the leases legally affirmed by the administration will have their full effect, if the adjudicators don't prefer to compromise with the owners or their representatives who will have obtained the lifting of the seizure.

Art 75—It proclaims that it is upon the respect of persons and property that the cultivation of land, all production, and all means of labor and all social order rests.

Art 76—It proclaims that every citizen owes his services to the land that nourishes him and that saw him born; to the maintenance of liberty equality and property every time the law calls him to defend them.

Art 77—The General-in-Chief Toussaint Louverture is and remains charged with sending the present Constitution for the approval of the French government. Nevertheless, and given the absence of laws, the urgency of escaping from this state of peril, the necessity of promptly re-establishing culture and the well expressed unanimous wish of the inhabitants of Saint-Domingue, the General-in-Chief is and remains invited, in the name of public good, to put it into effect in the entire expanse of the territory of the colony.

"Done at Port-Républicain, 19 Floreal year 9 of the one and indivisible French Republic."

Signed:

Borgella (president)

Raimond, Collet, Gaston Nogérée Lacour, Roxas, Mugnos, Mancebo, E Viart (Secretary).

"After having learned of the Constitution I give it my approbation. The invitation of the Central Assembly is an order for me. Consequently, I will have it passed on to the French government for its aproval. As for as its execution in the colony, the wish expressed by the CentralAssembly will be equally fulfilled and executed."

Given at Cap-Francais, 14 Messidor, year 9 of the one and indivisible French Republic.

General-in Chief: Toussaint Louverture

Samana	now a province of the Dominican Republic
Saone	Saona Island, close to the southeastern coast of the Hispaniola, in the Caribbean Sea and now part of the Dominican Republic
Tortuga, … , Ile-a-Vache	islands off the coast of Haiti
vacant successions	unclaimed inheritances, or those for which the heirs are unknown
Vendémiaire, … , Pluviose, …	months in the French Republican Calendar, which was in use in France and its possessions when the Haitian constitution was promulgated

DIPLOMATIC CORRESPONDENCE BETWEEN MUHAMMAD AL-KĀNAMĪ AND MUHAMMAD BELLO

"If [the Shaikh and the truth] disagree it is the truth which comes first."

Overview

This diplomatic correspondence took place between two Muslim leaders of nineteenth-century West Africa: Muhammad Bello of Sokoto and Shehu al-Hajj Muhammad al-Amīn ibn Muhammad al-Kānamī of Kanem-Borno. Bello was ruler of the Sokoto Caliphate, a newly created Islamic empire in what is now northern Nigeria, and al-Kānamī was an adviser to the ruling class of Kanem-Borno, an ancient Islamic empire formed around Lake Chad. The correspondence was the result of conflict between the two nations. Bello felt that Sokoto was justified in attacking Kanem-Borno, while al-Kānamī tried to point out the inconsistencies and hypocrisy in Sokoto's justification for war. To understand the content of these letters better, we need to examine the formation of the Sokoto Caliphate.

The Sokoto Caliphate took root in 1804 when a group of Muslim Fulani (a pastoral people who live throughout the savanna belt of West Africa) initiated a jihad (termed *jihād* in the document) under the leadership of Usuman dan Fodio against the city-state of Gobir, in Hausaland (contemporary northern Nigeria and southeastern Niger). Jihad is an Islamic concept meaning "struggle." A jihad can take a number of forms, including struggling against one's doubt or struggling against poverty in the community. In this case, the Fulani meant the struggle to be a violent one against "paganism" and bad Islam. Dan Fodio believed that the Hausa people were guilty of practicing "impure" Islam and that the kings of Hausaland did not rule according to the laws of the Qur'an, the Islamic sacred scripture. After they had gained control of Gobir, the followers of dan Fodio quickly conquered most of Hausaland and in 1810 established an Islamic theocracy (a form of government where the people believe their officials are divinely guided and God is their supreme ruler) called the Sokoto Caliphate. Soon Fulani settlers living in Kanem-Bornu, an Islamic nation to the east of Hausaland, began to claim that Kanem-Bornu was also ruled by a "bad" Muslim and composed of "impure" Muslims. They eventually insisted that the Muslims of Kanem-Bornu were so impure they were merely "pagans." With the blessing of Sokoto's leader-

ship, Fulani Muslims declared jihad and began attacking Kanem-Bornu.

In response to this hostility, a leader emerged in Kanem-Bornu named Shehu al-Hajj Muhammad al-Amīn ibn Muhammad al-Kānamī, a Muslim scholar and adviser to Kanem-Bornu's nobility. He began a lengthy correspondence with Usuman dan Fodio, which he continued later with dan Fodio's son and successor, Muhammad Bello, and with dan Fodio's brother, Abdullah. In the letters al-Kānamī criticizes the behavior of the Fulani and defends the people of Kanem-Bornu as faithful Muslims. Bello, in turn, defends the decision to attack Kanem-Bornu, insisting that the people and their king were idolaters. The correspondence between al-Kānamī and the leaders of Sokoto reveal debates over the legitimacy of Fulani claims against Kanem-Bornu, the consequences of the ensuing violence, their differing interpretations of Qur'anic law, and the struggle to reconcile Fulani imperialism with the expansion and reform of Islam in the region.

Context

The first significant presence of Islam in what is now Nigeria and Cameroon began in the eleventh century in the kingdom of Kanem and in the fourteenth century in the kingdom of Bornu. From those two states, later united to create Kanem-Bornu, Islam spread to the Hausa. Islam also entered Hausaland from the west when the Fulani, who had been followers of Islam for centuries, migrated to the region beginning in the fourteenth century. By that time, Kanem-Bornu boasted two impressive madrassas (Islamic universities). It is therefore plain that both the kingdoms of Kanem-Bornu and of the Fulani, who later built the empire of Sokoto, could claim a legitimate and long-standing devotion to Islam.

In the Hausa city-states and the kingdom of Kanem-Bornu, Islam was neither ubiquitous nor necessarily entirely "orthodox." Islam reached the region along the trade routes of the Sahara and was concentrated in urban centers. Acceptance of Islam by the local leadership had a number of benefits. Like many religions, Islam offered not only spiritual guidance but also a valuable source of social

1804

- The reformer Usuman dan Fodio moves his community to Gudu after being threatened by Gobir's leadership, and shortly later they declare jihad in Gobir; over the course of the next six years, the Fulani take control of most of Hausaland and some territory in neighboring countries, including that of Kanem-Bornu.

1809

- The capital of the Fulani empire is established at Sokoto.

1810

- Control of the empire is divided between dan Fodio's son, Muhammad Bello, and his brother Abdullah; Bello becomes emir at Sokoto and Abdullah at Gwandu. Correspondence begins between al-Kānamī and dan Fodio, Bello, and Abdullah regarding the conduct of the Fulani in Bornu.

1812

- Correspondence between Kanem-Bornu and Sokoto gradually comes to an end without satisfactorily resolving the conflict; hostility between the two continues for decades afterward.

and political power. Literacy and special spiritual knowledge gave leaders and elites more prestige and power within their communities. Islam provided strong diplomatic, economic, and intellectual connections to the larger Islamic world. However, in a region where a multiplicity of indigenous polytheistic faiths predated Islam's arrival, leaders would often endorse, or at least permit, practice of both indigenous religions and Islam. Even in the cases where rulers had converted to Islam, they still wanted to retain the support of non-Muslims in their kingdoms. They thus maintained at least some connection to indigenous religions, typically through the celebration of annual festivals or reverence of royal ancestors. They also often demonstrated leniency when it came to the blending of Islam with indigenous religious practices. Such syncretization was a frequent occurrence, and many worshipers, Muslims and non-Muslims alike, found both Islam and their indigenous faith efficacious. A blending of practices from Islam and indigenous religions could be found in the practice of wearing verses of the Qur'an about the neck as a protective amulet, in cults of spirit possession containing both Arabian and African spirits, and in the celebration of both African and Islamic festivals. Most people in the region were tolerant of such religious blending, and many even found it spiritually meaningful. Yet for a good many Muslims who viewed themselves as following an orthodox and "pure" form of Islam, such practices were a serious offense, a sacrilege and a pollution of Islam.

The Fulani were no exception, and once they settled in Hausaland, they quickly established a pattern of criticizing their Hausa neighbors for practicing "impure" Islam. They disapproved of such syncretic practices as spirit possession or the wearing of Qur'anic verses as amulets, and they condemned what they believed to be the lax morality of Hausa Muslims. The Fulani additionally complained of ethnic discrimination against them by the Hausa aristocracy. Even after generations of cohabitation, the Fulani were still considered alien to Hausaland. The Fulani, a pastoral people, were typically taxed at a higher rate and had limited access to grazing land, most of which was owned by the Hausa.

A reform movement, dedicated to "purifying" the region's Islam and improving the lot of the Fulani, emerged in the city-state of Gobir in the late eighteenth century under the leadership of Usuman dan Fodio. Dan Fodio had received a strong Qur'anic education and was famed as a brilliant scholar of Islam. He later served as a missionary for the Qadiriyya Sufi *tariqa* (brotherhood), which is among the oldest Sufi brotherhoods in the world with followers from South Asia to West Africa. Dan Fodio authored many books and papers outlining grievances against Gobir's rulers, criticizing the poor Islamic behavior of the people and characterizing what he believed to be the proper understanding of Islam and Islamic law. His most famous publication was the undated book *Kitab nur al-albab* (Light of Consciousness) which defined the characteristics of a good Muslim, a bad one, and an unbeliever. Dan Fodio also wrote poetry in Fulfulde (the language of the Fulani), Hausa, and Arabic that provided moral instruction on how to live a proper Muslim life.

Dan Fodio initially maintained a cooperative relationship with the Hausa leadership, even as he continued to regard Hausaland's Islam as corrupt. From 1789 to 1801 he maintained good relations with King Yakuba of Gobir, who feared his popular support. Yakuba granted freedom to preach, greater protection for Muslims, and lighter taxation for peasants. Yet by 1801 relations between dan Fodio and Yakuba's successor, Nafata, had deteriorated beyond repair. King Nafata outlawed religious meetings and declared that only individuals who had inherited Islam from their fathers could practice Islam. Such repressive efforts continued under Nafata's successor, Yunfa, who made an attempt on dan Fodio's life and threatened dan Fodio's community of followers at Degel. In 1804 dan Fodio performed *hijra*, in imitation of the migration of Muhammad and the early Muslim community from Mecca to Yathrib (Medina), by moving his community of followers from the village of Degel to Gudu.

Dan Fodio was not alone in his efforts to purge Islam of "impurities." His reform movement was part of an orthodox revival throughout the Islamic world in the eighteenth and nineteenth centuries that emphasized a literal interpretation of the Qur'an and a strict code of moral conduct. Similar revival movements occurred in the Arabian Peninsula. Through the travels of scholars, merchants, and pilgrims, many of these movements exchanged ideas and encouragement with one another. While it was informed by global currents of Islamic revival, dan Fodio's movement was principally grounded in local history, sour Hausa-Fulani relations, and his own prophetic experiences.

Emerging tension with Gobir was contemporaneous with a series of supernatural communications to dan Fodio from Muhammad, the founder of Islam, and 'Abd al-Qadir al-Jilani, the founder of Qadiriyya. Dan Fodio never claimed a direct prophetic revelation from Allah (the Arabic name for God), thus remaining within the bounds of Islamic theological orthodoxy. The most significant vision came in 1794, when dan Fodio believed he was handed the Sword of Truth by al-Qadir. The Sword was not a physical sword but a supernatural one that dan Fodio believed allowed its possessor to know true Islam from false Islam. He interpreted this to mean he had permission from Allah to declare a violent jihad, though he did not do so until 1804, shortly after the *hijra* to Gudu.

Dan Fodio's followers attacked Gobir shortly after their migration to Gudu and gained control of the city-state within a matter of a few years. Soon after, additional jihads were declared against neighboring Hausa city-states when they too were accused of practicing "impure" Islam. The Fulani quickly came to dominate much of Hausaland. Within just six years, from 1804 to 1810, a theocratic empire had been consolidated and its capital established at Sokoto. Dan Fodio withdrew from the political sphere, and rule of the immense empire was divided between his son, Muhammad Bello, and his brother, Abdullah. Bello became the emir at Sokoto in the east and Abdullah the emir at Gwandu in the west. Fulani conquest continued beyond the borders of Hausaland and came to include parts of Adamawa and Bauchi to the southeast, Nupe and Ilorin to the south, and Kanem-Bornu to the north and east. Kanem-Bornu was in a weakened state after centuries of external warfare and three significant famines in the mid-eighteenth century. The land lost to Sokoto was hotly contested and remained a chief source of much bitterness. In addition, the leadership of Kanem-Bornu had been closely allied with the kings of Hausaland. Ties between the Hausa and Kanem-Bornu remained close and continued to enrage the Fulani.

Very quickly, the Fulani began to attack the unconquered portion of Kanem-Bornu. The attackers included those Fulani who had lived in Kanem-Bornu before the initial wars and those who had also settled after the first conquest. More Fulani settlers were to follow as the second set of attacks took more land. They justified their attack in much the same way they had justified attacking Hausaland. As they had done in Hausaland, the Fulani accused the king and people of Kanem-Bornu of practicing an "impure" and corrupted Islam, as evidenced in illegal taxation, corruption in the courts, idolatrous practices, and the inappropriate conduct of women in public. Unlike Hausaland, however, Kanem-Bornu was additionally accused of unbelief, or paganism. This would become the primary "crime" attributed to Kanem-Bornu and was used to justify the many large-scale attacks by Sokoto directed by dan Fodio's son, Muhammad Bello.

A powerful leader emerged in Kanem-Bornu to meet the threat of Sokoto. Shehu al-Hajj Muhammad al-Amīn ibn Muhammad al-Kānamī was, like dan Fodio, a Muslim scholar, administrator, and soldier, and he too attracted a great following. During the initial jihad of dan Fodio, he had been instrumental in halting Fulani advances into Kanem-Bornu. After stopping Sokoto's initial advance, al-Kānamī became the voice of negotiations with dan Fodio (who later withdrew from political power to pursue spiritual matters) and then with Muhammad Bello and Abdullah when they assumed power. Correspondence between al- al-Kānamī and Bello lasted from 1810 to 1812 and was significant because Kanem-Bornu bordered the eastern portion of Sokoto, where Bello was emir. In his letters to Bello, al-Kānamī heavily criticized the Fulani attacks on Kanem-Bornu as disproportionate to their alleged crimes. He also denied that the people of Kanem-Bornu were guilty of "paganism." Further, he claimed that the Fulani were allowing themselves to become involved in sin by mistreating fellow Muslims, an accusation that the leaders of Sokoto did not take lightly.

About the Author

The authors of the Kanem-Bornu/Sokoto correspondence are Shehu al-Hajj Muhammad al-Amīn ibn Muhammad al-Kānamī and Emir Muhammad Bello. Al-Kānamī, born in 1776, was a Muslim scholar, soldier, administrator, political and religious leader, and adviser to Kanem-Bornu's nobility. During the jihad in neighboring Hausaland, he had led forces that both suppressed Fulani rebellion with-

Lake Chad, the site of the ancient Islamic empire of Kanem-Bornu (AP/Wide World Photos)

in Kanem-Bornu and turned back Fulani advances into the kingdom. In the course of his efforts, al-Kānamī virtually became the leader of Kanem-Bornu. As Fulani aggression within Kanem-Bornu increased, he began a series of letters to negotiate peace with Sokoto and to refute the charges of paganism made against the people and leaders of Kanem-Bornu.

Muhammad Bello was the son of Usuman dan Fodio, the leader of the Fulani jihad in Hausaland. Bello, like his father, was a Muslim scholar and had served as a field commander during the initial jihad. He was a skilled military strategist and a master of cavalry tactics. His prayers before battle reflected his conviction in the righteousness of the Fulani cause, asking that "God help us to pluck up the tents of the heathen from our land and set up the tents of the law" (Hiskett, p. 96). When the Sokoto Caliphate was consolidated, dan Fodio named him as successor and one of the two emirs of Sokoto, along with his brother, Abdullah.

Explanation and Analysis of the Document

The two diplomatic letters examined here were published by Muhammad Bello in his book *Infāq al-maysūr* (translated as *The Rise of the Sokoto Fulani*). The first letter, "The Case against the *Jihād*"—the first of the series published by Bello—was written by Shehu al-Hajj Muhammad al-Amīn ibn Muhammad al-Kānamī and makes the case against the Fulani jihad in Kanem-Bornu. In response to al-Kānamī's argument, Bello composed the following letter, "The Case against Bornu." This was the fifth in the series published by Bello. It defends the actions of the Fulani and makes the case against the people of Kanem-Bornu.

◆ "The Case against the *Jihād*"

In the opening lines of his letter, al-Kānamī presents himself humbly to the leadership in Sokoto, acknowledging his own sin and following up with statements of reverence to the Fulani *ulamā* (Islamic scholars, particularly those that interpret Islamic law). After this conciliatory introduction, he quickly describes the ongoing conflict between the Fulani and the people of Kanem-Bornu and the efforts of the Kanem-Bornu government to bring them to an end. Attempts to find a reason for Fulani aggression initially met with little success. In response to his letters to local Fulani leaders, al-Kānamī says he received only "a weak answer" and lists of some books that, after he examined them, still did not provide a satisfactory explanation. Meanwhile, the capital came under attack; as Fulani hostility increased, Kanem-Bornu had no choice but to retaliate.

In the next portion, al-Kānamī addresses the motivation he has since come to understand is responsible for the antagonism of the Fulani: the "paganism" of the inhabitants of Kanem-Bornu. He immediately refutes the accusation, pointing to the religious habits of the people of Kanem-Bornu as evidence as well as the contradiction of Fulani invaders praying in allegedly pagan temples (mosques) they have captured. Much of his letter is spent rebuking specific religious crimes that the Fulani have charged the people of Kanem-Bornu with committing. One such accusation concerns the performance of sacrifice in sacred places. While considered necessary by non-Muslims, it is viewed as a form of idolatry within Islam. Al-Kānamī insists that this is merely ignorance on the part of those who practice it; they engage in almsgiving, as is required of a dutiful Muslim, yet the practice had been harmlessly mixed with a preexisting tradition. With regard to other crimes, such as corruption in the courts and allowing women to appear in public with their heads uncovered, al-Kānamī agrees these are indeed disobedient and punishable actions that merit castigation. He therefore acknowledges the sins of his people but calls them just that—sins. He claims that the people of Kanem-Bornu are appropriately faithful but at the same time are mere mortals subject to error. This weakness no more makes them "pagans" than it made pagans of Egyptians or Syrians in ages past.

Al-Kānamī claims the Fulani response to Kanem-Bornu's alleged crimes was excessive to the point of becoming a sin in its execution. By acting in the extreme and ignoring the fact that religious transgressions do not equate with an absence of faith, he argues that the Fulani forgot that they were abusing their fellow Muslims. In this way, he makes clear that it was not just the motive for the Fulani attack on Kanem-Bornu that warranted a reprisal but also the methods they employed to achieve their ends.

The letter closes with criticism and a warning. Al-Kānamī questions not only the true motivation for Fulani aggression but also the need for violence to "purify" Islam. In this way, he implied that reforming Kanem-Bornu was merely a pretense, an effort to hide Sokoto's ambition for greater conquest. He warns Bello that by behaving in this manner, the Fulani were involving themselves in sin and points to the writings of dan Fodio that contradict their actions. His last lines express commitment to the truth, which he believes is on the side of Kanem-Bornu, and hope that God will preserve the people of Kanem-Bornu in the face of the aggression of the Fulani "whose striving goes astray in the present life, while they think that they are working good deeds."

◆ "The Case against Bornu"

In response to al-Kānamī's argument, Bello defends the actions of the Fulani and makes the case against the people of Kanem-Bornu. Bello opens his letter with praises to God for preserving Muslims from nonbelievers and providing them with the true knowledge of Qur'anic law, followed by praises for the Prophet Muhammad for protecting that truth despite adulteration by the deceptive and ignorant. This is followed by a greeting and Bello's recognition that Kanem-Bornu seeks to settle the conflict with the Fulani.

In the subsequent paragraphs, Bello defends Sokoto's support of the local Fulani who attacked Kanem-Bornu. He dismisses al-Kānamī's arguments as false and mere tools of mischief. He goes so far as to suggest that he should not have deigned to reply but that he felt compelled to address al-Kānamī's arguments in order to prevent the innocent and ignorant from being misled under al-Kānamī's guidance. He then explains that the leaders in Sokoto were willing to permit the attacks on Kanem-Bornu because they repeatedly received news that the residents of Kanem-Bornu behaved as pagans, worshiping trees, the river, and false idols. He points out that al-Kānamī recognizes the same facts in his letter. Rather than acknowledge the severity of this crime, however, Bello accuses al-Kānamī of trying to dismiss such habits as innocent traditions without religious connotations, a claim he does not believe warrants consideration by any thinking person. Such practices are what they are, Bello insists—acts of paganism.

Bello also points out the behavior of the emir of Kanem-Bornu, in particular, who he claims has harassed Fulani Muslims so severely that many of them had to flee the kingdom. He believes that this aggression is a reflection of both the emir's paganism and his alliance with the Hausa kings who had oppressed the Fulani. To approve of paganism, according to Bello, is paganism in and of itself, and if the sultan of a country is pagan, then his country follows suit. Therefore, any fighting against the emir of Kanem-Bornu, the kingdom, and its people is justified.

The tone of the letter shifts at this point from defensive and critical to somewhat conciliatory. While Bello continues to condemn the behavior of Kanem-Bornu, he advises al-Kānamī that if he is able to find evidence that they are repentant, the attacks on Kanem-Bornu will cease. He then says that reports have reached him suggesting that this may, in fact, be the case, and advises al-Kānamī that Sokoto will send their messenger to confirm these reports. Once confirmed, Bello suggests that a meeting be called in order to arrange a treaty between the two parties. Perhaps to prove that Sokoto, too, is eager for peace, Bello mentions that a raid that had been scheduled was deliberately delayed in order to pursue such reconciliation.

Bello then reiterates his defense of both his own actions and those of the Fulani. He dismisses al-Kānamī's allegation that their response was excessive or inappropriate and reminds him that it is quite legal to end immorality and

Modern-day Fulani (AP/Wide World Photos)

corruption. To simply say that others have made mistakes without being corrected is of no avail. The letter closes with a cautious optimism. Bello says that many attempts have been made to make contact with al-Kānamī to come to an accord, but they were met with no reply. He is quick, however, to redirect any blame for this from al-Kānamī himself, saying simply that "we think that probably our messages do not reach you, and that you do not receive intelligence of them." His last line emphasizes the hope for reconciliation and that God direct both parties to good.

Audience

Al-Kānamī and Bello made up the target audience of their mutual correspondence. Nonetheless, the correspondence was quite likely read, overheard, and discussed by others, as indicated by the frequent use of "we" in the text of letters from both sides. As the issue at hand was not only a religious matter but also a diplomatic one, both Bello and al-Kānamī would likely have sought the council of other *ulama*, advisers, and bureaucrats when considering the arguments presented and in crafting their responses to such arguments. Nonetheless, who else might have read or responded to the letters, aside from al-Kānamī and Bello, is purely speculative.

Impact

The correspondence between al-Kānamī and Bello did not ultimately come to any satisfactory conclusion. Neither side seemed to emerge victorious in the theological debate the letters inspired, though the correspondence continued over a period of approximately two years. The aggression between Sokoto and Kanem-Bornu persisted but gradually slowed to a stalemate. By the time of al-Kānamī's death in 1837, it had been reduced to squabbling over borders. The dialogue between the two leaders therefore seemed to have resolved nothing. Why, then, are these letters significant?

Perhaps most important, they offer a unique, first-person perspective on the difficulty in reconciling a religious reform movement with the imperial conquest that it ultimately became. In examining the relations between Sokoto and their neighbors after the success of the jihad, it becomes clear that the intentions of those involved were mixed at best and openly contradictory at worst. While the jihad had certainly been motivated by religious fervor, there was no shortage of personal ambition among those who had participated in it. Reforming Islam aside, there were powerful positions to be had, wealth to be plundered, and territory to be gained. In their rapid expansion, the Fulani left more than a few of their neighbors wondering if their efforts were more about politics, economics, and power

"If you say that you have done this to us because of our paganism, then I say that we are innocent of paganism, and it is far from our compound. If praying and the giving of alms, knowledge of God, fasting in Ramadān and the building of mosques is paganism, what is Islam?"

("The Case against the *Jihād*")

"Sin does not make anyone a pagan when he has confessed his faith. And if you had ordered the right and forbidden the wrong, and retired when the people did not desist, it would have been better than these present doings.... But your forbidding has involved you in sin, and brought evil on you and the Muslims in this world and then next."

("The Case against the *Jihād*")

"If this business does originate from him [Usuman dan Fodio], then I say that there is no power nor might save through God, the most high, the most glorious. Indeed we thought well of him. But now, as the saying is, we love the Shaikh and the truth when they agree. But if they disagree it is the truth which comes first."

("The Case against the *Jihād*")

"The verdict depends on what is seen. And God controls what is secret. Him whom we have seen sacrificing to rocks and trees we have charged with paganism."

("The Case against Bornu")

"May it be clear to you from what we have said of him that the Amir of Bornu has been known for his paganism. You also know that the law of a country is the law of its sultan. If he is a Muslim, then the country is dār al-Islām; if he is a pagan, then the country is dār kufr."

("The Case against Bornu")

"How can it be said that it is not legal, for him who is able, to reform immorality or put an end to corruption?"

("The Case against Bornu")

than about religion and morality. Al-Kānamī, in his letters to Sokoto, made this very point; in questioning their motives, he left dan Fodio, Bello, and likely other leaders of Sokoto rather uneasy. It introduced a moral crisis—to shed Muslim blood in the struggle against oppression and corruption was one thing, but to suggest that the cause had not been legitimate (if not in the case of Hausaland, then certainly in that of Kanem-Bornu) meant that Muslims on both sides had died for nothing. This disturbing thought perhaps explains Bello's vehemence in defending both the jihad and the actions of the Fulani in Kanem-Bornu in his responses to al-Kānamī. It was only by steadfastly maintaining that Islam was in need of reform both in Hausaland and in Kanem-Bornu and that such reform had to come at all costs that the leadership of Sokoto could justify the sacrifice of Muslim lives in either case.

The communication between these two Muslim leaders also highlights the multiplicity of interpretations of Islamic law and how those interpretations were sources of conflict among Muslims. Especially during a period of widespread reform in the Islamic world, the variations in interpretation were many, and frequently reformers found themselves unable to reconcile their beliefs with each other, much less with the everyday practices of ordinary Muslims. Then as now determining the legitimacy of one group's claims against another, and defining and gauging adherence to "orthodoxy," was rarely a simple matter and was always open to debate. The letters that al-Kānamī and Bello exchanged exemplify this difficulty.

Further Reading

■ Books

Adeleye, Rowland Aderemi. *Power and Diplomacy in Northern Nigeria, 1804–1906: The Sokoto Caliphate and Its Enemies.* New York: Humanities Press, 1971.

Falola, Toyin, and Matthew M. Heaton. *A History of Nigeria.* New York: Cambridge University Press, 2008.

Hiskett, Mervyn. *The Sword of Truth: The Life and Times of the Shehu Usuman dan Fodio,* 2nd ed. Evanston, Ill.: Northwestern University Press, 1994.

Hodgkin, Thomas. *Nigerian Perspectives: An Historical Anthology.* London: Oxford University Press, 1960.

Johnston, Hugh Anthony Stephen. *The Fulani Empire of Sokoto.* London: Oxford University Press, 1967.

—Allison Sellers and Joel E. Tishken

Questions for Further Study

1. What role did trade and economic activity play in the early spread of Islam?

2. The Sokoto Caliphate and Kanem-Bornu were in a state of war apparently because of the religious practices of the people of Kanem-Bornu. What other factors led to war between the two peoples? Were the motives of the Sokoto Caliphate purely religious?

3. Throughout world history, differing religious beliefs and practices have often merged (a process called "syncretism") when one nation or culture dominates another or when two cultures intermix. What types of religious practices and beliefs emerged from the blending of Islam and indigenous religions in this region of Africa?

4. What qualifies these letters—written two centuries ago in faraway Africa—as "milestone" documents? Why are they important, especially given that they did not eliminate hostilities? What can they tell modern readers about religious disputes?

5. Contrast this document with "Queen Victoria's Proclamation concerning India," written in 1858. What do the two documents, taken together, teach modern readers about the relationship between empire and religion?

Diplomatic Correspondence between Muhammad al-Kānamī and Muhammad Bello

I. Al-Kānamī: The Case against the *Jihād*

Praise be to God, Opener of the doors of guidance, Giver of the means of happiness. Prayer and peace be on him who was sent with the liberal religion, and on his people who prepared the way for the observance of His law, and interpreted it.

From him who is filthy with the dust of sin, wrapped in the cloak of shame, base and contemptible, Muḥammad al-Amin ibn Muḥammad al-Kānamī to the Fulani *"ulamā"* and their chiefs. Peace be on him who follows His guidance.

The reason for writing this letter is that when fate brought me to this country, I found the fire which was blazing between you and the people of the land. I asked the reason, and it was given as injustice by some and as religion by others. So according to our decision in the matter I wrote to those of your brothers who live near to us asking them the reason and instigation of their transgression, and they returned me a weak answer, not such as comes from an intelligent man, much less from a learned person, let alone a reformer. They listed the names of books, and we examined some of them, but we do not understand from them the things which they apparently understood. Then, while we were still perplexed, some of them attacked our capital, and the neighbouring Fulani came and camped near us. So we wrote to them a second time beseeching them in the name of God and Islam to desist from their evil doing. But they refused and attacked us. So, when our land was thus confined and we found no place even to dwell in, we rose in defence of ourselves, praying God to deliver us from the evil of their deeds; and we did what we did. Then when we found some respite, we desisted, and for the future God is all-knowing.

We believe in writing; even if it makes no impression on you, it is better than silence. Know that if an intelligent man accepts some question in order to understand it, he will give a straightforward answer to it.

Tell us therefore why you are fighting us and enslaving our free people. If you say that you have done this to us because of our paganism, then I say that we are innocent of paganism, and it is far from our compound. If praying and the giving of alms, knowledge of God, fasting in Ramadān and the building of mosques is paganism, what is Islam? These buildings in which you have been standing of a Friday, are they churches or synagogues or fire temples? If they were other than Muslim places of worship, then you would not pray in them when you capture them. Is this not a contradiction?

Among the biggest of your arguments for the paganism of the believers generally is the practice of the amirs of riding to certain places for the purpose of making alms-giving sacrifices there; the uncovering of the heads of free women; the taking of bribes; embezzlement of the property of orphans; oppression in the courts. But these five charges do not require you to do the things you are doing. As for this practice of the amirs, it is a disgraceful heresy and certainly blameworthy. It must be forbidden and disapproval of its perpetrators must be shown. But those who are guilty of it do not thereby become pagans; since not one of them claims that it is particularly efficacious, or intends by it to associate anything with God. On the contrary, the extent of their pretence is their ignorant idea that alms given in this way are better than otherwise. He who is versed in the books of *fiqh*, and has paid attention to the talk of the imams in their disputation—when deviation from the right road in matters of burial and slaughter are spoken of—will know the test of what we have said. Consider Damietta, a great Islamic city between Egypt and Syria, a place of learning and Islam: in it there is a tree, and the common people do to this tree as did the non-Arabs. But not one of the *"ulamā"* rises to fight them or has spoken of their paganism.

As for uncovering the head in free women, this is also *Ḥaram*, and the Qur'ān has prohibited it. But she who does it does not thereby become a pagan. It is denial which leads to paganism. Failing to do something while believing in it is rather to be described as disobedience requiring immediate repentance. If a free woman has prayed with the head uncovered, and the time passes, but she does not repeat the prayer in accordance with what we know they say in the books of *fiqh*, surely you do not believe that her prayer is not proper because she has thereby become a pagan?

The taking of bribes, embezzlement of the property of orphans and injustice in the courts are all major sins which God has forbidden. But sin does not make anyone a pagan when he has confessed his faith. And if you had ordered the right and forbidden the wrong, and retired when the people did not desist, it would have been better than these present doings. If ordering and forbidding are confined within their proper limits, they do not lead to anything more serious. But your forbidding has involved you in sin, and brought evil on you and the Muslims in this world and the next....

Since acts of immorality and disobedience without number have long been committed in all countries, then Egypt is like Bornu, only worse. So also is Syria and all the cities of Islam. There has been corruption, embezzlement of the property of orphans, oppression and heresy in these places from the time of the Bani Umayya [the Umayyad dynasty] right down to our own day. No age and no country is free from its share of heresy and sin. If, thereby, they all become pagan, then surely their books are useless. So how can you construct arguments based on what they say who are infidel according to you? Refuge from violence and discord in religion is with God....

We have indeed heard of things in the character of the Shaikh 'Uthmān ibn Fūdī, and seen things in his writings which are contrary to what you have done. If this business does originate from him, then I say that there is no power nor might save through God, the most high, the most glorious. Indeed we thought well of him. But now, as the saying is, we love the Shaikh and the truth when they agree. But if they disagree it is the truth which comes first. We pray God to preserve us from being those of whom He said:

Say: "Shall we tell you who will be
the greatest losers in their works?
Those whose striving goes astray
in the present life, while they think
that they are working good deeds."
And from being those of whom he also said:

But they split in their affair between them
into sects, each party rejoicing in
what is with them.

Peace.

II. Bello: *The Case against Bornu*

In the name of God, the compassionate, the merciful. Prayer of God be on him after whom there is no prophet. Praise be to God who has preserved the

religion of Islam by the laws in his Qur'ān for the believers who seek guidance; who has wiped out that which Satan has put in the hearts of those who rule them oppressively, and in whose hearts there is sickness, the hard-heartedness of the idolators; who has preserved the laws in the Qur'ān by his saying:

It is We who have sent down the Remembrance
and We watch over it.

Prayer and peace on our lord Muḥammad, lord of the prophets, the sayer who keeps the true knowledge from the false sayings of all its enemies, who preserves it from the alterations of the interpolators, the boastings of the triflers and the comments of ignorant people. Prayer and peace also on all his people and companions and on those who follow them in the better way until the day of judgment.

From Muḥammad Bello ibn Amīr al-Mu'minīn 'Uthmān ibn Fūdī to al-Ḥājj al-Amīn ibn Muḥammad al-Kānamī, peace and sincere greeting.

We have occupied ourselves with the letter which you wrote to those of our people who are your neighbours asking for an explanation of the true state of affairs. We have given it full consideration, and have understood from it what led to it. Briefly, we have understood from it that you desire us to follow the word of God, may He be exalted, when He says:

If two parties of the believers fight,
put things right between them.

Secondly you have put forward certain arguments.... But, by God, I tell you, my brother, that, if the Lord is kind to you, and you look on us with the eye of justice, it will be seemly for you to find that these are false arguments and mischief-making words, refutable contentions for the most part and worthless propositions. It is indeed seemly for me not to reply, but I am constrained to do so through solicitude for the ignorance of the *ṭalaba*, so that they may not follow you because of your great conceit and mischief-making, and think that you are right in this way of acting. My intention is neither childishness nor quarrelling.

This is so that you will learn in the first place that what made it proper for us to permit our people neighbouring on you to fight Bornu was the continual receipt of news (of which we mastered the contents) from those who mixed with the people of Bornu and knew their condition, to the following effect. It was that they make sacrifices to rocks and trees, and regard the river as the Copts did the Nile in the days of the Jāhilīya. It was also that they have shrines with their idols in them and with priests. We have seen the proof of this in your first letter where you say: 'Among the biggest of your arguments for the paganism of the believers generally is the practice of the amirs of riding to certain places for the purpose of making alms-giving sacrifices there.' Then you explained that they do not wish by this to associate anything with God; nor do they believe that it has influence on events, the extent of their claim being that alms given in this way are better than otherwise. But it is not hidden from the meanest intelligence that this claim warrants no consideration. The verdict depends on what is seen. And God controls what is secret. Him whom we have seen sacrificing to rocks and trees we have charged with paganism. These matters are among those for which we have charged Bornu with paganism.

For what caused the Amir of Bornu (according to what has reached us) to inflict harm on the believers among the Shaikh's people near to you until they were obliged to flee? What caused him to begin to fight them, unless he were in alliance with the Hausa kings to assist them? It is manifest that he would not have risen to assist the Hausa kings had he not approved of their religion. And certainly the approval of paganism is itself paganism. To fight them is per-

mitted, since the *jihād* against paganism is incumbent on all who are able.

May it be clear to you from what we have said of him that the Amir of Bornu has been known for his paganism. You also know that the law of a country is the law of its sultan. If he is a Muslim, then the country is *dār al-Islām*; if he is a pagan, then the country is *dār kufr*. Only those ignorant of the words of the "'*ulamā*'" will deny this....

If you had confined yourself to saying that the Bornuans had repented and desisted from what they were at, it would have been better than all this talk and clamour. For the latter is a weak argument for preventing the fighting to anyone who acknowledges the truth. But we did not know previously, and nothing reached us at all to show, that they had repented. However in the autumn of this year we received messages concerning you which indicated this. We have therefore sent our messenger to you in order that we may confirm this information, and so that he may bring back an account of the true state of affairs. If the matter is as we hear, then we shall despatch our messenger, Gidado Lima, to assemble our chiefs of the east. You will send those whom you please to conduct your affairs and whom you trust behind your back; and a meeting will take place in Siko. And those assembled will make a treaty according to such bonds and covenants as they find mutually acceptable, and fighting will stop. Let peace be established. In this

Glossary

amirs	in Islamic countries, rulers, tribal chiefs, or military commanders
Copts	an Egyptian people who first became Christians in the first century of the Common Era
fiqh	Islamic jurisprudence
haram	forbidden to Muslims
imams	those who lead prayers; also Muslim leaders with greater spiritual and civil authority
Jāhilīya	to Muslims, the period before the revelation of the Qur'an ("Qur'ān" in the document) to Muhammad
liberal	in this context, tolerant and universal
Ramadān	the ninth month of the Islamic year, whose sacredness is observed with daily fasts from dawn to sunset
talaba	Arabic word for "students"
this country	Kanem-Bornu's western territory, recently conquered by Sokoto
we did what we did	an oblique reference to attacking the Fulani, to retake their land

connection we have delayed raiding Bornu this year, though we intended to. If the matter is as I have said, namely that they have repented and desisted, then let the fighting stop, for it is repugnant to our relationship, and peace is necessary between us....

You say that generations of "*ulamā*" and reformers from among the imams have passed, and they have not used such arguments as these, nor charged the generality of believers with paganism, nor drawn the sword of oppression in this way, even though this heresy and immorality have been present in all countries in all ages. You say that the verses of the Qur'ān which we cite, indicating what are crimes in the sight of God, are not hidden from old women and children, let alone learned "*ulamā'*." You mention that we can do what the ancients did, though they were princes in God's name, but that more is not possible, since this generation is not created to be more virtuous or stronger or more learned than the first Muslims. The answer to this is that we have made war on Bornu only because of what I have already mentioned. There is nothing more; though it is permitted to struggle against even less than that, as will appear. The statements in your premises and the contentions you have used to elucidate them amount only to refutable arguments. How can it be said that it is not legal, for him who is able, to reform immorality or put an end to corruption? It is not right for an able man to point to learned men who in the past have not bothered to change it or speak of it. By my faith, that is of no avail....

We have indeed attempted many times to initiate with you the peace which you ask for, and we have not ceased to write to you concerning it every year. But we think that probably our messages do not reach you, and that you do not receive intelligence of them. Please God there may be a suitable reconciliation. May God direct us and you to the good.

Simón Bolívar (AP/Wide World Photos)

SIMÓN BOLÍVAR'S CARTAGENA MANIFESTO

1812

"Fly to avenge the dead, to give life to the dying, ease to the oppressed, and freedom to all."

Overview

The Cartagena Manifesto, written on December 15, 1812, was the work of Simón Bolívar, whose name survives as that of one of the chief liberators of the nations of South America from Spanish rule. Bolívar was Venezuelan, but after the collapse of his nation's First Republic, formed at the beginning of the Venezuelan War of Independence (1811–1823), he departed to live in exile in modern-day Colombia. In the city of Cartagena de Indias (Cartagena of the Indies), he wrote a manifesto outlining what he perceived to be the causes for the First Republic's collapse. In doing so, he implicitly outlined what he believed should be the shape of a future Venezuelan republic or of any South American republic. More explicitly, his goal in the manifesto was to seek support for an invasion of Venezuela to oust the Spanish.

The manifesto quickly became a key document in the larger context of the Spanish American wars of independence that took place in Mexico and South America from 1808 to 1829. At least in part as a consequence of the manifesto, and certainly in large part due to Bolívar's leadership, Venezuela effectively achieved its independence in 1821. Bolívar also lent aid to revolutions in other countries, helping to liberate Peru, Chile, Bolivia, and Argentina and thus earning the sobriquet "Liberator of Five Nations." Because of his role and those of numerous other revolutionaries, Spanish rule in continental Central and South America, which dated back to the late fifteenth century, came to an end. After the early nineteenth century's wave of revolutionary activity, only Puerto Rico and Cuba remained under Spanish control, a state of affairs that lasted until the Spanish-American War of 1898.

Discussions of South American history during this period are complicated by the nomenclature used to refer to the states. In the modern world, the various nations of South America—Argentina, Bolivia, Colombia, Ecuador, Paraguay, Peru, Uruguay, Venezuela, and others—are established independent countries. In the eighteenth and early nineteenth centuries, however, these nations were in essence provinces of larger polities ruled by Spain. Borders were shifting, and

Spain's territories were often carved up and recombined into new political entities. Venezuela, for example, began as a province of Spain's Viceroyalty of Peru. Later it was part of the Viceroyalty of New Granada and then what was called a captaincy general—all referring to administrative units of Spain's New World colonies. Accordingly, in historical context, modern country names such as "Venezuela" and "Peru" serve as shorthand devices for referring to the regions that would eventually become these nations.

Context

The deepest roots of the Cartagena Manifesto extend back to 1492 and Christopher Columbus's first voyage to the New World. In the name of the Catholic Church and the Spanish monarchs, colonization of the New World began on the island of Hispaniola. On his second voyage to the New World, Columbus brought along some fifteen hundred men and established La Isabela on Hispaniola, in today's Dominican Republic. Another settlement, Nueva Isabela, was built in 1496, but a hurricane destroyed it; it was rebuilt as Santo Domingo, which remains as the oldest permanent European settlement in the Americas. In 1513 Vasco Núñez de Balboa crossed the Isthmus of Panama, leading the first European expedition to the western coast of the New World and the Pacific Ocean. In Mexico the Spanish soon conquered the Aztec Empire, launching an invasion under Hernán Cortés in 1519 and declaring victory in 1521 after the fall of Tenochtitlán (rebuilt as Mexico City). In 1532 Spaniards under the command of Francisco Pizarro defeated the Incas at the Battle of Cajamarca, completing the conquest of Peru. Estimates hold that during the 1500s, about a quarter million Spaniards settled in the New World, with devastating effects on indigenous populations. In Mexico, for example, the indigenous population declined, according to some estimates, by about 90 percent during the century. Over the same period, the native population of Peru declined from about six and a half million to about one million.

As Spanish territories in the New World expanded, they were divided into what were called viceroyalties, each under the command of a governor-general. The first two were the

1542

- The Viceroyalty of Peru, encompassing Spain's South American colonies, is created.

1717

- **May 27**
  The Viceroyalty of New Granada is formed out of what would become Panama, Columbia, Ecuador, and Venezuela.

1783

- **July 24**
  Simón Bolívar is born in Caracas.

1810

- **April 19**
  The Caracas Junta, the municipal council of Caracas, deposes the governor-general of Venezuela.

1811

- **July 5**
  The Venezuelan congress declares the nation's independence from Spain and establishes the First Republic.

1812

- **March 26**
  The Caracas earthquake devastates large portions of republican-controlled Venezuela.

viceroyalties of New Spain and Peru. New Spain encompassed what is today California and the southwestern United States, Mexico, most of Central America, and the Caribbean islands. The Viceroyalty of Peru consisted essentially of all of Spain's South American holdings (with the notable exception of Brazil, which was a Portuguese colony). Later, in the eighteenth century, two additional viceroyalties were formed. In 1717 the Viceroyalty of New Granada was created out of what would become Panama, Columbia, Ecuador, and Venezuela. In 1776 the Viceroyalty of the Río de la Plata was formed out of what would become Argentina, Bolivia, Uruguay, and Paraguay. Thus, by the eighteenth century, a map of Spain's New World colonies would extend all the way from the southern tip of South America up through most of western South America, through Central America and the western regions of North America.

Spain's relationships with its Atlantic colonies were rarely entirely smooth. Spanish colonists in the New World grew to resent the high taxes they paid to the Spanish Crown as well as interference in their affairs by Spain, and they began to agitate for political independence. Many Latin American colonists were influenced by ideas coming out of the European Enlightenment, which, during the eighteenth century, questioned the legitimacy of hereditary succession and the divine right of kings to rule. These democratic notions began to gather momentum after England's American colonies declared their independence in 1776 and achieved victory in the Revolutionary War in 1783. Then, in 1789, the French Revolution overthrew the monarchy in France. The spirit of revolt moved to Central America with the Haitian Revolution, which began in 1791 and led to Haitian independence from France in 1804. The time was ripe for revolutionary movements to spread to Spain's American colonies. By and large, revolutionary agitation in Latin America was conducted among white settlers, with little regard for the wishes or aspirations of indigenous peoples; in fact, some indigenous peoples, such as the *llaneros* (cowboys) of Venezuela, who were often mixed Spanish and Indian, supported the Spanish monarchy.

A key event that triggered revolutionary movements in Latin America was the 1808 invasion of Spain by Napoléon Bonaparte in what is called the Peninsular War (referring to the Iberian Peninsula, which comprises Spain and Portugal). This campaign was part of a larger series of wars called the Napoleonic Wars, waged when Napoléon, having declared himself emperor of France, fought to topple hereditary monarchies and impose unified rule over Europe. The French invasion led to the complete breakdown of Spanish administration, both in Spain and in its colonies. What followed was a long period of warfare—both guerrilla and conventional—instability, turmoil, and uncertainty in Spain. The chief outcome of Napoléon's invasion, at least from the standpoint of the Americas, was a breakdown in communication between the colonies and Spain, which now no longer had the might necessary to enforce its control across the Atlantic.

Almost immediately, the Spanish colonies began to take action. The first effort to achieve independence in Venezuela occurred in 1810, when the municipal council in Caracas, the capital of the Captaincy General of Venezuela, launched a movement to depose the governor-general and set up a governing congress. Several of Venezuela's provinces quickly joined the "Caracas Junta," though numerous others did not. On July 5, 1811, the Venezuelan congress declared the nation's independence from Spain and established the First Republic. Meanwhile, revolutionary fervor spread to other Spanish colonies. In 1799 rebels in Mexico had launched an unsuccessful revolt called the Conspiracy of the Machetes. The spirit of rebellion survived in Mexico, and in September 1810 Mexico launched its war for independence from Spain, which it would achieve through the Treaty of Córdoba, signed in 1821. Also in 1810 the United Provinces of South America was formed. This state would become the United Provinces of the Río de la Plata, which in turn would eventually become the nation of Argentina. The United Provinces deployed armies, including the Army of the North, to liberate northern Argentina and Upper Peru (modern-day Bolivia). On November 5, 1811, a rebellion called the Primer Grito de Independencia, or "First Shout of Independence," erupted in El Salvador. The Spanish Empire in the New World was crumbling.

In Venezuela, matters did not go well for the infant First Republic. Civil war erupted between republicans and those who wanted to remain loyal to the Spanish monarchy. Two major provinces, Maracaibo and Guiana, as well as the district of Coro, refused to recognize the rebellious junta in Caracas. The republicans launched a military operation to bring Coro and Guayana to heel, but the operation failed—though republican forces did succeed in suppressing a rebellion against the republicans in Valencia. Meanwhile Spain, now under Napoléon's brother Joseph Bonaparte, imposed a blockade. A further setback for the republican government was an earthquake on March 26, 1812, which hit republican areas particularly hard and killed some fifteen thousand to twenty thousand people. Amid all this turmoil, Francisco de Miranda, the First Republic's political leader, was able to assume dictatorial powers, but he was unable to stop the advance of royalist troops under the command of Domingo de Monteverde. On July 25, 1812, royalists dealt a decisive defeat to the republicans at the Battle of San Mateo. Miranda signed a cease-fire agreement with Monteverde, effectively ending the First Republic.

One of the key leaders of the republican movement was Simón Bolívar, a young aristocrat who supported complete independence from Spain. Bolívar regarded Miranda's surrender as an act of treason. He arrested Miranda and turned him over to Monteverde, who ignored the terms of the cease-fire and arrested and executed many of the rebels. To escape Monteverde's reprisals, Bolívar fled to Cartagena de Indias, where he wrote the Cartagena Manifesto and planned an invasion of Venezuela.

About the Author

The author of the Cartagena Manifesto was Simón José Antonio de la Santísima Trinidad Bolívar y Palacios Ponte

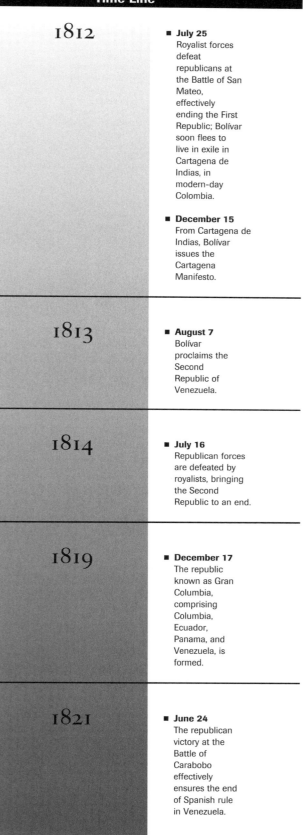

Time Line

1812

- **July 25**
  Royalist forces defeat republicans at the Battle of San Mateo, effectively ending the First Republic; Bolívar soon flees to live in exile in Cartagena de Indias, in modern-day Colombia.

- **December 15**
  From Cartagena de Indias, Bolívar issues the Cartagena Manifesto.

1813

- **August 7**
  Bolívar proclaims the Second Republic of Venezuela.

1814

- **July 16**
  Republican forces are defeated by royalists, bringing the Second Republic to an end.

1819

- **December 17**
  The republic known as Gran Columbia, comprising Columbia, Ecuador, Panama, and Venezuela, is formed.

1821

- **June 24**
  The republican victory at the Battle of Carabobo effectively ensures the end of Spanish rule in Venezuela.

Milestone Documents

1823

■ July 24
Venezuelan
republican
forces win the
Battle of Lake
Maracaibo
against Spain,
the last war of
the Venezuelan
War of
Independence.

1830

■ December 17
Bolívar dies of
tuberculosis at
Santa Marta,
Gran Colombia.

Blanco, known to history simply as Simón Bolívar. Bolívar was born in Caracas on July 24, 1783, to an aristocratic family that had made its immense fortune in sugar and mining, particularly of copper. He thus was a member of the caste called criollos, or people of pure Spanish descent born in the colonies. After completing his education in Spain and living for a time in France, he returned to Venezuela in 1807. After the Caracas Junta assumed control, he was dispatched to England as a diplomatic representative, but he returned to Venezuela in 1811. When republican forces surrendered to royalist forces in 1812, he fled to Cartagena, where he wrote the Cartagena Manifesto later that year.

Bolívar's life after 1812 was eventful. He was given a military command by the United Provinces of New Granada, and in 1813 he led an invasion of Venezuela known as the Admirable Campaign, liberating the provinces of Mérida, Barinas, Trujillo, and Caracas from Spanish rule. When he seized Caracas on August 6, 1813, he proclaimed the Second Republic and served as its president until it collapsed in 1814. After a series of successes and setbacks, including the need to flee to Jamaica and then to Haiti, Bolívar returned to fight for the political independence of New Granada. He led military campaigns that liberated Venezuela and Ecuador and then established the nation known as Gran Colombia (comprising Venezuela, Colombia, Panama, and Ecuador) on December 17, 1819, serving as the nation's first president. He was able to witness his dream of a sovereign Venezuela after republican forces won the Battle of Carabobo on June 24, 1821, ensuring his nation's independence. A later victory in the Battle of Lake Maracaibo on July 24, 1823, drove out the last vestiges of the Spanish.

On August 6, 1825, the Congress of Upper Peru created the nation of Bolivia—one of the few nations in the world named after a person. Bolívar had difficulty governing, however, and had to assume dictatorial powers to maintain some semblance of control of the fragile state. He resigned his presidency on April 27, 1830, and died of tuberculosis on December 17 that year in Santa Marta, Gran Colombia (now Colombia).

Explanation and Analysis of the Document

Bolívar addresses his manifesto specifically to the people of New Granada. His goal is to outline his experiences in Venezuela, particularly the collapse of the First Republic, with a view to helping the people of New Granada escape the state's errors. Essentially, he outlines five major problems with the First Republic: the ineffectiveness of the army, poor administration of public revenues, reliance on a weak federal system, the Caracas earthquake of 1812, and the opposition of the Catholic Church to republican views. He then outlines his reasons for wanting to launch an invasion of Venezuela.

◆ Paragraphs 1–14

The first section of the manifesto is sharply critical of the republican military. After brief introductory paragraphs, Bolívar launches into a discussion of the failure of the First Republic's military campaigns, particularly against the district of Coro. His tone is harsh. He refers to "the fatal adoption of a system of tolerance" that allowed Coro to resist republican rule. He then makes a startling statement regarding the governing council in Caracas: "The Council based its political policy on a mistaken understanding of humanity that does not allow any government to free by force stupid people who do not know the value of their rights." Bolívar was a liberator, but he was by instinct an aristocrat, and as such he was willing to impose his political vision even on those who did not share it. He then discusses what he regarded as misplaced idealism, referring to "ethereal republics" and "pious doctrine" where philosophers supplanted leaders and philanthropy supplanted law. Crimes against the new state were tolerated, thus allowing royalist supporters free rein in Venezuela. One consequence of this tolerance was that unchecked opposition prevented the First Republic from calling up veteran troops, leading to the creation of undisciplined militias that were not equal to the fight at hand. And because these militias were formed from the local laboring populations, the impact on agriculture was severe. He rejects the view that because earlier nations, from ancient Greece and Rome to the fledgling United States, did not need mercenary armies, Venezuela did not need them either. He counters this view by arguing that these states had "political virtues, austere habits, and military character" that the Venezuelans did not possess.

The collective impact of these failures was twofold. In paragraph 13, Bolívar argues that the First Republic's military was simply ineffective; enlistees lacked discipline, obedience, and even knowledge of the use of weapons. The forces were thus doomed to defeat. In paragraph 14, Bolívar notes that the republic's unwillingness to take harsh

Horseback riders follow the route taken by Simón Bolívar in 1821 in his defeat of Spanish forces in the battle of Carabobo, the last battle in the war for independence. (AP/Wide World Photos)

measures led to problems in the city of Valencia; although the republic subdued Valencia, there resulted a rivalry between city and country that allowed the Spanish to regain a foothold in Venezuela.

◆ Paragraph 15

Paragraph 15 briefly discusses the First Republic's poor administration of public revenues—"the dissipation of public revenues on frivolous and harmful items." For example, he cites the bloated salaries given to legions of public bureaucrats. The consequence of this overspending was that the First Republic had to issue its own paper currency. The currency, though, lacked the backing of goods and productive capacity. It was essentially worthless, with no "intrinsic value." Under such conditions of fiscal irresponsibility, many Venezuelans concluded that life was better under the Spanish than it was under the First Republic.

◆ Paragraphs 16–21

The core of Bolívar's argument is contained in this sequence of paragraphs. His chief objection to the First Republic was its "federal structure," a term that in Bolívar's usage means decentralization. In his view, too much power and authority were given to Venezuela's districts and cities,

and not enough was reserved for the central government. Interestingly, the fledgling United States had faced the same problem. Under the original Articles of Confederation, the nation's first constitution, power was decentralized. The nation was less a unified polity than a "confederation" of states. Centrifugal forces threatened to drive the independent states apart until the U.S. Constitution, in the form in which it survives today, strengthened the federal government—while also planting the seeds of the American Civil War, when regional factionalism would overcome allegiance to the nation. Venezuela experienced the same kind of factionalism during the First Republic and beyond, as local economic interests trumped allegiance to the national government.

Bolívar's position is clear: "Authorizing each man to rule himself breaks the social compact and characterizes nations in anarchy." He goes on to write that despite its being ideal in certain respects, "the federal system is nonetheless the most contrary to the interests of our nascent states," especially since "our citizens are not in a position to exert their rights fully, because they lack the political virtues that characterize the true republican." He defends this notion by appealing to the nature of the times. When a country is "prosperous and serene," it can afford to relinquish power to its citizens. But when a country is fighting both internal factionalism and a foreign enemy, the times require it to exhibit strength. One of the practical consequences of this diffusion of power in the First Republic was that the federal government and provincial authorities quarreled in Caracas about who was going to deploy troops while the Spanish poised to strike. The result was certain defeat. A second practical consequence was ineffectual elections. In Bolívar's view, the federal system encouraged divisiveness, for "popular elections conducted by the rustics of the countryside and by those engaged in intrigue in the cities" become obstacles because the rustics "are so ignorant that they vote mechanically" while those in the cities "are so ambitious that they turn everything into factionalism."

◆ **Paragraphs 22 and 23**

In these paragraphs Bolívar makes reference to the Caracas earthquake, which struck on March 26, 1812, killing some fifteen to twenty thousand people and causing widespread property damage. Because the earthquake was centered in republican-controlled areas of Venezuela, it represented a serious setback to the First Republic. While Bolívar acknowledges that the earthquake was the "immediate cause" of the collapse of the republic, he goes on to argue that its effects would not have been as devastating if there had been a strong central government to address the crisis. In essence, the earthquake helped to expose the weaknesses of the federal system of government of the First Republic.

◆ **Paragraph 24**

Paragraph 24 briefly apportions some of the blame for the collapse of the First Republic on the Catholic Church. Bolívar argues that Catholic priests aided those who promoted civil war and allowed the Spanish sanctuary in the country. He is particularly shocked by the fact that none of these "traitorous priests" were punished for their "heinous crimes"—again, a failing that he attributes to the weak and overly tolerant federal congress.

◆ **Paragraphs 25–42**

In the manifesto's final sequence of paragraphs, after reiterating the key points of his argument, Bolívar turns to the future by outlining how New Granada can learn from the mistakes made in Venezuela. He first insists that New Granada forces should invade and subdue Caracas. He draws his readers' attention again to the factionalism in Caracas, where distinct groups pursued their selfish ends at the expense of the republic, as had occurred in Coro. Bolívar argues that only by retaining control over Caracas could New Granada spread the spirit of revolution through South America. He then notes that because of events in Spain, it was likely that large numbers of Spanish immigrants would arrive in South America. These immigrants, acting in concert with seasoned military officers and soldiers, would be in a position to subvert South American independence. Bolívar goes on to claim that nothing can stop this immigration, and he raises the specter of a new Spanish army bent on conquest.

The only solution to this looming problem was "to pacify our rebellious provinces and then to take up our weapons against the enemy." He makes clear that fighting a purely defensive war would be ruinous to the country; the only alternative was to take the fight to the enemy. He calls the moment "propitious," for the Spanish were confined to their garrisons, which they had to defend. New Granada had to strike before Spanish reinforcements arrived. The manifesto closes with an inspirational call to action. Bolívar points out the obligation of New Granada to "chasten those audacious invaders" and "liberate the cradle of Colombian independence."

Audience

The audience for the Cartagena Manifesto consisted primarily of republicans in Venezuela and New Granada. The manifesto was Bolívar's first significant piece of political writing, and he used it to convince republicans of the errors they had made in forming the First Republic and confronting the challenges of uniting the provinces into a stable nation able to fend off its adversaries. Most directly, the manifesto represented Bolívar's request to New Granada, which he addresses in the opening paragraph, for permission to lead a New Granada army into Venezuela. A secondary audience, then, was military leaders. Bolívar believed that the defeat of the First Republic by royalist forces was in some measure his responsibility. Through the manifesto he wanted to rehabilitate his reputation among military leaders, for he was already planning his invasion of Venezuela, which would lead to the formation of the Second Republic. A third audience was the rest of South America, as he hoped to instruct other nations seeking independence and help them avoid the errors of the First Republic. A final audience was more broadly international. Bolívar knew that like any infant country Venezuela would need aid from foreign nations, such as the United States and Great Britain; indeed, British and Irish troops would fight in Venezuela after the collapse of the First Republic. With his manifesto, Bolívar hoped to convince international leaders that the political leadership of a republican Venezuela—specifically he himself—would have the necessary political heft to forge and maintain a new nation, one worthy of assistance from other nations that support the goal of independence.

Impact

In the short term, the Cartagena Manifesto had a profound impact. Bolívar won the support of New Granada and launched his Admirable Campaign on February 16, 1813. During the campaign, Bolívar issued a document called the Decree of War to the Death, in which he announced that any Spaniard who failed to support independence would be put to death. On July 22 his forces met and defeated the royalists at the Battle of Horcones. In August his army occupied Valencia and La Victoria, and the royalist government, established after the fall of the First Republic, surrendered, leading to the formation of the Sec-

"Motivated by a patriotic zeal, let me dare to address you, to outline for you the causes that led to Venezuela's destruction; flattering myself that the awful and exemplary lessons that extinguished Republic has given us persuade America to improve her conduct, correcting the errors of unity, strength, and energy that are manifested in her forms of government."

(Paragraph 3)

"The codes consulted by our magistrates were not those that could teach them the practical science of government but those that have formed certain visionaries who, imagining ethereal republics, have sought to attain political perfection, assuming the perfectibility of humankind. Thus we got philosophers for leaders; philanthropy for law, dialectics for tactics, and sophists for soldiers. With such a subversion of principles and things, the social order suffered enormously."

(Paragraph 7)

"The result provided Venezuela with harsh evidence of the error of their calculation, because the militiamen who went to meet the enemy, ignorant of the use of weapons and not being accustomed to discipline and obedience, were overwhelmed at the start of the last campaign, despite the heroic and extraordinary efforts made by their leaders to lead them to victory."

(Paragraph 13)

"Popular elections conducted by the rustics of the countryside and by those engaged in intrigue in the cities add a further obstacle to the practice of federation among us, because the former are so ignorant that they vote mechanically and the latter are so ambitious that they turn everything into factionalism."

(Paragraph 21)

"The influence of the church played a large part in the uprising of the towns and cities and the introduction of the enemies into the country, sacrilegiously abusing the sanctity of its ministry in aid of the promoters of civil war. However, we must candidly confess that these traitorous priests were encouraged to commit the heinous crimes of which they are justly accused simply because impunity for their crimes was absolute."

(Paragraph 24)

ond Republic—which itself ended up collapsing less than a year later. From 1817 to 1819, Bolívar was head of a rump government that created a legislative body called the Congress of Angostura, which wrote a constitution for Venezuela in 1819. Later, in the Battle of Lake Maracaibo on July 24, 1823, republicans drove out the last vestiges of the Spanish. Thus, Bolívar's dream of an independent Venezuelan Republic was realized. The official, formal name of the country became and remains the Bolivarian Republic of Venezuela.

In the longer term, Bolívar's goal of a free, unified, prosperous South America proved harder to realize. Although several nations gained their independence— largely through the efforts of Bolívar and numerous other republicans—factionalism, caste, and power plays undermined attempts at South American unity. Gran Colombia collapsed within a decade, and in the ensuing years the nations of South America fell under the control of caudillos, a term often translated as "strongmen" or "warlords." Thus, throughout the 1800s, South American nations—excepting Brazil, a stable nation under the Portuguese until 1889—were ruled by authoritarian dictators, and the century was one of revolts, coups, civil wars, and wars between states.

Further Reading

■ Books

Andrien, Kenneth J., and Lyman L. Johnson, eds. *The Political Economy of Spanish America in the Age of Revolution, 1750–1850.* Albuquerque: University of New Mexico Press, 1994.

Anna, Timothy. *Spain and the Loss of America.* Lincoln: University of Nebraska Press, 1983.

Archer, Christon I., ed. *The Wars of Independence in Spanish America.* Wilmington, Del.: Scholarly Resources, 2000.

Brading, David A. *The First America: The Spanish Monarchy, Creole Patriots, and the Liberal State, 1492–1867.* Cambridge, U.K.: Cambridge University Press, 1991.

Brown, Matthew. *Adventuring through Spanish Colonies: Simón Bolívar, Foreign Mercenaries and the Birth of New Nations.* Liverpool, U.K.: Liverpool University Press, 2006.

Chasteen, John Charles. *Americanos: Latin America's Struggle for Independence.* New York: Oxford University Press, 2008.

Costeloe, Michael P. *Response to Revolution: Imperial Spain and the Spanish American Revolutions, 1810–1840.* New York: Cambridge University Press, 1986.

Domínguez, Jorge I. *Insurrection or Loyalty: The Breakdown of the Spanish American Empire.* Cambridge, Mass.: Harvard University Press, 1980.

Francis, John Michael, ed. *Iberia and the Americas: Culture, Politics, and History: A Multidisciplinary Encyclopedia.* Santa Barbara, Calif.: ABC-CLIO, 2006.

Graham, Richard. *Independence in Latin America: A Comparative Approach,* 2nd ed. New York: McGraw-Hill, 1994.

Questions for Further Study

1. Compare and contrast the roles of Simón Bolívar in the Venezuelan independence movement and William of Orange in the Dutch independence movement, as reflected in the Dutch Declaration of Independence.

2. From a modern perspective, an examination of such documents as the Requerimiento, the Dutch Declaration of Independence, and the Cartagena Manifesto, along with the events surrounding them, creates an impression of Spanish rule as brutal and tyrannical. Imagine that you have been tasked with the job of defending the Spanish. How would you do so?

3. From one point of view, Bolívar's efforts were ultimately a failure, at least in part. Do you think that this diminishes his status as an important South American leader?

4. How would Bolívar have reacted to the Korean Declaration of Independence if he had had an opportunity to read it?

5. In the manifesto Bolívar makes reference to "stupid people" and "rustics"; in general, his attitude toward many Venezuelans seems haughty and aristocratic. How would you reconcile this attitude with his position as the "Liberator of Five Nations" and a hero in South America, where the monuments to him are almost uncountable?

Humphreys, Robert A., and John Lynch, eds. *The Origins of the Latin American Revolutions, 1808–1826.* New York: Knopf, 1965.

Kinsbruner, Jay. *The Spanish-American Independence Movement.* Huntington, N.Y.: R. E. Krieger, 1976.

———. *Independence in Spanish America: Civil Wars, Revolutions, and Underdevelopment*, 2nd ed. Albuquerque: University of New Mexico Press, 2000.

Lombardi, Cathryn L., John V. Lombardi, and K. Lynn Stoner. *Latin American History: A Teaching Atlas.* Madison: University of Wisconsin Press, 1983.

Lynch, John. *The Spanish American Revolutions, 1808–1826*, 2nd ed. New York: Norton, 1986.

———. *Caudillos in Spanish America, 1800–1850.* Oxford, U.K.: Clarendon Press, 1992.

———. *Simón Bolívar: A Life.* New Haven, Conn.: Yale University Press, 2007.

Rodríguez, Jaime E. *The Independence of Spanish America.* New York: Cambridge University Press, 1998.

Schmidt-Nowara, Christopher, and John M. Nieto-Phillips, eds. *Interpreting Spanish Colonialism: Empires, Nations, and Legends.* Albuquerque: University of New Mexico Press, 2005.

—Michael J. O'Neal

Simón Bolívar's Cartagena Manifesto

To spare New Granada the fate of Venezuela and save it from its present suffering are the objects of this report. Consent, my countrymen, to accept it with indulgence, in light of its praiseworthy intentions.

I am, Granadans, a child of unhappy Caracas, who having miraculously escaped from the midst of her physical and political ruins, always faithful to the liberal and just system proclaimed by my country, have come here to follow the standards of independence, so gloriously waving in these states.

Motivated by a patriotic zeal, let me dare to address you, to outline for you the causes that led to Venezuela's destruction; flattering myself that the awful and exemplary lessons that extinguished Republic has given us persuade America to improve her conduct, correcting the errors of unity, strength, and energy that are manifested in her forms of government.

The gravest mistake Venezuela made, when they entered the political arena, was without a doubt the fatal adoption of a system of tolerance—a system that was rejected by the whole sensible world as weak and ineffective but that was held to tenaciously and with unexampled blindness until the end.

The first evidence that our government gave of its foolish weakness manifested with respect to the subject city of Coro, when it refused to recognize the city's legitimacy, pronounced it insurgent, and harassed it as an enemy.

Instead of subjugating that defenseless city, which was ready to surrender when our maritime forces arrived, the Supreme Council allowed it to fortify itself and to put on such a respectable facade that it later succeeded in subjugating the whole Confederation, almost as easily as we had previously done. The Council based its political policy on a mistaken understanding of humanity that does not allow any government to free by force stupid people who do not know the value of their rights.

The codes consulted by our magistrates were not those that could teach them the practical science of government but those that have formed certain visionaries who, imagining ethereal republics, have sought to attain political perfection, assuming the perfectibility of humankind. Thus we got philosophers for leaders; philanthropy for law, dialectics for tactics, and sophists for soldiers. With such a subversion of principles and things, the social order suffered enormously, and, of course, the state ran by leaps and bounds to a universal solution, which was soon realized.

Hence was born the impunity of crimes against the state committed brazenly by the discontented, and especially on the part of our born and implacable enemy, the Spanish Europeans, remained in our country with the malicious intent of causing constant unrest and promoting as many conspiracies as our forgiving judges allowed, even if their attacks were so enormous that the public well-being was threatened.

The doctrine supporting this behavior stemmed from the philanthropic maxims of certain writers who defend the notion that no one has to take the life of a man, even one who has committed a crime against the state. In the shelter of this pious doctrine, a pardon followed every conspiracy, and after every pardon came another conspiracy, which in turn was forgiven because liberal governments must be distinguished by leniency. But this clemency is criminal and contributed more than anything else to tearing down the machinery that had not yet quite been established!

From this source stemmed the determined opposition to the calling up of veteran troops, disciplined and able to appear in the battlefield, as instructed, to defend liberty with success and glory. Instead, countless undisciplined militia were established, which, in addition to exhausting the funds of the national treasury with huge salaries, destroyed agriculture, driving the peasants away from their homes and making hateful the government that had forced them to take up arms and abandon their families.

Our statesmen tell us, "Republics have no need of men paid to maintain their freedom. All citizens are soldiers when the enemy attacks us. Greece, Rome, Venice, Genoa, Switzerland, Holland, and recently North America defeated their opponents without the help of mercenary troops always ready to support despotism and subjugate their fellow citizens."

The simple-minded were fascinated by these impolitic and inaccurate arguments, but they failed to convince the wise, who knew well the vast difference between the peoples, times, and customs of those republics and ours. It is true that those republics paid no standing armies, but in ancient times it was for the reason that they did not have any and instead entrusted their salvation and the glory of the States to their political virtues, austere habits, and military character, qualities that we are very far from possessing. As for modern republics that have shaken off the yoke of tyrants, it is well known that they have maintained a considerable number of veterans to assure their security—except North America, which being at peace with everyone and bounded by the sea has not had the need in recent years to sustain a full complement of veteran troops to defend its borders and squares.

The result provided Venezuela with harsh evidence of the error of their calculation, because the militiamen who went to meet the enemy, ignorant of the use of weapons and not being accustomed to discipline and obedience, were overwhelmed at the start of the last campaign, despite the heroic and extraordinary efforts made by their leaders to lead them to victory. This produced a general feeling of discouragement among the soldiers and officers, because it is a military truth that only hardened armies are capable of overcoming the first fateful events of a campaign. The inexperienced soldier believes that everything is lost if he is once defeated, because experience has not proved that courage, skill, and perseverance make up for bad fortune.

The subdivision of the disputed province of Caracas, planned and sanctioned by the federal congress, awakened and fostered a bitter rivalry between the cities and outlying areas and the capital, which—so said the congressmen, ambitious to dominate their districts—was the tyranny of the cities and the leech of the State. In this way the flames of civil war were fanned in Valencia and were never put out, even with the defeat of that city. Secretly the torch was passed from adjacent towns to Coro and Maracaibo and grew in intensity, in this way facilitating the entry of the Spanish, who brought about the downfall of Venezuela.

The dissipation of public revenues on frivolous and harmful items—particularly in salaries for countless clerks, secretaries, judges, magistrates, provincial and federal legislators—dealt a fatal blow to the Republic because it was forced to resort to the dangerous expedient of establishing a paper currency, without other security than the strength and anticipated income of the Confederation. This new currency appeared in the eyes of most people to be a gross violation of property rights, because they saw themselves as being robbed of objects of intrinsic value in exchange for others whose price was uncertain and even imaginary. Paper money put the finishing touches on the discontent of the stolid people of the interior, who called upon the Commander of the Spanish troops to come and rescue them from a currency that they viewed with more horror than slavery.

But what weakened the government of Venezuela the most was the federal structure they adopted, following the most exaggerated notions of human rights. Authorizing each man to rule himself breaks the social compact and characterizes nations in anarchy. Such was the true state of the Confederation. Each province was governed independently and, following this example, each city sought to claim the same powers and adopt the theory that all men and all peoples have the prerogative to establish at will the government that suits them.

Although it is the most perfect and most capable of providing human happiness in society, the federal system is nonetheless the most contrary to the interests of our nascent states. Generally speaking, our citizens are not in a position to exert their rights fully, because they lack the political virtues that characterize the true republican—virtues that are not acquired in absolute governments, where the rights and duties of citizenship are not recognized.

On the other hand, what country in the world, no matter how temperate and Republican it is, will be able to rule itself, in the middle of internal strife and foreign warfare, by a system as complicated and weak as the federal government? No, it is not possible to maintain order in the turmoil of fighting and factions. The government needs to adjust itself, so to speak, to the nature of the circumstances, the times, and the men that surround it. If they are prosperous and serene, it should be temperate and protective, but if they are dire and turbulent, it has to be harsh and arm itself with strength equal to the dangers, with no regard for laws or constitutions until happiness and peace are restored.

Caracas had to suffer much in light of the defects of the Confederation, which, far from aiding her, exhausted her wealth and military supplies and, when danger came, abandoned her to her fate—without help, with the smallest contingent. Moreover, it augmented the problems by fostering competition between the federal and provincial powers, which allowed the enemy to get to the heart of the State, before it had resolved the question of which troops—federal or provincial—should be dispatched to drive them back, when they already had occupied a large portion of the province. This fatal disagreement produced a delay that was terrible for our forces. They were defeated in San Carlos before the reinforcements necessary for victory arrived.

I believe that as long as we do not centralize our American governments, our enemies will gain the most comprehensive advantages. We will be inevitably involved in the horrors of civil strife and abjectly defeated by the handful of bandits who infest our region.

Popular elections conducted by the rustics of the countryside and by those engaged in intrigue in the cities add a further obstacle to the practice of federation among us, because the former are so ignorant that they vote mechanically and the latter are so ambitious that they turn everything into factionalism. So in Venezuela a free and fair election has never been seen, which put government in the hands of men who are uncommitted to the cause, inept, and immoral. The party spirit decided all matters, thus creating more chaos than the circumstances dictated. Our own divisions and not the Spanish forces, has turned us to slavery.

The earthquake of March 26 certainly was as upsetting physically as psychically and can properly be called the immediate cause of the ruin of Venezuela. But this same event could have occurred without producing such deadly effect if Caracas had then been governed by a single authority that, acting with speed and force, could have repaired the damage unfettered by the hindrances and rivalries that retarded the effect of these measures until the destruction had become so devastating that it was beyond help.

If Caracas, instead of a languid and ineffectual Confederation, had set up a simple government—the kind it required for its political and military circumstances, you would exist today, O Venezuela, and you would enjoy freedom.

After the earthquake, the influence of the church played a large part in the uprising of the towns and cities and the introduction of the enemies into the country, sacrilegiously abusing the sanctity of its ministry in aid of the promoters of civil war. However, we must candidly confess that these traitorous priests were encouraged to commit the heinous crimes of which they are justly accused simply because impunity for their crimes was absolute, a condition that Congress shockingly aided. The situation came to such a pass that from the time of the insurrection of the city of Valencia—the pacification of which cost the lives of a thousand men—not a single rebel was given over to the vengeance of the law.

All of them were left with their lives intact, and the majority also kept their property.

It follows from the foregoing that among the causes leading to the fall of Venezuela should be placed, first, the nature of its Constitution, which was, I repeat, as contrary to her own interests as it was favorable to those of her opponents. Second was the spirit of misanthropy that gripped our leaders. Third was the opposition to the establishment of a military force that could have saved the Republic and repelled the blows of the Spaniards. Fourth was the earthquake, accompanied by a fanaticism that succeeded in drawing from this phenomenon the most ominous interpretations. Finally, there were the internal factions that were, in fact, the deadly poison that had pushed the country into the grave.

These examples of mistakes and misfortunes are not entirely without value for the peoples of South America, who aspire to freedom and independence.

New Granada has seen the demise of Venezuela, so it should avoid the pitfalls that have destroyed her. To this end, I advocate the reconquest of Caracas as an essential measure for securing the safety of New Granada. At first glance, this project might seem irrelevant, costly, and perhaps impractical, but if we examine it more closely, attentively, and with foresight, it is impossible to ignore the necessity and not to implement it once its utility is established.

The first thing that speaks in support of this operation is the origin of the destruction of Caracas, which was none other than the contempt with which the city regarded the existence of an enemy that seemed inconsequential. It was not, considered in its true light.

Coro certainly could never have competed with Caracas, when compared with Caracas in terms of its intrinsic strength. But because, in the order of human events, it is not always the largest physical entity that tilts the political balance, but the one that has superior moral force, should not the government of Venezuela therefore have refrained from removing an enemy who, though seemingly weak, had the support of the province of Maracaibo, including all those bound to the Regency; the gold; and the cooperation of our eternal enemies, the Europeans who live among us; the clerical party, always addicted to its supporter and partner, despotism; and, above all, the confirmed regard of the ignorant and superstitious within the boundaries of our states. So, to dismantle the machinery of state, it required only one traitorous official to call in the enemy, after which the unprecedented and patriotic efforts of the advocates of Caracas could not prevent the collapse of a structure already toppling from the blow of a single man.

Applying the example of Venezuela to New Granada and expressing it mathematically as a ratio, we find that Coro is to Caracas as Caracas is to all America; consequently, the danger that threatens this country is due to the aforementioned formula, because Spain, possessing the territory of Venezuela, can easily obtain men and munitions of war such that, under the direction of leaders with experience against the masters of war, the French, they can penetrate from the provinces of Barinas and Maracaibo to the ends of America South.

Spain has many ambitious and courageous general officers, who, accustomed to dangers and privations, yearn to come here to find an empire to replace the one she just lost.

It is very likely that upon the decline of the Peninsula, there will be a prodigious emigration of all sorts of men, particularly cardinals, archbishops, bishops, canons, and revolutionary clerics capable not only of subverting our tender and languid States but also entangling the entire New World in a frightful anarchy. The religious influence, the rule of civil and military domination, and all the prestige they can use to seduce the human spirit are so many instruments available to subjugate these regions.

Nothing will prevent emigration from Spain. England is likely to assist the emigration of a group that weakens Bonaparte's forces in Spain and augments and strengthens their own power in America. Neither France nor America can stop it. Neither can we do so on our own; all of our countries lacking a respectable navy, our attempts will be in vain.

These defectors will indeed find a favorable reception in the ports of Venezuela, as they are reinforcing the oppressors of that country and supplying the means to undertake the conquest of independent states.

They will raise a force of fifteen or twenty thousand men who will promptly be brought to order by their leaders, officers, sergeants, corporals, and veteran soldiers. This army will be followed by another, even more fearsome—one consisting of ministers, ambassadors, counselors, judges, the entire church hierarchy, and the grandees of Spain, whose profession is deceit and intrigue and who will be decorated with flashy titles well suited to dazzle the crowd. They will engulf everything like a torrent, right down to the seeds and even the roots of the tree of freedom in Colombia. The troops will fight on the field, and the others will wage war

from their ministries by means of seduction and fanaticism.

Thus, we have no other recourse to guard against these calamities than to pacify our rebellious provinces and then to take up our weapons against the enemy and in this way to form soldiers and officials worthy to be called the pillars of the country.

Everything conspires to make us adopt this measure; without mentioning the urgent need for us to close the doors to the enemy, there are other very strong reasons for us to take the offensive. It would be an inexcusable political and military failure to fail to do so. We have been invaded, and we are therefore forced to drive the enemy back beyond the border. Moreover, it is a principle of the art of war that any defensive war is injurious and ruinous to the country that conducts it, because it weakens without hope of compensation. Conversely, fighting in enemy territory is always advantageous, for the sake of the good that results from harming the enemy. For this reason we must not, under any circumstances, go on the defensive.

We should also consider the current state of the enemy, which is in a very vulnerable position, having been deserted by most of its Creole soldiers and having, at just this time, to defend the patriotic garrison cities of Caracas, Puerto Cabello, La Guaira, Barcelona, Cumaná and Margarita, where they have their supplies. They do not dare abandon these positions, fearing a general uprising when they leave. So it would be impossible for our troops to arrive at the gates of Caracas without engaging in a pitched battle.

It is certain that as soon as we arrive in Venezuela thousands of brave patriots who are longing for our arrival to help them shake off the yoke of their tyrants will join us, uniting their forces with ours to defend freedom.

The nature of this campaign gives us the advantage of approaching Maracaibo by way of Santa Marta and Barinas by way of Cucuta.

Let us therefore take hold of this propitious moment. Do not allow reinforcements that might arrive at any time from Spain to entirely alter this strategic balance. Do not lose, perhaps forever, the providential opportunity to ensure the fortune of these states.

The honor of New Granada absolutely requires us to chasten those audacious invaders, pursuing them to their last stronghold. Because her glory depends on our undertaking the enterprise of marching to Venezuela, to liberate the cradle of Colombian independence, its martyrs and the worthy people of Caracas, whose cries are directed only to their beloved compatriots of Granada, whom they eagerly await as their redeemers. Let us hasten to break the chains of those victims who groan in the dungeons, ever hopeful of rescue by us. Do not betray their confidence; do not be insensitive to the cries of your brothers. Fly to avenge the dead, to give life to the dying, ease to the oppressed, and freedom to all.

Cartagena de Indias, 15 December 1812

Glossary

Creole	in this context, Spanish American
Peninsula	the Iberian Peninsula
Regency	French-dominated junta that briefly attempted to govern Spain's colonial possessions in South America
traitorous official	Francisco de Miranda

CARLSBAD DECREES

"The object ... is to [examine] the origins and the ... ramifications of the secret revolutionary and demagogic associations."

Overview

In July 1819 the Austrian foreign minister, Klemens von Metternich, persuaded representatives from a select group of the larger states of the German Confederation to issue a series of resolutions that imposed a rigid discipline on German universities, established restrictions on the German press, and created a commission of inquiry to root out revolutionary activity in the confederation's member states. (The confederation consisted of thirty-nine states, including the large and powerful Austrian Empire and the Kingdom of Prussia, several principalities and grand duchies, and four free cities.) The resolutions, created during a series of meetings in Carlsbad (in Bohemia, Austrian Empire), were a response to the growing unrest within university communities. The students and some members of the faculty were advancing liberal and nationalist philosophies current in the early nineteenth century. The incident that precipitated Metternich's action was the murder of August von Kotzebue, a conservative German literary figure, by Karl Ludwig Sand, a German student nationalist. Metternich used the murder as an excuse to suppress the growing nationalist and liberal influences in the German universities and to censor the press.

Context

German liberalism, which the Carlsbad Decrees were designed in part to suppress, had its roots in the liberalism of the Enlightenment. The classic formulation of liberalism in the Age of Enlightenment, John Locke's *Two Treatises of Government* (1690), argues that legitimate authority depends upon the consent of the governed. In economics, Adam Smith's *Wealth of Nations* rejected state interventionism in favor of laissez-faire and free-market economics. Coming out of the Enlightenment, liberalism emphasized individual rights and equality of opportunity. As liberalism developed during the first half of the nineteenth century, it stressed various aspects of the creed depending upon time and place. Political liberalism encompassed support for free-

dom of thought and speech, freedom of religious worship, limitations on the power of government via written constitutions that contained checks and balances, the rule of law, and the right of the individual to possess private property. Most German liberals favored a united Germany; they believed that a united Germany would provide a freer social and political order. German liberals looked to either Prussia or Austria to lead that national unification and, as a result, were more tolerant of a strong state or monarchical power.

Perhaps even more than liberalism, the Carlsbad Decrees were designed to address nationalism, which conservative German leaders viewed as destructive to their particularistic interests. Modern nationalism is largely a product of the intensity of feeling aroused during the French Revolution, which began in 1789. German nationalism was fueled by the ideas of such German philosophers as Johann Gottfried Herder, who called for the territorial unification of Germany, and Johann Gottlieb Fichte, who called for German self-sufficiency. Also fueling German nationalism was the humiliation the Austrian and Prussian armies had suffered at the hands of the French army during the Napoleonic Wars, which spanned the years 1803–1815 and were led by French emperor Napoléon Bonaparte. Napoléon's greatest victory in these wars, fought to bring Europe under one rule and to eliminate hereditary monarchies, was at the Battle of Austerlitz in 1805, when he defeated the Austrians (and Russians). At the Battle of Jena in 1806, he defeated the Prussian army. Napoléon's victories over Austria allowed him to impose his will on the German states. He created the Confederation of the Rhine (initially comprising sixteen German states) in July 1806 and then forced the dissolution of the Holy Roman Empire on August 1, 1806. His victories also permitted him to occupy Berlin on October 27, 1806, and in July 1807 he signed a treaty with Prussia that forced the Prussians to surrender about half the country's territory, reduce its standing army to forty thousand, and compelled them to pay a substantial indemnity and ally with France. The French victories and Napoléon's heavy-handed treatment of the occupied and allied German states stimulated in many a desire to be free of French influence and to be united in one state. The humiliation of Prussia began the reform of Prussia, which led to the modernization of the

1806

- **July 12**
  Napoléon proclaims the Confederation of the Rhine, a new German organization in central Europe to replace the Holy Roman Empire.

- **August 1**
  Napoléon announces that he will no longer recognize the existence of the Holy Roman Empire; Francis II, Holy Roman Emperor, declares that he will be known from that time on as Francis I, Emperor of Austria, a title he created two years earlier.

1813

- **October 16–19**
  Napoléon is defeated at the Battle of Leipzig (Battle of the Nations).

- **November 4**
  The allies opposing Napoléon formally dissolve the Confederation of the Rhine.

1814

- **November 1**
  The Congress of Vienna convenes.

1815

- **June 8**
  Participants at the Congress of Vienna announce the formation of the German Confederation.

- **June 12**
  German university students in Jena form a student association (one of the Burschenschaften) for the purpose of advancing liberal and patriotic ideals.

state under the prime ministers Heinrich Friedrich Karl vom und zum Stein (Baron Stein) and Karl August Hardenberg. Prussian modernization took advantage of a growing German nationalism directed against the French and their occupation of Prussia and other German states.

Napoléon's grip on Europe and the German states began to loosen as a result of his invasion of Russia in 1812, which ended in disaster. The defection of a number of the German states forced him to mount a campaign in 1813 to bring them back into the French sphere. The War of Liberation (Befreiungskriege), the German name for what is also called the War of the Sixth Coalition, culminated in the Battle of Leipzig, also known as the Battle of the Nations, on October 16–19, 1813. French forces were forced to withdraw from east of the Rhine, and the defeat eventually led to Napoléon's abdication on April 6, 1814.

The leaders of the European nations came together in November 1814 in Vienna to settle the many issues arising from this series of wars and the dissolution of the Holy Roman Empire. Peace meant the creation of a balance of power and an international framework that would ensure the future peace. The participants at Vienna sought to create a solution that the European states would accept. By embracing the forces of stability—conservatism, legitimacy, and the balance of power—the leaders at the Congress of Vienna wanted to suppress those forces that could disrupt the future status quo, forces such as nationalism and liberalism.

For the German states, the political result of the Congress of Vienna was the creation of the German Confederation. Signed on June 8, 1815, the Act of Confederation created an association of thirty-nine German states to replace the old Holy Roman Empire, which had encompassed more than three hundred. As part of the new confederation, a permanent diet (the Bundesversammlung, or Federal Convention) was established at Frankfurt. Under the presidency of Austria, this general assembly represented the sovereigns of each of the thirty-nine German states, not the people of those states. Under the constitution of the German Confederation, each state was to be independent in internal affairs, but war between the individual states was forbidden, and the consent of the confederacy was necessary for foreign war. The German Confederation had roughly the same boundaries as the Holy Roman Empire at the time of the French Revolution. The creation of the confederation frustrated the expressed desires of German nationalists.

German nationalism had blossomed during the Napoleonic Wars. The combination of nationalistic ideals, Romantic influences, and a hatred of the French and their occupation spurred support for the war against Napoléon. With the victory over the French, German students saw an opportunity to advance the nationalist cause. They founded the first of the student Burschenschaften (student fraternities) at Jena in June 1815; more were soon established at other German universities. The Burschenschaften, whose motto was "Honor, Liberty, Fatherland," fostered liberal and nationalistic ideals. The conservative leadership of the Germanic states offered no progress toward the students' goal of a united Germany. Therefore, students staged the Wartburg Festival in October 1817; it gave the nationalist students an opportunity to express their frustration with the leaders of the Germanic states for the lack of progress in the creation of a German nation. Over five hundred people celebrated the three hundredth anniversary of Martin Luther's posting of his *Ninety-five Theses* and the victory over Napoléon at the Battle of Leipzig. At the bonfire that marked the high point of the celebration, students consigned various symbols of the old order to the flames, including Kotzebue's *Geschichte des deutschen Reichs* (History of the German Empires). The festival was attended by Karl Ludwig Sand, who was a member of several of the Burschenschaften. This festival has been characterized as the first public protest against the decisions of the Congress of Vienna.

Two years later, in March 1819, Sand murdered Kotzebue, who was reputed to have ridiculed the Burschenschaften and whom Sand considered a traitor. Metternich used Kotzebue's murder to pressure the members of the German Confederation into acting against what were perceived to be threats against the conservative order established at the Congress of Vienna and to issue the Carlsbad Decrees. The Carlsbad Decrees proved to be Metternich's most effective weapon against the students and the press in the fight against liberalism and nationalism.

About the Author

Prince Klemens von Metternich (1773–1859) is generally credited as the author of the Carlsbad Decrees. More than any other European statesman of the time, Metternich, the Austrian foreign minister, epitomized the conservative point of view. Throughout his early career as a diplomat and politician, he gained a reputation for brashness and self-assurance in a variety of posts, including Austrian envoy to the elector of Saxony, ambassador to Berlin, and Austria's minister of state. He also acquired a reputation as something of a ladies' man amid charges that he had amorous relationships with Napoléon's stepdaughter and two of Napoléon's sisters. He ingratiated himself throughout Europe, but particularly in France. Metternich played a key role in diplomatic negotiations leading to the 1814 Treaty of Paris between France and the Sixth Coalition and as a delegate to the Congress of Vienna. In 1821 he was appointed chancellor of Austria, a position he held until 1848, when he resigned in the wake of liberal nationalist revolutionary activities across the Austrian Empire and within the German states.

The Carlsbad Decrees were part of Metternich's larger approach to the management of Europe through a diplomatic system. So closely is he associated with the period from the defeat of Napoléon in 1815 until the outbreak of revolutions in 1848 that those years are often referred to as the "Age of Metternich." Metternich used his considerable diplomatic skill to suppress revolutionary impulses that sought to disrupt the conservative status quo established after Napoléon's defeat.

Time Line

1817

- **October 18**
  German students attend the Wartburg Festival celebrating the tercentenary of Martin Luther's *Ninety-five Theses* and the victory over Napoléon at the Battle of Leipzig.

1819

- **March 23**
  Karl Ludwig Sand, a German university student, murders August von Kotzebue, a prominent conservative German dramatist, in Manheim.

- **August 6–31**
  The larger members of the German Confederation meet to address the issue of nationalist unrest and arrive at a series of resolutions.

- **September 20**
  The German Confederation formally adopts the Carlsbad Decrees.

- **October**
  The central commission of inquiry created by the Carlsbad Decrees and charged with investigating revolutionary activities in member states of the German Confederation holds its first meeting.

- **November 26**
  As a result of the Carlsbad Decrees, the members of the Jena Burschenschaft formally dissolve their organization; that same night many of the students form a secret society to carry on the spirit of the one that had been outlawed.

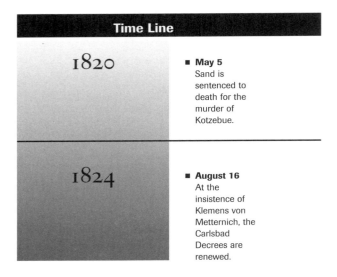

Time Line

1820
- **May 5**
  Sand is sentenced to death for the murder of Kotzebue.

1824
- **August 16**
  At the insistence of Klemens von Metternich, the Carlsbad Decrees are renewed.

Explanation and Analysis of the Document

At a special conference of selected ministers and envoys of the major states of the German Confederation held at Carlsbad, Bohemia, from August 6 through 31, 1819, Metternich sought to take advantage of the concern caused by recent revolutionary actions to take steps to suppress liberal and nationalist agitation in the German states. The most dramatic of those events was the assassination of the German literary figure August von Kotzebue by the university student Karl Sand. Metternich planned to use the specter of revolutionary agitation to persuade the assembled representatives of the urgent need for action. In his opening address, Metternich divided the business for discussion into two categories: first, matters of urgent importance needing to be addressed immediately—that is, the revolutionary agitation—and, second, questions affecting the fundamental constitution of the German Confederation. Over the course of the next twenty-three meetings, a unanimous consensus emerged concerning the need to suppress revolutionary activity. However, the assembled representatives of ten of the German states could not agree on the constitutional issues, so the Carlsbad Decrees addressed only the curbing of revolutionary activity. They were submitted to the Bundesversammlung (the Federal Convention) in September 1819 and formally adopted on September 20. The Carlsbad Decrees are divided into three distinct parts: those addressing the universities, those having to do with press censorship, and those concerning the formation of a central investigative commission to uncover revolutionary plots within the German Confederation.

◆ **"Provisional Decree Relative to the Measures to Be Taken concerning the Universities"**

Section 1 of the first decree directs the sovereign to appoint an "extraordinary commissioner" for each university. The commissioner was to reside at the university, enforce the existing regulations in the strictest fashion, and keep an eye on the faculty. The purpose of this oversight was to ensure that students maintained proper behavior and morals, and the extraordinary commissioners were given powers commensurate with their duties.

Section 2 directs members of the confederation to remove professors and other teachers who could be proved to have corrupted the minds of the youth with teachings that were "hostile to order and public tranquility." Section 2 further states that a professor or tutor who was removed from one university could not be employed at any other educational institution in the confederation. Section 3 directs that existing laws against secret or unauthorized student associations be rigorously enforced and extended to include the Burschenschaften. The decree instructs confederation members to refuse public employment to individuals who maintained their association with the student associations after the publication of the decree. Section 4 declares that a student dismissed from one university in the confederation was not to be admitted to any other university in the confederation. A student who left one university would not be allowed to enroll in another without an "attestation of his good conduct at the university he has left."

In summary, the "Measures to Be Taken concerning the Universities" required confederation members to appoint overseers to their universities, restricted the faculty to teaching only what the government deemed inoffensive, outlawed student organizations that were formed to promote liberalism and nationalism, prevented expelled students from enrolling in other universities, and ensured that students who did belong to the Burschenschaften would not be employed by members states of the German Confederation.

◆ **"Measures for Preventing the Abuses of the Press"**

Section 1 of the second decree requires all daily publications and periodicals of less than twenty pages to obtain the consent of the authorities to be published. Publications not covered by the new regulations remained under the jurisdiction of existing laws. Any German state was permitted to raise a complaint about a publication in any other state; the complaint would initiate proceedings against the author or the editor of the work.

Section 2 authorizes each state to adopt any necessary measures to administer the decree. Section 3 criticizes current laws on publishing in the German states, the implication being that the states should pass better ones. Section 4 holds each of the German states responsible for what was published in that state. The state in which the offending material was published was considered answerable not only to the offended state but also to all members of the German Confederation.

Section 5 exhorts member states to prevent press-related complaints from arising, so as to secure peace and harmony within the confederation. It requires the members of the Confederation to "devote their most serious attention" to the supervision of materials published within their boundaries. Section 6 allows a member state that perceived itself to be injured by writings published in another state and that was unsatisfied by the response of the other state to its complaints to take its case to the Federal Convention, which was to appoint a commission to investigate and rule on the matter. The findings of the commission were to be implemented. If a commission determined that a publication "compromised the dignity of the Germanic body, the safety of any of its members, or the internal peace of Germany," the Federal Convention was obligated to compel the state in which the offending material had been published to suppress that material. Thus, Section 6 allowed the members of the confederation, through the Federal Convention, to intervene in the internal workings of an individual member state.

Section 7 declares that if authors, editors, and publishers complied with the press restrictions, they would not be punished as individuals if the publication with which they were associated was suppressed by the Federal Convention, but editors were forbidden to publish anything similar for five years. Section 8 gives the members of the Confederation a deadline of six months in which to inform the Federal Convention of the measures they had implemented to carry out the press laws. Section 9 requires every work printed within the borders of the German Confederation to bear the name of its printer or editor. Works that did not were to be confiscated and the offending person or persons punished. Section 10 declares that the decree was to remain in force for five years from its initial publication and that before its expiration the diet was to give its attention to how article 18 of the Federal Constitution (governing the conduct of the press) could be used to limit the press in member states. Section 10 thereby sought to compel the Federal Convention to reconcile the federal constitution with the "Measure for Preventing the Abuses of the Press."

These measures were only partially successful. Standards were less draconian in the individual German states, and many authors and publishers found loopholes that enabled them to evade censorship. Nevertheless, it has been estimated that only about 25 percent of the books that were approved in Germany were also approved in Austria, suggesting that the censorship restrictions had a dampening effect on political discourse in Austria.

◆ "Decree Relative to the Formation of a Central Commission"

The "Decree Relative to the Formation of a Central Commission, for the Purpose of Ulterior Inquiry respecting Revolutionary Plots, Discovered in Some of the States of the Confederation" creates a commission to investigate revolutionary activities within the German states and their link to liberal and nationalist agitation outside the confederation. Article 1 establishes a seven-person commission to meet in Mainz ("Mentz" in the accompanying document) within fifteen days after the date of the decree; Article 2 charges the commission with seeking out those secret revolutionary associations that wanted to harm the confederation or its individual members. Articles 3 describes how commission members were to be appointed, while Article 4 names the qualifications required of commission members. Article 5 instructs the central commission to oversee all current and future investigations. Article 6 compels the

Klemens von Metternich (© Bettmann/CORBIS)

members of the Confederation to cooperate with commission. Article 7 gives the commission authority to examine any individual it deems necessary. Articles 8–10 regulate the proceedings of the commission.

A Prussian state police agency called the Immediate Investigation Commission, based in Berlin, had already begun collecting enormous amounts of information on dissidents and revolutionaries. The commission was headed by the municipal police chief, but it was under the authority of the chief police officer of the ministry of justice, Karl Albert von Kamptz. A law book that von Kamptz had written was one of the books that had been burned at the Wartburg Festival, and perhaps in retaliation he was obsessive about rooting out radicalism. The ministry maintained a number of prisons in and around Berlin, where revolutionaries were held and interrogated, their letters and papers were examined minutely, and reports were compiled. In a footnote, one of the compilers of these reports was E. T. A. Hoffman, one of Austria's foremost poets, who worked as a lawyer for the ministry of justice and who used information from his work in several of his books.

Audience

The audience for the Carlsbad Decrees was threefold: the member states of the German Confederation; the gen-

"The duty of this commissioner shall be to ... observe carefully the spirit with which the professors and the tutors are guided in their public and private lectures; to endeavour, ... to give the instruction a salutary direction, suited to the future destiny of the students, and to devote a constant attention to every thing which may tend to the maintenance of morality, good order and decency among the youths."

("Provisional Decree Relative to the Measures to Be Taken concerning the Universities," Section 1)

"The governments [of the confederation will] ... remove from their universities and other establishments of instruction, the professors and other public teachers, against whom it may be proved, that in departing from their duty, in overstepping the bounds of their duty, in abusing their legitimate influence over the minds of the youth ... they have shown themselves incapable of executing the important functions entrusted to them."

("Provisional Decree Relative to the Measures to Be Taken concerning the Universities," Section 2)

"Each government of the confederation is accountable for the writings published under its jurisdiction, and consequently for all those comprehended in the principle regulation of Art. I [Section 1]; and when these writings wound the dignity or safety of another state of the confederation, or make attacks upon its constitution or its administration, the government which tolerates them is responsible, not only to the state which suffers, directly therefrom, but to the whole confederation."

("Measures for Preventing the Abuses of the Press," Section 4)

"The object of this commission is, to make careful and detailed inquiries respecting the facts, the origins and the multiplied ramifications of the secret revolutionary and demagogic associations, directed against the political constitution and internal repose, as well of the confederation in general, as of the individual members thereof; of which indications more or less conclusive have been already discovered, or may result from ulterior researches."

("Decree Relative to the Formation of a Central Commission," Article 2)

"The central commission is authorized to examine every individual whom it may judge necessary."

("Decree Relative to the Formation of a Central Commission," Article 7) eral population of the German states, specifically those who would disrupt the peace by liberal or nationalist agitation; and the leaders of the European state system. Metternich sought to use the Carlsbad Decrees not only to suppress liberalism and nationalism but also to unify the German states. The decrees passed by the Federal Convention in September 1819 compelled the member nations to act in concert and to submit to the will of the majority. The decrees gave warning to those liberal and nationalist elements within the German states that activism would not be tolerated. Those who sought to disrupt the status quo would be punished. The decrees also gave notice to the European community that revolutionary agitation would not be tolerated in the German states, thereby encouraging other Europeans states to act similarly. This view was consistent with the conservative attitudes of the Great Powers of Europe.

Impact

The results of the Carlsbad Decrees were dramatic. The forces of German conservatism now had the weapons with which to combat liberalism and nationalism at a basic level. The decrees banned nationalist student organizations, forbade student activism on pain of expulsion, curtailed faculty involvement in liberal and nationalist causes, dismissed those faculty members who had been active, and prohibited publishing nationalist and liberal materials at any level. Still, as a result of the Carlsbad Decrees, the members of the Jena Burschenschaft dissolved their organization, but that same night many of the students formed a

secret society to carry on the spirit of the one that had been outlawed. As one historian of the period has written:

> During the remainder of Metternich's age, there appeared to be almost no progress at all, and in the long years of this stagnation the hopes of German liberals almost died. Spies and officials of the governments persecuted the men who had helped to liberate Germany from Napoleon, and who now looked forward to still better things. (Turner, p. 224)

Among those persecuted were the educator Friedrich Ludwig Jahn, who had founded the Prussian gymnastic societies; the poet Ernst Moritz Arndt; the writer Johann Joseph von Görres; and the philosopher Jakob Friedrich Fries. Metternich hoped to use the commission of inquiry to root out subversives in the German states. His belief that secret societies in Germany and throughout Europe were centrally organized was never proved. The commission functioned for nearly eight years, during which time proceedings were instituted against 161 individuals, forty-four of whom were acquitted.

In a larger sense, the Carlsbad Decrees provided Metternich with the ability to coerce those German states that were reluctant to follow his lead. By using the power of the confederation, Metternich was able to force a number of the more independent-minded states to adhere to his wishes. Through the Carlsbad Decrees and other actions, Metternich suppressed revolutionary impulses for a generation. The conservatives' use of secret police, coercion, and censorship prevailed until the continent-wide revolutionary

Questions for Further Study

1. Examine the Maastricht Treaty of European Union in the context of nationalism in Germany in the nineteenth century. What circumstances changed that made nationalism in Germany and elsewhere in Europe less pronounced, as reflected in the Maastricht Treaty?

2. Do you believe that it would be fair to trace German Nazism, as exemplified by Hitler's Proclamation to the German People and the Nuremberg Laws, to the nationalist impulse the Carlsbad Decrees attempted to suppress?

3. History as it is often studied examines major events and important historical people: the German Confederation, Metternich, the Napoleonic Wars, the Congress of Vienna, and so forth. How do you think the Carlsbad Decrees might have affected the daily lives of ordinary Germans—if at all?

4. In contemporary life, nationalism is often associated more with conservatives than liberals; liberals generally are more likely to view the world through an internationalist lens. What has changed between now and the early nineteenth century? Why would liberal students in Germany at that time have advocated a strong nationalist point of view?

5. To what extent do you think the Carlsbad Decrees contributed to the eruption of revolution throughout Europe in 1848? What lesson does this teach about censorship?

explosion of 1848, when revolts and insurrections for reform rocked France, Germany, Austria, Switzerland, Poland, Italy, and even Brazil in South America. The forces of liberalism and nationalism had been forestalled for over three decades, but the revolutionary eruption of 1848 ended Metternich's career and initiated a sequence of events that pitted Prussia and Austria against each other for the leadership of German unification. Metternich was able to delay German nationalism, but he could not eradicate it.

Further Reading

■ Books

Artz, Frederick B. *Reaction and Revolution, 1814–1832.* New York: Harper & Row, 1934. Reprint. New York: HarperCollins Publishers, 1977.

Billinger, Robert D., Jr. *Metternich and the German Question: States' Rights and Federal Duties, 1820–1834.* Newark, N.J.: University of Delaware Press, 1991.

Kissinger, Henry A. *The World Restored: Metternich, Castlereagh, and the Problems of Peace, 1812–22.* Boston: Houghton Mifflin, 1957.

Krüger, Peter, and Paul W. Schröder, eds. *The Transformation of European Politics, 1763–1848: Episode or Model in Modern History?* New York: Oxford University Press, 1996.

Turner, Edward Raymond. *Europe, 1789–1920.* Garden City, N.Y.: Doubleday, Page, 1920.

■ Web Sites

"The Memoirs of Prince Metternich." Humanities and Social Sciences Online (H Net) Web site.
    http://www.h-net.org/~habsweb/sourcetexts/mettsrc.htm.

—Stephen Balzarini

Carlsbad Decrees

Provisional Decree Relative to the Measures to Be Taken concerning the Universities

Sect. 1. The Sovereign shall make choice for each university of an extraordinary commissioner, furnished with suitable instructions and powers, residing in the place where the university is established; he may be either the actual curator, or any other person whom the government may think fit to appoint.

The duty of this commissioner shall be to watch over the most rigorous observation of the laws and disciplinary regulations; to observe carefully the spirit with which the professors and tutors are guided in their public and private lectures; to endeavour, without interfering directly in the scientific courses, or in the method of instruction, to give the instruction a salutary direction, suited to the future destiny of the students, and to devote a constant attention to every thing which may tend to the maintenance of morality, good order and decency among the youths.

Sect. 2. The governments of the states, members of the confederation, reciprocally engage to remove from their universities and other establishments of instruction, the professors and other public teachers, against whom it may be proved, that in departing from their duty, in overstepping the bounds of their duty, in abusing their legitimate influence over the minds of youth, by the propagation of pernicious dogmas, hostile to order and public tranquillity, or in sapping the foundation of existing establishments, they have shown themselves incapable of executing the important functions entrusted to them, without any obstacle whatever being allowed to impede the measure taken against them, so long as the present decree shall remain in force, and until definitive arrangements on this point be adopted.

A professor or tutor thus excluded, cannot be admitted in any other state of the confederation to any other establishment of public instruction.

Sect. 3. The laws long since made against secret or unauthorized associations at the universities, shall be maintained in all their force and rigour, and shall be particularly extended with so much the more severity against the well-known society formed some years ago under the name of the General Burgenschaft, as it has for its basis an idea, absolutely inadmissible, of community and continued correspondence between the different universities.

The governments shall mutually engage to admit to no public employment any individuals who may continue or enter into any of those associations after the publication of the present decree.

Sect. 4. No student who, by a decree of the Academic Senate confirmed by the government commissioner, or adopted on his application, shall be dismissed from a university, or who, in order to escape from such a sentence, shall withdraw himself, shall be received in any other university; and in general, no student shall be received at another university without a sufficient attestation of his good conduct at the university he has left.

Decree Relative to the Measures for Preventing the Abuses of the Press

Sect. 1. As long as the present decree shall be in force, no writing appearing in the form of a daily paper or periodical pamphlet, which does not contain more than 20 printed leaves, shall be issued from the press without the previous consent of the public authority.

The works not comprehended under this regulation shall continue to be regulated by the laws now existing, or which may be hereafter enacted; and if any work of the above-mentioned description shall give rise to a complaint on the part of any state of the confederation, the government to which the complaint may be addressed shall cause proceedings to be instituted in its name against the authors or editors of the said work.

Sect. 2. Each government is at liberty to adopt, for the maintenance and execution of the present decree, those measures which may appear the most suitable; it being well understood that these measures must be recognized proper to fulfil the object of the principal regulation of Art. 1.

Sect. 3. The present decree being called for by the necessity generally acknowledged of adopting some preventive measures against the abuse of the press in Germany, as long as this decree shall remain in force, the laws attributing to the tribunals the prosecution and punishment of the abuses and offences committed by the press, inasmuch as they apply to the writings specified in Art. 1, cannot be considered as sufficient in any state of the confederation.

Sect. 4. Each government of the confederation is accountable for the writings published under its jurisdiction, and consequently for all those comprehended in the principal regulation of Art. I; and when these writings wound the dignity or safety of another state of the confederation, or make attacks upon its constitution or its administration, the government which tolerates them is responsible, not only to the state which suffers directly therefrom, but to the whole confederation.

Sect. 5. In order that this responsibility, founded in the nature of the Germanic Union and inseparable from its preservation, may not give rise to disagreements which might compromise the amicable relations subsisting between the confederated states, all the members of the confederation must enter into a solemn engagement to devote their most serious attention to the superintendence which the present decree prescribes, and to exercise it in such a manner as to prevent as much as possible all reciprocal complaints and discussions.

Sect. 6. In order, however, to assure better the guarantee of the moral and political inviolability of the states of the confederation, which is the object of the present decree, it is to be understood, that in case a government believe itself injured by writings published under another government, and cannot obtain complete satisfaction by amicable and diplomatic representations, that government will be at liberty to prefer its complaint to the Diet, which, in such a case, will hold itself bound to appoint a commission to examine the writing which shall have been thus denounced, and if the report of the commission state it to be necessary, to command the suppression of the said writing, and also to prohibit its continuance if it be of the number of periodical publications.

The Diet will proceed also, without a previous denunciation, and of its own authority, against every publication comprised in the principal regulation of Art. I. in whatever state of Germany it may be published, if in the opinion of a commission appointed to consider thereof, it may have compromised the dignity of the Germanic body, the safety of any of its members, or the internal peace of Germany, without any recourse being afforded against the judgment given in such a case, which shall be carried into execution by the government that is responsible for the condemned publication.

Sect. 7. The editor of a journal, or other periodical publication, that may be suppressed by command of the Diet, shall not be allowed, during the space of five years, to conduct any similar publication in any states of the confederation.

The authors, editors and publishers of newspapers or periodical writings and others, mentioned in the first paragraph of Article 1, shall be, in other respects, upon submitting to the regulation of that article, free from all responsibility; and the judgments of the Diet, mentioned in the preceding article, will be directed only against the publications, without affecting individuals.

Sect. 8. The confederated states engage within six months to acquaint the Diet with the measures which each shall have adopted to carry into execution the first article of this decree.

Sect. 9. Every work printed in Germany, whether comprehended in the regulations of this decree or not, must bear the name of the printer or the editor; and if it be of the number of periodical publications, of the principal editor. Every work in circulation in any of the states of the confederation, with respect to which these conditions have not been complied with, will be seized and confiscated, and the person or persons who may have published and sold it condemned, according to the circumstances of the case, to the payment of fine, or some other punishment proportionate to the offence.

Sect. 10. The present decree shall remain in force during five years from the date of its publication. Before the term of its expiration the Diet will take in to mature consideration in what manner the 18th article of the federal act relative to the uniformity of laws on the conduct of the press in the confederated states, can be carried into execution, by definitively fixing the legal limits of the press in Germany.

Decree Relative to the Formation of a Central Commission, for the Purpose of Ulterior Inquiry respecting Revolutionary Plots, Discovered in some of the States of the Confederation

Art. 1. In 15 days from the date of this decree, an extraordinary commission of inquiry, appointed by the Diet and composed of 7 members, including the President, shall assemble in the city of Mentz, a fortress of the confederation.

2. The object of this commission is, to make careful and detailed inquiries respecting the facts, the origin and the multiplied ramifications of the secret

revolutionary and demagogic associations, directed against the political constitution and internal repose, as well of the confederation in general, as of the individual members thereof; of which indications more or less conclusive have been already discovered, or may result from ulterior researches.

3. The Diet elects by the plurality of suffrages the seven members of the confederation who are to appoint the members of the central commission.

4. None can be elected members of the central commission but civil officers, who in the state which appoints them are fulfilling, or have fulfilled, judicial functions, or have been engaged in preparing processes in important investigations.

5. In order to attain the end proposed, the central commission shall undertake the general direction of the local investigations which have already been commenced, or may hereafter be instituted.

6. All the members of the confederation, in the territories in which investigations of this nature have been already commenced, engaged to point out to the central commission, immediately after it shall be constituted, the local authorities to whom the investigations shall have been previously confided.

7. The central commission is authorized to examine every individual whom it may judge necessary. To secure his appearance, it will apply to the superior authority of the members of the confederation, or to the authorities who, in virtue of Art. 6, may be pointed out for this purpose.

Articles 8, 9, and 10, which conclude this decree, and the proposition of the Imperial Minister, consist merely of directions for regulating the routine proceedings of the central commission.

plurality of suffrages	the most votes (i.e., a majority was not required)
tutors	in this context, instructors of individual university students

TREATY OF CÓRDOBA

"This kingdom of America shall be recognized as a sovereign and independent nation and shall, in future, be called the Mexican Empire."

Overview

On August 24, 1821, Agustín de Iturbide, general of the Mexican Army of the Three Guarantees, and Juan O'Donojú, captain general of New Spain and representative of the Spanish Crown, signed the Treaty of Córdoba, which granted independence to Mexico. (The accompanying document uses the anglicized spelling "Cordova" and the variant spelling "O'Donnoju.") The treaty brought to a close the long and complex Mexican War of Independence (1810–1821).

The Mexican War of Independence occurred during has been called the "Age of Revolution," a period from roughly 1760 to 1830, during which revolutionary movements flowered on both sides of the Atlantic. Countries broke free of absolutist monarchies and established republics. Enlightenment thought, particularly ideas about human equality and the relationship between government and the governed, encouraged both social and political revolution and caused people to challenge the established social hierarchy and the role of religion in politics. The Mexican War of Independence proved to be much more conservative than many other contemporaneous revolutions. It began with both social and political elements but ended largely as a political revolution, gaining Mexico independence but leaving its society largely unchanged. Additionally, like most of the Latin American wars of independence, the relationship between the Catholic Church and the state was largely unquestioned. The Catholic Church retained much of its authority, special rights, and powers after Mexican independence.

Context

The Mexican War of Independence took place during a very turbulent time for the Spanish Empire. The colonies, increasingly unhappy with Spain, desired autonomy. At the same time, there was increasing social tension between the *criollos*, those of Spanish descent born in the New World, and the *peninsulares*, Spaniards from the mother country. The era saw the growth of *criollismo*, a

movement promoting pride in American origin and empowering the *criollo* population. *Peninsulares* predominated in the highest offices of the government and Catholic Church in the colonies, including Mexico, even though *criollos* outnumbered them by a factor of ten or more. Compounding this social tension was the legal, organized discrimination against others under the *sistema de castas* (caste system), which differentiated between individuals by their *calidad*, or "quality." Under this system, mestizos (people of mixed European and Indian heritage) and Indians were denied many of the rights enjoyed by both *peninsulares* and *criollos*.

Spain itself was entering a very troubled time. In 1808 France's Napoléon Bonaparte invaded Spain, deposed King Ferdinand VII, and installed his brother, Joseph Bonaparte, on the throne of Spain as Joseph I of Spain. This simultaneously diverted Spanish attention from the colonies and provided a rallying point for the fighters in the War of Mexican Independence and, indeed, for revolutionaries across the Americas. Many Spanish colonies broke away from the mother country when Napoleon deposed Ferdinand VII. The colonies cited Spanish law that declared that colonies belonged to the monarch, not to Spain. Therefore, the colonies would rule themselves while the "false king" was on the throne of Spain. By the time the Treaty of Valençay restored Ferdinand VII to the throne in December of 1813, the colonies had grown accustomed to governing themselves. The independence movements, including Mexico's, grew from this. For the next decade, Spain fought wars all over Latin America, trying to keep its crumbling empire together. Mexico was the first of Spain's American colonies to successfully break away.

The Mexican War of Independence began on September 16, 1810, with the "Grito de Dolores" (Cry of Dolores), a speech delivered by the *criollo* priest Miguel Hidalgo y Costilla, who called upon his parishioners in the community of Dolores to revolt. Hidalgo had long worked to improve the welfare of his parishioners, trying to stimulate the local economy and provide employment through practices such as grape cultivation and beekeeping. Hidalgo's goals in the revolution included social and economic reform that would benefit both *criollos* and Indians. Soon after Hidalgo gave the "Grito de Dolores" speech, the Bat-

1808

- Napoléon Bonaparte invades Spain and has his brother Joseph crowned king of Spain.

1810

- September 16 Miguel Hidalgo calls his parish to arms with the "Grito de Dolores."

1811

- July 30 Hidalgo is executed; José María Morelos assumes command of the army.

1813

- November 6 Members of the Congress of Chilpancingo sign the Solemn Act of the Declaration of Independence of Northern America.

1814

- October 22 Members of the Congress of Chilpancingo sign the Constitution of Apatzingán.

1815

- December 22 Morelos is executed.

- War degenerates into regional guerilla activity led by Guadalupe Victoria in Puebla and Vicente Guerrero in Oaxaca.

tle of Guanajuato, the first battle of the War of Independence, was fought.

The peasant army, only nominally under the direction of Hidalgo and his ally, Captain Ignacio Allende, proceeded to sack and loot the city, massacring both *peninsulares* and *criollos*. Although Hidalgo's army was largely successful for several months, within a year Hidalgo was captured, tried, and executed. After the death of Hidalgo, José María Morelos y Pavón arose as one of the leaders of the War of Independence. Like Hidalgo, Morelos was a priest who was dedicated to social reform. Under his leadership, the Congress of Chilpancingo was convened in 1813. In an initial document endorsed by Morelos, the Congress called for Mexican independence, the establishment of the Roman Catholic Church as the country's sole religion, division of government into executive, legislative, and judiciary branches, and the abolition of slavery and the ending of the *sistema de castas*. Morelos was captured and executed late in 1815.

From 1815 on, the war devolved into guerrilla activity led by Vicente Guerrero, Morelos's deputy, and Guadalupe Victoria, which continued until near the war's end in 1821. The guerrillas met with mixed success. In 1820 General Agustín de Iturbide was appointed to lead the royalist forces against the insurgents. The year 1820, however, also marked the outbreak of the Spanish Civil War, in which liberals sought to press constitutional reforms and limitations on the Spanish monarch. Faced with the loss of prestige, many conservative *criollos*, including Iturbide, chose to change allegiances and support the independence movement.

Iturbide's defection to the insurgents was codified in a document known as the Plan de Iguala, or the Plan of the Three Guarantees. Iturbide and Guerrero, the architects of the plan, agreed to unite their forces. The three guarantees that the plan laid out were Mexican independence, establishment of Roman Catholicism as the state religion, and legal codification of social equality through the abolition of the *sistema de castas*. Iturbide and Guerrero further agreed that Mexico would become a constitutional monarchy. The plan, signed on February 24, 1821, was the basis for the Treaty of Córdoba.

Iturbide, now head of the newly christened Army of the Three Guarantees, quickly cemented the insurgents' victory on the battlefield, which led to the resignation of Spain's highest-ranking political representative in New Spain, Juan O'Donojú. Iturbide and O'Donojú signed the Treaty of Córdoba on August 24, 1821, formalizing Mexican independence and establishing a constitutional monarchy.

In accordance with the treaty, Ferdinand VII was called upon to become king of Mexico. When he refused, the throne was offered to other members of his family, each of whom also declined, refusing to recognize Mexican independence. The Spanish legislature also declined to recognize Mexican independence, declaring it illegal on February 13, 1822. Ultimately, Iturbide himself assumed the throne. After a short reign (1822–1823), Iturbide was overthrown by General Antonio López de Santa Anna and

Guadalupe Victoria, who called for the establishment of a republic. Spain tried to retake Mexico several times, most significantly through an invasion from Cuba in June 1829. Mexican forces defeated the invaders, and Spain was compelled to recognize Mexican independence in 1830.

About the Author

Agustín de Iturbide helped to craft two of the documents that were foundational for the establishment of an independent Mexico: the Plan de Iguala and the Treaty of Córdoba. Iturbide was born into a high-status *criollo* family in Valladolid, New Spain (in the modern-day state of Michoacán, Mexico). He entered the army at an early age, and when the Mexican War of Independence broke out, he chose to fight for Spain, becoming one of the most important leaders of the royalist army. He fought against the insurgents with mixed success; ultimately, however, Iturbide was never able to defeat the insurgent leader Guerrero. This, coupled with the adoption in Spain of a liberal, republican constitution, led him to break with the royalist army and join with the insurgents.

When the new revolutionary government was unable to find a member of the Bourbon dynasty who was willing to take the crown of Mexico, Iturbide took the throne, becoming Emperor Agustín I. The nature of Iturbide's rise to power is hotly debated: some argue that he assumed the crown at the behest of his troops and the people of Mexico. Others contend that Iturbide's rise to power was nothing more than a coup and that public support for him was largely manufactured. Agustín I's reign was very short (1822–1823), and he was quickly overthrown in favor of a more liberal, republican form of government. Sent into exile in 1823, Iturbide tried to return in 1824, only to be arrested and executed.

Other authors of the treaty and its antecedent, the Plan de Iguala, include Vicente Guerrero and Juan O'Donojú. Guerrero was born in 1782 in Tixtla, a town in the Sierra Madre del Sur, a mountain range in southern Mexico. He joined the revolt against Spanish rule in 1810, rising through the ranks to become lieutenant colonel by 1812. Guerrero was one of the most effective commanders for the insurgents in the War of Mexican Independence and fought successfully against Iturbide before they joined forces to form the Army of the Three Guarantees. After the Treaty of Córdoba was signed, Guerrero initially supported Iturbide as Emperor Agustín I. Iturbide's support of the wealthy *criollos*, however, turned Guerrero against him. Guerrero allied with Antonio López de Santa Anna to overthrow Iturbide, and Mexico became a republic. Guerrero was elected Mexico's second president in 1829. Later that year he was deposed by his vice president, Anastasio Bustamante y Oseguera, who had him executed in 1831.

O'Donojú was born of Irish descent in Seville, Spain, in 1762, joining the army at an early age. In 1814 he was appointed minister of war and then became aide de camp to Ferdinand VII. He served as the last viceroy of Mexico from

Time Line

1820

- **November**
  General Agustín de Iturbide leads the Spanish army against Guerrero's troops.

1821

- **February 24**
  Iturbide and Guerrero join forces and sign the Plan de Iguala; the combined army is known as the Army of the Three Guarantees.

- **August 24**
  The Treaty of Córdoba signed.

1822

- **July 21**
  Iturbide is proclaimed Emperor Agustín I.

- **February 13**
  The Spanish legislature declares the Treaty of Córdoba illegal.

1823

- General Antonio López de Santa Anna and Guadalupe Victoria overthrow Iturbide.

- **April 8**
  The Mexican congress exiles Iturbide to Italy.

1824

- **October**
  Guadalupe Victoria is elected the first president of Mexico.

1824

■ Iturbide comes back to Mexico from exile, tries to recapture his throne, and is captured and executed.

1829

■ **June–September** In Spain's most significant attempt to retake Mexico, Spanish troops led by General Isidro Barradas invade Mexico from Cuba but are repulsed.

1830

■ Spain recognizes Mexican independence.

July to September 1821. Upon his arrival in Mexico in July, he found tremendous support among the population for Iturbide and the Army of the Three Guarantees. O'Donojú, realizing that he had little hope of holding the colony for Spain, called for a meeting with Iturbide. The resulting treaty was modeled closely on the Plan de Iguala. The only real change between the treaty and the plan was the provision that if none of the members of the royal family of Spain would take the Mexican crown, the Mexican congress would choose the ruler. Some historians argue that this provision resulted from a collaboration between Iturbide and O'Donojú and that the two intended for Iturbide to assume the crown from the very beginning. After the signing of the treaty, O'Donojú supervised the removal of Spanish troops from the country. He died of pleurisy in October of 1821.

Explanation and Analysis of the Document

The two paragraphs and fourteen articles of the Treaty of Córdoba outline not only Mexico's new government but also the way in which Mexico should make the transition from war to peace with the establishment of a provisional government. The treaty sets up a constitutional monarchy and calls upon King Ferdinand VII of Spain to become the crowned head of Mexico. The treaty looks to the Plan de Iguala as a guideline, referencing the plan often. In particular, the treaty establishes the "three guarantees" of the Plan de Iguala: constitutional monarchy, establishment of Roman Catholicism as the nation's sole religion, and social equality under the law. These three guarantees were also known as "independence,

religion, and union," and the three colors of the Mexican flag, designed by Iturbide, symbolize these guarantees: green for independence, white for religion, and red for union.

◆ **Paragraphs 1 and 2**

The Treaty of Córdoba begins with a statement of when and where it was signed and the names and titles of its signatories, establishing that it is a legal document. Paragraph 2 outlines the general provisions of the treaty and the condition of Mexico at the time of the treaty. It declares Mexico's independence from Spain, giving the reasons why Mexico has made the declaration and citing its power to do so. Mexico, it asserts, has effectively won the struggle for independence on the battlefield. Therefore, Juan O'Donojú, "desirous of … reconciling the interests of Old and New Spain," has agreed to meet with Iturbide. Both parties state that they are interested in continuing a relationship but say that the relationship must be altered. Mexico will be an independent country but one that still recognizes and celebrates its Spanish roots.

◆ **Articles 1–17**

The remainder of the treaty lays out the way in which Mexico was to establish itself as an independent nation. First and most important, Mexico was to be an independent, sovereign nation referred to as the Mexican Empire. Second, Mexico would be a constitutional monarchy. That is, Mexico would have a monarch, but the monarch's powers would be limited by a constitution. By establishing itself as a constitutional monarchy, Mexico followed in the political steps of Spain and other European powers.

The third and fourth articles outline how the king of Mexico was to be chosen and where his court would be established. The throne of Mexico was to be located in Mexico City, and Mexico City was to be the capital of the empire. The throne was to be offered first to Ferdinand VII of Spain. Should he decline the throne, it was to be offered to Ferdinand's brothers, heirs to the Spanish throne. The desire of Iturbide and other *criollos* to maintain a relationship with Spain is evident here. The treaty provided for Mexico to be governed by the Spanish monarch himself but as a sovereign nation, not a colony; failing that, another member of the Bourbon royal family was to be offered the throne. However, the treaty recognized that Ferdinand and his brothers might refuse the throne: in that case, the Cortes, Mexico's new legislative body, was to choose the monarch. Some historians have suggested that Iturbide himself was behind the wording of this provision; they argue that Iturbide planned from the very beginning to assume the throne himself. Although this is a possibility, there is no direct evidence that it is so.

The fifth article outlines the manner in which Ferdinand VII of Spain was to be notified of Mexico's independence. It also details how the offer of the crown of Mexico should be delivered. The article asks Ferdinand, should he himself refuse the Mexican throne, to encourage one of his brothers to accept the throne for the economic good of both Spain and Mexico and to reaffirm the ties between the

Boy sitting at the foot of a statue of the Mexican hero José Morelos in Cuernavaca, Mexico (AP/Wide World Photos)

Miguel Hidalgo's skull lies along with the skulls of three other founding fathers of Mexico in a glass case in a crypt underneath the monument for the Angel of Independence in Mexico City. (AP/Wide World Photos)

nations. Mexicans, it asserts, "wish to see themselves … united to the Spaniards."

The sixth through twelfth articles concern the interim government that would govern Mexico until such time as both the king and legislature were vested with power. The temporary government was to be known as the Provisional Junta. The Junta was to be made up of "eminent" men of the empire, including Juan O'Donojú. Here again we can see the Mexican desire to maintain an active relationship with Spain. The six articles charge the Junta with several responsibilities and duties, the first being to choose three people to govern as regent—that is, to be the executive power of the government until a monarch ascended the throne.

The Junta (and, by extension, the regents they chose) were to be charged with governing the Mexican Empire by the provisions outlined in the Plan de Iguala. Much of the Treaty of Córdoba concerns the first of the three guarantees of the Plan: the establishment of a constitutional monarchy. Here, the second and third guarantees are referenced. The Junta was to ensure that Roman Catholicism became the state religion of Mexico and that the *sistema de castas* was abolished. As the Plan de Iguala states in article 11, in Mexico, "all the inhabitants of the country are citizens, and equal, and the door of advancement is open to virtue and merit" (http://historicaltextarchive.com/sections.php?op=viewarticle&artid=538).

The thirteenth and fourteenth articles outline how the regency and Junta was to be governed until the throne was filled and the Cortes convened. The regency was to govern as the executive body; the Junta was empowered to act as the legislative body. Moreover, the regency and the Junta were charged with determining how members of the Cortes would be chosen. Article 13 references the Plan de Iguala (article 7) again, saying specifically that the primary duty of the Junta, after its nomination, would be to "proceed to the convocation of the Cortes."

The last two articles concern the rights of individuals to remain in or to leave Mexico and Spain. The fifteenth article guarantees Europeans' right to leave Mexico if they so chose, provided, of course, that they paid their debts and were not serving a criminal sentence. Moreover, it asserts that Americans residing in Spain had the right to relocate

"*Lieut.-Gen. Don Juan O'Donnoju ... invited the First Chief of the imperial army, Don Augustín de Iturbide to an interview in order to discuss the great question of independence, disentangling without destroying the bonds which had connected the two Continents.*"

(Paragraph 2)

"*This kingdom of America shall be recognized as a sovereign and independent nation and shall, in future, be called the Mexican Empire.*"

(Articles 1)

"*Conformably to the spirit of the 'Plan of Iguala,' an assembly shall be immediately named, composed of men the most eminent in the empire ... men marked out by the general opinion, whose number may be sufficiently considerable to insure by their collective knowledge the safety of the resolutions which they may take in pursuance of the powers and authority granted them by the following articles.*"

(Article 6)

"*The Provisional Junta, as soon as it is installed, shall govern ad interim according to the existing laws, so far as they may not be contrary to the 'Plan of Iguala' and until the Cortes shall have framed the constitution of the state.*"

(Article 12)

"*The occupation of the capital by the Peninsular troops being an obstacle to the execution of this treaty, it is indispensable to have it removed ... Don Juan O'Donnoju agrees to exercise his authority for the evacuation of the capital by the said troops without loss of blood, and upon the terms of an honorable capitulation.*"

(Article 17)

to Mexico. The sixteenth article imposes limits on article 15: Any public figure, civil or military, who opposed Mexican independence would be exiled from Mexico.

Finally, O'Donojú agrees, in article 17, to evacuate the royalist army occupying Mexico City. The article makes two pointed statements: First, it acknowledges that the royal army had fought bravely. Second, it notes that although General Iturbide was not using military power to force the Spanish army to leave, he and his army were more than capable of doing so.

Audience

The audience of the Treaty of Córdoba was threefold. First, the audience was the Mexican people. The treaty confirmed that they had achieved independence, and it assured them that the transfer of power would be peaceful and that the new government would adhere to the three guarantees of the Plan de Iguala. The document was also, of course, a notification to the Spanish Crown that the colony of Mexico had successfully broken away from the mother country. It notified the Crown of the terms that its representative had agreed to and offered the Mexican throne to the Bourbon dynasty of Spain.

Finally, the document also served as notification to a hemispheric and global audience. The Mexican War of Independence was part of a larger struggle against the Spanish Crown; other Latin American colonies took heart from Mexico's success and redoubled their own efforts. Mexico joined two other newly established American nations, the United States and Haiti, both of which had also fought for independence. On a global scale, by signing the Treaty of Córdoba, Mexico entered into world politics, becoming a sovereign nation.

Impact

Although the Treaty of Córdoba established Mexican independence and allowed for a peaceful transition of power at the war's end, it did not ensure lasting changes in Mexico. Socioculturally, even though the *sistema de castas* had been abolished, the social hierarchy, in fact, remained. Race and color still determined one's place in society, with those of European descent at the top and those of Indian and African ancestry at the bottom. Widespread change that brought greater equality came during the mid-nine-

teenth-century period known as La Reforma (the Reform), under the leadership of the Zapotec Indian Benito Pablo Juárez, who sought to ensure that social equality and equality under the law would be enforced and would become part of the greater Mexican culture.

In economic terms, haciendas (plantations) were still the basis of much of the economy and remained in the hands of the elite. Politically, the constitutional monarchy that the treaty established did not last. Iturbide was overthrown within a year, and the Mexican Empire was no more. Over the course of the next century, the government of Mexico would undergo many changes, including becoming a federal republic, a centralist republic, and a dictatorship. The Mexican Revolution of 1910 eventually established the modern state of Mexico.

Throughout the period from the establishment of the Mexican Empire through the formation of the modern state of Mexico, the second of the three guarantees affirmed by the Treaty of Córdoba, namely, the establishment of Catholicism as the state religion, remained important in Mexican politics and culture. Culturally, Catholicism remained (and still remains) the dominant religion of Mexico. The Catholic Church maintained much political power in Mexico after independence because of its status as a state religion. It also retained a voice in politics in Mexico, and its clergy maintained many of the rights and privileges that they had enjoyed in the colonial era. For example, members of the clergy were exempt from having to stand trial in civil courts, even if charged with a violation of civil law. Instead, they were tried in an ecclesiastical court. The special privileges of the clergy were not contest-

Questions for Further Study

1. What factors in the late eighteenth and early nineteenth centuries contributed to the crumbling of Spain's Empire in the New World, which had predominated since Christopher Columbus's 1492 voyage?

2. What role did caste, or social class, play in the genesis of the Mexican Revolution? Did the revolution solve the issues surrounding caste?

3. Compare the origins, course, and outcome of the Mexican Revolution with other, similar social revolts in Latin American and Caribbean countries at the time. Entries to consult include Emiliano Zapata's Plan of Ayala, Fidel Castro's *History Will Absolve Me*, and Juan Perón's "Twenty Fundamental Truths of Justicialism." What factors did the rebellions have in common? How did they differ?

4. Many former colonies throughout the world have been eager to throw off their colonial oppressors in their desire for independence. Mexico, however, wanted to retain a Spanish monarch and maintain a close relationship with Spain. Why?

5. Trace the course of events from the Treaty of Córdoba to the 1848 Treaty of Guadalupe Hidalgo, which officially ended the Mexican-American War. How did the course of events in those decades permanently affect Mexico?

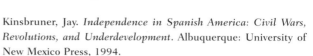

ed until thirty years later, during La Reforma. The influence of the Catholic Church in politics was largely brought to an end one hundred years later, during the Mexican Revolution of 1910.

Further Reading

▪ Articles

Anna, Timothy E. "Inventing Mexico: Provincehood and Nationhood after Independence." *Bulletin of Latin American Research* 15, no. 1 (1996): 7–17.

———. "The Rule of Agustin de Iturbide: A Reappraisal." *Journal of Latin American Studies* 17, no. 1 (May 1985): 79–110.

Van Young, Eric. "Agrarian Rebellion and Defense of Community: Meaning and Collective Violence in Late Colonial and Independence-Era Mexico." *Journal of Social History* 27, no. 2 (Winter 1993): 245–269.

▪ Books

Henderson, Timothy J. *The Mexican Wars for Independence.* New York: Hill and Wang, 2009.

Kinsbruner, Jay. *Independence in Spanish America: Civil Wars, Revolutions, and Underdevelopment.* Albuquerque: University of New Mexico Press, 1994.

Van Young, Eric. *The Other Rebellion: Popular Violence, Ideology, and the Mexican Struggle for Independence, 1810–1821.* Stanford, Calif.: Stanford University Press, 2001.

▪ Web Sites

"The Plan de Iguala." Historical Text Archive Web site. http://historicaltextarchive.com/sections.php?op=viewarticle& artid=538.

—Tamara Shircliff-Spike

TREATY OF CÓRDOBA

Agreement on the Independent Kingdom of Mexico 24 Aug 1821

Treaty concluded in the Town of Cordova on the 24th of August, 1821, between Don Juan O'Donnoju, Lieutenant-General of the Armies of Spain, and Don Augustín de Iturbide, First Chief of the Imperial Mexican Army of the "Three Guarantees."

New Spain having declared herself independent of the mother country; possessing an army to support this declaration; her provinces having decided in its favour; the capital wherein the legitimate authority had been deposed being besieged; the cities of Vera Cruz and Acapulco alone remaining to the European government ungarrisoned, and without the means of resisting a well directed siege of any duration, Lieut.-Gen. Don Juan O'Donnoju arrived at the first, named port in the character and quality of Captain General and first political chief of this kingdom, appointed by his most Catholic Majesty, and being desirous of avoiding the evils that necessarily fall upon the people in changes of this description, and of reconciling the interests of Old and New Spain, he invited the First Chief of the imperial army, Don Augustín de Iturbide to an interview in order to discuss the great question of independence, disentangling without destroying the bonds which had connected the two Continents. This interview took place in the town of Cordova, on the 24th of August, 1821, and the former under the character with which he came invested, and the latter as representing the Mexican empire, having conferred at large upon the interests of each nation, looking to their actual condition and to recent occurrences, agreed to the following Articles, which they signed in duplicate, for their better preservation, each party keeping an original for greater security and validity.

1st. This kingdom of America shall be recognised as a sovereign and independent nation and shall, in future, be called the Mexican Empire.

2d. The government of the empire shall be monarchical, limited by a constitution.

3d. Ferdinand VII, Catholic king of Spain, shall, in the first place, be called to the throne of the Mexican Empire, (on taking the oath prescribed in the 10th Article of the plan) and on his refusal and denial, his brother, the most serene infante Don Car-los; on his refusal and denial, the most serene infante Don Francisco de Paula; on his refusal and denial, the most serene Don Carlos Luis, infante of Spain, formely heir of Tuscany, now of Lucca; and upon his renunciation and denial, the person whom the Cortes of the empire shall designate.

4th. The emperor shall fix his court in Mexico, which shall be the capital of the empire.

5th. Two commissioners shall be named by his excellency Señor O'Donnoju, and these shall proceed to the court of Spain, and place in the hands of his Majesty king Ferdinand VII a copy of this treaty, and a memorial which shall accompany it, for the purpose of affording information to his Majesty with respect to antecedent circumstances, whilst the Cortes of the empire offer him the crown with all the formalities and guarantees which a matter of so much importance requires; and they supplicate his Majesty, that on the occurrence of the case provided for in Article 3, he would be pleased to communicate it to the most serene infantes called to the crown in the same article, in the order in which they are so named; and that his Majesty would be pleased to interpose his influence and prevail on one of the members of his august family to proceed to this empire, inasmuch as the prosperity of both nations would be thereby promoted, and as the Mexicans would feel satisfaction in thus strengthening the bands of friendship, with which they may be, and wish to see themselves, united to the Spaniards.

6th. Conformably to the spirit of the "Plan of Iguala," an assembly shall be immediately named, composed of men the most eminent in the empire for their virtues, their station, rank, fortune, and influence; men marked out by the general opinion, whose number may be sufficiently considerable to insure by their collective knowledge the safety of the resolutions which they may take in pursuance of the powers and authority granted them by the following articles.

7th. The assembly mentioned in the preceding article shall be called the "Provisional Junta of Government."

8th. Lieutenant-General Don Juan O'Donnoju shall be a member of the Provisional Junta of Government, in consideration of its being expedient that a person of his rank should take an active and immediate part in the government, and of the indispensable necessity of excluding some of the individuals mentioned in the above Plan of Iguala, conformably to its own spirit.

9th. The Provisional Junta of Government shall have a president elected by itself from its own body, or from without it, to be determined by the absolute plurality of votes; and if on the first scrutiny the votes be found equal, a second scrutiny shall take place, which shall embrace those two who shall have received the greatest number of votes.

10th. The first act of the Provisional Junta shall be the drawing up of a manifesto of its installation, and the motives of its assemblage, together with whatever explanations it may deem convenient and proper for the information of the country, with respect to the public interests, and the mode to be adopted in the election of deputies for the Cortes, of which more shall be said hereafter.

11th. The Provisional Junta of Government after the election of its president, shall name a regency composed of three persons selected from its own body, or from without it, in whom shall be vested the executive power, and who shall govern in the name and on behalf of the monarch till the vacant throne be filled.

12th. The Provisional Junta, as soon as it is installed, shall govern ad interim according to the existing laws, so far as they may not be contrary to the "Plan of Iguala" and until the Cortes shall have framed the constitution of the state.

13th. The regency immediately on its nomination, shall proceed to the convocation of the Cortes in the manner which shall be prescribed by the Provisional Junta of Government, conformably to the spirit of Article No. 7 in the aforesaid "Plan."

14th. The executive power is vested in the regency, and the legislative in the Cortes; but as some time must elapse before the latter can assemble, and in order that the executive and legislative powers should not remain in the hands of one body, the junta shall be empowered to legislate; in the first place, where cases occur which are too pressing to wait till the assemblage of the Cortes, and then the junta shall proceed in concert with the regency; and, in the second place, to assist the regency in its determinations in the character of an auxiliary and consultative body.

15th. Every individual who is domiciled amongst any community, shall, on an alteration taking place in the system of government, or on the country passing under the dominion of another prince, be at full liberty to remove himself, together with his effects, to whatever country he chooses, without any person having the right to deprive him of such liberty, unless he have contracted some obligation with the community to which lie had belonged, by the commission of a crime, or by any other of those modes which publicists have laid down; this applies to the Europeans residing in New Spain, and to the Americans residing in the Peninsula. Consequently it will be at their option to remain, adopting either country, or to demand their passports (which cannot be denied them) for permission to leave the kingdom at such time as may be appointed beforehand, carrying with them their families and property; but paying on the latter the regular export duties now in force, or which may hereafter be established by the competent authority.

16th. The option granted in the foregoing article shall not extend to persons in public situations, whether civil or military, known to be disaffected to Mexican independence; such persons shall necessarily quit the empire within the time which shall be allotted by the regency, taking with them their effects after having paid the duties, as stated in the preceding article.

17th. The occupation of the capital by the Peninsular troops being an obstacle to the execution of this treaty, it is indispensable to have it removed. But as the Commander-in-Chief of the imperial army fully participating in the sentiments of the Mexican nation, does not wish to attain this object by force, for which, however, he has more than ample means at his command, notwithstanding the known valour and constancy of the Peninsular troops, who are not in a

Glossary

infante	a younger brother of Ferdinand VII
Peninsular troops	equivalent to the imperial army of Spain
regency	in this context, the temporary executive body described in the 11th article

situation to maintain themselves against the system adopted by the nation at large, Don Juan O'Donnoju agrees to exercise his authority for the evacuation of the capital by the said troops without loss of blood, and upon the terms of an honourable capitulation.

Augustán de Iturbide, Juan O'Donnoju. (a true copy.)
Jose Dominguez. Dated in the Town Of Cordova, 24th August, 1821

ACT FOR THE ABOLITION OF SLAVERY THROUGHOUT THE BRITISH COLONIES

"All such persons [held in slavery] should be manumitted and set free."

Overview

The year 1833 was a watershed in the history of humankind owing to the passage of the far-reaching Slavery Abolition Act by the British parliament, a decree that abolished slavery throughout the British Empire. Great Britain was the world's foremost superpower at that time, a nation of great international authority with a history of slave trading and keeping, and the abolition act was the first legal ruling by a national government to ban slavery within its colonies. It therefore set a precedent for all other imperialistic countries to follow, setting forth into law the concept that freedom is a natural right of all human beings.

Although it was not the first rule banning slavery within the British colonial context—as such a law was passed in the British colony of Upper Canada in 1793—the Slavery Abolition Act of 1833 was a major political turning point in British and global history that arose as a result of a lengthy process of protest and legal progress. The abolition act evolved from earlier British law such as the Slave Trade Act of 1807 and was the fruition of campaigns by persons and groups who began opposing the institution of enslavement in earlier decades. Central to the opposition were associations like the Religious Society of Friends, known as the Quakers, who vigorously sought antislavery support from the late eighteenth century onward, such as through the publication of journals outlining the immorality of slavery. It is in this context that the 1833 turning point came about.

Context

From as early as the mid-eighteenth century, discussion regarding the abolition of slavery in Britain was already vigorous, with calls being made to ban the institution in accord with the spreading conviction that slavery was a blight on civilized society. Many persons of religious conviction had long protested the trafficking of what was then commonly referred to as "men-bodies," and by the last quarter of the eighteenth century many abolitionist groups had been formed both in Britain and

in its colonies in North America. Prominent associations and religious groups thus joined forces with the newly formed antislavery societies to integrate previously detached religious, moral, and economic arguments against slavery.

In colonies such as Pennsylvania, groups like the Society for the Relief of Free Negroes Unlawfully Held in Bondage (established in 1775) and the successor Pennsylvania Society for Promoting the Abolition of Slavery (founded in 1784) formed part of a lobby seeking to emancipate slaves. Particularly vocal in the movement to liberate slaves were the Quakers, who described slavery as being "a hellish sin" and "the greatest sin in the world" and as arising from "the belly of hell" (Davis, p. 291). Highly motivated in pursuing the eradication of slavery, the Quakers saw their political influence increase through the second half of the eighteenth century. In the colonies and Britain alike, Quakers pressured public authorities to change existing laws and also attempted to influence those in positions of economic power to reconsider the practice of slavery. They furthermore established initially small but subsequently powerful locally organized groups, held public debates, and published abolitionist propaganda.

A small but greatly influential abolitionist association in Britain was the Society for Effecting the Abolition of the Slave Trade (SEAST), which at the time of its establishment in 1787 consisted of only twelve people. Among them were the noted abolitionists Thomas Clarkson, author of a pamphlet entitled *A Summary View of the Slave Trade and of the Probable Consequences of Its Abolition* (1787), and William Wilberforce, a young and energetic member of Parliament. Initially, SEAST members had limited access to public political channels; most were Quakers and thus, as members of a nondenominational religious group, were legally forbidden from sitting in positions of public political responsibility. Nonetheless, the group circumnavigated barriers to the political arena by finding non-Quaker allies who could broaden the abolitionist cause and also act as mouthpieces for the movement. For example, the Anglican Church and SEAST forged a union based on common moral values. The clergy of the Anglican Church then disseminated antislavery messages from pulpits up and down the country and

1772

- **June 22**
Lord Chief
Justice William
Murray, Earl of
Mansfield, rules
that English law
does not
support slavery.

1775

- **April 14**
North America's
first abolitionist
group, the
Society for the
Relief of Free
Negroes
Unlawfully Held
in Bondage, is
established in
Philadelphia, the
capital of the
British colony of
Pennsylvania.

1780

- **October 31**
William Wilberforce
becomes the
member of
Parliament for
Kingston upon Hull.

1781

- **November 29–
December 1**
In crossing the
Atlantic, the
crew of the
overcrowded
British slave
ship *Zong* throw
more than one
hundred
Africans
overboard prior
to arriving in
Jamaica,
causing outrage
in Britain.

1787

- **May 22**
The Society for
Effecting the
Abolition of the
Slave Trade is
founded in London,
becoming a potent
force in the quest
to abolish slavery
until its demise in
1797.

helped promote abolitionism among politicians of pious temperament, drawing on the close alliance between the church and the state at that time.

Broad political shifts leading up to 1833 greatly affected the perceptions and beliefs at the foundation of Britain's antislavery ideology and the actions of people endorsing them. The 1780s bore witness to a new political exploit in Britain, political lobbying, which for the first time permitted individuals and groups to more directly persuade members of Parliament to consider alternative perspectives on a variety of political matters. With the passage of the Slave Trade Act of 1807, the trading of slaves was no longer permitted, although the keeping of slaves was still allowed. In the ensuing years, the dissemination of antislavery sentiment was evident not only in the forming of more abolitionist groups, such as the Society for the Mitigation and Gradual Abolition of Slavery throughout the British Dominions, but also in the signing of treaties between Britain and European countries such as Spain, Portugal, the Netherlands, and Sweden to abolish slave trading. The Slave Trade Act of 1824 struck out at British financial institutions still involved in the international trafficking of slaves.

While historians commonly acknowledge the significance of the legal landmarks leading to the Slavery Abolition Act of 1833, far less attention has been given to the evolution of the values of the antislavery groups who helped manufacture these groundbreaking legal rulings. The contribution of the Quakers to abolitionism is recognized, but persons of various backgrounds and convictions were drawn into the British movement owing not only to religion but also to the shifting ideological climate of the late eighteenth century, which granted new opportunities for British citizens to confront existing philosophical, cultural, and legal frameworks. The underpinnings of abolitionism thus may be seen as derived from the emergence of new human opinions tied to the Enlightenment, industrialization, and capitalism, with its concept of free labor.

Certain individuals made great contributions to the British antislavery movement. Of note were Olaudah Equiano and Mary Prince, Africans who had their life stories published; Hannah More, a writer and philanthropist; James Ramsay, a priest who helped deepen the moral argument for abolition; and Beilby Porteus, an Anglican reformer who gained national fame in 1783 for a sermon that criticized the church for ignoring the plight of slaves. What was unique and important about this generation was that they sought not merely to temper slavery but further to put a complete end to it, and they inspired others to speak out, so that by the early 1800s the abolitionist movement comprised far more than a small circle of propagandists connected to religious groups or elite politicians. Among those who broadened the popularity of the movement were James Stephen, a lawyer who assisted greatly in drafting the 1807 slave trade bill; Granville Sharp, a businessman opposed to the injustices of slavery; and Elizabeth Heyrick, a philanthropist.

In early 1833 a proposal was presented to the houses of Parliament suggesting an end to slavery in the British Empire. Other such bills had been introduced before, but the 1833 proposal was met with three months of ultimately positive debate. In July of that year the abolitionist proposition was approved—and just three days after receiving the news that the bill had won parliamentary approval, William Wilberforce, its inspiration, passed away. Although he had retired from the public political arena, Wilberforce, a voice of British abolitionism for almost fifty years, was universally credited with the penning of the bill that became the Slavery Abolition Act of 1833. Many other persons, such as Thomas Fowell Buxton, who from the early 1820s became the British abolitionist movement leader, and persons belonging to the Society for Effecting the Abolition of the Slave Trade, likely had an influence on the form of the emancipation bill, as it was known before being presented to Parliament. Many of its clauses were probably derived from the original abolitionist motions that Wilberforce had offered to Parliament in the 1790s.

Employed as a member of Parliament from October 1780 until February 1825 for three successive constituencies, Wilberforce acquired the reputation of a reformer by as early as the mid-1780s. In 1787 he was instrumental in the formation of SEAST, Britain's first abolitionist society, and at the suggestion of Prime Minister William Pitt the Younger he was also asked to become the parliamentary leader of the abolitionist movement. He thus attained the status of Britain's most vocal abolitionist elected official and, against a lack of wider political commitment to abolitionism within Parliament, endeavored to effect the emancipation of those in enslavement. In Parliament on May 12, 1789, he gave what is still widely considered one of the most eloquent speeches in British political history, a talk calling for what was in "the interests not of this country, nor of Europe alone, but of the whole world": the ending of slavery (Cobbett, column 41).

Strong in religious and moral character and yet highly skilled in political maneuvers, Wilberforce, along with Thomas Clarkson, was a key motivating force in bringing about the abolition of slavery. Although best known for his parliamentary activities, including the seemingly countless bills associated with slave trading, slave registration, and slave keeping that he put forward, Wilberforce's greatest legacy was the 1833 abolition bill, which, given to Parliament eight years after his retirement, acknowledged his tireless humanitarian work. Following Wilberforce's death in July 1833, the Slavery Abolition Act not only freed over eight hundred thousand slaves in the British colonies but also established for the world at the highest political level the principle of granting human rights for all. Through the transitions in global society since the 1830s, Wilberforce's name still represents the promotion of social action and social rights and the ethical drive to reshape attitudes and laws when necessary so as to ensure that social equity is not compromised.

Time Line

1788

- **January 28**
  Bristol becomes the first provincial British city to set up a committee to abolish slave trading.

1789

- **May 12**
  Wilberforce delivers his first major abolitionist speech before Parliament, an oration that receives widespread media attention.

1791

- **April 18**
  Wilberforce presents to the House of Commons a bill to abolish the slave trade, but it is defeated by a vote of 163 to 88.

1792

- **April 2**
  Wilberforce introduces another parliamentary bill proposing abolition.

1793

- **February 1**
  War with France is declared, and abolitionism, perceived as a philosophical ally of the French Revolution, consequently declines in popularity.

- **July 9**
  Upper Canada, a British colony, passes the Act against Slavery to ensure the equal treatment of Native Americans, Africans, and Europeans.

1804

- **June**
Wilberforce introduces a bill in parliament to end slave trading.

1806

- **May 23**
The Foreign Slave Trade Act is passed to prohibit British subjects from transporting slaves to the territory of any foreign (non-British) state.

1807

- **March 25**
The British parliament votes to abolish the trading of slaves between colonies by passing the Slave Trade Act.

1817

- **September 23**
Spain and Britain sign a treaty prohibiting slave trading, the first of a series of such pacts between European nations.

1823

- **May 15**
A debate begins in Parliament on a motion for the "Mitigation and Gradual Abolition of Slavery throughout the British Dominions."

1824

- **June 24**
The Slave Trade Act of 1824 is passed, making slave trading a criminal offense and striking out at insurance and mortgage companies engaged in slave trading.

Explanation and Analysis of the Document

Approved by Parliament on August 28, 1833, the Slavery Abolition Act was a law that promised much for those kept in captivity in British colonies. As is typical of legal edicts, the act was meticulously composed and includes numerous detailed sections. While the media of the era reported extensively on the act's freeing of slaves, far less was noted regarding its many other clauses.

◆ Core Principles

The Slavery Abolition Act was founded upon three principles, which made up its "long title": "the abolition of slavery throughout the British colonies; for promoting the industry of the manumitted slaves; and for compensating the persons hitherto entitled to the services of such slaves" (*Yorkshireman*, p. 288). With regard to the first principle, the opening clause of the act states that *"divers Persons are holden in Slavery within divers of his Majesty's Colonies, and it is just and expedient that all such Persons should be manumitted and set free."* On liberating persons from captivity, the act subsequently remarks that "a reasonable compensation should be made to persons hitherto entitled to the services of such Slaves for the loss which they will incur by being deprived of their right to such services." In short, former slave owners are entitled to financial recompense for their loss of human capital. What exactly a "reasonable" financial sum would amount to is not stated, but, in total, £20 million was to be handed out by Parliament to cover all reparation claims by former slave owners.

The first section proceeds to appreciate "the new state and relations of society therein" that shall be produced within the colonial context. However, so as to allow for colonial societies to prepare to adopt the law and in turn adapt to the new social situation it would create, the act specifies that "a short interval should elapse before such Manumission should take effect." To assist in this adaptation phase, slave owners were compelled to register their slaves between August 28, 1833—the date when the law was passed by Parliament—and August 1, 1834—the date when royal assent was awarded. Once these persons were registered, they were obliged to continue to work for their slave masters but now with legal rights through their new status as "apprenticed Labourers." This labor system was to end before August 1, 1840, when workers were given the legal right to work where they pleased.

◆ Registered Workers

With regard to the apprenticeship system, former slaves were divided into three categories. As noted in section IV, the first group was known as *"praedial apprenticed Labourers attached to the soil,"* encompassing individuals employed in the agricultural-industrial sector ("praedial," or "predial" relating to the land or products from the land). The second group, *"praedial apprenticed Labourers not attached to the soil,"* comprised persons employed in the manufacturing sector. *"Non-praedial apprenticed Labourers,"* the third category, included persons in the domestic service industry or clerks, among others. Irrespective of their class of apprenticeship, former slaves were to work from 1834 until 1840—the period of adjustment to the "new state and relations of society" prior to full manumission. The abolition act is explicit in stating in section I that freedom was to be awarded in August 1834 to those slaves younger than six years old. Very young children had no labor status under the new law, but all those older than six were to be given the new standing of "apprenticed Labourers"; they would continue to serve their former colonial masters as paid employees for no more than forty-five hours per week until no later than August 1, 1840. Persons of infirm body or mind, and very young children, could not be registered as apprentices.

The abolition act of 1833 did not apply to all parts of the British Empire. The decree states in section LXIV that "nothing in this Act contained doth or shall extend to any of the Territories in the Possession of the East India Company, or the Island of Ceylon, or to the Island of Saint Helena." Furthermore, as noted in section LXV, while broadly enacted on August 1, 1834, the act was not to take effect until four months afterward within the colony of the Cape of Good Hope and until six months afterward in Mauritius. The act's immediate direct application was in Bermuda, the Bahamas, Jamaica, Honduras, the Virgin Islands, Antigua, Montserrat, Nevis, Saint Christopher, Dominica, Barbados, Grenada, Saint Vincent's Tobago (as it was then called), Saint Lucia, Trinidad, and British Guyana.

◆ **Social Welfare**

Regarding the social alteration period of 1834 to 1840, certain clauses in the act address the welfare of those previously enslaved. As stated in section VII, once former slaves were registered as apprentices, their former masters were liable "to provide for the maintenance" of the individual. While on the one hand this obliged former slave masters to physically look after their apprentices—with the act granting, for example, the provision of medication and food and freedoms such as access to medical assistance—the decree also deals with matters relating to the mental well-being of liberated slaves. The act states in section IX that the lawful transfer of newly registered apprentices from one estate or plantation to another should not "be injurious to the health or welfare" of the apprentices. One way in which freed people's contentment was to be ensured was through the maintenance of family units. A laborer, his or her spouse, their children, and other immediate family members could not be separated. In addition, with respect to the moral welfare of those liberated, clauses of the act encourage the promotion of habits of industry, good conduct, and piety. For instance, the act states in section XXI that an apprentice would be able to undertake religious worship on Sundays "at his or her free Will or Pleasure … at full liberty so to do without any Let, Denial, or Interruption whatsoever."

◆ **Freedom and Social Control**

In managing the mental and emotional well-being of emancipated persons, such as by granting freedom of worship, the act indicated a fundamental transition in governmental attitudes among the British colonizers toward those they colonized. Incidentally, the act thus established a number of channels that also allowed for the social control of the colonized populations. To begin with, by offering freedom of worship, which basically meant the right to go to church, the British were legally promoting the Christianizing of local populations. Christianity played another vital role in helping to link the colonizer with the colonized by educating all parties to the benefits of freedom, which among other effects encouraged the workforce to toil with great spirit and diligence, which, it was believed, would make them much better off and happier.

Time Line

1825
- **February**
  Wilberforce retires from Parliament.

1830
- **September 14**
  Having won the general election with a reformist agenda, the Whig Party gains control of Parliament.

1831
- **December 25**
  A major slave revolt breaks out in Jamaica, fueling debate about the keeping of slaves.

1832
- **June 7**
  The Reform Act of 1832 is passed, leading to changes in the national voting system and great reductions in parliamentary corruption.

1833
- **August 28**
  The British parliament passes the Slavery Abolition Act.

Engraving of the African slave trade (1791) (© Museum of London)

Of prime significance to the British process of supporting the provision of liberty in its colonies was the apprentice system, which, in light of the structure of the 1833 act, offered previously enslaved individuals freedom but in a highly regulated way. The British placed so much importance on the apprentice system in part owing to their lack of empirical knowledge relating to the freeing of slaves; that is, the British did not know how the completely open process of liberating slaves was going to turn out. Hence, they created a law that immediately awarded not complete free will but rather a limited sense of independence, which after a short period of time (in 1840) would indeed be replaced by a social and economic system granting even fewer restrictions. Relevant in this regard was the British desire to preserve plantation economies and maintain the stable, industrious workforces upon which the colonies so greatly relied. The challenge, therefore, was to compose an act that could allow freedoms while concurrently indoctrinating freed persons with industrious work habits and prevalent social values, which would then be internalized. Toward this end, the act endeavored to placate both slaves and plantation owners, a colonial class who feared the demise of their authority in a social and economic system founded upon the discontinued institution of slavery. Likewise, the British want-

ed the freed slaves to grow accustomed to working for wages under British law in the new post-enslavement social and economic structure. Religion and the apprentice system were crucial means of promoting this agenda.

Audience

The initial audience of the 1833 emancipation bill, the motion that was passed into law a few months later as the Slavery Abolition Act, consisted of the members of Parliament who belonged to the assembly of the House of Commons as well as peers in the House of Lords. As such, the act was formed to appease the political community and the broad opinions they held. Vital to its promotion was not only the increasingly widespread desire to ban slavery but also the provision of mechanisms to ensure the preservation of local colonial societies and economies. As such it was composed to satisfy a variety of parliamentarians so that a broad enough consensus could be reached to ensure its passage into law, such that it could grant, if not straightaway permit, the liberty of persons in enslavement in the British colonies.

Beyond the politicians needed to legally enact the initial proposal for change, the foremost audiences were those

"Whereas divers Persons are holden in Slavery within divers of his Majesty's Colonies, and it is just and expedient that all such persons should be manumitted and set free."

(Section I)

"And be it further enacted, That during the continuance of any such Apprenticeship, as aforesaid, the Person or Persons for the time being entitled to the services of every such apprenticed Labourer shall be, and is and are, hereby required to supply him or her with ... Food, Clothing, Lodging, Medicine, Medical Attendance, and such other Maintenance and Allowances."

(Section XI)

"And whereas, towards compensating the Persons at present entitled to the Services of the Slaves, to be manumitted and set free by virtue of this Act, for the Loss of such Services, His Majesty's most dutiful and loyal Subjects the Commons of Great Britain and Ireland in Parliament assembled, have resolved to give and grant to His Majesty the Sum of Twenty Millions Pounds Sterling."

(Section XXIV)

"And be it further enacted, That the said Commissioners shall proceed to apportion the said Sum into Nineteen different Shares, which shall be respectively assigned to the several British Colonies or Possessions hereinafter mentioned (that is to say,) the Bermuda Islands, the Bahama Islands, Jamaica, Honduras, the Virgin Islands, Antigua, Montserrat, Nevis, Saint Christopher's, Dominica, Barbadoes, Grenada, Saint Vincent's Tobago, Saint Lucia, Trinadad, British Guiana, the Cape of Good Hope, and Mauritius."

(Section XLV)

whom it would directly effect: the colonizers, in particular the slave owners who were to receive financial compensation, and those once enslaved, who were to be freed. A third important audience consisted of the persons who controlled the structure of colonial economies. Hence, provision was made in the act to ensure that plantation workers stayed on the land at least temporarily, albeit now under a system of freedoms and the status of apprenticed laborers.

Impact

Great Britain's Slavery Abolition Act of 1833 openly proclaimed the beginning of the end of the Western world's activities in slavery, a denouement that was ultimately fulfilled throughout the developed and colonized world. The quest for the passage of the abolition act brought together various reformers—who perhaps would have never united otherwise—under a common cause and established a progressive context in which persons wishing to improve the lot of the downtrodden could operate. The act itself was the drawing of a battle line as to what was socially, economically, and racially tolerable—an assertion that the removal of enslavement and the awarding of freedom could be effected by law and should be protected in law. As slavery was closely tied to racism, the one being both cause and effect of the other, slavery's defeat ensured the evolution of intolerance to racism as well as associated poverty and inequality. The act's success relied not just upon parliamentary approval but furthermore upon reconciliation between all in society, and without such understanding, full social freedom can never be achieved. The greatest legacy of the act may be its serving as a historical inspiration to all those seeking to rid the world of oppression and to banish injustices from modern society. One piece of legal change in 1833 redefined how all human beings should think about, allow, and preserve liberty, teaching that all human life has a value that money cannot buy.

Further Reading

■ **Articles**

Lorimer, Douglas. "Black Slaves and English Liberty: A Re-examination of Racial Slavery in England." *Immigrants and Minorities* 3, no. 2 (July 1984): 121–150.

"Pro Patria." *The Yorkshireman, a Religious and Literary Journal by a Friend* 115 (1837): 287–301.

Temperley, Howard. "Capitalism, Slavery and Ideology." *Past and Present* 75 (1977): 94–118.

Tyson, Thomas N., David Oldroyd, and Richard K. Fleischman. "Accounting, Coercion and Social Control during Apprenticeship: Converting Slave Workers to Wage Workers in the British West Indies, c. 1834–1838." *Accounting Historians Journal* 32, no. 2 (2005): 201–231.

■ **Books**

Cobbett, William. *The Parliamentary History of England: From the Norman Conquest, in 1066, to the year 1803.* Vol. 28: *1789–1791.* London: T. C. Hansard, 1803.

Davis, David Brion. *The Problem of Slavery in Western Cultures.* New York: Oxford University Press, 2008.

Walvin, James. *Black Ivory: Slavery in the British Empire.* Oxford, UK: Blackwell Publishers, 2001.

Williams, Eric. *Capitalism and Slavery.* London: Deutsch, 1964.

■ **Web Sites**

"The Abolition of the Slave Trade." New York Public Library Schomburg Center for Research in Black Culture Web site.
  http://abolition.nypl.org/print/abolition/.

"Abolition of the Slave Trade 1807." BBC Web site/British History Web site.
  http://www.bbc.co.uk/history/british/abolition/.

Questions for Further Study

1. How was a relatively small religious group like the Quakers, who lacked access to political office in England, able to exert such a disproportionate influence on the antislavery movement?

2. What impact, if any, do you think Britain's abolition of slavery had on policies with regard to slavery in the United States?

3. The act exempted territories in the possession of the British East India Company from its provisions. Read the entry titled Queen Victoria's Proclamation concerning India and explain why the company may have been exempted from the terms of the act.

4. Why do you think Great Britain rather than some other nation became the world's leader in the process of abolishing slavery? Were there particular qualities in the makeup of British thought or British politics that enabled the antislavery movement to strike deep roots in that country?

5. Drawing on the entry titled Nelson Mandela's Inaugural Address, compare the process of abolishing slavery in Britain's colonies with the process of abolishing the apartheid system of South Africa.

"William Wilberforce's 1789 Abolition Speech." Acton Institute Birth of Freedom Web site.
  http://www.thebirthoffreedom.com/william-wilberforce-s-1789-abolition-speech.

"William Wilberforce (1759–1833)." Brycchan Carey's British Abolitionists Web site.
  http://www.brycchancarey.com/abolition/wilberforce.htm.

—Ian Morley

Milestone Documents

ACT FOR THE ABOLITION OF SLAVERY THROUGHOUT THE BRITISH COLONIES

Whereas divers Persons are holden in Slavery within divers of his Majesty's Colonies, and it is just and expedient that all such Persons should be manumitted and set free, and that a reasonable compensation should be made to the persons hitherto entitled to the services of such Slaves for the loss which they will incur by being deprived of their right to such services: And whereas it is also expedient that provision should be made for promoting the industry and securing the good conduct of the persons so to be manumitted, for a limited period after such their Manumission: And whereas it is necessary that the laws now in force in the said several Colonies should forthwith be adapted to the new state and relations of society therein, which will follow upon such general manumission as aforesaid of the said Slaves; and that in order to afford the necessary time for such adaptation of the said laws, a short interval should elapse before such Manumission should take effect: Be it therefore enacted—*That from and after the First Day of August One thousand eight hundred and thirty-four, all Persons* who in conformity with the laws now in force in the said Colonies respectively shall on or before the first Day *August* One thousand eight hundred and thirty-four *have been duly registered as slaves in any such colony,* and who on the said First day of *August* One thousand eight hundred and thirty four shall be actually within any such Colony, and who shall by such registries appear to be on the said First Day of *August* One thousand eight hundred thirty-four *of the full age of six Years or upwards, shall* by force and virtue of this act, and without the previous execution of any Indenture of Apprenticeship, or other deed or instrument for that purposes aforesaid, every Slave engaged in his ordinary Occupation on the Seas shall be deemed and taken to be within the Colony to which such Slave shall belong.

II. And be it further enacted, That during the Continuance of the Apprenticeship of any such apprenticed Labourer, such person or persons shall be entitled to the services of such apprenticed Labourer as would, for the time being, have been entitled to his or her services as a Slave if this Act had not been made.

III. Provided also, and be it further enacted, That all Slaves who may at any time previous to the paus-ing of this Act have been brought with the consent of their possessors, and all apprenticed Labourers who may hereafter with the like consent be brought, into any part of the United Kingdom of *Great Britain* and *Ireland,* shall from and after the passing of this Act be absolutely and entirely free to all intents and purposes whatsoever.

IV. And whereas it is expedient that all such apprenticed Labourers should, for the purposes herein-after mentioned, be divided into *Three districts Classes,* the First of such Classes consisting of *prædial apprenticed Labourers attached to the soil,* and comprising all persons who in their state of Slavery were usually employed in Agriculture, or in the Manufacture of Colonial produce or otherwise, upon lands belonging to their owners; the Second of such Classes consisting of *prædial apprenticed Labourers not attached* to the soil, and comprising all persons who in their state of Slavery were usually employed in Agriculture, or in the Manufacture of Colonial Produce or otherwise upon lands not belonging to their owners; and the Third of such Classes consisting of *non-prædial apprenticed Labourers,* and comprising all apprenticed Labourers not included within either of the Two preceding Classes: Be it therefore enacted, That such Division as aforesaid of the said apprenticed Labourers into such Classes as aforesaid shall be carried into effected in such manner and forms, and subject to such Rules and Regulations, as shall for that purpose be established under such Authority, and in and by such Acts of Assembly, Ordinance or Orders in Council, as herein-after mentioned: Provided always, that no persons of the Age of Twelve Years and upwards shall by or by virtue of any such Act of Assembly, Ordinance, or Order in Council, be included in either of the said Two Classes of prædial apprenticed Labourers, unless such person shall for Twelve Calendar Months at the least next before the passing of this present Act have been habitually employed in Agriculture, or in the Manufacture of Colonial Produce.

V. And be it further enacted, *That no person* who by virtue of this Act, or of any such Act of Assembly, or Order in Council as aforesaid, shall *become a prædial apprenticed Labourer,* whether attached or not attached to the soil, *shall continue in such Appren-*

ticeship beyond the *First Day of August One Thousand Eight hundred and Forty*; and that during such his or her Apprenticeship *no such prædial apprenticed Labourer*, whether attached or not to the soil, *shall be bound or liable*, by virtue of such Apprenticeship, *to perform any labour* in the service of his or her Employer, or Employers, *for more than forty-five Hours in the whole in the whole in any One Week.*

VI. And be it further enacted, *That no Person* who by virtue of this Act or of any such Act of Assembly, Ordinance, or Order in Council as aforesaid, shall *become a non-prædial apprenticed labourer, shall continue in such Apprenticeship beyond the First Day of August One Thousand Eight Hundred and Thirty-Eight.*

VII. And be it further enacted, *That if, before any such Apprenticeship shall have expired, the Person* or persons entitled for and during the reminder of any such term to the services of such apprenticed Labourer *shall be desirous to discharge him or her from such Apprenticeship, it shall be lawful for such person or persons so to do* by any deed or instrument to be by him, her, or them for that purpose made and executed; which deed or instrument shall be in such form, and shall be executed and recorded in such manner and with such solemnities, as shall for that purpose be prescribed under such authority, and in and by such Acts of Assembly, Ordinances, or Orders in Council, as herein-after mentioned: Provided nevertheless, that *if any Person so discharged* from any such Apprenticeship by any such voluntary act as aforesaid, *shall at that time be of the age of fifty years or upwards, or shall be then* labouring under any such disease or mental or bodily infirmity, as may render him or her *incapable of earning his or her Subsistence, then and in every such case the Person* or Persons so discharging any such apprenticed labourer, as aforesaid, *shall continue and be liable to provide for the maintenance of such apprenticed Labourer* during the remaining term of such apprenticed Labourer had not been discharged therefrom.

VIII. And be it further enacted, *That it shall be lawful for any such apprenticed Labourer to purchase his or her discharge* from such Apprenticeship, even *without the consent*, or in opposition, if necessary, to the will *of the Person or Persons entitled to his or her Services, upon payment to such Person or Persons of the appraised values of such services*; which Appraisement shall be effected, and which purchase money shall be paid and applied, and which discharge shall be given and executed; in such manner and form, and upon, under, and subject to such conditions, as

shall be prescribed under such Authority, and by such Acts of Assembly, Ordinances, or Orders in Council, as are herein-after mentioned.

IX. And be it further enacted, *That no apprenticed Labourer shall be subject or liable to be removed from the Colony* to which he or she may belong; and that *no prædial apprenticed Labourer*, who may in manner aforesaid become attached to the soil *shall be subject or liable to perform any Labour* in the service of his or her employer or employers, *except upon or in or about the Works and Business of the Plantations* or Estates to which such prædial apprenticed Labourer shall have been attached, or on which he or she shall have been usually employed on or previously to the First Day of *August* One thousand eight hundred and thirty-four: Provided nevertheless, that, *with the consent in writing of any Two or more Justices* of the Peace holding such special commission as herein-after mentioned, *it shall be lawful for the Person* or Persons, entitled to the services of any such attached prædial apprenticed Labourer or Labourers, *to transfer his or their services to any other Estate or Plantation within the same Colony*, to such person or persons belonging; which written consent shall in no case be given, or be of any validity, unless any such Justices of the Peace shall first have ascertained, that such transfer would *not have the effect of separating any such attached prædial apprenticed Labourer from his or her wife or Husband, Parent or Child*, or from any person or persons reputed to bear any such relation to him or her, and that such transfer *would not probably be injurious to the health or welfare* of such attached prædial apprenticed Labourer; and such written consent to any such removal shall be expressed in such terms, and shall be in each case given, attested, and recorded in such manner, as shall for that purpose be prescribed under such Authority, and by such Acts of Assembly, Ordinances, and Orders in Council, as herein-after mentioned.

X. And be it further enacted and declared, *That the Right or Interest of any Employer*, or Employers, to and in the services of any such apprenticed Labourers as aforesaid *shall pass and be transferable by Bargain and Sale*, Contract, Deed, Conveyance, Will, or Descent, according to such rules and in such manner as shall for that purpose be provided by any such Acts of Assembly, Ordinances, or Orders in Council as herein-after mentioned; provided that *no such apprenticed Labourer shall,* by virtue of any such Bargain and Sale, Contract, Deed, Conveyance, Will, or Descent, *be subject or liable to be separated from his Wife or Husband, Parent or Child,* or from any person or persons reputed to bear any such relation to him or her.

XI. And be it further enacted, That during the continuance of any such Apprenticeship, as aforesaid, *the Person or Persons* for the time being entitled to the services of every such apprenticed Labourer *shall be, and is and are, hereby required to supply him or her with such Food, Clothing, Lodging, Medicine, Medical Attendance*, and such other Maintenance and Allowances, as *by any law now in force in the Colony* to which such apprenticed Labourer may belong, *an owner is required to apply* to and for any Slave being of the same Age and Sex as such apprenticed Labourer shall be; *and in cases in which the Food* of any such prædial apprenticed Labourer *shall be supplied*, not by the delivery to him or her of Provisions, but *by the Cultivation by such prædial apprenticed Labourer of Ground set apart for the Growth of Provisions*, the person or persons entitled to his or her services shall and is or are hereby *required to provide such prædial apprenticed Labourer with Ground adequate*, both in Quantity and Quality, for his or her support, and within a reasonable distance of his or her usual place of abode, *and to allow* to such prædial apprenticed Labourer, from and out of the annual time during which he or she may be required to labour, after the rate of Forty-five Hours per week as aforesaid, in the service of such of his Employer or Employers, *such a Portion of Time as shall be adequate for the proper Cultivation of such Ground*, and for the raising and securing the Crops thereon grown; the actual extent of which Ground, and the Distance thereof from the place of residence of the prædial apprenticed Labourer for whose use it may be so allotted, and the length of time to be deducted for the Cultivation of the said Ground from the said annual Time, shall and may, in each of the Colonies aforesaid, be regulated under such Authorities, and by such Acts of Assembly, Ordinances, or Orders in Council as herein-after mentioned.

XII. And be it further enacted, That, subject to the obligations imposed by this Act, or to be imposed by any such Act of General Assembly, Ordinance, or Order in Council as herein-after mentioned, upon such apprenticed Labourers as aforesaid, *all and every the Persons who on the said First Day of August One Thousand Eight Hundred and Thirty Four shall be holden in Slavery within any such British Colony as aforesaid shall, upon and from and after the said First Day of August One Thousand Eight Hundred and Thirty Four, become and be to all intents and purposes free and discharged of and from all manner of Slavery, and shall be absolutely and forever manumitted; and that the Children thereafter to be born to any such*

persons, and the Offspring of such Children, shall in like manner be free from their Birth: and that from and after the First Day of August One Thousand Eight Hundred and Thirty Four Slavery shall be, and is hereby utterly and for ever abolished and declared unlawful, throughout the British Colonies, Plantations, and Possessions Abroad.

XIII. Children below the Age of Six, on 1st of August, 1834, or born after that time to any Female Apprentice, if destitute, may be bound out by any Special Magistrate as an Apprentice to the Person entitled to the Services of the said Mother; but at the Date of such Indentures the Apprentice must be under 12 Years of Age. Indentures to continue in force until the Child has completed his or her 21st Year and no longer.

XIV. His Majesty, or any Governor by his Authority, may appoint Justices of the Peace by Special Commission, to give effect to this Act and to all Colonial Laws to be made in pursuance of this Act; and no other qualification necessary. Such Justices may also be included in the General Commission of the Peace.

XV. His Majesty may grant Salaries to Special Justices. Lists of such Persons to be laid before Parliament.

XVI. Recital of various Regulations necessary for giving Effect to this Act. This Act not to prevent the Enactment, by Colonial Assemblies or by His Majesty in Council, of the Laws necessary for establishing such Regulations. Provisions repugnant to this Act contained in any such Colonial Law void.

XVII. *Such Colonial Acts may not authorize the Whipping or other Punishment of the Labourer by the Employer's Authority.*

XVIII. Colonial Acts or Orders in Council not to authorize any Justices, except those having Special Commissions, to act in execution thereof.

XIX. Justices having Special Commissions to exercise exclusive Jurisdiction between apprenticed Labourers and their Employers. Jurisdiction of Supreme Courts preserved.

XX. Provided also, and be it further enacted, That no apprenticed Labourer shall, by any such Act of Assembly, Ordinance, or Order in Council as aforesaid, be declared or rendered liable for and in respect of any offence by him or her committed, or for any cause or upon any ground or pretext whatsoever, except as hereafter is mentioned, to any Prolongation of his or her Term of Apprenticeship, or to any new or additional Apprenticeship, or to any such additional Labour as shall impose upon any such apprenticed Labourer the Obligation of working in the Service, or for the Benefit, of the Person or Persons entitled to his or her Services, for more than fifteen extra Hours in the whole in any One Week, but every such Enactment, Regulation, Provision, Rule or Order shall be and is hereby declared null and void and of no effect: Provided nevertheless, that any such Act of Assembly, Ordinance, or Order in Council as aforesaid may contain Provisions for compelling any apprenticed Labourer who shall, during his or her Apprenticeship, wilfully absent himself or herself from the Service of his or her Employer, either to serve his or her Employer after the expiration of his or her Apprenticeship, for so long a time as he or she shall have so absented himself or herself from such Service, or to make satisfaction to his or her Employer for the Loss sustained by such Absence (except so far as he or she shall have made Satisfaction for such Absence, either out of such extra Hours as aforesaid, or otherwise), but nevertheless so that such extra Service or Compensation shall not be compellable, after the Expiration of Seven Years next after the Termination of the Apprenticeship of each Apprentice.

XXI. Provided always, and be it hereby further enacted, That neither under the Provisions of this Act, nor under the obligations imposed by this Act, or to be imposed by any Act of any General Assembly, Ordinance, or Order in Council, shall any apprenticed Labourer be compelled or compellable to labour on *Sundays*, except in Works of Necessity or in Domestic Services, or in the Protection of Property, or in tending of Cattle, nor shall any apprenticed Labourer be liable to be hindered or prevented from attending anywhere on *Sundays* for Religions Worship, at his or her free Will or Pleasure, but shall be at full liberty so to do without any Let, Denial, or Interruption whatsoever.

XXII. Nothing herein to interfere with any Colonial laws, by which apprenticed Labourers may be exempted from, or disqualified for, certain Military or Civil Services and Franchises.

XXIII. Acts passed by Local Legislatures with similar but improved Enactments to this Act to supersede this Act on being confirmed by His Majesty in Council.

XXIV. And whereas, *towards compensating the Persons at present entitled to the Services of the Slaves,* to be manumitted and set free by virtue of this Act, for the Loss of such Services, His Majesty's most dutiful and loyal Subjects the Commons of Great Britain and Ireland in Parliament assembled, *have resolved to give and grant to His Majesty the Sum of Twenty Mil-*

lions Pounds Sterling, &c. [with the usual provisions for raising it by Government Annuities, Sec. XXV., XXVI., XXVII., and XXVIII.]

XXIX. Monies raised to be paid to an Account at the Bank, called *the West India Compensation Account.*

XXIX., XXXI., XXXII., Further Provisions as to the Government Annuities.

XXXIII. And for the Distribution of the said Compensation Fund, and for the Apportionment thereof amongst the several Persons who may prefer Claims thereon, be it enacted, that it shall and may be lawful for His Majesty from time to time, by a Commission under the Great Seal of the United Kingdom, to constitute and appoint such Persons, not being less than Five, as to His Majesty shall seem meet, to be Commissioners of Arbitration for inquiring into and deciding upon the Claims to Compensation which may be preferred to them under this Act.

XXXIV. Commissioners to be sworn.

XXXV. Meetings of the Commissioners, and appointment of the subordinate Officers. Officers to be sworn.

XXXVI. Any three Commissioners to be a Quorum.

XXXVII. And be it further enacted, That no Remuneration shall be given for and in respect of the Execution of the said Commission to such of the said Commissioners as shall be Members of either House of Parliament, nor to say Number exceeding Three of the said Commissioners.

XXXVIII. And whereas it may be necessary that Assistant Commissioners should be appointed, to act in aid of and under the Directions of the Commissioners appointed by this Act in the said several Colonies; be it therefore enacted, That the Governor and the Attorney General or other chief Law Adviser of the Government of the said Colonies respectively shall, with any Two or more resident Inhabitants for each of such Colonies, to be nominated during pleasure by the Governor thereof, be Commissioners for the Colony to which they respectively belong, to act in aid of the Commissioners under this Act in all such Cases and in relation to all Matters and Things which shall be referred to them by the said Commissioners, and for all such Purposes shall have and use and exercise all the Powers and Authorities of the said Commissioners; and such Assistant Commissioners shall take an Oath, to be administered to the Governor by the Chief Justice or any Judge of the said Colonies respectively, and to the other Assistant Commissioners by the Governor thereof, that they will well and truly and impartially execute the Powers and Authorities given to them as such Assistant Commissioners, in the several Matters and Things which shall be referred or submitted to them under the Provisions of this Act; and the said Assistant Commissioners shall, in all Matters which shall be referred to them by the Commissioners, transmit to the said Commissioners a full Statement of the several Matters which shall have been given in evidence before them, and true Copies of such written Evidence as shall have been received by them, and thereupon the said Commissioners shall proceed to adjudicate upon the same, and upon such other Evidence, if any, as may be laid before them.

XXXIX. Issue of Money for Payment of the Expense of the Commission.

XL. Commissioners may compel the Attendance and Examination of Witnesses.

XLI. and XLII. Commissioners authorized to take Examinations on Oath.

XLIII. Exemption from Postage of Letters on the Business of the Commission.

XLIV. No part of the Compensation to be applicable to any Colony unless His Majesty, by Order in Council, shall have first declared that adequate Provision has been made by the Legislature thereof. Such Orders to be published, and laid before Parliament.

XLV. And be it further enacted, That the said Commissioners shall proceed to apportion the said Sum into Nineteen different Shares, which shall be respectively assigned to the several British Colonies or Possessions herein-after mentioned (that is to say,) the Bermuda Islands, the Bahama Islands, Jamaica, Honduras, the Virgin Islands, Antigua, Montserrat, Nevis, Saint Christopher's, Dominica, Barbadoes, Grenada, Saint Vincent's Tobago, Saint Lucia, Trinadad, British Guiana, the Cape of Good Hope, and Mauritius; and in making such Apportionment of the said Funds between the said several Colonies the said Commissioners shall, and are hereby required to have regard to the number of Slaves, belonging to or settled in each of such Colonies, as the same may appear and are stated according to the latest Returns made in the Office of the Registrar of Slaves in England, appointed in pursuance and under the Authority of an Act passed in the Fifty-ninth Year of his late Majesty King George the Third, intituled *An Act for establishing a Registry of Colonial Slaves in Great Britain, and for making further Provision with respect to the Removal of Slaves from the British Colonie*; and the said Commissioners shall and they are hereby further

required, in making such Apportionment as aforesaid, to have regard to the Prices for which, on an average of Eight Years ending on the Thirty-first Day of December One Thousand Eight Hundred and Thirty, Slaves have been sold in each of the Colonies aforesaid respectively, excluding from consideration any such sales in which they shall have sufficient reason to suppose that such slaves were sold or purchased under any Reservation, or subject to any express or tacit Condition affecting the Price thereof; and the said Commissioners shall then proceed to ascertain, in reference to each Colony, what Amount of Sterling Money will represent the average Value of a slave therein for the Period of Eight Years: and the total Number of the Slaves in each Colony being multiplied into the Amount of Sterling Money so representing such average Value as aforesaid of a Slave therein, the Product of such Multiplication shall be ascertained for each Colony separately; and the said Twenty Millions of Pounds Sterling shall then be assigned to, and apportioned amongst the said several Colonies rateably, and in proportion to the product so ascertained for each respectively.

XLVI. No Compensation to be allowed for Persons illegally held in Slavery.

XLVII. And whereas it is necessary that Provision should be made for the Apportionment amongst the Proprietors of the Slaves to be manumitted by virtue of this Act, in each of the said Colonies respectively of that part of the said compensation fund which shall be so assigned as aforesaid to each of the respective Colonies: And whereas the necessary Rules for that Purpose cannot be properly or safely established until after full inquiry shall have been made, into the several Circumstances which ought to be taken into consideration in making such Apportionment; be it therefore enacted, That it shall be the duty of the said Commissioners, and they are hereby authorized and required to institute a full and exact inquiry into all the circumstances connected with each of the said several Colonies which in the judgment of the said Commissioners ought, in Justice and Equity, to regulate or affect the Apportionment within the same of that part of the said general Compensation Fund, which shall in manner aforesaid be assigned to each of the said Colonies respectively; and especially such Commissioners shall have regard to the relative value of prædial Slaves, and of unattached Slaves, in every such Colony: and such Commissioners shall distinguish such Slaves, whether prædial or unattached, into as many distinct Classes as, regard being had to the circumstances of each

Colony shall appear just; and such Commissioners shall with all practicable precision, ascertain and fix the average Value of a Slave in each of the Classes into which the Slaves in any such Colony shall be so divided; and the said Commissioners shall also proceed to inquire and consider of the Principles according to which the Compensation to be allotted in respect to any Slave or Body of Slaves ought, according to the Rules of Law and Equity, to be distributed amongst Persons who, as Owners or Creditors, Legatees or Annuitants, may have any joint or common Interest in any such Slave or Slaves, or may be entitled to, or interested in such Slave or Slaves, either in Possession, Remainder, Reversion, or Expectancy; and the said Commissioners shall also proceed to inquire and consider of the Principles upon which, and the Manner in which, Provision might be most effectually made for the Protection of any Interest in any such Compensation Money which may belong to or be vested in any married Women, Infants, Lunatics, or Persons of insane or unsound Mind, or Persons beyond the Seas, or labouring under any other legal or natural Disability or Incapacity, and according to what Rules, and in what Manner, and under what Authority Trustees should, when necessary, be appointed for the safe Custody, for the Benefit of any Person or Persons, of any such Compensation Fund or any Part thereof, and for regulating the Duties of such Trustees, and providing them with a fair and reasonable Indemnity; and the said Commissioners shall also inquire and consider upon what Principles, according to the established Rules of Law and Equity in similar Cases, the Succession to such Funds should be regulated upon the Death of any Person entitled thereto who may die intestate; and the said Commissioners shall and they are also authorised and required to consider of any other question which it may be necessary to investigate in order to establish just and equitable Rules for the Apportionment of such Compensation Money amongst the Persons seised of, or entitled to, or having any Mortgage, Charge, Incumbrance, Judgment, or Lien upon, or any Claim to, or Right or Interest in, any Slave or Slaves so to be manumitted as aforesaid, at the Time of such their Manumission; and having made all such Inquiries, and having taken all such Matters and Things as aforesaid into their Consideration, the said Commissioners shall and are hereby required to proceed to draw up and frame all such general Rules, regard being had to the Laws and Usages in force in each Colony respectively, as to them may seem best adapt-

ed in each Colony respectively, for securing the just and equitable Distribution of the said Funds amongst or for the Benefit of such several Persons as aforesaid, and for the Protection of such Funds, and for the Appointment and Indemnification of such Trustees as aforesaid; and such general rules when so framed, and when agreed Upon by the said Commissioners, shall by them be subscribed with their respective Hands and Seals, and transmitted to the Lord President of His Majesty's Council, to be by him laid before His Majesty in Council; and so from Time to Time as often as any further general Rules should be so framed and agreed to for the Purposes aforesaid or any of them.

XLVIII. Rules to be published in the London Gazette, with a Notice that Appeals will be received against their Establishment.

XLIX. His Majesty in Council may hear such Appeals, and thereupon confirm or disallow any general Rule so appealed against.

L. In absence of Appeal, His Majesty in Council may confirm, rescind, or amend such Rules.

LI. Rules when confirmed by His Majesty shall be recited in the confirmatory Order in Council, and enrolled in Chancery.

LII. Rules so enrolled may be removed or amended.

LIII. Rules when confirmed and enrolled shall be of the same validity as if enacted by Parliament.

LIV. Rules so enrolled shall be observed by the Commissioners in making their Awards.

LV. Persons interested in any Slaves manumitted by this Act may prefer Claims before the Commissioners, who are to make rules for the Conduct of all Proceedings under the Commission.

LVI. Commissioners to adjudicate on all Claims preferred to them. Appeal may be made against adjudication. His Majesty in Council may make Rules for the Regulation of such Appeals. In adverse Claims, any Claimant interested in the Adjudication may undertake its defence.

And be it further enacted, That the said Commissioners shall proceed in the Manner to be prescribed by any such general Rules as last aforesaid, to inquire into and adjudicate upon any such Claims as may be so preferred to them, and shall upon each such Claim make their Adjudication and Award in such Manner and Form as shall be prescribed by any such last-mentioned general Rules; and if any Person interested in, or affected by, any such Adjudication or Award shall be dissatisfied therewith, it shall be lawful for such Person to appeal therefrom to His

Majesty in Council, and Notice of any such Appeal shall be served upon the said Commissioners, who shall thereupon undertake the Defence thereof; and it shall be competent to His Majesty in Council to make and establish all such Rules and Regulations as to his Majesty shall seem meet, respecting the time and manner of preferring and proceeding upon such appeals, and respecting the Course to be observed in defending the same, which Rules shall be so framed as to promote, as far as may be consistent with Justice, all practicable Economy and Dispatch in the proceedings upon the decision thereof; and in cases in which any Two or more Persons shall have preferred before the said Commissioners adverse or opposing Claims, and in which any or either of such Persons shall be interested to sustain the adjudications or award of such Commissioners thereupon, then and in every such case it shall be lawful for any Person or Persons so interested, to undertake the defence of any such appeal in lieu and instead of the said Commissioners.

LVII. His Majesty in Council may confirm or disallow, or alter or remit, Adjudications appealed against.

LVIII. Failing any Appeal, the Award of the Commissioners final.

LIX. And be it further enacted, That the Lord High Treasurer, or the Commissioners of His Majesty's Treasury, or any Three or more of them, for the time being, may order and direct to be issued and paid out of the said Sum of Twenty Millions of Pounds Sterling any Sum or Sums of Money for the Payment of Salaries to Commissioners, Officers, Clerks, and other Persons acting in relation to such Compensation in the Execution of this Act, and for discharging such incidental Expences as shall necessarily attend the same, in such manner as the Lord High Treasurer, or Commissioners of the Treasury, or any Three or more of them, shall from time to time think fit and reasonable; and an Account of such Expense shall be annually laid before Parliament.

LX. And be it enacted, That a Certificate containing a List of the Names and Designations of the several Persons in whose favour any Sum or Sums of Money shall be awarded front time to time under the Provision of this Act by the Commissioners, as herein-before mentioned, shall be signed by Three or more of the said Commissioners, who shall forthwith transmit the same to His Majesty's Principal Secretary of State then having Charge of the Affairs of the said Colonies, for his Approbation and Signature, who shall, when he shall have signed the same,

transmit it to the Commissioners of His Majesty's Treasury; and the said Commissioners of the Treasury, or any Three of such Commissioners, shall thereupon, by Warrant under their Hands, authorize the Commissioners for the Reduction of the National Debt to pay the said Sums, out of the Monies standing upon their Account in the Books of the said Bank under the Title of "The West India Compensation Account," to the Persons named in such Certificate; and the said Commissioners for the Reduction of the National Debt, or the Comptroller General or Assistant Comptroller General acting under the said Commissioners, are hereby required to pay all such Sums of Money to the Persons named therein, under such Forms and Regulations as the said Commissioners for the Reduction of the National Debt shall think fit to adopt for that Purpose.

LXI. And whereas in some of the Colonies aforesaid a certain Statute, made in the Thirteenth and Fourteenth Years of King Charles the Second, intituled "An Act for preventing the Mischiefs and Dangers that may arise by certain Persons called Quakers and others refusing to take lawful Oaths"; and a certain other Statute made in the Seventeenth Year of King Charles the Second, intituled "An Act for restraining Nonconformists from inhabiting in Corporations"; and a certain other Statute, made in the Twenty-second Year of King Charles the Second, intituled "An Act to prevent and suppress seditious Conventicles"; and a certain other Statute, made in the First and Second Year of King William and Queen Mary, intituled "An Act for exempting Their Majesty's Protestant Subjects dissenting from the Church of England from the Penalties of certain Laws"; and a certain other Statute, made in the Tenth Year of Queen Anne, intituled "An Act for preserving the Protestant Religion by better securing the Church of England as by Law established; and for confirming the Toleration granted to Protestant Dissenters by an Act intituled 'An Act for exempting Their Majesty's Protestant Subjects dissenting from the Church of England from the Penalties of certain Laws,' and for supplying the Defects thereof; and for the further securing the Protestant Succession, by requiring the Practisers of the Law in North Britain to take the Oaths and subscribe the Declaration therein Mentioned"; or some one of those Statutes, or some Parts thereof or of some of them, have and hath been adopted, and are or is in force; be it further enacted, That in such of the Colonies aforesaid in which the said several Statutes or any of them, or any Parts thereof or any of them, have or hath been adopted and are or is in force, a certain Statute made in the Fifty-second Year of His late Majesty King George the Third, intituled "An Act to repeal certain Acts and amend other acts relating to Religious Worship and Assemblies, and Persons teaching or preaching therein," shall be and is hereby declared to be in force, as fully and effectually as if such Colonies had been expressly named and enumerated for that Purpose in such last-recited Statute: Provided nevertheless, that in the said several Colonies, to which the said Act of His late Majesty King George the Third is so extended and declared applicable as aforesaid, any Two or more Justices of the Peace holding any such Special Commission as aforesaid shall have, exercise, and enjoy all and every the Jurisdiction, Powers, and Authorities whatsoever, which by force and virtue of the said Act are within the Realm of England had, exercised, and enjoyed by the several Justices of the Peace, and, by the General and Quarter Sessions therein mentioned.

LXII. His Majesty in Council may make all necessary Laws for giving effect to this Act in the Settlement of Honduras.

LXIII And be it further enacted, that within the Meaning and for the Purposes of this Act every Person who for the Time being shall be in the lawful Administration of the Government of any of the said Colonies shall be taken to be the Governor thereof.

LXIV. And be it further enacted, That nothing in this Act contained doth or shall extend to any of the Territories in the Possession of the East India Company, or to the Island of Ceylon, or to the Island of Saint Helena.

LXV. And be it further enacted, That in the Colonies of the Cape of Good Hope and Mauritius the several Parts of this Act shall take effect and come into operation, or shall cease to operate and to be in force, as the case may be, at Periods more remote than the respective Periods herein-before for such Purposes limited by the following Intervals of Time; *videlicet*, by Four Calendar Months in the Colony of the Cape of Good Hope, and by Six Calendar Months in the Colony of the Mauritius.

LXVI. And be it further enacted and declared, That within the Meaning and for the Purposes of this Act all Islands and Territories dependent upon any of the Colonies aforesaid, and constituting Parts of the same Colonial Government, shall respectively be taken to be Parts of such respective Colonies.

Glossary

Descent	inheritance
enrolled in Chancery	officially registered
his Majesty's Colonies	colonies existing during the reign of William IV
Indenture of Apprenticeship	work contract specifying a relationship that includes material support but not necessarily a salary
manumitted and set free	liberated and emancipated, meaning both set free and set free from slavery
Nonconformists	persons not conforming to the Church of England; also Protestants
seditious Conventicles	meetings for the purpose of plotting insurrection or rebellion
seised of	having acquired ownership of
Twenty Millions of Pounds Sterling	approximately £1,500,000,000